D1539963

FOR DUMMIES™ BESTSELLING BOOK SERIES

Visual Studio® .NET All-in-One Desk Reference For Dummies®

Cheat Sheet

What's New in Visual Basic .NET

In addition to the basic features, such as variables, data types, constants, arrays, enumerations, operators, expressions, statements, and procedures, some of the new features of Visual Basic .NET are

- **Assemblies:** An EXE or a DLL file that forms the basis of deployment, version control, reuse, and security permissions of an application.
- **Namespaces:** The components of assemblies, namespaces primarily organize the objects present in the assemblies. An assembly can contain more than one namespace.
- **Adding references:** You need to add a reference to the external object that you want to use in your current application.
- **Attributes:** The tags that are used to provide additional information about the elements defined in a Visual Basic .NET program. Some of the most common uses of attributes are
  - To explain COM properties for classes, interfaces, and methods
  - To explain assemblies
  - To specify security requirements of methods
  - To specify features required to enforce security
- **Inheritance:** Enables you to create classes that are derived from some other classes known as base classes. Inheritance provides you the advantage of defining a class only once. You can then reuse this functionality by deriving new classes from this class.
- **Windows Forms:** With a new forms package called Windows Forms, Visual Basic .NET allows the developers to inherit a form from an existing form.
- **Structured exception handling:** Enables you to create more efficient and robust error handlers by using structured exception handling, which allows you to detect and remove errors at runtime.
- **Multithreading:** Enables your applications to handle multiple tasks simultaneously.

Visual C# .NET Features

Visual C# (pronounced Visual C *sharp*) is Microsoft's new generation programming language that integrates the flexibility of C++ with the short development cycle of Visual Basic. These features, along with an array of new features, make Visual C# more than just the sum of Visual Basic and C++. Some of the features of Visual C# are

- **Garbage collection:** The function of the garbage collector, provided by Visual C#, is to check for the objects not being used by an application and to delete them from memory.
- **Value/reference type system:** According to the value/reference type system, the standard data types, enumerations, and structures are called value types. Interfaces, classes, and delegates are called reference types. This type system provides the advantage of eliminating a number of memory bugs and simplifying object manipulation.
- **Unified declaration and definition of class methods:** The unified declaration and definition of class methods alleviates you from creating multiple files — one for declaration and the other for definition.
- **Delegates:** A type-safe and secure object that contains a reference to a method. The advantage of using delegates is that it is helpful in anonymous invocation, which means that the method to be invoked is not known at compile time.
- **Simple thread synchronization:** Enables you to created multithreaded applications.
- **Versioning:** You need to explicitly override the members of a base class in a derived class. This revision creates a new version without affecting the existing program.
- **Interoperability:** Visual C# applications are platform-independent.
- **Access to native-code:** Visual C# allows a developer to programmatically view the native code.
- **Attributes:** A declarative tag that you can use to describe various entities in your programs.

Visual Studio® .NET All-in-One Desk Reference For Dummies®

Cheat Sheet

A Quick Glance at Visual Basic .NET Language Changes

Here we briefly describe some of the language changes in Visual Basic .NET.

Variable declaration changes

In Visual Basic .NET, you can declare multiple variables in a single line without specifying the type of each variable.

Array changes

- By default, the lower bound of an array is 0, which cannot be modified.
- You cannot create fixed-sized arrays in Visual Basic .NET.
- You cannot use the `ReDim` statement for declaring arrays for the first time. You can use this statement only for resizing an array.

Data type changes

Following are the changes in the usage of data types in Visual Basic .NET:

- Visual Basic .NET doesn't support the `Currency` data type. Instead, the `Decimal` data type can be used to store currency values.
- In Visual Basic 6.0, a date was stored in the `Double` data type. However, Visual Basic .NET provides the `DateTime` data type to store the values in the date format.
- In Visual Basic 6.0, the `Variant` data type is used to store data of any type. In Visual Basic .NET, the `Object` data type is used to store data of any type.

Logical operator changes

As opposed to Visual Basic 6.0, where `And`, `Or`, `Not`, and `Xor` are used to perform the logical and bitwise operations, in Visual Basic .NET, `And`, `Or`, `Not`, and `Xor` can only perform logical operations. To perform bitwise operations, you use `BitAnd`, `BitOr`, `BitNot`, and `BitXor` operators.

Cheat Sheet $2.95 value. Item 1626-4.
For more information about Hungry Minds, call 1-800-762-2974.

...FOR DUMMIES™

References for the Rest of Us!®

BESTSELLING BOOK SERIES

Are you intimidated and confused by computers? Do you find that traditional manuals are overloaded with technical details you'll never use? Do your friends and family always call you to fix simple problems on their PCs? Then the For Dummies® computer book series from Hungry Minds, Inc. is for you.

For Dummies books are written for those frustrated computer users who know they aren't really dumb but find that PC hardware, software, and indeed the unique vocabulary of computing make them feel helpless. For Dummies books use a lighthearted approach, a down-to-earth style, and even cartoons and humorous icons to dispel computer novices' fears and build their confidence. Lighthearted but not lightweight, these books are a perfect survival guide for anyone forced to use a computer.

"I like my copy so much I told friends; now they bought copies."

— Irene C., Orwell, Ohio

"Quick, concise, nontechnical, and humorous."

— Jay A., Elburn, Illinois

"Thanks, I needed this book. Now I can sleep at night."

— Robin F., British Columbia, Canada

Already, millions of satisfied readers agree. They have made For Dummies books the #1 introductory level computer book series and have written asking for more. So, if you're looking for the most fun and easy way to learn about computers, look to For Dummies books to give you a helping hand.

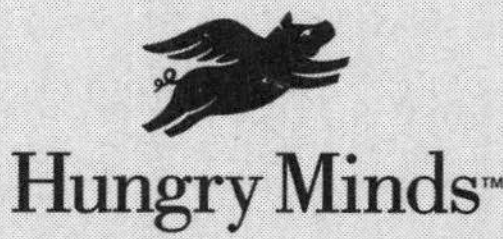

1/01

Visual Studio® .NET
ALL-IN-ONE DESK REFERENCE
FOR
DUMMIES®

Nitin Pandey, NIIT
Yesh Singhal, NIIT
Mridula Parihar, NIIT

Best-Selling Books • Digital Downloads • e-Books • Answer Networks • e-Newsletters • Branded Web Sites • e-Learning

New York, NY ◆ Cleveland, OH ◆ Indianapolis, IN

Visual Studio® .NET All-in-One Desk Reference For Dummies®

Published by
Hungry Minds, Inc.
909 Third Avenue
New York, NY 10022
www.hungryminds.com
www.dummies.com

Library of Congress Control Number: 2002100097

ISBN: 0-7645-1626-4

Printed in the United States of America

10 9 8 7 6 5 4 3 2 1

1O/SQ/QT/QS/IN

Distributed in the United States by Hungry Minds, Inc.

Distributed by CDG Books Canada Inc. for Canada; by Transworld Publishers Limited in the United Kingdom; by IDG Norge Books for Norway; by IDG Sweden Books for Sweden; by IDG Books Australia Publishing Corporation Pty. Ltd. for Australia and New Zealand; by TransQuest Publishers Pte Ltd. for Singapore, Malaysia, Thailand, Indonesia, and Hong Kong; by Gotop Information Inc. for Taiwan; by ICG Muse, Inc. for Japan; by Intersoft for South Africa; by Eyrolles for France; by International Thomson Publishing for Germany, Austria and Switzerland; by Distribuidora Cuspide for Argentina; by LR International for Brazil; by Galileo Libros for Chile; by Ediciones ZETA S.C.R. Ltda. for Peru; by WS Computer Publishing Corporation, Inc., for the Philippines; by Contemporanea de Ediciones for Venezuela; by Express Computer Distributors for the Caribbean and West Indies; by Micronesia Media Distributor, Inc. for Micronesia; by Chips Computadoras S.A. de C.V. for Mexico; by Editorial Norma de Panama S.A. for Panama; by American Bookshops for Finland.

For general information on Hungry Minds' products and services please contact our Customer Care Department within the U.S. at 800-762-2974, outside the U.S. at 317-572-3993 or fax 317-572-4002.

For sales inquiries and reseller information, including discounts, premium and bulk quantity sales, and foreign-language translations, please contact our Customer Care Department at 800-434-3422, fax 317-572-4002, or write to Hungry Minds, Inc., Attn: Customer Care Department, 10475 Crosspoint Boulevard, Indianapolis, IN 46256.

For information on licensing foreign or domestic rights, please contact our Sub-Rights Customer Care Department at 212-884-5000.

For information on using Hungry Minds' products and services in the classroom or for ordering examination copies, please contact our Educational Sales Department at 800-434-2086 or fax 317-572-4005.

For press review copies, author interviews, or other publicity information, please contact our Public Relations Department at 317-572-3168 or fax 317-572-4168.

For authorization to photocopy items for corporate, personal, or educational use, please contact Copyright Clearance Center, 222 Rosewood Drive, Danvers, MA 01923, or fax 978-750-4470.

About the Authors

Mridula Parihar has a Masters degree in Applied Operations Research from Delhi University, India. She is a Microsoft Certified Solution Developer (MCSD) and has approximately two and a half years work experience with NIIT Ltd. She spent her first year in Career Education Group (CEG) of NIIT. In the CEG group, she taught NIIT students and was involved in scheduling and managing resources. For the past one and a half years, Mridula has been working in Knowledge Solutions Business (KSB) of NIIT, where she's had the opportunity to work on varied technical projects. She has been involved in design, development, testing, and implementation of instructor-led training courses. Her primary responsibilities include instructional review, technical review, and ensuring ISO compliance. For the past ten months, Mridula has been involved in textbook writing on various technical subjects, such as TCP/IP and .NET.

When Mridula isn't programming, reading, or writing, you can find her playing badminton, one of her favorite outdoor games.

Yesh Singhal has a Bachelors degree in Physics (Honors) from Delhi University, India. He has completed the three-year GNIIT course, and he's a Microsoft Certified Solution Developer (MCSD) with approximately two and a half years work experience with NIIT Ltd. Yesh spent his first year in Career Education Group (CEG) of NIIT, where he was involved in training NIIT students. He was also extensively involved in scheduling and managing resources. For the past one and a half years, Yesh has had the opportunity to work on various technical projects in Knowledge Solutions Business (KSB) of NIIT. He was involved in design, development, testing, and implementation of instructor-led training courses, such as those for Crystal Reports 8.0 and Fireworks 3.0. His primary responsibilities include instructional review, technical review, and ensuring ISO compliance. For the past four months, Yesh has been involved in textbook writing on technical subjects such as .NET.

Yesh likes partying and loves the game of cricket. When Yesh isn't working, you can catch him watching cricket or hanging out with friends.

Nitin Pandey is a subject matter expert at NIIT. Before joining NIIT two years ago, he completed his Bachelors in Chemistry Honors.

Nitin has been in touch with the latest technologies for the last three years. Some of the technologies that he has worked on include Commerce Server 2000, BizTalk Server 2000, and of course, Visual Studio .NET.

Dedication

Like all my books, this book is also dedicated to my Supreme Guide, the Almighty. In addition, I dedicate this book to my Mom and Daddy who have always been a constant source of energy and encouragement for me. Also, I must thank my brothers, Amit and Abhay, who have always given their constant support to me.

— Mridula Parihar

This book is dedicated to my mom, wife, and brother. Mom has been an inspiration to me. Every time I was down with work pressure, I used to see a book written by her and was instantly recharged with energy. My wife, Manisha, has been incredibly patient with my busy schedule during the writing of this book and provided me with the much-needed mental support. And last — but not least — my brother, Ruchien, who, always curious to see my book, innocently asked, "When is your book getting published?" This question filled me with an enthusiasm to complete the book as soon as possible.

— Yesh Singhal

I dedicate this book to all those at NIIT who helped this book see the light of the day.

— Nitin Pandey

Authors' Acknowledgments

First and foremost I would like to thank my Supreme Guide, the Almighty, who has always guided me in the right direction.

Then, I would like to acknowledge the time and effort put in by the teams at both ends: NIIT and Hungry Minds, Inc. At NIIT, I would like to convey my special thanks to Ms. Anita Sastry, the project manager. Without her valuable contribution and support, this book wouldn't have been possible. Also, I would like to thank Nitin and Yesh, my co-authors, for their cordial support. Thank you once again for giving a helping hand when it was needed the most.

At Hungry Minds, my special thanks go to the acquisitions editor, Mary Corder, who gave me the opportunity to write this book, and to the project editor, Linda Morris. Also, I would like to acknowledge the technical editor, Greg Guntle, and the copy editor, Teresa Artman, for their valuable input and constant support. Thank you all for your valuable contributions, without which this book wouldn't be possible.

Thank you mom and daddy for your support and care while I was busy writing. My special thanks go to my brothers, Amit and Abhay, who have always been by my side whenever I needed their support. Thank you both of you.

— Mridula Parihar

Thank you Anita Sastry, project manager with NIIT Ltd., for giving me an opportunity to write this book.

Also, I would like to thank our acquisitions editor, Mary Corder, and our project editor, Linda Morris, who helped in the creation of this book. A special thanks also goes to Greg Guntle, the technical editor, and Teresa Artman, the copy editor. Also, I would like to mention my coauthors, Nitin and Mridula, for their constant comments and feedback that helped me improved the quality of the book. Nitin, you are a morale booster. Thanks for being so.

This acknowledgement won't be complete without the mention of my family, who always provided me with the strength without which this book would not have been finished.

— Yesh Singhal

Foremost, I would like to thank my project manager, Ms. Anita Sastry, for her patience and support through the project. I honor her commitment to quality that helped me improve the quality of chapters as they went by. But for Ms. Anita's efforts, we would not have been able to complete this book on time.

My special thanks go to the project editor, Ms. Linda Morris, and copy editor, Ms. Teresa Artman. They've been most enthusiastic and eager to help us out with this book. Their feedback and suggestions during author reviews were indeed valuable and helped us bring this book in its present shape. It's been wonderful working with them.

Finally, this book has meant long working hours and working weekends for all of us. It would not have been possible for me without the robust support of all my family members. They have been very supportive and understanding in my endeavors for this book. Therefore, my very special thanks to my parents, my brother and sister-in-law, my two sisters, and my brother-in-law; not to forget the one year old!

— Nitin Pandey

Publisher's Acknowledgments

We're proud of this book; please send us your comments through our Hungry Minds Online Registration Form located at www.dummies.com.

Some of the people who helped bring this book to market include the following:

Acquisitions, Editorial, and Media Development

Project Editor: Linda Morris

Acquisitions Editor: Mary C. Corder

Copy Editors: Teresa Artman, Nicole A. Laux

Technical Editor: Greg Guntle

Editorial Manager: Constance Carlisle

Editorial Assistant: Amanda Foxworth

Production

Project Coordinator: Dale White

Layout and Graphics: Joyce Haughey, Gabriele McCann, Barry Offringa, Jacque Schneider, Betty Schulte, Jeremey Unger, Mary J. Virgin, Erin Zeltner

Proofreaders: Andy Hollandbeck, Arielle Carole Mennelle

Indexer: Richard Shrout

General and Administrative

Hungry Minds Technology Publishing Group: Richard Swadley, Senior Vice President and Publisher; Mary Bednarek, Vice President and Publisher, Networking; Joseph Wikert, Vice President and Publisher, Web Development Group; Mary C. Corder, Editorial Director, Dummies Technology; Andy Cummings, Publishing Director, Dummies Technology; Barry Pruett, Publishing Director, Visual/Graphic Design

Hungry Minds Manufacturing: Ivor Parker, Vice President, Manufacturing

Hungry Minds Marketing: John Helmus, Assistant Vice President, Director of Marketing

Hungry Minds Production for Branded Press: Debbie Stailey, Production Director

Hungry Minds Sales: Michael Violano, Vice President, International Sales and Sub Rights

Contents at a Glance

Book V: Visual C# .NET 413

Book VI: Associated Technologies and Enhancements 507

Book VII: Creating and Deploying Web Services and Other Visual Studio .NET Solutions 799

Index 887

Cartoons at a Glance

By Rich Tennant

The 5th Wave
By Rich Tennant
IT WAS THE LAST TIME EMILY SERVED ALPHABET SOUP TO HER WORD PUZZLE PLAYING HUSBAND.
ADO.NET... XML... DAO...
Obsessive... fanatical... fixated...Ooo-compulsive...

page 69

The 5th Wave
By Rich Tennant
My job consists of working with Visual C#.NET all day.

page 413

The 5th Wave
By Rich Tennant
C++

"It was at this point in time that there appeared to be some sort of mass insanity."

page 263

The 5th Wave
By Rich Tennant
History was about to repeat itself as Charlie Van Gogh, Visual Basic.NET programmer and great-nephew of Vincent Van Gogh is assigned the job of designing a user interface for his company's new database program.
Sorry Chuck-management is still rejecting your latest designs.

page 507

The 5th Wave
By Rich Tennant

"Excuse me – is anyone here NOT talking about the .NET initiative?"

page 7

The 5th Wave
By Rich Tennant
How to Deploy Your Web Service

"Can't I just give you riches or something?"

page 799

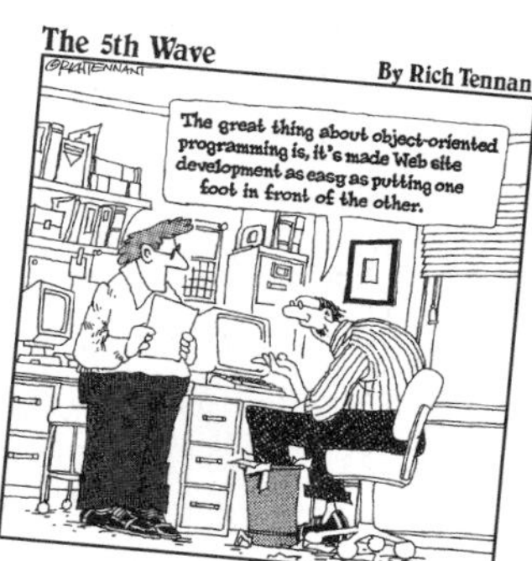

The 5th Wave
By Rich Tennant
The great thing about object-oriented programming is, it's made Web site development as easy as putting one foot in front of the other.

page 97

Cartoon Information:

Fax: 978-546-7747

E-Mail: richtennant@the5thwave.com

World Wide Web: www.the5thwave.com

Table of Contents

Book V: Visual C# .NET....413

Book VI: Associated Technologies and Enhancements.....507

Introduction

Welcome to the latest Microsoft product, Visual Studio .NET, which unleashes the next generation of application development. Visual Studio .NET provides a complete development environment in which you can develop a variety of applications ranging from Windows applications to ASP.NET Web applications and Web services. Visual Studio .NET provides you a number of programming languages to choose from for developing applications, enabling you to leverage your current development skills instead of needing to refrain.

In *Visual Studio .NET All-in-One Desk Reference For Dummies*, we take a straightforward approach to telling you about Visual Studio .NET and the different programming languages that it offers. Besides giving you lots of concepts in plain and simple English, we've included lots of code samples that help you put the concepts to work. The goal of this book is to take the anxiety and stress out of mastering the assortment of technologies available with Visual Studio .NET. We hope that you find the book a clear and straightforward resource for exploring Visual Studio .NET.

About This Book

This book is your friendly and approachable guide that will help you master Visual Studio .NET. The way this book is organized makes you grasp the technologies easier and faster. This book, however, isn't meant to be read from front to back. The book is divided into seven mini books — each mini book focusing on a specific technology. Each chapter in each mini book is divided into sections, each of which is self-contained. Here are some of the topics that we cover in this book:

- Key components of the .NET Framework
- An overview of Visual Studio .NET along with its installation
- The Visual Studio .NET IDE
- Features of Visual Basic .NET, Visual C++ .NET, and Visual C#
- Application development using Visual Basic .NET, Visual C++ .NET, and Visual C#
- ASP.NET Web application development
- ASP.NET Web services development
- Application deployment

Conventions Used in This Book

Keeping things consistent makes them easier to understand. In this book, those consistent elements are *conventions*. Notice how the word *convention* is in italics? In this book, we put new terms in italics, and then we define them so that you know what they mean.

This book contains lots of code. All code in this book appears in monofont type, as shown here:

```
MsgBox("Hello World")
```

When URLs (Web addresses) appear within a paragraph, they appear in monofont and look like this: `www.microsoft.com`.

Any programming keywords or method names used within a paragraph also appear in monofont type, like this: `Display_Details`.

What You Don't Have to Read

When you read this book, remember that it is not meant to be read from front to back. However, when you read a specific chapter, it is advisable to read the entire content of a section. But, if you read a chapter just for reference, you can very well skip sidebars without missing crucial information.

Foolish Assumptions

Making foolish assumptions can make a fool out of the person who makes them. Throwing caution to the wind, we make a few assumptions about you, the readers of this book:

- You're already familiar with programming languages in the previous version of Visual Studio, Visual Studio 6.0.
- You have a basic knowledge of HTML and XML.
- You know the difference between Web browsers and Web servers.
- You have a basic understanding of Internet Information Server (IIS).

In addition to these assumptions, we also assume that you've installed Visual Studio .NET software on your computer. It'll be great if you have a working Internet connection because you can then directly download the applications provided in this book from `www.dummies.com/extras/VS.NETAllinOne`.

How This Book Is Organized

We've divided *Visual Studio .NET All-in-One Desk Reference For Dummies* into seven mini books. Each mini book covers a different technology separately. Organizing the book as an assortment of several books facilitates your search for the topics that you want to explore. Any time that you require help or information on a specific topic, use the table of contents to locate your topic. This section provides a breakdown of the mini books and what you'll find in each of them.

Book I: Visual Studio .NET Overview

Book 1 provides you an overview of Visual Studio .NET, where you'll find answers to some of your most fundamental questions:

- ✦ What is the .NET initiative?
- ✦ What are the components of Visual Studio .NET?
- ✦ How do you install Visual Studio .NET?

Book II: Using the Visual Studio .NET IDE

Book 2 is a good resource to get you started with Visual Studio .NET. In this book, you'll get a closer look of the common Integrated Development Environment (IDE) provided with Visual Studio .NET. This book takes you through the complete Visual Studio .NET interface and tells you how to use the various IDE tools.

Book III: Visual Basic .NET

Book 3 introduces you to the new features of Visual Basic .NET. Additionally, this book delves into the programming intricacies with Visual Basic .NET. Some of the areas that we explore in this book are

- ✦ Windows Forms
- ✦ Variables
- ✦ Program flow control
- ✦ Procedures
- ✦ Classes
- ✦ Error handling
- ✦ Database applications with Visual Basic .NET

Book IV: Visual C++ .NET

Book 4 is a perfect resource for you to explore programming with Visual C++ .NET. Some of the topics that we cover in this book are

- ✦ MFC applications
- ✦ Database applications with Visual C++ .NET
- ✦ ATL server projects
- ✦ Managed extensions in C++

Additionally, this book teaches you how to debug and handle exceptions in Visual C++ .NET applications. You can also read about upgrading the existing application to Visual C++ .NET applications.

Book V: Visual C# .NET

This book gets you started with Visual C#. In addition to providing a basic language feature, this book tells you how to create Windows applications and Windows services by using Visual C#.

Book VI: Associated Technologies and Enhancements

This book is a good guide for you to explore the field of programming for the Web with ASP.NET. The book builds a solid ground for ASP.NET and gets you started with it. We cover the following major topics in this book:

- ✦ Web Forms and the Web Forms Server controls
- ✦ Data binding with server controls
- ✦ Mobile Web applications
- ✦ Using ADO .NET
- ✦ HTTP handlers
- ✦ Caching
- ✦ Application security

Book VII: Creating and Deploying Web Services and Other Visual Studio .NET Solutions

Book 7 presents advanced features of Visual Studio .NET in such a simple manner that you'll easily master these advanced features while being tempted to discover them. This book teaches you how to create Web services and Web service clients. Additionally, you'll find out how to deploy different types of applications created in Visual Studio .NET.

Icons Used in This Book

To make your experience with the book easier, we use various icons in the margins of the book to indicate particular points of interest.

This icon flags technical details that are informative and interesting but not critical to write code in any of the .NET languages. You can skip these if you want.

This icon marks important directions to keep you out of trouble. These paragraphs contain facts that can keep you from having nightmares.

This icon flags useful information that acts as a hint or a tip for performing certain tasks in an easy and efficient manner.

This icon is a friendly reminder or a marker for something that you want to make sure that you cache in your memory for later use. Don't skip these gentle reminders.

Where to Go from Here

Just as Visual Studio .NET is a single product that hosts multiple technologies, *Visual Studio .NET All-in-One Desk Reference For Dummies* is certainly a great collection of multiple books that provides you with several of these technologies. Now, you're ready to use this book and discover different technologies that Visual Studio .NET hosts. No doubt, the table of contents stands as a ready reference to navigate you to your topic of interest.

We wish you good luck on your journey to explore the host of technologies with Visual Studio .NET.

Enjoy!

Book I

Visual Studio .NET Overview

"Excuse me – is anyone here NOT talking about the .NET initiative?"

Contents at a Glance

Chapter 1: Exploring the .NET Initiative

In This Chapter

- Finding out about the .NET initiative
- Getting to know products in the .NET suite

Visual Studio .NET is the result of the .NET initiative — an initiative that didn't originate on its own but was brought about by you and me, the customers. We brought about this initiative through increased collaboration, mostly through the Internet, and partly through other communication channels. Increased collaboration resulted in a gradual shift from desktop computing to distributed computing. Microsoft, as always, was quick to realize this shift and launched its .NET initiative to capitalize on it. The .NET initiative gained momentum in the second quarter of 2000 and brought about the development of new applications and services.

In this chapter, we explore the world of .NET, discussing the products and services associated with .NET and discovering how Visual Studio .NET takes the lead role in the .NET initiative.

Understanding the .NET Initiative

Today, users often encounter on a daily basis applications that are user-friendly but not platform-independent. For example, when you visit a Web site, you can register on the site and that registration information can be used by the Web site administrator to offer customized products. The same is pertinent for applications, such as Microsoft Word, installed on your computer in which you can store your preferences. Comparatively, if you have two applications running on different platforms (such as Linux and Windows together), they may not offer complete interoperability — meaning that you can't run Windows applications on a Linux platform.

You can therefore conclude that customizing an application for a user is easy, but you have very limited options for customizing an application for another. The .NET initiative aims to bridge this customizability gap between applications.

But what are the benefits of customizing one application for another? If you've not experimented with applications that communicate with each other, you may not know all their benefits. Application interoperability enables you to access existing data and functionality from different applications that may run on different platforms.

Take this idea a little further: If an application exposes its functionality over the Internet, your application can access the Internet application from anywhere. Thus, you've got two applications that talk over the Internet. This is exactly what .NET tries to achieve.

Check out how .NET enables applications to communicate with one another. As an example, take two applications that need to interoperate, looking closely at some of the inherent barriers and how they're overcome.

- **Geography:** Applications that need to interoperate can be located in different parts of the world.
- **Platform:** Applications may run on different platforms.
- **Language:** These applications may have been developed in different programming languages without the slightest degree of similarity.

Consider possible solutions to these obstacles. The simplest solution that we (and probably you, too) can think for the geographical requirement is to run the applications through the Internet. The Internet is the fastest and the easiest way to break geographical barriers. For the platform problem, you need to have a common language that can make the two applications talk with each other. XML (eXtensible Markup Language) has fast emerged as this common language and is also the industry standard for describing and transporting data. Therefore, XML is used to exchange data and information between .NET applications. XML also solves the language difference problem. Even if applications don't understand each other's language, they can communicate as long as they are based on XML.

Thus, you can create applications that don't require user interaction but still communicate with each other to serve a common purpose. We call these applications *services* to distinguish them from the applications that we normally use. See how smart you already are? You now know three important keywords to use together: XML, Web (or Internet), and services — XML Web services! XML Web services are the most significant outcome of the .NET initiative.

With XML Web services, you can provide software products as services. Users don't need to purchase software. Instead, they can subscribe to a service and use the service as long as they need it. Microsoft is coming up with its own set of Web services, known as My Services. These services are based on the Microsoft Passport authentication service, the same service that runs Hotmail.

The .NET initiative includes a suite of products, from .NET Enterprise servers to the Visual Studio .NET development platform, that are centered on XML Web services. But before we move on to a description of these products, let us examine two main benefits that the .NET initiative offers.

Interoperation of client devices

Microsoft software, such as Windows CE .NET and Windows XP, can be used to operate handheld computers, laptops, and PCs. (Windows CE .NET is the next version of Windows CE that's used for wireless communication.) Windows XP extensively uses XML to implement features such as remote assistance and Web publishing. On the other hand, Windows CE .NET supports XML 3.0, thereby enabling you to access Web services over mobile devices. Therefore, by using these software products, you can access Web services on client devices, such as laptops and handhelds. Web services can provide important data to these client devices so that the data is easily accessible.

Enhancements to user experience

.NET offers a good opportunity to enhance user experiences. In fact, this is the essential quality of the .NET initiative. Imagine the convenience to a customer who doesn't have to stop at the next ATM to transfer money from one bank account to another. Such user experiences are possible by using XML Web services. Examples of some existing XML Web services that enhance user experiences are the Microsoft Passport authentication service, and the Remote Assistance feature of Windows XP.

Solution providers can subscribe to the Microsoft Passport authentication service to enable Passport authentication on their Web sites. When you log on to a Passport-enabled Web site, your log-on information is stored on your computer as a cookie. When you browse to another Passport-enabled site, the cookie enables the other site to recognize you as an authenticated user and provide customized services. This mechanism is depicted in Figure 1-1.

The advantages of the Passport authentication service extend beyond just being able to use the same log-on information on more than one site. The user and the service provider can derive many advantages, including

- **Ease of deployment:** A solution provider subscribing to the Microsoft Passport authentication service doesn't have to deploy the infrastructure to host and maintain the authentication service. This saves deployment and operational costs.
- **Customized service:** The information provided by a user on one Web site can be accessed on another site. Consequently, solution providers can offer a complete package of services customized for specific users.

✦ **Better market coverage:** If a solution provider is associated with a well-known service, the market coverage of the solution provider is enhanced. For example, if you trust the Microsoft Passport authentication service, you can be confident when supplying sensitive information, such as a credit card number, to a Web site that uses this service.

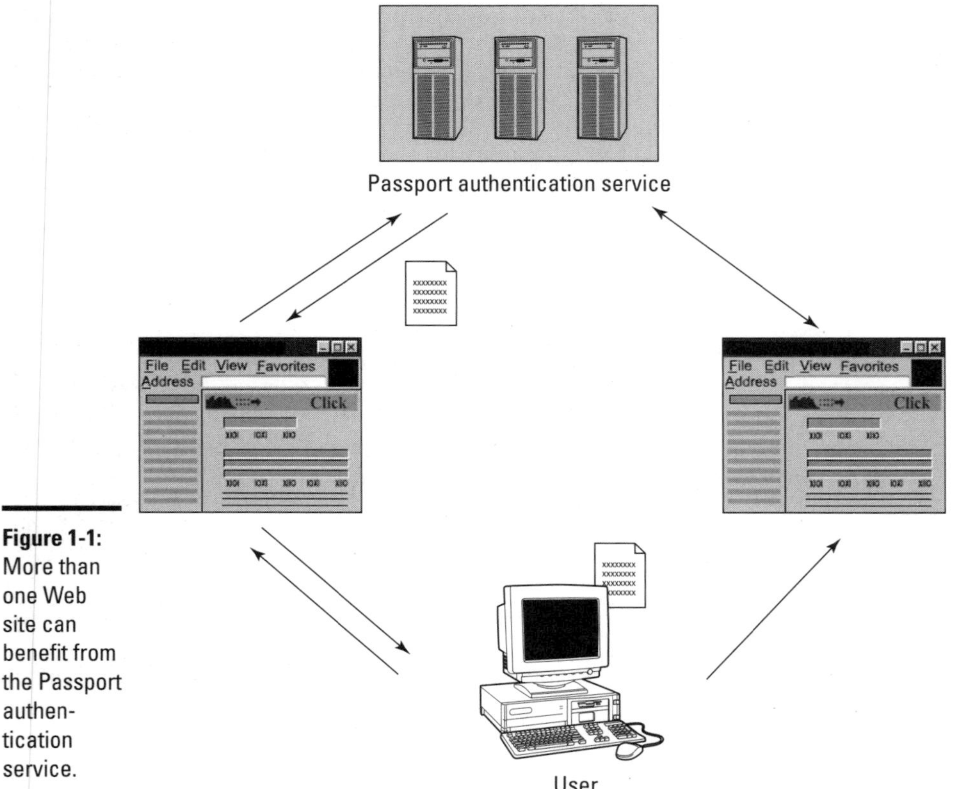

Figure 1-1: More than one Web site can benefit from the Passport authentication service.

Products in the .NET Suite

Microsoft developed a range of products and services for its .NET initiative. Ranging from operating systems to Enterprise servers and development platforms, Microsoft offers a complete suite to build and deploy applications for the .NET initiative. We cover these products briefly in the following sections.

.NET Enterprise servers

The .NET initiative, upon complete implementation, will require many processes to run all applications simultaneously and manage the flow of information between applications and services.

Microsoft developed .NET Enterprise servers as a set of servers to help you achieve high interoperability and availability. The .NET Enterprise servers are Windows.NET Server, Application Center 2000, BizTalk Server 2000, Commerce Server 2000, Content Management Server 2001, Exchange Server 2000, Host Integration Server 2000, Internet Security and Acceleration Server 2000, Mobile Information 2001 Server, SharePoint Portal Server 2001, and SQL Server 2000. In Figure 1-2, you can view each of these servers along with their roles in the .NET Enterprise environment.

Corporate Connectivity to Internet	B2B amd B2C	Business Communication	Content Management and Collaboration	Data and Data Management
ISA Server 2000	BizTalk Server 2000	Mobile Information 2001 Server	Content Management Server 2001	SQL Server 2000
	Commerce Server 2000	Exchange Server 2000	SharePoint Portal Server 2001	Host Integration Server 2000

Windows.NET Server | Application Center 2000

Operating Systems

Figure 1-2: Each .NET Enterprise server has a specific role.

We briefly describe each of these servers here.

Windows.NET Server

Windows.NET Server is the operating system for other .NET Enterprise servers. It has a native support for XML and SOAP (Simple Object Access Protocol). The server also integrates with the Microsoft Passport service so that users can use a single log-on ID for accessing all sites that subscribe to this service.

SOAP is an XML-based protocol that's used for exchanging information in a distributed setup. The protocol includes three parts that describe the message that's being transmitted and the rules to process the message.

Application Center 2000

Microsoft Application Center 2000 is a high-availability management and deployment tool for Web applications built on Microsoft Windows 2000. Application Center 2000 provides clustering and is designed for customers who need Web applications with high scalability and availability.

A *cluster* is a group of servers that works like a single unit. By implementing clustering, Application Center 2000 exposes a group of Web servers as a single server on the Internet. If one or more servers in the cluster fail, other servers can take the incoming traffic and prevent a site from going offline.

Application Center 2000 supports Network Load Balancing (NLB) and Component Load Balancing (CLB). NLB is the same as a cluster of Web servers. NLB enables Application Center 2000 to remove a server from a network when that server fails. CLB organizes and manages Web and COM+ applications by using a centralized management console.

BizTalk Server 2000

The advent of .NET has created a key business requirement for the integration of business processes running across different organizations. BizTalk Server 2000 enables you to accomplish exactly that. The server provides extensive support for XML and uses advanced technologies, such as Visio 2000, to describe business processes. BizTalk Server 2000 presents advanced capabilities to manage and exchange data in the XML format as well as access data in non-XML format.

Commerce Server 2000

Commerce Server 2000 is the Microsoft solution to the high customizability needs of e-commerce Web sites. Organizations are deploying Commerce Server 2000 to deliver personalized content to users. The strength of the software is in its ability to provide customized solutions to businesses.

Microsoft also provides two solution sites with Commerce Server 2000. These sites can be used to develop business-to-business (B2B) and business-to-commerce (B2C) Web sites. The coding of solution sites and other Web sites deployed on Commerce Server 2000 is done using Active Server Pages (ASPs). Therefore, Commerce Server 2000 provides a good opportunity to create Web applications in ASP.NET for deploying Commerce Server Web sites.

Content Management Server 2001

Content Management Server 2001 is used to manage content published on Web sites. The server includes sample Web sites and the customization code that you can use to create dynamic Web sites to deploy content.

These Web sites can include presentation templates that help you plan site design and layout. You can apply different presentation templates to quickly change the appearance of a site.

Content Management Server 2001 integrates with other .NET Enterprise Servers, such as Windows 2000 Advanced Server, Microsoft SQL Server 2000, and Microsoft Commerce Server 2000.

Exchange Server 2000

Exchange Server 2000 is used to manage networking and messaging infrastructure. The server offers built-in calendar services, contact and task management capabilities, and discussion groups. When an organization deploys Exchange Server 2000, users can access their e-mail messages, schedules, and contacts through any Web browser. This eliminates constraints to information availability.

Exchange Server 2000 also offers extensive development opportunities. These include unified support for XML that enables vendors to develop solutions for Exchange users. Users can employ these solutions to access important information on devices such as mobile phones and palmtops.

Host Integration Server 2000

Microsoft Host Integration Server 2000 can help you access data from legacy systems. Thus, data on systems such as AS/400, Unix, and DB2 can be made available for an enterprise solution. By using Host Integration Server 2000, you can create distributed applications that best utilize the information on host systems.

Internet Security and Acceleration Server 2000

Internet Security and Acceleration Server 2000 (ISA Server 2000) is used to manage corporate connectivity to the Internet. As the name suggests, ISA Server imparts security and accelerated speed during Internet access.

To enable security with ISA Server 2000, a system administrator can limit the Web sites accessible to corporate employees. The server has built-in security mechanisms to prevent unauthorized users from accessing a corporate network and breaching its security.

ISA Server 2000 also speeds up Internet access by caching Web pages that are visited frequently. Consequently, when a user requests for a cached Web page, the page is retrieved from the internal cache instead of the Web site. This enables organizations to save expenses of unnecessary connectivity to the Internet.

Mobile Information 2001 Server

Microsoft Mobile Information 2001 Server (MIS 2001) is a gateway for mobile users to access their corporate data and the intranet. MIS 2001 also includes Outline Mobile Access in its integrated package. This enables users to access information, such as e-mail messages, tasks, calendars, and contacts on mobile devices by using Microsoft Outlook.

SharePoint Portal Server 2001

SharePoint Portal Server 2001 helps you create Web portals for collating information from different sources into a central location. SharePoint Portal Server 2001 offers a number of features, such as version tracking, document publishing, and controlling role-based access to help you streamline document management.

Just like Visual SourceSafe 6.0 (VSS), SharePoint Portal Server 2001 records the history of a document to help you track changes and eliminate the possibility of a user changing another user's modifications. To edit a document, a user must first check out the document. This prevents other users from changing the document until the first user checks it in. Each time that a document is checked in, a new version number is assigned to the document and the previous version is archived.

SQL Server 2000

Microsoft SQL Server 2000 is a relational database management system (RDBMS) that provides improved turnaround time, lower transaction costs, and high availability. SQL Server 2000 provides a graphical user interface (GUI) and a development environment for creating data-driven applications.

SQL Server 2000 has built-in support for the XML format. You can import XML-format data to databases and export data from database tables to an XML format. XML processing capabilities make SQL Server 2000 an effective solution for providing data access in XML Web services.

.NET Framework

The .NET Framework is a platform for creating XML Web services. It provides the necessary classes, namespaces, and assemblies to create such applications. The .NET Framework consists of three components:

- **Common language runtime (CLR):** The common language runtime manages execution of code at runtime. The CLR ensures efficient memory and thread management and safety of the executing code. CLR is so named because it ensures interoperability between programming code that's written in different Visual Studio .NET applications. As a result, you can run an application coded in one language in another language. You can read more about cross-language interoperability in Book 1, Chapter 2.

- **Class library:** The .NET Framework includes the class library that has a comprehensive collection of object-oriented classes that you can use to develop Windows and Web applications.
- **ASP.NET:** ASP.NET is an important component of the .NET Framework. ASP.NET provides advanced capabilities, such as efficient database access and easy-to-use Application and Session state capabilities. ASP.NET applications can be created using any .NET language, such as Visual Basic .NET or Visual C# .NET (that's *C sharp*, not *C pound*)

By including ASP.NET in .NET Framework, Microsoft ensures that you can code in ASP.NET without using the Visual Studio .NET development platform. However, you'll find it easier to code ASP applications in Visual Studio .NET because Visual Studio .NET provides server controls that make it easy to code.

A simple way to shift from your existing ASP applications to ASP.NET is by changing the file extensions from `.asp` to `.aspx`. This ensures that your application runs in the .NET Framework environment. Subsequently, you can update the code incrementally to optimize your application for Visual Studio .NET.

See Book 1, Chapter 2 for the details on the components of the .NET Framework that we describe here.

The .NET Framework is essentially the backbone of all your endeavors in Visual Studio .NET although you may not directly use it in your journey through Visual Studio .NET. This framework provides key components that are used by Visual Studio .NET to achieve interoperability and tight integration between programming languages. For example, you use the classes of the .NET Framework to develop Visual Studio .NET applications.

Visual Studio .NET

Visual Studio .NET, the Microsoft platform for developing Web services and Windows applications, comprises a number of languages that share a common set of classes and a development environment. The platform consists of Visual Basic .NET, Visual C#, Visual FoxPro, and Visual C++ .NET.

Take a look at the bigger picture of the .NET initiative to help you see its components, Visual Studio .NET and the .NET Framework, in the right perspective. Figure 1-3 depicts the role of Visual Studio .NET in the .NET initiative.

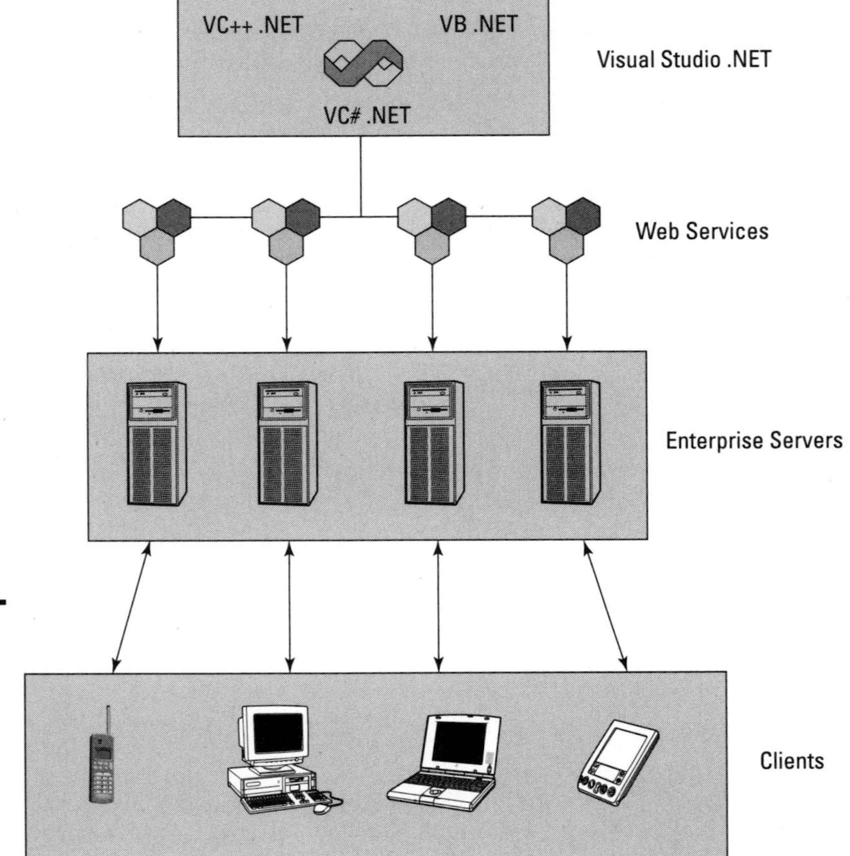

Figure 1-3: Visual Studio .NET is an important component of the .NET initiative.

Note these two immediate advantages of Visual Studio .NET. (For more on the advantages of Visual Studio .NET, turn to Book 1, Chapter 4.)

✦ **Common IDE across languages:** All Visual Studio .NET languages have the same IDE (Integrated Development Environment). Therefore, after you grasp the basics of working on one language, it's easy to switch to and share tools and applications across languages. This is a feature distinct from Visual Studio 6.0, in which Visual Basic and Visual InterDev have an IDE different from that of other languages. We discuss more on IDE in Book 2.

- **Easy ASP programming:** Visual Studio .NET also compliments ASP.NET programming in the .NET Framework. For example, when you use Visual Studio .NET to create ASP.NET Web applications, you can take advantage of tools such as WYSIWYG (what you see is what you get) editors for Web pages and code-aware editors for statement completion to develop your application. Visual Studio .NET also enables you to compile and debug your ASP.NET application when you create it. These features give you a welcome break from the tedious process of manually creating ASP Web pages by using a text editor, such as Notepad, and then deploying applications on IIS (Internet Information Services).

WYSIWYG editors enable you to know the output of your application as you design it. For example, if you use Microsoft FrontPage 2000, you'll know how your Web page will look as you create it.

Chapter 2: Key Components of the .NET Framework

In This Chapter

- **Using common language runtime**
- **Understanding class library**
- **Developing applications with ASP.NET**

In Chapter 1, Book 1, we introduce you to the .NET Framework, discussing the components of .NET Framework: common language runtime (CLR), class library, and ASP.NET. If you're curious to find out about the usefulness of these components for your Visual Studio .NET application, read this chapter for a detailed description of the .NET Framework components. Here we present how CLR enables you to interoperate applications, and we give you information on the constituents of class library and the applications that you can develop in ASP.NET.

Common Language Runtime

Runtime can be described as a reduced version of a program. A runtime enables you to execute the program but not develop it. For example, you can execute a Visual Basic 6.0 program by using the Visual Basic runtime called VBRun, but you can't develop applications by using this runtime. In Visual Studio 6.0, each programming language has a separate runtime. This complicates the process of achieving interoperability between applications because each application executes in a unique domain.

The development of Visual Studio .NET helped to overcome this problem. The introduction of CLR simplifies the task of providing cross-language interoperability and enhanced exception handling. CLR manages application execution and provides services to impart memory management, thread management, and so on.

In addition to imparting language interoperability, CLR simplifies the development of applications. In this section, you can learn about the functions of CLR at the time of design and execution of an application.

The CLR at design time

During design, the CLR automates routinely performed tasks, such as memory management. As a result, you can concentrate on the functionality that you need to build in your application instead of worrying about the state of variables and objects in your application. In the earlier versions of Visual Studio, references to objects had to be managed manually. For example, you needed to use the `AddReference` and `Release` methods, respectively, to add and remove references from objects. Incorrect implementation of these methods could result in the early release of an object or the accumulation of released objects in memory. These problems have been effectively solved in Visual Studio .NET by new mechanisms such as garbage collection. You can read about garbage collection in Book 1, Chapter 3.

The CLR also provides features, such as reflection, that simplify the development of COM-based applications. *Reflection* is a namespace that contains classes and interfaces to expose the functionality of COM objects. You can know the loaded types, methods, and fields of objects by using this namespace. We discuss namespaces later in this chapter in the section "Class Library."

The CLR at runtime

Code that targets the CLR is known as *managed code*. Managed code is written by using some specific classes and types, which we discuss later within this section. The runtime enables you to achieve application language interoperability for managed code. Language interoperability enables the code written in one language to access and interpret the code written in another language. If you write managed code, the CLR provides the following support:

- **Enhanced exception handling:** Exception handling for managed code is consistent across applications. Therefore, you can create an application in one language and debug it in another language. You may need to do this when you create controls in one language and include them in a project in another language. Find more information on exception handling in Book 1, Chapter 3.
- **Interoperable types:** In .NET Framework, types encapsulate data structures and perform input and output. In managed code, you can inherit implementation of one type from another or invoke methods that are defined in other types.

The CLR includes a common type system that defines a standard set of data types and specifies the rules for creating new data types. To write managed code, you need to use the data types provided by the common type system.

Although the code written using the data types of the common type system is targeted at the CLR, the code doesn't guarantee interoperability across applications. For instance, suppose you have two applications, one of which supports unsigned integers and one that doesn't. In such a case, the two applications aren't interoperable.

How, then, is application interoperability guaranteed? The common language specification, another subset of the CLR, guarantees interoperability. The common language specification includes only those common type system data types and language features that are compatible across all languages. Therefore, the common language specification is available across all applications. Figure 2-1 shows the relationship between the .NET Framework, the common type system, and the common language specification.

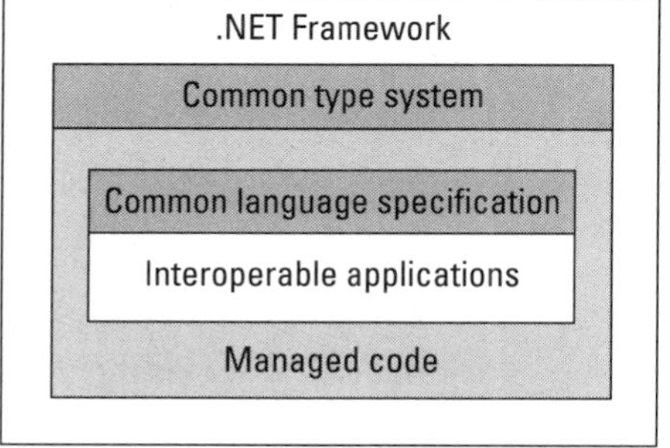

Figure 2-1: Relationship between managed code, the common type system, and the common language specification.

As a starting point, we begin with a concise stand-alone description of the common type system and the common language specification. These concepts will come in handy when you need to develop interoperable applications.

Common type system

Compilers of the .NET Framework use runtime services to define data types and make method calls. Therefore, to develop interoperable applications, you have to specify a set of rules for defining objects and data types. The common type system defines a framework for type safety and code execution and also provides an object-oriented model for programming.

Common language specification

Objects present a good opportunity to reuse code. If you need to use objects across applications, you need to ensure that the objects expose only the features that are common with other languages. The common language specification defines a set of such common features. The components that include only the features of common language specification (CLS) are known as *CLS-compliant components*.

You can easily write CLS-compliant code because most of the members of the .NET Framework library are CLS-compliant. For members that aren't CLS-compliant, an alternative is always available. For example, the `UInt32` type isn't CLS-compliant. However, a CLS-compliant type — `Int32` — for the `UInt32` type is available. As you write your code, you can look up documentation of the software to ensure that all types used in your application are CLS-compliant.

Class Library

A *class library* is an application programming interface (API) that you use to develop applications. An API provides you the ability to interact with the operating system or use specialized functions to encode your program. An example of an API or a class library is the Microsoft Foundation Classes (MFC), which are used in Visual C++ 6.0.

The .NET Framework includes a base class library, which includes classes, interfaces, and value types that provide access to system functionality. An important feature of the .NET Framework class library is that it provides a unified set of functions across different languages. The same class library can be used for development in Visual C++ as well as Visual Basic. This is an advantage for Visual Basic developers who earlier didn't have access to such class libraries. You can develop anything from simple command-line interface applications to complex mobile data access applications using the .NET Framework class library.

The class library provided by the .NET Framework is organized into namespaces, which are provided by assemblies. You need to understand what assemblies and namespaces are all about so that those `imports System.Console` or `using System.Console` statements that you may encounter in your first application don't look like ancient Greek to you (as they did to us!). Read through this section to understand namespaces and assemblies and some of the common classes of the `System` namespace.

Assemblies

An *assembly* provides information on the implementation of types. An assembly is a collection of types and resources that function in association to achieve the required functionality. Namespaces are also stored in assemblies. When you need to include a namespace in your application, you need to include the assembly file that contains the namespace.

All types, references, and versions are scoped within an assembly. For example, any type that you declare in an assembly doesn't hold good outside the assembly. Similarly, each type declared in an assembly has the same version as the assembly.

Namespaces

The .NET Framework class library is available as a collection of namespaces. Namespaces contain types, such as classes and enumerations, which are used in a program. When you create an application, you import one or more namespaces for the types that you need to use in a program. Also, your application is organized as a namespace so that your application can be identified programmatically and used in other programs. Another advantage of namespaces is that you can use multiple classes with the same name in an application as long as these classes exist in different namespaces.

To identify namespaces and types present in them, the .NET Framework separates the two with a dot (`.`). This also helps you build and understand the hierarchy of namespaces when you code a program. For example, the `System.Console` statement represents the `Console` class in the `System` namespace. Similarly, the `System.Collections.Queue` statement represents the `Queue` class in the `System.Collections` namespace.

Now it starts to make a bit more sense. Look at `using System.Console`. Here, you're adding a reference to the assembly that contains the `Console` class of the `System` namespace. Next, you can use the methods of the `Console` class in your program. The `Console` class is used to read and write characters from a console. The `using System.Console` statement is in the Visual C# syntax. The same syntax in Visual Basic is `imports System.Console`.

Console-based applications run from the command prompt.

Namespaces available with Visual Studio .NET begin with either the keyword `System` or `Microsoft`.

System namespace

The `System` namespace contains the fundamental types of the .NET Framework. When a data type of the .NET Framework is expected, you need to import the appropriate namespace into your program.

You need to include the `System` namespace in most of your programs.

Table 2-1 lists important classes of the `System` namespace along with their descriptions.

Table 2-1 Important Classes of the System Namespace

Class	*Description*
`System.Array`	This class provides methods for managing arrays. It is the base class for all arrays in the Common Language Runtime.
`System.Console`	This class provides methods for standard input, output, and error messages in console-based applications.
`System.Convert`	This class provides methods to convert base data types from one type to another. For example, you can convert from `Int32` type to `Char`.
`System.Math`	You have all the trigonometric, logarithmic, and arithmetic functions available in the `Math` class.
`System.Random`	The `Random` class generates random numbers that satisfy a statistical criterion.
`System.String`	The `String` class represents a string of characters. The string, after it's created, can't be modified. When you assign a new value to the string, a new instance of this class is returned.

In addition to classes, the `System` namespace provides a number of interfaces and structures for managing applications.

Microsoft namespace

The `Microsoft` namespace provides a collection of namespaces developed by Microsoft but which are not directly related to Visual Studio .NET. For example, the `Microsoft.Word` namespace represents the Microsoft Word class library. Although this class library isn't directly related to Visual Studio .NET, you can include a reference to this namespace and manipulate Microsoft Word documents by using the methods of this namespace.

ASP.NET

ASP.NET is the next version of Microsoft Active Server Pages (ASP). ASP.NET offers a new programming model to enable Web developers to create Web sites easily. It brings along a whole new approach to the world of ASP. The most important advantage of ASP.NET is that, unlike its earlier version, ASP.NET is object-oriented and enables you to create an application in any programming language. Another advantage is that your application is compiled in the .NET Framework environment.

Applications created in ASP.NET

You can create three types of applications in ASP.NET:

- **Web applications:** Web applications are used to create powerful HyperText Markup Language (HTML) pages. Web sites that you develop in ASP.NET fall in this category. These applications can be developed in any of the Visual Studio .NET languages. When you use Visual Studio .NET, you can use its visual interface to arrange controls on your form. You can also separate your programming code from the HTML code. For example, after you enclose it in <% and %> tags, you don't have to place the code specifying the click of a button on an HTML page. You can place the code in a separate file, just as you place the code for Windows Forms.
- **Web services:** Web services enable you to remotely access the functionality of a server. These applications don't directly interact with the user and therefore don't have a user interface. Web services are XML-based and are, consequently, platform-independent. These services can be accessed by a remote service running on any platform.
- **Server controls:** In certain situations, you may have pieces of code that are to be reused. For example, you may have a well-designed form that you need to implement on many Web pages. An easy way to do this is to create a server control that can be used like any other control on your Web page. You can create a server control in one language and use it in an ASP application that's being developed in another language.

All controls that you import in an ASP application are actually server controls.

Advantages of ASP.NET over ASP

ASP.NET offers the following advantages over ASP:

- **Compiled code:** In contrast to ASP 3.0, ASP.NET code is compiled. Therefore, unlike ASP 3.0 applications, ASP.NET applications run as compiled applications. This feature allows you to implement early binding or Just-in-Time (JIT) compilation. You can read more about JIT in Book 1, Chapter 3.
- **Efficient data access:** Data access is a very important feature of ASP. ASP.NET provides server controls, such as the DataGrid and DataList controls, for easy access of data from databases.
- **Optimized state management:** *State* is an attribute that's maintained over a period of time. For example, you may need to maintain user preferences until a user is logged on to your site. ASP.NET offers three types of states for Web applications: application, session, and user. Although state management was possible in ASP 3.0 as well, ASP.NET includes a new type of state management — view state management. In view state management, the state of a Web page, its attributes, and its content is cached so that this information can be retrieved from the cache for improving efficiency.

- **Improved caching:** *Caching* is a process in which data is retrieved from a database and stored in an intermediate object called a cache. When a user request is issued, data can be retrieved from the cache. This process saves unnecessary calls to the database, consequently improving response time as well as improving performance. ASP.NET includes a complete API to implement caching in your Web application.
- **Easy update to applications:** To update an application in ASP, you need to shut down the Web server or unload an application from memory. In ASP.NET, a Web server doesn't lock application files and the files can be updated even when a Web application is online. This is especially useful for applications that need to be updated frequently.
- **Multiple audience targeting:** In ASP.NET, the same page can provide specific services to a range of audiences. An application can detect the device accessing it and deliver content to the device accordingly. For example, a Web application might deliver text-only content to a mobile phone but rich-dynamic content to an Internet Explorer 6.0 Web browser.
- **Object-oriented programming:** For those of you who love object-oriented programming, you can freak out in ASP.NET because programming in ASP.NET is very efficient compared with programming in any other language.

Upgrading from ASP to ASP.NET

To upgrade to ASP.NET, you can either rewrite the code in Visual Studio .NET or simply change the extension of the file from `.asp` to `.aspx`. Each method has its own set of advantages and disadvantages, which we briefly describe here:

- **Create a new application in Visual Studio .NET:** When you create a new application from scratch, you may need to maintain two versions (one in ASP and one in ASP.NET) of your ASP code until the ASP.NET application is finalized. However, this method provides you an opportunity to enhance the functionality of your Web application and to reorganize your application interface. You can also take advantage of the new controls included in ASP.NET.
- **Upgrade the existing application by changing the file extension:** When you upgrade the existing application, your site remains functional, and you can add new ASP.NET code or enhance the existing functionality incrementally. This saves development effort. The development process tends to be long and unstructured, however, and you may end up spending more effort than you would creating the new application.

Chapter 3: Application Execution in the .NET Framework

In This Chapter

- **Optimized code execution**
- **Enhanced code debugging and monitoring**

If you've wondered how you can benefit from the new features of .NET Framework, you've landed at the right place. This chapter describes the benefits to your application when it runs in the .NET Framework. The chapter also starts you out on what it takes to configure your application to reap these benefits. The chapter ends with the debugging and performance monitoring capabilities of Visual Studio .NET.

Optimized Code Execution

In this section, you can learn how the .NET Framework manages your application internally and how some of the common problems in the earlier programming languages are automatically taken care of. We also examine the mechanism of side-by-side execution, a mechanism in which you can simultaneously run multiple versions of an application.

When your application runs in the .NET Framework, the application benefits from the ability of the framework to control the execution of your code. The framework ensures that the variables and objects that you use in your application are automatically removed from memory when no longer required.

To optimize the execution of code, the .NET Framework implements just-in-time (JIT) compilation and garbage collection. JIT compilation ensures that your application is fast and doesn't consume unnecessary memory. The garbage collector ensures that the programming objects don't stay in memory after their utility is over. At the same time, it ensures that an object in use isn't accidentally removed from memory.

Although JIT compilation and garbage collection happen automatically, you can write code better if you know the implementation of these concepts. Hang with us to read how these concepts are implemented.

JIT compilation

.NET applications developed using managed code can be run on multiple platforms. Managed code is written by using the types provided by the common type system of the .NET Framework. Read more about managed code in Book 1, Chapter 2. Applications that run on multiple platforms need to follow a distinct mechanism by which they can run according to the operating system. The applications don't run themselves; the compiler compiles the applications into a usable form. Follow along as we describe the path from the time that your application is compiled and finally runs in the .NET Framework:

1. **After you design your application and compile it, the compiler changes the managed code into a set of CPU-independent instructions known as Microsoft Intermediate Language (MSIL).**

   The MSIL code includes instructions for managing calls to methods on objects as well as other detailed instructions regarding assembly information and so on.

2. **When your application is ready to run on a platform, the MSIL code is compiled into a code that the operating system can interpret. Subsequently, the code is run.**

   This is akin to an interpreter identifying the language that you understand and conveying to you information in that language.

   The MSIL code is converted to *native code*, code that the operating system can interpret, just before the application executes. Otherwise, the code is stored in MSIL format.

3. **In the last step of this process, the JIT compiler compiles the MSIL code into a CPU-specific code.**

   The resultant code is native code and can run on the intended platform.

In Figure 3-1, see an illustration of a chain of compilation steps leading to the role of the JIT compiler.

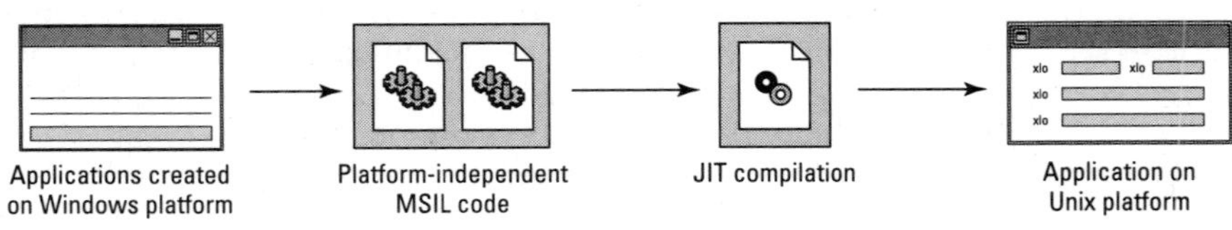

Figure 3-1: Your code travels a long way before it's run.

The function of the JIT compiler is more than merely compiling the MSIL code into a usable form. You may (or may not) realize that there's no fun in compiling all the code before execution when some of it may not be required at all. For example, you might develop a game in which the fifth level is very different from the fourth level. What's the point compiling code for the fifth level and loading it into memory when the user might not even reach that level? This is exactly what the JIT compiler avoids.

The JIT compiler compiles code on demand. When code is required during execution, the JIT compiler compiles it into native code and stores it in memory. The stored code can be invoked in all future calls. In this way, the JIT compiler ensures that your program doesn't tax the system resources and runs as efficiently as possible.

Garbage collection

In the .NET Framework, the garbage collector performs the tasks of a cleaner. The garbage collector ensures that objects no longer required by your program are automatically cleared from the memory. To understand the mechanism by which the garbage collector decides which objects need to be removed from the memory, you need to know how memory is allocated when a managed application runs.

When you run an application, the runtime creates an address space in which your application needs to be run. As new objects are created in the application, the runtime fills up continuous memory locations in the address space. This leads to the formation of a heap of objects that are in use. This heap is known as a *managed heap*.

When the address space allotted to your application is completely occupied, no more objects can be created unless some space is created. The garbage collector now comes into picture. The garbage collector scans the address space and clears the memory of objects that are no longer required by the application.

The garbage collector removes objects not required by your program *only when* the managed heap is full. After the heap is scanned and the unnecessary objects cleared, it again goes dormant. The intermittent role of garbage collector ensures that the performance overhead is reduced to a minimum.

To ensure that the object about to be cleared from memory is no longer in use by the application, garbage collector follows a simple mechanism. Every application has roots that point to the objects in a managed heap that they reference. The JIT compiler maintains a list of roots in use by an application. This list is available to the garbage collector. The garbage collector uses roots to try and reach objects in the managed heap from the application. Objects that aren't reachable by the roots are not in use by the program. These objects are cleared, and the memory is released.

Figure 3-2 shows the chain of events that lead to the removal of unused objects by the garbage collector when the managed heap is completely occupied.

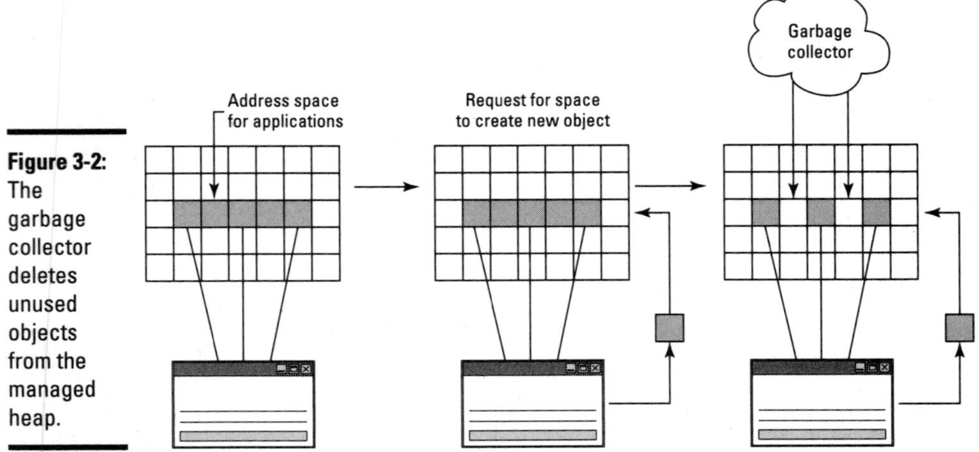

Figure 3-2: The garbage collector deletes unused objects from the managed heap.

If you need to perform some cleanup before removing an object, you might want to close down some network or Web server connections before an object is released. To enable you to do so, the .NET Framework offers the `Close`, `Dispose`, or `Finalize` events depending on the language that you use for writing code. These events are fired when the garbage collector is about to remove an object from the managed heap. Thus, you can write the code for cleanup in the methods for these events.

Side-by-side execution

Side-by-side execution enables you to run multiple versions of the same assembly simultaneously. Think of this as running two versions of Visual Studio, Visual Studio 6.0, and Visual Studio .NET on one computer. Such a capability did not exist in the earlier versions of Visual Studio. However, that's possible now.

If your code is optimized for side-by-side execution, you don't have to worry about the backward compatibility of your application because the assembly required to run the previous version of the software will always be available.

You need to remember a number of aspects when you code for supporting multiple versions. We examine these aspects when we deal with the various programming languages. Refer to the respective minibook for the programming language in which you want to explore this feature. (That is, if you're interested in reading more about this feature and Visual C++, head to Book 4.)

Side-by-side execution is possible because the version of the assembly is stored within the assembly itself. When your application executes, by default it searches for the version of the assembly that was used to create the application. It's only when the same version isn't found that the application searches for another version that can run the code.

Enhanced Code Debugging and Monitoring

All Visual Studio .NET languages use the same debugger. Consequently, you can debug Visual Basic .NET code in Visual C# and vice versa. In addition, you can attach a debugger to an application created in multiple languages and debug it. These are just some debugging options. In Visual Studio .NET, you not only debug your applications but also monitor and optimize them. In this section, we briefly examine the debugging and monitoring options in Visual Studio .NET. To provide some background information, though, we first look at the debugging classes in the .NET Framework.

Classes for debugging in Visual Studio .NET

The debugging classes of the .NET Framework are used for debugging Visual Studio .NET applications. All these classes are stored in the `System.Diagnostics` namespace. Apart from the usual debugging options carried forward from Visual Studio 6.0, the `System.Diagnostics` namespace provides classes that allow you to write to event logs and monitor system performance. Some of the important classes of the `System.Diagnostics` namespace are

- **`Debug`:** The `Debug` class includes methods for debugging applications. For example, the `Assert` method of this class checks for a condition and displays a message if the condition is `FALSE`.
- **`Debugger`:** The `Debugger` class allows you to communicate with the debugger and check its state. For example, the `IsAttached` method of the `Debugger` class checks whether a debugger is attached to the application.

- `EventLog`: The `EventLog` class allows you to access the event logs in Windows 2000. You can read and write events to the log or respond to events generated in the log by another application.
- `PerformanceCounter`: *Performance counters* are graphs that indicate the performance of an application. These counters are available on Windows server systems. You can use the `PerformanceCounter` class to read application performance-related data from performance counters and write data to customized performance counters.
- `Process`: Applications have processes associated with them when they run. For example, Microsoft Word has the `Winword.exe` process associated with it. By using the methods of the `Process` class, you can manage processes on your computer or another computer.
- `Trace`: The `Trace` class enables you to trace the execution of your code. When you trace your code, you can prevent errors when your application runs. To trace your code, you test for the success of an operation by using an assertion statement. If the operation requested by the assertion statement fails, the statement throws an exception. The exception indicates that the operation didn't yield the required output. You can handle the exception with another chunk of code to prevent unexpected termination of your program. For example, you can write the code to open a file as an assertion. If the requested file doesn't exist, your program throws an exception. You can handle this exception and inform the user that the requested file doesn't exist.

Methods of debugging in Visual Studio .NET

Debugging in Visual Studio .NET isn't restricted to debugging the application that you're developing; it offers much more than that. For instance, if you know that an application on another computer isn't running correctly, you can debug it from your computer remotely.

Some of the debugging options available in Visual Studio .NET are

- **Debugging across languages:** If you have an application that's created using two applications, such as Visual Basic .NET and Visual C#, you can debug the code of both applications in any one of the languages. As a result, you don't have to split the application and debug it in different languages.
- **Debugging a running process:** You can attach a debugger to a running process and debug it. The process that you need to debug may not be created on the .NET development platform. For example, as shown in Figure 3-3, the Visual Studio .NET platform lists all processes that are running on your computer. You can select a process and debug it.

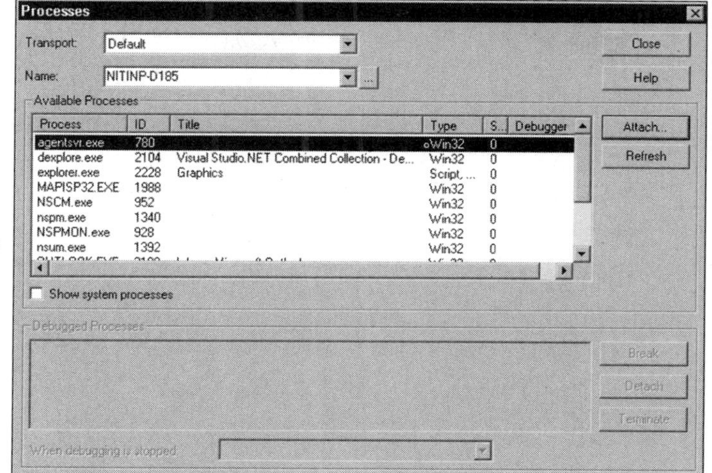

Figure 3-3: Use the Processes dialog box to select any process and debug it.

✦ **Debugging ASP.NET Web applications:** You can debug ASP.NET Web applications almost as easily as you debug Windows applications. One difference, however, is that if you want to debug ASP.NET Web applications on a remote server, you need to be a member of the Debugging Users group on the remote server.

Chapter 4: Exploring Visual Studio .NET

In This Chapter

- **Programming languages in Visual Studio .NET**
- **Applications commonly developed in Visual Studio .NET**

Visual Studio .NET bundles several good languages into one suite. In this chapter, we drill into the unique features and advantages of these languages. In addition, we introduce you to the applications developed in these languages.

After reading this chapter, you can jump into the world of Visual Studio .NET without fear. This chapter will help you gain knowledge on Visual Studio .NET so that you can select a language of your choice and develop an application suitable for your requirements.

Programming Languages in Visual Studio .NET

Visual Studio .NET is designed to eliminate the lapses and discrepancies of the earlier versions of Visual Studio languages. For example, Visual C++ 6.0 was the epitome of an object-oriented programming language. But in the Visual Studio .NET suite, if your friend can do object-oriented programming in Visual C++, so can you, in Visual Basic. In addition, you can use Visual C#, which incorporates the best of Visual C++ and Visual Basic to create fancy applications. And to top it all, you can create an application by using a multiplex of applications — a custom control created in Visual Basic that's used in Visual C#.

Visual Studio .NET offers many opportunities. Read on as we identify the different languages in Visual Studio .NET. We begin with the new entrant — Visual C#.

Visual C#: The new entrant

Visual C#, pronounced *Visual C Sharp*, is a new object-oriented programming language in the .NET suite. Visual C# includes the best of all programming languages. Languages such as Visual C++ enable you to create high-end applications that communicate with the underlying operating system using low-level system calls. These applications are very useful and effective but require a lot of time and effort for development. In contrast, Visual Basic applications can be developed quickly but they aren't as functional and powerful as Visual C++ .NET applications.

The search for an easy, productive, and very powerful programming language led to the birth of Visual C#. Visual C# incorporates the best features of Visual C++ and Visual Basic. Visual C# enables you to write *unmanaged* code, which is code that doesn't target the common language runtime (CLR). The code can bypass the .NET Framework application programming interface (API) and make direct calls to the operating system. This makes it as powerful as Visual C++. At the same time, Visual C# has the same IDE (Integrated Development Environment) and uses the same class libraries as Visual Basic .NET. Therefore, you can develop Windows applications or Web forms in Visual C# as easily as in Visual Basic .NET. In fact, the IDE is common across all Visual Studio .NET languages. The common IDE of Visual C#, Visual Basic .NET, and Visual C++ .NET is shown in Figure 4-1.

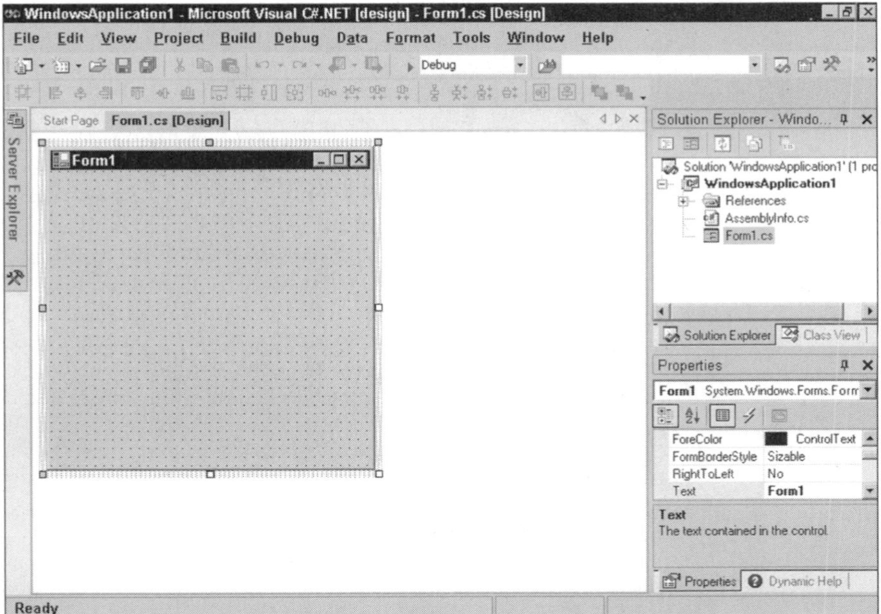

Figure 4-1: Visual Studio IDE — the common IDE for all .NET languages.

Some of the features of Visual C# are that it

- **Uses the .NET Framework Library:** Visual C# developers need to use the class library provided by the .NET Framework for creating C# applications. Therefore, you can write managed code targeted at the CLR. This enables your application to derive the benefits of both CLR and the .NET Framework.
- **Uses Web standards:** Visual C# provides a built-in support for Internet standards, such as HyperText Markup Language (HTML), extensible Markup Language (XML), and SOAP (Simple Object Access Protocol). You can convert Windows applications created in Visual C# to Web applications. In addition, you can start Visual C# programs from the Internet and access them on any platform through the HyperText Transfer Protocol (HTTP) protocol.
- **Eliminates common programming errors:** Visual C# has built-in support to prevent common programming errors. For example, pointers were a major cause for instability of programs in Visual C++. Pointers were a problem for developers who had to constantly keep track of when to use pointers (`->`), scope resolution (`::`), or dot (`.`). C# provides a solution to this problem by using a dot (`.`) for all referencing members, classes, or namespaces.

  If you're porting a program from Visual C++ to Visual C#, you can still use pointers within a specially marked chunk of code.

- **Is object-oriented:** All types in the Visual C# language are objects. Primitive data types such as `Int` are also treated like objects in Visual C#. You can combine these objects into namespaces and access them programmatically.
- **Helps develop applications quickly:** Visual C# has an intuitive user interface that allows you to develop applications quickly. You can use code wizards to add classes, methods, and properties to your application. The code generated by these wizards blends with the existing classes easily. In addition, common features such as statement completion enable you to complete code statements easily and prevent common errors.
- **Manages system resources efficiently:** Visual C# provides built-in mechanisms to optimize the utilization of system resources. These mechanisms have been derived from the .NET Framework. For example, the garbage collector ensures that memory is utilized optimally. In addition, Visual C# eliminates the need for variable initialization because it initializes variables automatically.
- **Provides built-in support for versioning:** Visual C# provides built-in support for versioning, thus minimizing the chances of errors when software components are updated. For example, when you update software, you need to override functions explicitly. This ensures that a function that must be used in the updated components isn't accidentally overridden.

- **Provides compatibility with Windows APIs:** Visual C# supports all APIs that are commonly used on the Windows platform. For example, C APIs are integrated with Visual C#.
- **Is simple and stable:** This important feature of C# is worth a mention. C# is simple, efficient, and stable. C# was developed to provide a stable and productive programming language. These features of C# make it the optimal language for development of Web applications and COM programs.
- **Supports console-based programming:** Programming in C# is primarily done in Visual Studio .NET. However, you can also use a text editor and create your own programs from scratch. To compile these programs, Visual Studio .NET provides the console-based compiler `CSC.EXE`.

A *console-based compiler* compiles applications from the command prompt.

Visual Basic .NET: A new experience

Ever since Visual Basic was developed 10 years ago, it's been a favorite of amateur programmers and enterprise developers. Beginning with Visual Basic 1.0 to Visual Basic .NET (7.0), the development cycle of Visual Basic has involved a number of versions but all of them were simple and resulted in high productivity. Visual Basic .NET was developed after radical changes in Visual Basic 6.0 but retained the advantages of Visual Basic 6.0.

If you've been using Visual Basic 6.0 for programming, you have a lot to learn in Visual Basic .NET. As we guide you through your efforts, you'll soon realize that it's worth the effort. Visual Basic .NET provides a development environment that is unified with other .NET languages and is also object-oriented. In addition, you can create Web applications and XML Web services in Visual Basic .NET. You'll also find it easier to interoperate Visual Basic .NET applications with the applications in the other languages of the .NET suite.

In this section, we introduce you to Visual Basic .NET and its advantages.

Some important changes have been incorporated in Visual Basic to develop Visual Basic .NET. Some of these features of Visual Basic .NET are that it

- **Is object-oriented:** Visual Basic .NET is object-oriented. All managed types in Visual Basic are derived from the `System.Object` class. As your requirements dictate, you can choose to use object-oriented features or the seemingly nonobject-oriented model of Visual Basic .NET for programming.
- **Supports server-side programming:** Visual Basic .NET has simplified server-side programming. Server Explorer, which is included in the Visual Studio IDE, makes it easy to develop server-side components and Web applications.

- **Supports inheritance:** A direct implication of object-oriented features of Visual Basic 6.0 is the support for inheritance. You can now create a form and inherit from it to create another one that adds to its functionality.
- **Supports overloading:** Visual Basic .NET supports operator and function overloading. You can create more than one `Sub` or function with the same name but different parameters. This method is beneficial when you want to apply the same programming logic for different data types.
- **Doesn't support control arrays:** Visual Basic .NET doesn't support control arrays because the architecture of the .NET Framework doesn't support control arrays. However, you can achieve the functionality of control arrays by using delegated events, which we discuss more in Book 5, Chapter 1.
- **Offers an integrated development environment:** The development environment of Visual Basic .NET is integrated with that of other .NET languages, Visual C#, and Visual C++ .NET. This has proved advantageous for all Visual Studio .NET programming languages. For example, a developer using Visual C# will find it easy to switch to Visual Basic .NET and vice versa.
- **Integrates with the CLR:** Visual Basic .NET integrates with the .NET Framework and generates code that's targeted at the CLR. The classes and data types used in Visual Basic .NET are from the .NET Framework. Therefore, Visual Basic .NET applications can achieve interoperability with other Visual Studio .NET applications that also derive from the .NET Framework class library.
- **Supports console-based programming:** Just as in Visual C#, you can do console-based programming in Visual Basic .NET. Visual Basic .NET provides the VBC.EXE compiler to compile console-based applications.
- **Provides advanced controls:** Visual Basic .NET provides advanced controls for high-level programming. For example, the `FileSystemWatcher` control monitors a directory for the presence of a file or a type of files. When the expected type of file is added to the directory, an event is fired and the corresponding code is executed.

Upgrading from Visual Basic to Visual Basic .NET

Visual Basic .NET offers an upgrade wizard to upgrade Visual Basic 6.0 applications to Visual Basic .NET. This wizard also creates an upgrade report that includes an outline of the tasks to be performed manually to complete the process of upgrade. To run the wizard, open your Visual Basic 6.0 application in Visual Studio .NET. The wizard is automatically launched, as shown in Figure 4-2. Find out how to use this wizard in Book 3, Chapter 1.

Figure 4-2: The Visual Basic Upgrade Wizard.

If you don't want to upgrade your program, you can create a new one by using the best features of Visual Basic .NET and Visual Basic 6.0. Visual Basic .NET provides a compatibility library that enables Visual Basic .NET applications to communicate with Visual Basic 6.0 applications. For example, Visual Basic .NET doesn't offer the `DriveListBox` control. However, this control can be added from the compatibility library and used in a Visual Basic .NET program.

Visual C++ .NET: More powerful than ever

Visual C++ .NET is a remarkable update of Visual C++ 6.0. The new language offers greater capabilities for developing high-end enterprise applications. In Visual Studio .NET, Visual C++ .NET differs slightly from other languages. This is because Visual C++ .NET allows you to program without using the .NET Framework. Thus, Visual C++ .NET applications can be created in the native Windows model. Such a feature doesn't exist in other Visual Studio .NET languages; it's been retained in Visual C++ because of the high flexibility that it offers.

In addition to new features included in Visual C++, Microsoft enhanced the existing functionality of Visual C++ and created managed extensions that enable you to write managed code. *Managed code*, as we discuss in Book 1, Chapter 2, is code that uses the .NET Framework class library and is targeted at the CLR.

This section lists the features and advantages of Visual C++ .NET. Here we also provide a brief overview of the migration of code from Visual C++ 6.0 to Visual C++ .NET.

Managed applications can interoperate with applications in other languages of the .NET Framework. Managed applications are created by using managed extensions for C++. However, these benefits are also available for unmanaged applications in Visual C++ because these applications can access the classes of the .NET Framework. A conceptual model that shows how unmanaged and managed applications are related is shown in Figure 4-3.

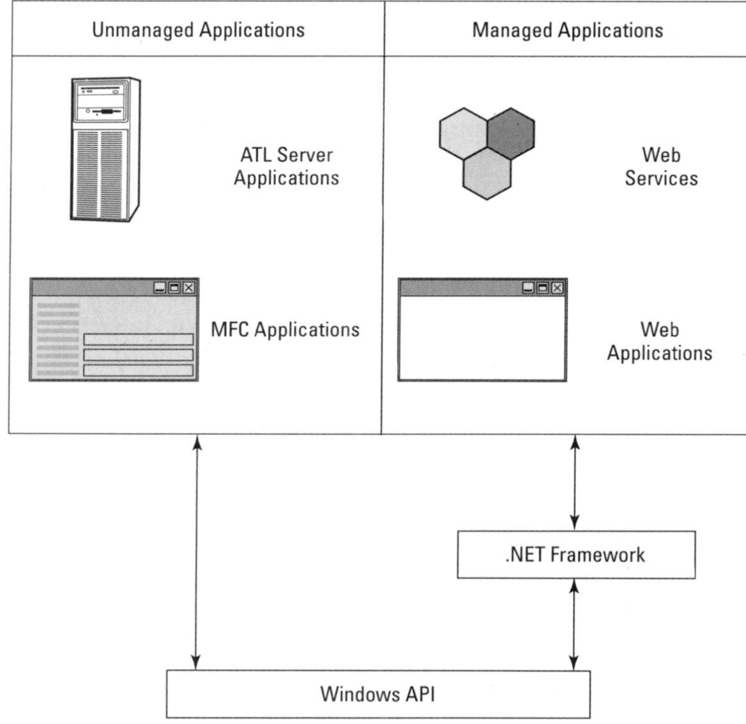

Figure 4-3: Unmanaged and managed applications in Visual C++ .NET.

Unmanaged applications

Visual C++ .NET includes many enhancements to Visual C++ 6.0. The Active Template Library (ATL) has been enhanced in the new ATL Server. The enhancements to ATL Server are that it

✦ **Supports thread pooling:** IIS can run only a limited number of threads for an Internet application. ATL Server runs in IIS (Internet Information Services) and has its own internal set of threads. Therefore, the number of threads available to run an application increases. This substantially improves application performance.

- **Saves session state:** ATL Server automatically saves session states in memory between client calls. You can write code to save this session state on a database or at another convenient location.
- **Supports server-to-server applications:** ATL Server includes an HTTP client that allows you to invoke XML Web services on other servers.
- **Provides strong monitoring features:** ATL Server enables you to build mail services that can send an e-mail alert for error notification. You can also create performance counters that can be installed in the Windows 2000 Performance Monitor service.
- **Is customizable:** The source code for ATL Server is included in the software. Therefore, you can customize the code to your advantage.

In addition to ATL Server, Microsoft Foundation Classes (MFC) is also updated. These updates enable you to access the latest Windows platform enhancements and ensure that the MFC-generated code is faster and smaller in size.

Managed extensions in C++

Managed extensions in C++ help you write applications for the .NET Framework. When you write managed code, you use the classes of the .NET Framework, which are available across all Visual Studio .NET languages. Therefore, your application can interoperate with applications in other languages of Visual Studio .NET.

In a Visual C++ .NET application, managed and unmanaged code can exist in a single application. Therefore, you can have the benefits of both worlds. You can decide which code is best placed in the .NET Framework and which code is best executed outside the framework.

Check out Book 4 to read more about managed extensions in C++.

Upgrading from Visual C++ 6.0 to Visual C++ .NET

Both managed and unmanaged code can coexist within an application. Therefore, you can upgrade your application incrementally. Upgrading is not a major concern because you can access .NET Framework classes from unmanaged code also.

You have two options when you upgrade Visual C++ applications. You can continue using the same application and create new wrapper functions to interoperate your application with other applications of the .NET Framework. Alternatively, you can migrate each component to .NET one by one. In the latter case, your application continues to run in the new environment while the application is being upgraded.

Which one should I choose?

If you're new to all programming languages in Visual Studio, or if you're equally comfortable (or uncomfortable) with all Visual Studio languages, then you're an exception! You might as well skip to the next section because the language that you select is only constrained by the application requirements. For the rest of you, the choice is simple.

If you're familiar with Visual Basic, you'll either select Visual Basic .NET or Visual C#. In most cases, Visual Basic .NET should meet your requirements. Therefore, go ahead and hone your technical skills in Visual Basic .NET. You can also begin with Visual C# if you're good at object-oriented programming and need to develop powerful applications involving low-level system programming.

If you're familiar with Visual C++, you'll certainly want to explore Visual C++ .NET. But you should first explore Visual C#: It's equally powerful and simplifies application development. You can switch to Visual C# for some of the conventional applications that you develop in Visual C++ 6.0. You'll probably end up using a combination of Visual C# and Visual C++ .NET, depending upon your application requirements.

Visual C# has the same interface and programming logic as those of Visual Basic .NET and Visual C++ .NET. Therefore, it shouldn't pose a problem for you to shift to Visual C#.

Applications Commonly Developed in Visual Studio .NET

Visual Studio .NET can be used to develop a wide range of applications ranging from console applications to Web services. We briefly discuss these applications in Book 1, Chapter 1, but here we get into the nitty-gritty.

In this section, we describe the following types of applications:

- Console applications
- Windows applications
- ASP.NET Web applications
- Web services

A number of other applications, such as the Windows Control library and Web Control library, are also created in Visual Studio .NET. However, these applications usually support one of the main applications that we name in the preceding list. We discuss each additional application in the corresponding book for the language used to create them. For example, to create a custom control in ASP.NET, you can refer to Book 6, Chapter 4. To create an ATL (Active Template Library) Server application, refer to Book 4, Chapter 5.

Console applications

Console applications run on console. For example, any application that you invoke from the command prompt is a console-based application. These applications lack a graphical user interface and run as a single executable file. The output of a console application is shown in Figure 4-4.

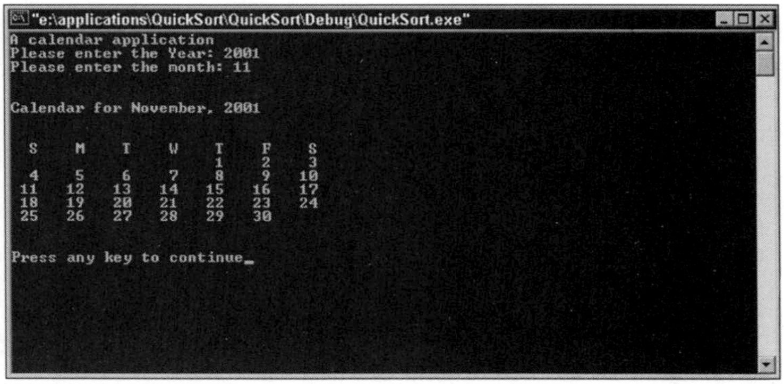

Figure 4-4: A console-based application runs from the command prompt.

Visual Studio .NET includes a Console Application project template that creates a class file and adds necessary system references — for example, references to the `System.Console`, `System.Data`, and `System.XML` namespaces.

Windows applications

Windows applications usually execute on a stand-alone computer. These applications are often self-contained and depend on the processing power of the computer running them. Examples of Windows applications are common word processing software and computer games. A sample Windows application is shown in Figure 4-5.

Visual Studio .NET includes Windows Forms. Windows Forms provide an object-oriented framework that you use to create Windows applications. You generally add Windows Forms controls on Windows Forms and create your application.

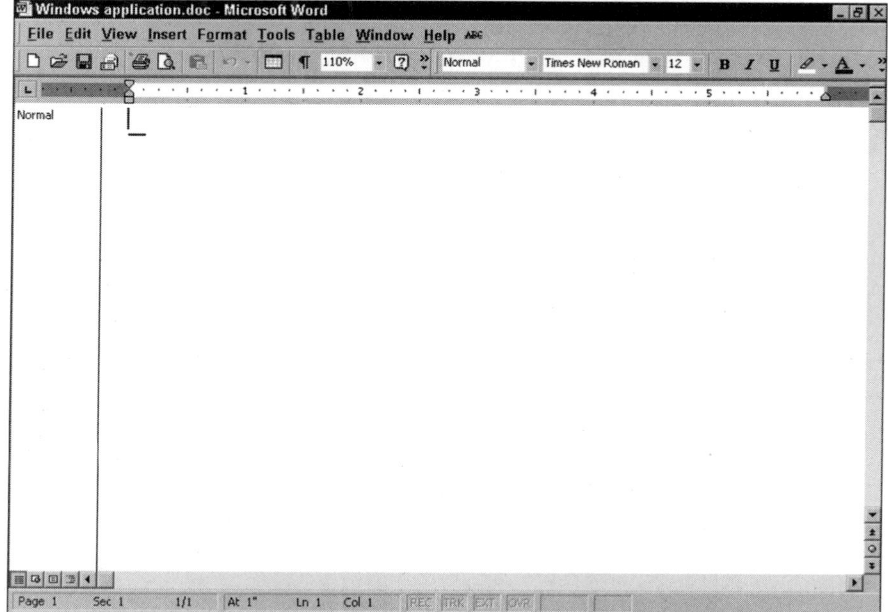

Figure 4-5: A Windows application runs on a stand-alone computer.

You can create applications by using Windows Forms in any Visual Studio .NET programming language. Each language has the same Windows Application template.

Web applications

Web applications are deployed on the Internet and accessed by using a Web browser. Web services provide the advantage of zero distribution costs because the user needs only a browser to access the application. In addition, an application, after it's upgraded, is instantly available to all users. The Web application is developed in Visual Studio .NET and deployed on the Web server, after which it is accessed by a Web browser, such as Internet Explorer. The sample output of a Web application, as seen in a Web browser, is shown in Figure 4-6.

Visual Studio .NET provides the ASP.NET Web Application project template to create a Web application. The ASP.NET Web Application project provides Web forms used to create the visual interface of the application and write the code for processing user interactions. Web Forms also allow you to separate the business logic code from the HTML code used to draw a page for a user.

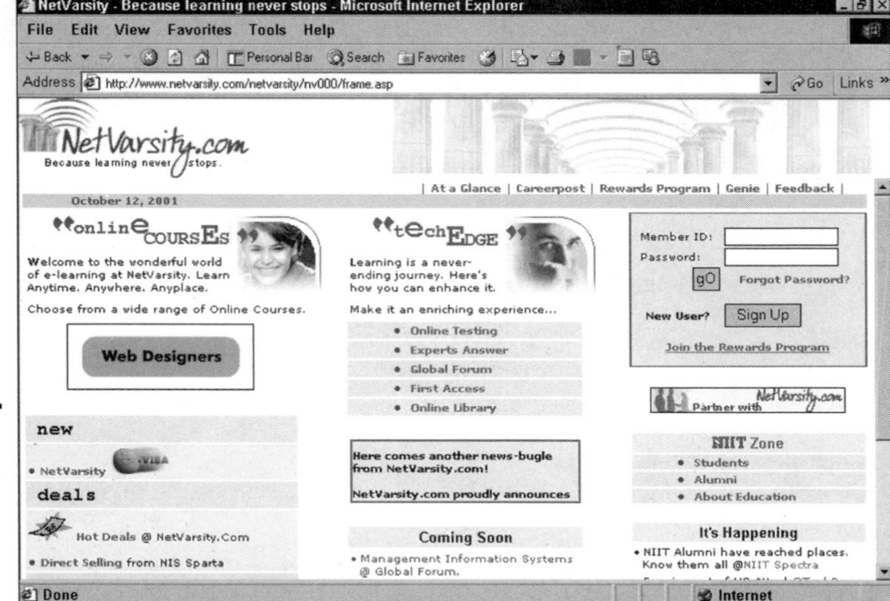

Figure 4-6: A Web application is accessed over the Internet.

Web services

Web services, which are used to exchange data between applications by using XML, are the most talked-about application of Visual Studio .NET.

Web services don't have a user interface. Visual Studio .NET provides the ASP.NET Web Service template to create Web services. Web services can use all the advantages of the .NET Framework. An example of a Web service is the Microsoft Passport authentication service. This service allows you to use Passport authentication for validating users who visit your Web site. For more about Web services, refer to Book 7.

Chapter 5: Application Development Cycle in Visual Studio .NET

In This Chapter

- Planning by defining your needs
- Designing an application
- Developing a prototype
- Testing and debugging your application

When you realize that your business needs aren't being met by your current application, you realize that you must develop a new one. You visualize and refine this need specifically in terms of your requirements, which are further characterized in the form of application design. The design forms the basis for developing the application. Finally, you test and implement your application. This progression is the lifecycle of application development.

In this chapter, we describe a software development cycle in detail, which is divided into four phases: planning, designing, developing, and testing and debugging. As we move through each of these stages, we describe tasks that are pertinent for a developer so that you'll understand the role of Visual Studio .NET in each stage.

Planning Your Application

The first step of any development cycle is the planning stage. Here you identify your application need(s). During this stage, you pin down the rationale behind developing an application and the end objective to be achieved.

After you define the need for an application, you must estimate the time required for completing the project. Strive to determine a realistic time frame for a project to ensure that your application isn't outdated by the time it sees the light of day.

To determine a realistic timeframe, you should use a number of parameters, such as the time taken by a similar application that may have been developed in the past and the skill set of the developers who would venture into creating the application.

Next, you define the features and functions of your software product. Remember to keep flexible enough to possibly alter the scope of your product functionality to roll it out within the desired time frame. For example, suppose you need to develop an appraisal application for the assessment of employees in your organization, and this form has a datasheet. Although you may want to automatically include the name of an employee's supervisor in that datasheet, you may not be able to accomplish this addition without jeopardizing the application's timetable.

Next, you define the roles and responsibilities for all members of the team working on the project. For example, the Project Manager could be responsible for coordination between the development and support teams involved in the project. Or you may be the one responsible for training the development team on the .NET Framework.

After you define these roles and responsibilities comes the most important step in planning. You need to choose the development language for your application. The choice of a language depends on a number of factors, including these two important ones:

✦ **Development time:** The time required to develop an application depends upon the language that you select. For example, developing simple client applications in Visual Basic .NET is less time-consuming compared to developing similar applications in Visual C++ .NET.

✦ **Skills available:** Before you begin developing software, you need to assess the skill set available for programming languages. To develop software in Visual C++ .NET, we recommend that you employ experts in this language. Developers proficient in Visual Basic .NET may experience a few hiccups when taking up such a project.

These factors present an inherent problem. Seldom are all developers conversant in the same programming language. When you use Visual Studio .NET, you don't have to use one programming language; different development teams can develop components of the application on different platforms. These components are subsequently integrated to obtain the all-in-one final product. This scales down the development time because many developers can simultaneously help create the application.

After you choose the requirements for the project, it's time to design the product.

Designing Your Application

The second step of the application development cycle is the design phase. This is the time for brainstorming and evaluating the pros and cons for each feature in your application. An effective design ensures that you're able to code efficiently according to application requirements in the development stage. Such a design also ensures high productivity by leaving no scope for repeat work that may arise because of errors. To create a competent design:

1. **Finalize your requirements:** Furnish and finalize all requirements early in the design stage of the development cycle. Begin by organizing a brainstorming session to examine all possible requirements. Next, consult a group of experts to finalize the requirements. Finally, based on the input from your experts, an architect creates the logical design of the software, and you, the developer, create the physical design to implement the logic.
2. **Create a prototype:** An easy way to ensure that the physical design meets the requisites of the project is to create a software prototype. The prototype is a sample application that describes the functionality of the software. As an example, consider the appraisal system that we discuss in the previous section. The prototype for this application has the visual interface of the application and also enables you to specify sample values that yield an arbitrary result. In such a prototype, start with a dummy user and analyze whether the application meets your requirements. See such a prototype in Figure 5-1 where we have a dummy user, Suzan. In the actual software, this name may be retrieved from the user's login ID.

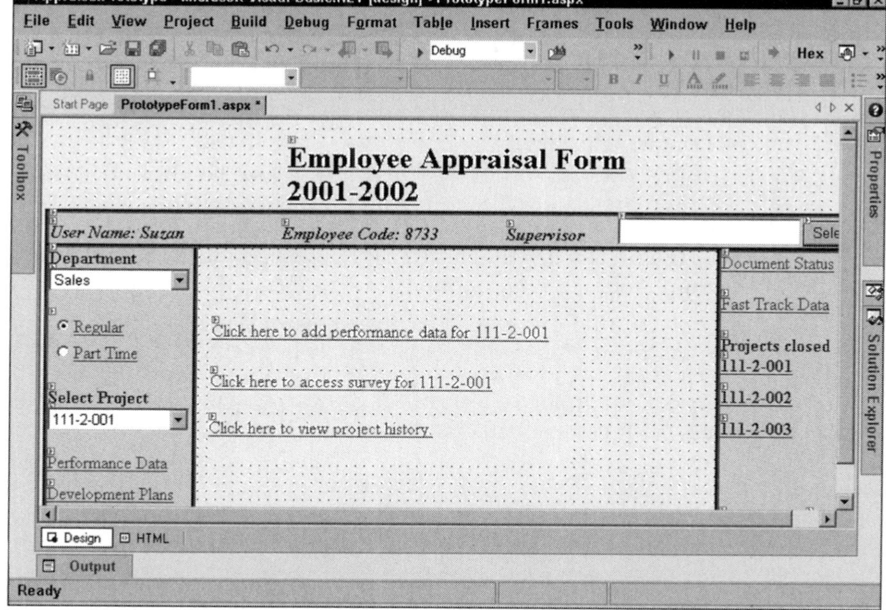

Figure 5-1: A prototype helps you visualize your application before you create it.

Developing a prototype helps all project team members get a feel of the final product. Your prototype also helps you foresee any additional requirements that you might have missed otherwise.

You can use the prototype to determine the required functionality that may already be present in one form or another. For instance, in the same example, the component that you use to log on a user to the appraisal system may already be present, automatically logging on a user to the system through an existing Windows 2000 domain account. Reusability of such existing components helps you to significantly cut down the development effort. Recycle when you can.

Because Visual Studio .NET enables you to create the prototype in any language, you have more freedom during the design stage. Suppose you want to use your prototype for developing the final software but the prototype is written in a language other than what will be used for the final application. Visual Studio .NET gives you the choice of selecting any language for the final software, regardless of the language in which you create your prototype.

Additionally, as you discover through the course of this book, Visual Studio .NET enables you to achieve interoperability with existing applications and application components. Therefore, you don't end up spending unnecessary time attaining interoperability.

Developing Your Application

After you plan and design your application, you're ready for the third stage of the development cycle: development. In this stage, individual teams usually work on different features of the application. When using Visual Studio .NET, the development teams can work in multiple languages, which is a great freedom. These teams can also integrate existing applications with the new one. After the development team has developed all the components, the components are integrated to create the final application.

In the developing stage, you complete the functionality and the user interface, if applicable, of the application. Although a formal testing round for the application follows this phase, you can do an initial round of tests to ensure that each component of the software functions accurately.

Most of the Visual Studio .NET tools and functionality are put to use in the developing stage. Visual Studio .NET provides a number of enterprise templates that you can use as starting points for creating applications. *Enterprise templates* are predefined projects that are shipped with Visual Studio .NET. They provide a good starting point for you to create your application. Some of the templates available for creating a new project are shown in Figure 5-2. You can read about using enterprise templates in the language of your choice by reading the minibook for that language. For example, to use enterprise templates of Visual C++ .NET, refer to Book 4, Chapter 1.

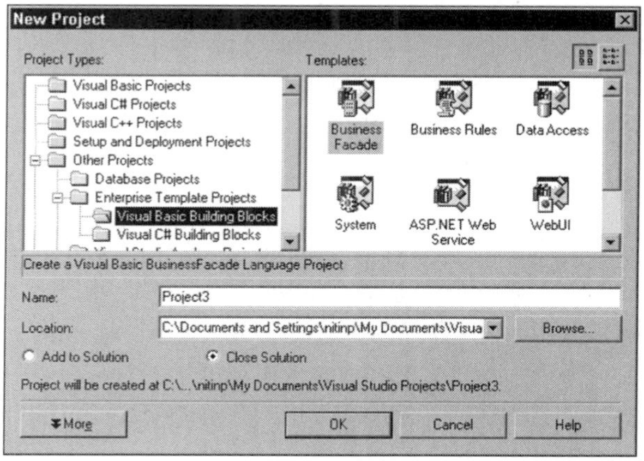

Figure 5-2: Use enterprise templates to create a new application.

In the development stage, you also need to ensure that all members of the development team follow a standard pattern of coding. The code needs to be well commented so that any developer of the team can easily debug it. If the development team is large, you also need to assign responsibilities to ensure that the team is able to coordinate its development efforts. This ensures consistency in the interface design, function and method declaration, and code implementation.

One advantage that Visual Studio .NET offers is that it enables you to share projects easily. For example, instead of having to import a form into a new project as you did in Visual Basic 6.0, you can inherit a form in Visual Basic .NET. Similarly, the Visual Studio .NET projects that you create are stored as namespaces. Therefore, you can use the classes of an application in the same manner that you use the classes provided by Visual Studio .NET. You can read about namespaces in Book 1, Chapter 2 and inheritance of classes in Book 3, Chapter 8.

Testing and Debugging Your Application

Testing and debugging is the final and usually the most important stage in an application's development. To ensure that your application is bug-free, follow these steps:

1. **Create a test plan.**

   Use a test plan to ensure that all functionality in an application is tested for its accuracy. The test plan includes cases that define what needs to be tested in an application, and these cases provide a benchmark for testing your application.

2. **Implement the test plan.**

   Tests that are detailed in the test plan can be of two types:

   - **Glass box testing:** Developers perform *glass box testing*, in which they examine the application code to ensure that it's bug-free. This process is often time-consuming because you traverse the code of the entire application.

     Glass box testing can be very time-consuming. To ensure that it doesn't jeopardize your project schedule, plan for it when you create the timetable of your project.

   - **Black box testing:** Testers perform *black box testing*, during which a tester only needs to know about the input for the application and the required output. This type of testing takes less time than glass box testing.

3. **Create a bug report.**

   Based on the tests carried out, you create a bug report. From the bug report, you can isolate tasks that can be added to the task list in Visual Studio .NET. You can list the tasks in this task list in a variety of ways. For example, you may refer to the exact line or method where the bug exists or you may write generic comments that need to be implemented across the application. See a sample task list in Figure 5-3.

Figure 5-3: A task list from a bug report is an easy way to organize your work.

Task List - 5 tasks

!		✔	Description	File	Line
		☐	Change alignment of the Save button		
↓		☐	Change form background		
!		☐	This link does not seem to work		
	◆		TODO This seems to be out of place	c:\inetpub\wwwroot\...\PrototypeForm1.aspx.vb	49
	◆		TODO Validate this code	c:\inetpub\wwwroot\...\PrototypeForm1.aspx.vb	53

4. **Fix the bugs.**

   You're ready to debug after you test your code and create a bug report. While debugging the code, you should fix all bugs and get them verified by a tester. Visual Studio .NET offers extensive debugging support. We discuss some of the possible debugging actions in Book 1, Chapter 3.

Check out the complete testing and debugging cycle in Figure 5-4. Note that the cycle may be repeated several times until no bugs are found in the application.

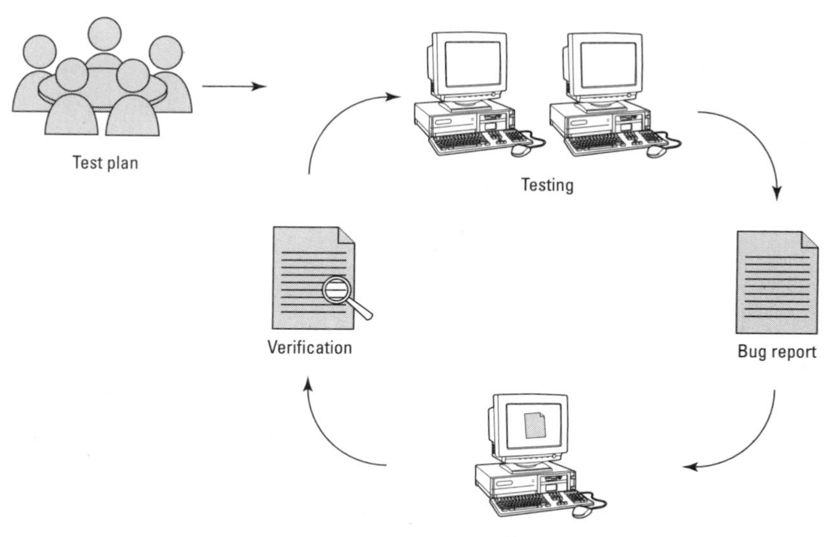

Figure 5-4: The testing and debugging cycle for ensuring a bug-free application.

When debugging code, you can use a number of strategies depending upon the types of error that you encounter. Errors can be categorized as logical errors and obvious syntactical errors:

- **Logical errors:** *Logical errors* occur because of incorrect programming logic. Incorrect programming logic occurs when you nod off to sleep while coding the application. For example, you may have a logical error that increases a value instead of decreasing it. Logical errors can be tricky to catch because they aren't detected during development. However, they often cause your program to stop responding at runtime. At worst, these errors may go undetected even at runtime and may cost you a fortune when you need to replace the faulty application.
- **Syntactical errors:** *Syntactical errors* are syntax errors or misspelled words that may creep in when you write the code. Such errors are easy to detect because the compiler points them out when you code your application.

To eliminate any possibility of logical errors, write modular code. *Modular code* spans across multiple functions, helping you attribute a bug to one function instead of a large chunk of code. Debugging a function is easier than debugging a large segment of code.

To detect a bug, you can use debugging tools available in Visual Studio .NET. Some of these tools include the Watch window, the Immediate window, and the Locals window. These windows enable you to view the state of an application and the expected output when your application runs. Read about how to use these tools in the chapters on debugging — Book 3, Chapter 9 and Book 4, Chapter 8.

Chapter 6: Installing Visual Studio .NET

In This Chapter

- **Discovering the system requirements for installing Visual Studio .NET**
- **Installing Visual Studio .NET**

In this chapter, we walk you through installing Visual Studio .NET. Its simple installation procedure is wizard-based and has minimal user interaction.

Before you install Visual Studio. NET, you need to ensure that your computer fulfills the minimum system requirements. In addition, to be able to run Visual Studio .NET, you also need to install a number of components, such as Internet Explorer 6.0, on your computer. However, these components are also provided in the installation package as a separate Windows Component Update CD-ROM.

System Requirements for Installing Visual Studio .NET

Visual Studio .NET includes four editions: Professional, Enterprise Developer, Enterprise Architect, and Academic. These editions differ in the number of components that are included in the installation package. For example, the Enterprise Developer edition includes the developer editors of Commerce Server 2000 and BizTalk Server 2000, which are not included in the Professional edition. For a detailed list of components that are available in each edition, refer to the Visual Studio .NET documentation, which is installed with Visual Studio .NET.

In this book, we use the Professional edition of Visual Studio .NET. Don't worry if you are using another version of Visual Studio .NET — all the features and tasks that we explain in this book work equally well in the other editions of Visual Studio .NET.

Some system requirements for installing Visual Studio .NET, such as the available disk space and the prerequisite software, depend upon the components that you want to install. However, for best performance with any component that you install, you should use a fast computer (600 MHz or more) and have a screen resolution of at least 800 x 600 pixels. We list the detailed hardware and software requirements in this section.

Hardware requirements

The recommended hardware requirements for installing Visual Studio .NET are

- 256MB RAM
- 600 MHz Pentium II microprocessor
- 3.5GB available hard disk space
- 52X CD-ROM drive
- Internet connection (required for checking software updates)

Software requirements

To install Visual Studio .NET, you need to use one of the following operating systems:

- Windows NT 4.0 (Server or Workstation)
- Windows 2000 (Server or Professional)
- Windows XP Professional
- Windows .NET Server

Windows NT 4.0 does not support ASP.NET. Therefore, if you plan to create ASP.NET applications, use Windows 2000 or Windows XP.

To run server components, you need to install Internet Information Services (IIS) 5.0. IIS is automatically installed when you install Windows 2000 Server or Windows NT Server (with Service Pack 6a). However, you need to separately install IIS 5.0 on a computer that runs a desktop operating system, such as Windows 2000 Professional.

IIS is Microsoft's solution for building and hosting Web sites. You typically host Web sites developed by using Active Server Pages (ASP) or Internet Server Application Programming Interface (ISAPI) on IIS.

You also need the following components to install Visual Studio .NET:

- Windows 2000 Server Service Pack 2 or Microsoft Windows NT 4.0 Service Pack 6a (depending upon the operating system that you're running)
- Microsoft FrontPage 2000 Server Extensions Service Release 1.2
- Microsoft Windows Installer 2.0
- Microsoft Windows Management Infrastructure
- Microsoft FrontPage 2000 Web Extensions Client

- Setup Runtime Files
- Microsoft Internet Explorer 6.0 and Internet Tools
- Microsoft Data Access Components 2.7
- Microsoft Jet 4.0 Service Pack 3
- Microsoft .NET Framework

The earlier versions of most of the components are installed along with the Windows operating system. When you install Visual Studio .NET, you just need to upgrade these software items. You can install the latest versions of the preceding Windows components on your computer by using the Windows Component Update CD-ROM that accompanies the installation package.

Preparing to Install Visual Studio .NET

The procedure for installing Visual Studio .NET is automated. You gotta like that! All you need to do is to run Setup, specify the destination folder, and then insert the required CD-ROM when you're prompted to do so.

In this section, we cover the procedure for updating Windows components and installing Visual Studio .NET.

Installing the prerequisite software

The number of CD-ROMs included in the Visual Studio .NET installation kit varies depending on the version of Visual Studio .NET that you are installing. Visual Studio .NET is also available in a DVD (Digital Versatile Disks)-ROM, in which case all the installation files are on just one DVD-ROM. If you are installing Visual Studio .NET from CD-ROMs, the last CD-ROM has the Windows components updates. (When installing from a DVD-ROM, don't worry about the location of the Windows component update. It'll be on the DVD!)

When you begin the installation, start with the first CD-ROM (or the DVD-ROM). The automated set-up process then prompts you for subsequent CD-ROMs as they're required.

To install Windows component updates:

1. **Insert the first CD-ROM in your computer's CD-ROM (or the DVD-ROM) drive to begin the installation.**

   The first CD should have the label CD 1 on it.

   The Visual Studio .NET Setup detects your system configuration and prompts you to first install the missing Windows 2000 components, if any.

If you're one of those computer wizards who always runs the latest components, you might not need to update your Windows configuration. In that case, the Setup directly takes you to the installation of Visual Studio .NET. If this is you, proceed directly to the "Installing Visual Studio .NET" section.

Check out Figure 6-1 for the first window of Setup. The Windows Component Update option will be highlighted, as shown in Figure 6-1, when one or more components on your computer aren't updated to match the required versions. All components that are not updated on the computer appear in the list.

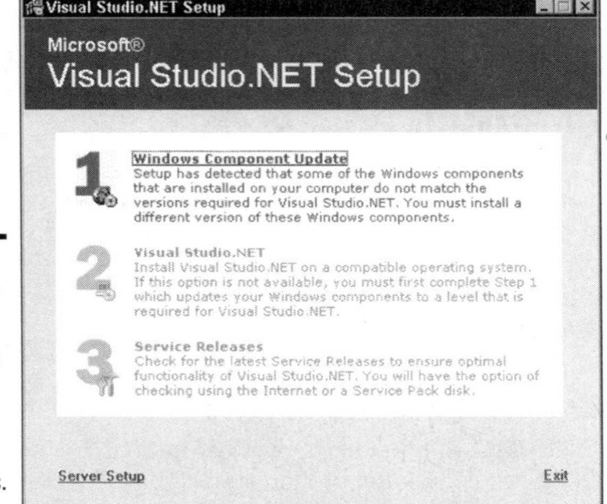

Figure 6-1: The Setup screen prompts you to install updated Windows components.

2. **Click the Windows Component Update link.**

   Setup prompts you to insert the Windows Component Update CD-ROM.

3. **Insert the Windows Component Update CD-ROM into your computer's CD-ROM drive and click OK.**

   The End User License Agreement screen appears (as shown in Figure 6-2).

4. **Select the I Accept the Agreement radio button and click Continue.**

You can click Continue only after you accept the license agreement. Think of it this way: If you don't accept the agreement, you're done and you don't need this book anymore!

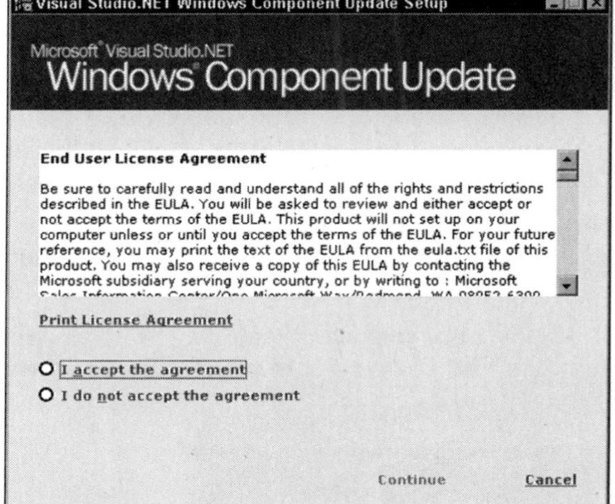

Figure 6-2: Accept the license agreement before you proceed.

The next screen displays a list of the Windows components that need to be upgraded on your computer to complete a successful installation. Additionally, the needed-to-be-installed components for which your computer needs to restart are marked with "information" icons to their left; see Figure 6-3.

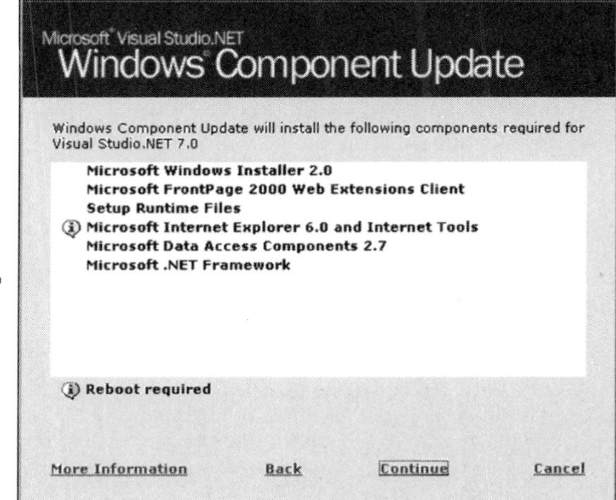

Figure 6-3: Setup even tells you what it will install for you.

5. **Click Continue to proceed with the installation.**

   When you upgrade your Windows components, your computer will automatically restart several times before the Windows update components are completely installed. To avoid specifying log-on information each time that your computer restarts, you can specify this information in the Optional Automatic Log On screen, as shown in Figure 6-4.

   REMEMBER: Feel safe specifying log-on information in the Optional Automatic Log On screen. When Setup is complete, the information is automatically cleared.

6. **Specify your log-on information by entering your password in the Password text box and retyping it in the Confirm password textbox.**

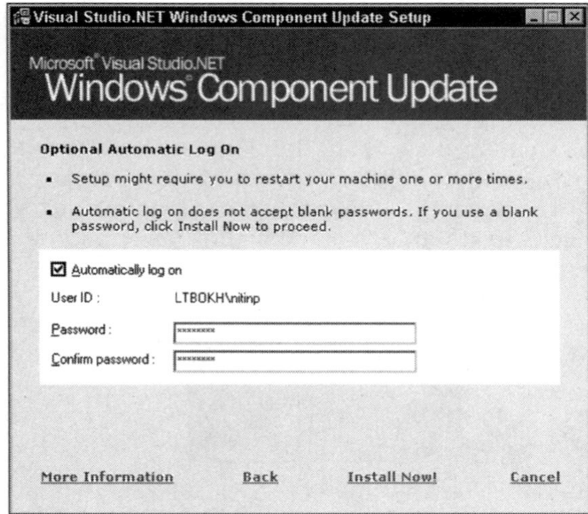

Figure 6-4: Avoid logging on each time that your computer restarts during installation.

7. **Click the Install Now! link.**

   The Setup program completes the upgrade of those Windows components that need to be updated.

   After windows components are updated on your computer, the Setup screen shown in Figure 6-1 reappears. This time, the Visual Studio .NET option (to install Visual Studio .NET) is enabled.

Installing Visual Studio .NET

After you upgrade any needed Windows components on your computer — or if they're already updated — Setup begins the installation of Visual Studio .NET. You see the same screen shown in Figure 6-1, but the second option, Visual Studio .NET, is highlighted. Follow these easy steps for installation:

1. **Click the Visual Studio .NET option on the Setup window.**

   Unless it's already there, you're prompted to insert the Visual Studio .NET CD-ROM 1 in your computer's CD-ROM drive.

2. **Insert the Visual Studio .NET CD-ROM 1 in your computer's CD-ROM drive and click OK.**

   The End User License Agreement screen appears, as shown in Figure 6-5. Notice that your name automatically appears in the Your Name text box. If that's not your name, your computer probably didn't recognize you! In such cases, change the name to reflect yours.

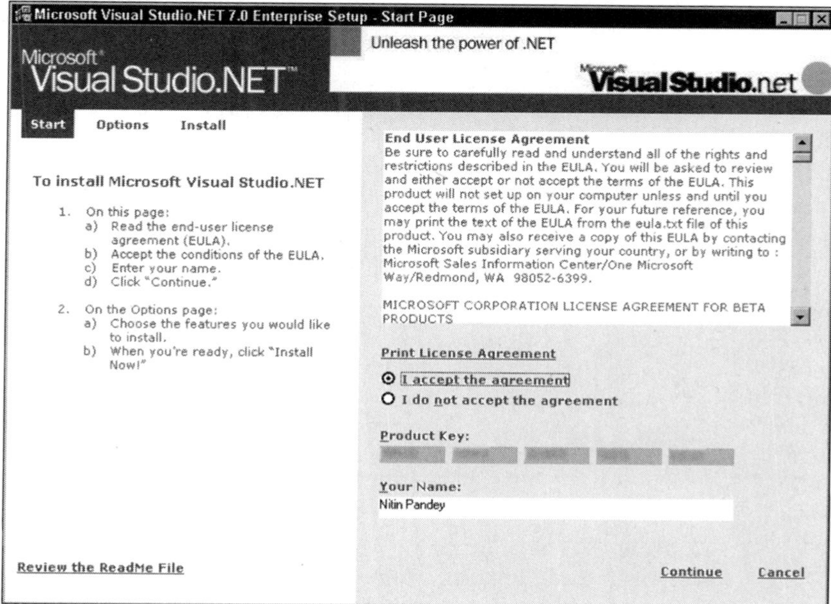

Figure 6-5: Take the bait and accept the license agreement.

3. **Select the I Accept the Agreement radio button and click Continue.**

   In the Options Page window that opens, select the components that you want to install and then specify the destination of those files. Here you can also read a feature description of the components and see how much free space your hard drive still has.

   In the left side of the Options Page window, shown in Figure 6-6, select the check boxes for the components that you want to install. Choose from such options as Language Tools and Server Components. Then, if you want, you can change the location of files in the Path text box by typing in a new location or by selecting a new location by clicking the ellipsis button (...).

4. **Select the components that you want to install and click the Install Now! link.**

The Visual Studio .NET installation begins. Setup shows the time remaining for the installation to complete (which is fairly accurate) and prompts you to insert the appropriate CD-ROMs as and when they're required.

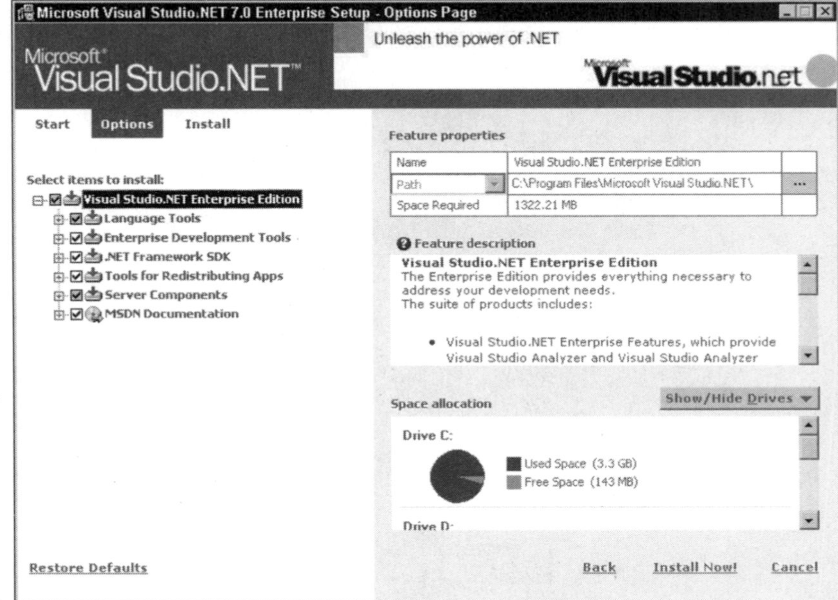

Figure 6-6: Select the components you want and specify file location.

That's all you need to do for installing Visual Studio .NET. The installation is error-free and generally takes about one hour. After the installation is complete, you get a message notifying the same. Thereafter, you have the option of going to the Microsoft Web site to check for upgrades to Visual Studio .NET. You don't have to navigate to the site yourself. Instead, use the smart way: Click the Service Releases link that you see on the Visual Studio .NET Setup screen in Figure 6-1.

If, for any reason, you need to cancel Visual Studio .NET setup, click the Cancel link when it appears in the setup program while Visual Studio .NET is being installed. If you choose to cancel the setup, the Setup program runs a script to undo the changes that it made to your system.

Index

Symbols

A

B

C

D

T

U

V

W-X-Y-Z

Book II

Using the Visual Studio .NET IDE

The 5th Wave
By Rich Tennant
IT WAS THE LAST TIME EMILY SERVED ALPHABET SOUP TO HER WORD PUZZLE PLAYING HUSBAND.
ADO.NET... XML.... DAO...
Obsessive... fanatical... fixated...Ooo-compulsive...

Contents at a Glance

Chapter 1: Meet the Visual Studio Interface

In This Chapter

- Exploring tools in IDE
- Managing windows
- Designing applications

Visual Studio .NET is the latest feather in the Microsoft cap. Microsoft introduced this suite to help you build a variety of applications, including Web, desktop, and mobile. In addition, the tools in this package can help you create Web services. And the languages that constitute Visual Studio .NET are real gems. Moreover, the integrated development environment (IDE) that these languages share is superb, and features of the IDE enable you to create required applications in a jiffy. In this chapter, we take you on a trip through all these features.

Exploring Tools in IDE

Visual Studio .NET is an integrated package of various software development tools of Microsoft. The package contains an assortment of tools, such as Visual Basic, Visual C++, Visual C#, and MSDN (Microsoft Developer Network), bound together. All now share a common IDE, giving you the advantage of tools that are easily accessible across all Visual Studio .NET languages. This flexibility simplifies any task that you perform in the Visual Studio .NET environment. Read on to discover some of the more frequently used tools of IDE.

Start Page

When you launch Visual Studio .NET, the first screen that appears is the Start Page. From this page, you access existing projects or create new ones. Sure, any IDE has a Start Page. But what's so great about the Visual Studio .NET Start Page is that it contains various links to help you, including one to search for information on MSDN Online. You can use this information to work efficiently with Visual Studio .NET. Choose from links to an Online Community where you can indulge in discussions with your colleagues or maybe What's New for the latest in product news.

You can also customize the appearance of IDE by specifying your preferences from the Start Page. For example, you can specify a keyboard mapping scheme or window layout that you like. To select your preferences, click My Profile and make appropriate changes. A sample Start Page is shown in Figure 1-1.

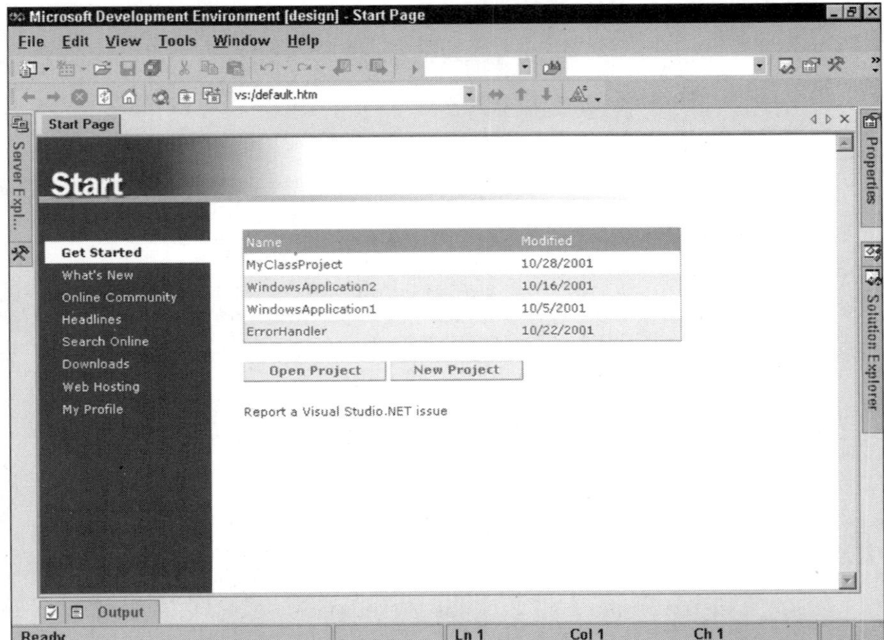

Figure 1-1: Where it all begins: the Start Page.

To launch Visual Studio .NET, choose Start⇨Programs⇨Microsoft Visual Studio.NET⇨Microsoft Visual Studio.NET.

Solution Explorer

Because a project can contain a number of files, you may need to frequently switch from one file to another. As a convenience tool, the IDE provides Solution Explorer to display all projects along with their respective files. A *solution* is a collection of all projects and files needed for an application. The Solution Explorer displays these files in a tree-view format, as shown in Figure 1-2. To open a file, double-click the filename in the Solution Explorer.

To open Solution Explorer, choose View⇨Solution Explorer. The Solution Explorer contains a toolbar with buttons specific to the selected file in the tree view. For example, if you select the `Form1.vb` file, the toolbar shows the View Designer button because the form has an interface, which you can design using the designer. However, if you select the `Module1.vb` file, the toolbar doesn't display the View Designer button because it doesn't have an interface.

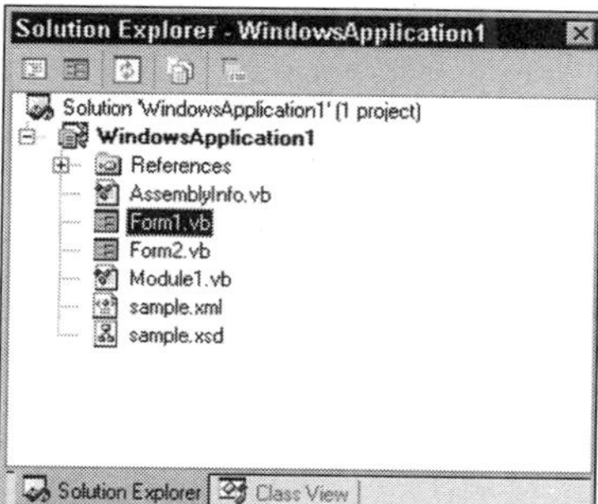

Figure 1-2: Manage the files in a solution with Solution Explorer.

Some of the commonly displayed buttons are View Code, Show All Files, and Properties. Click the View Code button to open the selected file in the Code Editor, the Show All Files button to display all files that are hidden or excluded from the project, and the Properties button to display the Properties window for the selected file.

Toolbox

The Toolbox is a storehouse of controls that you use to design applications. The controls present in the Toolbox are categorized into groups, such as Windows Forms controls, Data controls, Components, and HyperText Markup Language (HTML) elements. The controls that are a part of the Toolbox may vary depending on the designer or editor you're working in. For example, if you're working in the Windows Forms designer, all Windows Forms controls are available. However, when you're in the Code Editor, the Windows Forms controls aren't present. Figure 1-3 shows the Toolbox, which appears every time you open an application.

A nifty advanced feature of the Toolbox is that you can store a code snippet inside it. Just select the code and drag it to the Toolbox; then you can use this code later.

Read more about the Toolbox in Book 3, Chapter 2.

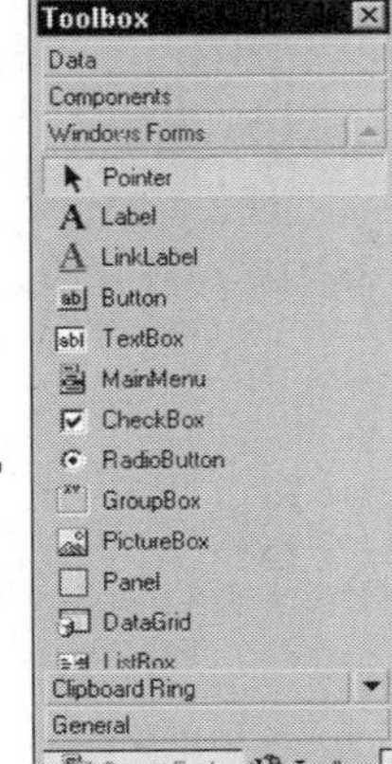

Figure 1-3: Use Toolbox controls when designing.

Server Explorer

Server Explorer is the server-development console that helps you manage a computer. Of course, you need to have permissions for accessing the required computer. Server Explorer also helps you get connected with servers and explore their resources. By default, Server Explorer appears on the left side of the IDE.

You can use Server Explorer to establish connections with SQL Server and other databases. This explorer also helps you access the available XML Web services on a server.

Server Explorer displays items in a tree-view format. Server Explorer contains two main nodes, Data Connections and Servers. The *Data Connections* node lists all database connections that you create. The *Servers* node lists the servers that you can currently use, as shown in Figure 1-4.

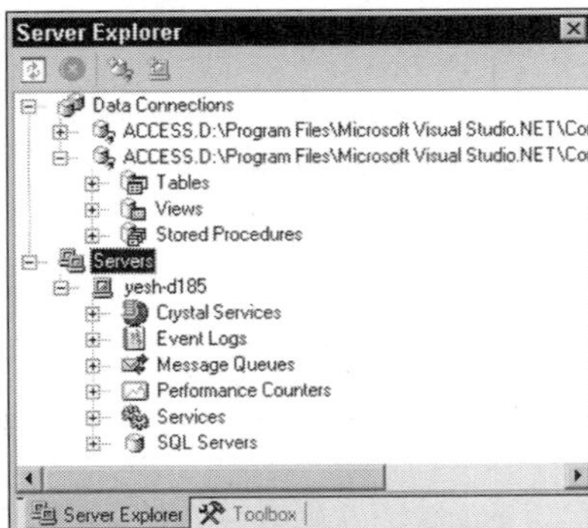

Figure 1-4: Connect with computers and databases with Server Explorer.

Task List

Another distinct feature in Visual Studio .NET is that you can mark code within your application with comments. To do so, you use a Task List, which you access by choosing View➪Show Tasks➪Comment. Add your comments to the Task List by typing them directly in the list that appears. These comments are then displayed in a tabular format. For example, you can include comments that describe the state of the code. This may help in situations when some other developer needs to work on your project.

In addition, the Task List displays errors and warnings when you compile an application. If you double-click an error, the Task List takes you to that part of code that contains the error. See Figure 1-5 for the Task List along with an error message.

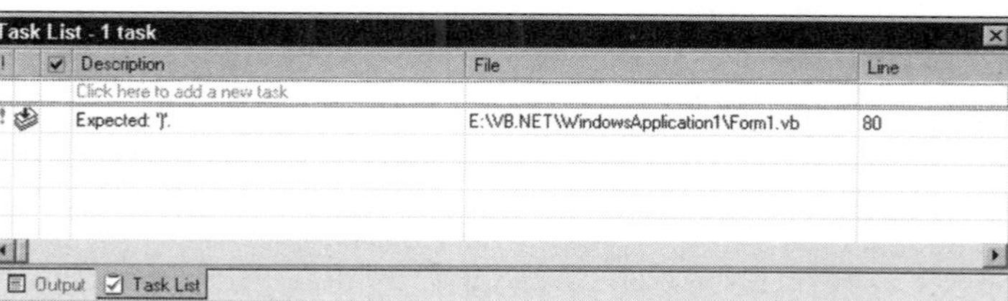

Figure 1-5: Leave notes and locate errors with the Task List.

Dynamic Help

With the introduction of Dynamic Help, Visual Studio .NET offers an amazing feature that displays additional information links on the topic that you're currently working on. These links change when you work on other topics.

Dynamic Help constantly examines your movements. For example, this feature tracks the selections that you make, notes the position of the cursor, and notes the items, such as controls that you're working with. Dynamic Help then searches for the appropriate topics on MSDN Online and shows a link for the same. For example, in Figure 1-6, the cursor is positioned on the `MessageBox` word and the Dynamic Help window displays links to related topics.

Command Window

You can use Command Window (see Figure 1-7) to directly access the menu commands available in the IDE. To access a command, you need to type the command in this window. For example, the command shown in Figure 1-7 displays the Add New Item dialog box. To make Command Window available, choose View➪Other Windows➪Command Window.

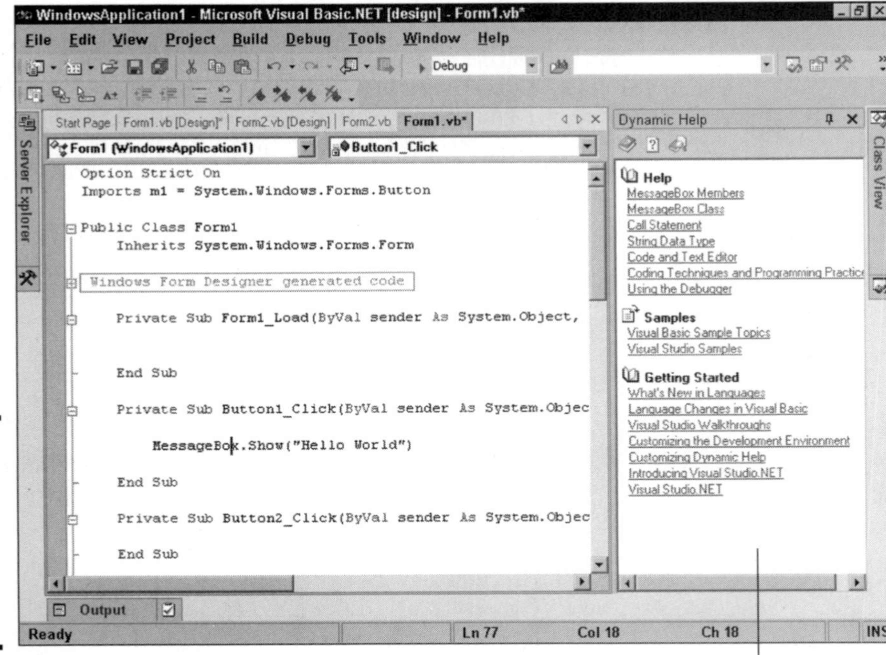

Figure 1-6: The Dynamic Help window is always on watch.

Command Window has two modes: Command and Immediate. Use the Command mode to execute Visual Studio commands directly without using the menus. Use the Immediate mode to debug applications. The Immediate mode also helps you evaluate expressions or manipulate variables.

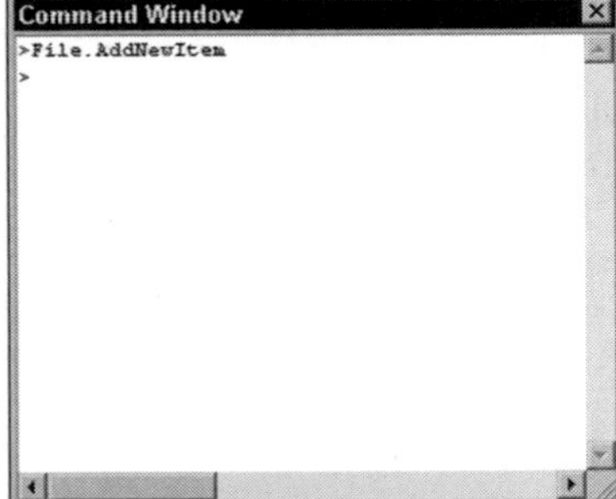

Figure 1-7: Execute menu commands in shortcuts in the Command window.

IntelliSense

The IntelliSense feature provides options that help you write correct syntax. Some options that comprise IntelliSense include providing a list of members and parameter information, completing the statements automatically, and matching braces. This feature invokes automatically while you're keying in the code. This helps making applications easier and less prone to errors.

The IntelliSense feature in Visual Studio .NET can handle HTML and eXtensible Markup Language (XML) as well as the compiled programming languages. This is a major help to Web developers.

Managing Windows

While working with your application, you use a number of windows. For example, you need the Solution Explorer to switch between files, the Toolbox to add controls to the form, and the Task List to detect any errors. However, after you open all these windows, your project appears completely cluttered, leaving you with little space to view the Code Editor. In such situations, use window management features provided by the IDE to maximize the screen space and make your project window more viewable.

Hiding windows automatically

Use the Auto Hide feature to hide a window when it's not in use. The hidden window is then displayed as a tab along the edges of the IDE. To view the hidden window again, just point to the appropriate tab with your mouse pointer. The Auto Hide feature is applicable to various tools of IDE, such as Solution Explorer, Toolbox, and Task List.

Enable or disable the Auto Hide feature by toggling its pushpin icon. The pushpin icon is located next to the standard Close (X) button of the various IDE tools, such as Solution Explorer, Toolbox, and Task List.

Docking windows

In Visual Studio .NET, you can drag any window in the IDE to wherever you want. Attach windows with others or let them remain freestanding. If you attach (dock) one window to another, they enter the tab-linked mode, meaning that the attached windows are displayed as tabs in a single window.

Arranging files as tabs

While working in an application, you might open several files. You can use the Solution Explorer to switch between these files. In addition, Visual Studio .NET has a new feature that displays all the open document windows as tabs within the IDE. Now, to switch to any particular window, you just have to click the corresponding tab.

Navigating in the IDE

Thanks to the Back and Forward buttons, the IDE also enables you to navigate through open windows. These buttons are similar in function to the Back and Forward buttons in a Web browser.

Check out all these windows management features in Figure 1-8.

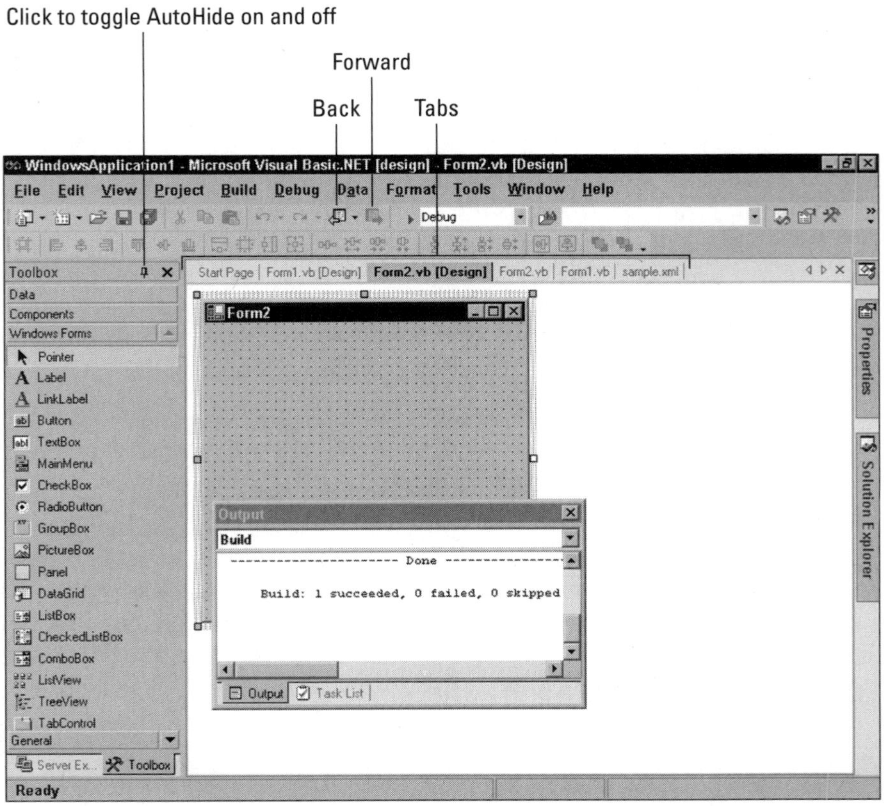

Figure 1-8: Managing windows is easy with the Visual Studio .NET IDE.

Designing Applications with Ease

The Visual Studio .NET designers — including the Web Form Designer, Windows Forms Designer, Component Designer, and XML Designer — help you to create your applications with ease.

Web Form Designer

Use the Web Form Designer to create ASP.NET Web applications without writing HTML code. With this designer, you can add and arrange controls on a form. In addition, you can use the designer to code events of the controls that you add. While designing a form with the Web Form Designer, add controls to the form by using the Web Forms, Data, HTML, and Components tab of the Toolbox. A sample Web Form Designer is shown in Figure 1-9. This designer is available whenever you create a Web application using Visual Studio .NET.

When you're in the Web Form Designer, you can switch to the Code Editor or the HTML source, or display the page in a browser. To make your choice, right-click the designer and choose the appropriate option by clicking it from the pop-up menu that appears.

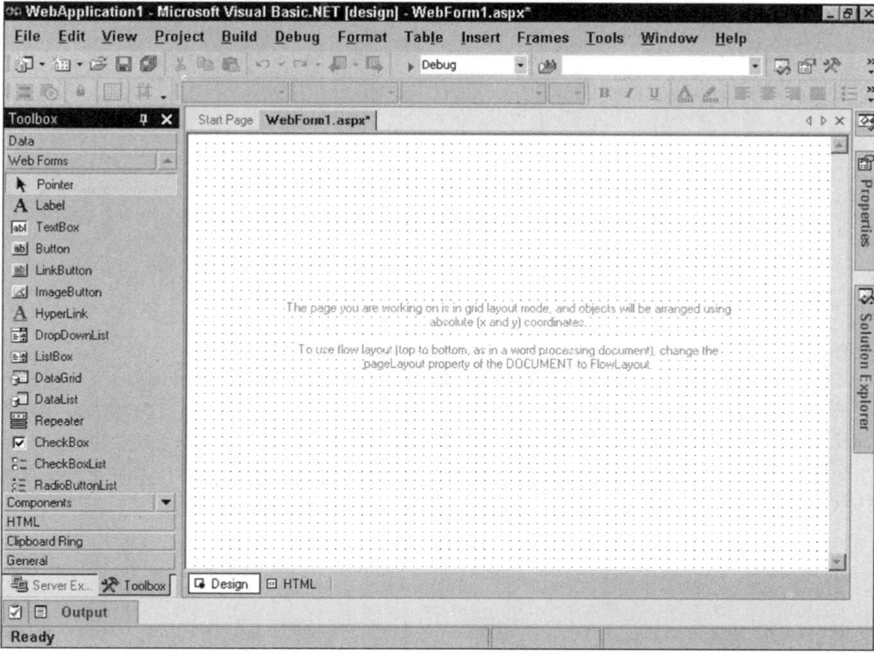

Figure 1-9: Design Web applications with the Web Form Designer.

Use the Code Editor window to enter and edit text. You can view this window by right-clicking the designer or control and choosing View Code from the pop-up menu that appears.

Read more about controls in Book 3, Chapter 3.

Windows Forms Designer

Use the Windows Forms Designer to create Windows applications. Here you can add and arrange controls and write code for them. In the Windows Forms Designer, you can also add controls from the Windows Forms, Data, and Components tab of the Toolbox. A sample Windows Forms Designer is shown in Figure 1-10. This designer becomes available when you create a Windows application using Visual Studio .NET.

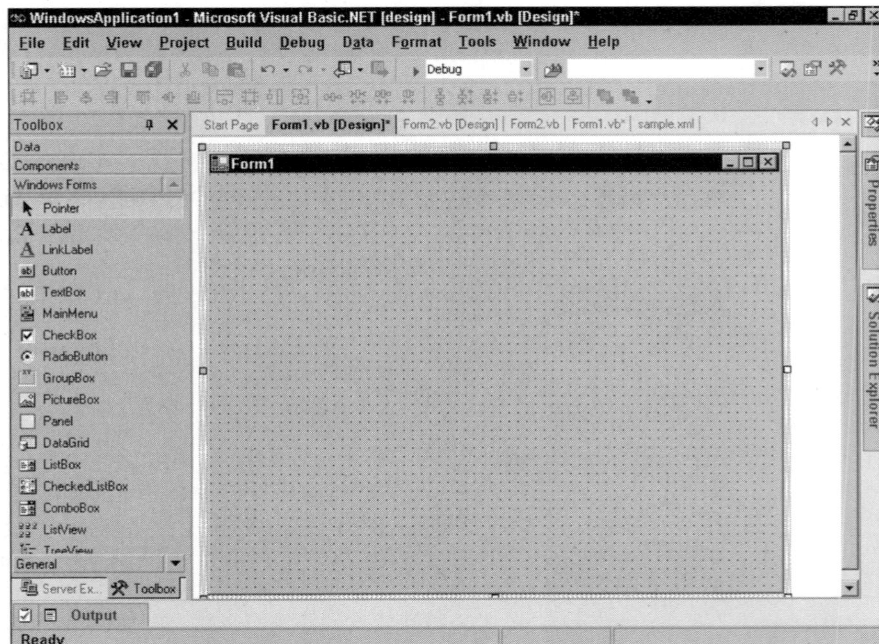

Figure 1-10: Design Windows application with the Windows Forms Designer.

Component Designer

Use the Component Designer to manipulate non-visual components such as the `OpenFileDialog` control. Components lacking a user interface are *non-visual components*. The Component Designer is actually the Tray that appears at the bottom of the Web Form and Windows Forms designers. For example, when you add an `OpenFileDialog` control to a Windows Form, the control sits in the Tray at the bottom (as shown in Figure 1-11), which is the Component Designer. Here you can set the properties of this control. Moreover, you can add code for the `OpenFileDialog` control by using this designer. To add the code, right-click the designer and choose View Code from the pop-up menu that appears.

XML Designer

Use the XML Designer to manipulate XML Schemas, ADO.NET datasets, and XML documents. This designer is visible only when you add an XML Schema, an XML file, or a dataset. The XML Designer has three views: Schema view, Data view, and XML view.

The Schema view helps you create and modify XML schemas. The Data view displays the schema associated with an XML file in a data grid; in this view, you can directly edit the data. The XML view helps you work with the XML code. See the Data view of the XML designer in Figure 1-12. Switch between different views by choosing the appropriate option present at the bottom of the designer.

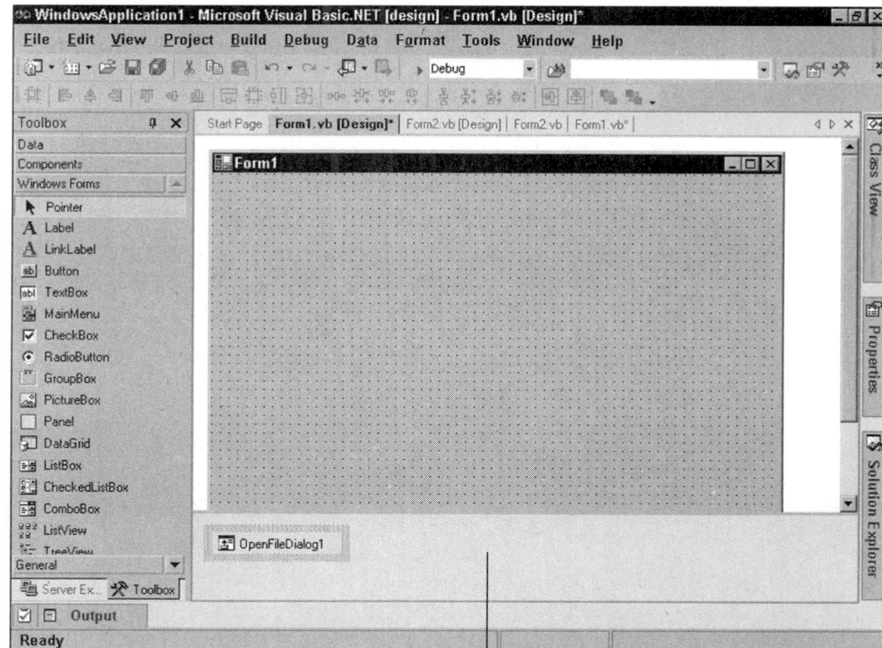

Figure 1-11: Add and configure non-visual controls from the Component Designer.

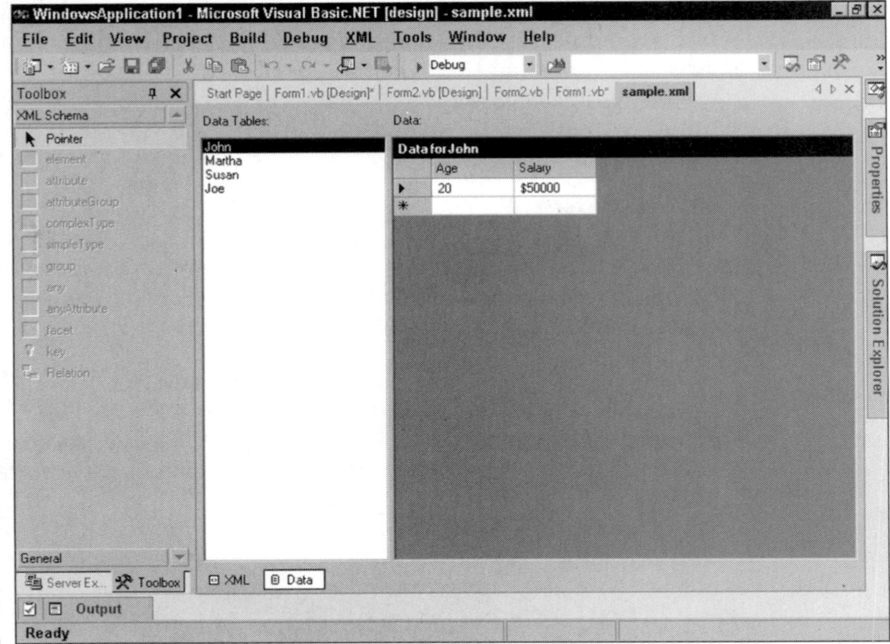

Figure 1-12: Get XML-compliant; use the XML Designer.

Chapter 2: Customizing Your Development Environment

In This Chapter

- **Using the Options dialog box**
- **Using the Customize dialog box**

Visual Studio .NET is a user-friendly package. Microsoft developed this suite realizing that you need to work in an environment that suits your taste. You can tailor the Integrated Development Environment (IDE) just like you want with the Visual Studio .NET Options and Customize dialog boxes. In this chapter, we discuss the major elements of each and how to customize your IDE with the tools that you find within them.

Options Dialog Box

You use the Options dialog box to customize the integrated development environment. With this dialog box, you can specify a default location to save your projects and manipulate the layout of the IDE. You can also specify keyboard mappings as well as font and color for the user interface elements by using this dialog box.

To display the Options dialog box, choose Tools⇨Options. This dialog box is divided into two panes (see the upcoming Figure 2-1). The left pane contains various folders, such as Environment, Text Editor, Debugging, and HTML Designer. Each folder contains a number of pages that display related topics. For example, the Environment folder contains Dynamic Help and Help pages. The right pane of the Options dialog box displays the options present in the page selected in the left pane. To display the options of a page, click the page name in the left pane.

The Environment folder contains various pages that help you customize numerous elements and tools present in the IDE. Before moving on to a more detailed discussion of the Environment folder, we first briefly describe each of the folders present in the Options dialog box:

- **Source Control:** Specifies settings for the various source control roles, including Visual SourceSafe, Team Development, and Independent Developer.
- **Text Editor:** Specifies settings for the Code/Text Editor.

- **Analyzer:** Specifies settings for Visual Studio Analyzer.
- **Database Tools:** Specifies settings for projects containing databases.
- **Debugging:** Specifies various debugging options.
- **HTML Designer:** Manipulates the view in which various HTML, Active Server, and Web Form pages open up in the HTML Designer.
- **Projects:** Specifies whether the VC++ builds are to be logged. You can also use this folder to find out the time taken by the build.
- **Windows Forms Designer:** Specifies various grid settings of a Windows Forms.
- **XML Designer:** Specifies the default view in which the XML Designer starts.

In the following sections, we look at the different pages present in the Environment folder.

- **General page:** Use the General page (as shown in Figure 2-1) to change the default settings of the IDE, including:
  - To specify whether the IDE should support MDI (Multiple Document Interface) environment or tabbed documents. If you're working in the tabbed document environment, the document opened last is visible and all other documents, which were previously opened, appear as tabs at the top. When you work in MDI environment, only the last open document is visible.
  - To display the Status bar in the IDE.
  - To specify the item to be displayed at the startup. By default, the IDE displays the Start Page. However, you can display the New Project or the Open Project dialog box.

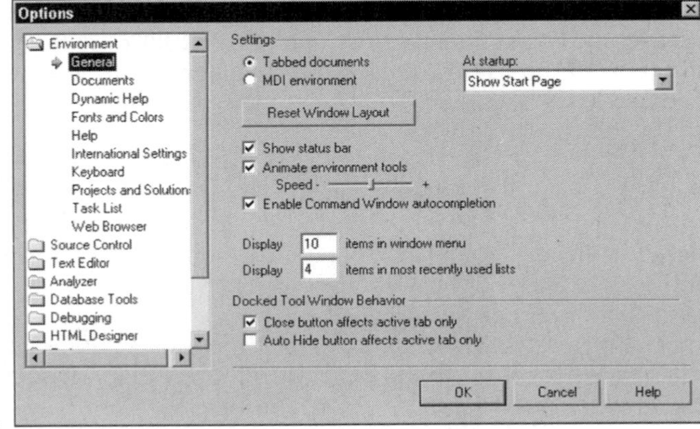

Figure 2-1: Change default settings by using the General page.

✦ **Documents page:** Use the Documents page (see Figure 2-2) to monitor documents and files in the IDE. A few uses of this page are

- To track whether any changes have been made to a document or file outside the IDE. To do so, check the Detect When File Is Changed Outside the Environment check box.
- To specify that read-only files can be edited. However, you need to save this file with a new name. To do so, check the Allow Editing of Read-only Files, Warn When Attempt to Save check box.
- To display message boxes during the Find and Replace options.

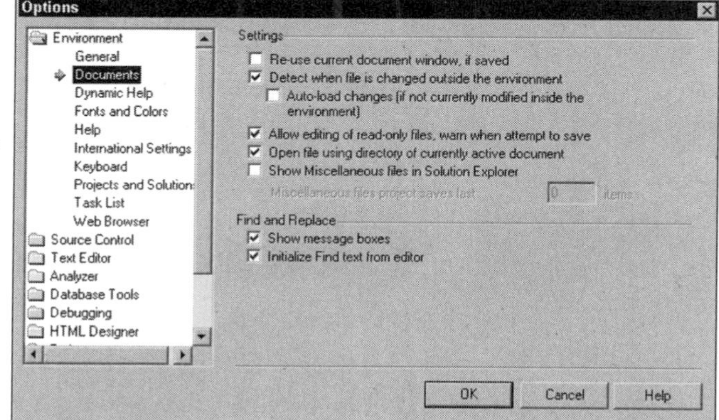

Figure 2-2: Monitor your documents with Documents page options.

✦ **Dynamic Help page:** Use the Dynamic Help (see Figure 2-3) page to customize the Dynamic Help window as you want. For example, you can use this page to specify the number, type, and order of links displayed in the Dynamic Help window.

The Dynamic Help page contains two lists: Categories and Topic Types. The Categories list contains various groups of topics, such as Training, Help, and Samples. The Topic Types list contains topics, such as Article, Reference, and Syntax, for each category.

Customize the Dynamic Help window by selecting or clearing appropriate topics. You can limit the number of links displayed in the window and also specify the type of links. For example, you can set the Dynamic Help window to display links for the selections only or for the user interface elements that you're currently working with.

✦ **Fonts and Colors page:** Use the Fonts and Colors page to customize font and color settings for elements with a user interface, such as the Text Editor. Figure 2-4 shows the Fonts and Colors page of the Options dialog box.

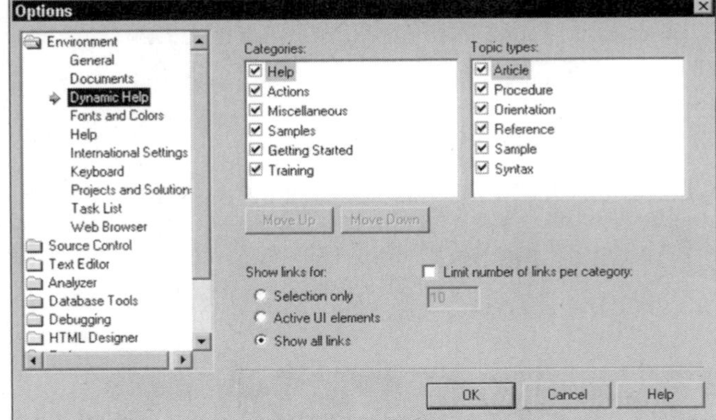

Figure 2-3: Customize the Dynamic Help window.

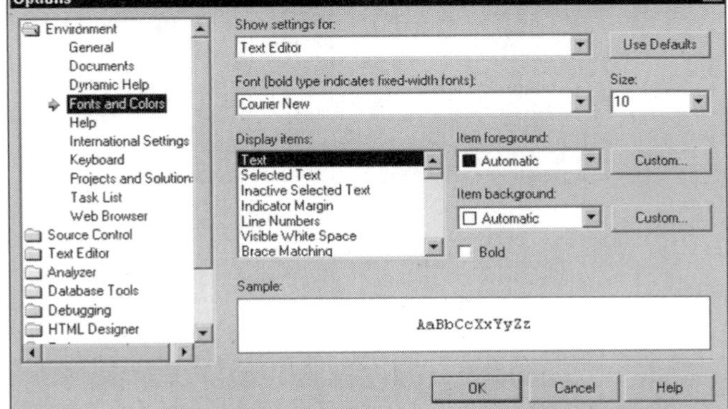

Figure 2-4: Specify custom fonts and colors here.

✦ **Help page:** Use the Help page (see Figure 2-5) to specify the language in which the Help installed on your computer displays. This page also enables you to specify whether the Help topics should be displayed in the IDE or in a separate window. To specify, use either the Internal Help or the External Help radio buttons.

✦ **International Settings page:** Use the International Settings page (Figure 2-6) to specify a language for the IDE. This comes in handy if you have many language versions of the IDE installed on your computer.

✦ **Keyboard page:** Use the Keyboard page (see Figure 2-7) to specify the keyboard settings for the IDE and for keyboard shortcuts for several frequently used commands.

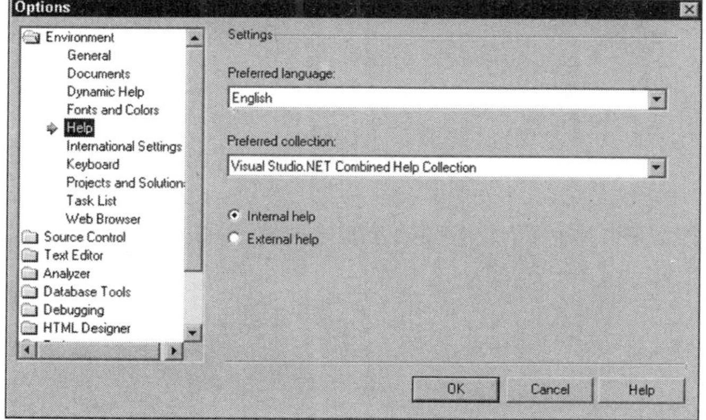

Figure 2-5: Specify Help options from the Help page.

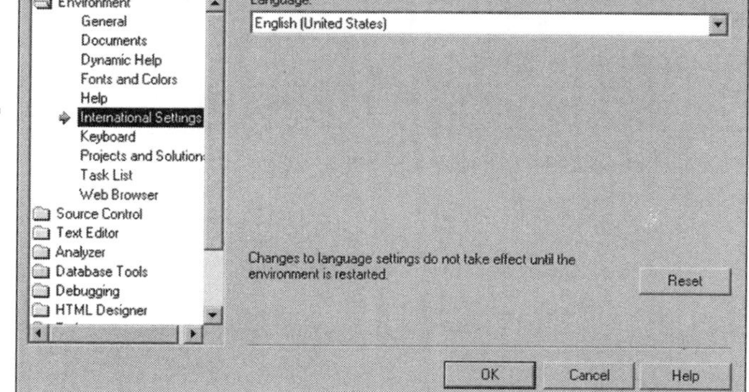

Figure 2-6: Specify the IDE language with the International Settings page.

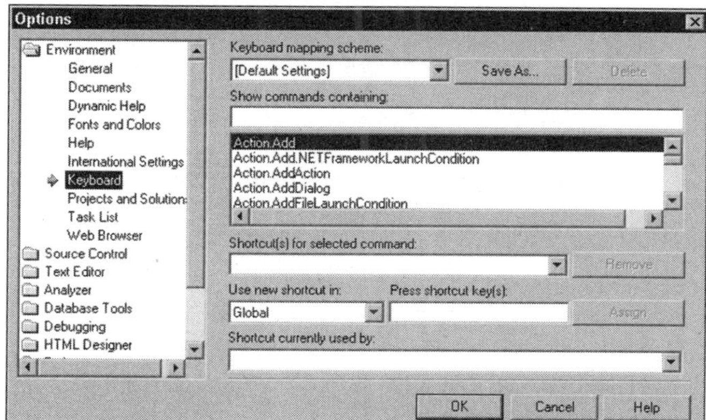

Figure 2-7: Specify keyboard mappings here.

✦ **Projects and Solutions page:** Use the Projects and Solutions page (as shown in Figure 2-8) to specify a location for storing your projects. The page also helps you specify that when you build or run an application, the computer should automatically save open documents, prompt the user to save such documents, or doesn't need to save the open documents.

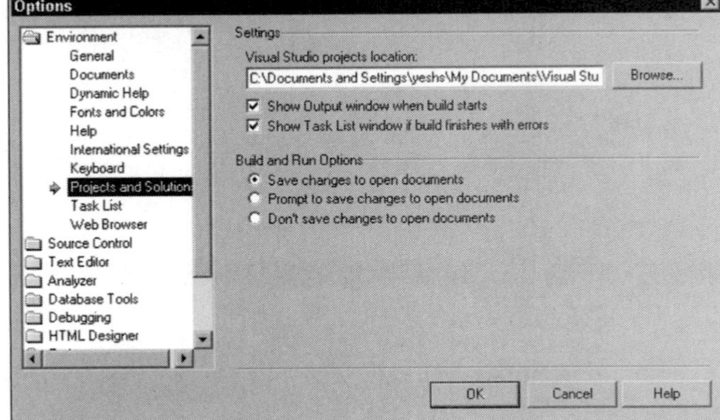

Figure 2-8: Customize projects and solutions with the Projects and Solutions page.

✦ **Task List page:** Use the Task List page (Figure 2-9) to specify options for adding, deleting, and modifying comments in the Task List.

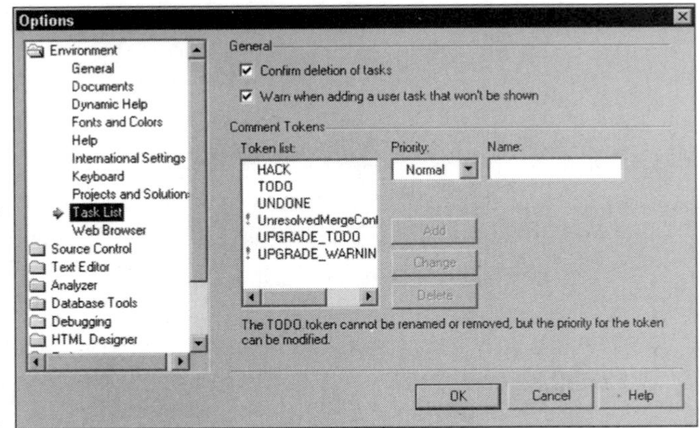

Figure 2-9: Manage your Task List comments here.

✦ **Web Browser page:** Use the Web Browser (Figure 2-10) page to customize the internal Web browser of Visual Studio and Internet Explorer.

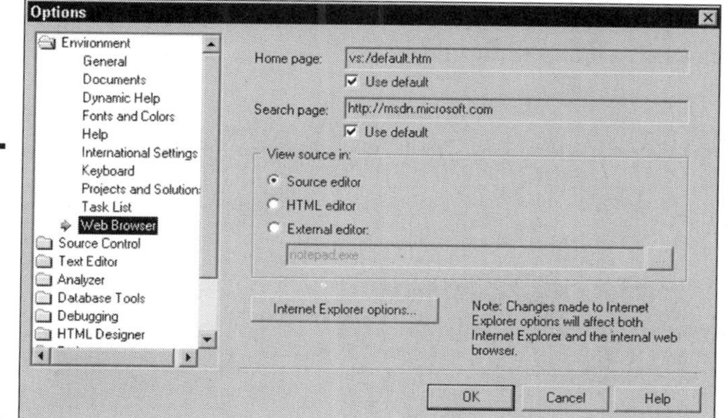

Figure 2-10: Customize browser settings with the Web Browser page.

To change the internal Web browser of Visual Studio .NET, follow these steps:

1. **Under Home page (refer to Figure 2-10), uncheck the Use Default.**

   Notice that the Home page text box becomes enabled.

2. **In the Home page text box, type** http://msdn.microsoft.com.

3. **Close Visual Studio .NET and then start it again.**

   The home page of `msdn.Microsoft.com` appears instead of the Start Page.

Customize Dialog Box

Use features of the Customize dialog box to manipulate the toolbars present in the IDE. This dialog box enables you to create your own toolbars, add or remove buttons from the existing toolbars, and modify the appearance of the toolbars.

To display the Customize dialog box, choose Tools⇨Customize. The Customize dialog box contains three tabs: Toolbars, Commands, and Options.

Toolbars tab

You use the Toolbars tab to perform the following tasks:

- ✦ Create new toolbars.
- ✦ Rename existing toolbars.
- ✦ Delete existing toolbars.
- ✦ Reset existing toolbars by removing any changes that you made.

Figure 2-11 shows the Toolbars tab of the Customize dialog box.

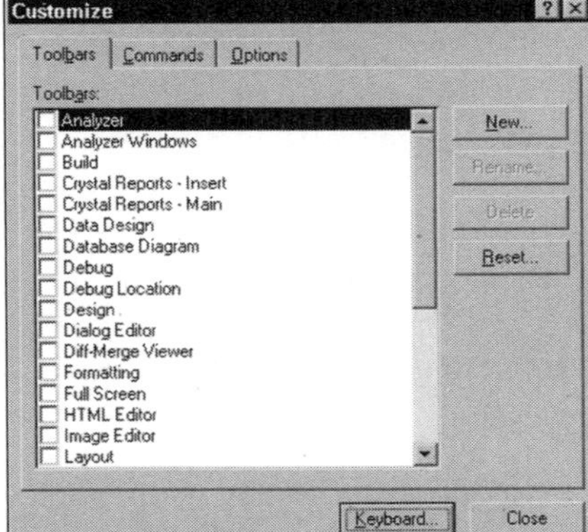

Figure 2-11: Customize the toolbars in the IDE by using the Toolbars tab.

To create a toolbar:

1. **Choose Tools⇨Customize to display the Customize dialog box.**
2. **Click the Toolbars tab to make it active.**
3. **Click the New button to display the New Toolbar dialog box, as shown in Figure 2-12.**

Figure 2-12: Create custom toolbars.

4. **In the Toolbar Name text box, type** My Toolbar **and click OK.**

   A toolbar named `My Toolbar` appears in the IDE.

After creating a toolbar, you need to add buttons to it from the Commands tab.

Commands tab

You use the Commands tab to add frequently used commands to toolbars. As shown in Figure 2-13, the Commands tab contains two lists: Categories and Commands. The Categories list displays various groups of commands, such as File and Edit. The Command list displays commands in a selected category. For example, the File category contains the New Project and New File commands.

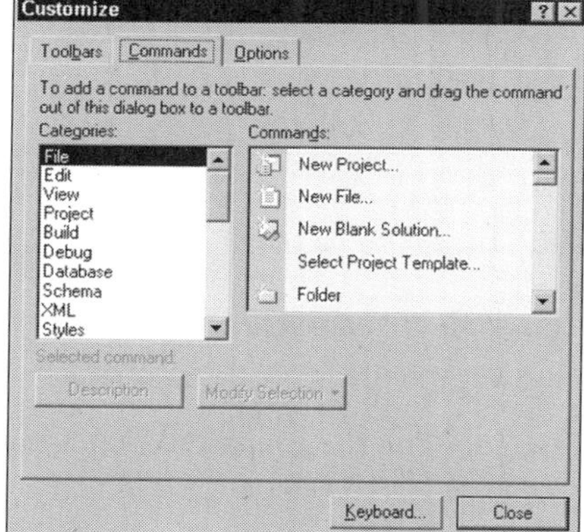

Figure 2-13: Add toolbar commands from the Commands tab.

To add the Close command, of the File category, to the toolbar (`My Toolbar`) that we create in the previous section:

1. **Switch to the Commands tab of the Customize dialog box.**
2. **Ensure that File is selected in the Categories list.**
3. **From the Command list, click Close to select it.**
4. **Drag the Close command and drop it on** `My Toolbar`**.**

   Notice that the Close command button appears on My Toolbar. You can now use this command to close the documents.

Options tab

Use the Options tab to customize the appearance of toolbars and menu bars. For example, you can specify an animation, such as a slide-down, for a menu. Figure 2-14 displays the Options tab.

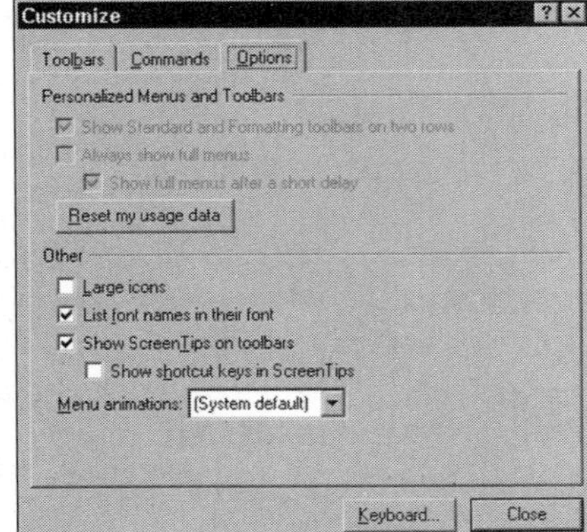

Figure 2-14: Customize toolbars and menu bar appearance here.

To add an animation to the menus available in IDE:

1. **Switch to the Options tab of the Customize dialog box.**
2. **From the Menu Animations list, click Slide to select it.**
3. **Click the Close button to close the Customize dialog box.**
4. **Click the File menu.**

   Notice that the menu slides down.

Index

A

B

C

D

E

R-S

T

V

W

X-Y-Z

Book III

Visual Basic .NET

The 5th Wave
By Rich Tennant
©RICHTENNANT
The great thing about object-oriented programming is, it's made Web site development as easy as putting one foot in front of the other.

Contents at a Glance

Chapter 1: Introduction to Visual Basic .NET

In This Chapter

- **Exploring the features of Visual Basic .NET**
- **Attending a short course on language changes in Visual Basic .NET**
- **Upgrading your projects from Visual Basic 6.0 to Visual Basic .NET**

One of the most powerful tools available in the .NET Framework is Visual Basic .NET. Delivering the ability to develop applications quickly and effectively, it's also now a complete object-oriented language you can use to develop Windows and Web applications. With the introduction of object orientation, Visual Basic .NET allows you to reuse existing functionality, thus saving your precious time. Visual Basic.NET is the next generation of the Visual Basic language.

Visual Basic .NET is somewhat different from Visual Basic 6.0 in syntax. You can upgrade your existing Visual Basic 6.0 applications to Visual Basic .NET by using the Visual Basic Upgrade Wizard.

In this chapter, we discuss the very basics of Visual Basic .NET, throw in a little history on Visual Basic .NET and its ancestor Visual Basic 6.0, and introduce you to the methods for converting your existing Visual Basic 6.0 applications to Visual Basic .NET.

Exploring Visual Basic .NET

Visual Basic .NET is based on the .NET Framework, which is Microsoft's latest initiative for enhanced security, efficient memory management, and easy deployment of applications. The .NET Framework is known for its interoperability across applications, which allows you to reuse existing components created in a programming language other than yours. Visual Basic .NET, the new generation of Visual Basic, provides an easy and fast way to create applications based on the .NET Framework.

Visual Basic .NET is now a powerful object-oriented programming language with features such as inheritance, interfaces, and overloading. Other useful features include structured exception handling and multithreading. Before we get to the toys — the new features — here's the skinny on the basic features of the Visual Basic .NET language.

Starting with the basics

If you're new to programming, read through the following for the scoop on the basic concepts used in a programming language. You advanced smarties can skip this part, or maybe give in to the temptation to read a refresher. These concepts aren't unique to Visual Basic, but you need to know them.

- **Variable:** A *variable* is a memory location that's used to store data. A variable is referred by a name and can store data of a particular data type. The data stored in a variable can change at any point in a program.
- **Data types:** The *data type* refers to the kind of data, such as numbers or text. Visual Basic .NET provides you with various data types such as `Integer`, `String`, `Byte`, and `Date`.
- **Constant:** A *constant* is similar to a variable and is used to store a value. The only difference between the two is that the value stored in a constant always remains the same. A constant is also assigned a name and is of a particular data type.
- **Array:** An *array* is a set of variables with the same name. You refer to these variables by specifying their *index position*, which is the position of the variable in the array. Visual Basic .NET enables you to create single- and multi-dimensional arrays as well as to resize the array at runtime.
- **Enumeration:** An *enumeration* is a set of related constants. For example, you can have an enumeration that contains constants that are used to specify colors, such as `Black`, `Red`, `Yellow`, and `Green`. Visual Basic .NET provides you a number of enumerations. You'll learn about them as and when you use them.
- **Operators:** An *operator* is a symbol used to perform operations on constants and variables. Visual Basic .NET provides you with arithmetic, logical, and concatenation operators to perform operations with constants and variables.
- **Expression:** A combination of variables, constants, and operators, an *expression* returns a value.
- **Statement:** A *statement* is a combination of variables, constants, operators, expressions, and keywords.

A *keyword* is a term with a special meaning. For example, the `Dim` keyword is used to declare a variable.

Visual Basic .NET provides two types of statements:

  - **Declaration statements:** These statements are used to declare a variable, a constant, or a procedure.
  - **Executable statements:** These statements are used to perform an action. For example, a statement used to assign a value to a variable is an executable statement.

- **Procedure:** A *procedure* is a set of statements that are used to perform a specific task.

These programming concepts are also a part of earlier versions of the Visual Basic programming language.

Exploring new features of Visual Basic .NET

You'll really like the new features of Visual Basic .NET. Microsoft added such goodies as inheritance and structured exception handling. Visual Basic .NET basically uses the same syntax as Visual Basic 6.0 except for some changes, which we detail in the upcoming section "Discovering Visual Basic .NET Language Changes."

Let's look at some of the new features of Visual Basic .NET.

Using assemblies as building blocks

An *assembly* is an EXE or a DLL file that forms the basis of deployment, version control, reuse, and security permissions of an application. Simply put, an assembly is a building block of the .NET Framework. An advanced version of type libraries, which existed in previous versions of Visual Basic, an assembly contains information contained in the type libraries and also all the essential ingredients required for an application or a component.

What's cool: Because an assembly contains all information about the content, version, and dependencies of an application, your application is less dependent on registry values. Assemblies reduces DLL conflicts, making your applications easier to deploy.

To use an assembly, you need to add a reference to it; read about this in the upcoming section "Adding references to an object."

Using namespaces for identifying types

A *namespace* contains types, such as classes, structures, enumerations, and interfaces. You can utilize these types in your applications. Namespaces are components of assemblies and primarily organize the objects present in the assemblies. An assembly can contain more than one namespace.

What's cool: With the introduction of namespaces, you can now create classes with the same names. However, these classes need to be present in different namespaces. Moreover, while referencing a class, you need to precede it with the name of the namespace separated by a dot. For example, you can create two classes named Class1, which are present in Namespace1 and Namespace2. Now, you reference Class1 present in Namespace1, as shown below.

```
Namespace1.Class1
```

Similarly, to access Class1 in Namespace2, use the following statement.

```
Namespace2.Class1
```

All namespaces begin with either the word *System* or *Microsoft*. System namespaces are developed by the .NET Framework Software Development Kit (SDK) team, and the Microsoft namespaces are developed by other groups at Microsoft, such as the team responsible for the development of MS Office. These other groups are not directly involved in the development of Visual Studio .NET.

Some frequently used namespaces are

- `Microsoft.VisualBasic`: Contains classes (such as `VBCodeProvider`) used to compile and execute Visual Basic applications.
- `System`: Contains classes and base classes (such as `Array`, `String`, and `Type`) with commonly used data types, events, and interfaces, such as `String`.
- `System.Windows.Forms`: Contains classes (such as `Button` and `CheckBox`) that enable you to create Windows-based applications containing various controls, such as buttons and check boxes.

Hierarchies of namespaces are written with dots (periods; .) inserted between any two levels. For example, `System.Windows.Forms` represents the `Forms` namespace, which is contained in the `Windows` namespace. The `Windows` namespace, in turn, is present in the `System` namespace. Read more on namespaces in Book 1, Chapter 2.

Read through the following sections to discover how the objects that you provide by a namespace or an assembly can be used in your application. For this, you need to add a reference to that object.

Adding references to an object

To use objects that are external to your current application, you need to add a reference to that object by selecting the `Add Reference` menu item from the `Project` menu present in the Visual Studio .NET IDE (Integrated Development Environment). For example, you created a spell checker object in some application. Now, if you need to use this spell checker object in some other application, then you can add a reference to this object in the current application. After adding a reference to a namespace, you can use the `Imports` statement to refer to the namespaces available in that assembly. The syntax of an `Imports` statement is

```
Imports [Alias =] Namespace
```

In the preceding syntax, `Alias` refers to an alternate (short) name of the namespace. The `Namespace` refers to the name of the namespace being referred. The alias name is useful in situations where the hierarchy of a particular namespace is long and difficult to remember. For example, instead of writing `System.Windows.Forms.Button` over and again, you can give an alias, say `MyButton`, and use this alias to refer to properties and events of the `Button` class. The code for such an alias looks like this:

```
Imports MyButton = System.Windows.Forms.Button
```

This statement is placed at the beginning of the code.

You can't begin an alias name with special characters, such as @ and #.

Adding attribute tags to elements

Attributes are the tags introduced with Visual Studio .NET that you use to provide additional information about the elements you define in a Visual Basic .NET program. This information can be utilized by other applications, such as the Visual Basic .NET compiler, to determine the usage of objects that you provide in your application. The advantage of using attributes is that they enable you to expand the functionality of your application without requiring changes in the compiler. Some of the most common uses of the attributes are to

- Explain `COM` properties for classes, interfaces, and methods by using attributes, such as `ComRegisterFunctionAttribute` and `ComImportAttribute`
- Explain assemblies by using attributes, such as `AssemblyVersionAttribute` and `AssemblyCultureAttribute`
- Specify security requirements of methods by creating your own attributes that define the permissions required to execute a procedure
- Specify features required to enforce security by creating your own attributes that define these features

Maximizing inheritance for code reuse

When you utilize inheritance, Visual Basic .NET enables you to reuse code, thus reducing your application development time. *Inheritance* means that you can create classes that are derived from some other classes, known as *base* classes. These derived classes can utilize the methods and properties defined in the base class; or, if need be, they create their own methods and properties if required.

Inheritance provides you the advantage of defining a class only once. You can then reuse this functionality over and over again by deriving new classes from this class. The introduction of inheritance in Visual Basic .NET makes it par with other programming languages, as previous versions of Visual Basic doesn't support inheritance.

Inheriting forms with visual inheritance

Visual Basic .NET introduces a new forms package called Windows Forms that enables developers to inherit a form from an existing form. Offering the advantage of enhanced productivity and code reuse, this feature, called *visual inheritance,* is helpful in situations where a company decides to provide a standard user interface, such as a common set of buttons, across forms contained in all its applications. In this scenario, you need to create only one form with all the required controls and code. Now, using visual inheritance, you can inherit a number of new forms from this form. Each of the inherited forms will contain the same set of controls and code, thus saving your valuable time.

Detecting error handlers more efficiently

You can use Visual Basic .NET to create more efficient and robust error handlers by using structured exception handling, which helps you to detect and remove errors at runtime. To do this, Visual Basic .NET uses the `Try...Catch...Finally` statements. This type of error handling enhances the performance of your application, as you can act smart and handle all the possible errors that might occur in your application.

Maximizing multithreading

Visual Basic .NET introduces multithreading to enable your applications to handle multiple tasks simultaneously. This improves application responsiveness to the user input because the user interaction part can run on one thread and the part that requires processor use can run on a different thread.

Discovering Visual Basic .NET Language Changes

Change is always a bit unsettling. Of course, Visual Basic .NET has its share of language changes, too, but they're not that awful and really make a good bit of sense. In a nutshell, here's why Microsoft changed what it did.

- To make the language simpler to understand and easier to use
- To reduce the errors, such as syntax errors, that occur while writing code
- To make the code more readable by automatic indentation
- To make debugging programs easier by introducing structured exception handling
- To add the features that users requested, such as inheritance

One great thing about Visual Basic .NET is that it does allow you to upgrade applications that you created in Visual Basic 6.0. You do need to take care of a number of things before you actually start upgrading, which you can read about in the upcoming section "Upgrading to Visual Basic .NET."

Read on to discover the language changes introduced in Visual Basic .NET with respect to its immediate predecessor, Visual Basic 6.0. Microsoft made changes to arrays, string, data types, logical operator, control flow, and variable declaration. If you're new to programming, you can skip this section.

Changes in arrays

Changes that have occurred in implementing arrays in Visual Basic .NET affect declaration, size declaration, and the `ReDim` statement.

Declaration

In Visual Basic .NET, the lower bound of an array is 0 and you can't change it because it doesn't support the `Option Base` statement. This change has been introduced to bring Visual Basic .NET to par with other programming languages.

In Visual Basic 6.0, the lower bound of an array is 0 by default. However, you can change this bound by using the `Option Base` statement.

Size declaration

In Visual Basic.NET, you cannot create fixed size arrays. The previously mentioned statement will be written as

```
Dim MyArr(10) As String
```

Or

```
Dim MyArr() As String= New String (10) {}
```

You can resize these arrays by using the `ReDim` statement.

In Visual Basic 6.0, you declare an array like this:

```
Dim MyArr(0 To 10) As String
```

In the preceding statement, the array `MyArr` is a *fixed-size* array, and you can't modify it by using the `ReDim` statement.

ReDim statement

In Visual Basic .NET, you can use the `ReDim` statement only for resizing an array.

In Visual Basic 6.0, you can use the `ReDim` statement to declare an array for the first time.

Changes in strings

The changes for implementing strings in Visual Basic .NET affect length declaration.

In Visual Basic .NET, you can't specify the length of a string. You can, however, declare a string like this:

```
Dim MyStr As String
```

In Visual Basic 6.0, the length of a string can be specified. For example,

```
Dim MyStr As String * 10
```

In the preceding statement, the length of the string `MyStr` is `10`.

Data type changes

The changes in the usage of data types in Visual Basic .NET include the following:

- **Visual Basic .NET uses the `Decimal` data type to store currency values.**

  In Visual Basic 6.0, you use the `Currency` data type to store currency values.

- **Visual Basic .NET provides the `DateTime` data type to store the values. in the date format.**

  In Visual Basic 6.0, you store a date in the `Double` data type.

- **Visual Basic .NET uses the `Object` data type to store data of any type.**

  In Visual Basic 6.0, you store data of any type in the `Variant` data type.

Changes for logical operators

In Visual Basic .NET, `And`, `Or`, `Not`, and `Xor` can only perform logical operations. To perform bitwise operations, you use `BitAnd`, `BitOr`, `BitNot`, and `BitXor` operators.

Read more about logical operators in Book 3, Chapter 5.

In Visual Basic 6.0, `And`, `Or`, `Not`, and `Xor` are used to perform the logical *and* bitwise operations.

Changes for control flow statements

The following have changes for control flow statements used in Visual Basic .NET.

- **In Visual Basic .NET, the `While...Wend` loop has changed to `While...End While`.**

  In Visual Basic 6.0, you use the `While...Wend` loop to execute a set of statements repeatedly while a condition is `true`.

- **In Visual Basic. NET, the `GoSub` statement is not supported. You can call procedures by using the `Call` statement.**

  In Visual Basic 6.0, you used the `GoSub` statement to call a subprocedure form within a procedure.

Changes for variable declarations

In Visual Basic .NET, you can declare multiple variables in a single line without specifying the type of each variable. Therefore, Statements `1` and `2` in the following code snippets declare two variables of the type `Integer`.

In Visual Basic 6.0, you needed to specify data types for each variable that you declare, especially when you declare multiple variables in a single line. For example:

```
Dim Var1, Var2 As Integer     'Statement 1
```

In the preceding statement, the `Var1` is of type `Variant` and `Var2` is of the type `Integer`. Therefore, to specify the data types of both the variables as `Integer`, you need to use the following statement:

```
Dim Var1 As Integer, Var2 As Integer   'Statement 2
```

Upgrading to Visual Basic .NET

Visual Basic.NET is designed to take full advantage of the features of the .NET Framework. Visual Basic is one of the most powerful tools used to develop Windows-based applications and now it contains features that make it a robust tool for creating Web sites. However, you cannot migrate your existing applications based on previous versions to the .NET version without undertaking a few updates. Here are some key points that you should consider before upgrading your existing applications.

Finding what needs updating for Visual Basic .NET

The following list contains some of the features that were part of Visual Basic 6.0 but are no longer supported by Visual Basic .NET:

- **OLE Container Control**
- **Dynamic Data Exchange (DDE)**
- **Data control and Remote Data control**
- **Visual Basic 5.0 Windows Common Controls**
- **Dynamic HyperText Markup Language (DHTML) applications**
- **ActiveX documents**
- **Web classes**

If your applications use any of the features listed previously, you should change it to a parallel present in Visual Basic .NET. For example, Visual Basic 5.0 Windows Common Controls need to be upgraded to version 6 controls, and ActiveX documents need to be rewritten as User Controls. This might take a significant amount of time, but you can't avoid it. This amount of time depends on the amount of rework required in the application. You can get a fair idea of the rework by looking at issues listed in the Upgrade Report, which are discussed in the upcoming section "Using the Visual Basic Upgrade Wizard". In addition, some of the features of Visual Basic 6.0 might not have any parallel in Visual Basic .NET. DHTML applications are such victims. In such situations, you should leave the application in its original version.

The fact that some of the features used in Visual Basic 6.0 are not supported by Visual Basic .NET shouldn't disturb you because Visual Studio 6.0 and Visual Basic .NET can coexist on the same computer. Hence, your applications created in Visual Basic 6.0 can coexist with the ones created in the .NET version.

You do have tools at your disposal to help with these updates as you upgrade your existing applications. Visual Basic .NET provides you with the Visual Basic Upgrade Wizard to help.

Using the Visual Basic Upgrade Wizard

To utilize the full potential of the .NET Framework, use the Visual Basic Upgrade Wizard to upgrade the projects that you created in Visual Basic 6.0. In addition to making upgrades easy, using this wizard doesn't make changes to your original application but creates a new Visual Basic .NET application. Note that you may be required to make some changes in the new .NET application because the Upgrade Wizard doesn't upgrade each and every thing present.

After you complete your updates, the Upgrade Wizard provides an upgrade report. The upgrade report, in HTML format, contains a list of issues that weren't covered by the Upgrade Wizard, such as the `GoSub` statement is not supported. These are the issues that are not supported by Visual Basic .NET. You need to fix these before executing the project.

Follow along to begin the process to upgrade an existing application:

1. **In Visual Basic 6.0, open the required project and choose File➪Make *<project_name>* where *<project_name>* is the actual name of your project.**
2. **Start Visual Studio .NET by clicking the Open Project button.**

   The Open Project dialog box opens.
3. **Select the appropriate project file (look for a `.vbp` file extension) of the Visual Basic 6.0 project that you want to update and then click the Open button.**

   The Visual Basic Upgrade Wizard – Page 1 of 5 appears, as shown in Figure 1-1.

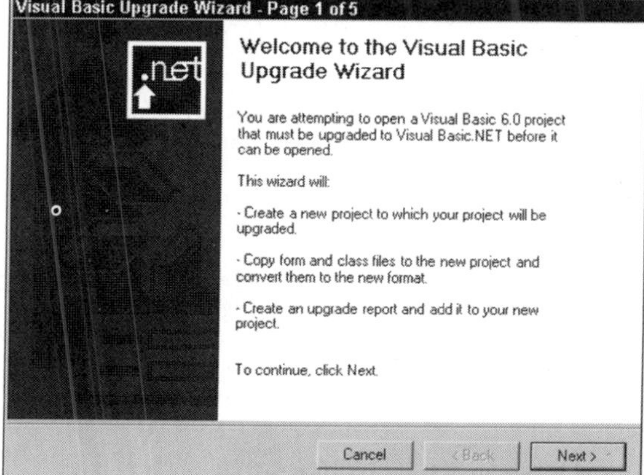

Figure 1-1: Beginning your Visual Basic upgrade with the wizard.

4. **Click the Next button to move to the second page of the wizard, as shown in Figure 1-2.**

   Specify the appropriate options for upgrade. These options might be different depending on the project that you're upgrading. For example, you may be queried whether you want to upgrade a project file to an EXE or a DLL file.

   In addition, a Generate default interfaces for all public classes check box is also present that helps you generate interfaces for the public classes present in your application.

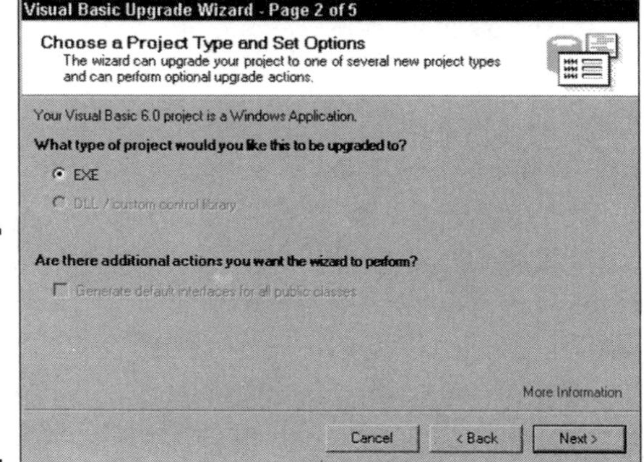

Figure 1-2: Choosing your upgrade from the wizard.

5. **After you make your initial selections, click the Next button to move to the third page of the wizard, as shown in Figure 1-3.**

   Here you type in or browse to specify the location that you want for your new project.

   If the folder that you specify doesn't exist, the Upgrade Wizard displays a Warning message box prompting you to create one. If you need to create a new folder:

   In the Warning message box, click the Yes button to create a new folder. The fourth page of the wizard appears.

6. **After you establish your project location without creating a new folder, click the Next button to move to the fourth page of the wizard, as shown in Figure 1-4.**

   This page lets you know that the Upgrade Wizard is now ready to start upgrading.

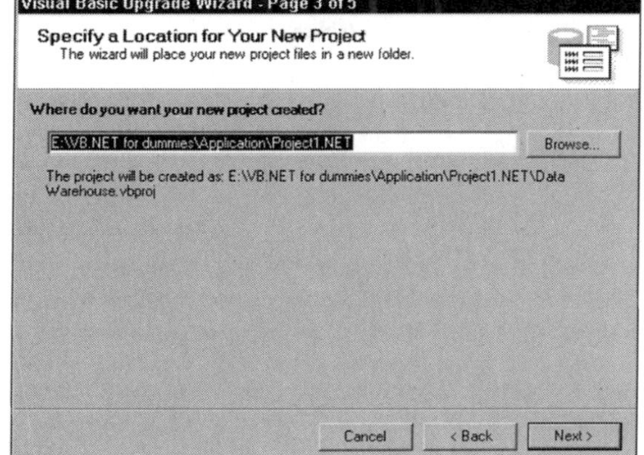

Figure 1-3: Specify your project location in the wizard's third page.

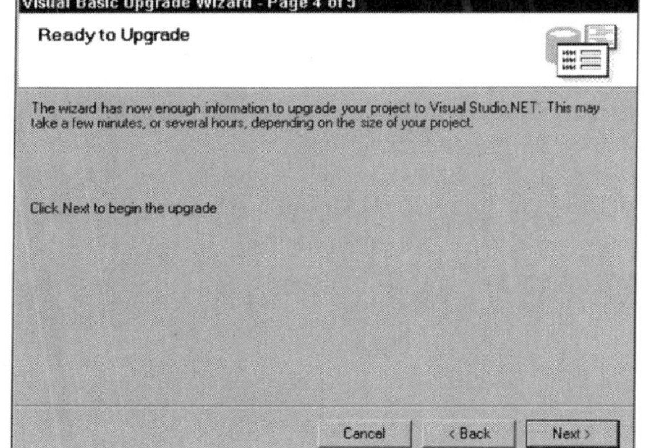

Figure 1-4: Almost home.

7. **Click the Next button to start the upgrading process.**

   Page 5 of 5 of the Upgrade Wizard appears, as shown in Figure 1-5. The page displays the status of process and time remaining for the upgrade.

   When the upgrade is complete, the Upgrade Wizard disappears and your new project appears in the Solution Explorer that is visible on the right side of the IDE.

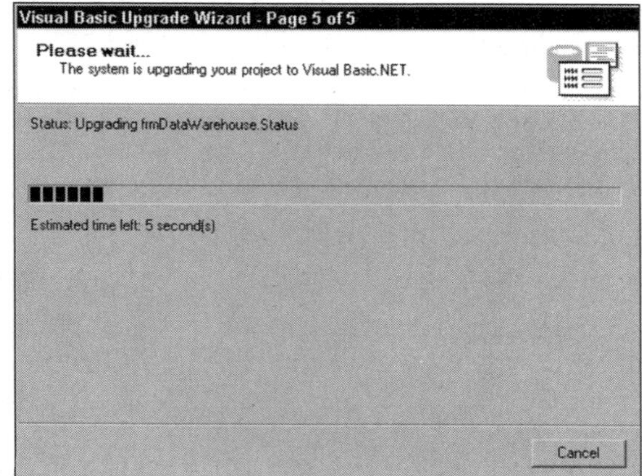

Figure 1-5: Houston, we have an upgrade in progress.

8. **In the Solution Explorer, double-click the file `_UpgradeReport.htm`.**

   The upgrade report for the project appears, as shown in Figure 1-6. You need to correct any errors cited in this report. You should also check the warnings for their possible effects on your applications.

Start Page | Browse - Data...pgrade Report

List of Project Files

New Filename	Original Filename	File Type	Status	Errors	Warnings	Total Issues
(Global Issues)				0	0	0
Global update issues: None						
Data Warehouse.vb	Data Warehouse.frm	Form	Upgraded with issues	0	33	33

Upgrade Issues for Data Warehouse.frm:

#	Severity	Location	Object Type	Object Name	Property	Description
1	Runtime Warning	Command1_Click				Couldn't resolve default property of object strConn.
2	Runtime Warning	Command1_Click				Couldn't resolve default property of object cnnConnection.Open.
3	Runtime Warning	Command1_Click				Couldn't resolve default property of object strConn.
4	Runtime Warning	Command1_Click				Couldn't resolve default property of object cmdCommand.ActiveConnection.
5	Runtime Warning	Command1_Click				Couldn't resolve default property of object cmdCommand.CommandText.
6	Runtime Warning	Command1_Click				Couldn't resolve default property of object cmdCommand.Execute.
7	Runtime Warning	Command1_Click				Couldn't resolve default property of object recNew.Open.
8	Runtime Warning	Command1_Click				Couldn't resolve default property of object recNew

Figure 1-6: Check for errors in your update report.

   If your update went through successfully — or after any errors needing correction are repaired — you're now ready to execute your application.

9. **Choose Debug⇨Start, and you're off with your updated project.**

Chapter 2: Windows Forms: The First Step

In This Chapter

- Introducing Windows Forms
- Working with Windows Forms
- Creating inherited Windows Forms

The basis of any Visual Basic .NET application is forms. Microsoft has introduced a new forms package — Windows Forms — that comes packed with a number of enhancements over its predecessors. In this chapter, you read about Windows Forms, create a traditional "Hello World" application, and discover how to create forms easily by using inheritance.

A *form* is a window that appears while you're working with an application. In addition, the dialog boxes and message boxes that you encounter when using different applications are also forms. A form provides user interaction by allowing you to display information to and accept information from the user.

Windows Forms

Windows Forms is the new forms package that comes bundled with the .NET Framework. Windows Forms enables your Windows-based applications to fully utilize the user interface features of the Windows operating system. Windows Forms also supports various new features, such as common application framework, managed execution environment, integrated security, and object-oriented design principles. These forms also provide support for Web services by using eXtensible Markup Language (XML) and for database applications by using ADO.NET.

The applications that you build using Windows Forms are based on the `System.Windows.Forms` namespace. This namespace includes classes, such as `Form`, `Menu`, and `Clipboard`, which help you implement and manipulate forms, menus, and clipboard support in your applications. Just like all other objects present in the .NET Framework, forms are also instances of classes. Actually, when you create a form in the Windows Forms Designer, a class is created, which is derived from `System.Windows.Forms.Form`. When you display this form at runtime, an instance of the class is created. You can read more on namespaces in Book 1, Chapter 2.

Read on to discover some differences between Windows Forms and the forms in the earlier version of Visual Basic.

Form Changes in Visual Basic .NET

Windows Forms has introduced some changes in the usage of forms. Some of these changes include

- **Form naming:** In Visual Basic 6.0, you specify a name for the form by using the `Name` property of the form. However, in Visual Basic .NET, you need to set the `File Name` property of the class file of a form.
- **Start-up position of the form:** In Visual Basic 6.0, you specify the start-up position of the form by using the Layout window or the `Startup` property in the Properties window. In Visual Basic .NET, you can set the `StartPosition` property in the Properties window.
- **Alignment and size of the controls on the form:** In Visual Basic 6.0, you select all the controls by clicking on them. All the selected controls were aligned and sized based on the last control that you selected. In Visual Basic .NET, all the selected controls are aligned and the size is based on the size of the first control that you select.
- **Tab order for the controls on the form:** In Visual Basic 6.0, you used to select the control and set the `TabIndex` property of the control. In Visual Basic .NET, you set tab order by choosing View⇨Tab Order. All the controls on the form now contain a number that displays their tab positions. To set the tab order, just click the control in the desired order.
- **Modality of a form:** In Visual Basic 6.0, you use the `Show` method to display a form and use the constant `vbModal` to display a modal dialog box. In Visual Basic .NET, you use the `ShowDialog` method to display a form as a modal dialog box. A *modal dialog box* is a dialog box that doesn't allow you to work with any application until you close it.

Working with Windows Forms

If you've already worked with Visual Basic, welcome back to the somewhat similar look and feel. All you need to do is to create a new project and get going. You use the Windows Forms Designer for designing your applications. To create a Windows application, you need to perform the following steps:

1. **Create a new Windows Application project.**

   To accomplish this task, read the following section "Creating a new Windows Application project."

2. **Design the form at design time by using the Properties window.**

   To find out how to accomplish this task, read the section "Customizing Windows Forms" later in this chapter.

3. **Add controls to the form.**

   Read how to add controls to a form in Book 3, Chapter 3.

   You can also add MDI (Multiple Document Interface) forms, provide drag-and-drop support, utilize system clipboard — and most importantly, provide help in your applications — depending on the necessity and requirement. We discuss these topics in more depth in Book 3, Chapter 4.

Get started now by creating a new Windows Application project.

Creating a new Windows Application project

To create a new application, follow these steps:

1. **Launch Visual Studio .NET by choosing Start⇨Programs⇨Microsoft Visual Studio .NET 7.0⇨Microsoft Visual Studio .NET 7.0.**

   The Start Page appears.

2. **Click the New Project button.**

3. **In the New Project dialog box that appears, under Project Types, click the Visual Basic Projects folder to display its contents.**

   This folder contains various templates that you can use to create various applications, such as Windows Application, by using Visual Basic.

4. **In the New Project dialog box, under Templates, click Windows Application to select it.**

   You create a new Windows Application project.

5. **In the Name box, type a name for the project.**

   For this example, use the name `MyApplication`.

6. **In the Location box, specify the appropriate location where this project will be stored.**

7. **Click OK to create the application.**

   Observe the Solution Explorer. It displays the project and the files contained in this project in a tree view. The project contains a form named `Form1` by default.

After you create a project, you might need to add new forms to it. Read the following section for details on adding forms to a project.

Adding forms to a project

When you create a new application, the application contains one form by default. However, you can add more forms to it by using either of the following two methods:

1. **In Solution Explorer, right-click the project name.**

   For example, if you named the project `MyApplication`, right-click `MyApplication`. Read more on Solution Explorer in Book 2, Chapter 1.

2. **From the pop-up menu that appears, choose Add⇨Add Windows Form.**

   The Add New Item dialog box appears, as shown in Figure 2-1. The Title bar of the dialog box also displays the name of the current project.

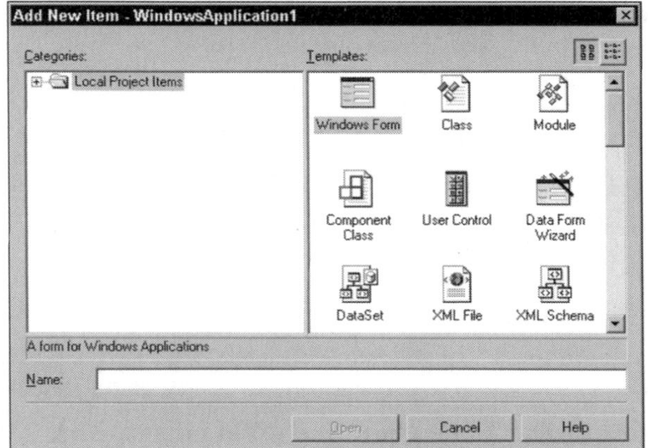

Figure 2-1: The Add New Item dialog box.

3. **In the Name text box, type an appropriate name for the form and then click the Open button.**

   A form with the specified name appears in the project.

Or

1. **Choose Project⇨Add Windows Form.**
2. **In the Name text box of the Add New Item dialog box, type an appropriate name for the form, and then click the Open button.**

   A form with the specified name appears in the project.

After you create a Windows Application project and then add the requisite number of forms to it, it's time to design or customize these forms. Read the following section to understand various steps involved in the process.

Customizing Windows forms

While developing applications in Visual Basic .NET, you may need to manipulate a form's appearance. For example, you may need to alter the size of a form or apply a different border style. You can easily do so by using the properties provided by a form. You can set these properties either at design time by using the Properties window or at runtime in the code. You can also force one form to appear on top of another.

Setting the size of Windows forms

If you need to change the size of the form, Visual Basic .NET enables you to resize a form at both the design time and runtime.

- At **design time**, you can resize a form either
  - Manually, by clicking and dragging sizing handles that appear on the form border.
  - By specifying the size in the Size field of the Properties window, which is present at the lower-right corner of the IDE. Specify the width and height dimensions, separated by a comma, in the Size field of the Property window. Or you can specify width and height separately by expanding the Size field and then filling the Width and Height properties. To expand the Size field, click the plus icon next to it.

If the Properties window isn't available, choose View⇨Properties Window to display it.

- At **runtime**, you can resize a form by
  - Specifying the values for the `Size` property in the code. The following statement shows the syntax:

```
MyForm.Size = New Size(200,200)
```

  - Specifying the width and height of the form. The following code statements illustrates the syntax:

```
'Specify the Width of the form
MyForm.Size = New Size(200, MyForm.Size.Width)
'Specify the Height of the form
MyForm.Size = New Size(200, MyForm.Size.Height)
```

  - Setting the height and width of the form in the code, like this:

```
MyForm.Width = 200
MyForm.Height = 200
```

Changing borders of Windows forms

You can change the appearance of your Windows Forms by applying a border style to it. Visual Basic .NET provides you with a number of border styles, such as `FixedDialog` and `Sizable`. To change the border style of a form, use the `FormBorderStyle` property, with which you can also control the resizing behavior of your form. For example, if you specify the border style as `FixedDialog`, you can't resize the form.

You can set this property either at design time (in the Properties window) or at runtime (in the code). The following statement sets the border style of the form to `FixedDialog`.

```
MyForm.FormBorderStyle = FormBorderStyle.FixedDialog
```

Making a Windows Forms appear on top

In your application, you may require a form to appear on top of other forms. For example, you might want the splash screen of your application to appear on top when the application starts. Achieve this by setting the `TopMost` property to `True` either in the Properties window or in the code, as we've done in the following snippet:

```
MyForm.TopMost = True
```

Creating a sample application

For a little practice, create a sample application by following these steps:

1. **Create a new Windows Application project named `MyFirstApplication`.**

   You can read the details for creating a new Windows Application project in the section "Creating a new Windows Application project." The `MyFirstApplication` project contains a blank form named `Form1`.

2. **Click `Form1` to select it.**

   The Properties window displays the properties of this form. You now customize your form by using this window.

3. **In the Text field of the Properties window, type** My First Form.

   `My First Form` now appears in the title bar of the form.

   The Text field (in the Properties window) actually represents the `Text` property of the form. Use this property to specify a caption (which appears in the Title bar of the form) for the form.

4. **In the Properties window, select `FixedDialog` from the `FormBorderStyle` list.**

5. **In the Properties window, select `False` from the `MaximizeBox` list.**

   Note that the Maximize button is now disabled.

6. **In the Properties window, select `False` from the `MinimizeBox` list.**

   The Minimize and Maximize buttons disappear from the form, as shown in Figure 2-2.

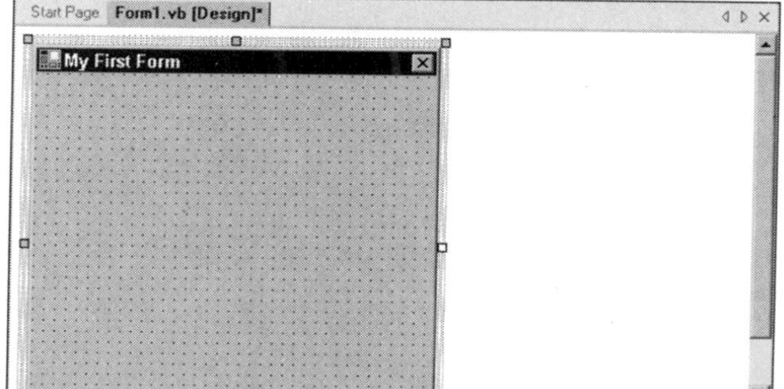

Figure 2-2: Creating a sample form.

7. **Double-click the form to open the Code window.**

   This puts you in the `Form1_Load` event, which occurs as soon as the form is loaded while executing.

8. **At the position of the insertion point, type the following:** MsgBox("Hello World").

   The preceding statement will display a message box with text `"Hello World"`. Read more about message boxes in Book 3, Chapter 4. You can refer to Figure 2-3 for the exact position of the syntax.

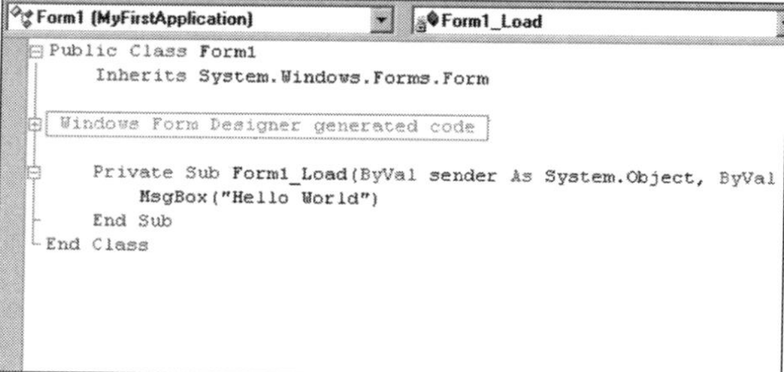

Figure 2-3: Type in your message here.

9. **Execute the application by choosing Start from the Debug menu.**

   A message box appears, as shown in Figure 2-4.

Figure 2-4: Your new message box.

10. **Click OK to close the message box.**

    The form that you created appears.

11. **Close the form.**

Now that you've created an application, look at the ways to create forms easily and quickly.

Creating Inherited Windows Forms

After putting in a lot of sweat, you designed a form containing a number of controls. Your supervisor appreciated your handiwork so much that you were rewarded with the task of designing another form. Luckily for you, this form is similar to the previous form except for some minor changes. Let Visual Basic .NET come to your rescue, helping you duplicate a form without having to re-create it — just inherit the new form from the desired form and make the required changes.

In order to inherit a form, you need to

- **Build the file or namespace that contains the form into an EXE or DLL file.**
- **Add a reference for the namespace to the class inheriting the form.**

You can inherit a form from another either by writing appropriate code or by using the `Inheritance Picker` dialog box.

Inheriting by coding

To inherit a form through coding, just perform the following steps:

1. **Add a reference to the namespace that you need to inherit from. For example, if you need to inherit a form from a form, which is present in the `WindowsApplication1` project, add the following line at the beginning of the code:**

    ```
    Imports WindowsApplication1
    ```

    You can read more on namespaces in Book 1, Chapter 2.

In case you're inheriting a form from another form that exists in the same project, you can skip this step. In addition, you need to build the application before moving on to the next step.

2. **In the class definition, specify the form to inherit from by using the** `Inherits` **keyword:**

```
Public Class MyNewForm Inherits
   WindowsApplication1.MyBaseForm
```

Read more about the `Inherits` keyword in Book 3, Chapter 8, where we lead you through the concept of inheritance.

Inheriting via Inheritance Picker

You can inherit a form from an existing form by using the Inheritance Picker dialog box; just follow these steps:

1. **Choose Project⇨Add Inherited Form to display the Add New Item dialog box.**
2. **In the Name box of the Add New Item dialog box, type an appropriate name for the new form and click Open.**

   The Inheritance Picker dialog box appears, as shown in Figure 2-5.

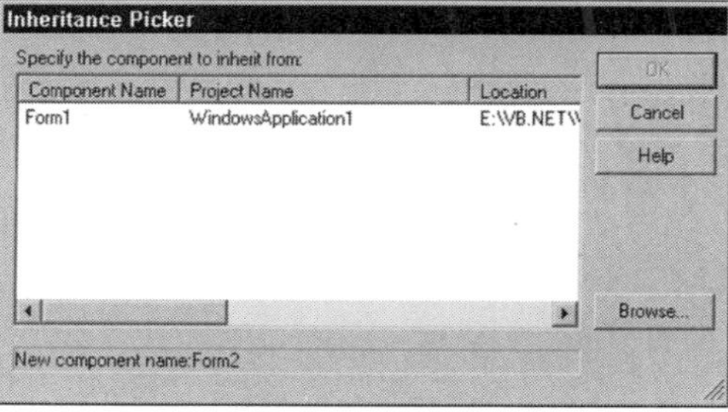

Figure 2-5: Set inheritance from the Inheritance Picker dialog box.

   The Specify the Component to Inherit From list displays all the components in the current application. This list displays components only if the application has been built; otherwise, the dialog box displays a message that the current application contains no components that can be inherited from.

3. **To inherit a component present in some other application, click the Browse button.**

   The Select a File Which Contains a Component to Inherit From dialog box appears, as shown in Figure 2-6. In this dialog box, select the component and click Open to move back to the Inheritance Picker dialog box.

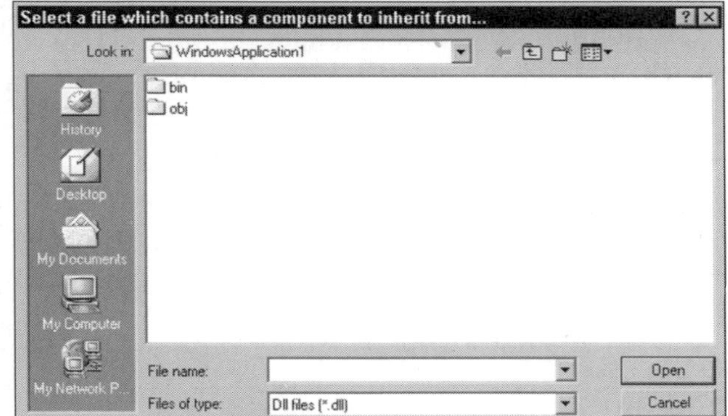

Figure 2-6: Inherit a component in a different application.

To inherit from a form in the current application, you skip Steps 3 and 4. In addition, you need to build the application by choosing Build➪Build.

4. **Click the appropriate EXE or DLL file to select it, and then click Open to return to the Inheritance Picker dialog box.**

   The name of the component appears in the Specify the Component to Inherit From list.

5. **Click the appropriate component to select it, and then click OK to add it to your project.**

   If this component has a user interface, then the inherited form will contain all the controls present on the original form along with a glyph. The *glyph* is an icon that appears in the upper-left corner of all the controls present on the inherited form.

Next, consolidate your learning by implementing this in the `MyFirstApplication` project.

Continuing with the sample application

In this section, we show you how to implement the concept of inheritance in the application that we show you how to create in the previous section. To inherit a form via coding, just follow these steps:

1. **In the Toolbox, which is present at the left edge of IDE, click the Windows Forms tab.**
2. **In the Toolbox, double-click Button to add it to** `Form1`**.**

   A Button with the caption Button 1 appears on the form. You can position the button on the form by clicking and dragging it. Don't worry, we cover details of adding controls to a form in Book 3, Chapter 3.

3. **Add a new form named `Form2`. You'll now inherit `Form2` from `Form1` via coding.**

   Read the details of adding new forms to a project in the section "Adding forms to a project" earlier in this chapter.

4. **Right-click anywhere in `Form2`.**

5. **From the pop-up menu that appears, choose View Code to display the class definition of `Form2`.**

   You'll learn more about classes in Book 3, Chapter 8.

6. **Modify the class definition of `Form2` to the one shown here:**

```
Public Class Form2
    Inherits Form1
```

7. **Switch to the design view of the form.**

   A message box displaying Hello World appears. This indicates that the code present in the existing form is also copied to the new form. In addition, note that `Form2` (as shown in Figure 2-7) also contains a button, `Button1`, with an icon (called a glyph) present in its upper-left corner.

   You can now make any other changes to `Form2` per your requirement.

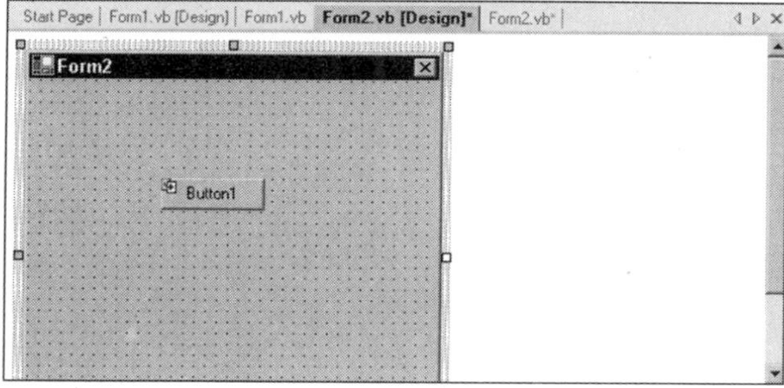

Figure 2-7: Form2 is ready in a flash.

Chapter 3: Working with Controls

In This Chapter

- **Adding controls to Windows forms**
- **Arranging controls on Windows forms**
- **Discovering other useful controls**

Unless you've created applications that only have dialog boxes and input boxes, you're bound to have used user interface controls in your career as an application developer. Any text box, list, label, or menu that you frequently encounter while working in Windows is a *user control*. Without a user control in Windows forms, a user running your application can only stare at a blank form, expecting something to happen.

Visual Studio .NET provides a number of controls that you can add to a form to make it visually appealing and enhance its functionality. For example, consider the annoyance of a user who has to provide her name, age, and address in three separate input boxes. Simplify her life by adding three text boxes on a form and using the form to accept data. Better still, provide a list of options that the user can select from: This saves your users from having to type in their data and also reduces the likelihood of introducing typos.

In this chapter, we explore the common controls available for a Windows form, as well as some common uses of these controls. We also walk you through the creation of a basic form and show you how to make it visually appealing.

Adding Controls to Windows Forms

In Visual Basic 6.0, the controls for a form are stored in a `Controls` collection. However, to provide interoperability across .NET applications, these controls are now placed in a common resource pool that can be used across applications. This common resource pool is the `System.Windows.Forms.Control.ControlCollection` class. Controls that you add to a form are retrieved from this class.

After you add controls to a form, they're available in the `ControlCollection` class of a form. Use the methods and collections of the `ControlCollection` class to add and remove controls at runtime. For example, if you need to first accept country information from a user and then display another list with the names of the provinces in that country, use the `ControlCollection` class and add the control at runtime.

In this section, we describe the procedure to add controls to the form at design time and runtime.

Adding controls at design time

Adding controls to a form at design time is simple. To add controls, simply use the options in the Toolbox. (See Figure 3-1.) By default, the Toolbox is visible on the left side of the screen. If it mysteriously disappears, make it visible again by selecting the Toolbox option from the View menu (or use the keyboard shortcut Ctrl+Alt+X).

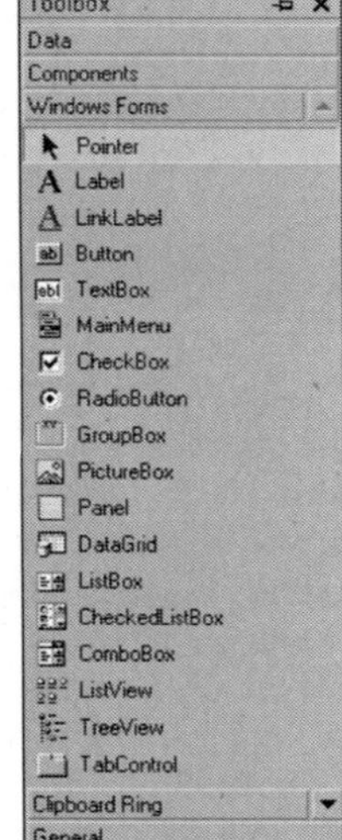

Figure 3-1: Use the Toolbox to add controls.

The controls available in the Toolbox are grouped into different categories for easy accessibility. The controls for each category are organized in the separate tabs of the Toolbox. You can switch to the appropriate category by clicking the appropriate tab. To view the controls under the Data category, for example, click the Data tab. The Toolbox includes a number of other categories; we highlight the important ones here:

- **Data:** The Data category includes controls that you use to access and manage data sources. For example, you can use the `DataView` control to retrieve data from a table in a database and then sort and filter it.
- **Components:** The Components category includes controls that you use to optimize the performance of your application. This category also contains controls that help you monitor the file events. To monitor a directory for the presence of a file, for example, use the `FileSystemWatcher` control. This control can monitor a directory or

its subdirectories for a specific file. When the file is found, you can write code to send the file to multiple recipients or analyze it and store the information in a database.

- **Windows Forms:** The Windows Forms category includes all the controls that you can include on the visual interface of a form. For example, this category includes the `TextBox` and the `MainMenu` controls used to add text boxes and menu options to a form.
- **Clipboard Ring:** Use the Clipboard Ring category to store text items in memory. Any code that you copy or cut from the `Code Editor` window is placed in this category. This category is especially useful when you want to move multiple code snippets from one part of the editor window to another.
- **General:** The General category contains only the Pointer tool. However, you can add controls, commonly used in your project, to this category. When you open the Toolbox, by default, the General category is visible.

After you become familiar with the Toolbox control categories, you're ready to add controls to a Windows form. The controls that you add to a Windows form either do or don't have a user interface; those that don't are hidden in the background. The hidden controls are used to perform back-end tasks. For example, the `Timer` control isn't visible to a user, but you can use it to invoke a function at a periodic interval.

To better differentiate visible and hidden controls, we discuss them separately, and then we move on to discuss adding ActiveX controls to a Windows form.

Adding user interface controls

The best way to learn how to add user interface controls is to create a sample application that uses these controls. For this example, we create an Employee Details form, which is used to accept an employee's name, gender, date of hire, and department. The controls that we use in the form are

- `Label`: For labeling the text box, radio button, and the other controls used on the form.
- `TextBox`: For entering the employee name.
- `RadioButton`: For entering the employee gender.
- `GroupBox`: For grouping the preceding radio buttons.
- `ListBox`: For creating a list of departments in the company to select from.
- `DateTimePicker`: For entering the date of hire of the employee.

Adding a label and a text box

Now you can create a new Windows application. The first screen of the application appears with a blank form. Add the employee name field to the form. To add a label and text box for the employee name, follow these steps:

1. **Access the Toolbox by choosing View⇨Toolbox.**

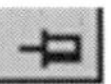

2. **Turn off the Auto Hide feature by clicking the pushpin icon next to the Close button of the Toolbox.**

   The Auto Hide feature gives you more space to work in because the name and icon of an auto-hidden window are visible as a tab on the edge of the IDE (Integrated Development Environment). When you point to this window, the contents are visible. However, as soon as the focus shifts away from this window, or in other words, when another window comes to the front, the window (with Auto Hide feature) again slides back to the tab. When you click the pushpin icon to disable the Auto Hide feature, the pushpin icon changes from vertical to horizontal.

3. **In the Toolbox, click the Windows Forms tab.**

   A list of controls available for the form appears.

4. **Click the `Label` control and drag it onto the form.**

   Alternatively, you can click the control: The shape of the pointer changes. Click and drag the pointer on the form to draw a label of appropriate size.

5. **Open the Properties window by selecting the `Label` control and then choosing View⇨Properties Window. (Or, select the Label control and press F4.)**

   Each form and its controls has properties that must be set, which you do in the Properties window. You can view the Properties window for any control by using any of the methods that we describe in this numbered list.

   For a label, you need to set its `Text` and `Name` properties. Check out Figure 3-2 to see the Properties window for the control that you now add.

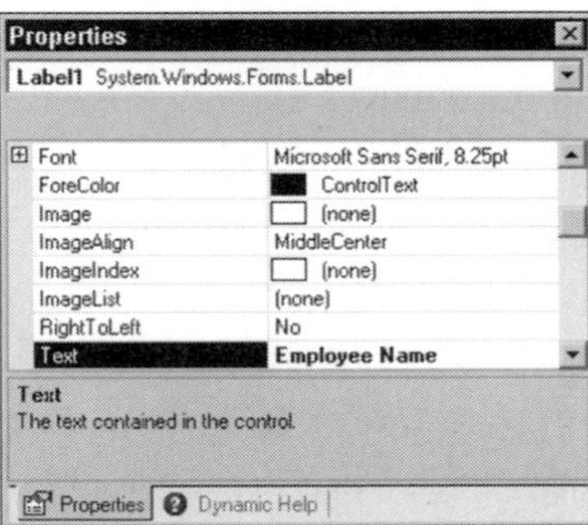

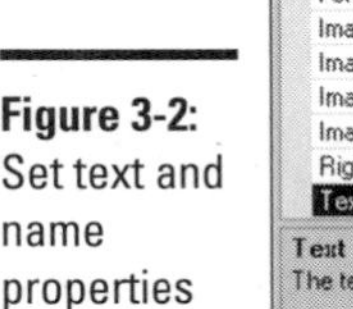

Figure 3-2: Set text and name properties here.

6. **Specify a caption for the label in the Text field by typing the caption in the right column of the Properties window. Additionally, specify a name, such as `EmployeeNameLabel`, for the label in the Name field.**

   You use this name to identify the control in the code.

7. **To add a text box to the form to accept the employee's name, click and drag the `TextBox` control from the Toolbox to the form.**

   In this case, name the text box as `NameTextBox`. After you add the label and the text box to the form, the form appears as shown in Figure 3-3.

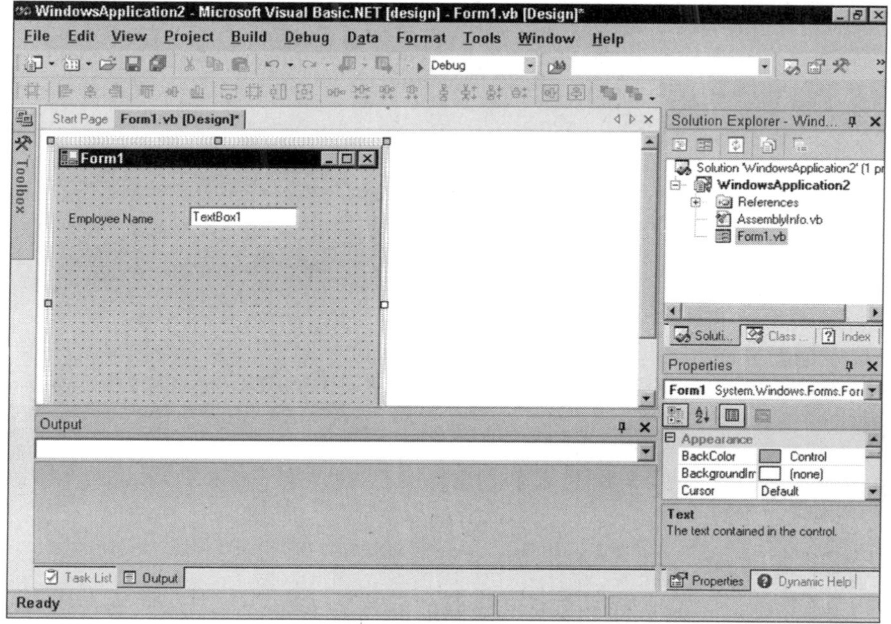

Figure 3-3: Add a label and a text box to a form.

8. **Highlight and delete the text that initially appears in the Text property of the text box by editing the Text field in the Properties window of the Text Box.**

   In this case, you delete `TextBox1` because you need to initially display a blank text box to the user so that the employee can enter his name in the text box.

Adding a group box and radio buttons

After you set the text and name fields, you're ready to add a group box and two radio buttons to the form to format the employee gender selection. You want to use a group box because the user has to select from only one of the two available options for the gender: (ahem) Male or Female. A group box helps you do exactly that. Another reason that developers use group boxes is to group controls into logical sections and thus enhance the user interface. Use the following steps to add a group box and two radio buttons to the form:

1. **Click and drag a `GroupBox` control from the Toolbox to the form.**
2. **In the Properties windows, specify Gender for the `Text` property of the group box.**

   To bring up the Properties window, select the group box and choose View➪Properties Window.
3. **Click and drag the `RadioButton` control to the form, in the Gender group box, twice — once for Male and once for Female.**
4. **Label each radio button accordingly by setting the `Text` property.**

   In this case, name the radio buttons `MaleRadioButton` and `FemaleRadioButton`.

Finishing your form

To finish this form, add a list box that gives users the option of selecting their department from a list of set choices: This strategy ensures that users enter their department name in a consistent format.

To add a list box that lists all the departments in the organization, click and drag a `ListBox` control from the toolbox to the form. Next, drag a Label icon to the form and label the list box as Department by using a Label control. Also, name the list box as `DepartmentListBox`.

To add department names to the Department list, you could use the Items collection in the Properties window, but we have a better way. We add items to the list when the form is about to be displayed at runtime (which we discuss later in the chapter, in the "Adding controls at runtime" section). This method is useful because in real life, you'll probably add items to the list from the output of a database table or probably from output from another data source. For now, we skip over adding items to the list, proceeding to the next step: adding a calendar to record the hire date. The steps to add a `DateTimePicker` control are

1. **Drag a `DateTimePicker` control to the form.**
2. **Name this control `DatePicker`.**
3. **Click and drag a Label control from the Toolbox to the form and set its `Text` property to `Date of Hire`.**

   You'll use this to label the `DateTimePicker` control. Read more on using the Label control in the "Adding a label and a text box" section.

4. **Select a value from the calendar provided with the `MinDate` property of the control.**

The `MinDate` property enables you to restrict the lower bound date of the control. For example, you can't have an employee who joined on a date before the date when the company was established. Therefore, the `MinDate` should be the date when the company was established. In this case, take the value as January 4, 1999.

The `MaxDate` must be the current date because you can't enter the hire date of an employee who will join your company in the future. (Neat trick if you could, though.) But here's the catch: If you specify a `MaxDate` as the current date and then a user opens the form one year from now, the calendar control will display the date on which the form was created, not the date on which the form was opened. If the user tries to input a date of hire that falls after the date when the form was created, an error message displays. The solution is to set the current date when the user is about to display the form, which we discuss after we finish working with controls. Don't worry about setting the `MaxDate` property right now.

Finally, to accept the user input, you need to add a Submit button users can click after they fill out the form. Also, add a Reset button so that the user can reset the contents of the form if desired.

To create a button, click and drag a `Button` control from the Toolbox to the form. Next, label the button Submit by using the `Text` property of the button. Name the button `SubmitButton` by using the `Name` property. Repeat the process to create a Reset button. Name the button `ResetButton`. We show you how to give these buttons functionality later in the section, "Adding the code for your form."

See the form as it appears after adding these controls in Figure 3-4.

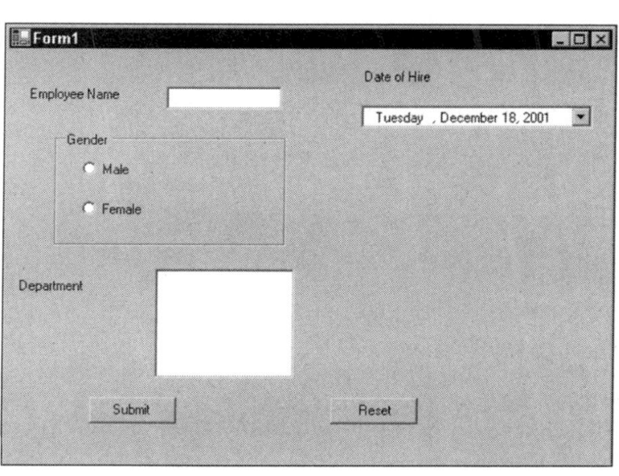

Figure 3-4: Your new form is set to accept employee details.

You may notice that lot of space is left on the form below the `DateTimePicker` control (see the right side of Figure 3-4). This space is intentional because this control behaves like a drop-down menu, popping up into a complete month's calendar when you click its down arrow. Look for this feature when you run the form.

Icing the cake with menus and bars

After you take care of all the functionality that you desire on the form, provide the user with some user-friendly features, such as menus and dialog boxes, for variety and visual appeal. You can begin to enhance the form a little by adding a small menu and a status bar to the form.

A menu contains various useful commands that display only when the user points or clicks at it. For example, most Windows-based applications contain a File menu that contains commands to create, open, and save files.

If you've added a menu in Visual Basic 6.0, you understand how this example demonstrates the superiority of Visual Basic .NET over Visual Basic 6.0. Visual Basic .NET provides you a `MainMenu` control to add menus to your applications. This control is easy to use and has more pleasing design capabilities. Say good-bye to the good old Menu Editor. Instead, do the following:

1. **From the Toolbox, add a `MainMenu` control to the form by clicking and dragging the control.**

   A menu item appears on the top-left side of the form, named `MenuItem1`.

   When you add a `MainMenu` control to the form, note that the control doesn't appear on the form. Instead, the icon for the `MainMenu` control appears in a space below the form and a text entry area appears on the form. The area in which the icon appears is the *Tray*, as shown in Figure 3-5. When you run the form, the `MainMenu` control isn't shown on the screen. Instead, its output — the menu — is displayed on the screen.

2. **In the text entry area that appears on the screen, type** File**.**

   This is the first menu. When you type the first menu item, two text entry areas emerge from the menu, as shown in Figure 3-6.

   The text entry area on the right of the first menu item is for the next menu item, and the text entry area below the first menu item is for the submenu. Thus, you can easily visualize your menu while you create it. Our example creates a File menu that has two options: Reset and Exit, as shown in Figure 3-7. Name these menu items `ResetMenu` and `ExitMenu` by using the Name field in the Properties window.

Of course, when you create your own menu, add whatever is suitable for your application. The next important control to create is the `StatusBar` control.

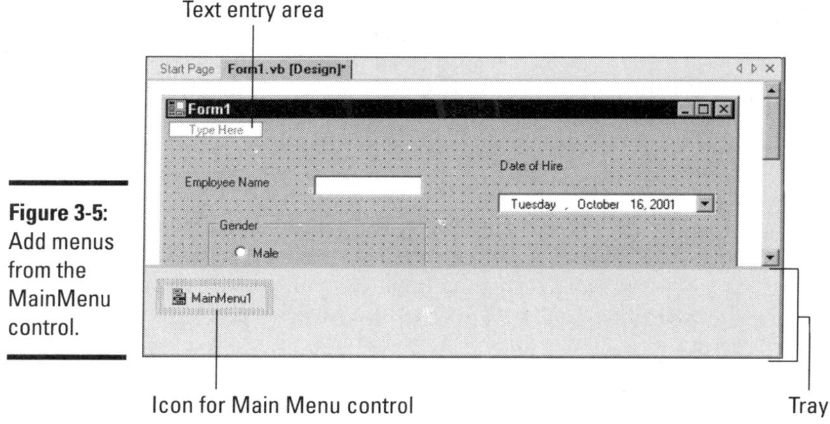

Figure 3-5: Add menus from the MainMenu control.

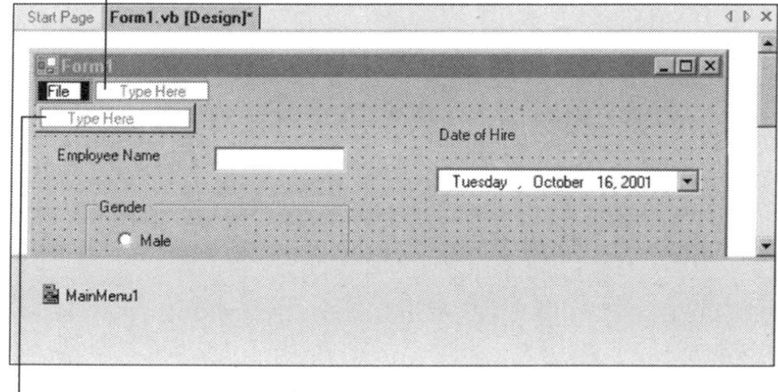

Figure 3-6: Adding a menu to your form is simple.

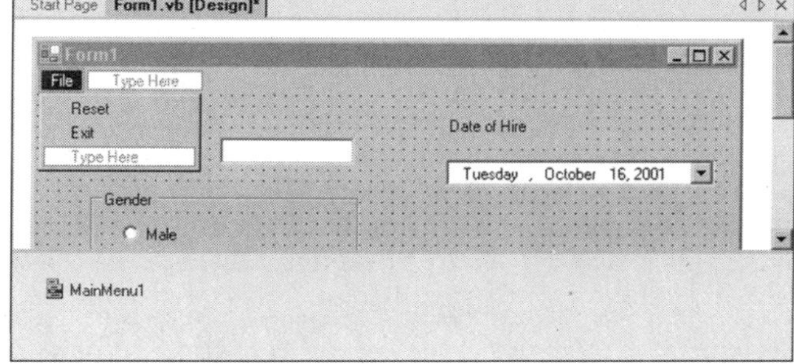

Figure 3-7: A sample menu with its options.

A *status bar*, which is used to provide information about the current state of an application, appears at the bottom of the screen. For example, in Microsoft Word, the status bar displays the page number, paragraph number, the line number, and much more. To add a status bar to your application, follow these steps:

1. **Click and drag the `StatusBar` control from the Toolbox to the form.**

   You might need to scroll down the controls list because the `StatusBar` control isn't visible.

   A status bar typically consists of a number of panels that divide a status bar into a number of parts. These parts are used to display different text simultaneously. For example, if you had just one area on the status bar, you could only display one message at a time, and when you displayed the next, the first one would get erased. Avoid this by having two panels that display two different messages simultaneously.

2. **Click the Status bar to select it and open the Properties window (or choose View⇨Properties Window).**

3. **Set the `ShowPanels` property to `TRUE`.**

   This ensures that the panels are visible when you run the form.

4. **Select the Panels property and click the ellipsis (...) next to it, as shown in Figure 3-8.**

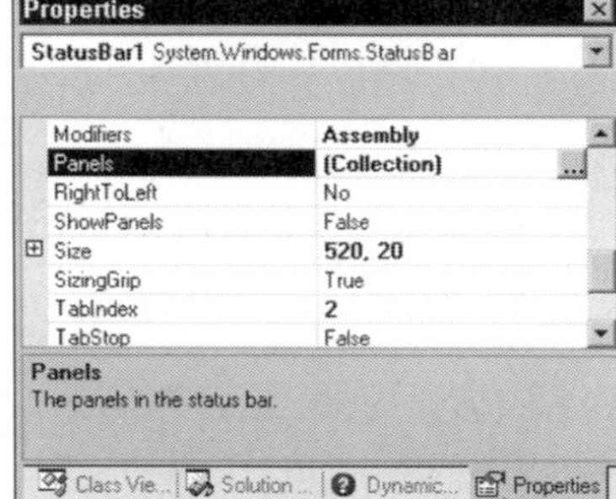

Figure 3-8: The Panels property.

   The Panels property of a status bar stores a collection of panels.

5. **In the StatusBarPanel Collection Editor dialog box that appears, add as many panels as you want by clicking the Add button.**

   Each time that you click the Add button, a new panel is added to the status bar and you can edit its properties. The first panel, called `CustomMessage`, is added to the status bar as shown in Figure 3-9.

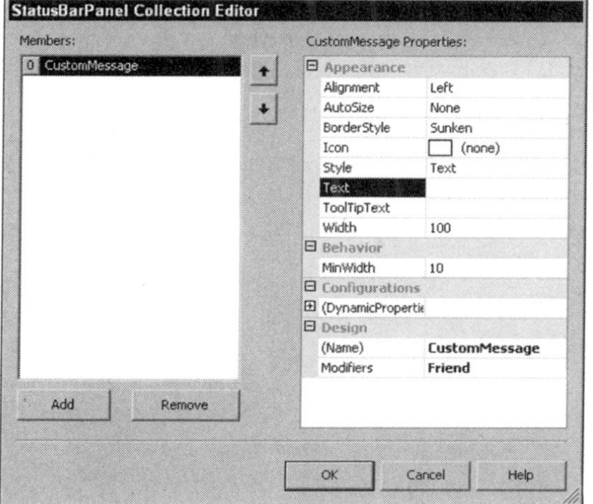

Figure 3-9: Add panels to a status bar with the Collection editor.

Adding the code for your form

After you add controls on the form, your next step is to examine the code to initialize the form and accept values from a user. When a form is about to be displayed, the following items need initialization:

- The Employee Name field should have a maximum character limit of 15.
- The Department list should contain a list of departments.
- The Hire Date list should not accept dates later than the current date.

To perform these initializations, you add code for the `Load` event of the form. To add this code, double-click anywhere on the form that's not a control. You are automatically taken to the Code Editor window.

The Code Editor window is displayed in Figure 3-10. This window is different from the conventional Code Editor window of Visual Basic 6.0, featuring new elements such as class declarations and some Windows Forms Designer-generated code.

In Visual Basic .NET, each form is a class. When you run the form, you instantiate the class and call its `Show` method to display the form. The difference is that the methods and variables of a class are *encapsulated*, which means that they are hidden from the code outside the class. (Don't worry, we talk about encapsulation more in Book 3, Chapter 8.) Another advantage is that the functions that you declare for a form can be used in another form without loading and displaying the other form. All you need to do is to create a new instance of the other form and access the public functions. You can read more on accessing another form in Book 3, Chapter 4.

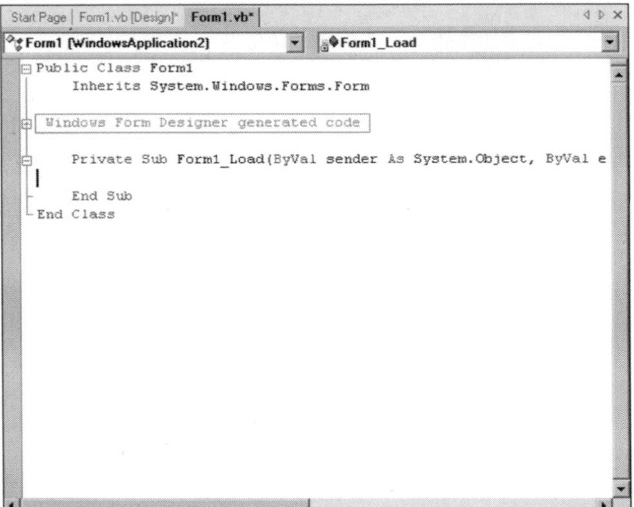

Figure 3-10: The Code Editor window.

The code for the `Load` event of the form is

```
Private Sub Form1_Load(ByVal sender As System.Object,
        ByVal e As System.EventArgs) Handles MyBase.Load
    NameTextBox.MaxLength = 15
    DepartmentListBox.Items.Add("Sales")
    DepartmentListBox.Items.Add("Product Development")
    DepartmentListBox.Items.Add("Tech Support")
    DepartmentListBox.Items.Add("Human Relations")
    DatePicker.MaxDate = DateTime.Today
    StatusBar1.Panels(0).Text = "Please enter your name"
End Sub
```

In the preceding code, the `Today` function of the `DateTime` class is used to set the `MaxDate` property of the `DatePicker` control to the current date. The `DatePicker` control represents the hire date of an employee. Also, the preceding code limits the name field to 15 characters and lists the options in the Department list box.

Next, you need to code for the Submit and Reset buttons. You also need to code for the menu options. The functionality of the Reset button and the Reset menu option is identical — you give users two options for performing the same task. Define a method, Reset, that can be called for the `Click` event of the Reset button as well as the Reset menu option. The method is required within the form only, so you can declare its scope as `private`. The definition of the Reset method is given below:

```
Private Sub Reset()
    NameTextBox.Text = ""
```

```
        DepartmentListBox.ClearSelected()
        DatePicker.Text = DateTime.Today
        MaleRadioButton.Checked = False
        FemaleRadioButton.Checked = False
        NameTextBox.Focus()
  End Sub
```

This method can now be called in the Click event of the Reset button and menu option. The definitions of the methods for the Reset button and the Reset menu are given below:

```
Private Sub ResetButton_Click(ByVal sender As
          System.Object, ByVal e As System.EventArgs)
          Handles ResetButton.Click
      Reset()
End Sub

Private Sub ResetMenu_Click(ByVal sender As
          System.Object, ByVal e As System.EventArgs)
          Handles ResetMenu.Click
      Reset()
End Sub
```

You can add the method (or procedure) for handling the Click event of a button by double-clicking the appropriate button. When you do so, the Code window (or Code Editor) shows up with a procedure that'll handle the click event. You can write the required code statements in this procedure. For more about procedures, check out Book 3, Chapter 7; for more about events, take a look at Book 3, Chapter 8.

The following code — for the Submit button — first ensures that the user has entered correct values in all controls and then retrieves the values entered in different controls, displaying them in a message box. Notice that the message box is displayed by using the Show method of the MessageBox class.

```
Private Sub SubmitButton_Click(ByVal sender As _
  System.Object, ByVal e As System.EventArgs) _
  Handles SubmitButton.Click

Dim gender As String
If NameTextBox.Text = "" Or DepartmentListBox.Text = "" Then
   MessageBox.Show("Please specify the name " & _
    "and department of the employee")
   Exit Sub
End If
If MaleRadioButton.Checked Then
   gender = "Male"
ElseIf FemaleRadioButton.Checked Then
   gender = "Female"
Else
   MessageBox.Show("Please select a gender.")
```

```
      MaleRadioButton.Focus()
      Exit Sub
   End If
   MessageBox.Show("Employee Name: " & NameTextBox.Text _&
     Chr(13) & _"Gender: " & gender & Chr(13) & _
     Date of Hire: " & DatePicker.Text & Chr(13) & _
     "Department: " & DepartmentListBox.Text, _
     "Employee Details", MessageBoxButtons.OK,_
     MessageBoxIcon.Information)
End Sub
```

Now create code for the Exit menu item. When a user clicks the Exit button, the application should terminate. The code for the Exit button is

```
Private Sub ExitMenu_Click(ByVal sender As
          System.Object, ByVal e As System.EventArgs)
          Handles ExitMenu.Click
      Application.Exit()
End Sub
```

You can now display the form. Select the Start option from the Debug menu, and the form appears as shown in Figure 3-11. We expanded the `DateTimePicker` control in the figure.

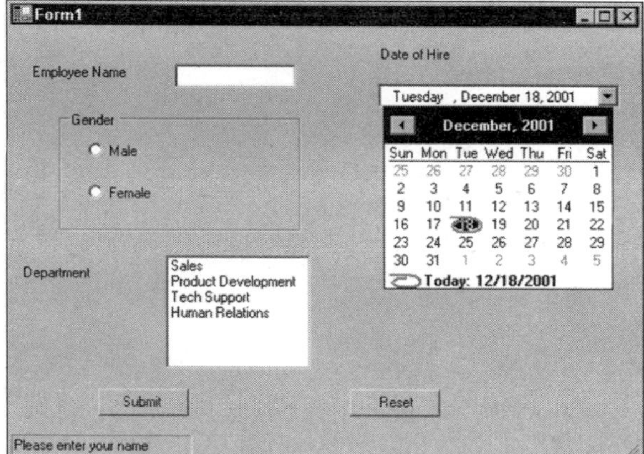

Figure 3-11: The final employee details form has functional and visual elements.

Adding nonuser-interface controls

Some controls don't have a user interface: that is, they're hidden from the user. Such controls, although invisible to the user, are necessary for performing background functions, such as periodically executing a task. An example of such a control is the `Timer` control. This control periodically generates the `Tick` event. You can write a code to enable your program to perform a task whenever the `Tick` event is generated. In this way, you can periodically execute a task.

When you add a control without a user interface to a form, the control is placed in a Tray. In Figure 3-12, you can see the Timer control added to the form; the control is placed in the Tray.

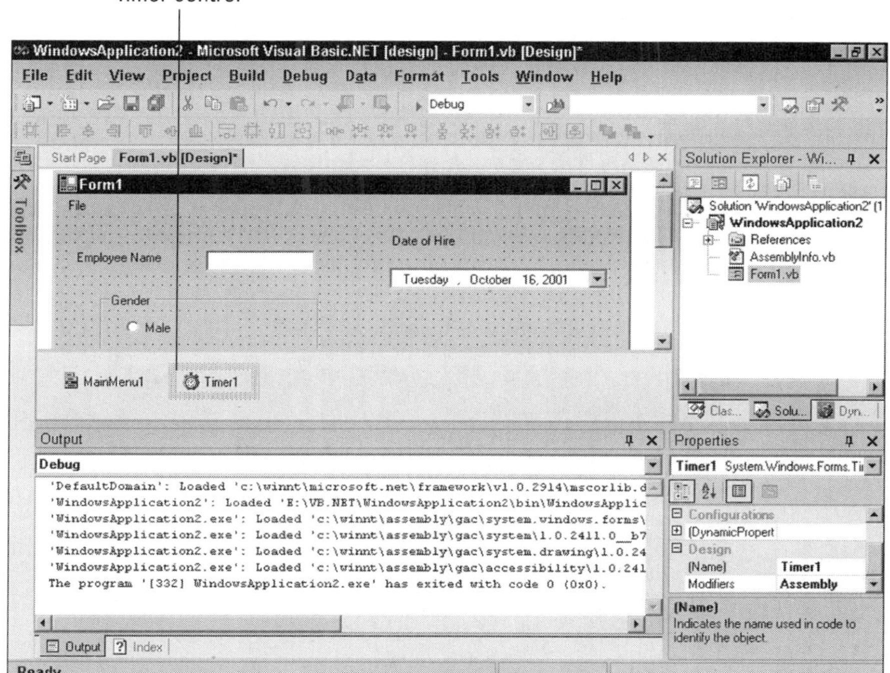

Figure 3-12: The Timer control sits in the Tray.

You can write code to display the current time in the status bar every ten seconds. To display the time, simply write the following code in the `Tick` event of the Timer.

```
Private Sub Timer1_Tick(ByVal sender As
      System.Object, ByVal e As System.EventArgs)
      Handles Timer1.Tick
        StatusBar1.Panels(0).Text = DateTime.Now
    End Sub
```

Additionally, specify the `Interval` property of the Timer as 10000 and set the `Enabled` property to `True`. We specify 10000 because the time is specified in milliseconds. Now the status bar displays the current time every ten seconds.

In addition to the controls that we discuss here, you can add many other controls to the form. The scope of this book makes it practically impossible to include every control here. However, we include a brief description of some commonly used controls in the section "Other useful controls" — enough to get you started.

Adding ActiveX controls

In Visual Basic 6.0, you add ActiveX controls to a form by using the Components menu item in the Project menu. You can achieve the same functionality in Visual Basic .NET in a different way. You first add the ActiveX control to the Toolbox and then you can use it as you would use any other control available in the Toolbox. To add the control to the Toolbox, perform the following:

1. **Choose Tools⇨Customize Toolbox.**

   The Customize Toolbox dialog box appears, as displayed in Figure 3-13. This dialog box has two tabs: the COM Components tab and the .NET Framework Components tab. The COM Components tab provides a list of COM components that are registered on your computer.

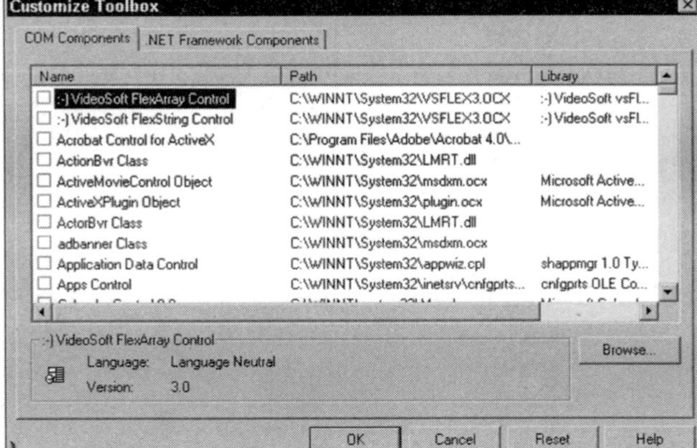

Figure 3-13: Add ActiveX controls from the Customize Toolbox dialog box.

2. **From the COM Components tab, select the required COM Component(s) and click OK.**

In fact, all the existing controls available in the Toolbox are included in the Customize Toolbox dialog box. If you select the .NET Framework Components tab, you see all the controls of the Toolbox listed here. This means that you can customize the Toolbox by selecting or deselecting components in this tab, giving you some level of customization.

After you add a component to the Toolbox, you can use it on the form like any other Toolbox control. Visual Basic .NET adds all the required references to your project.

Adding controls at runtime

Just like you can add controls at design time, you can also add controls at runtime. For example, you may include conditional logic in your program to ask for the state of a user only if the user is from the United States. Just create the second list box for listing the state and hide the list unless it's needed. Alternatively, you can create a list box at runtime. The second method improves memory utilization by loading controls only when they are needed. The code to add a `ListBox` control to the form at runtime is

```
Dim StateList As New Windows.Forms.ListBox()
        StateList.Location = New Point(248, 104)
        Me.Controls.Add(StateList)
```

The preceding code creates a `ListBox` control, specifies its position, and adds the control to the collection of controls available to the form.

Just like you can add the `ListBox` control to the form, you can add other controls in the Code Editor window. You won't have any problems selecting the correct control and specifying the correct syntax for its methods thanks to the Statement Completion feature of Visual Basic .NET. This feature prompts you with the correct syntax of methods and lists available methods and properties while you type. Just press the Tab key to accept an entry. Additionally, the editor also warns you if you type an invalid statement.

Arranging Controls in Windows Forms

When you add controls to a form, Visual Basic .NET provides a number of options for you to arrange these controls professionally. First of all, the dots that you see on the interface of the form help you align the controls. You can use the alignment options in Visual Basic .NET to align the controls correctly.

Additionally, you can set the Tab order for the controls. *Tab order* is the order in which controls are selected when the users move through the controls by pressing the Tab key.

You can also anchor, dock, and layer controls. Anchoring controls specifies how the controls are positioned when a form is resized. Docking controls specifies the position and manner in which the controls are docked to the edge of the container. Layering specifies the order of visibility of controls. In this section, we look at mechanisms for all these alignment tools.

Aligning controls

To align controls on a form, select one or more controls by using the Shift key and then using the options in the Format menu in the IDE. The Format menu presents a number of options:

- **Align:** Align two or more controls with the Align option. You can align the left, right, top, or bottom of controls and also snap controls to the grid (the dotted lines on the form) by using Align.
- **Make Same Size:** Text boxes look most appealing when they're the same size. To do this, use the Make Same Size menu item. This menu presents options to match the width, height, or both, of two or more controls.
- **Horizontal Spacing** and **Vertical Spacing:** Use the Horizontal Spacing and Vertical Spacing menu items to make three or more controls horizontally and vertically equidistant.
- **Center in Form:** Use the Center in Form menu item to place controls on the horizontal or vertical center of the form.
- **Order:** Use the Order menu to place controls one above the other. You can send a control behind the other or bring it in front of the other by using this menu item. The order menu helps you in layering the controls.

Specifying Tab order

Specifying Tab order of controls was a tedious task in Visual Basic 6.0. You had to specify values separately for the `TabOrder` property of controls. In Visual Basic .NET, specifying the tab order is very simple:

1. **From the View menu, choose Tab Order.**

   Numbers appear onscreen for each control, as shown in Figure 3-14. These numbers represent the order in which the user proceeds through the controls by pressing the Tab key.

2. **To change the Tab order, just click the controls in the order in which you want to select them.**

Notice that the numbers that appear on the controls change to the order in which you select the controls.

Anchoring controls

Throughout this chapter, we place controls where we want them on our form to make our form visually appealing — that is, until we actually run the form. When we maximize the form, all that careful placement was for naught, as Figure 3-15 shows. Now the form looks bare, and the layout is not at all what we want.

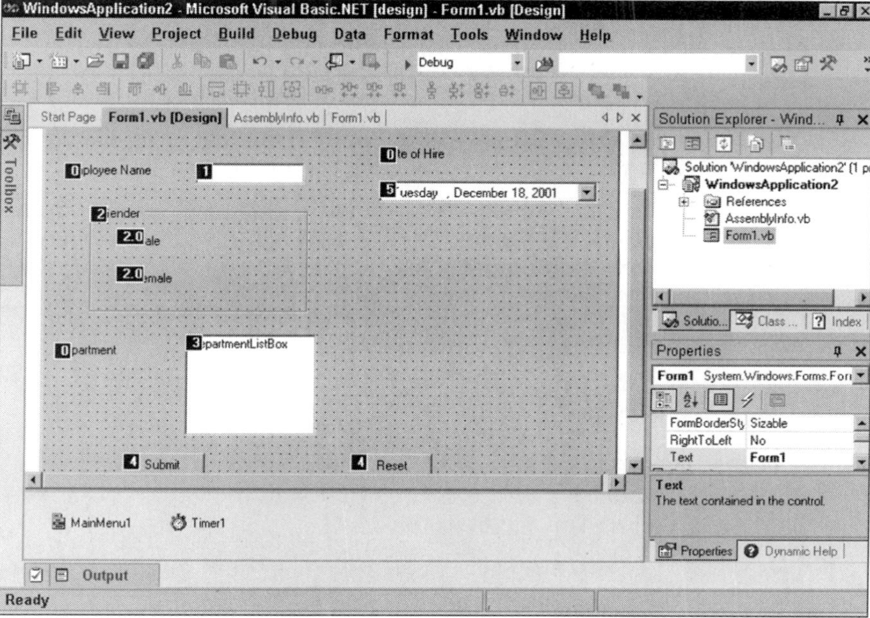

Figure 3-14: Change Tab order from the View menu.

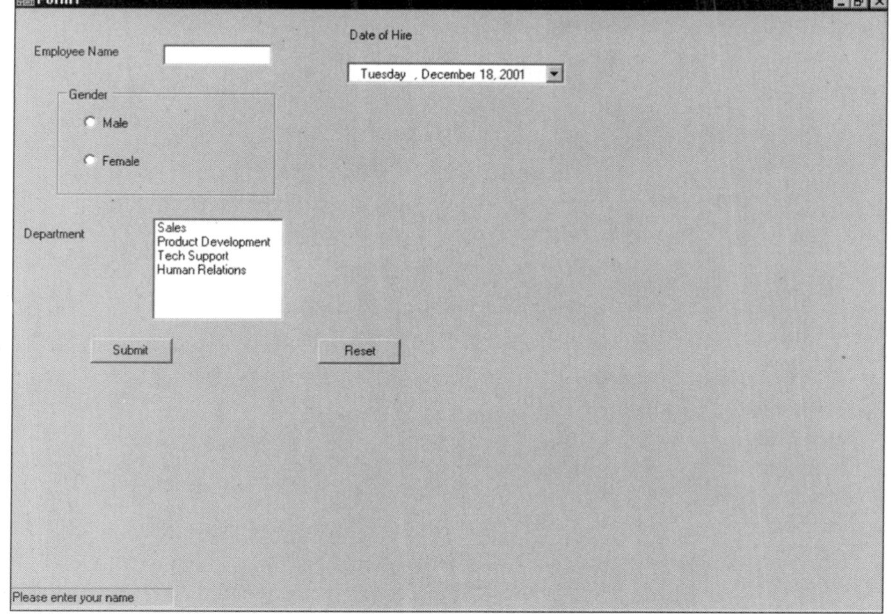

Figure 3-15: Maximizing controls without anchoring them will change your form's look.

This is where anchoring is useful. When you anchor controls, their position relative to the form is fixed. Thus, if the form increases in size, the controls change their positions to remain where they were so that the controls on the left of the screen remain at that position and the controls on the right side of the screen move to the right of the resized form. To anchor your form's controls, follow these steps:

1. **Click the controls for accepting the name, gender, department, and submitting the form while holding down the Shift key to select all of them simultaneously.**
2. **Pull up the Properties window by selecting View⇨Properties Window.**
3. **In the Properties window, in the Anchor property, select Top, Left, (see the far right side of Figure 3-16).**

   This anchors these controls at the Top Left of the form.
4. **Similarly, for the Reset button and the `DateTimePicker` control, select Top, Right as the anchor.**

5. **Perform the same steps to anchor the status bar as Bottom, Left, Right.**

   The status bar should always remain at the bottom of the screen.

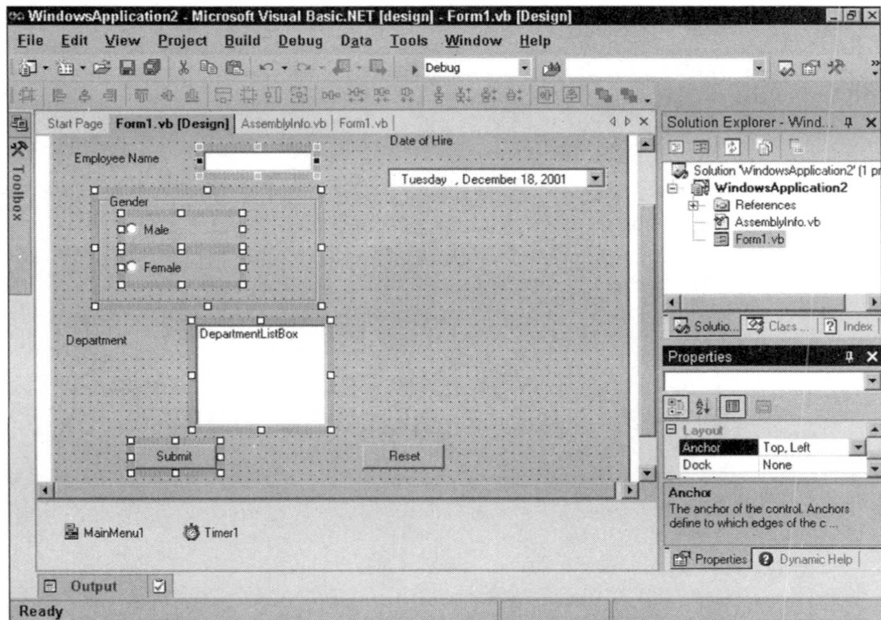

Figure 3-16: Anchor your controls from the Properties window.

After you first anchor the control and then maximize the form, the controls appear as shown in Figure 3-17. Compare the difference in form appearance with Figure 3-16.

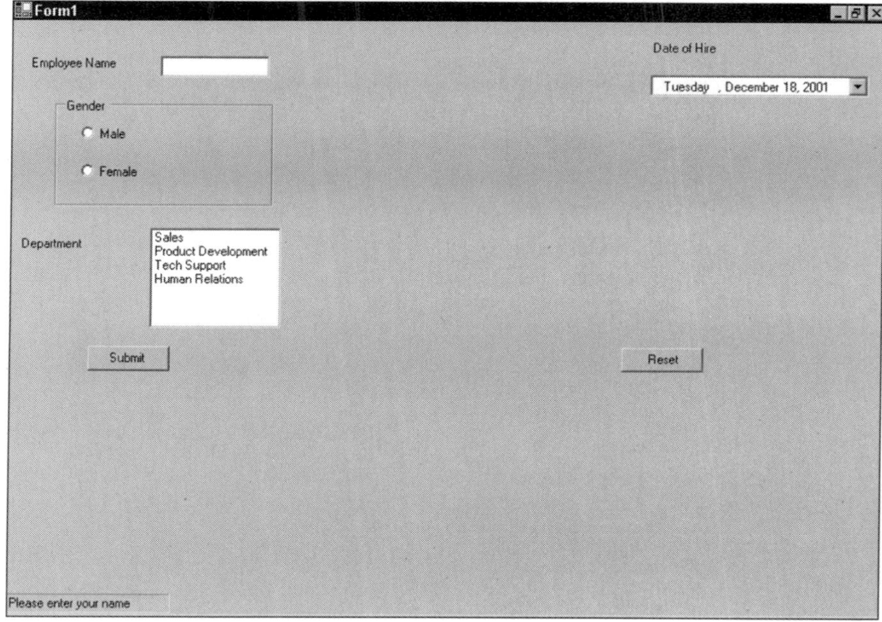

Figure 3-17: Anchor your controls first and then maximize the form.

Docking controls

Study a Windows Explorer window and note two things. One, the control displaying the Folder hierarchy is fixed to the left edge; second, the control displaying the contents of these folders is fixed to the right edge of the window. Whether you maximize the window or resize it, these controls remain docked to their respective edges. You can also dock the controls present in your forms to the edges. You can also make them fill the container, which is the form or another control that contains the control.

If you dock the control to one particular edge, such as Left or Right, the respective edge of the control is resized equal to the size of the container's edge. However, if you specify Fill, then the size of the container becomes equal to the container. Use the following steps to dock controls:

1. **Observe the two radio buttons in the form we've created so far in this chapter.**

   The buttons aren't docked with the Gender group box, as you can see in Figure 3-18. So that you can easily see that these buttons aren't docked, we selected both radio buttons in Figure 3-18.

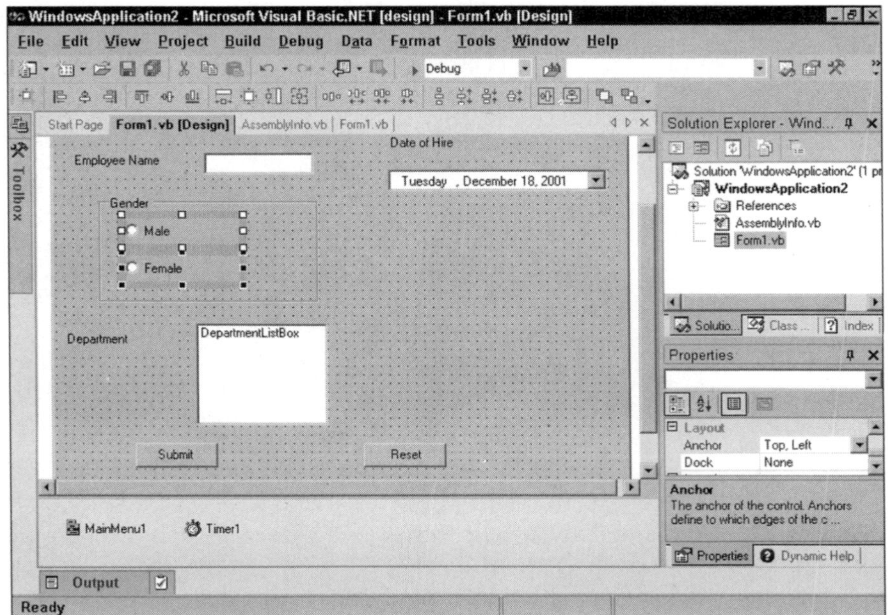

Figure 3-18: Undocked radio buttons.

2. **Click the Male radio button control to select it.**

   Note that the Male radio button is docked with the Top edge of the Gender group box.

3. **In the Properties window, set the Dock field to Top.**
4. **Similarly, set the Dock field for the Female radio button to Bottom.**

   The Female radio button is now docked with the Bottom edge of the Gender group box (see Figure 3-19).

Layering controls

All the forms and the controls obey the z-order of placements, in which controls are layered on the basis of form's depth. That is, the control that was added last is visible. However, at times you might need to alter the order of the controls in which they're placed.

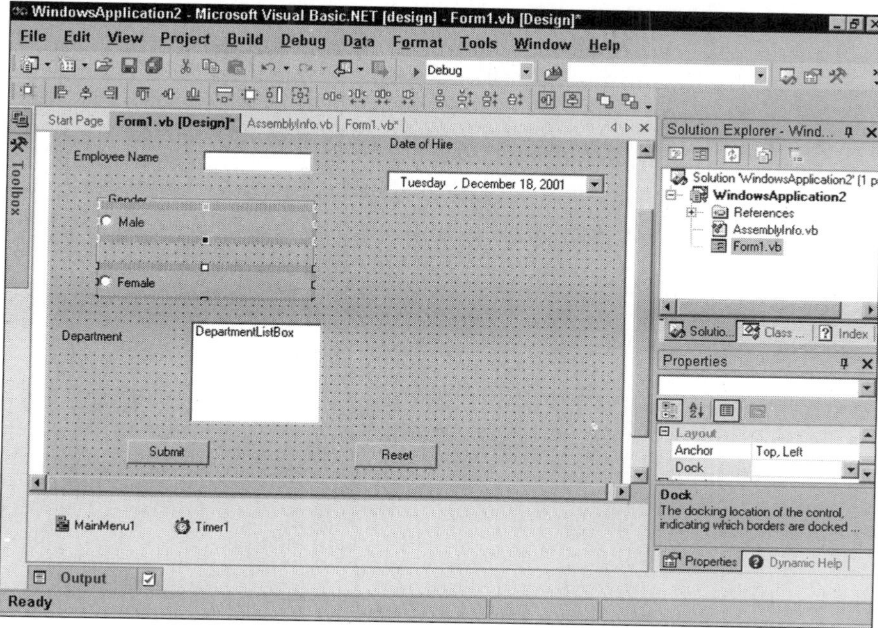

Figure 3-19: Docked radio buttons.

To understand this better, just repeat the process of adding group box and radio buttons to the form, but add the radio buttons first and then add the group box. The result is that the radio buttons aren't visible because the group box is on top of them. In such a situation, you can use layering. Here's how to layer your controls:

1. **Add two radio buttons to a form.**
2. **Add a group box to the form, putting this box on top of the radio buttons.**

   Notice that the radio buttons aren't visible.
3. **Click the group box to select it.**
4. **From the Format menu, choose Order➪Send to Back.**

   Both radio buttons are now visible.

Other Useful Controls

In earlier sections of this chapter, we discuss several basic controls, such as `Label`, `TextBox`, and `Button`. Visual Basic .NET provides a number of other useful controls. In the following sections, we list these controls in a series of tables. Of course, whether you use these controls entirely depends on the application that you want to create. Therefore, you may be interested in a set of controls that provide certain functionality. The controls are grouped into different categories for easy navigability.

List-related controls

To manage lists, use the list-related controls that we describe in Table 3-1.

Table 3-1 List-Related Controls

Control	*Description*
`CheckedListBox`	Displays a list of items with a check box next to each item in the list.
`ComboBox`	Displays a list of drop-down items. You can add items to the list.
`ListBox`	Displays a list of predefined items in a list.
`ListView`	Displays a list of icons with their names.
`NumericUpDown`	Displays a list of numeric values.

Print-related controls

Use print-related controls to manage page set up and to print data or graphics. These controls are given in Table 3-2.

Table 3-2 Print-Related Controls

Control	*Description*
`PageSetupDialog`	Displays a dialog box to set up a page for printing.
`PrintDialog`	Displays the Print dialog box.
`PrintDocument`	Displays options to prepare a document for printing.
`PrintPreviewDialog`	Previews a document before you print it.

File- and data-related controls

The following file- and data-related controls relate to file and data management operations:

- `DataGrid`: Displays data from a data source, such as Microsoft SQL Server, in a tabular format.
- `OpenFileDialog`: Displays a conventional Open dialog box.
- `SaveFileDialog`: Specifies a name and location to save a file.

Option selection-related controls

The controls that relate to clicking buttons and selecting options are

- `Button`: Displays clickable buttons.
- `CheckBox`: Displays options as check boxes.
- `RadioButton`: Displays options as radio buttons.

Menu- and toolbar-related controls

Use menu and toolbar controls to display menu items on forms, menus and buttons on a toolbar, tool tips, and specialized menus; see Table 3-3 for details.

Table 3-3 Menu- and Toolbar-Related Controls

Control	*Description*
`MainMenu`	Displays menu items on forms.
`ToolBar`	Displays menus and buttons on a toolbar.
`ToolTip`	Displays tool tips when the user points at controls.
`ContextMenu`	Displays specialized menus that are associated with controls on the form.

Date- and time-related controls

Visual Basic .NET provides the following two controls for managing date and time:

- `DateTimePicker`: Provides dates in the form of a calendar that a user can select from.
- `MonthCalendar`: Displays date and month information that a user can manage.

Font- and color-related controls

The two controls you use to select fonts and colors are

- `ColorDialog`: Displays a color palette from which the user can select a color.
- `FontDialog`: Displays the fonts installed on the computer.

Text input- and text display- related controls

Use text input and text display controls to display text as labels, labels as hyperlinks, and to enable users to enter and format text. See Table 3-4 for these controls.

Table 3-4 Text Input- and Text Display-Related Controls

Control	*Description*
`Label`	Displays text as labels for other controls.
`LinkLabel`	Displays labels in the hyperlink style.
`RichTextBox`	Allows users to enter and format text.
`TextBox`	Allows users to enter plain text.

Picture-related controls

Controls related to managing pictures and images are

- ✦ `ImageList`: Displays images on controls such as toolbars and status bars.
- ✦ `PictureBox`: Displays images in multiple graphic formats.

Notification controls

Use notification controls to notify a user about an event, its progress, or its status. You also use these controls to notify programs periodically. These controls are given in Table 3-5.

Table 3-5 Notification Controls

Control	*Description*
`NotifyIcon`	Displays notification icons for processes that run in the background.
`ProgressBar`	Displays the progress of a time-consuming action.
`StatusBar`	Displays status information about a program or a control.
`Timer`	Raises an event periodically.

Miscellaneous controls

In this section are all those controls that don't truly belong in any of the above categories. Just because they're unique, though, don't dismiss them: They're gems. These controls are given in Table 3-6.

Table 3-6 Miscellaneous Controls

Control	*Description*
`DomainUpDown`	Displays text that a user can browse and select.
`ErrorProvider`	Displays information about errors.
`HelpProvider`	Associates a help file with an application.
`HscrollBar`	Provides a horizontal scrollbar.
`VscrollBar`	Provides a vertical scrollbar.
`Splitter`	Provides a mechanism to resize controls.
`TabControl`	Provides multiple tabs to optimize space utilization while displaying controls.
`TreeView`	Provides a hierarchical view to display nodes and subnodes.

Chapter 4: Windows Forms: Moving Ahead

In This Chapter

- Working with dialog boxes
- Working with MDI forms
- Implementing the drag-and-drop operations
- Utilizing the clipboard
- Providing help

Windows Forms constitutes the basic structure for user interaction. Going beyond simple forms used for accepting and displaying information, you can put the power of Windows Forms to work, creating applications that contain MDI forms, have drag-and-drop features, and provide clipboard support. You can even include help files in your applications.

You're in the right place to read all about implementing dialog boxes, MDI forms, drag-and-drop operations, clipboard support, and HTML help files.

Working with Dialog Boxes

Among the most useful features of the Windows environment is its ability to provide a number of *dialog boxes,* which are forms with features that perform certain tasks to make your life easier. We've probably used the basic dialog boxes to open, save, or print a file about a trillion times. Dialog boxes are also used to display certain messages from time to time, such as a *Are you really sure you want to do that?* kind of message.

A dialog box is called from a form and is generally used to accept some values from the user, which are required for some operation by the calling form. A dialog box returns a value to the calling form, which indicates the operation performed by the user. Visual Basic .NET provides you with the `MessageBox.Show` and the `MsgBox` functions to display message boxes in your applications.

Most dialog boxes don't allow you to continue working with the application until you close them. One such example is the Open dialog box. Such dialog boxes are called *modal* dialog boxes. However, you can have *modeless* dialog boxes that allow you to work with the rest of the application.

Some basic features of a dialog box include

- ✦ Dialog boxes generally don't have minimize and the maximize buttons, menu bars, and scroll bars.
- ✦ Dialog boxes can't be resized.

Read on to discover how to create dialog boxes in Visual Basic .NET.

Creating dialog boxes

You can include your own dialog boxes in applications by following the steps listed below:

1. **Create a new Windows Application project. Name this project as AdvWindows.**

   This project contains a form named `Form1`. Read more on creating a new Windows Application project in Book 3, Chapter 2.

2. **In the Toolbox that appears on the left side of the IDE, double-click Button, to add a button to Form1.**

   Read more on adding controls to a form in Book 3, Chapter 3.

3. **Click and drag the button to an appropriate location.**
4. **Click the button to display its properties in the Properties window that appears on the right side of the IDE.**
5. **In the `Text` field, enter `Display` to change the caption of the button.**
6. **Add a new Windows Form to your project. You use this form as a dialog box.**

   The name of this form is `Form2`. You can learn to add Windows Forms to your project in Book 3, Chapter 2.

7. **Click to display the properties of the form in the Properties window.**
8. **In the Properties window, enter `FormDialog` in the Name field.**
9. **In the Properties window, in the `FormBorderStyle` list, select `FixedDialog`.**

   This sets the `FormBorderStyle` property of the form.

10. **In the Properties window, in the `MinimizeBox` and `MaximizeBox` lists, select `False`.**

This sets the MinimizeBox and MaximizeBox properties of the form.

11. **Display a modal dialog box by using the `ShowDialog` method.**

The syntax of the `ShowDialog` method is

```
Dim Form_Obj As New Form_Name()
Form_Obj.ShowDialog()
```

12. **Add the following code to the `Click` event of the Display button to display the dialog box.**

```
Dim FrmObj As New FormDialog()
FrmObj.ShowDialog()
```

13. **Choose Debug⇨Start to execute the application.**

`Form1` shows up.

14. **Click the Display button.**

The dialog box (or FormDialog) that you created shows up.

The above example displays a blank dialog box. You can add controls to this dialog box just like you would add controls to a form. You can learn to add controls to a form in Book 3, Chapter 3.

In the following section, we discuss the details of implementing the complete functionality of a dialog box.

Retrieving the dialog box result

You're undoubtedly familiar with the standard Display Properties dialog box in Windows that you use to specify your desktop properties, such as Appearance, Screen Saver, and Background. You fiddle with your settings how you want and then either click OK to accept your changes or click the Cancel button when you realize you really don't want that Barney wallpaper after all. You'll probably encounter something similar in your Visual Basic .NET applications where the calling form needs to take different actions based on the return values of a dialog box. If you're like us, though, you always kind of wonder in the back of your mind how to implement this concept in your application.

Verifying dialog box functionality with Visual Basic .NET is really pretty simple. All you need to do is to specify certain properties.

To retrieve the result of a dialog box, use the `DialogResult` property of the form. You set this property by specifying a member of the `DialogResult` enumeration as the value. The `DialogResult` enumeration contains members that represent the return value of a dialog box, such as clickable OK and Cancel buttons. You set the DialogResult property of the buttons on the dialog box, which in turn sets the DialogResult property of the form. Here's the drill:

1. **In Solution Explorer that appears on the right-side of IDE, double-click Form2.vb to display the dialog box (named FormDialog) that you created in the section "Creating dialog boxes."**

   Read more on Solution Explorer in Book 2, Chapter 1.

2. **Add two buttons to the `FormDialog` form. Name these buttons as OK and Cancel.**

   You can read more on adding buttons to a form in Book 3, Chapter 3.

3. **Click the OK button to display its properties in the Properties window.**

4. **In the Properties window, from the `DialogResult` list, select `OK`.**

   This sets the DialogResult property of the OK button.

5. **Repeat steps 3 and 4 to set the DialogResult property of the Cancel button to `Cancel`.**

6. **Write the code to check for the result (of the dialog box) in the `Click` event of the `Display` button of `Form1`.**

   The code is

   ```
   Dim FrmObj As New FormDialog()
   'Display the dialog box and check for OK button
   If FrmObj.ShowDialog() = DialogResult.OK Then
      MessageBox.Show("You clicked the OK button")
   Else
      MessageBox.Show("You clicked the Cancel button")
   End If
   ```

We mention earlier that the message boxes that you often encounter are also dialog boxes. However, you don't have to create your own message boxes because Visual Basic .NET provides you with a class named MessageBox to implement message boxes in your applications.

Displaying message boxes

You use the Show method of the MessageBox class to display message boxes in your applications. This message box can contain text, buttons, and icons.

```
MessageBox.Show("Hello World", "Message",
   MessageBoxButtons.OK, MessageBoxIcon.Exclamation)
```

The preceding statement displays a message box (as shown in Figure 4-1) with the text `Hello World`. `Message` appears as the caption. This message box also contains the `OK` button and an `Exclamation` icon.

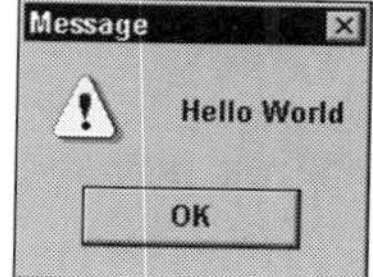

Figure 4-1: A simple sample message box.

The `MessageBoxButtons` is an enumeration that contains constants for displaying various buttons, such as `OK`, `Cancel`, `Yes`, and `No`, in a message box.

The `MessageBoxIcon` is an enumeration that contains constants to display icons, such as `Exclamation`, `Asterisk`, and `Error`, in a message box.

In addition to the `MessageBox.Show` method, you can use the `MsgBox` function that was used in the earlier versions of Visual Basic.

The syntax of the `MsgBox` function is the same. However, it now uses an enumeration named `MsgBoxStyle` to specify the buttons, icons, and modality of the dialog box. For example, the above example can be rewritten by using the `MsgBox` function as

```
MsgBox("Hello World", MsgBoxStyle.Exclamation, "Message")
```


Working with MDI Forms

In Microsoft (MS) Word, you can open a number of documents simultaneously. In MS Paint, conversely, you can only open a single document at a time. Word is an MDI application, and MS Paint is an SDI application. MDI, Multiple Document Interface, refers to an interface in which you can work simultaneously with a number of windows . SDI, or Single Document Interface, means that only one window can be opened at a time.

You can make your Visual Basic .NET applications MDI by creating MDI forms. However, in MDI applications created using Visual Basic .NET, multiple forms open inside one main form. Forms that contain other forms or, in other words, act as the container form are called *MDI parent* forms and the forms that are contained are called *MDI child* forms.

Read the next section to discover how to add an MDI parent to the Windows application that you created in the previous section.

Creating MDI parent and child forms

To create an MDI parent form:

1. **Add a new Windows Form to the AdvWindows project.**

   A form named Form3 is added to the project. To learn how to add a new form to your project, read Book 3, Chapter 2.

2. **Click Form3 to display its properties in the Properties window.**
3. **In the Properties window, enter `MyMDIForm` in the Name field.**

   This specifies the name of the form as MyMDIForm.

4. **In the Properties window, from the `IsMDIContainer` list of the form, select `True`.**

   This makes MyMDIForm the MDI parent form. After you add a MDI parent form, you need to implement a way in which you can open the child forms. To do so, you use the MainMenu control present in the Toolbox.

   In this case, you create a menu named Display that contains two menu items, Form1 and Form Dialog to display these forms (already contained in your application) respectively.

5. **In the Toolbox, double-click the MainMenu control to add a menu to your application.**

   Read Book 3, Chapter 3 to learn about adding menus to your applications.

6. **In the text entry area that appears on the screen, type** Display.
7. **Add menu items Form1 and Form Dialog under the Display menu.**

   You can use these menu items to call the appropriate child forms.

You now set the already existing forms in your application as MDI child.

1. **In MyMDIForm, double-click the Form1 menu item to add a corresponding event handler for its `Click` event.**

   The event handler named `MenuItem2_Click` shows up.

2. **Now, you set the `MDIParent` property of the `Form1` form and write code to display this form at the click of the menu item.**

   The `MDIParent` property of the form determines the parent form of the current form. The following code statements illustrates the use of this property.

Add this code to the event handler.

```
'Create an object of the Form1
Dim ChldFrm1 As New Form1()
'Specify the MDIParent
ChldFrm1.MDIParent = Me
'Display the form
ChldFrm1.Show()
```

3. **Repeat Step 1 to create an event handler for the `Form Dialog` menu item.**

4. **Now, you set the `MDIParent` property of the `FormDialog` form and write code to display this form at the click of the menu item. The code to do so is given below.**

   Add this code to the corresponding event handler:

```
Dim ChldFrm2 As New FormDialog()
'Specify the MDIParent
ChldFrm2.MDIParent = Me
'Display the form
ChldFrm2.Show()
```

5. **In Solution Explorer, right-click AdvWindows to display a pop-up menu.**

   You now set MyMDIForm (the MDI parent) as the start-up form.

6. **In the pop-up menu, click Properties to display the Property Pages for the AdvWindows project.**

7. **From the Startup object list, select MyMDIForm.**

8. **Execute the application and test both the menu items by clicking them.**

Similarly, add more forms to this project as needed and attach them with menus.

Arranging child forms

Use Visual Basic .NET to implement the Windows-like functionality of arranging the open child forms in your applications. You can arrange the child forms by either cascading or tiling (horizontally or vertically). You can also arrange the child form icons in the lower portion of the MDI parent. To arrange child windows:

1. **In Solution Explorer, double-click Form3.vb to activate the MyMDIForm.**

   This form currently contains the Display menu.

2. **Click the Display menu.**

   The text placeholder for the next menu shows up to the right of the Display menu.

3. **In this text placeholder, type `Window` to create a new menu.**

4. **In the text placeholder that appears under the** `Window` **menu, type Cascade.**

5. **Repeat step 4 to add the** `Tile Horizontal`**,** `Tile Vertical`**, and** `Arrange Icons` **menu items.**

   Read more on adding menus and menu items in Book 3, Chapter 3.

6. **You use the** `LayoutMDI` **method of the MDI parent form to arrange the child forms within it.**

   It takes the type of layout as a parameter.

7. **To specify this parameter, use the** `MDILayout` **enumeration.**

   The `MDILayout` enumeration contains constants to specify the type of arrangement of the child forms.

8. **Add an event handler for the** `Click` **event of the** `Cascade` **menu item and add the following code.**

   ```
   Me.LayoutMDI (MDILayout.Cascade)
   ```

   In the preceding statement, all the open child forms are cascaded within the parent form, as shown in Figure 4-2. Similarly, write code for all the layout menu items.

9. **Execute the application.**

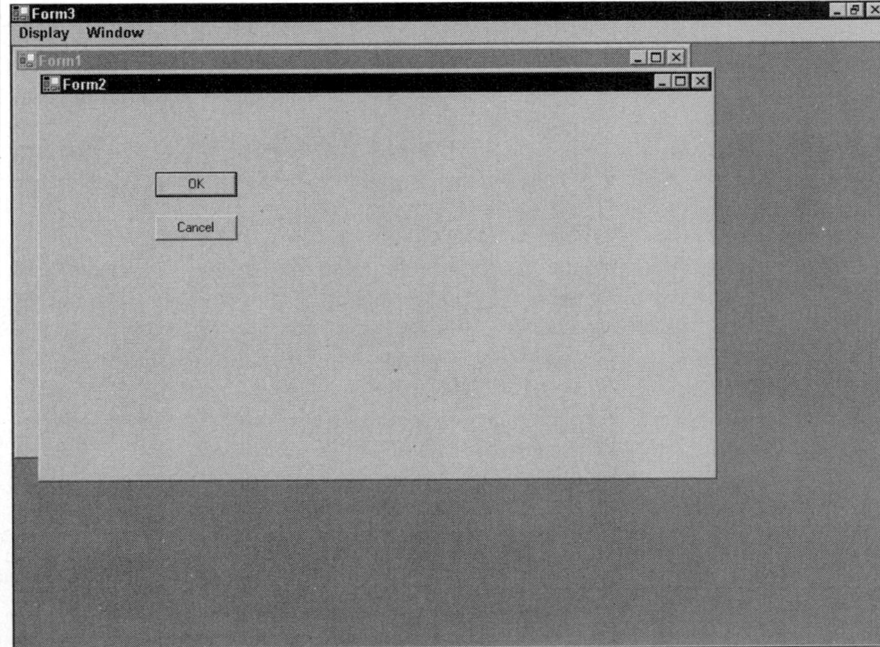

Figure 4-2: An MDIForm displaying cascaded child forms.

10. **Display Form1 and Form Dialog forms by clicking the respective menu items.**

11. **Select Window➪Cascade.**

    Both the forms are cascaded.

Implementing Drag-and-Drop Operations

You can add drag-and-drop capability to the applications that you create by using Visual Basic .NET. For implementing drag-and-drop operations in your application, you need to trap a number of events, such as `DragDrop` and `DragEnter`. These events contain various arguments that help you perform the drag-and-drop operations smoothly.

Drag operation

To implement the drag capability in your application, you need to handle events that will occur when you start moving the object. Let's look at the steps involved in a drag-and-drop operation, and the events that help you do so.

1. Start the drag operation. To indicate the start of a drag operation, use the `MouseDown` event of the source control, which occurs when you press the mouse button. *Source control* is a control from which the data is to be dragged. You can also use any other event to indicate the start of a drag operation. To actually start the drag, use the `DoDragDrop` method inside the appropriate event.
2. Check the type of data being dragged and specify the effect that will be applied when the drop happens. To perform this operation, use the `DragEnter` event of the target control, which occurs when you drag an object in the bounds of a control. *Target control* is a control on which the data is to be dropped.
3. Retrieve the data being dragged. To do so, use the `DragDrop` event of the target control, which occurs on the completion of a drag-and-drop operation. I'll discuss the `DoDragDrop` method that we mentioned earlier.

DoDragDrop method

The `DoDragDrop` method is used to begin the drag-and-drop operation. This method takes two parameters:

- **The data to be dragged**
- **The effects of the drag-and-drop operation**

  The `DragDropEffects` enumeration helps you specify these effects.

The following statement illustrates the use of DoDragDrop method.

```
txtDrag.DoDragDrop(txtDrag.Text, DragDropEffects.Copy)
```

In the preceding statement, the DoDragDrop method of a text box named txtDrag is called. The text contained in the text box is being dragged and the effect to be applied is Copy, which means that the data will be copied to the destination control.

To understand drag-and-drop operations better, let's now implement it. Before doing so, let's do some preparations first.

1. **Create a new Windows Application project. Give an appropriate name to this project.**
2. **Name the form as frmDragDrop and design it, as shown in Figure 4-3.**

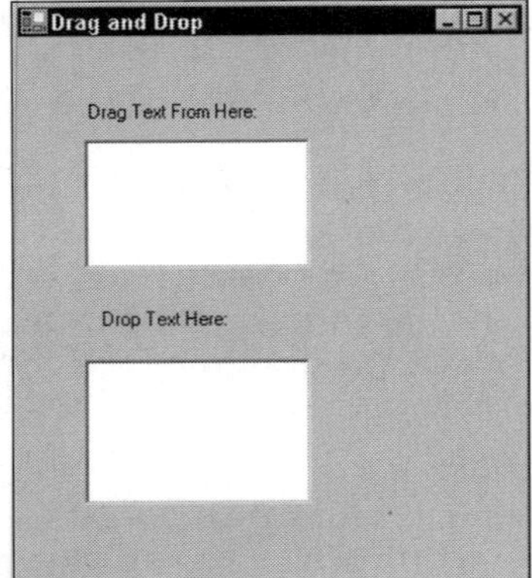

Figure 4-3: Beginning a drag-and-drop operation.

To learn adding controls to a form, read Book 3, Chapter 3. Table 4-1 lists the text boxes present on the form, with their names and functions.

Table 4-1 Names and Functions of Text Boxes

Caption	*Name*	*Function*
Drag Text From Here	txtDrag	Contains the text to be dragged.
Drop Text Here	txtDrop	The text dragged will be dropped in this text box.

In this form, you provide the functionality that enables a user to drag the contents of the txtDrag text box to the txtDrop text box.

TIP: To specify a name for a text box, click the appropriate text box to select it and set the Name field in the Properties window.

3. **Set the `Multiline` property of both text boxes to true.**

   To do so, in the Properties window from the `Multiline` list, select `True`.

4. **Add the following code to the `MouseDown` event of the txtDrag text box.**

```
Private Sub txtDrag_MouseDown(ByVal sender As Object,
   ByVal e As System.Windows.Forms.MouseEventArgs)
Handles
   txtDrag.MouseDown
'Start the drag and drop operation
  txtDrag.DoDragDrop(txtDrag.Text,
DragDropEffects.Copy)
End Sub
```

The `MouseEventArgs` class used in the preceding code is used to make available the data for `MouseDown`, `MouseUp`, and `MouseMove` events. This data could be something like, for example, which mouse button was pressed.

Let's look at steps to trap the `MouseDown` event of the txtDrag text box.

1. **Double-click Form1 to view the Code window.**
2. **In the Class Name list, as shown in Figure 4-4, click txtDrag.**
3. **In the Method Name list, as shown in Figure 4-5, click MouseDown.**

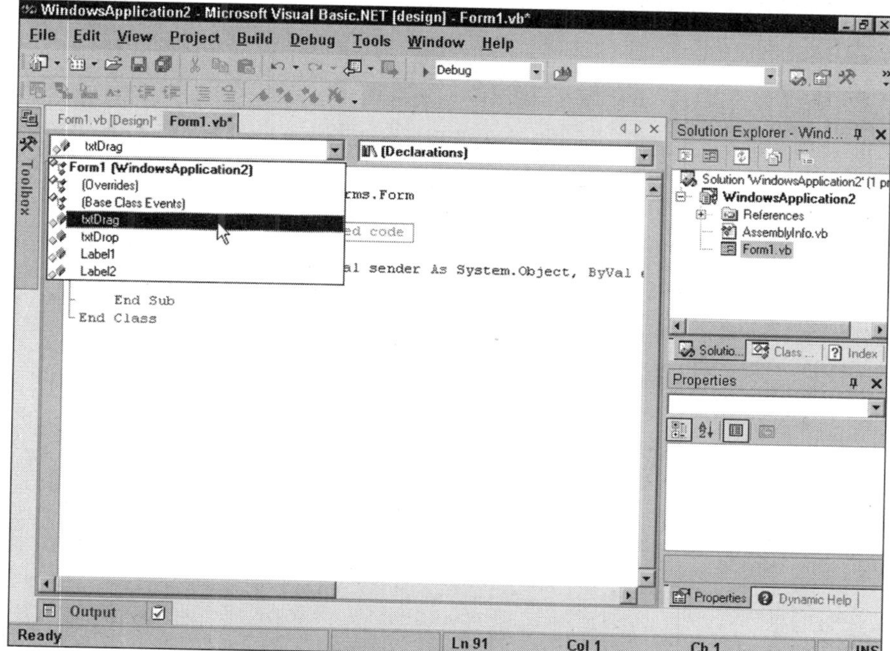

Figure 4-4: Specify the control by using the Class Name list.

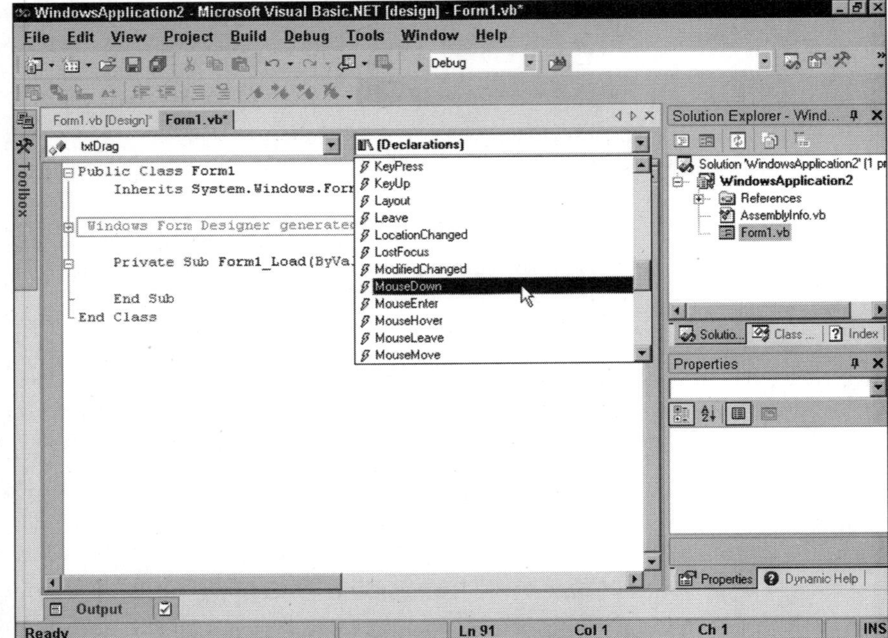

Figure 4-5: Specify the event by using the Method Name list.

The `txtDrag_MouseDown` event appears in the Code window.

Drop operation

Using a drag-and-drop operation also necessitates moving data to a destination or target location, which is usually a control such as a text box. To implement the drop operation, perform the following steps:

1. **Click txtDrop to select it.**
2. **In the Properties window, from the `AllowDrop` list, select `True`.**

   This sets the `AllowDrop` property of the text box to true.
3. **Handle the `DragEnter` event of the destination control.**

   To learn handling an event of a control, look for the Technical Stuff icon in the "Drag operation" section earlier in this chapter.

   The `DragEnter` event occurs when an object is being dragged into a controls area. In this event, you need to check the type of the data being dropped. After the type checking, you need to specify the effect that will be applied when the drop happens.

To understand this better, look at the DragEnter event of the destination text box named txtDrop.

```
Private Sub txtDrop_DragEnter(ByVal sender As Object,
  ByVal e As System.Windows.Forms.DragEventArgs) Handles
  txtDrop.DragEnter
   If (e.Data.GetDataPresent(DataFormats.Text)) Then
      e.Effect = DragDropEffects.Move
   Else
      e.Effect = DragDropEffects.None
   End If
End Sub
```

In the preceding code sample, the DragEventArgs class is used to make the data available for the DragDrop, DragEnter, or DragOver event.

- **The If...Then...Else statement is used to check the type of data. If the type of data is text, the effect to be applied is to move it. Otherwise, no action is to be taken.**

  Learn more about these statements in Book 3, Chapter 6.

- **The GetDataPresent method is used to determine whether the available data can be converted or be associated with the specified format.**

  You can use the DataFormats.Format class to specify the format or type of data. For example, DataFormats.Text specifies the ANSI text format.

After checking the type of data, you need to specify the effect that will be applied to the data being dropped (in this case, it is copied). You can do this by setting the Effect property of the DragEventArgs class by using the DragDropEffects enumeration.

The last step for performing a drop is to retrieve the data being dragged. You do so in the DragDrop event of the destination control. The DragDrop event occurs when a drag-and-drop operation is completed.

Consider the following code sample:

```
Private Sub txtDrop_DragDrop(ByVal sender As Object, ByVal
  e As System.Windows.Forms.DragEventArgs) Handles
  txtDrop.DragDrop
'Set the data in the txtDrop text box
   txtDrop.Text =
     CStr(e.Data.GetData(DataFormats.Text))
   TxtDrag.Text = ""
End Sub
```

In the preceding syntax, the `GetData` method is used to obtain the data associated with the specified format (in this case, text). The format of the data is the parameter for the `GetData` method. To specify the format, you use the `DataFormats.Format` class, where `Format` is replaced with the actual format name.

Utilizing the Clipboard

You're undoubtedly familiar with the Cut, Copy, and Paste operations that you perform in any word processing application. When you use the Cut or Copy commands, the data is temporarily placed on the clipboard. You can then paste this data at any other point. Visual Basic .NET provides you with the `Clipboard` class that helps you in utilizing the system clipboard. This class provides methods that help you place data to and retrieve data from the clipboard. The following section walks you through the usage of these methods.

Setting data on the clipboard

You use the `SetDataObject` method of the `Clipboard` class to place data on the system clipboard. The following statement illustrates placing data on the clipboard:

```
Clipboard.SetDataObject(txtClipboard.Text)
```

In the preceding statement, contents of the text box `txtClipboard` are placed onto the clipboard.

The best way to understand a concept is to put it in practice. Thus, we continue with the application that we created in the section "Implementing Drag-and-Drop Operations." To begin with, perform the following steps:

1. **Add a new Windows Form to the project.**

   To get more information on adding forms to a project, read Book 3, Chapter 2.

2. **Make this form the startup form.**

   To learn making a form appear at startup of an application, read the section "Creating MDI parent and child forms." You can also refer to Book 3, Chapter 2.

3. **Design the form as shown in Figure 4-6.**

   To learn adding controls to a form, read Book 3, Chapter 3. Name the various text boxes as shown in Table 4-2.

Table 4-2	Names of Text Boxes
Caption	*Name*
Copy	TxtClipboard
Paste	TxtPaste

4. **In the Properties window, set the `Multiline` property of both the text boxes to true.**
5. **Double-click the Copy button to view the `Button1_Click` event of the Copy button in the Code window.**
6. **In the event handler, add the following code.**

```
Clipboard.SetDataObject(txtClipboard.Text)
```

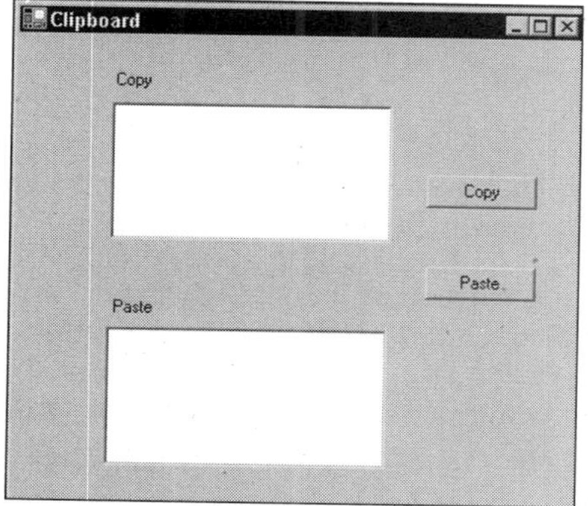

Figure 4-6: A sample form to perform clipboard operation.

Let's now move on to retrieving data placed on the clipboard.

Getting data from the clipboard

You use the `GetDataObject` method to retrieve the data placed on the system clipboard. This method returns data by using the `IDataObject` interface. This interface is used to retrieve the data available in a number of formats, such as text or .rtf. To practice retrieving data, let's continue with our application.

1. **Double-click the Paste button to view the event handler for its Click event (`Button2_Click`).**
2. **Add the following code to the `Button2_Click` event handler.**

```
 'Create an object that implements IDataObject
Dim Contents As IDataObject
'Initialize the object with the value store in clipboard
```

```
Contents = Clipboard.GetDataObject()
'Check for the format of the data
If (Contents.GetDataPresent(DataFormats.Text)) Then
'Set the text box txtPaste with the value
   txtPaste.Text =
     CStr(Contents.GetData(DataFormats.Text))
End If
```

In the preceding code sample, the contents of the clipboard are placed on the text box `txtPaste`.

3. **Choose Debug⇨Start to execute the application and add some contents to the `txtCopy` text box.**
4. **Click the Copy button.**

   This places the contents of the `txtCopy` text box on the clipboard.
5. **Click the Paste button.**

   The contents of the `txtCopy` text box are copied to the `txtPaste` text box.

Providing Help

You can make your applications more user-friendly by providing help regarding the various options and commands available in your application. Visual Basic .NET provides the `HelpProvider` control for displaying help. By using this control, you can incorporate two types of help in your applications. These are

- **Displaying a help file in HyperText Markup Language (HTML) format.**

  This file might contain steps for performing some task or notes on some topic related to the application.
- **Displaying pop-up help.**

  This kind of help is similar to the What's This help provided in many applications, such as MS Word.

The following section provides information on incorporating help in your applications.

Displaying a help file

Visual Basic. NET enables you to display an HTMLHelp1.x, HTMLHelp2.0, or HTML help file in your applications. Read through the following steps for information on including help file in your applications.

In the following steps, use the application that you created in the section "Implementing Drag-and-Drop Operations."

1. **In Solution Explorer, double-click Form2 to activate it.**
2. **In the Toolbox, double-click the `HelpProvider` control to add it to the form.**

   The HelpProvider1 appears in the Tray at the bottom of the form.
3. **Click HelpProvider1 to select it.**
4. **In the Properties window, set the `HelpNamespace` field to specify the name of the `.chm`, `.col`, or `.htm` file that contains help.**

   This sets the `HelpNamespace` property, which indicates the name of the help file to be opened. For example, you can specify the file name as C:\Help.htm.

   The `.chm` files are the compiled html files and the `.col` files are the html help files.
5. **On the form, click the Copy button to select it.**

   You'll provide assistance for this button.
6. **In the Properties window, set the `HelpKeyword` property.**

   The `HelpKeyword` property contains the string that is used to retrieve information for the specific control. This string is passed by the `HelpProvider` control to the help file for picking up the appropriate topic.
7. **In the Properties window, set the `HelpNavigator` property to an appropriate value.**

   Use the `HelpNavigator` to determine the manner in which the `HelpKeyword` property is passed to the help file. You use the `HelpNavigator` enumeration to specify a value for this property. Some of the members of this enumeration are `Index`, `Find`, and `TableOfContents`. `Index` specifies that the index of the help file is to be displayed. `Find` specifies that the search page of the help file is to be displayed. `TableOfContents` specifies that the table of contents of the specified file is to be displayed.
8. **Choose Debug⇨Start to execute the application.**
9. **Set the focus on the Copy button and press F1.**

   The associated help file opens in the browser window. A sample help file is shown in Figure 4-7.

To set focus on a control, you can click on it.

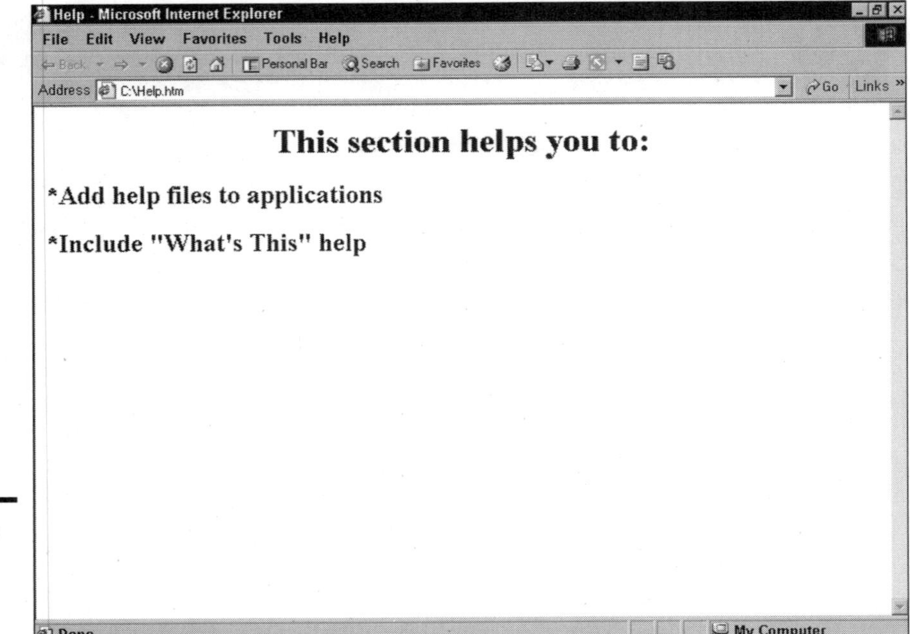

Figure 4-7: Creating a sample Help file.

Displaying What's This help

In a number of dialog boxes, a Help button appears next to the Close button. If you click this button and then click on any control present on the dialog box, a brief description of that control pops up. This is referred to as *What's This* help. Note that we're specifically discussing dialog boxes and not forms.

- **Because a dialog box doesn't contain the Maximize and Minimize buttons, the Help button can be displayed.**

  However, the forms do have Minimize and Maximize buttons. Hence, the forms can't have What's This help.

- **Dialog boxes are mostly modal, meaning that they don't allow you to continue work with any application unless they're closed.**

  In this situation, it's difficult to display help in another window. Therefore, What's This help is more suitable for dialog boxes.

Follow these steps to incorporate this help feature in your ongoing application.

1. **In Solution Explorer, double-click Form2 to activate it.**
2. **In the Properties window, from the MinimizeBox list, select False.**

3. **In the Properties window, from the MaximizeBox list, select False.**

   Note that your form now contains only the Close button. Now, you display the What's This help button.

4. **In the Properties window, from the** `HelpButton` **list, select** `True`**.**

   A help button with a question mark appears on the right side of the title bar of the form. You can refer to this button as your Help button.

5. **Click the Copy button to select it.**

   You provide help for this button.

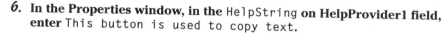

6. **In the Properties window, in the** `HelpString` **on HelpProvider1 field, enter** `This button is used to copy text.`

   TIP: The `HelpString` property contains text that is displayed onscreen as help for the control at runtime.

   TIP: This property is available only if you've added a HelpProvider control to the form. Note that we are using the HelpProvider1 control that was used in the previous section.

7. **To display this help, execute the application (choose Debug⇨Start).**

   Click the Help button present on the Title bar.

8. **Click the Copy button.**

   The text that you specified appears, as shown in Figure 4-8.

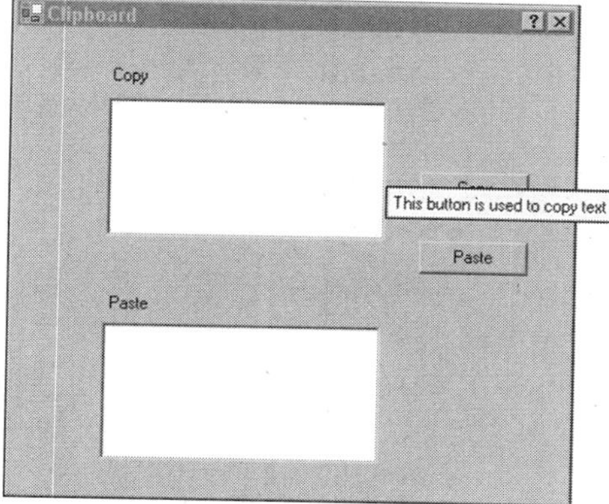

Figure 4-8: Creating a What's This help button.

Chapter 5: Variables: The .NET Lingo

In This Chapter

- ✓ **Traversing the A to Z of variables**
- ✓ **Discovering arrays**
- ✓ **Using more strings**

After you create the basic design of your application by using Windows Forms and controls, the next logical step is to write the code. This code helps your application perform the required tasks that you outline when you design it. While performing these tasks, your application obviously needs to handle data, which could be of different types, such as numeric or text. You need to make your application adapt to the type of data supplied to it as well as store this data. If this sounds like a tall order, don't worry: You can rely on Visual Basic .NET to help.

Visual Basic .NET provides a number of data types that make handling different types of data child's play. With Visual Basic .NET, you can create variables to store this data and arrays to store similar types of data together.

In this chapter, you learn about the different data types supported by Visual Basic .NET. We also introduce you to the fundamentals of creating variables and arrays and discuss the `String` class in depth.

Creating Variables Made Easy

Sometimes you may need to temporarily store data in your application. Consider an application used in a department store. The clerk at the payment counter enters the price and the quantity purchased by a customer, and the application then calculates the total price of all purchases, displaying it to the clerk. In such applications, the value entered by the clerk needs to be stored for calculation. In addition, the result of the calculation should also be stored for display. You create variables to store such values.

A *variable* is a memory location that stores data temporarily. In an application, you can repeatedly initialize a variable with a value. Before initializing, however, you need to declare variables. Visual Basic .NET provides you with an option to declare variables, implicitly or explicitly. *Implicit declaration* enables you to use variables without any formal declaration, whereas *explicit declaration* requires you to declare variables before using them.

Declaring implicit variables

The implicit declaration of variables doesn't actually involve any declaration: You use the variables without declaring them. For example, you can use the following statement in your programs:

```
Implicit_Variable = 10
```

The preceding statement stores `10` in the variable `Implicit_Variable`. However, for such statements to be valid, you need to turn `Option Explicit` off. Use the `Option Explicit` statement to make sure that variables are declared before they're used. The syntax of the `Option Explicit` statement is

```
Option Explicit [On | Off]
```

If you use `On` with the `Option Explicit` statement, you need to declare a variable. When you use `Off`, you can use variables without declaring them. By default, `Option Explicit` is `On`.

You can also set the value for the `Option Explicit` statement by following these steps:

1. **In Solution Explorer, right-click the project name.**
2. **From the pop-up menu that appears, choose Properties to display the Property Pages for the project.**
3. **Under Common Properties, click Build to select it.**
4. **Under Complier Defaults, select the appropriate value (On or Off) from the Option Explicit list.**

After you set a value for this option by using the preceding steps, Visual Basic .NET checks for the declaration of all variables at compile time.

We don't recommend using the implicit declaration because it can make your programs malfunction. For example, suppose that you use a variable in your program without declaring it. If you happen to misspell that variable at some other point in the same program, your program won't give you any error because of implicit declaration. Instead, a new variable will be created and will be used, which might lead to unexpected results.

Declaring explicit variables

The explicit declaration compels you to declare all the variables that you use in your programs. You use the `Dim` statement to declare variables, as shown in the following statement:

```
Dim Name_Variable [As Type_of_Variable]
```

In the preceding syntax, `Name_Variable` refers to the name of the variable and `Type_of_Variable` refers to the type of data that the variable can store. You specify the type of data by using data types. For more on data types and how to specify them, read the next section.

Understanding data types

You can store any type of data in a variable. However, only certain operations can be performed on the data of a particular type. To help illustrate this, we build on the department store application from earlier (see the section "Creating Variables Made Easy"). To calculate the total amount payable by a customer, the application requires that the data is stored in numeric format. If you extend the application to store the name and address of customers, those values must be provided in text format. To further complicate this application, the address can contain both numerals and alphabets. To store data in its respective format(s), you use data types.

Visual Basic .NET provides you with data types to handle numeric, text, byte, Boolean, and date time data. In addition, Visual Basic .NET provides the `Object` data type, which can store any type of data.

Numeric data types

Visual Basic .NET provides you with `Integer`, `Long`, and `Short` data types to store numerals. To store floating-point numbers, you can use `Single`, `Double`, and `Decimal` data types.

All these data types differ in the range that they support. For example, `Integer` is used for 32-bit numbers, `Short` for 16-bit numbers, and `Long` for 64-bit numbers.

Text data types

Visual Basic .NET provides `Char` and `String` data types to store text data. The `Char` data type can store only a single character, and the `String` data type is used to store a string of characters. In addition, the `String` type variables can store alphanumeric data.

Miscellaneous data types

In addition, Visual Basic .NET also provides you with `Byte`, `Boolean`, and `Date` data types. Use the `Byte` data type to store binary data and ASCII values of characters in numeric form. Use the `Boolean` data type to store data with only two possible values (`True` or `False`) and the `Date` data type to store date and time values.

A handy general-purpose data type is `Object`, in which you can store any type of data, such as `Boolean`, `Integer`, or `String`.

Refer to the `Dim` statement syntax in the earlier section "Declaring explicit variables." Remember that specifying the type of a variable is optional. If you skip the type of variable in declaration, the variable automatically assumes the `Object` data type.

After you declare and initialize a variable, you can use the name of this variable to insert the value contained in that variable at a specific point in code. To understand this better, consider the following example that illustrates declaring, initializing, and using variables:

```
'Declare variables
Dim MyVar As String
'Initializing variable
MyVar = "Hello"
'Using Variable
MessageBox.Show(MyVar)
```

When you need to use variables throughout your application or within one procedure, you need to specify the scope of the variable.

Specifying the scope of variables

The variables that you declare by using the `Dim` statement can be used only in the current procedure. A *procedure* is a set of statements used to perform some specific task. All the code in Visual Basic .NET is organized within procedures. (Read more about procedures in Book 3, Chapter 7.) Visual Basic .NET allows you to create public and private variables.

- **Public variables** can be used across *modules* (collections of procedures), which can be declared at the module level only. To make a variable public, use the `Public` keyword, as shown in the following syntax.

  ```
  Public Name_of_Variable As Type_of_Variable
  ```

- **Private variables** can be used only in the module in which they are declared. Additionally, the private variables can be declared only at the module level. To make a variable private, you use the `Private` keyword.

  ```
  Private Name_of_Variable As Type_of_Variable
  ```

The variables that you declare in a procedure are destroyed as soon as the execution of procedure is over, and the value stored in the variable is also destroyed. However, you can retain the value stored in a variable even after the execution of procedure by using the `Static` keyword. The following syntax describes the usage of the `Static` keyword.

```
Static Name_of_Variable As Type_of_Variable
```

Changing the Data Type of Variables

You may sometime need to change the type of data stored in a variable in your applications. For example, you may need to convert a number to text or vice versa.

Suppose that you have application containing five text boxes to accept five numbers from the user. The application then calculates and displays the sum. However, when you try to save the numbers entered by the user in `Integer` variables, Visual Basic .NET doesn't like that, stating that implicit conversion from `String` to `Integer` isn't allowed. In Visual Basic .NET, you need to explicitly convert data of one type to another. Converting one data type to another is known as *type conversion*. Visual Basic .NET allows two types of conversions:

- **Widening conversions** are carried out without any data loss and are always successful, such as when you change the data type from `Short` to `Integer`.
- **Narrowing conversions** may cause data loss and may or may not be successful, such as when you try to convert an `Integer` to `Short`.

TIP

If a narrowing conversion isn't successful, Visual Basic .NET displays an error message. We recommend that you use widening conversions.

Visual Basic .NET provides you with various functions that allow you to convert one type of data to another, such as `CStr` and `CInt`. The `CStr` and `CInt` functions are used to convert the supplied data to `String` and `Integer`, respectively. These functions are also called *cast operators*; conversions involving the use of cast operators are *explicit conversions*.

Type conversion is also possible without the use of cast operators; this type of conversion is *implicit conversion*. Both widening and narrowing conversions can be explicit or implicit. The `Option Strict` statement is useful for performing type conversions successfully.

Use the `Option Strict` statement to ensure that the implicit conversions involving any loss of data don't occur. The syntax of the `Option Strict` statement is

```
Option Strict [On | Off]
```

If you set `Option Strict` to `On`, the data type of variables is checked before conversion. If you set it to `Off`, implicit type conversions can happen. By default, `Option Strict` is `On`. When set to `On`, the `Option Strict` statement requires explicit declaration of variables.

You can also set the value for the `Option Strict` statement by following these steps:

1. **In the Solution Explorer, right-click the project name.**
2. **From the pop-up menu that appears, choose Properties to display the Property Pages for the project.**
3. **Under Common Properties, click Build to select it.**
4. **Under Complier Defaults, select the appropriate value (On or Off) from the Option Strict list.**

After you set a value for this option by using the preceding steps, Visual Basic .NET checks for all the implicit conversions at compile time.

Operating on Variables

You manipulate data stored in variables with Visual Basic .NET arithmetic, relational, and logical operators. An *operator* is a symbol that's used to perform an operation on two expressions, as follows:

✦ **Arithmetic operators:** Use arithmetic operators to perform mathematical operations, such as multiplication and addition. Some commonly used arithmetic operators are `*`, `+`, `\`, and `-`.

Relational operators: Use relational operators to compare two values or expressions. These operators return a Boolean value of `True` or `False`. Some commonly used relational operators are `=`, `< >`, `<`, `>`, `<=`, and `>=`.

Logical operators: Use logical operators to perform logical evaluation of Boolean expressions. Some commonly used logical operators are `And`, `Or`, and `Not`. In addition, Visual Basic .NET also provides `AndAlso` and `OrElse` operators. See Table 5-1 for a description of these logical operators.

Table 5-1 Logical Operators

Operator	Definition	Description
`And`	Use the `And` operator to perform logical conjunctions. This operator evaluates all the expressions.	If a Boolean comparison comprises two Boolean expressions joined by `And`, the result is `True` *only if* both the expressions return `True`.
`Or`	Use the `Or` operator to perform logical disjunctions. This operator evaluates all the expressions.	If a Boolean comparison comprises two Boolean expressions joined by `Or`, the result is `True` even *only if* one of the expressions returns `True`.
`Not`	Use the `Not` operator to perform logical negations.	If a Boolean expression uses `Not`, the result of the expression is negated. For example, the value `True` becomes `False` after the use of `Not` operator.
`AndAlso`	Use the `AndAlso` operator as a short-circuit form of the `And` operator.	If the first expression evaluates to `False`, the remaining expressions are not evaluated and the result is `False`.
`OrElse`	The `OrElse` operator is a short-circuit form of the `Or` operator.	If the first expression evaluates to `True`, the remaining expressions are not evaluated and the result is `True`.

Arrays — Go Ahead and Store More

Earlier in this chapter, we discuss that you use variables to temporarily store data. However, when you need to store a large amount of related data, you can't rely on variables. Now, you must be thinking, why not? To understand this, suppose that your supervisor asks you to create an application that stores the name of all the possible *For Dummies* books — that's a lot of titles. You could create a number of variables and store the book names within them . . . but this forces you to create a variable for each title, giving them apt names, and remembering all those variable names. How painful. Visual Basic .NET provides you with a better and easier way out: using arrays to store related data.

An *array* refers to contiguous memory locations that are used to store multiple values of the same type. In other words, an array is a collection of multiple variables having a common name, and all those variables are of a similar data type. You can refer to any variable in an array by using an index number, which indicates the position of the variable in the array. You can call these variables as elements of an array. The total number of elements in an array is the *array length*.

In Visual Basic .NET, you can create two types of arrays:

- A *single-dimensional array* is an array that can store one type of data only. For example, you can create an array that stores the names of the books.
- A *multidimensional array* can store this data along with additional information about this data. For example, if you need to store the price of each book along with the book title, you can create a two-dimensional array that stores book titles in one-dimension and prices of the corresponding books in a second dimension.

Visual Basic .NET, however, allows you to create arrays with more than two dimensions. In Visual Basic .NET, you can create arrays with up to 32 dimensions.

You can resize arrays in Visual Basic .NET depending on your requirements. The `System.Array` class simplifies working with arrays, and the `Array` class contains functions you can use to manipulate arrays.

Creating arrays

Creating arrays is simple, just like creating variables — with a slight modification. The syntax is

```
Dim Name_Array (Total_Elements) [As Type_of_Element]
```

In the preceding syntax,

- `Name_Array` is the name of the array.
- `Total_Elements` is the number of elements that the array can contain.
- `Type_of_Elements` is the data type of the array.

Here's the code for an array named `Books` of size `50` and data type `String`.

```
Dim Books(50) As String
```

The array created by the preceding statement is a single-dimensional array. Read more about single-dimensional arrays in the next section.

Single-dimensional arrays

As the name suggests, a single-dimensional array can store data in only one dimension, which means that the data belongs to one particular category.

For example, you can create a single-dimensional array to store names of all the employees in a company, or names of all the books published by a particular publishing house.

Look at the code snippet (that we use in the previous section) to create a single-dimensional array that stores names of all the books:

```
Dim Books(50) As String      'Statement 1
```

From the preceding code snippet, can you tell how many elements the `Books` array can store? The answer is 51 because the starting position of variables in an array is `0`.

An alternate way of creating the same array is

```
Dim Books() As String = New String(50) {}
```

The preceding statement also creates an array named `Books` of size `50` and type `String`. The `New` keyword used in the preceding statement reserves memory for the array at the time of declaration. This process is also referred to as *assigning memory to an array*. If we create an array by using `Statement 1` (in the first code snippet), then the memory is assigned when you initialize the array with values. The following section introduces you to the details of initializing arrays.

Here's yet another method of creating an array. This method helps you simultaneously create and initialize arrays:

```
Dim Books() As String = {"XML For Dummies", "Office 2000 For
     Dummies", "Visual Studio .NET For Dummies"}
```

Multidimensional arrays

Continuing with the book inventory example, suppose that your supervisor asks you to also store the price of the book along with the book title. To solve this problem, you can create two arrays: one that stores book titles and a second one that stores book prices. However, this method isn't very useful because you need to refer two arrays, and that's time consuming because you need to write code to manipulate both the arrays simultaneously. In addition, you need to map the corresponding indexes of both arrays. For example, if you're displaying a book's title, then the price of this book should be displayed. This require lots of work. The easy way out is to create an array with two dimensions and then store the data at one place. The syntax for creating a two-dimensional array is

```
Dim BooksPrice(50, 50) As String
```

The preceding statement declares an array of type String having two dimensions of size 50 each. Use the first dimension to store the book title and the second dimension to store the corresponding price. The following code sample specifies book titles and prices.

```
'Store XML FOR DUMMIES at index position (0,0)
BooksPrice(0,0) = "XML For Dummies"
'Store the price of XML For Dummies at index position (0,1)
BooksPrice(0,1) = "$50"
'Store Office XP For Dummies at index position (1,0)
BooksPrice(1,0) = "Office XP For Dummies"
'Store the price of Office XP For Dummies at index position
   '(1,1)
BooksPrice(1,1) = "$30
'Store Visual Studio .NET For Dummies at index position (2,
   0)
BooksPrice(2,0) = "Visual Studio .NET For Dummies"
'Store the price of Visual Studio .NET For Dummies at index
   position (2,1)
BooksPrice(2,1) = "$60"
```

Similarly, you can create arrays having more than two dimensions. Consider for example, a three-dimensional array.

```
Dim SampleArray(5, 5, 5) As String
```

The number of dimensions in an array is the *rank* of the array. The size of each dimension can vary. For example, you can define an array like this:

```
Dim SampleArray(5, 4, 3) As String
```

Assigning values to an array

After you create an array, you need to assign values to it, as shown in the following code:

```
Books(0) = "XML For Dummies"
Books(1) = "Office XP For Dummies"
. . .
Books(50) = "Visual Studio .NET For Dummies"
```

In the preceding example,

- ✦ At index position 0 of the array is the book *XML For Dummies.*
- ✦ At index position 1 of the array is the book *Office XP For Dummies.*
- ✦ At index position 50 of the array is the book *Visual Studio .NET For Dummies.*

You can retrieve the values stored at a particular index position by specifying the index position along with the array name. For example, to retrieve the value stored at index position 1, you can use the following statement.

```
Dim Var As String
Var = Books(1)
'Displays Office XP For Dummies
MessageBox.Show(Var)
```

After you finish working with arrays, you should release the memory assigned to the array. To do so, you use the Erase statement. The syntax is

```
Erase Books
```

Resizing arrays

You can also use Visual Basic .NET to resize arrays. In our running book inventory example, the array Books that we create in the previous section to store book details was of size 50. However, the number of books that you need to store in this array might be more than 50 — say 70. In such a situation, you can create a dynamic array (resize the existing array) by using the ReDim statement.

ReDim statement

You use a ReDim statement to resize an array, which is already declared. However, you don't have to declare size at this time. Building on our book inventory example, you can use the following statement to resize the Books array so that it contains 70 elements.

```
ReDim Books(70)
```

You can also resize multidimensional arrays by using the ReDim statement. However, the ReDim statement doesn't allow you to change the number of dimensions and the data type of an array.

Any array that you resize by using the ReDim statement loses all its existing data.

Preserve keyword

If you need to retain the existing data that you lose by using a ReDim statement, use the Preserve keyword.

```
ReDim Preserve Books(70)
```

You can use the `Preserve` keyword for multidimensional arrays as well. However, you can only modify the size of the last dimension of a multidimensional array.

Consider the `BooksPrice` array that we create in the "Multidimensional arrays" section:

```
Dim BooksPrice(10, 1) As String
```

Suppose that you try to resize this array like this:

```
ReDim Preserve BooksPrice(15, 15)
```

An error is generated because you tried to change the size of both dimensions of the `Booksprice` array while using the `Preserve` keyword. Only the rightmost dimension of the array can be changed.

Manipulating arrays with the System.Array class

Manipulate arrays in Visual Basic .NET with the `Array` class, which is contained inside the `System` namespace. Some functions of this class include `GetUpperBound`, `GetLowerBound`, and `GetLength`.

GetUpperBound function

While working with arrays, you might need to find the length of an array or find the upper bound of the array. The *upper bound* of an array is the number of elements that you specify when declaring an array. Use the `GetUpperBound` function to find the upper bound of the specified dimension of an array. The syntax of the `GetUpperBound` function is

```
Name_Array.GetUpperBound(Dimension)
```

In the preceding syntax, `Name_Array` refers to the name of the array for which you need to find the upper bound of the specified `Dimension`. Consider the following example:

```
UpperBound = Books.GetUpperBound(0)
```

In the preceding example, the upper bound value of the first dimension of the `Books` array is stored in the variable `UpperBound`.

The upper bound of an array can also be defined as the number of elements contained in the array minus one because the array index starts at zero.

GetLowerBound function

Use the `GetLowerBound` function to determine the lower bound of the specified dimension of an array. However, the lower bound of all the dimensions in an array is fixed to zero.

```
Name_Array.GetLowerBound(Dimension)
```

In the preceding syntax, `Name_Array` refers to the name for which you need to find the lower bound of the specified `Dimension`. Consider the following example:

```
LowerBound = Books.GetLowerBound(1)
```

In the preceding example, the lower bound value of the second dimension of the array `Books` is stored in the variable `LowerBound`.

GetLength function

Use the `GetLength` function to help you determine the number of elements (length) in the specified dimension of an array.

```
Name_Array.GetLength(Dimension)
```

In the preceding syntax, `Name_Array` refers to the name for which you need to determine the length of the specified `Dimension`. Consider the following example:

```
Length = Books.GetLength(0)
```

In the preceding example, the number of elements in the first dimension of the `Books` array is stored in the variable `Length`.

Tying It All Together

Sometimes it's best to show how lots of small things can come together to help you achieve your application goals. The following example illustrates using all the functions that we have discussed so far in this chapter. We recommend that you go back and read any section you may have skipped before perusing the following.

```
 'Create and initialize an array
Dim myarry() As String = {"Jan", "Feb", "March"}
MessageBox.Show("The lower bound of this array is " & _
   myarry.GetLowerBound(0))
```

```
MessageBox.Show("The upper bound of this array is " & _
   myarry.GetUpperBound(0))
MessageBox.Show("The Length of this array is " & _
   myarry.GetLength(0))
MessageBox.Show("The value stored at index position 0 is " &
   myarry(0))
MessageBox.Show("The value stored at index position 1 is " &
   myarry(1))
MessageBox.Show("The value stored at index position 2 is " &
   myarry(2))
'Resize the array without Preserve keyword
ReDim myarry(6)
myarry(3) = "April"
myarry(4) = "May"
'No Value is displayed
MessageBox.Show("Value stored at index position 0 is " & _
   myarry(0))
MessageBox.Show("Value stored at index position 1 is " & _
   myarry(1))
MessageBox.Show("Value stored at index position 2 is " & _
   myarry(2))
'April is displayed
MessageBox.Show("Value stored at index position 3 is " & _
   myarry(3))
'May is displayed
MessageBox.Show("Value stored at index position 4 is " & _
   myarry(4))
'Resize the array by using the Preserve keyword
ReDim Preserve myarry(6)
myarry(0) = "Jan"
myarry(1) = "Feb"
myarry(2) = "March"
'Jan is displayed
MessageBox.Show("Value stored at index position 0 is " & _
   myarry(0))
'Feb is displayed
MessageBox.Show("Value stored at index position 1 is " & _
   myarry(1))
'March is displayed
MessageBox.Show("Value stored at index position 2 is " & _
   myarry(2))
'April is displayed
MessageBox.Show("Value stored at index position 3 is " & _
   myarry(3))
'May is displayed
MessageBox.Show("Value stored at index position 4 " _
   "is " & myarry(4))
```

In the preceding example, we declare an array to store the names of months. The example first displays the lower bound, the upper bound, and the length of this array. Then it displays the contents of the array. Because we first resize the array without using the Preserve keyword, it loses all its existing contents. After we resize the array with the Preserve keyword, all the contents that we add are safe.

Employing Strings to Handle Text Data

Use the Visual Basic .NET String class when you want your programs to handle data in text format. Strings, which represent a collection of characters, are widely used in day-to-day applications, such as storing names and addresses of employees. Some commonly performed operations on strings include:

- **Comparing strings:** For example, an application asks a user to logon. To check the authenticity of a user, this application then compares the values entered with the ones stored in the database.
- **Concatenating strings:** For example, an application accepts the address of a user in multiple columns, such as Address1, Address2, City, State, and Country, and then displays the complete address as one single string for verification.
- **Finding the length of strings:** For example, an application needs to ensure that the value entered in the phone number column is of correct length. To check this, the application needs to find out the length of the value entered in the phone number field.

The String class has methods and properties that help you play with strings in your applications. The String class provides two types of methods:

- **Shared methods** don't require an instance of the String class to work. You access these methods by using the following syntax.

  ```
  String.MethodName
  ```

  In the preceding syntax, MethodName is the method that you need to access.

- **Instance methods** do require an instance of the String class to work. You access these methods by using the following syntax.

  ```
  'Create an instance of a string
  Dim String1 As String
  'Accessing the method
  String1.MethodName
  ```

We can't cover all the methods provided by the String class in this chapter, but we do cover the most commonly used methods and properties.

String.Compare method

The `String.Compare` method is used to compare two strings for equality. This method returns an integer value that indicates the result of comparison. If the result is negative, the first string is smaller than the second string. If the result is positive, the first string is greater than the second string. And, if the result is zero, the two strings are equal. The following example illustrates using this method.

```
Dim String1, String2 As String
Dim Result As Integer
String1 = "Hello"
String2 = "World"
Result = String.Compare(String1, String2)
'The Result is -1
MessageBox.Show(Result)
```

A cool feature about `String.Compare` is that it provides you with an option to match case while comparing strings. The most common use of this feature is to validate a user's password, which is case-sensitive.

String.Concat method

Use the `String.Concat` method to concatenate a series of strings. Concatenation means to join two or more strings.

```
Dim String1, String2 As String
Dim Result As String
String1 = "Hello"
String2 = "World"
Result = String.Concat(String1, String2)
'The Result is HelloWorld
MessageBox.Show(Result)
```

You can also use the operators & and + to concatenate two strings. These operators are called *concatenation operators*. To understand the usage, consider the following code sample:

```
MessageBox.Show("Hello" + "World")
```

String.Copy method

Use the `String.Copy` method to copy the contents of a given `String` variable to a second variable. You can use this method to prevent yourself from doing repeated work. For example, after you accept the company name from an employee, you can copy this value to the details of the remaining employees.

```
Dim String1, String2 As String
String1 = "Hello World"
String2 = String.Copy(String1)
'String2 now contains Hello World
MessageBox.Show(String2)
```

String.Replace method

While entering data in an application, you might enter an incorrect spelling of the company name. In such a situation, use the `String.Replace` method to replace either characters or strings within the given strings.

```
Dim String1, String2 As String
String1 = "Hello Wld"
'Replace Wld by World
String2 = String1.Replace("Wld", "World")
'String2 now contains Hello World
MessageBox.Show(String2)
```

String.Substring method

Use the `String.Substring` method to extract substrings from a given string. For example, suppose that you need to display the initials of an employee. In such a situation, you can extract first characters from the first name and last name fields respectively.

The `String.Substring` method takes the index position where the substring should start and the length of the substring as arguments.

```
Dim String1, String2 As String
String1 = "Hello World"
'Extract World from Hello World
String2 = String1.Substring(6, 5)
'String2 now contains World
MessageBox.Show(String2)
```

String.Length property

Use the `String.Length` property to find the number of characters in a string. Here's how to use this property:

```
Dim String1 As String
Dim Result As Integer
String1 = "Hello World"
Result = String1.Length
'The Result is 11
MessageBox.Show(CStr(Result))
```

Chapter 6: Controlling Program Flow

In This Chapter

- ✔ **Discovering decision structures**
- ✔ **Understanding loop structures**

You design an application to perform certain tasks, such as taking input from a user, performing calculations based on this input, and displaying the result to the user. You then write programs to accomplish all these tasks. To perform calculations, these programs might depend on the result of some conditions, or they might need to repeat certain statements repeatedly. In addition, you will undoubtedly encounter situations when a user may enter incorrect or incomplete data or is perhaps required to enter the data more than once. As a safety net, you should design programs that can be used to perform tasks in such situations, using Visual Basic .NET to help you construct decision and loop structures.

Implementing Decision Structures

In your programs, you may need to handle certain situations where the program must be able to make decisions based on user input. For example, even if a user enters incomplete or incorrect information, you want to design your program so that it can perform its next step, such as to inform the user of an entry error, assume some default value, or exit the program. To specify the next logical step to be performed in a specific situation, use Visual Basic .NET decision structures, such as the `If...Then...Else` and `Select...Case` statements.

Using If...Then...Else statements

You use an `If...Then...Else` statement when you need to execute statement(s) depending on the result of an expression that returns a Boolean value, such as if you determine the type of the figure based on the number of sides it has. You can divide these statements into two: single-line and multiple-line. The single-line statement allows you to check for a condition in one line whereas the multiple-line helps you check for complex conditions. In the upcoming section, we discuss these two categories of the `If...Then...Else` statements.

Single-line statement

You use the single-line form of the If...Then...Else statements in situations where a relatively small number of statements needs to be executed based on a condition. Check out the following simple syntax:

```
If Condition Then Statement1[:Statement2] [Else Statement]
```

The optional part of the code (which you can skip) is enclosed in square brackets.

In the preceding syntax, Condition is the expression, which is evaluated. If the condition returns true, the statements following Then are executed. If the condition return false, the statements following Else are executed. You can skip the Else part in an If...Then...Else statement when you need to check only one particular condition.

Using the same elements as the previous example, the single-line form looks like this:

```
If sides = 3 Then MessageBox.Show("The figure is a Triangle")
   Else MessageBox.Show("The figure is not a Triangle")
```

In a single-line If...Then...Else statement, you can include multiple statements by separating the statements with colons (:).

Here's an example:

```
If sides = 3 Then Angle = "Triangle" : MessageBox.Show(Angle)
```

However, if you do choose to include a number of statements in a single-line If...Then...Else statement, the readability of the code decreases. In such situations, you should use the multiple-line If...Then...Else statements to make it easier to read.

Multiple-line statements

The following code lists the syntax of a multiple-line If...Then...Else statement:

```
If Condition Then
   Statement(s)
[Else
   Statements(s)]
End If
```

Note that unlike a single-line statement, the end of the multiple-line `If...Then...Else` statement is marked by an `End If` statement.

Consider this basic example: We want to determine whether a figure is a triangle by defining the number of sides that it has.

```
If sides = 3 Then
   MessageBox.Show("The figure is a Triangle")
Else
   MessageBox.Show("The figure is not a Triangle")
End If
```

In certain situations, you might need to evaluate an expression and check the result in a number of values. Use an `ElseIf` statement within a statement to handle such situations. The syntax of using an `ElseIf` statement is as follows:

```
If Condition1 Then
   Statement1(s)
[ElseIf Condition2 Then
   Statement2(s)]
[Else
   Statements(s)]
End If
```

In the preceding syntax, `Condition1` is evaluated; if it returns `false`, the control moves to the `Condition2`. If `Condition2` returns `true`, the statement set `Statement2` is executed. Otherwise, the statements following the `Else` statement are executed.

Look over this example that uses an `ElseIf` in a `If...Then...Else` statement. Using this enables you to define a variety of figures by the number of sides that they have:

```
If sides = 3 Then
   MessageBox.Show("The figure is a Triangle")
ElseIf sides = 4 Then
   MessageBox.Show("The figure is a Quadrilateral")
ElseIf sides = 5 Then
   MessageBox.Show("The figure is a Pentagon")
ElseIf sides = 6 Then
   MessageBox.Show("The figure is a Hexagon")
ElseIf sides = 7 Then
   MessageBox.Show("The figure is a Heptagon")
Else
   MessageBox.Show("Incorrect value entered")
End If
```

In the preceding example, the value of the variable `sides` is checked in multiple values and the name of the figure is displayed accordingly.

Nested statements

You can also use a `If...Then...Else` statement within another `If...Then...Else` statement. These types of statements are *nested statements*. These statements are helpful in situations where you need to check for certain conditions and, based on the result of these conditions, you need to check some other conditions.

For example, consider an application that is used to calculate discount. The discount varies from item to item. In addition, depending on the quantity bought, a particular item has different levels of discount. Here, you'll check the first condition (name of the item) by using an `If...Then...Else` statement and within this condition, you need to check the second condition (quantity bought) by nesting an `If...Then...Else` statement inside the first statement. Using nested statements help your code execute faster. This is because the nested conditions are executed only when the main condition is true.

You can have as many levels of nested statements as you require. However, a large number of nested loops might reduce the readability of the program.

Suppose that you also want to be able to identify a figure that has less than three sides. Nest that condition first to separate out those occurrences.

```
If sides < 3 Then
   If sides = 1 Then
      MessageBox.Show("This is a Line")
   ElseIf sides = 2 Then
      MessageBox.Show("This is an Angle")
   End If
ElseIf sides = 3 Then
   MessageBox.Show("This is a Triangle")
Else
   MessageBox.Show("The figure is a Polygon")
End If
```

Opting for Select...Case statements

Use `Select...Case` statements to add decision-making capability to your applications. Just like an `If...Then...Else` statement, you can use the `Select...Case` statement to execute a set of statements based on the result of an expression. For example, you can use the `Select...Case` statement to find out the type of figure depending on the number of sides instead of an `If...Then...Else` statement.

`Select...Case` statements increase the readability of the code as compared to the `If...Then...Else` statements.

Note the following differences, however, between the two:

✦ The expression of a `Select...Case` statement does not return a Boolean value.

✦ A `Select...Case` statement evaluates an expression only once.

(You can use an `If...Then...Else` statement to evaluate different expressions by using `ElseIf` statements.)

The syntax of a `Select...Case` statement is

```
Select Case Expression
   Case expressionlist
[Case Else
   [Statement(s)]
End Select
```

The `End Select` statement marks the end of a `Select...Case` statement.

In the preceding syntax, the `Expression` is evaluated and the result is compared with the constants or expressions specified in the `expressionlist`. If the result doesn't match any of the specified values, the statements specified after the `Case Else` statement are executed.

Here's how to rewrite the example that we mention in the `If...Then...Else` statement section by using the `Select...Case` statement. By using this statement, you write less code, which adds to the readability of the code.

```
Select Case sides

Case 3
   MessageBox.Show("The figure is a Triangle")
Case 4
   MessageBox.Show("The figure is a Quadrilateral")
Case 5
   MessageBox.Show("The figure is a Pentagon")
Case 6
   MessageBox.Show("The figure is a Hexagon")
Case 7
   MessageBox.Show("The figure is a Heptagon")
Case Else
   MessageBox.Show("Incorrect value entered")
End Select
```

You can also nest one `Select...Case` statement inside another.

Loop Structures

If the values entered by a user in an application are incorrect, you may need to repeat the whole task of entering values all over again.

Consider an application that accepts a log-in name and password from a user. If the user enters an incorrect value, the application should prompt the user to re-enter the new (correct) values. This prompting process should repeat until the values entered are correct. For example, if a user enters invalid characters, such as numbers in her name, you need to prompt her until the values she enters are correct. In such situations, use the looping structures provided by Visual Basic .NET.

The looping structures enable you to execute a set of statements repeatedly. You can choose from a number of structures, such as the `While...End While`, `Do...Loop`, and `For...Next` statement. Each has a specific purpose, and we examine each of them in the upcoming sections.

Utilizing a While...End While statement

Use the `While...End While` statement to specify that a set of statements is to be repeated as long as the condition is `true`. For example, you can use the `While...End While` statement to repeat a set of statements that populate a `ListBox` control on the form with the values stored inside a database. This set of statements is repeated as long as any value remains in the database. Following is the syntax of a simple `While...End While` statement:

```
While Condition
   Statement(s)
   [Exit While]
End While
```

You use the `Exit While` statement to exit from a `While...End While` loop.

In the preceding syntax, the `Condition` is an expression that returns a Boolean value. The `Condition` is evaluated at the beginning of the loop; if it returns `true`, the statements following the `Condition` are executed.

For example:

```
Dim Ctr As Integer
Ctr = 1
While Ctr <=5
   Dim Num As Integer
   Num = CInt(InputBox("Enter a number"))
```

```
    If Num Mod 2 = 0 Then
       MessageBox.Show("Even Number")
    Else
       MessageBox.Show("Not an Even Number")
    End If
    Ctr = Ctr + 1
End While
```

In this example, a number is accepted from the user and a message indicating whether (or not) the number that's displayed to the user is even.

Using a Do...Loop statement

Use the `Do...Loop` statement to specify that a set of statements is to be repeated based on the value of a condition. For example, you can use a `Do...Loop` statement to repeat, five times, a set of statements that accepts a number from a user and displays whether the number entered is even or odd. Using a `Do...Loop` statement enables you to repeat a set of statements as long as a given condition is `true` *or* while the condition is `false`. In addition, the `Do...Loop` statement also provides you the flexibility of checking the condition before executing the loop or checking the condition after the loop has executed at least once.

The syntax of a `Do...Loop` statement for checking a condition before executing a loop is as follows:


```
Do While|Until Condition
   Statement(s)
   [Exit Do]
Loop
```

TIP

Use an `Exit Do` statement to exit the `Do...Loop` statement.

Using the `While` keyword allows you to repeat the statements while the condition is `true` and using the `Until` keyword allows you to repeat the statements while the condition is `false`.

TIP

You can only use one of these keywords (`While` or `Until`) at a time.

The syntax of a `Do...Loop` statement for checking a condition after the statements are executed once is

```
Do
   Statement(s)
   [Exit Do]
Loop While|Until Condition
```

Now, rewrite the example from the previous section (where we cover While...End While loops) by using the Do...Loop statement, as shown here:

```
Dim Ctr As Integer
Ctr = 1
'Repeat the loop five times
Do While Ctr <=5
   Dim Num As Integer
   Num = CInt(InputBox("Enter a number"))
   If Num Mod 2 = 0 Then
      MessageBox.Show("Even Number")
   Else
      MessageBox.Show("Not an Even Number")
   End If
   Ctr = Ctr + 1
Loop
```

In the preceding code sample, a Do...Loop statement is used to accept five numbers from the user. The variable Ctr is used to count the numbers entered. The program then displays whether the number entered is an even number. This process is repeated five times.

Choosing a For...Next statement

You use the For...Next statement to execute a set of statements a definite number of times. For example, you can use a For...Next statement to accept 10 numbers from a user and display their sum. The syntax of a For...Next statement is as follows:

```
For Counter = Begin To End [Step]
   Statement(s)
   [Exit For]
Next [Counter]
```

Use an Exit For statement to exit the For...Next loop.

In the preceding syntax:

- Counter is a numeric variable.
- Begin refers to the initial value of the counter, and End refers to the end or the final value of the counter. The To keyword is used to specify the range.
- Step refers to the increment value of the counter.

  You can use a negative value for Step. If you omit Step, its default is set to a positive 1.

✦ The Next statement is used to mark the end of the For...Next loop. When the program encounters the ending Next statement, the value specified as a step is added to the Counter and the next iteration of the loop takes place. Although you can skip mentioning the name of the Counter with the Next statement, we recommend that you do so.

Rewrite the example used in the previous section by using the For...Next statement.

```
Dim Ctr As Integer

For Ctr = 1 To 5 Step 1
   Dim Num As Integer
   Num = CInt(InputBox("Enter a number"))
   If Num <= 0 Then
      MessageBox.Show("Incorrect Number")
      Exit For
   ElseIf Num Mod 2 = 0 Then
      MessageBox.Show("Even Number")
   Else
      MessageBox.Show("Not an Even Number")
   End If
Next Ctr
```

Now, if a user enters a number less than or equal to zero, the loop displays an error message and exits from the loop.

Using a For Each...Next statement

Use a For Each...Next statement to execute a set of statements for each element in an array or a collection. For example, consider an array that stores the name of employees. Now, to display all the names stored in this array, you can use a For Each...Next statement. The syntax for a For Each...Next statement is as follows:

```
For Each Element In Group
   Statement(s)
   Exit For
Next [Counter]
```

Use a Next statement to mark the end of a For Each...Next loop.

In this syntax:

✦ Element refers to the elements of the array or collection.

  A *collection* is a group of similar items having properties and methods. An array is a group of variables that are referred to by the same name.

✦ Group refers to the array or collection.

To understand this better, consider the following example:

```
Dim Name() As String = { "James", "Martha", "Shirley", "Jim",
   "Mike"}
Dim Element As String
For Each Element In Name
   MessageBox.Show (Element)
Next
```

In this example, `Name` is an array of type `String`. `Element` is a `String` variable. The `For Each...Next` statement is used to display in a message box each of the names stored in the array `Name`.

Chapter 7: Procedures in Visual Basic .NET

In This Chapter

- **Introducing the Sub, Function, and Property procedures**
- **Working with procedures by defining arguments, optional arrays, and parameter arrays**

After you determine how you want to configure control flow statements, you're ready to configure Visual Basic .NET procedures. All the code written in Visual Basic .NET is organized within procedures, which make the code easy to understand and work with. Imagine a code containing thousands of statements: To make a small change, you need to go through the entire code and make the change in many places, which is a difficult and time-consuming task. You can prevent such situations by using procedures in your code.

Procedures 101

A *procedure* is a set of statements that perform a specific task, such as organizing your code by breaking it into smaller logical chunks. For example, in an employee details form, you can create one procedure to accept the details of an employee and a second one to display the details. A procedure is marked by a declaration statement, which contains the name of the procedure and an `End` statement.

Procedures are great because they allow the reuse of code and because you can call a procedure from different locations within an application. For example, you can create a procedure that checks whether a user has entered a value in a text box. You can call this procedure from different locations in your forms instead of rewriting the code everywhere.

To perform certain tasks, a procedure might require some input values or *arguments*, which are a series of values that the procedure can work on. Consider a procedure that checks whether a text box is empty. The procedure needs to accept the name of the text box as a parameter, and you supply this value to the procedure as an argument.

You can create three types of procedures in Visual Basic. NET: Sub, Function, and Property. All of these procedures can be started with a Call statement and ended with an Exit statement.

Starting a procedure with a Call statement

You use the Call statement to call a procedure. The following statement shows the usage of the Call statement:

```
[Call] Procedure_Name([Argument(s)])
```

In the preceding syntax, the Call statement is enclosed in square brackets, which implies that you can also call a procedure without using the Call statement. Therefore, to call the procedure that we created earlier, you can use one of the following statements:

```
Call Accept_Details()
```

or

```
Accept_Details()
```

If the procedure accepts arguments, you need to pass them in the Call statement.

Ending a procedure with an Exit statement

You may come across a situation when you don't need to execute the entire code written in a procedure. For example, if a user enters an incorrect choice, the statements mentioned in the procedure shouldn't be executed. You use the Exit statement to exit from a procedure, meaning that the statements (in a procedure) after the Exit statement aren't executed. This statement can be placed after any statement inside a procedure. The following statement shows the usage of the Exit statement.

```
Exit Sub
```

Sub procedures

A Sub procedure contains a set of statements that are used to perform a specific task, such as accepting or displaying the details of an employee. These procedures don't return a value. A Sub procedure is marked by the Sub and End Sub statements, and it can accept arguments. The syntax of a Sub procedure is

```
Sub Procedure_Name([Argument(s)])
...
End Sub
```

In the above syntax, Arguments refers to the values passed to the procedure. For example, the Sub procedure used to display the details of a particular employee in a form might accept the employee code as an argument. The procedure then uses this argument to display the details of the required employee. A Sub procedure may or may not require arguments. Here's how you create a procedure.

```
Sub Accept_Details()
   Dim Code, Name As String
   Code = InputBox("Enter the code of the customer")
   Name = InputBox("Enter the name of the customer")
End Sub
```

In the preceding sample, the procedure Accept_Details is used to accept the details of the customer from the user. We discuss the usage of arguments in a procedure in the upcoming section "Declaring an argument."

Function procedures

A Function procedure is similar to a Sub procedure except that it returns a value to the calling code. A Function procedure is marked by the Function and End Function statements, and this procedure can also accept arguments. For example, a Function procedure can accept the salary details of an employee and then calculate and return the deductions to be made. The syntax of a Function procedure is


```
Function Procedure_Name([Arguments]) As Data_Type
...
...
End Function
```

In the preceding syntax, Data_Type refers to the type of the return value.

The value returned by a procedure is called its *return value*. You can trap this value in one of two ways:

✦ **Assign the return value to the function itself.**

  ```
  Procedure_Name = Expression
  ```

  Consider the following code.

  ```
  Function Display_Details() As String
     Dim Code, Name, Result As String
     Code = InputBox("Enter the code of the customer")
     Name = InputBox("Enter the name of the customer")
     Display_Details = Code + Name
  End Sub
  ```

  In the preceding code, the user is prompted to enter the code and the name of the customer. The Function procedure then returns both these values by assigning it to the Function name.

✦ **Use the Return statement to specify the return value.**

```
Return Expression
```

Consider the following code.

```
Function Display_Details() As String
   Dim Code, Name, Result As String
   Code = InputBox("Enter the code of the customer")
   Name = InputBox("Enter the name of the customer")
   Return Code + Name
End Sub
```

In the preceding code, the user is prompted to enter the code and the name of the customer. The Function procedure then returns both these values by using the Return statement.

To call a Function procedure, specify the name of the procedure in an expression. In the following example, Result is a variable with a same data type as that of the Function procedure.

```
Result = Procedure_Name()
```

For example,

```
Dim Result As String
Result = Display_Details()
```

In the preceding code, the Display_Details procedure is called and the value returned by this function is stored in the variable Result.

You can exit from a Function procedure by using the Exit statement.

Property procedures

Use the Property procedure to assign and read values to and from the property of an object or a class. For example, you can create one class for customers and then make the code and name of the customer the properties of this class. You can then use this class to accept and display details of a customer.

A Property procedure consists of the Get and Set procedures.

Using the Get procedure

Use the Get procedure to read the value stored in a property. You can do this by performing either of the following two tasks:

✦ Assign the value to the property.

✦ Use the Return keyword to return the value.

The syntax of the Get procedure is as follows:

```
 'Use the Get statement to return the property value
Get
   PropertyName = Variable
'The preceding statement is equivalent to the following
   statement
   Return Variable
End Get
```

In the preceding syntax, Variable refers to the class or object variable.

For example,

```
Get
   Customer_Name = strName
End Get
```

The preceding syntax creates a Get procedure for the property Customer_Name.

Using the Set procedure

Use the Set procedure to assign a value to a property. This procedure accepts the value to be stored as an argument. The Set procedure is executed whenever there is a change in property value, and its syntax is

```
 'Use the Set statement to return the property value
Set (ByVal Value As Type)
   Variable = Value
End Set
```

In the preceding syntax, Variable refers to the class or object variable.

For example,

```
Set (ByVal Value As Type)
   strName = Value
End Set
```

The preceding syntax creates a Set procedure for the property Customer_Name.

Read more about the ByVal keyword later in the upcoming section "Passing arguments by value."

Generally, a Property procedure contains both the Get and Set procedures. However, both these procedures can exist on their own depending upon whether the property is read-only (Get) or write-only (Set). Check out this syntax of a complete Property procedure.

```
Property PropertyName() As DataType
   Get
   ...
   End Get
   Set(ByVal Value As Datatype)
   ...
   End Set
End Property
```

Now look at the complete code for creating the Customer_Name property.

```
Property Customer_Name() As String
   Get
     Customer_Name = strName
   End Get
   Set(ByVal Value As String)
     strName = Value
   End Set
End Property
```

The Property procedures can also be referred to as *property accessors*.

For a better understanding of the Property procedures, read up on classes in Book 3, Chapter 8.

Working with Procedures

Earlier in this chapter, we discuss arguments of a procedure, which are the values supplied to a procedure. In this section, we explain using arguments in your procedures. The first step when using arguments is to declare them.

After you declare an argument, you then pass values to the argument. Visual Basic .NET allows you to pass these values in two ways, by value or by reference. Read the upcoming section to get introduced to the concept of arguments.

Declaring an argument

Before you use argument in a procedure, you need to declare them. The declaration of an argument includes its name and data type. You use the As clause in the procedure declaration to specify the data type for an argument. Consider the following example:

```
Function CalcPercentage (ByVal Score As Integer) As Integer
   ...
   ...
End Function
```

In the preceding syntax, the CalcPercentage function accepts Score as an argument, which is of the type Integer. ByVal is used to specify the manner in which the arguments are passed.

The process of calling this procedure is as follows:

```
Score_Obtained = CInt(InputBox("Enter your score"))
'Let's assume user enters 80
Result = CalcPercentage(Score_Obtained)
MessageBox.Show(Score_Obtained)
```

In the preceding example, the code accepts a value from the user and stores it in a variable Score_Obtained. This code then calls the procedure CalcPercentage and passes this variable as an argument to the procedure. The code that calls a procedure is referred to as *calling code*.

Read the following sections to discover how to pass arguments in a procedure.

You can avoid mentioning the data type of the arguments if Option Strict is Off. The Option Strict statement ensures that converting one type of data to another doesn't involve any data loss. Read more about the Option Strict statement in Book 3, Chapter 5. However, if you specify data type for one argument, you need to do it for all the arguments.

Passing arguments

In Visual Basic, you need to specify the manner in which arguments are passed to a procedure. You can pass arguments either by value or by reference.

Passing arguments by value

You use the ByVal keyword to pass the arguments by value. If you pass arguments by value, the procedure can't modify the contents of the variables passed by the calling codes as arguments to the procedure because when you pass variables by value, a separate copy of the variables is created by the procedure. Check out the following snippet, in which a Function procedure is used to increase the score of each student by 10.

```
Function IncreaseScore(ByVal Score As Integer) As Integer
   Score = Score + 10
   Return Score
End Function
```

Now, consider the following statements that accept the score of a student and then calls this procedure.

```
Dim Result, Score_Obtained As Integer
Score_Obtained = CInt(InputBox("Enter your score"))
'Let's assume user enters 80
Result = IncreaseScore(Score_Obtained)
'After executing the preceding statement, value of
   'the Score_Obtained variable will still be 80
MessageBox.Show(Score_Obtained)
```

In the preceding statement, the function `IncreaseScore` can't modify the contents of the variable `Score_Obtained` because it is passed by value and the procedure creates a second copy of this variable.

Passing arguments by reference

You use the `ByRef` keyword to pass arguments by reference. If you pass arguments by reference, the procedure can modify the contents of the variables passed by the calling codes as arguments to the procedure. This is because when you pass arguments this way, only a reference to the memory address of the variable used by the calling code is passed. (By comparison, passing arguments by value cannot modify the contents of the variables used by the calling code as arguments to the procedure.) Consider the following function definition:

```
Function IncreaseScore(ByRef Score As Integer) As Integer
   Score = Score + 10
   Return Score
End Function
```

Now, consider the following statements that accept the score of a student and then calls this procedure.

```
Dim Result, Score_Obtained As Integer
Score_Obtained = CInt(InputBox("Enter your score"))
'Let's assume user enters 80
Result = IncreaseScore(Score_Obtained)
'After executing the preceding statement, value of
   the Score_Obtained variable will now be 90
MessageBox.Show(Score_Obtained)
```

In the preceding statement, the function `IncreaseScore` can modify the contents of the variable `Score_Obtained` because only a reference is passed to this variable.

Using optional arguments

You'll find times when you need to create procedures that accept a number of values. However, at the time of execution, it's not necessary to pass all these values, such as when you have a procedure that accepts customer details such as Code, Name, Address, and Phone. Each customer might not enter his phone number. In such situations, Visual Basic allows you to create procedures that have optional arguments. *Optional arguments* are the arguments that may or may not be passed when you call the procedure.

Use the `Optional` keyword to specify an argument as optional. You do need to specify a default value for an optional argument, which should be a constant. And, all the arguments that come after an optional argument need to be optional.

Consider the following example that illustrates the use of the `Optional` keyword:

```
Sub CustDetails (ByVal Code As String, ByVal Name As
   String, Optional ByVal Country As String = "USA")

End Sub
```

In the preceding example, the `CustDetails` procedure accepts three arguments: `Code`, `Name`, and `Country`. Here `Country` is an optional argument and its default value is `USA`. You can call this procedure as shown below:

```
Call CustDetails ("001", "John", "UK")
```

Or

```
Call CustDetails ("002", "Jim")
```

In the preceding statement, no value is provided for `Country`. Therefore, the procedure assigns the default value to it.

Creating parameter arrays

You also might need to pass an indefinite number of arguments in a procedure. In such a situation, you can use a *parameter array,* which allows a procedure to accept an array of values as argument. Use the `ParamArray` keyword to specify a parameter array.

```
Sub OrderDetails (ByVal Name As String, ByVal ParamArray
   Products() As String)
```

In the preceding statement, the procedure `OrderDetails` accepts the name and the products required by a customer as arguments. Because a customer can order more than one product at a time, a parameter array named `Products` that can accept a number of strings is declared. To call the above procedure, you can use the following statement:

```
OrderDetails ("John", "Toys", "Flowers")
```

In the preceding statement, the procedure `OrderDetails` is called with three arguments. The first argument is the name of the customer, and the remaining two are the products ordered by the customer.

Only one parameter array can be present in a procedure and it should be handled (by the code) as a single-dimensional array. A single-dimensional array is a set of contiguous memory spaces used to store data of similar type. Read more on arrays in Book 3, Chapter 5. The parameter array needs to be the last argument of the procedure; it is optional by default. In fact, the parameter array can be the only optional argument for a procedure.

Overloading procedures

Overloading procedures means creating procedures having same names but differing in the type, number, and position of arguments. For example, you may have an application that accepts orders from a customer, identifying that customer either by Code, Name, or both. For this, you as a programmer can create three different procedures that all accept different parameters. The real problem is naming these procedures. If you give them all different names, it's difficult to memorize all of them. As a solution, you can create overloaded procedures, such as the `OrderDetails` procedure in the following examples:

```
Sub OrderDetails (ByVal Code As String, ByVal ParamArray
   Products() As String)
...
End Sub
```

In the preceding syntax, the procedure `OrderDetails` accepts `Code` and `Products` as arguments.

```
Sub OrderDetails (ByVal Name As String, ByVal ParamArray
   Products() As String)
...
End Sub
```

In the preceding syntax, the procedure `OrderDetails` accept `Name` and `Products` as arguments.

```
Sub OrderDetails (ByVal Code As String, ByVal Name As String,
   ByVal ParamArray Products() As String)
...
End Sub
```

In the preceding syntax, the procedure `OrderDetails` accept `Code`, `Name` and `Products` as arguments.

Chapter 8: Implementing VB .NET Classes

In This Chapter

- Understanding the object-oriented programming technique
- Implementing object-oriented programming in Visual Basic .NET
- Creating your own classes
- Assigning inheritance in classes

Previous versions of Visual Basic allowed you to create classes. However, you weren't allowed to inherit classes — the most basic requirement of object-oriented programming. Don't worry, Visual Basic .NET is now an object-oriented programming language, providing you the flexibility of using existing classes or creating your own classes from scratch. It allows you to reuse existing classes by inheriting new ones from them. Unlike previous versions, Visual Basic .NET doesn't have any classes of its own. It uses the classes provided by the class library present in the .NET Framework. Read more on the class library in Book 1, Chapter 1.

In this chapter, we discuss the basic concepts of object-oriented programming. Then we walk you through creating your own classes by implementing object-oriented programming in Visual Basic .NET. Finally, we show you how to implement inheritance in your applications.

`MyClassProject` is available for download from `www.dummies.com/extras/VS.NETAllinOne`.

Discovering Object-Oriented Programming

The concept of object-oriented programming (OOP), as the name suggests, is based entirely on an object. An object can be anything around you, such as a personal computer (PC), a wrist watch, or even this book that you're reading. An *object* is any entity that has a unique identity, possesses a state, and displays certain behavior.

The identity of an object is defined from those specific features that distinguish it from other similar or dissimilar objects. Think of your PC: Various parts of your PC, such as its processor and hard drive, have unique serial numbers that differentiate it from other computers, even those with similar configurations. The state of an object is characterized by certain attributes. Your PC is characterized by attributes, such as its processor speed, RAM, and hard drive capacity. Behavior refers to the change in the characteristics of an object with time.

To simplify our discussion on objects, we categorize objects with common attributes into groups. For example, laptops, handhelds, and desktops are all computers. All share common characteristics, such as a processor, RAM, and a hard drive, and all are used for processing information. Thus, we can conclude that the laptops, handhelds, and desktops belong to a class named computers. On the basis of this example, we define a class. A *class* is a set of objects that has common attributes and display similar behavior. Classes and objects form the building blocks of object-oriented programming.

Features of object-oriented programming

When you plan to purchase a PC, you're probably interested in its processor speed, RAM, or storage capacity, but couldn't care less about its guts — that is, the electronic gadgetry within the computer. Similarly, object-oriented programming works with only the essential details of an object and ignores the nonessential ones. This concept is called *abstraction*, which, in a way, reduces the complexity of an object.

You ignore non-essential details by hiding them. For example, when you work on your PC, you can't see the processes going on within the PC. All these processes are encapsulated. *Encapsulation* refers to hiding the non-essential details of an object. Encapsulation, also called *information hiding*, is a way to implement abstraction.

Another important feature of object-oriented programming is inheritance. *Inheritance*, in general, means that an entity derives a set of attributes from another entity. For example, a child inherits a father's legacy. Apply this concept to object-oriented programming, and inheritance means deriving an object or a class from another class.

To order a PC, you can either call the company or an authorized dealer. When you call the company directly, the company checks for vendors in your region and makes necessary arrangements to deliver the computer; conversely, a dealer takes your order and then contacts the company. In this example, the company and the dealer are two different objects that react differently to the same call. In object-oriented programming terminology, this is polymorphism. *Polymorphism* means that multiple objects or classes can be substituted for each other even though they react differently to similar attributes or behaviors.

The object-oriented programming concept supports abstraction, encapsulation, inheritance, and polymorphism.

Advantages of object-oriented programming

The key advantages of object-oriented methodology are

- **Code reuse:** You can create classes once and use them repeatedly in several applications.
- **Ease in changing an existing program:** Just create any necessary new parts for the program and plug them into the existing program.

Visual Basic .NET and Object-Oriented Programming

The controls that you use to design your forms in Visual Basic .NET are represented by classes. When you drag a control from the Toolbox to a form, you create an object of the respective class. Even the form that you use is a class; when you display this form at execution, an object is created. So if you've used Visual Basic .NET, you've already experienced using its object-oriented features even though you didn't notice it. You can read more on the Toolbox in Book 3, Chapter 3.

Understanding objects and classes

As we state in the previous section "Discovering Object-Oriented Programming," an object is the basic unit of object-oriented programming. Containing code and data, each object is characterized by properties, methods, and events, which are used to manipulate the data present in the object. All these characteristics are defined by the class from which the object is created. Therefore, an object is also called an *instance* of a class.

You can create multiple objects of the same class. Consequently, all these objects share the same characteristics although their values may differ. To get started with implementing object-oriented programming, first look at the process of creating objects.

Creating objects

You create objects the same way that you create variables — by using the `Dim` statement. The syntax is

```
Dim ObjName As ClassName
```

where `ObjName` refers to the name of the object and `ClassName` refers to the name of the class from which the object will be created. However, the object created using the preceding syntax can't refer to the properties and methods of the class. To make this possible, you use the `New` keyword. Therefore, rewrite the above statement as

```
Dim ObjName As New ClassName
```

The New keyword is used to assign memory to an object.

Properties

A *property* is an attribute that describes an object. For example, the *Text* property of a Button object describes the function of the button. You can refer to a property like this:

```
ObjName.Property
```

Now you can assign or retrieve values from an object like you do with variables. For reference, consider the following syntax:

```
'Assign a value
ObjName.Property = Value
'Retrieve the stored value
Value = ObjName.Property
```

Implement the preceding syntax in an example.

```
'Assign a caption to the button
Button1.Text = "Add Details"
'Store the caption of Button1 in the Caption variable
Caption = Button1.Text
```

Methods

To perform certain operations, an object uses the procedures defined in a class. These procedures are called *methods*. For example, the Button object uses the Focus method to set control on itself. A method is accessed the same way that you access the properties.

```
ObjName.Method()
```

For example,

```
'Set the focus on Button1
Button1.Focus()
```

Events

You can also attach an event with an object. An *event* is an action that causes a procedure to execute: for example, the Click event of a button. Here are the actions in the life cycle of an event.

- **Declare events to create them:** To declare an event, you use the Event keyword. You declare events within classes. The syntax is

  ```
  Event SampleEvent()
  ```

✦ **Specify an event raiser:** Any object that raises an event is an *event sender.* To specify that an object raises events, use the `WithEvents` keyword in the object declaration. The syntax is

```
Dim WithEvents Obj As Class
```

✦ **Handle events with care:** A procedure executed when an event occurs is an *event handler.* To specify an event managed by an event handler, use the `Handles` statement. The syntax is

```
Sun EventHandlerName() Handles Obj.SampleEvent
```

✦ **Raise the event:** In order to execute a procedure associated with an event, you need to raise the event by using the `RaiseEvent` keyword. The syntax is

```
RaiseEvent SampleEvent()
```

Creating Classes

Visual Basic .NET provides a number of classes that developers can use in their applications. In addition, Visual Basic .NET enables developers to create their own classes from scratch. Here we take you through the process of creating a class and its members.

Declaring a class

In the earlier section "Features of object-oriented programming," we introduce an example of a computer to understand OOP. We continue this running example as we create a class named `Computer` as a part of this exercise.

1. **Create a new Windows Application project.**

   Read more about creating new Windows Application projects in Book 3, Chapter 2.

2. **Name the project** `MyClassProject`**.**

   Check out Book 3, Chapter 2.

3. **Design the form as shown in Figure 8-1.**

   We talk about adding controls to a form in Book 3, Chapter 3.

4. **Using Table 8-1 as a reference, name the various controls.**

   In addition, set the `Multiline` property of `txtRecommendations` to `True` and the `Text` property of the form to `Computer`.

   You need to add a class to your project.

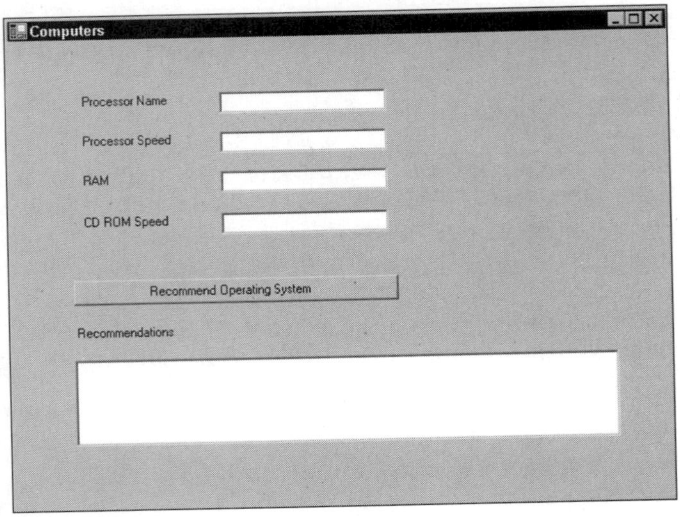

Figure 8-1: Preparing to create classes.

5. **From the Project menu present on the IDE, create a new class by clicking the Add Class menu item.**

   The Add New Item dialog box appears.

6. **Under Templates, click Class to select it.**

7. **Name the class by typing** Computer **in the Name box; click Open.**

   A new file — `Computer.vb` — is added to your project and contains the following statements:

   ```
   Public Class Computer

   End Class
   ```

   In the preceding statements, the `Class` statement is used to declare a class. The `Public` keyword specifies that the class can be accessed anywhere without any restrictions. The `End Class` statement marks the end of the class.

The preceding step completes a part of class declaration. As we mention in the earlier section "Understanding objects and classes," a class contains properties and methods, which we discuss in the upcoming sections.

Table 8-1 Control Names on Sample Form

Control	*Labeled As*	*Name*
`TextBox`	Processor Name	`txtProcessorName`
`TextBox`	Processor Speed	`txtProcessorSpeed`

Control	Labeled As	Name
TextBox	RAM	txtRAM
TextBox	CD ROM Speed	txtCDSpeed
Button	Recommend Operating System	btnRecommendations
TextBox	Recommendations	txtRecommendations

Creating properties and methods

Each class has its own set of properties and methods. For example, the `Computer` class that you create in the previous section can have properties such as processor name, processor speed, RAM, and CD-ROM speed. The class can also have a method that helps you decide the operating system to use depending on these properties. Before actually creating properties and methods, look at the steps involved in the procedure.

Creating properties

The following steps help you create a property:

1. **Declare the property by using the `Property` statement in the class.**

   The `Property` statement also declares the procedures to assign and read values from a property. These procedures are known as *property* procedures. The syntax is

   ```
   'The Property statement declares a property
   Property PropertyName () As DataType

   End Property
   ```

   The `End Property` statement marks the end of a property procedure.

2. **Assign values to a property by using the `Set` procedure inside the `Property` statement.**

   This procedure is executed as soon as the property value changes. The `Set` procedure takes the property value as a parameter. The `End Set` statement marks the end of the `Set` procedure. The syntax is

   ```
   'The Set statement returns the property value
      Set (ByVal value As Type)
         ClassVariable = value
      End Set
   ```

3. **Read the value stored in the property by using the `Get` procedure inside the `Property` statement.**

You can make this procedure return the value of a property in two ways: first, by using the `Return` keyword; and second, by assigning the value to the property.

```
'The Get statement returns the property value
 Get
    PropertyName = ClassVariable

    'The above statement is equivalent to the following
       'statement
    Return ClassVariable

 End Get
```

Now put the pieces together and complete the picture.

```
Property PropertyName () As DataType
   Get
      PropertyName = ClassVariable
   End Get
   Set (ByVal value As Type)
      ClassVariable = value
   End Set
End Property
```

Next you create the properties for the `Computer` class: `ProcessorName`, `ProcessorSpeed`, `RAM`, and `CDSpeed`. To do so, attach the following code to the `Computer.vb` file precisely between the `Class` and `End Class` statements.

```
'Declare class variables
Dim varPName, varPSpeed, varRAM, varCDSpeed As String

'Create properties
Property ProcessorName() As String
    Get
      ProcessorName = varPName
    End Get
    Set(ByVal Value As String)
      varPName = Value
    End Set
End Property

Property ProcessorSpeed() As String
    Get
      ProcessorSpeed = varPSpeed
    End Get
    Set(ByVal Value As String)
      varPSpeed = Value
    End Set
End Property
```

```
Property RAM() As String
    Get
      RAM = varRAM
    End Get
    Set(ByVal Value As String)
      varRAM = Value
    End Set
End Property

Property CDSpeed() As String
    Get
      CDSpeed = varCDSpeed
    End Get
    Set(ByVal Value As String)
      varCDSpeed = Value
    End Set
End Property
```

After you complete creating properties, you can move on to creating methods.

Creating methods

A *method* is simply a procedure used to perform certain operation. For a refresher on working with procedures, see Book 3, Chapter 7.

In this exercise, we create a method that recommends an operating system depending on the property values specified by a user.


```
Public Overridable Function Recommendation(ByVal PName As _
    String, ByVal PSpeed As String, ByVal vRAM As String, _
    ByVal vCDSpeed As String) As String
        Dim Result As String
        Result = "The given specifications are:"
        Result = Result & Chr(13) & Chr(10)
        Result = Result & "Processor Name: " & PName
        Result = Result & Chr(13) & Chr(10)
        Result = Result & "Processor Speed: " & PSpeed
        Result = Result & Chr(13) & Chr(10)
        Result = Result & "RAM: " & vRAM
        Result = Result & "CD Speed: " & vCDSpeed
        Result = Result & Chr(13) & Chr(10)
        Result = Result & "We recommend using Windows XP!!"
        Result = Result & Chr(13) & Chr(10)
        Result = Result & "Happy Working!!"
        Return Result
    End Function
```

Place the preceding code just before the `End Class` statement. The only remaining step is to implement the functionality of the class in your form.

Attaching a class with a form

After you complete creating the properties and methods of a class, you implement the functionality of this class in a form.

In order to access the properties and methods of a class, you need to create an object of this class.

In this case, attach the following code to the `Click` event of the `btnRecommendations` button.

```
'Create an object of the Computer class
Dim ObjComp As New Computer()

'Initialize the properties of the class
ObjComp.ProcessorName = txtProcessorName.Text
ObjComp.ProcessorSpeed = txtProcessorSpeed.Text
ObjComp.RAM = txtRAM.Text
ObjComp.CDSpeed = txtCDSpeed.Text

'Call the Recommendation method()
txtRecommendations.Text = ObjComp.Recommendation _
   (ObjComp.ProcessorName, ObjComp.ProcessorSpeed, _
    ObjComp.RAM, ObjComp.CDSpeed)
```

Your application is ready and awaits its execution! Go ahead and execute it by entering a few values to see the output. For your reference, we executed the application; a sample output is shown in Figure 8-2.

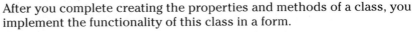

Figure 8-2: Making classes is child's play.

Implementing Inheritance

The sole purpose of creating classes is to use their functionality time and again. This saves your precious time. Visual Basic .NET has an important concept — *inheritance* — that helps you use the functionality of a class repeatedly. With inheritance, you can derive new classes from existing ones. Creating classes in this manner gives you a chance to utilize all the properties and methods of the class from which you derived a new class. The new class is the *child* class or the *derived* class; the existing class is the *parent* class or *base* class.

Some of the important statements and modifiers that help you implement inheritance include the following:

- **In order to implement inheritance, the most important step is to specify a base class for the new class.**

  Use the `Inherits` statement to do so. Read the following code to get the hang of the `Inherits` statement.

  ```
  'Declare a class named CorporateComputer
  Class CorporateComputer
     'Specify the base class as Computer
     Inherits Computer
  End Class
  ```

- **In certain situations, you may not want a class to be used as a base class.**

  For example, in your application, you want users to employ the existing classes. However, you don't want them to inherit from these classes in the applications that they create. In such situations, use the `NotInheritable` modifier to restrict users from inheriting the existing classes.

  ```
  'Declare a class named Computer
  NotInheritable Class Computer
  ```

  The preceding statement makes the class `Computer` non-inheritable.

- **To specify that a class can be used only as a base class, use the `MustInherit` modifier.**

  This modifier specifies that you can't instantiate this class. To utilize this class, you need to inherit from it. See the syntax to declare a class as a must-inherit type:

  ```
  'Declare a class named Computer
  MustInherit Class Computer
  ```

  The preceding statement declares the `Computer` class as `MustInherit`.

Visual Basic .NET also enables you to reuse properties and methods defined in a base class. Some modifiers that help you do so are

- **Overridable:** Using this modifier specifies that a property or a method defined in a class can be overridden in a derived class.
- **Overrides:** Using this modifier specifies that a given property or method in a child class overrides a property or a method defined using the Overridable modifier in the base class.
- **NotOverridable:** Using this modifier does not allow a property or a method to be overridden in a child class.
- **MustOverride:** Using this modifier makes it compulsory for a property or a method to be overridden in a derived class. A method declared using the MustOverride keyword contains only the declaration statement. For example, a Sub method contains only the Sub MethodName statement and no other statement — not even the End Sub statement.

Reconsidering our running example of the Computer class, we use this class as the base class to create two new child classes: CorporateComputer and HomeComputer.

Before you begin implementation, you need to make certain changes to the existing application, which we describe in the following list:

- **Change 1**
  1. Add a ComboBox control (used to display a drop-down list) to the form, as shown in Figure 8-3. Name it cmbCategory.

     This shows up as the Computer Category drop-down list (upper-right side).
  2. Attach the following code to the Load event of the form:

     ```
     cmbCategory.Items.Add("Corporate Computer")
     cmbCategory.Items.Add("Home Computer")
     ```

     This code adds the Corporate Computer and Home Computer items to the combo box as soon as the form shows up.
- **Change 2**
  1. Make the methods of the Computer class as overridable by using the Overridable keyword.
  2. Make the following changes in the Recommendation method:

     ```
     Public Overridable Function Recommendation(ByVal PName _
         As String, ByVal PSpeed As String, ByVal vRAM As _
         String, ByVal vCDSpeed As String) As String
     ```

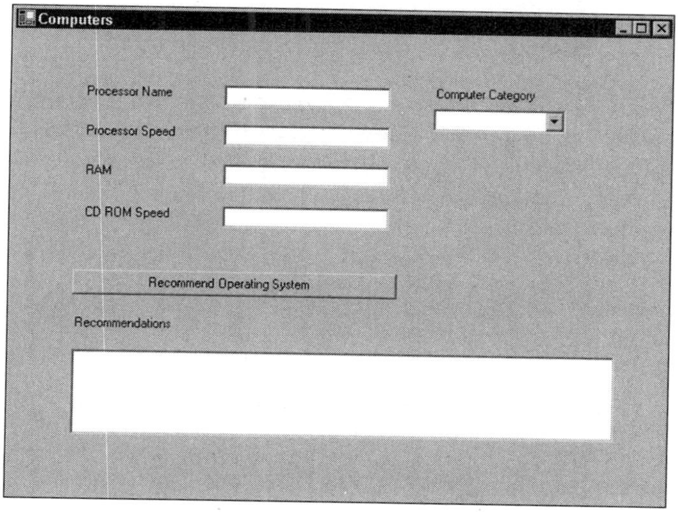

Figure 8-3: Making changes to implement inheritance.

Creating child classes

The first step to implement inheritance is the creation of child classes. To create child classes:

1. **Create a new class named** `CorporateComputer`.

   To create a new class, choose Project⇨Add Class and name the class `CorporateComputer`.

   In this case, specify the `Computer` class as the base class. See the following code:

   ```
   Public Class CorporateComputer
       Inherits Computer
   End Class
   ```

2. **Create another class named** `HomeComputer`.

   Specify the class computer as the base class by using the following code:

   ```
   Public Class HomeComputer
       Inherits Computer
   End Class
   ```

After you create child classes, you can override the methods defined in the base class.

Overriding methods of a base class

As we describe in the earlier section "Implementing Inheritance," you use the `Overrides` keyword to override the methods of a base class. In this case, you override the Recommendation method of the Computer class; just follow these steps:

1. **Override the Recommendation method by placing the following code in the CorporateComputer.vb file after the Inherits Computer statement.**

```
Public Overrides Function Recommendation(ByVal
      PName As _
String, ByVal PSpeed As String, ByVal vRAM
      As String, _
ByVal vCDSpeed As String) As String
     Dim Result As String
     Result = "The given specifications are:"
     Result = Result & Chr(13) & Chr(10)
     Result = Result & "Processor Name: " & PName
     Result = Result & Chr(13) & Chr(10)
     Result = Result & "Processor Speed: " & PSpeed
     Result = Result & Chr(13) & Chr(10)
     Result = Result & "RAM: " & vRAM
     Result = Result & Chr(13) & Chr(10)
     Result = Result & "CD Speed: " & vCDSpeed
     Result = Result & Chr(13) & Chr(10)
     'Recommend to use the Professional edition of
Windows XP
     Result = Result & "We recommend using Windows XP" _
       " Professional Edition!!"
     Result = Result & Chr(13) & Chr(10)
     Result = Result & "Happy Working!!"
     Return Result
    End Function
```

The preceding method recommends the use of the Windows XP Professional edition for corporate computers.

2. **Add the following code to define the Recommendation method for the HomeComputer class.**

```
Public Overrides Function Recommendation(ByVal
      PName As _
    String, ByVal PSpeed As String, ByVal vRAM As_
    String, ByVal vCDSpeed As String) As String
     Dim Result As String
     Result = "The given specifications are:"
     Result = Result & Chr(13) & Chr(10)
     Result = Result & "Processor Name: " & PName
     Result = Result & Chr(13) & Chr(10)
     Result = Result & "Processor Speed: " & PSpeed
     Result = Result & Chr(13) & Chr(10)
```

```
        Result = Result & "RAM: " & vRAM
        Result = Result & Chr(13) & Chr(10)
        Result = Result & "CD Speed: " & vCDSpeed
        Result = Result & Chr(13) & Chr(10)
        'Recommend to use the Home edition of Windows XP
        Result = Result & "We recommend using Windows XP" _
          " Home edition!!"
        Result = Result & Chr(13) & Chr(10)
        Result = Result & "Happy Working!!"
        Return Result
    End Function
```

The preceding method recommends the use of the Windows XP Home edition for home computers.

The only task remaining is to implement the functionality of all these classes in your form.

Implementing class functionality in forms

Building on our running example, depending on the category selected by the user, your form will display the appropriate recommendation. For example, if the selected computer category is `Corporate Computer`, then the recommendation is to use the Windows XP Professional edition.

To begin, add the following procedure to the form.

```
Private Sub CallRecommendations(ByVal Obj As Computer)
    txtRecommendations.Text = Obj.Recommendation _
      (Obj.ProcessorName, Obj.ProcessorSpeed, Obj.RAM, _
      Obj.CDSpeed)
End Sub
```

This procedure accepts an object of the `Computer` class and then calls the `Recommendation` method. However, you can also pass the objects of the `CorporateComputer` and `HomeComputer` classes in this method because these classes are the child classes of the `Computer` class. The advantage to this method is that you can derive further classes from the `Computer` class and you don't need to change the `CallRecommendations` method.

The `CallRecommendations` method also displays an important feature of object-oriented programming — polymorphism. You can pass an object of any of the three classes that you create as an argument to the `CallRecommendations` method. However, depending on the type of object, the appropriate `Recommendation` method is called, which displays different messages.

The only task remaining is to check the category selected by the user. To perform this task, you need to make some minor changes to the code given in the Click event of the btnRecommendation button. Change that code to the code shown here:

```
'Create an object of the Computer class

'Call the appropriate Recommendations method()
If cmbCategory.Text = "Corporate Computer" Then
    Dim objCC As New CorporateComputer()
'Initialize the properties of the class
    objCC.ProcessorName = txtProcessorName.Text
    objCC.ProcessorSpeed = txtProcessorSpeed.Text
    objCC.RAM = txtRAM.Text
    objCC.CDSpeed = txtCDSpeed.Text
'Call the Recommendation method of CorporateComputer class
    CallRecommendations(objCC)
ElseIf cmbCategory.Text = "Home Computer" Then
    Dim objHC As New HomeComputer()
'Initialize the properties of the class
    objHC.ProcessorName = txtProcessorName.Text
    objHC.ProcessorSpeed = txtProcessorSpeed.Text
    objHC.RAM = txtRAM.Text
    objHC.CDSpeed = txtCDSpeed.Text
'Call the Recommendation method of CorporateComputer class
    CallRecommendations(objHC)
End If
```

In the preceding code, if the user selects the Corporate Computer option, then an object of the CorporateComputer class is created and passed as an argument to the CallRecommendations method. And, if the user selects the Home Computer option, an object of the HomeComputer class is created and passed as an argument to the CallRecommendations method. This method then calls the Recommendation method of the appropriate child class.

If you followed along with us for the entire chapter, your application is ready. Execute it and test it by entering different values.

Chapter 9: Handling Errors in Visual Basic .NET

In This Chapter

- Introducing errors
- Handling program errors
- Tracing program errors

Every programmer's nightmare is writing a great program with vigor and zeal, executing it for your supervisor, and waiting anxiously for the accolades to roll in. Then your program crashes and all your hopes with it (with your supervisor looking on, of course) when it gets stuck at some point. In your horror, you realize that you didn't catch an error, such as some incorrect syntax or logic.

Save yourself from the night sweats by relying on Visual Basic .NET to help you write programs that don't crash when they encounter an error. Visual Basic .NET has the capability to tell you the cause of an error and then provide options to either rectify the errors or terminate your program peacefully.

In this chapter, we discuss the types of errors you can encounter and various error-handling techniques. We also detail how you can use Visual Basic .NET to make your programs work without crashing — even if they have errors — and how to trace your programming errors so that you can fix them.

Identifying Error Types

Even though you write a program that you assume to be error-free, inevitably we all make mistakes. You know you're in trouble when you execute your program and it won't build. Rats. Even when you think that you've removed all the errors and execute the program again, you get some obnoxious error messages and then the program terminates or gets stuck again. Double rats. Time to put Visual Basic .NET to work to determine what type of error you have. Errors come in three flavors: syntax, runtime, and logic.

In Visual Basic .NET, an error is also called an *exception*.

Syntax errors

Errors that you create while keying in code — such as misspelling a keyword — are *syntax errors*. Visual Basic .NET checks for syntax errors in your code while you type the code, enabling you to fix them as and when you create them. Just look for a wavy line under the mistyped word as your visual clue that something's amiss. Check out Figure 9-1 — compare the two variable declarations and note the different spellings of the final word *Integer*. The wavy line under the word *Integr* in the second line indicates an error.

```
Dim FirstVariable As Integer
Dim SecondVariable As Integr
```

Figure 9-1: Visual Basic .NET points out syntax errors with a wavy underline.

Runtime errors

Errors that occur only when the code is executed are *runtime errors*. These errors aren't caused by incorrect syntax but because you forgot to initialize some variables or assign memory to an object.

Consider the syntax to create an object of a class:

```
Dim Object1 As Class1
```

This code contains no syntax error. However, when you try to execute the following statement:

```
Object1.Class1Method1
```

Visual Basic .NET generates an error message, as shown in Figure 9-2. This error is generated because you didn't mention the keyword `New` while creating `Object1`. You must appreciate Visual Studio .NET as it tells you what you did wrong. You can get more details, such as location of error, by clicking the Details button in the error message box.

Logic errors

Errors that make your program produce undesired output are *logic errors*. For example, if you forget to mention the statement for incrementing the counter variable while working with loops in a program, you don't get an error but your program goes into an infinite loop. Not good.

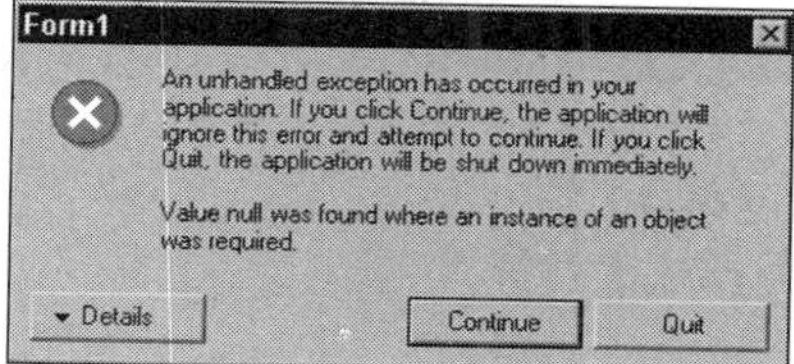

Figure 9-2: Visual Basic .NET generates runtime error messages.

Handling Errors in Programs

As annoying as errors in your programs are, tracing errors so that you can fix them is the most difficult part because you don't necessarily know the location of the error.

When a program encounters an error, it generally terminates abruptly without showing any result or *goes into a hang*, which means that the application stops responding. By writing code to handle these errors, you can make your applications continue working even after they encounter an error. Visual Basic .NET provides structured and unstructured exception handling techniques to plan for and trap all possible errors.

Structured exception handling

Structured exception handling involves the use of the `Try...Catch...Finally` statement within the code to handle errors in a program. The syntax of this statement is

```
Try
   'The statements that might generate an error
   Statement(s)
Catch [condition]
   'The statements written here are executed when the
   'statements listed in the Try block fail and the filter
   'specified is True. The filter is optional.
   Statement(s)
Finally
   'The statements in this block execute before the End Try
   'statement
   Statement(s)
End Try
```

In the preceding syntax, the `Try` block contains statements that may generate some error. If an error is generated, the condition specified in the `Catch` block is tested; then, if a condition matching the error is found, the control is transferred to the first statement following the `Catch`. However, if no match is found, the code generates an error. You can specify multiple `Catch` blocks in a `Try...Catch...Finally` statement. The statements specified in the `Finally` block are executed before the end of the `Try...Catch...Finally` statement.

The following example illustrates the use of the `Try...Catch...Finally` statement.

```
'Declare an array.
Dim Months() As String = {"Jan", "Feb", "Mar", "Apr", "May"}
Dim Counter As Integer = 0
'Set up an error trap
Try
   For Counter = 0 To 6
     'Cause an "Index out of range" error.
     MessageBox.Show(Months(Counter))
   Next Counter
   'Exception When Counter > 5
   'Catch the exception.
   Catch Excl As System.IndexOutOfRangeException
     'Show the error message.
     MessageBox.Show(Excl.ToString)
   Finally
     Erase Months
End Try
```

In the preceding example, an array named `Months` is declared to store the names of months. The `For...Next` statement is used to display the elements stored in this array. The array contains five elements, whereas the `For...Next` statement is repeated six times. Doing so generates the `IndexOutOfRangeException`, which is then handled by using the `Try...Catch...Finally` statement. When the exception occurs, a message box appears indicating the error. This message box is displayed in Figure 9-3. To test this code, place it in the `Click` event of a button. Read more on buttons in Book 3, Chapter 3.

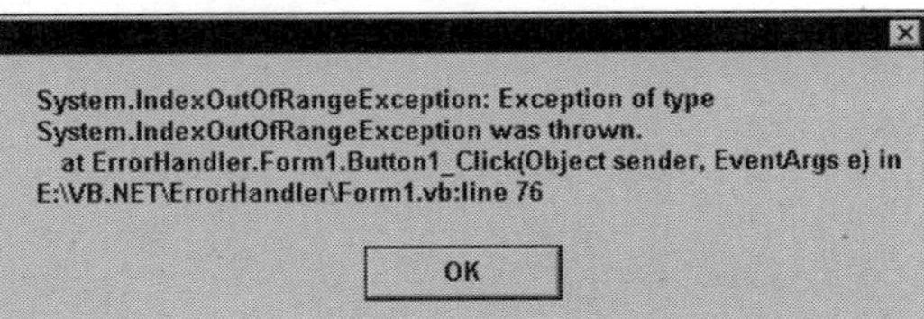

System.IndexOutOfRangeException: Exception of type
System.IndexOutOfRangeException was thrown.
at ErrorHandler.Form1.Button1_Click(Object sender, EventArgs e) in
E:\VB.NET\ErrorHandler\Form1.vb:line 76
OK

Figure 9-3: The error message box displays the cause and location of your error.

Unstructured exception handling

Unstructured exception handling involves the use of the On Error statement to handle errors. You specify the line number or label as an argument to this statement. This line number or label points to a set of statements that are used for error handling. This set of statements is an *error-handling routine*. Use an On Error statement at the beginning of a set of statements, such as a procedure. If an error occurs, the control shifts to the line specified with the On Error statement.

Suppose that you call Procedure B from Procedure A. Procedure A contains code for unstructured exception handling, but Procedure B doesn't contain any such code. If Procedure B generates an exception, this exception moves to Procedure A and the control shifts to the specified line. You can use two forms of the On Error statement. These are

- ✦ The On Error GoTo Line statement

  In the preceding statement, Line is generally a label that indicates the line you want to shift the control to.

- ✦ The On Error Resume Next statement

On Error GoTo Line statement

When using an On Error GoTo Line statement, you place the code to handle error after the line that you specify as an argument. This line may refer to a line number or a label. The line argument should be in the same procedure. Look at the following example:

```
'Unstructured exception handling
On Error GoTo ErrorCode
Dim Months() As String = {"Jan", "Feb", "Mar", "Apr", "May"}
Dim Counter As Integer = 0
For Counter = 0 To 6
   'Cause an "Index out of range" error.
   MessageBox.Show(Months(Counter))
Next Counter
'Exit the procedure if there is no error.
Exit Sub
ErrorCode:
   MessageBox.Show("Please check the code")
```

In the preceding example, we use the On Error statement to handle the exceptions. As soon as an exception is raised, the control moves to the code following the ErrorCode line label. In this case, the code displays an error message. Notice the presence of the `Exit Sub` statement in the code. We include this to prevent the error-handling code from executing in case no exception is raised.

In the above-mentioned code, only a general error message is displayed. This message does not provide any information regarding type or location of error. Visual Basic .NET provides the cool `Err` object to help you out in such situations. The `Err` object contains the details of the errors generated at runtime. The `Err` object contains properties, such as `Number` and `Description`, to help you get information about the error. The `Number` property contains a numeric value that displays the number assigned by Visual Studio .NET to that error. The `Description` property contains the error message associated with the corresponding `Number` property. You can modify the preceding code as shown here:

```
'Unstructured exception handling
On Error GoTo ErrorCode
Dim Months() As String = {"Jan", "Feb", "Mar", "Apr", "May"}
Dim Counter As Integer = 0
For Counter = 0 To 6
   ' Cause an "Index out of range" error.
   MessageBox.Show(Months(Counter))
Next Counter
'Exit the procedure if there is no error
Exit Sub
ErrorCode:
   MessageBox.Show("The following error occurred:" & Chr(13)
     & Chr(10) & Err.Number & " " & Err.Description)
```

The preceding example gives the description of the error by using `Err.Description` property.

The `Chr` function returns the character for the specified code. `Chr(10)` returns the linefeed character and `Chr(13)` returns a carriage return character. The *linefeed character* leaves a blank line, and the *carriage return character* moves the following text to the new line. You use these, simultaneously, to display the following text in a new line.

You can also use the following options with the `On Error` statement:

- ✦ Use the `On Error GoTo 0` statement to disable the error-handling routine in the given procedure.
- ✦ Use the `On Error GoTo -1` statement to disable the exception raised in the procedure.

  If you don't use –1 with this statement, the exception is disabled as soon as the procedure containing the exception ends.

On Error Resume Next statement

The `On Error Resume Next` statement moves the control to the line next to the error-causing line. The syntax of this statement is

```
On Error Resume Next
```

You can also use the `Resume`, `Resume Next`, and `Resume Line` statements without the `On Error` statement:

- ✦ Use the `Resume` statement to move the control back to the statement that generated the error.
- ✦ Use the `Resume Next` statement to move the control to the line following the one that caused the error.
- ✦ Use the `Resume Line` statement to move the control to the specified line.

To better understand the usage of these statements, consider the following error-handling routine:

```
ErrorCode:
   MessageBox.Show(Err.Description)
   Resume Next
```

The preceding error-handling routine displays the description of the error and then moves the control to the line following the one that generated the error.

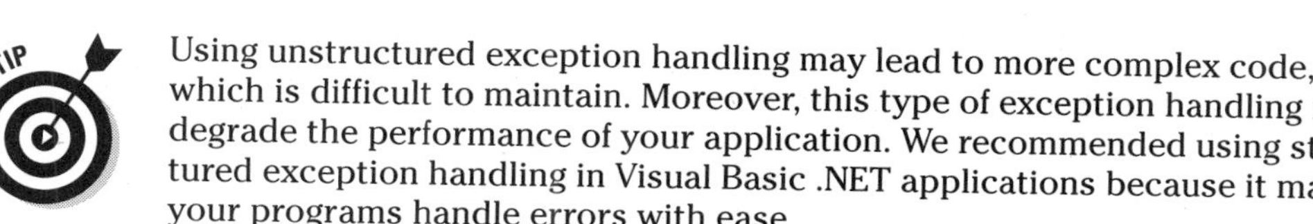

Using unstructured exception handling may lead to more complex code, which is difficult to maintain. Moreover, this type of exception handling may degrade the performance of your application. We recommended using structured exception handling in Visual Basic .NET applications because it makes your programs handle errors with ease.

Tracing Errors in Programs

Being able to handle errors is only part of the equation, though. You also need to locate them and then remove them. Employ Visual Basic .NET to help you in your error searches.

Finding errors can be an uphill task. Of course, eliminating syntax errors isn't that tough because Visual Basic .NET warns you about the syntax errors in a program while you key in the code. As an added useful feature, though, Visual Basic .NET also lists these errors in the Output window after you execute a program. To identify the code that's causing the error, just double-click the respective error.

Problems start, however, when you can't see the error. And, compilers also skip some errors because they are syntactically correct. Call on Visual Basic .NET to help sniff out and trace these hidden bugs.

The process of finding errors in a program is *debugging*.

Visual Basic .NET provides a powerful debugger that makes error-free code a reality. This debugger provides various tools that help you halt your application (enter break mode), examine your program at runtime, and also make changes. Some of these tools are the Autos window, the Locals window, the Watch window, the QuickWatch dialog box, and the Call Stack window.

Gimme a break (mode)

To access most of the Visual Basic .NET debugging tools, your application needs to be in break mode. In Visual Basic .NET, any error that occurs can halt the execution of an application. When this stoppage happens, an application is in *break mode*.

Your program may enter the break mode automatically if it encounters

- **An error**
- **A `Stop` statement**

  Use the `Stop` statement within the code to make your application enter the break mode.
- **A breakpoint**

  A *breakpoint* is a point from where the application enters the break mode. To add or remove breakpoints in your applications, choose the New Breakpoint option from the Debug menu. Visual Basic .NET has four types of breakpoints:

  - **Function breakpoint** halts the application when the program reaches a specific point in a given function.
  - **File breakpoint** halts the application when the program reaches a specific point in a given file.
  - **Address breakpoint** halts the application when the program reaches a specific memory address.
  - **Data breakpoint** halts the application when the value of a variable changes.

After break mode suspends the application execution, it takes you to the Code window. There you can monitor the status of your application by utilizing various tools, such as Watch window and Autos window. For example, you can test the value contained in a variable or an expression or see whether the procedures are executing in the correct order.

To test the value contained in a variable or an expression, you can also manually break an application's execution — that is, force an application to enter break mode — by

- **Choosing Break All from the Debug menu**
- **Pressing Ctrl+Break simultaneously**

When you're in break mode, you'll see the DataTips pop-up information box quite often. As its name suggests, this box pops up every time that you click or point to a variable or select an expression in the Code window, displaying the value stored in a variable or an expression. See an example of such a display in Figure 9-4.

```
Private Sub Button2_Click(ByVal sender As System.Object, ByV
    'On Error Goto ErrorCode
    Dim Months() As String = {"Jan", "Feb", "Mar", "Apr", "M
    Dim Counter As Integer = 0
    ' Set up structured error handling.
    For Counter = 0 To 4
        ' Cause a "Index out of range" error.
        MessageBox.Show(Months(Counter))
    Next Counter
    'Exit Sub  [Counter = 0]

    'Dim a As OpenFileDialog
    'a.ShowDialog()
```

DataTip pop-up box

Figure 9-4: View the contents of a variable by pointing to the variable.

After you pinpoint an error in break mode, Visual Basic .NET allows you to modify the values of variables and properties and then continue execution. We like that. Use the Watch windows and the QuickWatch dialog box to check and correct expressions for errors. Use the Autos window and the Locals windows to modify values of variables. Use the Call Stack window to verify code sequence from the Call Stack.

Watch window

Use the Watch window to check the values of expressions and variables in your code.

Your application needs to be in break mode to make use of the Watch window.

You can launch the Watch window in either of the following two ways:

- **Choose Debug⇨Windows⇨Watch.**
- **Choose the Watch 1, Watch 2, Watch 3, or Watch 4 option from the Debug⇨Windows⇨Watch submenu.**

  You can choose these options in any order. Choosing any of the four options displays a new Watch window with a caption that corresponds to the caption of the selected option. For example, if you select Watch 1, a window title Watch 1 displays.

As you can see in Figure 9-5, the Watch window contains three columns:

- The **Name** column displays the name of the variables.
- The **Value** column displays the current value.
- The **Type** column displays the data type of the variable.

After a Watch window is displayed, you need to add to it a variable that you want to evaluate. Right-click the appropriate variable in the Code window; from the pop-up menu that appears, click Add Watch.

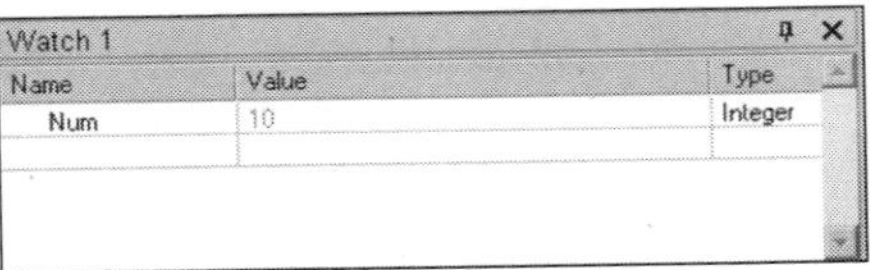

Figure 9-5: Contents of a variable in the Watch window.

Follow these steps as we walk you through monitoring a variable in the Watch window:

1. **Create a new Windows application.**

   Read more on creating a new Windows application in Book 3, Chapter 2.

2. **Create a button on the form.**

   Read more on creating a button in Book 3, Chapter 3.

3. **Attach the following code to the `Click` event of the button:**

   ```
   Dim Num, ctr As Integer
   For ctr = 1 To 5
      Num = Num + CInt(InputBox("Enter a number"))
   Next ctr
   ```

4. **Click at the location (left margin of the Code window) specified by the mouse pointer in Figure 9-6 to insert a breakpoint in the code.**

For more on breakpoints, see the earlier section "Gimme a break (mode)."

```
Dim Num, ctr As Integer
For ctr = 1 To 5
    Num = Num + CInt(InputBox("Enter a number"))
Next ctr
```

Figure 9-6: Click the left margin of the Code window to insert a breakpoint.

Look for a solid red circle to appear in the left margin, indicating that the breakpoint is now enabled. The complete expression should also now be highlighted in red.

5. **Execute the application and click the button that you create in Step 2.**

   The application enters the break mode. The point at which you inserted the breakpoint should appear highlighted in yellow.

6. **Choose Debug➪Windows➪Watch➪Watch 1.**

   The Watch 1 window appears.

7. **In the Code window, right-click the `Num` variable.**

8. **From the shortcut menu that appears, click Add Watch.**

   The `Num` variable appears in the Watch 1 window.

9. **From the Debug menu, click Continue.**

   The application displays an InputBox, which prompts the user to enter a value. It contains a text box to accept this value. In this case, it prompts the user to accept a number.

10. **Enter any number and click OK.**

    The number that you enter appears in the Value column of the Watch 1 window. (Refer to the left side of Figure 9-5 to see this column.)

In addition to monitoring values, you can also edit the values by using the Watch window. In the Value column, just double-click the entry that you want to modify and make the necessary changes there.

The Watch window is closed automatically, as soon as you end the application. To end the application, choose Debug➪Stop Debugging. In addition, you can close the Watch window manually by clicking the standard Close (X) button present in the upper-right corner of this window.

QuickWatch dialog box

You can also use the QuickWatch dialog box to monitor the value of variables. This dialog box is available only in break mode.

To activate the QuickWatch dialog box, choose the QuickWatch option from the Debug menu. In the QuickWatch dialog box, the Expression text box is used to specify the name of a variable or an expression and the Recalculate button is used to calculate the value of variables or expressions. The Add Watch button is used to add the variable or expression entered in the Expression text box to the Watch window.

See a sample QuickWatch dialog box in Figure 9-7.

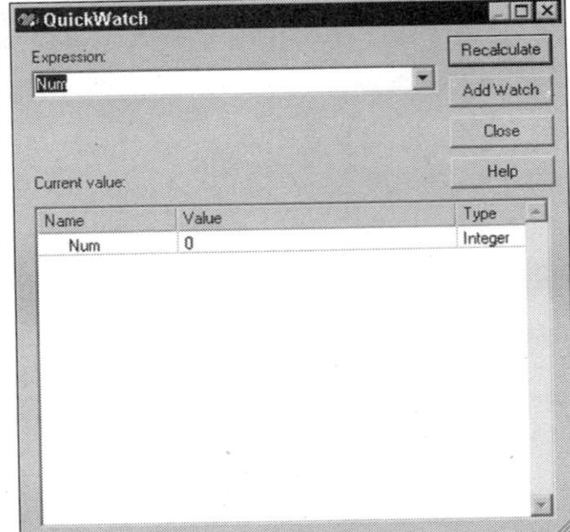

Figure 9-7: Monitor a variable's values from the QuickWatch dialog box.

To add a variable to the QuickWatch dialog box, right-click the appropriate variable in the code window. From the shortcut menu that appears, choose QuickWatch.

Autos window

You can also use the Autos window to modify the value of a variable. The Autos window displays the name of all the variables in the currently selected statement, in addition to the previous statement. Like the Watch window, this window contains the three columns Name, Value, and Type.

To launch the Autos window (see Figure 9-8), choose Debug➪Windows➪Autos. The Autos window is available only in the break mode.

Autos

Name	Value	Type
Num	0	Integer
ctr	1	Integer

Figure 9-8: Modify a variable's value from the Autos window.

Locals window

The Locals window displays the variables local to the current execution location, such as a procedure. This window also allows you to modify the value of a variable. Like the Watch and Autos windows, this window contains the three columns Name, Value, and Type.

To launch the Locals window (see Figure 9-9), choose Debug➪Windows➪Locals. The Locals window is available only in the break mode.

Locals

Name	Value	Type
⊞ Me	{ErrorHandler.Form1}	ErrorHan(
⊞ sender	{System.Windows.Forms.Button}	Object
⊞ e	{System.EventArgs}	System.E
ctr	1	Integer
Num	0	Integer

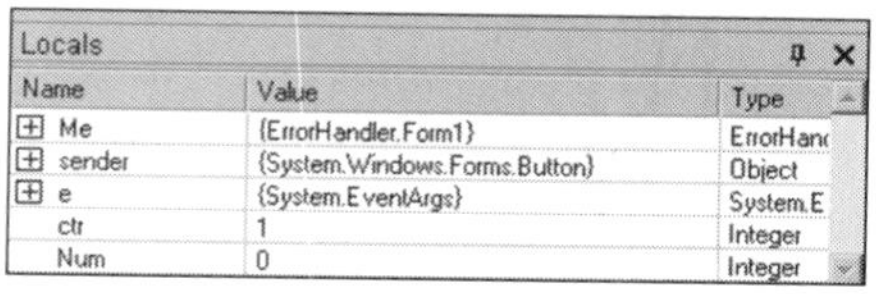

Figure 9-9: Modify a variable's value from the Locals window.

Call Stack window

The Call Stack window displays a list of procedure calls that are active. *Active procedures* are the ones that are currently loaded in the memory. You can use this window to verify whether the code follows the correct sequence of procedures. This window is visible only in the break mode.

To show this window (see Figure 9-10), choose Debug➪Windows➪Call Stack.

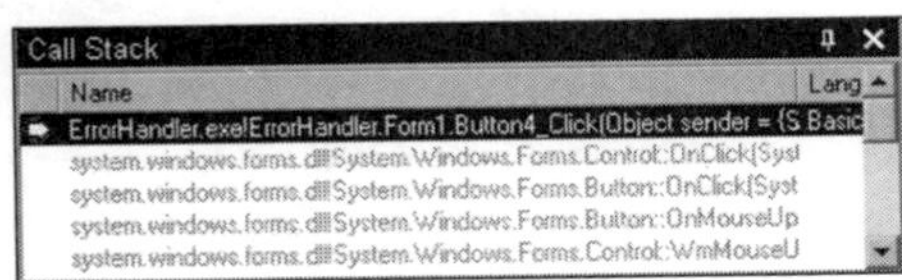

Figure 9-10: Verify code sequence from the Call Stack window.

Chapter 10: Accessing a Database

In This Chapter

- **Introducing ADO.NET**
- **Setting up a data adapter**
- **Storing data in a dataset**
- **Adding and binding controls**

Microsoft's .NET initiative revolves around the concept of interoperable applications, including database-driven applications. ADO.NET is the latest Microsoft tool for accessing data stored in databases. Visual Basic .NET utilizes the power of ADO.NET to build strong and interoperable applications with enhanced performance.

In this chapter, we present the basics of ADO.NET and its various components. We show you how to set up a data adapter, store your data, and then move on to creating an application for accessing data. Consider us your tour guide of two of the most important reasons that you create an application: to store and to access data.

ADO.NET 101

ADO.NET makes interoperable and scalable data access a reality. ADO.NET is the latest version of ActiveX Data Objects (ADO), which was used in the previous version of Visual Basic to access data. We like using ADO.NET because

- **ADO.NET transfers data in eXtensible Markup Language (XML) format.**

  Benefits

  - Data is accessible by any application that understands XML.
  - Applications developed using ADO.NET are interoperable with others that aren't based on ADO.NET.

✦ **ADO.NET uses a disconnected architecture, which means that once you retrieve records from a database, the connection between the application and database is terminated.**

Benefits

• You need a connection with the database only at the time that you save or retrieve records.

• The database is accessible by a large number of users, which increases the scalability of your applications.

ADO.NET Components

When based on ADO.NET, a database-driven application of Visual Basic .NET consists of the Windows Forms, DataSet, Data Adapters, Data Connection, and Data Source components. See their relationships in Figure 10-1.

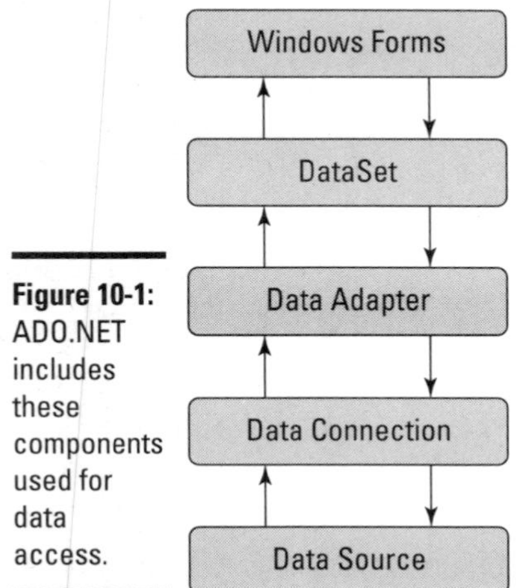

Figure 10-1: ADO.NET includes these components used for data access.

✦ **Windows Forms:** Use the Windows Forms to provide a user interface to your database-driven applications. (For the scoop on Windows Forms, read through Chapters 2, 3, and 4 of Book 3.)

✦ **DataSet:** Use a DataSet to store the data that you retrieve from a data source.

A dataset is only a storehouse: It can't actually transfer data to and from a data source. Actually, datasets are responsible for the disconnected architecture that we mention in the previous section. Read the architecture of ADO.NET in Book 6, Chapter 11. (For more on datasets, read the following section.)

✦ **Data Adapter:** Use a data adapter to transfer data to and from a data source. Think of a data adapter as a cargo company that picks up data from the data source, drops it into a dataset, picks it back up from the dataset, and then takes it back to the data source. (For more on data adapters, read the following section "Data adapters.")

✦ **Data Connection:** Use a data connection to establish a connection between a dataset and a data source.

TECHNICAL STUFF

When you configure a data adapter in your application, the connection with the data source is automatically established.

✦ **Data Source:** A data source generally represents a database. ADO.NET provides you the flexibility to work with various types of databases, such as a Microsoft Access or a SQL (Structured Query Language) Server database.

Datasets

In the .NET Framework, data is retrieved from the database and stored in an intermediate location as a dataset. A dataset is structurally similar to a relational database, containing the table(s) that you require. In addition, a dataset also contains information about the relationships between tables and the constraints that you define on these tables. The structure of a dataset, which includes tables, relationships, and constraints, is contained in an XML schema.

A dataset can be typed or untyped. A *typed dataset* is the one that acts upon the information stored in the XML schema file. An *untyped dataset* is the one that doesn't have any information stored in the XML file. We recommend that you use typed datasets because Visual Studio .NET provides more tools that support typed datasets. Moreover, using typed datasets makes dataset programming easy and less susceptible to errors.

An advantage when using datasets is that after the required data is retrieved, the connection with the database is terminated. This makes the database free for other applications to access. Another important advantage to datasets is that they store data in XML format, which makes the data accessible by any other application.

The `DataSet` class represents a dataset. This class contains objects that represent the tables, relations, and constraints present in a database.

To fill a dataset with data, you use a data adapter.

Data adapters

You use a data adapter to perform the following two operations:

- ✦ Reading data from a data source into a dataset (filling a dataset).
- ✦ Writing data back to the data source with modifications, if any.

A *data adapter* is a combination of data commands and data connection objects. The *data command* object helps you specify the data to be moved into a dataset: You can use SQL commands or stored procedures as commands. The *data connection* object helps you establish a connection between a dataset and a data source.

The `DataAdapter` class represents a data adapter. By using a data adapter, you connect to an SQL Server database or any other database, such as Access. For this, Visual Studio .NET provides the `SqlDataAdapter` and the `OleDbDataAdapter` classes.

- ✦ Use `SqlDataAdapter` to connect with SQL Server version 7.0 or higher databases. This class works in conjunction with the `SqlCommand` and `SqlConnection` classes to specify the commands and establish the data connection.
- ✦ Use `OleDbDataAdapter` with any data source provided by an OLE DB provider, such as MS Access. This class works in conjunction with the `OleDbCommand` and `OleDbConnection` classes to specify the commands and establish the connection.

Both of these classes contain properties that help you perform read, add, update, and delete operations in a database. The following describes these properties:

- ✦ **`SelectCommand`:** Use this property to retrieve records from a table in a database.
- ✦ **`InsertCommand`:** Use this property to add new records in a table in a database.
- ✦ **`UpdateCommand`:** Use this property to make changes to the existing records in a table.
- ✦ **`DeleteCommand`:** Use this property to delete records from a table in a database.

These properties are actually instances of the `OleDbCommand` or the `SqlCommand` class. You can manipulate these properties either at runtime or design time.

The `SqlDataAdapter` and `OleDbDataAdapter` classes provide the `Fill` method used to retrieve records in a database. This method takes the name of the dataset as a parameter. The syntax is

```
MyDataAdapter.Fill(MyDataSet)
```

Read more about Data Adapters in Book 6, Chapter 11.

Displaying Data on a Form

Time for the rubber to hit the road — creating an application that picks up records from a data source and displays them in Windows Forms.

To keep it simple, break the process of accessing data into these steps:

1. Set up the data adapter.
2. Generate a dataset.
3. Add and bind controls.

TIP

You should perform these steps in order.

Follow along as we create an application named `MyDataAccess`. This application will access the data stored in an Access database. Then we show you how to display this data in a `DataGrid` control. (You use the `DataGrid` control to display the data in a report format.)

Setting up a data adapter

Use the following steps to set up a data adapter for your project.

1. **Create a new Windows application and name this project MyDataAccess.**
2. **In the Toolbox, switch to the Data tab.**
3. **From the Data tab of the Toolbox, click and drag the `OleDbDataAdapter` control onto the form.**

   The welcome screen of the Data Adapter Configuration Wizard appears. Use this wizard to help you set up the data adapter.
4. **Click the Next button on the wizard welcome screen to move to the next screen.**

   From this screen, you specify the data connection object for the data adapter.

5. **In the second wizard window, click the New Connection button.**

   The Data Link Properties dialog box appears, as shown in Figure 10-2. By default, the Connection tab is active.

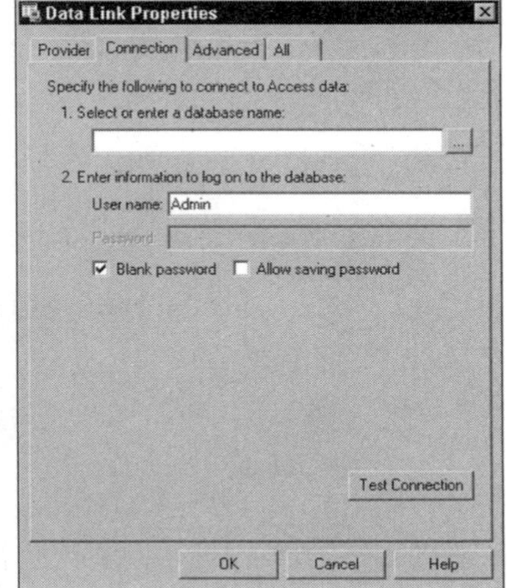

Figure 10-2: Establish a connection by using the Data Link Properties dialog box.

6. **Click the Provider tab of the Data Link Properties dialog box.**

7. **From the OLE DB Provider(s) list, click Microsoft Jet 4.0 OLE DB Provider to select it.**

   This step specifies that your application will use a Microsoft Access database.

8. **Click the Next button to activate the Connection tab of the Data Link Properties dialog box.**

   In the first text box (labeled `1. Select or Enter a Database Name`), you're prompted to enter a database name.

9. **In this text box, enter the following:** C:\Program Files\Microsoft Office\Office\Samples\Northwind.mdb.

   The drive letter in the preceding line may differ on your computer depending on where you have MS Office installed.

10. **In the section** `2. Enter Information to Log on to the Database`**, enter** Admin **in the User Name text box and select (check) the Blank Password check box.**

11. **Click the Test Connection button.**

    The Microsoft Data Link message box appears telling you that the connection was successfully established.

    In case the message box indicates that the connection isn't successful, check the path of the database.

12. **Click OK to close the Microsoft Data Link message box.**

    The Data Link Properties dialog box displays again.

13. **Click OK to close the Data Link Properties dialog box and to return to the Data Adapter Configuration Wizard.**

    As shown in Figure 10-3, the Which Data Connection Should the Data Adapter Use? list box contains the path and the name of the database that you select.

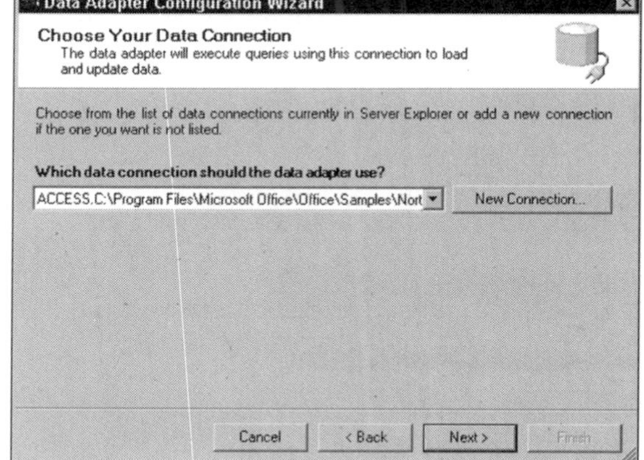

Figure 10-3: The Data Adapter Configuration Wizard displays the path and name of the database.

14. **In the wizard window, click the Next button to move to its next screen.**

    In this screen, you specify the data command object for your application. Ensure that the Use SQL Statements radio button is selected.

15. **Click the Next button to move to the next wizard screen.**

    In this screen, you specify the data that you need. To specify this data, write a query in the large text area, as shown in the middle of Figure 10-4. Either type the query there directly or use the Query Builder to build the query.

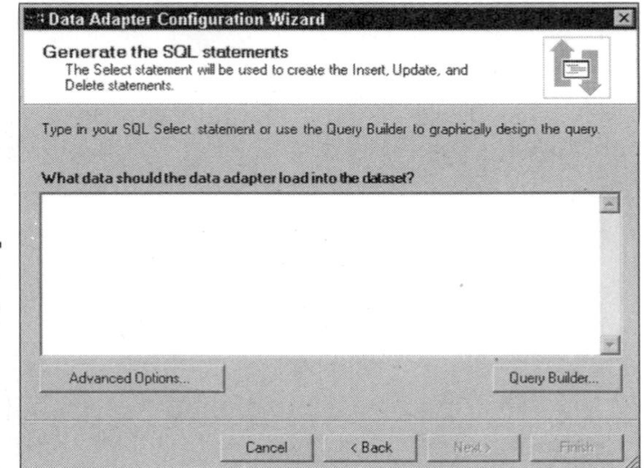

Figure 10-4: Specify your query to display the data that you want.

16. If you choose to use the Query Builder, click the Query Builder button.

The Query Builder appears (see Figure 10-5) with the Add Table dialog box actively displayed on top of it.

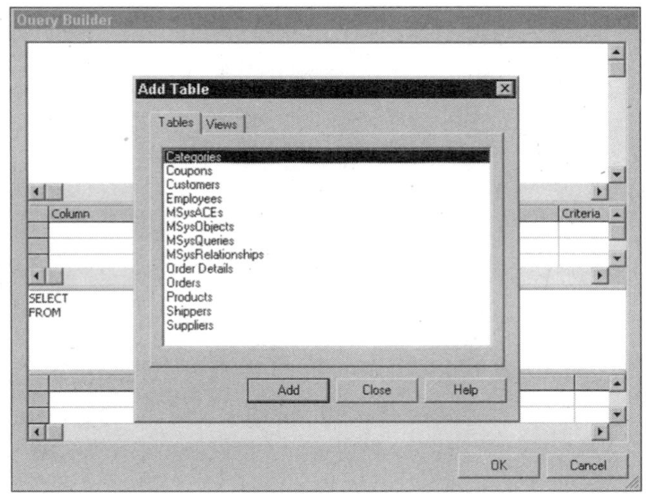

Figure 10-5: Use Query Builder to simplify building a query.

17. From the Tables tab of the Add Table dialog box, select Employees and click the Add button.

The Employees table appears in the box at the top of the Query Builder.

18. **Click the Close button to close the Add Table dialog box.**

    The Query Builder dialog box becomes active.

19. **In the Employees table in the Query Builder, select EmployeeID, FirstName, LastName, and HireDate by placing a check mark next to each.**

    The Query Builder automatically generates the query, as shown in Figure 10-6.

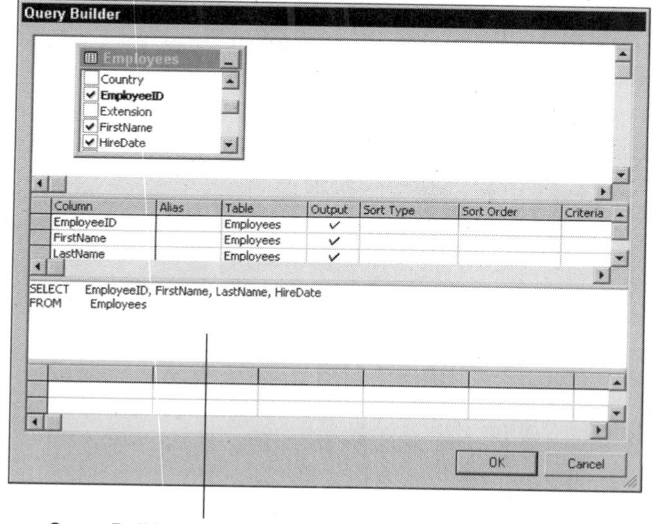

Figure 10-6: Generate a query with the Query Builder.

20. **Click OK to close the Query Builder and return to the configuration wizard.**

    The configuration wizard now displays the name of the fields and the table to be present in the data adapter.

21. **Click the Next button to move to the next wizard screen.**

    The screen displays that you successfully configured the data adapter.

    TIP: In some cases, the wizard displays a message telling you that the wizard detected some problems while configuring the data adapter. One of the reasons for this problem is an incorrect query, which might happen if you type the query manually.

22. **Click the Finish button to complete the wizard.**

    Observe that the form and that the `OleDbDataAdapter1` and `OleDbConnection1` objects appear in the Tray at the bottom of the form.

Storing data in a dataset

After you set up a data adapter, you can generate a dataset and bind it with controls. This is a piece of cake compared with setting up a data adapter.

After you establish a connection with the database and specify the data to be retrieved, you need to store it in a dataset. To generate a dataset:

1. **From the Data menu, select Generate Dataset.**

   The Generate Dataset dialog box appears, as shown in Figure 10-7.

   To make this command successful, ensure that focus is on the form. This is because if the focus is not on the form, the Generate Dataset command is not available in the Data menu.

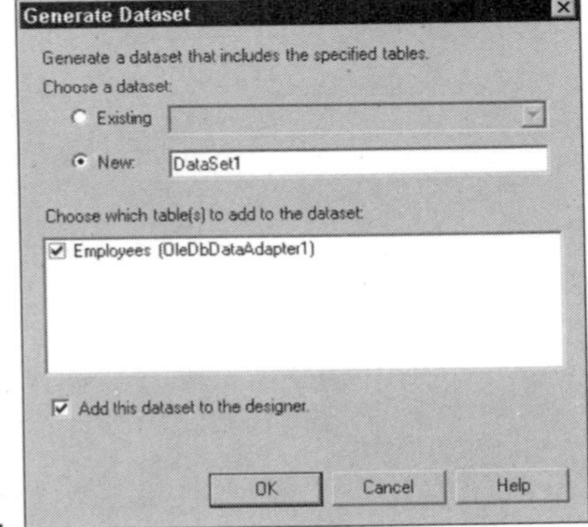

Figure 10-7: Specify tables for a dataset with the Generate Dataset dialog box.

   To set focus on a form, click it.

2. **In the Generate Dataset dialog box, select the New radio button.**
3. **Note that the text box to the right of the New radio button contains DataSet1, which is the default name of the dataset. Type an appropriate name for the dataset.**

   For this example, type **dsEmployees**.

   In the Choose Which Table(s) to Add to the Dataset list, the Employees table is selected (with a check mark next to it).

4. **Click OK to complete the process and close the dialog box.**

   DsEmployees1 appears in the Tray.

   The prefix Ds indicates that it is a dataset.

Adding and binding controls

After you generate a dataset, you want to display this data to the user. To display data, create a form that contains the required controls, such as `DataGrid` or `Text Box`, and then bind these controls with the dataset. For more on adding controls to a form, read through Book 3, Chapter 3. Read the next section to discover how to bind a control.

Binding a DataGrid control

Use a `DataGrid` control to display the data in a report format. To bind this control with the dataset, set the `DataSource` and `DataMember` properties. Use the `DataSource` property to determine the data source, such as dataset, that contains the required data. Use the `DataMember` property to determine the appropriate data member, such as a table present in the dataset, of the data source.

Displaying data in a `DataGrid` control, however, reduces the readability of the data. And, if you have more columns than what can fit in the grid, you're forced to scroll to see all the columns.

To bind the DataGrid control:

1. **From the Windows Forms tab of the Toolbox, click and drag a `DataGrid` control to the form.**
2. **Click the `DataGrid` control to display its properties in the Properties window.**
3. **In the DataSource field of the Properties window, select DsEmployees1.**

   In this case, the DsEmployees1 dataset is the data source.
4. **In the DataMember field, click Employees to select it.**

   In this case, you need to display the records present in the Employees table.

   The data grid now displays the field's headings, as shown in Figure 10-8, contained in the data source.
5. **Click the `DataGrid` control to select it.**
6. **Click and drag the sizing handles on the DataGrid control to resize it so that you can view all the columns.**
7. **Choose Debug⇨Start to execute the application.**

   Note that the data grid doesn't yet contain any records, as you can see by the `(null)` entry in each column of Figure 10-9. We haven't yet written the code to populate the grid.

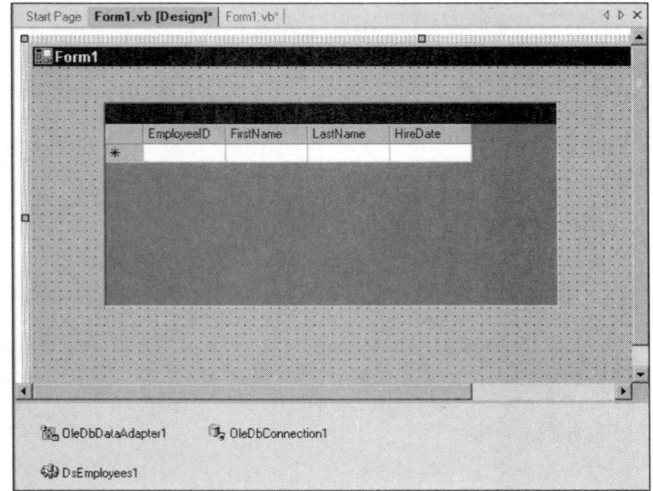

Figure 10-8: Bind the DataGrid control with the data source.

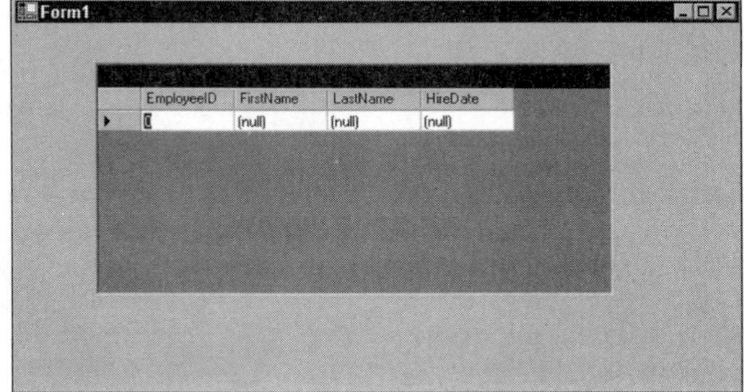

Figure 10-9: An unpopulated data grid.

8. **To populate the data grid, add the following code to the** `Load` **event of Form1.**

```
'Clear any existing data in the dataset
DsEmployees1.Clear()
'Fill the dataset with the data present in the data
source
OleDbDataAdapter1.Fill(DsEmployees1)
```

To view the `Load` event of the form, open the form in the Design view and double-click it.

9. **Choose Debug⇨Start to execute the application again.**

   The data grid now displays the records present in the Employees table, as shown in Figure 10-10.

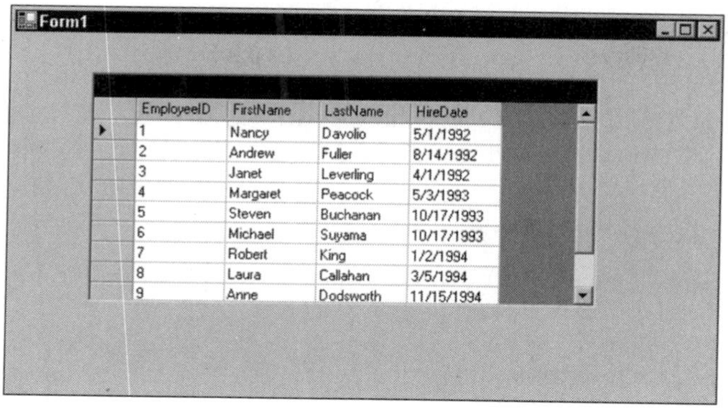

Form1

EmployeeID	FirstName	LastName	HireDate
1	Nancy	Davolio	5/1/1992
2	Andrew	Fuller	8/14/1992
3	Janet	Leverling	4/1/1992
4	Margaret	Peacock	5/3/1993
5	Steven	Buchanan	10/17/1993
6	Michael	Suyama	10/17/1993
7	Robert	King	1/2/1994
8	Laura	Callahan	3/5/1994
9	Anne	Dodsworth	11/15/1994

Figure 10-10: Fill the grid by using the Fill method of the Data-Adapter class.

Read the next section to learn how to bind a text box.

Binding the TextBox control

Because displaying data in a DataGrid control takes away the readability of the data and can add more columns than you can see at once, you may choose to use a TextBox control. When you choose this control, you can add to the visual appearance of your data access application by using multiple controls, such as text boxes, radio buttons, and list boxes to display a single record. For example, you can use text boxes to display an employee ID and name.

To bind a text box with a dataset, you use the DataBindings property. This property adds the Binding object to the ControlBindingsCollection of the text box. The Binding object represents the binding between the property of a control, such as text box and the property of an object, such as EmployeeID property of the Employees object. ControlBindingsCollection is the collection of data binding of a control. The syntax to bind the Text property of a text box with a dataset is

```
TextBox1.DataBindings.Add("Text", dsEmployees1,
   "Employees.EmployeeID")
```

In the preceding statement,

- `Text` **is the property of the text box with which you need to bind the** `EmployeeID` **property of the** `Employees` **object.**
- `dsEmployees1` **is the name of the dataset object.**
- `Employees.EmployeeID` **is the property with which you need to bind the** `Text` **property of the text box.**

To test this statement, create a text box. Then add the given statement to the `Load` event of the form. Finally, execute the application.

Or you can take the easy road and use the Visual Basic .NET Data Form Wizard. Works for us. Find out how in the next section, lazy bones.

Data Form Wizard

Use the Data Form Wizard to easily create forms having data-bound controls. The Data Form Wizard helps you

- **Generate a dataset.**
- **Establish a connection with the data source.**
- **Specify the tables to populate the dataset.**
- **Specify the columns present in the table to be displayed on the form.**
- **Display all the records in a grid format or single record in individual controls.**

The Data Form Wizard uses the `OleDbDataAdapter` and `OleDbConnection` by default. The advantage of using these is that you have access to any data source, such as SQL Server or Access. When you choose to display single records in individual controls, the Data Form Wizard provides you with options to display controls to add, delete, and navigate records.

To use the Data Form Wizard:

1. **In the Project menu present in the IDE, click Add New Item.**

   The Add New Item dialog box appears.

2. **From the Templates list of Add New Item dialog box, click Data Form Wizard to select it.**

3. **Enter an appropriate name to the form in the Name text box and click the Open button.**

   In this case, the name of the form is DataForm1. The welcome screen of the Data Form Wizard appears.

4. **Click the Next button.**

   The next wizard screen appears. Here you specify a dataset for your project.

5. **Select the Create a New Dataset Named radio button.**

6. **In the text box beneath Create a New Dataset Named, enter** dsEmp **for the name of the dataset.**

   See Figure 10-11.

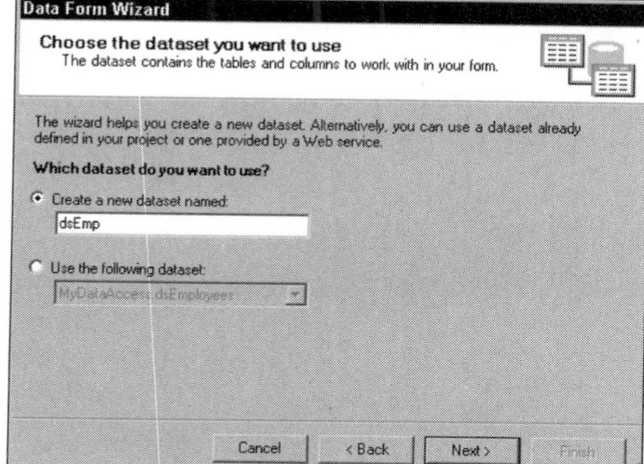

Figure 10-11: Specify the dataset with the Data Form Wizard.

7. **Click the Next button.**

   The next wizard screen appears, in which you establish a connection with the data source. You can create a new connection by repeating the steps that you performed in the section "Setting up a data adapter." However, you can also use the already existing connections that appear in the Which Connection Should the Wizard Use list.

   In this example, from the Which connection should the wizard use list, select the connection that you created in the previous section. For reference, see Figure 10-3.

8. **Click the Next button.**

   The next wizard screen appears, in which you select the tables to populate the dataset.

   In this example, add Employees under Tables in the Selected Item(s) list, as shown on the right-hand side of Figure 10-12.

   [>] To add the table, select the appropriate table in the Available Item(s) list (left-hand side of this wizard screen) and then click the center-window button with the > symbol.

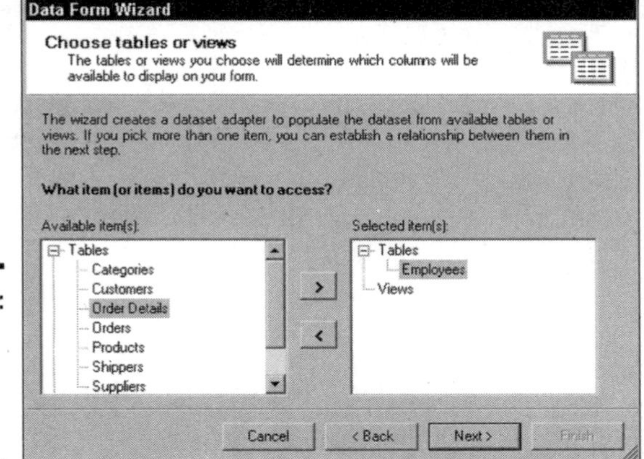

Figure 10-12: Specify a table for your dataset.

9. **Click the Next button.**

   The next wizard screen appears, in which you are prompted to specify the columns that you want displayed on the form.

   By default, all the columns are selected, as shown in Figure 10-13. If you want to remove any column, deselect (uncheck) the column name under the Columns list.

   In this case, we display all the columns on the form.

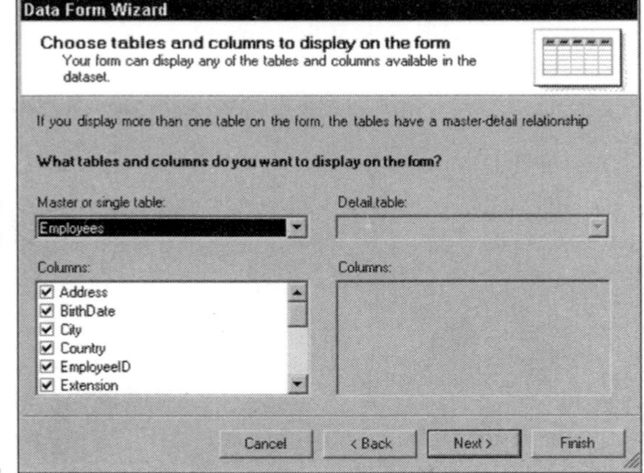

Figure 10-13: Specify the columns that you want to display on your form.

10. **Click the Next button.**

    The next wizard screen appears, in which you are prompted to specify the display style. See Figure 10-14.

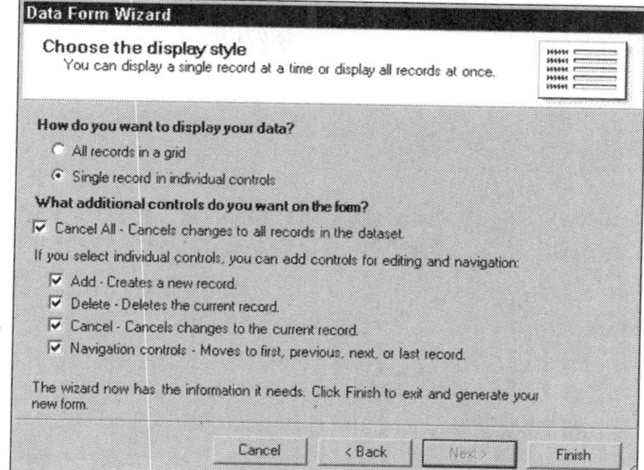

Figure 10-14: Specify the type of display.

You can display the records either in a grid format or display one record in individual controls.

11. **To display records individually, select the Single Record in Individual Controls radio button.**

    When you select this radio button, the wizard also provides you with check boxes with which you can insert controls to add, delete, and navigate records. In addition, you can also cancel all the changes made to a record.

    After you complete this step, the wizard is ready to generate the required form with all the specifications that you provide.

12. **Click the Finish button.**

    The form appears with all the required controls, as shown in Figure 10-15.

13. **Make this form your start-up form.**

14. **Choose Debug⇨Start to execute the application.**

1. To display a form at startup, right-click the project name (`MyDataAccess`) in Solution Explorer, which is present on the right-side of the IDE.
2. From the pop-up menu that appears, click Properties to display the project property pages.
3. From the Startup object list, click the appropriate form to select it (DataForm1).
4. Click OK to close the Property Pages of the MyDataAccess project.

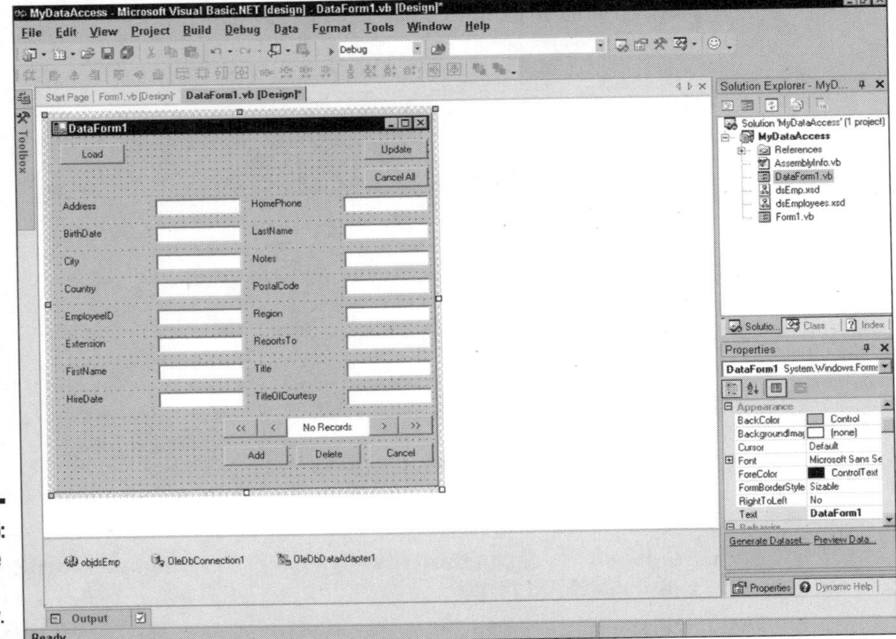

Figure 10-15: Your sample form in design view.

15. Click the Load button present at the top of the form.

The first record appears in the respective controls, as shown in Figure 10-16. You can now work in your form by using the various controls.

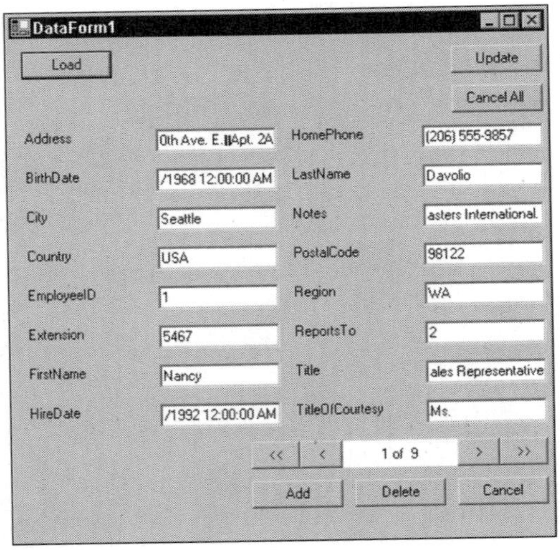

Figure 10-16: Your data appears in your form.

Index

A

B

C

D

M

N

O

P

Q

R

S

T

U

V

W-X-Y-Z

Book IV

Visual C++ .NET

"It was at this point in time that there appeared to be some sort of mass insanity."

Contents at a Glance

Chapter 1: Introducing Visual C++ .NET

In This Chapter

- **Getting to know Visual C++ .NET**
- **Exploring application creation methods**
- **Discovering Visual C++ .NET project template types**

If you've programmed using Visual C++ 6.0, Visual C++ .NET will appear familiar to you. In the .NET suite, Visual C++ is perhaps the only language for which knowledge of the earlier version enables you to get started easily in .NET. Most Visual C++ 6.0 features are retained in Visual C++ .NET. Even if you're a novice Visual C++ programmer, welcome aboard.

In this chapter, we briefly describe the new features of Visual C++ .NET and then move on to explain the enhancements to some of the existing Visual C++ 6.0 features. We also look at creating applications in Visual C++ .NET and explore its many project templates.

Discovering Visual C++ .NET

Although Microsoft continues to add enhancements to its programming languages (such as Visual Basic), Visual C++ has always been regarded as a complex language meant only for expert developers: Visual C++ is too powerful of a language to be simplified to the core. In the .NET version of Visual C++, the traditional features of Visual C++ are enhanced but the language is simpler.

Visual C++ .NET has improved libraries, faster applications, and more efficient debugging functionality than its predecessor. In addition, Visual C++ .NET introduces managed extensions for Visual C++. *Managed extensions* comprise a set of language extensions for Visual C++ that help you write Visual C++ applications for the .NET Framework.

With Visual C++ .NET, you have the flexibility to develop your applications the way that you want to. Because applications are developed with traditional Visual C++ libraries, these applications can run without using the .NET Framework classes. Also, applications developed with managed extensions use the .NET Framework.

Enhancements and new features in Visual C++ .NET

A number of enhancements in Visual C++ .NET make it more efficient and easier to use than its earlier version. In Visual Studio .NET, the integrated development environment (IDE) across languages in the .NET suite is common. This IDE is slightly different from the IDE of Visual C++ 6.0.

You'll notice some differences in the menu options used for performing familiar tasks. For example, to add a resource to your project in Visual C++ 6.0, you had to choose the Insert⇨Resource menu option. In Visual C++ .NET, you choose Project⇨Add Resource. These minor modifications shouldn't pose a problem for you; the more that you use the new IDE, the more you get used to it.

Do pay close attention, though, to the advanced features in Visual C++ .NET. In Visual C++ .NET, you can develop applications by using Microsoft Foundation Classes (MFC), Active Template Library (ATL) Server classes, or standard Visual C++ API functions.

The enhancements in the Visual C++ classes and functions are

- **Shared classes in Visual C++ .NET:** In Visual C++ 6.0, if you had to use common MFC classes (such as `CPoint` and `CRect`) in an ATL Server application, you had to add MFC dependencies to your project. You don't have to do this in Visual C++ .NET because common MFC classes (such as `CPoint`, `CRect`, `CSize`, and `CString`) are shared. These classes are MFC-independent, and you can access them from any Visual C++ application.

  The `CString` class is rewritten as a shared class in Visual C++ .NET. The shared class is named `CStringT` and has advanced features, such as character manipulation and string searching. The original `CString` class is also available, but remember that it's MFC-dependent.

- **Unified event handling:** In Visual C++ 6.0, you had to implement event handling for native and COM classes in different ways. This is different for Visual C++ .NET, which implements the same event-handling method across all class types in Visual C++. This provides consistency in the methods to implement event handling in C++, COM, and managed classes.

- **Enhanced MFC classes:** Visual C++ .NET includes new MFC classes and functions that improve the existing MFC infrastructure. The new MFC classes help you edit Dynamic HyperText Markup Language (DHTML) components and create windowless controls. MFC also includes additional functions that enable you to accept date entries beyond the year 2038. Read about the use of MFC classes in programming in Book 4, Chapters 3 and 4.

- **Extended Class View:** The Class View is extended in Visual C++ .NET. As shown in Figure 1-1, the new Class View appears as a class tree like it did in Visual C++ 6.0. However, from the Class View in Visual C++ .NET, you can access code wizards to add member functions, member variables, and classes. You can also use the Class View to implement interfaces and add Performance Monitor objects and counters to your project.

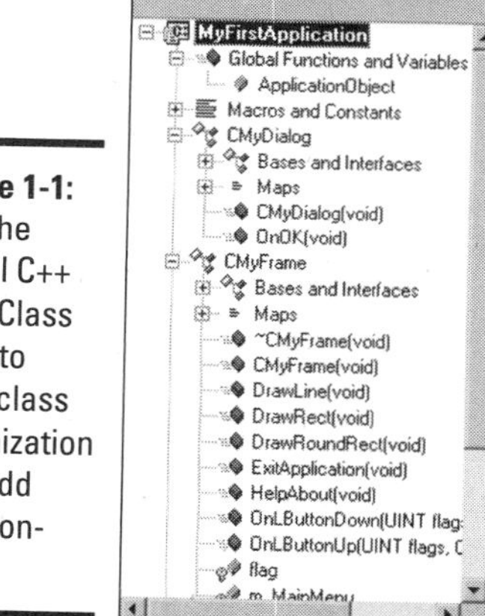

Figure 1-1: Use the Visual C++ .NET Class View to view class organization and add functionality.

Performance Monitor is a system analyzer with which you can determine the usage of system resources. This system analyzer comprises objects, such as `Processor` and `Memory`, and counters to these objects, such as `%User Time` and `Pages/sec`. You can use the information regarding the performance of system objects to analyze the performance of your computer and identify problems.

- **Integrated debugger:** Some basic debugging enhancements make debugging Visual C++ .NET applications a truly interesting experience. Whether you view a list of breakpoints in a docked window or use new compiler switches, the new debugger simplifies it all for you. Find out more about debugging and breakpoints in Book 4, Chapter 8.

In addition to these enhancements, Visual C++ .NET includes the following new features:

- **Programming with attributes:** Attributes are new to Visual C++ .NET. An *attribute* is a declaration that simplifies COM programming in Visual C++ .NET. When a compiler builds your application containing attributes, it considers the attributes as C++ keywords. When the compiler comes across these keywords, it inserts the appropriate code in the compiled file. For example, when you apply an `event_receiver` attribute to a class, the compiler uses this attribute to create an event sink for your class.

- **New ATL Server:** Visual C++ .NET includes the new ATL Server that enables you to create and deploy a wide range of applications on the Internet. ATL Server is a wonderful tool that you can use to develop Web applications and Web services because that's the primary focus of its functions. ATL Server also enables you to easily develop other applications, such as Simple Mail Transport Protocol (SMTP) mail applications. Find out more about ATL Server applications in Book 4, Chapter 5.
- **Compiler switches:** Visual C++ .NET includes compiler switches that enable you to easily switch compiling and debugging options. For example, while compiling your application, you can apply the `/clr` compiler switch to use or omit managed extensions for compiling your application. Similarly, you can turn the `/RTC` switch on to eliminate common coding errors before executing your application. Read through Book 4, Chapter 7 for more detail on compilation switches.

Managed extension enhancements

Managed extensions — synonymous with *managed applications* — bring Visual C++ .NET into the scope of the .NET Framework. Introducing managed extensions in C++ was necessary to enable C++ applications to easily access components from .NET compatible languages. The advantage of developing applications by using managed extensions is that these applications benefit from execution in the common language runtime (CLR) environment.

These application types use different classes, have distinct configuration settings, and often have unique functions. We recommend that you study them in more depth individually. To read about managed applications, peruse Book 4, Chapters 6 and 7. For more about the common language runtime, read Book 1, Chapter 2.

Managed extension brings the following enhancements to Visual C++ .NET:

- **Easy access to .NET Framework classes:** With managed extensions, you can access classes of the .NET Framework as simply as you access any other class of Visual C++.
- **Easy migration of the existing code:** Managed extensions enable you to easily migrate the existing code to the .NET Framework because your C++ application can support managed or unmanaged code. Instead of writing the code afresh for the .NET Framework, you can migrate your code incrementally to the .NET Framework, keeping your application running as the migration occurs.
- **Easy creation of applications in multiple languages:** Managed extensions provide support for the .NET Framework, thus offering an opportunity to create applications by using multiple programming languages. You can create a Web service in Visual C++ .NET and access it from a client application developed in Visual Basic .NET.

Exploring the Many Applications Creation Methods

In earlier sections of this chapter, you can read how to create seemingly similar applications by using different methods in Visual C++ .NET. For example, you can create a text editor by using native C++ functions, MFC classes, or managed extensions. This flexibility is an interesting feature of programming in Visual C++ .NET. But here's the feature that we like the best: You can create a program that uses a mix of managed classes and other classes of C++. Thus, you benefit from the .NET Framework while programming at ease in MFC.

In this section, we examine a Hello World application that's written in two ways — with managed extensions and with using conventional Visual C++ functions.

Hello World with managed extensions

Writing a Hello World application in managed extensions is simple. First look at the code for the application and what each statement in the code implies. The code for the application in managed extensions is

```
#include "stdafx.h"
#using <mscorlib.dll>
using namespace System;
int main(void)
{
    Console::WriteLine("Hello World from managed extensions
        in C++!!");
    return 0;
}
```

A description of each line of the preceding code is as follows:

✦ **The first line `#include "stdafx.h"` includes the `"stdafx.h"` file into your project.**

  This file builds a precompiled types file to compile and execute your code in a short time duration.

  If you build your application on the command prompt, you can omit the `#include "stdafx.h"` directive. However, your code runs faster when you use precompiled types provided by the `"stdafx.h"` file.

✦ **The second line `#using <mscorlib.dll>` imports a prebuilt type library that has the namespaces provided by managed extensions into your program.**

✦ **On the third line, the `using namespace System;` directive enables you to import the `system` namespace into your program.**

After importing the System namespace, you can use its classes without specifying their paths. (Get more information on namespaces in Book 1, Chapter 1.) For example, if you don't import the system namespace into your program, you have to write the Console::WriteLine statement as System.Console::WriteLine. Imagine how tedious this task becomes when you have 100 such statements in your code.

- **The main function of the program (Line 4) is the entry point for your application. The application executes and uses the WriteLine method of the Console class.**

  This method produces an output — *Hello World from managed extensions in C++!!* — at the command prompt.

Hello World without managed extensions

The conventional Hello World application in Visual C++ .NET isn't any different from the Hello World applications developed using Visual C++ 6.0. One such Hello World application is

```
#include "stdafx.h"
#include <stdio.h>
int _tmain(int argc, _TCHAR* argv[])
{
   printf("Hello World from the world of Visual
   C++!!");
   return 0;
}
```

This application uses the printf function defined in the stdio.h header file to produce the output — *Hello World from the world of Visual C++!!* — at the command prompt.

Although you can achieve similar outputs by using two different types of applications developed in Visual C++ .NET, your preference of programming using managed extensions and unmanaged code depends entirely upon the interoperability and manageability requirements of your application.

Apart from the two applications that we discuss here, Visual C++ .NET gives you the ability to create many others, including ATL, MFC, and managed projects.

Exploring Project Templates in Visual C++ .NET

Visual C++ .NET offers you many project types. Choose File⇨New⇨Project, and check out all the project templates in the Visual C++ Projects section of New Project dialog box that appears. (See Figure 1-2.)

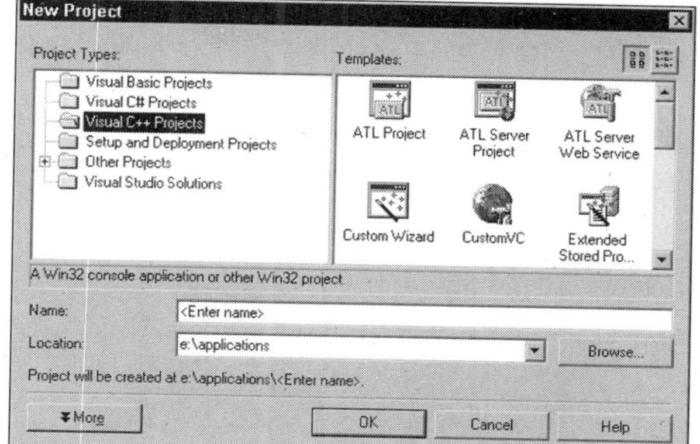

Figure 1-2: Choices, choices: So many Visual C++ .NET application templates.

The Visual C++ .NET project types are categorized into three projects: ATL projects, MFC projects, and managed extensions projects. All these projects are available as project templates. (Project templates are similar to Microsoft Word templates with predefined styles from which you create a document.) Apart from the project templates are some templates that really don't fall into any category.

ATL projects

The three ATL project templates in Visual C++ .NET are

- **ATL Project:** Use this template to create a project that uses Active Template Library. The project uses ATL classes that simplify writing COM objects that are small in size and fast in execution.
- **ATL Server Project:** Use this template to create Web applications that use ATL Server.
- **ATL Server Web Service:** Use this template to create Web services by using ATL Server. This project template includes the same wizard that the ATL Server Project template uses. However, the wizards differ in their configuration settings.

You can read about ATL projects in Book 4, Chapter 5.

MFC projects

Just like ATL projects, Visual C++ .NET has three project templates for MFC applications. These templates are

- **MFC Application:** Use the MFC Application template to create a wide range of Windows applications. The names of the applications that you create by the wizard are pretty self-explanatory.
  - Dialog-based applications
  - Form-based applications
  - Explorer style applications
  - Web browser style applications
  - Database access applications

  Find more on MFC applications in Book 4, Chapter 3.
- **MFC DLL:** Use the MFC DLL template project to create a dynamic link library (DLL) that can be used to share one or more functions in multiple applications. (Of course, you wouldn't create a DLL for sharing one function!)
- **MFC ActiveX Control:** You can group a set of controls into an ActiveX control and use it as a unit in your projects. Create such an ActiveX control from the MFC ActiveX control template.
- **MFC ISAPI Extension Dll:** The MFC ISAPI Extension Dll project creates an Internet Information Server (IIS) API extension (ISAPI extension). An ISAPI extension is installed in IIS and responds to HTTP requests from client computers.

Managed projects

The following managed extensions-based project templates are available in Visual C++ .NET:

- **Managed C++ Empty Project:** The Managed C++ Empty Project template creates an empty project with configuration settings necessary to compile a Visual C++ application in the managed environment. Use this project when you want to port your existing Visual C++ application to the managed environment.
- **Managed C++ Application:** This template creates a managed application that can execute in the .NET Framework environment.
- **Managed C++ Class Library:** Just like you can create a MFC DLL that can be used in multiple applications, you can create a class library by using the Managed C++ Application template and use it across applications. This template is different from the template for the MFC DLL because a class library created by using the Managed C++ Class Library template runs in the managed environment.

- **Managed C++ Web Service:** As the name suggests, the Managed C++ Web Service template helps you create a Web service by using managed extensions for Visual C++ .NET.

Other project templates

Visual C++ .NET also includes some project templates used for creating applications that don't utilize ATL, MFC, or managed extensions. These project templates are used for two reasons. First, because they're based on native C++ libraries, you can create varied applications. Second, because you code most of the functionality of the program, you've more control over your project, getting exactly what you want. These application templates are

- **Win32 Project:** Use the Win32 Project template to create command prompt applications, Windows applications, DLLs, and static libraries. This template enables you to build an application by beginning from scratch, adding the required functionality to fit your application needs.
- **Custom Wizard:** Use the Custom Wizard template to create your own wizards. With this template, you can create those easy-to-use wizards that you frequently encounter in different applications, such as your own Visual Studio .NET application.
- **Makefile Project:** If you're one of those adventurous developers who prefer programming from the command prompt, you must specify build settings for your application for Visual C++ .NET IDE to recognize the application. To specify these settings, you use the Makefile project template.
- **Extended Stored Procedure Dll:** An Extended Stored Procedure Dll project creates a stored procedure to be executed on a SQL Server. An extended stored procedure is similar to a SQL Server stored procedure, but the extended procedure uses Windows APIs. In addition, an extended stored procedure runs optimally because it runs as a separate process. This is in contrast to an ordinary stored procedure, which runs along with the SQL Server in the same process.

Chapter 2: Creating Good Old Windows Applications

In This Chapter

- Creating a window
- Adding a menu
- Displaying dialog boxes
- Painting the screen

Windows applications run on a standalone computer. Whatever resources a Windows application needs should be available on the computer on which the application is installed. Windows applications can be as simple as a blank window that a user stares at or as complex as a complete development suite. Most of the applications that you run on your computer are Windows applications. Also, it is relatively easy to install and use Windows applications because they often don't need any additional resources such as connectivity to the Internet or databases. To create a Windows application of any complexity, you must first know the basics of creating an application.

Visual Studio .NET provides an easy way to create Windows applications. All that it takes to create a window is to open a project template and write a few lines of code. In this chapter, we walk you through creating a Windows application by using the Win32 Project template. We also give you the lowdown on how to add functionality to your application, such as using menus and dialog boxes. Check out the end of the chapter for a quick lesson on finger-painting . . . um, we mean screen painting. (Smocks are optional.)

Creating a Window

Face it: The Windows interface is based on windows. These helpful little critters are everywhere. Application designers like them because they're easy to create and easy to adapt to specific functionality needs. Users like windows because they offer lots of useful tools, such as instructions, warnings, and connect-the-dot kinds of tools to make choices (radio buttons and check boxes) or enter information (text boxes). In a window, users can control an application and switch from one application to another. In a nutshell, a window is the boundary in which your application runs.

In this section, we take you through the steps to create a window. The window that you create in this section, and subsequently the application that you finally turn out with, can be downloaded from `http://www.dummies.com/extras/VS.NETAllinOne`. The name of the application is MyFirstApplication. If you hang with us to the end of this section, you'll have a window that's displayed on the screen when a user executes your application. Hey — ya gotta start somewhere, right?

Launching a new project

To create a window from scratch, you use the Win32 Project template. The steps for launching a new project are

1. **Launch the Microsoft Visual Studio .NET development environment.**

   The start page of Visual Studio .NET appears.

   If you've changed the settings of the development environment, it may open the project that you most recently created. Not to worry: You can work within that project just as well as in a new one.

2. **To create a new project, choose File⇨New⇨Project or press Ctrl+Shift+N.**

   The New Project dialog box appears.

   If you have an existing project open when you create a new one, the existing project automatically closes as your new project is created.

3. **In the New Project dialog box, click Visual C++ Projects (from the Project Types list) and then click the Win32 Project icon in the Templates box.**

   See Figure 2-1.

   Just like the Win32 application wizard, you have other application wizards in Visual C++.NET for different application types. To create another type of application, you would select one of the other icons in the Templates box.

4. **Still in the New Project dialog box, enter the name** MyFirstApplication **for your project in the Name text box and then click OK.**

   You can also specify a new location for your project in the Location text box or click the Browse button to navigate to a new location.

   The Win32 Project template launches the Win32 Application Wizard. This wizard has two sections — the Overview section and the Application Settings section — as shown in Figure 2-2. We refer to these sections as the wizard screens.

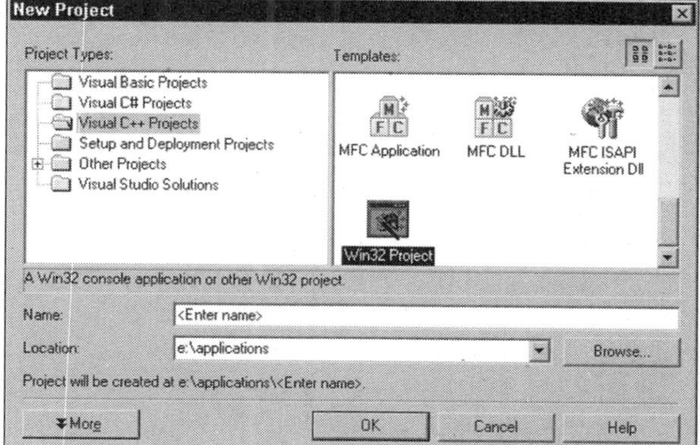

Figure 2-1: Begin to create a window here.

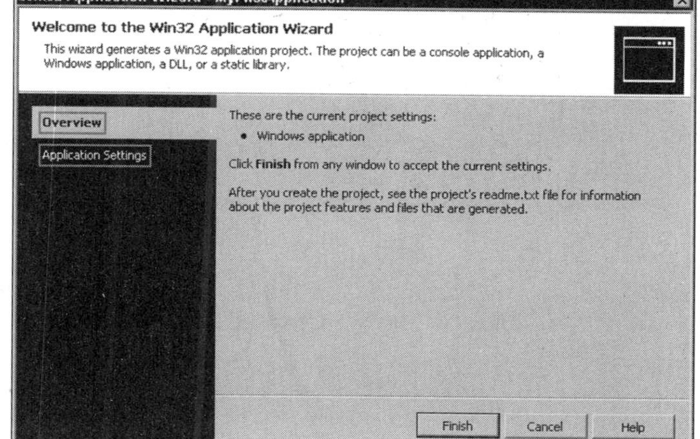

Figure 2-2: Use the Win32 Application Wizard to help you create a window.

5. **Click Application Settings to specify the type of application.**

   The Application Settings wizard screen opens. (See Figure 2-3.) Here you specify the type of application that you want to create. (Read through Book 4, Chapter 1 for a discussion on application types.) For a Windows application, you select the Windows application radio button. However, we will create a Windows application by using a blank project so that you can understand the code that goes into creating the application.

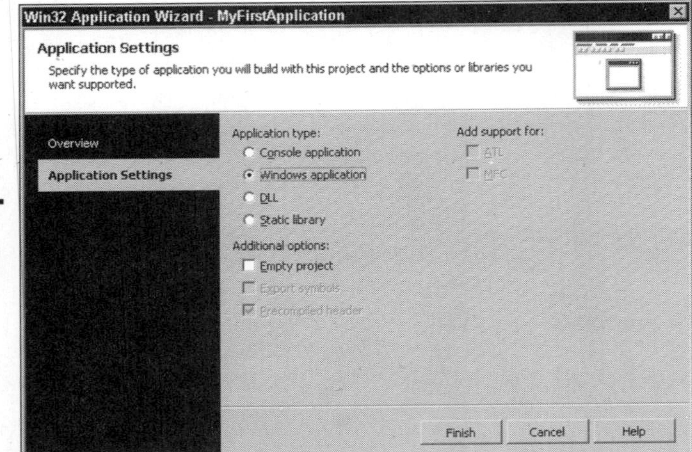

Figure 2-3: Specify the application type from the Application Settings page.

6. **Select the Empty Project check box to create a blank project and click the Finish button.**

   The Empty Project option creates a project that has no code or source files added to it. If you don't select Empty Project, the application wizard adds the code necessary to create a blank window.

When you click Finish, the application wizard creates a blank project for you. You are now ready to code a new Windows application right from scratch.

Creating classes for your application

After you open your new project, you need to give it a little class: that is, add some classes to it. You need to derive a class from the `CFrameWnd` class, which gives you the power to create a window for an application. The class has all the necessary message handlers and functions to control messages that are directed to a window.

To add a class in your project that's derived from the `CFrameWnd` class, perform the following steps:

1. **Choose Project⇨Add Class.**

   The Add Class dialog box appears.

   In the title bar of this dialog box, notice that the project name is appended to the title. In this example, the dialog box title is Add Class - MyFirstApplication. See Figure 2-4.

2. **From the Add Class - MyFirstApplication dialog box, click the Generic C++ Class icon and then click the Open button.**

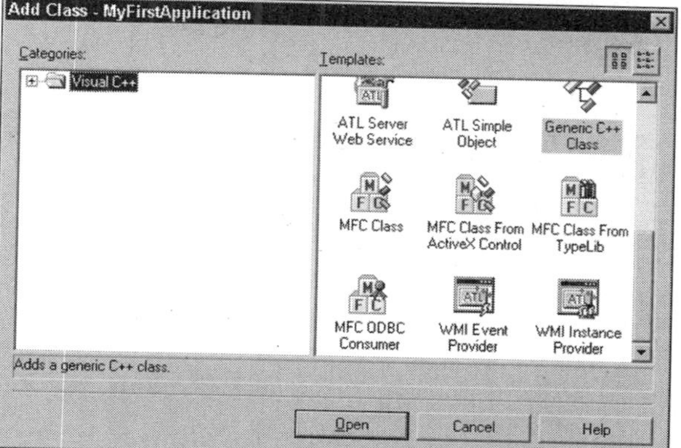

Figure 2-4: The Add Class dialog box shows the types of classes that you can add to your project.

The Generic C++ Class Wizard dialog box appears, as shown in Figure 2-5.

The Generic C++ Class is a common class that you can include in any project and give a desired functionality.

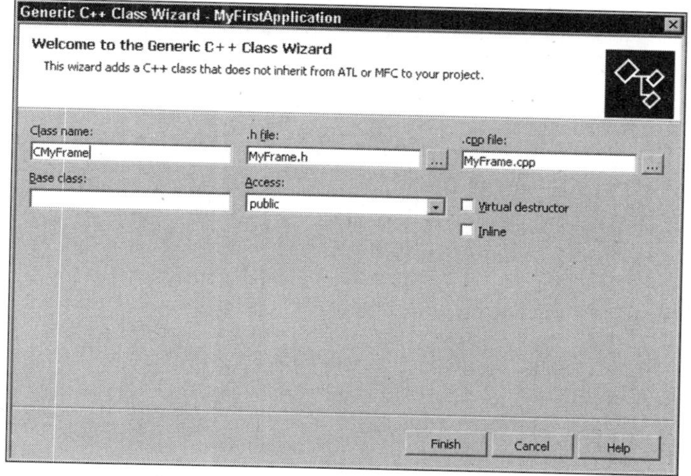

Figure 2-5: Specify the class name, and the wizard specifies the header and CPP file names.

3. **In the Generic C++ Class Wizard dialog box, enter the class name** CMyFrame **in the Class Name text box.**

   Check this out: As you type **CMyFrame** in the Class Name text box, the name of the header and CPP files appear automatically in the dialog box's `.h` file and `.cpp` file text boxes, respectively. These names are taken from the name of the class after excluding the first C in the class name. For example, if you enter **CMyFrame.h** as the name of the class, the name of the header file becomes MyFrame.h.

4. **In the Base Class text box, enter the name** CFrameWnd **and click the Finish button.**

   The class wizard creates and opens the header and CPP files for your project. You are back to your project, with the header and CPP files open. Notice that the constructor and destructor for your class are already declared in the header file. That's half your job done! All you need to do is to implement the functionality for these in the CPP file.

5. **Select the MyFrame.cpp file from the project workspace.**

   If you can't find the MyFrame.cpp file, locate and open it from the Solution Explorer under the Source Files option. (You can access the Solution Explorer from the View menu.)

6. **Change the code for the constructor of your class in the MyFrame.cpp file.**

   The changed code should read like this:

```
CMyFrame::CMyFrame(void)
{
    Create(NULL,"Sample Window");
}
```

The `Create` function used in the code example above creates a window and attaches it to the `CFrameWnd` object. (You will create an object of the `CFrameWnd`-derived class in the next set of tasks later in this section.) The `Create` function takes the following two parameters:

- **A null-terminated string with the name of the Windows class.**

  If you specify the value `NULL`, as we do in the code example above, the predefined attributes in the `CFrameWnd` class are used. Therefore, you no longer need to specify how your Window should look or what mouse pointer it should use. Makes our job simpler!

- **The name that appears in the title bar of the window.**

  For example, `Sample Window` appears as the caption of your window when you run your application.

After deriving a class from the `CFrameWnd` class, you need to derive a class from the `CWinApp`. After the `CFrameWnd`-derived class creates your window, the `CWinApp` class displays it to the user. The `CWinApp` class includes an `InitInstance` method that initializes your application the first time that it's run. You then override the `InitInstance` method to create a window object for your application and then display it to the user.

To derive a class from the `CWinApp` class, you use the Class Wizard as you derive a class from `CFrameWnd`. The only differences in these steps are that you

- Specify CWinApp as the base class.
- Specify CMyWindow as the class name for the derived class.

When you create the CMyWindow class, it's defined in the MyWindow.h and the MyWindow.cpp files.

After deriving your class from CWinApp, override the InitInstance function of the CWinApp class. The InitInstance function initializes your application when your program is run. To override the InitInstance function:

1. **Declare the InitInstance function in the MyWindow.h header file.**

   You declare the InitInstance function in the header file of the CWinApp-derived class. For example, substitute the code in your MyWindow.h header file with the following:

   ```
   #pragma once
   #include "afxwin.h"

   class CMyWindow :
      public CWinApp
   {
   public:
      BOOL InitInstance();
   };
   ```

   In the above code, we remove the declarations for the constructor and destructor of the class because we don't need to define them. In addition, we add the declaration for the InitInstance function.

2. **Override the InitInstance function in the MyWindow.cpp file.**

   You override the InitInstance function in the CPP file of the CWinApp-derived class. The code for the InitInstance function is

   ```
   BOOL CMyWindow::InitInstance()
   {
      CMyFrame *MyFrameObject;
      MyFrameObject = new CMyFrame;
      m_pMainWnd=MyFrameObject;
      MyFrameObject->ShowWindow(SW_SHOWMAXIMIZED);
      return TRUE;
   }
   ```

   In the code given above, we create an object of the CMyFrame class. Next, we associate the m_pMainWnd member variable of the CWinApp-derived class with this object. (We discuss the implementation of the code given above immediately after we complete coding our window.) However, the CMyWindow class can't recognize the CMyFrame class unless the two are declared together. To remedy this, include the CFrameWnd-derived class file (MyFrame.h) into the CWinApp-derived class file so that your application can recognize the CMyFrame class in the CMyWindow class.

3. **Specify the following statement just before the `InitInstance` function in the MyWindow.cpp file:**

   ```
   #include "MyFrame.h"
   ```

4. **Create an object of the `CWinApp`-derived class by specifying the following code at the end of the MyWindow.cpp file:**

   ```
   CMyWindow ApplicationObject;
   ```

   When you run the program, the object is created and the `InitInstance` function is invoked to display a window on the screen.

You're done with your application. Before you run the application, revisit the `InitInstance` function that we define in Step 2 above. In the new definition of the `InitInstance` function, you create an instance of the `CFrameWnd`-derived class (`MyFrame` in our case). Next, you assign this object to the `m_pMainWnd` member variable of the `CWinApp`-derived class. The `m_pMainWnd` member variable points to your application's window as long as you don't close the window.

Finally, you use the `ShowWindow` method of the `CFrameWnd` class to display the window. The function has one parameter: `nCmdShow`. A value of `SW_SHOWMAXIMIZED` for this parameter shows the window in a maximized state, filling your entire screen.

Give different values to the `nCmdShow` parameter and your windows will appear in different sizes. For example, `SW_MINIMIZE` minimizes your window after displaying it. Some other values are `SW_SHOWNORMAL` and `SW_SHOWRESTORE`.

Compiling and running your application

After you create your application, compile it and run it. The `CWinApp` and `CFrameWnd` classes require the MFC library for execution. You need to change the project settings to enable the compiler to use these libraries. Changing the compilation settings is easy. Follow these steps, and you're on your way to running your first application.

MFC library is a collection of classes and data types that are available to any application that uses the library. Because CWinApp and CFrameWnd are a part of the MFC library, you need to add the library to your application.

1. **In Solution Explorer, under the name of the solution, right-click MyFirstApplication (which is the name of your project) and click Properties in the shortcut menu.**

   If Solution Explorer isn't visible, open it by clicking View⇨Solution Explorer.

   The MyFirstApplication Property Pages dialog box appears.

2. **In the MyFirstApplication Property Pages dialog box, click the Use MFC in a Shared DLL option from the Use of MFC list, as shown in Figure 2-6.**

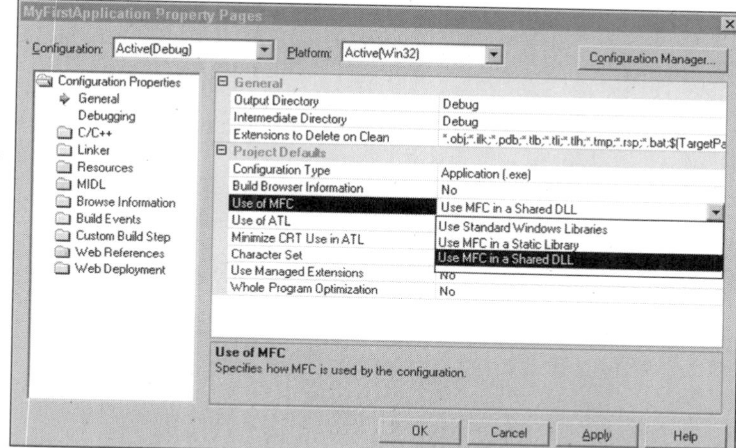

Figure 2-6: The property pages for your project allow you to specify a number of options.

After you select the option to use MFC libraries, these libraries are available to the compiler and linker when your application is compiled and executed.

After the compiler compiles your application, a linker links your application to the runtime files necessary to run your application, so that your application can execute successfully.

3. **Click OK to close the MyFirstApplication Property Pages dialog box.**

After changing the project properties, compile the application by choosing Build➪Build Solution (or press Ctrl+Shift+B). The Output window appears and notifies you of any errors. After compiling your application, choose Debug➪Start (or press F5).

Even if you start your application before compiling it, Visual Studio .NET will prompt you to build your application, after which the application will automatically execute. Therefore, pressing start to run your application even when you haven't compiled it is the quicker way.

The first window that you create in Visual C++ .NET appears on the screen: It will look like the one shown in Figure 2-7 (unless you've outwitted us by adding some advanced programming code).

Figure 2-7: Your first window fills the screen.

Rather sparse, isn't it? Add some functional elements to it quick, before folks start calling you Mother Hubbard.

Adding a Menu

Use the Visual C++ .NET Resource Editor to add resources to your project. Any bitmap, cursor, dialog box, menu, or toolbar that you add to your project is a *resource*. After you add a resource file to your project, you create a menu. When you finish creating the menu, attach it to your application programmatically. In this section, we show you how to do both.

Adding resources and creating a menu

To create a menu for your application, you add a new resource file to your application and then create a menu within the resource file. Perform the following steps to create a menu for your application:

1. **Choose Project⇨Add Resource.**

   The Add Resource dialog box appears; see Figure 2-8.

   An easy way to add a resource to your project is to right-click the project in Solution Explorer. From the shortcut menu, choose Add⇨Add Resource.

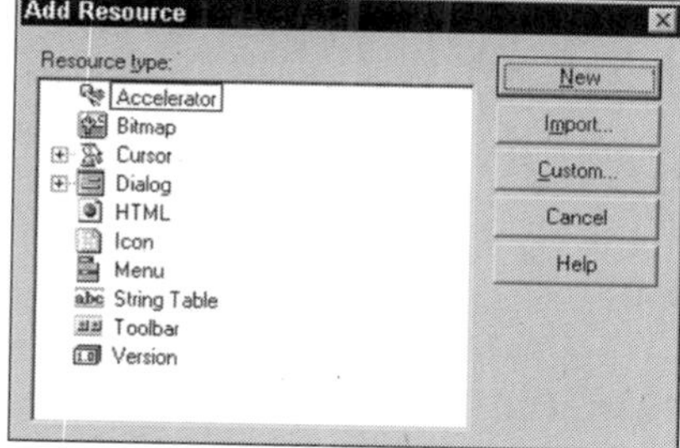

Figure 2-8: Choose resources from the Add Resource dialog box.

2. **In the Add Resource dialog box, select the Menu icon and then click the New button to create a new menu.**

   The Resource View appears. In this view, all the resources of your project are listed. As shown in Figure 2-9, a new menu appears in this view. You build on this menu by adding menu names and menu options.

   Notice the text box with the text `Type Here` (left-hand side): Here you enter the first menu name.

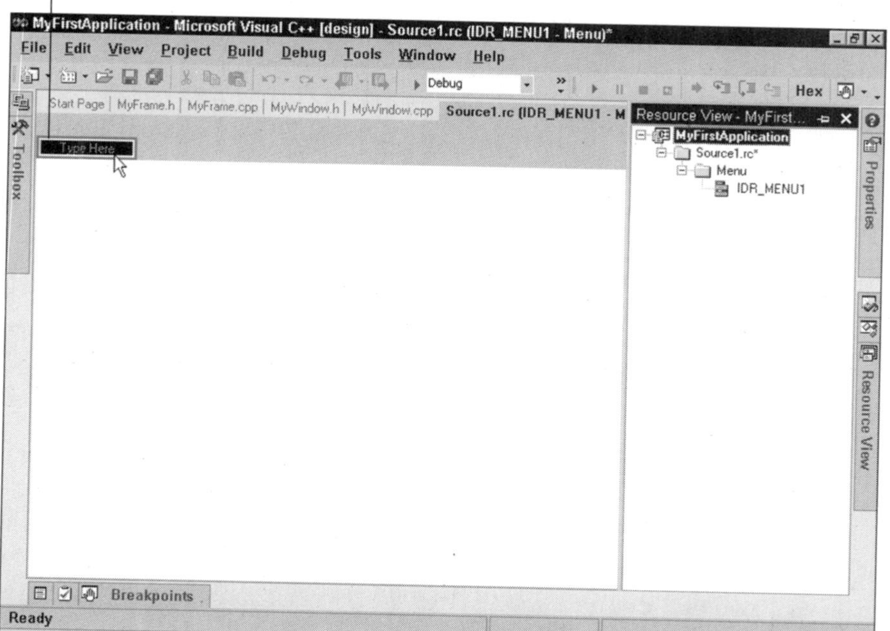

Figure 2-9: Building your menu.

3. **Click the text box containing** `Type Here` **and enter (type in)** File**, which represents the first menu.**

   As you type the word *File*, note that two new text boxes emerge from the new File menu — one to the right of it and one below it — as shown in Figure 2-10. The one to the right is the next menu item and the one below File is the menu option.

   In the menu that we're creating for our application, we have three menus: File, Insert, and Help. The File menu has one menu option: Exit.

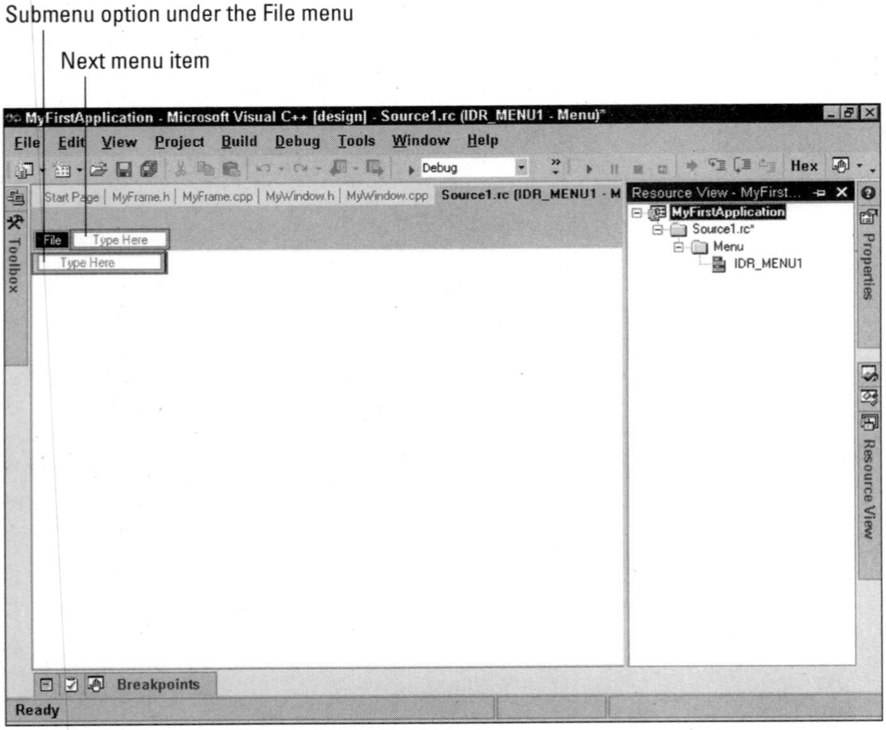

Submenu option under the File menu

Next menu item

Figure 2-10: After you specify the first menu name, text boxes appear for other menu names and options.

4. **Enter** Exit **for the name of the File menu option; make sure that you use the text box below where you see** `File`**.**

   Just as you create the first menu (File), you can create other menu names. In this example, add two more menu names — Help and Insert. Add About My Application as the only menu option for the Help menu. For the Insert menu, add Line, Rectangle, and Rounded Rectangle as the menu options. See Figure 2-11 to see how the menu looks.

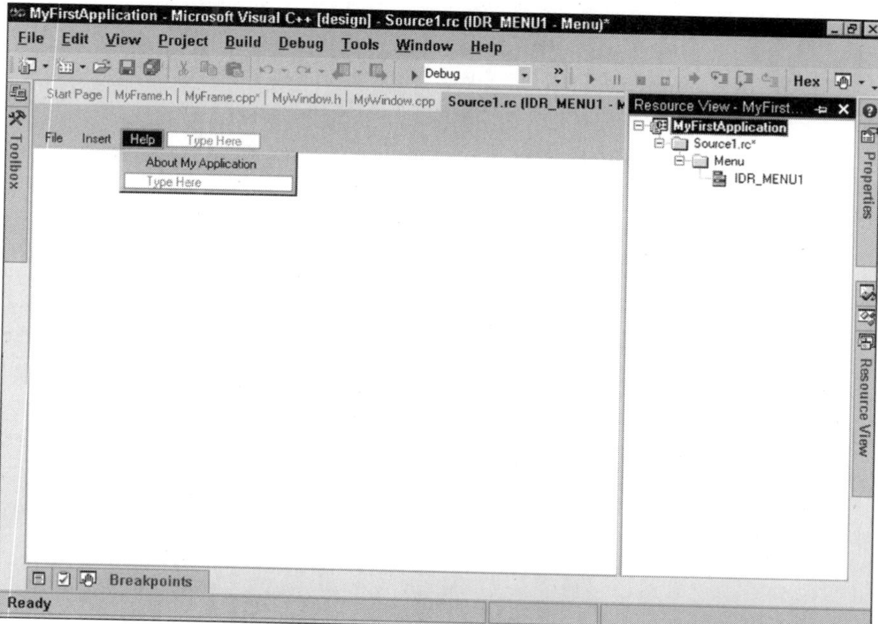

Figure 2-11: A menu with File, Insert, and Help menu items.

To make it easy to code the menu handlers for the Rounded Rectangle and About My Application menu options, we have changed the ID of these menu options to ID_INSERT_ROUND_RECTANGLE and ID_HELP_ABOUT respectively. You can change the name of these menu options by selecting the menu options and pressing F4 to open the Properties window. In the Properties window, you can change the ID of the menu option in the ID field.

5. **When you add all the menu items that you want, attach it to your application.**

   See the next section to learn how to attach a menu to an application.

   Only after you attach a menu is it visible when your application executes.

Attaching a menu

To attach a menu to your application, you use the `CMenu` class. The `CMenu` class represents the top-level menu and menu options. Follow these steps to attach the menu to your application:

1. **Declare a pointer to the `CMenu` class in the `CFrameWnd`-derived class (`CMyFrame`).**

   The following code snippet declares a protected pointer to the `CMyFrame` class in the `MyFrame.h` header file.

A protected pointer is accessible only within the class or from classes that are derived from the class in which the pointer is declared. On the other hand, a regular pointer can be accessed from any class.

```
protected: CMenu *m_MainMenu;
```

2. **In the constructor of the `CMyFrame` class, instantiate the `CMenu` object and call its `LoadMenu` function to load the menu.**

   The `LoadMenu` function of the `CMenu` class accepts the resource ID of the menu as a parameter. The resource ID is an integer. To convert it into a type that's recognizable by the `LoadMenu` function, you use the `MAKEINTRESOURCE` macro. The complete code of the constructor of the `CMyFrame` class, which you need to write in the MyFrame.cpp file, is

```
CMyFrame::CMyFrame(void)
{
    Create(NULL,"Sample Window");
    m_MainMenu= new CMenu;
    m_MainMenu->LoadMenu(MAKEINTRESOURCE(IDR_MENU1));
    SetMenu(m_MainMenu);
}
```

   In the code given above, the ID of the menu is `IDR_MENU1`. You can find this name in Resource View; refer to Figure 2-11.

After you insert the above code for the menu, your menu is visible when you run your application. However, notice that all menu options are disabled. To enable all menu options, add a few lines of code, which we give you in the steps immediately preceding the section "Displaying Dialog Boxes."

Defining message maps

All the menu options in your application are disabled because you don't yet have message maps defined for any menu option. *Message maps* join Windows messages to functions that handle these messages for your application. They serve as a link between functions in your application and the Windows messages for each user interaction. To trap the menu options (record the menu options clicked by the user) that a user clicks, you need to define message maps.

Adding message maps to your application involves two steps: declaring the message map by using the DECLARE_MESSAGE_MAP directive, and defining the message maps by using the BEGIN_MESSAGE_MAP directive. To declare message maps for your application, follow this sequence of steps:

1. **Declare the message map by using the `DECLARE_MESSAGE_MAP` macro at the end of your `CFrameWnd`-derived class.**

   There is no semicolon (;) after the message map declaration.

2. **Define the message map by using the `BEGIN_MESSAGE_MAP` macro.**

   You define the message map outside the class. This macro accepts two parameters: the name of the derived class and the name of the parent class. In our example, the two parameters are `CMyFrame` and `CFrameWnd`, respectively.

3. **Define the message map entries.**

   Message map entries can be generated for Windows messages (such as mouse clicks) or for application messages (such as clicking menu options). The message map entries for the two are slightly different:

   - For **Windows messages**, you specify the keyword `ON_WM_` followed by the action. For a left mouse button click, for example, specify `ON_WM_LBUTTONDOWN` as the message map.
   - For **messages generated when you click controls in applications**, the message map entries take the `ON_COMMAND` macro. This macro associates the ID of a control to a member function of the class for the message map. For example, to associate the Exit option in the File menu with a `ExitApplication` function, specify the message map entry as `ON_COMMAND(ID_FILE_EXIT, ExitApplication)`.

4. **End the definition of message map by specifying the `END_MESSAGE_MAP` macro.**

To define message maps, you need to know the IDs of each menu option. You can find these by right-clicking a menu item that you're creating in the menu editor and selecting Properties from the shortcut menu that appears. When you do so, the Properties window for the control appears. The control ID appears in the ID field of this window. As we continue our example, we add message maps to our application.

Adding message maps

After you define a message map, you need to add it to your application.

1. **Declare the message map in the region below the keyword public of the MyFrame.h file and also declare all the functions that you need to implement in your class.**

   For more on declaring a message map, see the earlier section "Defining message maps."

   The following code snippet declares the message maps and the required functions. These functions are the functions that will be invoked when the user selects menu options. For example, the `ExitApplication()` function will be invoked when the user selects the File⇨Edit option.

   ```
   void ExitApplication();
   void DrawLine();
   ```

```
void DrawRect();
void DrawRoundRect();
void HelpAbout();
DECLARE_MESSAGE_MAP()
```

2. **Create the message map for all menu options by specifying the following code outside your class in the MyFrame.cpp file:**

```
BEGIN_MESSAGE_MAP(CMyFrame, CFrameWnd)
ON_COMMAND(ID_FILE_EXIT,ExitApplication)
    ON_COMMAND(ID_INSERT_LINE,DrawLine)
    ON_COMMAND(ID_INSERT_RECTANGLE,DrawRect)
    ON_COMMAND(ID_INSERT_ROUND_RECTANGLE,DrawRoundRect)
    ON_COMMAND(ID_HELP_ABOUT,HelpAbout)
END_MESSAGE_MAP()
```

You can type the above code in the MyFrame.cpp file but don't enclose it in any function. Also, while typing the code, don't place a semicolon after the message map entries.

3. **Include the resource header file into your project by specifying the following line of code in the `MyFrame.h` header file:**

```
#include "resource.h"
```

Almost done. If you just can't resist the urge to run your application and see how your menu looks, you must define each function to handle menu options. For the time being, until we finish the next two sections, you can create blank functions for handling each menu option.

4. **Declare blank functions for all menu handlers, one below the other, in the MyFrame.cpp file in the same manner as mentioned below:**

```
void CMyFrame::ExitApplication()
{
}
```

All menu options in your application are now enabled. Run the application and check out your menu handiwork.

After you write the code for these functions, it's time to move on to displaying dialog boxes and painting the client area of the window.

Displaying Dialog Boxes

MFC provides a `CDialog` class that needs to be associated with all dialog boxes in your application. A dialog box is a resource; to read about resources, see the earlier section "Adding a Menu." It stands to reason that you create a dialog box in Resource Editor and then attach it to your application. In this section, we help you create a dialog box for a Help➪About menu and attach it to your project by using the `CDialog` class.

Creating the dialog box

To create a dialog box, perform these simple steps:

1. **Choose Project⇨Add Resource.**

   The Add Resource dialog box appears. (Refer to Figure 2-8.)

2. **In the Add Resource dialog box, select Dialog and click the New button.**

   A new dialog box is created for your project and it is assigned an ID, which is the word IDD_Dialog followed by a number that is obtained by adding one to the number of dialog boxes already present in your application.

3. **Access the Toolbox by choosing View⇨Toolbox or by pressing Ctrl+Alt+X.**

   You can skip this step if the Toolbox is already visible.

4. **Place controls on the dialog box to describe your application.**

   In this step, use your creativity to name your dialog box as descriptively as possible. For the sake of simplicity, we add a `Static Text` control to our dialog box and specify its caption — `My First Application for Learning Visual C++ .NET`. We also remove the Cancel button by selecting the button and pressing the Delete key because a Help⇨About dialog box does not need the Cancel button. Finally, we resize the dialog box by dragging its corners to remove the blank space on the dialog box. The completed dialog box is shown in Figure 2-12.

You can also change the caption of the Help⇨About dialog box. To do so, click the dialog box and press F4 to open the Properties window. In the Properties window, change the text that appears in the Caption property.

After you create your dialog box, you need to attach it to your application.

Creating a class for the dialog box

The dialog box that we create in the previous section is a modal dialog box. A *modal dialog box* doesn't allow a user to perform any other action in the application while the dialog box is visible onscreen. Thus, the user has to close the dialog box before he or she proceeds with the application.

You can also create a modeless dialog box. When these are displayed onscreen, the user can work with other features of the application. For example, the Find and Replace dialog box that appears in a Microsoft Word application is a modeless dialog box.

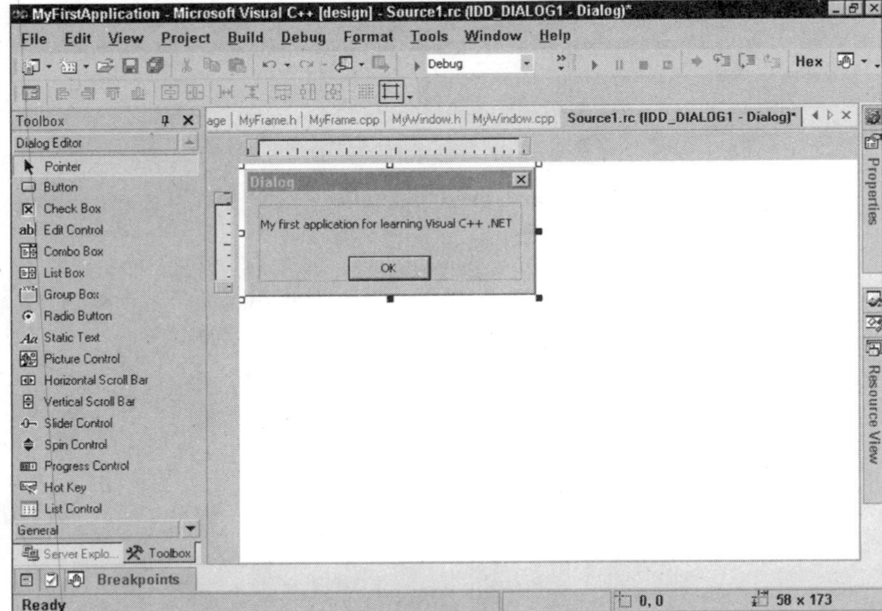

Figure 2-12: The completed dialog box for the Help⇨About My Application menu option.

To display a modal dialog box, you first create a class for your dialog box. The class is derived from the `CDialog` class. To create the class for your dialog box, perform these steps:

1. **Open Solution Explorer by choosing View⇨Solution Explorer.**
2. **Right-click the name of the application (MyFirstApplication) and choose Add⇨Add Class from the shortcut menu.**

   The Add Class - MyFirstApplication dialog box appears.
3. **In the Add Class - MyFirstApplication dialog box, select Generic C++ Class and click the Open button.**

   The Generic C++ Class Wizard for the application appears.
4. **Enter** CMyDialog **in the Class Name text box.**
5. **Enter** Enter **in the Base Class text box.**

   The completed Generic C++ Class Wizard - MyFirstApplication dialog box is shown in Figure 2-13.
6. **Click the Finish button to create the** `CMyDialog` **class.**

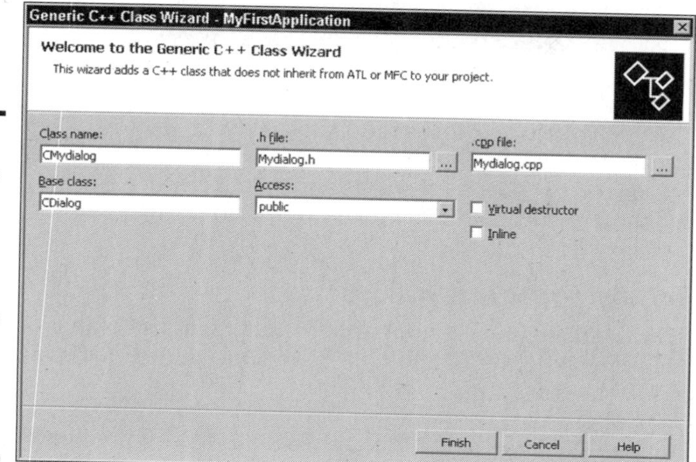

Figure 2-13: The Generic C++ Class Wizard - MyFirst-Application dialog box is also used to add a class for your dialog box.

7. **Change the header file of the `CMyDialog` class (MyDialog.h) to match the following code:**

```
#pragma once
#include "afxwin.h"
#include "resource.h"

class CMyDialog :
    public CDialog
{
public:
    CMyDialog():CDialog(IDD_DIALOG1)
    {
    }
    void OnOK();
    DECLARE_MESSAGE_MAP()
};
```

In the code given above, we overload the constructor of the `CDialog` class with the ID of the dialog box as the parameter. We also declare the message map for the `CMyDialog` class.

8. **In the CPP file of the `CMyDialog` class (MyDialog.cpp), change the code to match the following code:**

```
#include "mydialog.h"

BEGIN_MESSAGE_MAP(CMyDialog,CDialog)
   ON_COMMAND(IDOK,OnOK)
END_MESSAGE_MAP()

void CMyDialog::OnOK()
{
```

```
        EndDialog(TRUE);
    }
```

In the above code, when the user clicks OK, the `EndDialog` function of the `CDialog` class closes the dialog box.

Your dialog box is now ready to be shown onscreen. Read on to discover how to show the dialog box in your application.

Showing the dialog box

To show the dialog box in your application, create an object of the `CMyDialog` class and call its `DoModal` member function. Follow these steps to display the dialog box:

1. **Include the MyDialog.h header file into the MyFrame.CPP file by specifying the following statement:**

   ```
   #include "MyDialog.h"
   ```

   The dialog box needs to appear when the user chooses Help⇨About My Application. The function for handling this menu option is `HelpAbout`. Therefore, write the code for displaying the dialog box in this function.

2. **Write the following code in the `HelpAbout` function in the MyFrame.cpp file:**

   ```
   void CMyFrame::HelpAbout()
   {
       CMyDialog a;
       a.DoModal();
   }
   ```

   In the above code, you're creating an object of the `CMyDialog` class and calling its `DoModal` function.

The dialog box is now ready to be displayed. Before you run the application, you need to write the code for the File⇨Exit function. Insert the following function in the MyFrame.cpp file for exiting the application:

```
void CMyFrame::ExitApplication()
{
    exit(0);
}
```

Execute the application. The File⇨Exit and Help⇨About My Application menu options are now functional. The dialog box that you create for the Help⇨About My Application menu option is shown in Figure 2-14.

Now you need to make the Insert menu functional. We jump into that right away, in the following "Painting the Screen" section.

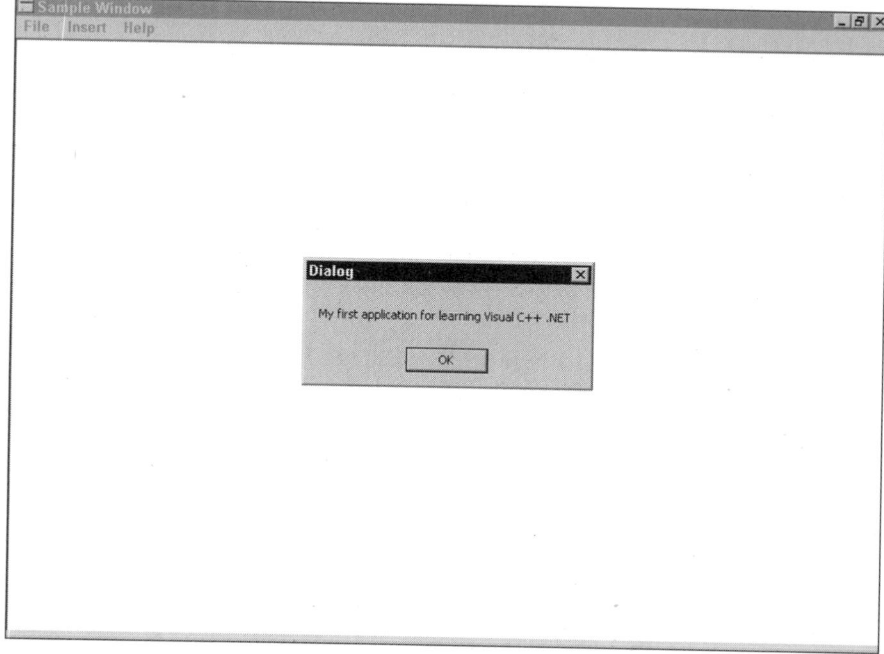

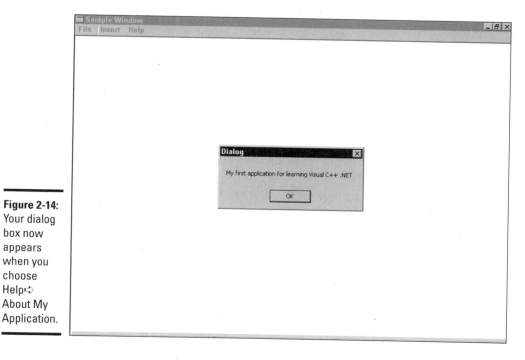

Figure 2-14: Your dialog box now appears when you choose Help➪About My Application.

Painting the Screen

Please don't start literally painting the screen after reading this section's title. That'll certainly be the end of this book and the end of your computer screen! In this section, you get the chance to explore the artiste inside you in a different manner. You can paint the screen in different colors, drawing all sorts of different shapes.

Instruments of drawing

MFC provides the `CDC` class for displaying the output of an application on the screen. The `CDC` class interacts with the *device context*, which is a Windows data structure with the required hardware information to output information on the screen.

The *device context* is a link between a Windows application, the device driver of an output device, and the output device. It takes care of issues related to the display of information, such as the available screen size and the screen resolution.

A number of classes are derived from the `CDC` class. We concentrate on the `CClientDC` class that you use to access the client area of our window: the drawing board.

Apart from the CClientDC class, MFC provides the CPen and the CBrush classes to draw shapes on the screen. (There are other drawing objects, such as CPalette and CBitmap, which are used for obtaining color palettes and fonts installed on the computer, but these are the ones we discuss here.)

When you draw figures on the screen, follow this sequence of steps:

1. **Create objects of the CPen and the CBrush class for drawing in the client area of the screen.**
2. **Create a brush by using the CreateSolidBrush function of the CBrush class.**
3. **Draw the shape by loading the brush into an object derived from the CClientDC class and using the LineTo, Rectangle, or RoundRect functions of the CClientDC class to create lines, rectangles, and rounded rectangles, respectively.**

We delve into these steps in detail, in the following section, "Drawing on the screen."

Drawing on the screen

After you create your drawing instruments, use the CBrush and the CClientDC classes to draw shapes in the client area of our window. Perform these steps:

1. **Declare the following variables in the protected region of the MyFrame.h header file:**

   ```
   CBrush *newBrush, *oldBrush;
   bool flag;
   int shape; //1=line, 2=rect, 3=circle
   POINT p1, p2;
   ```

   The flag variable is used to determine whether the user has clicked any menu option. When the user clicks a menu option, the shape variable identifies whether a line, rectangle, or round rectangle is to be drawn. Its value depends upon the menu option selected by the user. In addition, p1 and p2 are used to record the start point and the end point of the shapes.

2. **Add the following functions to the MyFrame.h header file:**

   ```
   void OnLButtonDown(UINT flags,CPoint Point1);
   void OnLButtonUp(UINT flags,CPoint Point2);
   ```

   These functions are used for responding to the events generated when a user clicks and releases the mouse. Our application draws onscreen from the point where the user clicks and up to the point where the user releases the mouse.

3. **In the message maps for the** `CMyFrame` **class (in the MyFrame.cpp file), add the following code:**

```
ON_WM_LBUTTONDOWN()
ON_WM_LBUTTONUP()
```

4. **In the MyFrame.cpp file, in the functions that respond to the Line, Rectangle, and Rounded Rectangle menu options, specify the following code:**

```
void CMyFrame::DrawLine()
{
    flag=true;
    shape=1;
}
void CMyFrame::DrawRect()
{
    flag=true;
    shape=2;
}
void CMyFrame::DrawRoundRect()
{
    flag=true;
    shape=3;
}
```

When the user selects a menu option from the Insert menu, the value of flag changes to `true`. When the user clicks the mouse in the client area of the window, the location where the user clicks needs to be assigned to the point `p1`.

5. **Specify the following code in the** `OnLButtonDown` **function (in the MyFrame.cpp file):**

```
void CMyFrame::OnLButtonDown(UINT flags,CPoint Point1)
{
    if (flag==true)
        p1=Point1;
}
```

6. **Specify the following code in the** `OnLButtonUp` **function:**

```
void CMyFrame::OnLButtonUp(UINT flags,CPoint Point2)
{
    if (flag==true)
    {
        CClientDC CurDC(this);
        //this pointer is the instance of a class
        //currently in use
        newBrush = new CBrush;
        oldBrush = new CBrush;
        newBrush->CreateSolidBrush(RGB(129,97,245));
        oldBrush=CurDC.SelectObject(newBrush);
```

```
        switch(shape)
        {
        case 1:
            CurDC.MoveTo(p1);
            CurDC.LineTo(Point2);
            flag=false;
            break;
        case 2:

CurDC.Rectangle(p1.x,p1.y,Point2.x,Point2.y);
            flag=false;
            break;
        case 3:

CurDC.RoundRect(p1.x,p1.y,Point2.x,Point2.y,17,17);
            flag=false;
            break;
        default:
                CurDC.MoveTo(p1);
                CurDC.LineTo(Point2);
                flag=false;
        }
        CurDC.SelectObject(oldBrush);
    }
}
```

Although the code above seems long, it's simple. All that you're doing is checking which menu option the user has clicked. Depending upon the menu option clicked, you are using a function to draw the shape on the screen. Some functions in the code above that deserve special mention are

- **`CreateSolidBrush`:** The `CreateSolidBrush` function uses the RGB (red, green, blue) macro to load a color into the brush. The color that we select is a shade of blue (`129,97,245`).
- **`SelectObject`:** The `SelectObject` function of the `CClientDC` class selects one object into the device context and discards the existing object of that type. In our application, this function loads the new brush and discards the existing brush, which is stored in the `oldBrush` object so that it can be loaded back after we're through with our work.
- **`MoveTo`:** The `MoveTo` function moves the device context to the desired start position of the line.
- **`LineTo`:** The `LineTo` function draws a line from the `MoveTo` position up to the `LineTo` position.

The final outcome of your efforts is a paint application that allows you to draw shapes on the client window. Go ahead and explore the painter in you. See our results in Figure 2-15.

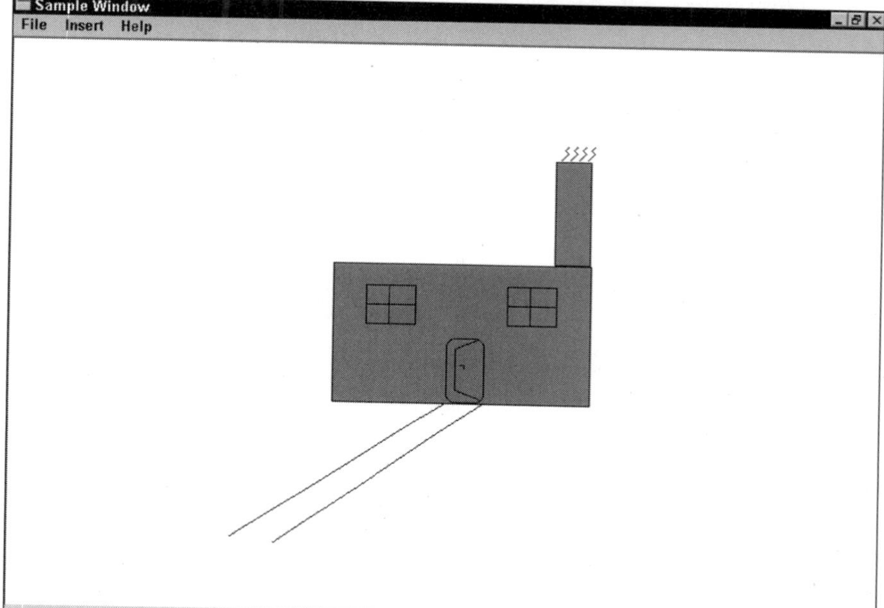

Figure 2-15: Home, sweet home!

Chapter 3: Creating MFC Applications the Easy Way

In This Chapter

- **Using the Microsoft Foundation Classes Application Wizard**
- **Digging into Microsoft Foundation Classes Application Wizard code**
- **Customizing and developing your application**

To simplify creating an application, we introduce you to the Microsoft Foundation Classes (MFC) Application Wizard. The MFC Application Wizard, which is a component of Visual C++ .NET, helps you create a wide range of applications, such as applications that connect to databases and applications that allow users to edit documents, that are based on the MFC. Here we steer you through the ways of the wizard and help you create a customized application on the basic framework designed by the wizard.

If you've already read Book 4, Chapter 2 (on creating Windows applications), you know that we traverse a number of steps to create a simple application. You're gonna love this wizard when you see how it can simplify your life.

Making Magic with the MFC Application Wizard

The MFC Application Wizard, like all wizards, comprises a number of screens that walk you through steps. This wizard is great for creating an application that's as close to your requirements as possible without spending unnecessary time writing code for a task. After you step through the wizard, you can customize the resulting application to your exact requirements. Follow along as we use the wizard to create an MFC application. The application that we create here, MFC1, can be obtained from the Hungry Minds Web site at `http://www.dummies.com/extras/VS.NETAllinOne`.

Invoking the wizard

Follow these steps to invoke the MFC Application Wizard (how very Harry Potter):

1. **Launch the Visual Studio .NET development environment by choosing Start⇨Programs⇨Microsoft Visual Studio.NET⇨Microsoft Visual Studio.NET.**

2. **Choose File⇨New⇨Project (or press Ctrl+Shift+N).**

   The New Project dialog box appears.

3. **In the New Project dialog box, click Visual C++ Projects in the Project Types list and click the MFC Application icon in the Templates list.**

4. **In the Name text box, enter** MFC1 **for the name of the project.**

   If desired, you can also change the location of the project directory by specifying a new path in the Location text box.

   The default location for the new project is the same as the location in which you had created your previous project. If this is the first project that you're creating, the location is your My Documents folder.

5. **Click OK to launch the wizard.**

   Visual Studio .NET launches the MFC Application Wizard.

If you've worked in Visual C++ 6.0, the wizard will be familiar. Most of the options in the new Application Wizard are similar to the options in the earlier version. However, note one significant difference: In Visual C++ .NET, all screens are listed in the same dialog box, and you can click a screen title to display the screen. (The Application Wizard in Visual C++ 6.0 moves from one screen to another when you click the Next button.) To understand this better, check out the wizard Overview screen of Figure 3-1. Here you can also see the list of other wizard screens (on the left side).

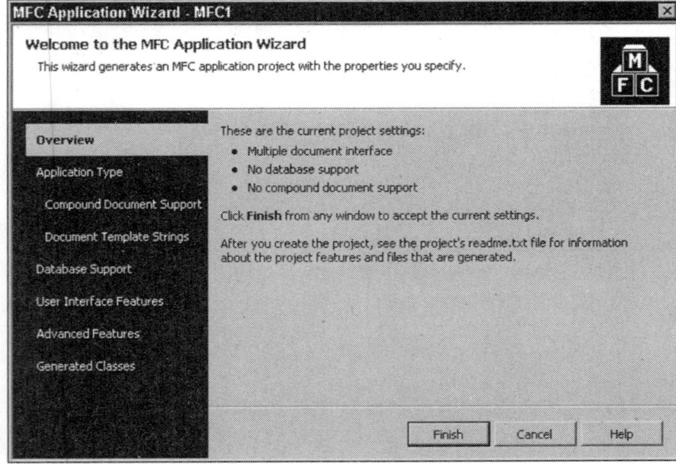

Figure 3-1: The Overview screen of the Application Wizard lists new application settings.

Creating an application with the wizard

The project settings in the wizard Overview screen summarize the settings to create a new application. These settings are based on the options selected in other screens of the wizard.

To create a customized application, select the relevant options in the various screens of the wizard. Follow these series of steps to run through the wizard.

1. **Select the Application Type screen of the wizard.**

   The Application Type screen, shown in Figure 3-2, prompts you to specify: an application type (single or multiple document interface, dialog-based, or multiple top-level documents); the layout of your project style (Windows Explorer or MFC standard); whether you want to link MFC as a shared DLL to your application; and whether your application will support the Document/View architecture. (We discuss more about this architecture in the next section.)

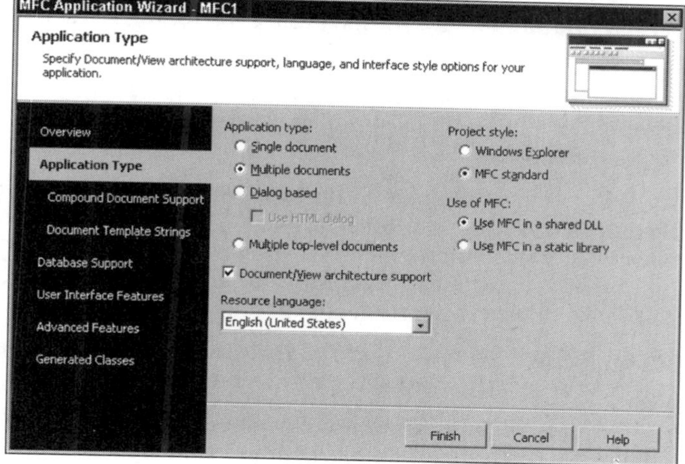

Figure 3-2: Specify application type and other project options here.

The main difference between multiple- and single-document applications is that you can open multiple child windows in a multiple document interface (MDI) application; comparatively, in a single document interface (SDI) application, you can open only one child window at a time.

2. **In the Application Type screen, select both the Single Document radio button and the Document/View Architecture Support check box and move to the next screen.**

Both screens beneath Application Type — Compound Document Support and Document Template Strings — are made available only when you select the Document/View Architecture Support check box in the Application Type Window.

3. **Select the Compound Document Support screen.**

   Find this screen choice immediately below Application Type, on the left side of the wizard screen.

   The Compound Document Support screen is used to specify whether you want to provide compound document support in your application. Compound document support enables your application to function as a container. A container application can accept items that are dragged to it. For example, if you drag text to the Microsoft Outlook window, a new mail message with the text that you dragged to the window is composed. Microsoft Outlook is an example of a container application.

   By default, your application doesn't support compound documents. You need not enable this support for your present application.

4. **Retain the default options of the Compound Document Support screen and then click the Document Template Strings screen of the wizard (found beneath Application Type on the wizard screen).**

   In the case of your form-based application, you don't need to support compound documents because you don't need your application to accept information that's supplied from other programs that are open on your computer.

   In the Document Template Strings screen (see Figure 3-3), you associate file extensions with your application. For example, the `.doc` extension is associated with a Microsoft Word application. You can also change the caption of your application window in this screen. The default caption for the window is the same as the name of your application.

5. **Retain the default options in the Document Template Strings screen and then select the next screen — Database Support.**

   In the Database Support screen, you specify the data source and the database support required for your application. When you include database support for your application, you're able to retrieve data from a database table and display it in your form. (For a more detailed discussion on database connectivity, peruse Book 4, Chapter 4.)

6. **Skip to the next screen: User Interface Features.**

   In the User Interface Features screen (Figure 3-4), you specify features of the user interface for your application. Instead of creating an application and then changing its interface manually, use the options in this screen to easily change the appearance of your application. As you can see in Figure 3-4, you have numerous user interface features to choose from, including main and child frame styles, toolbars, and dialog title.

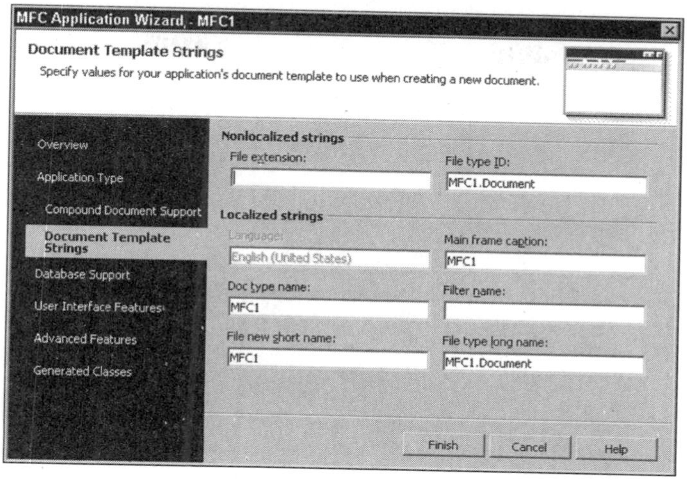

Figure 3-3: Associate filenames and specify the caption for your application here.

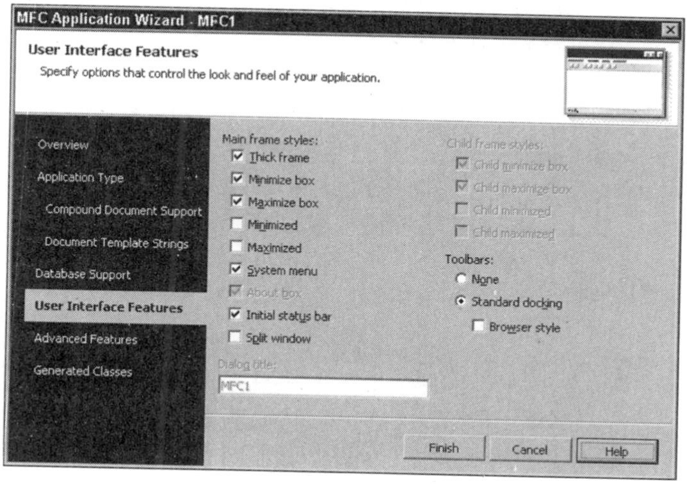

Figure 3-4: Change your application appearance in the User Interface Features screen.

7. **Retain the default options in the User Interface Features screen and then select the Advanced Features screen.**

   In the Advanced Features screen, you specify whether your application includes help and printing support. You can also select options to configure applications that operate over a TCP/IP network and also provide other such features, such as support for mail services. Also in this screen, the default options provide you with solutions to fit your basic application needs.

8. **Retain the default options in the Advanced Features screen and then select the final screen of the Application Wizard: Generated Classes.**

The Generated Classes screen is the most important screen of the Application Wizard. In this screen, you specify the base classes from which the view of your application is derived. The base class that you select determines the interface of your application. For example, if you select `CEditView` as the base class, your application will have the interface of a text editor. Similarly, if you select `CFormView` or `CHtmlView` as the base class, your application will have a form- or Web page-based interface, respectively.

9. **Select `CFormView` from the Base Class drop-down list for the `MFC1View` class, as shown in Figure 3-5.**

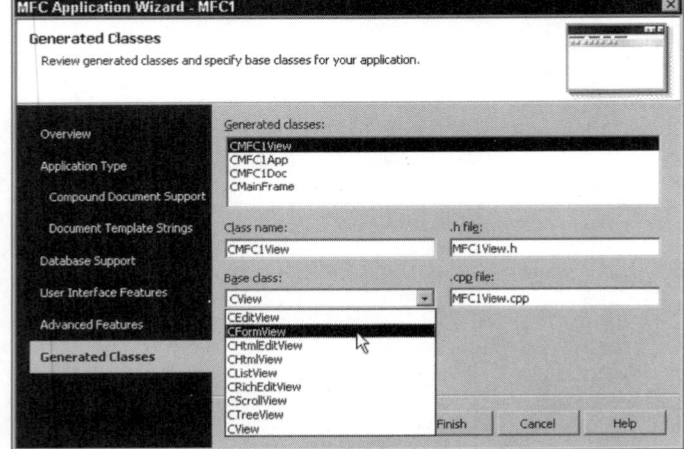

Figure 3-5: Select a class view in the Generated Classes screen.

When the view of your application is derived from the `CFormView` class, your application is form-based.

10. **Click the Finish button of the Generated Classes screen to complete the wizard and create your application.**

    You get a message that you can't print form-based documents. At this stage, you don't need that support (unless you want to print black text on a dark gray page).

11. **Click the Yes button to continue with your application.**

You can skip between wizard screens to change project settings; you don't have to progress through all screens in order. Note that each wizard screen has its own Finish button.

After you finish using the Application Wizard, you have an almost complete application at your disposal. You can now run the application to see its output.

Running the new application

To build and run your application, perform these steps:

1. **Choose Build⇨Build (or press Ctrl+Shift+B).**

   Your application is compiled. Build errors, if you have any, are displayed. Because applications generated by the Application Wizard don't have errors, you shouldn't get any errors (unless you've outsmarted the wizard!).

2. **Run your application by choosing Debug⇨Start.**

   The output of your application should look like Figure 3-6.

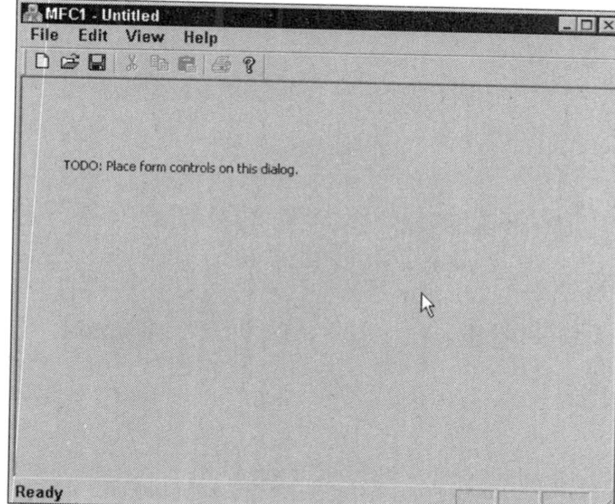

Figure 3-6: Your application derived from the CFormView class.

That's all there is to it; you've completed the application. As you can see, your application looks great, but you can't use it immediately. Keep reading to see how to turn it into a useful creation.

When you select a different base class to derive the view of your application, you create an entirely different interface. To give you an insight into the different types of interfaces, we compiled applications derived from each of the view-related classes in the Application Wizard. A collage of these applications is shown in Figure 3-7.

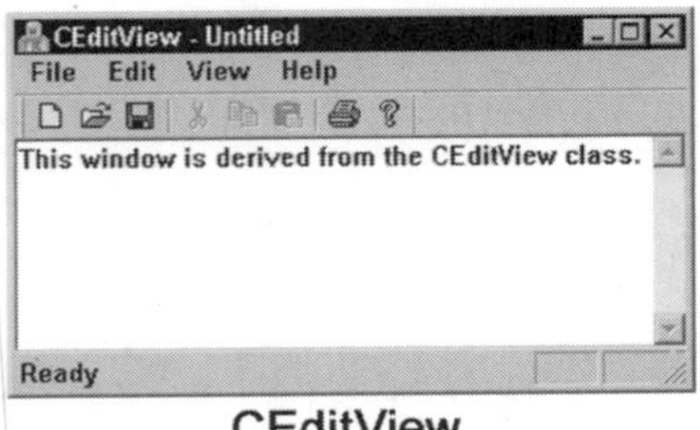

CEditView

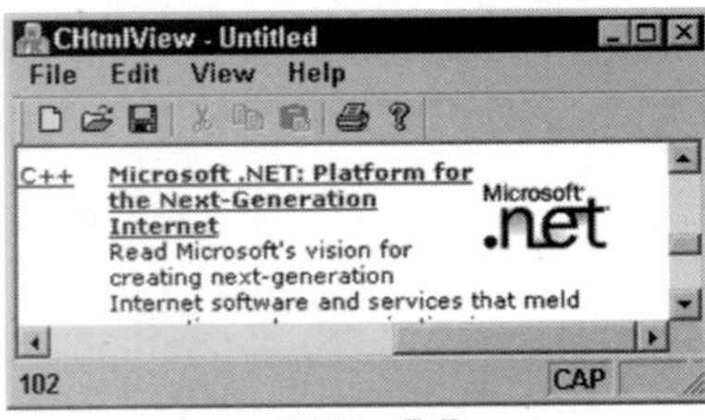

CHtmlView

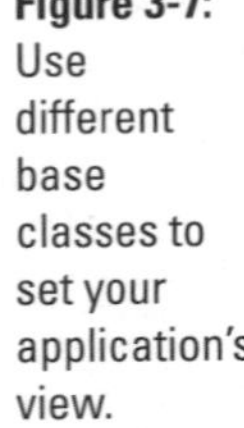

Figure 3-7: Use different base classes to set your application's view.

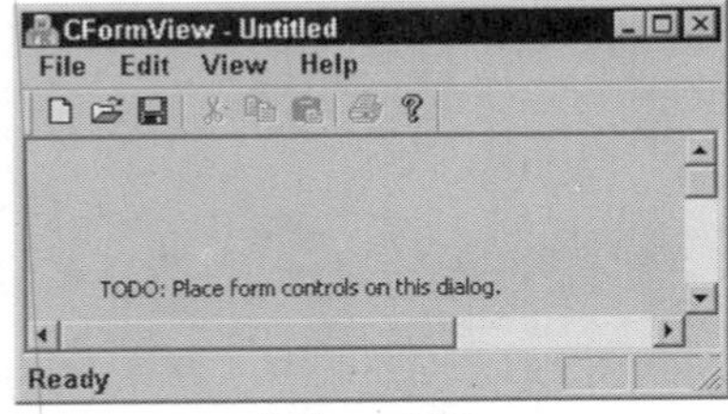

CFormView

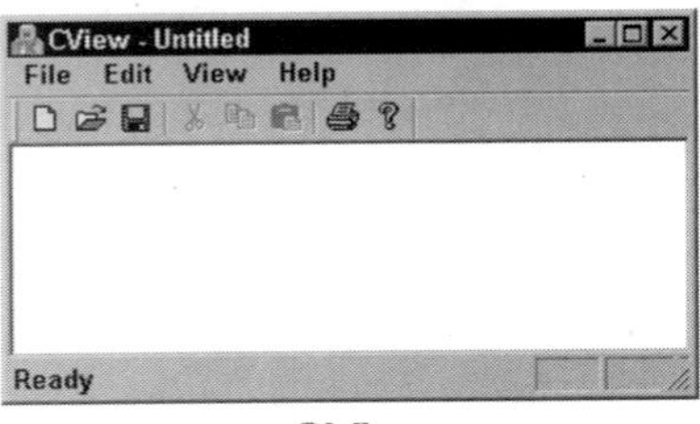

CView

Digging into the Code Generated by the Application Wizard

Try examining the code generated by the MFC Application Wizard. Thank your lucky stars that you didn't have to write such complex code all by yourself. However, you need to understand this code to help develop your application.

In this section, we discuss in detail the code generated by the Application Wizard. This section will come in handy when you get down to editing and customizing your application code according to your requirements.

Classes generated by the MFC Application Wizard

To explore the classes generated by the MFC Application Wizard, switch to Class View of the project by choosing View⇨Class View.

The Class View for the MFC1 project, which we create in the previous section, is shown in Figure 3-8.

Notice that the following classes have been created for your project:

✦ **`CAboutDlg`:** Use the `CAboutDlg` class for displaying the About MFC1 dialog box when a user choose Help⇨About MFC1. You derive the `CAboutDlg` class from the `CDialog` class. You can read how to implement the `CDialog` class in Book 4, Chapter 2.

- `CMainFrame`: The `CMainFrame` class is derived from the `CFrameWnd` class. The `CMainFrame` class manages creating and destroying windows for your application. This class also creates a toolbar and a status bar for your application and manages the layout of child windows.
- `CMFC1App`: Use the `CMFC1App` class, derived from the `CWinApp` class, to derive a Windows application object. Read more about using the `CWinApp` class in Book 4, Chapter 2.
- `CMFC1Doc`: The `CMFC1Doc` class is derived from the `CDocument` class, which represents data that needs to be displayed to a user. We discuss this class in detail in the next section "CDocument class."
- `CMFC1View`: The `CMFC1View` class is derived from the `CFormView` class. (We select this class when we run the Application Wizard in the earlier section "Creating an application with the wizard.") The `CMFC1View` class creates a form for your application and displays data retrieved by the `CMFC1Doc` class. The `CFormView` class, which is used as the base class here, is further derived from the `CView` class. We describe this class in the upcoming section "CView class."

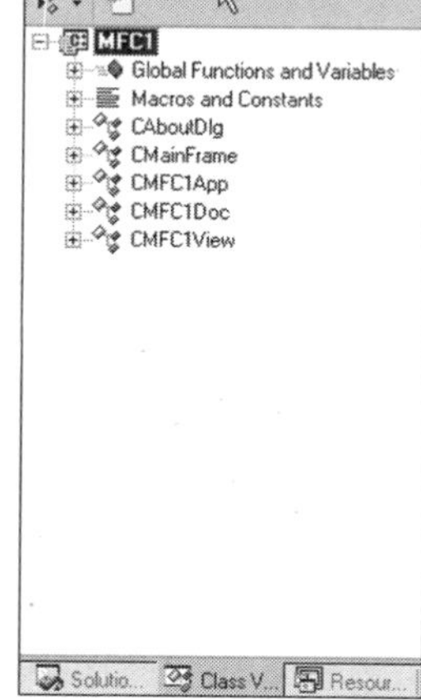

Figure 3-8: Use Class View to identify classes in an application.

CDocument class

The `CDocument` class manages file-related issues. For example, when you choose File⇨Save or File⇨Save As, in effect you call the `OnSaveDocument` function of the `CDocument` class that saves the document's data. The tasks performed directly or indirectly by the `CDocument` class are

- Creating new documents
- Saving and retrieving documents from hard drives
- Determining whether a document is modified
- Closing documents

CView class

After the `CDocument` class retrieves data, it needs to be displayed to the user. To display data, an MFC application uses the `CView` class and its derived classes. The `CView` class includes functions, such as `OnDraw` and `OnChar`, that help draw images and display text in the client area of the application.

When a view needs to communicate with a document to send or receive data, the view uses the `GetDocument` function. This function returns a pointer to the document associated with the view.

MFC classes and the document/view architecture

The document/view architecture provides a framework for creating document-based programs. When you create programs based on this architecture, you can segregate the user interface from the back-end operations. Therefore, the `CDocument` class isn't responsible for presenting data to the user. This class only stores and retrieves data from a document. The `CView` class and its derived classes display data to the user. See Figure 3-9 for a depiction of the role of different classes in the document/view architecture.

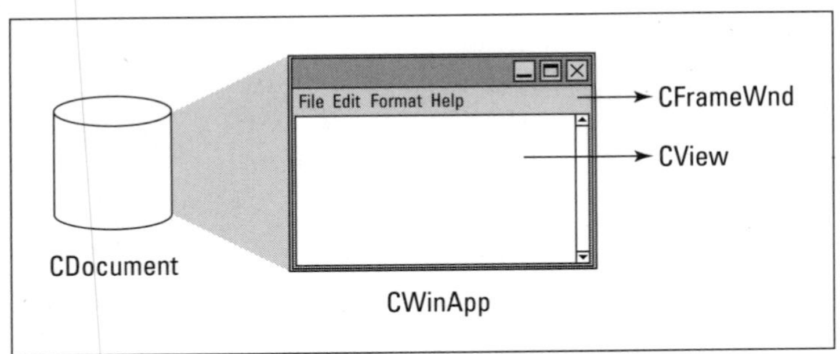

Figure 3-9: Different classes have different roles in the document/view architecture.

In an application based on the document/view architecture, the following sequence of steps occur when you run an application:

1. The `CWinApp`-derived class creates the Window application object for your application.
2. The `CFrameWnd`-derived class creates the framework for your application.
3. The `CView`-derived class creates the view for the application, which is attached to the application by the `CFrameWnd`-derived class.
4. The `CDocument`-derived class loads a document and passes data to the `CView`-derived class, which is then displayed to the user.

Where you should write code for the application

After running the Application Wizard, you need to write code for any additional functionality required in the application. If you attempt to add code manually, you might have a difficult time determining the correct location of code insertion. Here, the code wizards of Visual C++ .NET come to your rescue.

You can use the code wizards to add member variables, member functions, and event handlers to your application. For member functions and event handlers, the code wizard writes the function declaration in the header file and defines the function in the .cpp file. You just need to write the code for the function in the given placeholder.

Customizing and Developing Your Application

An application does what you want it to only after you customize it. Here's how to customize your sample application, MFC1, for accepting information from a user.

Adding controls to the form

You begin with customizing your application's interface. Building on our running example, you customize the user interface by adding controls to the form named `IDD_MFC1_FORM` that displays when you first run the application. Just a few steps and the user interface of your application is ready:

1. **Choose View⇨Resource View to open Resource View of your application.**

   The Resource View displays resources, such as menus, dialog boxes, and icons, that are included in your application.
2. **In Resource View, double-click IDD_MFC1_FORM in the Dialog section to open your form in Dialog Editor.**

Dialog Editor (shown in Figure 3-10) is used for adding controls to a dialog box.

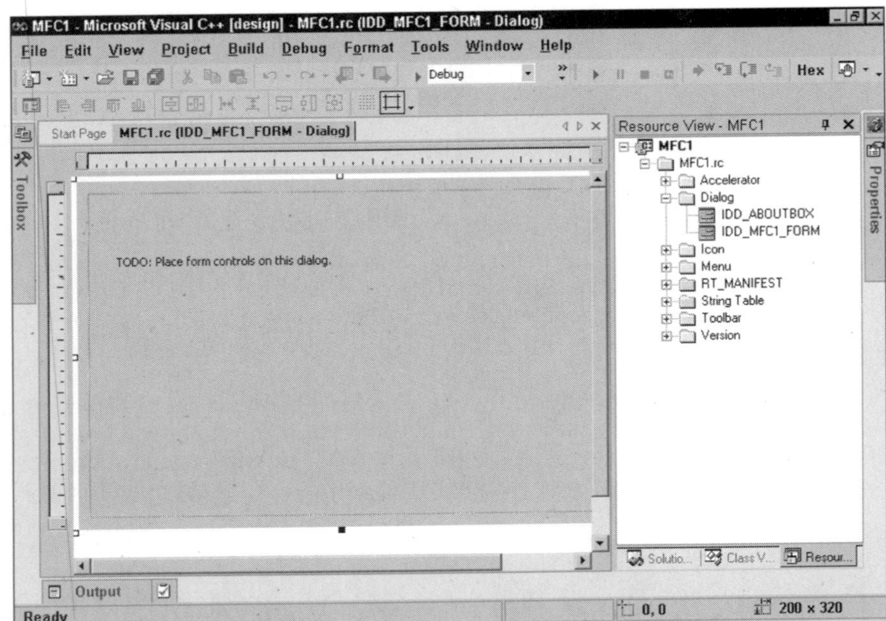

Figure 3-10: Add controls to your form in Dialog Editor.

3. **Open the Toolbox by choosing View⇨Toolbox.**

   The Toolbox has all controls that you would possibly add to your form. For our application, we add a few `Static Text`, `Edit Control`, and `Button` controls to our form. For more on the Toolbox and adding controls, read through Book 3, Chapter 3.

4. **From the Toolbox, add controls to the form to make it resemble the form shown in Figure 3-11.**

The ID of the `Static Text` and `Group Box` controls included on the form in Figure 3-11 has not been changed. However, for other controls, their ID — and in some cases, their properties also — have been changed to make them easy to code. These controls, along with any properties that have been changed, are listed in Table 3-1.

You need to change the ID of controls you add to the application to the ones given in Table 3-1.

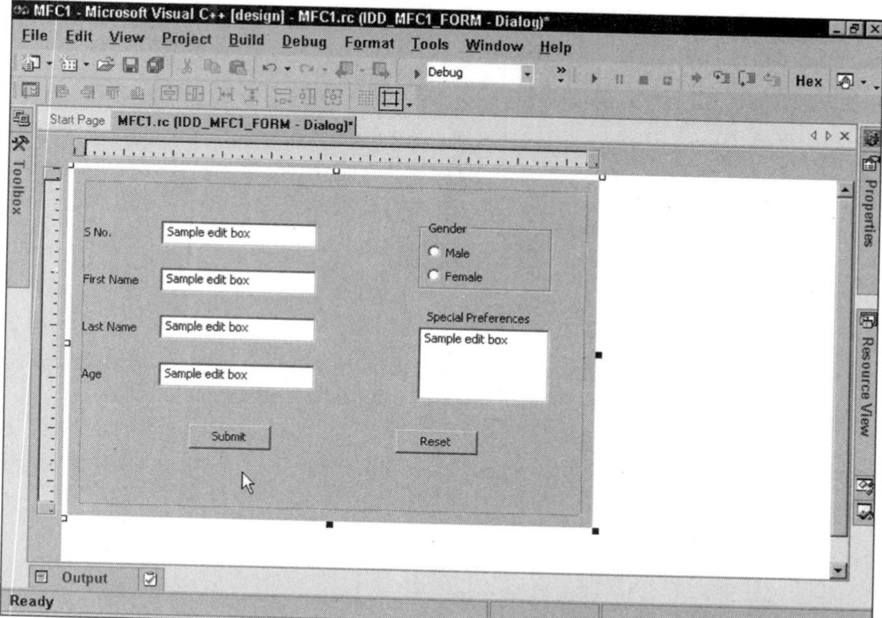

Figure 3-11: Your completed form should resemble this form.

Table 3-1 Controls Added on the User Form

Control ID	*Control Type*	*Default Properties Changed*
`IDC_SNO`	Edit Control	None
`IDC_FNAME`	Edit Control	None
`IDC_LNAME`	Edit Control	None
`IDC_AGE`	Edit Control	None
`IDC_MALE`	Radio Button	Tabstop=`True`
`IDC_FEMALE`	Radio Button	Tabstop=`True`
`IDC_PREF`	Edit Control	Multiline=`True`
`IDC_SUBMIT`	Button	None
`IDC_RESET`	Button	None

After adding controls to the form, you specify the *tab order* — the order in which the controls on a form are selected when a user presses the Tab key.

To specify the tab order, choose Format➪Tab Order and click the controls in the same order that you want them to be selected in the form. When finished, press the Escape key or choose the same menu option (Format➪Tab Order).

Exchanging data between controls and member variables

You can gather data and initialize controls easily by associating the controls on a form with application variables. The member variables for each control serve as a layer of interaction between the application and a form.

Add member variables to the controls in your form. When you do so, notice that the DDX and the DDV mechanisms (for exchanging and validating data) are automatically implemented. Perform these steps to add member variables to the form:

1. **In the form, right-click the S No. text box and click the Add Variable menu option from the shortcut menu that appears.**

   This launches the Add Member Variable Wizard for adding a new variable to the form. The first screen of the wizard is shown in Figure 3-12.

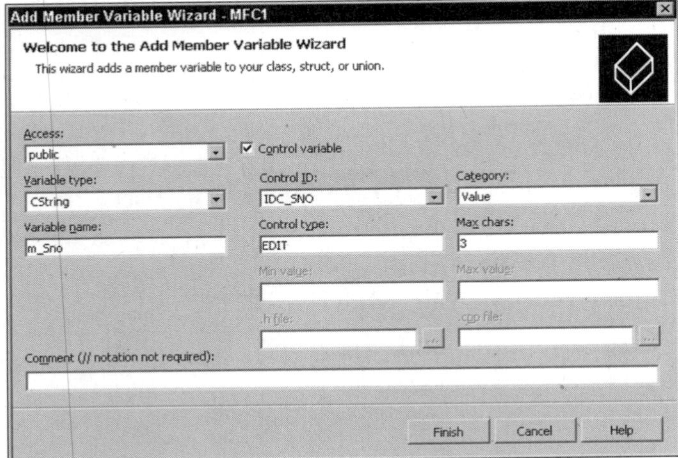

Figure 3-12: Use the Add Member Variable Wizard to associate controls with member variables.

2. **In the Add Member Variable Wizard screen, select Value from the Category drop-down list and enter** m_Sno **as the name of the variable in the Variable Name text box.**

   Notice that when you select Value from the Category list, the Variable type field automatically uses the data type that's closest to the intended use of a control. However, in some cases, you may need to specify a value for the data type that's different from the default value. For example, the data type for a text box changes to `CString`. However, if you want to store numeric data in the text box, you need to change the data type to `int`.

3. **Enter 3 as a value in the Max Chars text field.**

   The value 3 ensures that the control doesn't accept more than three characters.

4. **Click the Finish button to create the member variable.**

   The Add Member Variable Wizard opens the `MFC1View.cpp` and `MFC1View.h` files. Note that the variable has been automatically created in the `MFC1View.h` file. The DDX and DDV mechanisms for the control have been implemented in the `MFC1View.cpp` file by the following code:

   ```
   void CMFC1View::DoDataExchange(CDataExchange* pDX)
   {
       CFormView::DoDataExchange(pDX);
       DDX_Text(pDX, IDC_SNO, m_Sno);
       DDV_MaxChars(pDX, m_Sno, 3);
   }
   ```

   The above code ensures that the `IDC_SNO` variable is associated with the `m_Sno` variable and the maximum number of characters allowed in the `IDC_SNO` control is 3.

   Files that have the .h extension are header files and files with .cpp extension are source files. A header file is used to include other files into a project, declare classes, and declare function prototypes. A source file is used to code the implementation of classes and functions defined in a header file.

5. **Repeat Steps 2, 3, and 4 to create member variables for the other controls.**

   For each member variable that you add, you need to select Value from the Category drop-down list and specify a different name and a different value for the maximum number of characters. The values for each control are listed in Table 3-2.

DDX and DDV

After associating controls with member variables, you can use the DDX (Dialog Data Exchange) and DDV (Dialog Data Validation) mechanisms to initialize controls and validate data in a control, respectively. The implementation of the DDV mechanism should immediately follow the implementation of the DDX mechanism.

In the DDX mechanism, your application calls the UpdateData function of the CWnd class to exchange data between controls and variables. The UpdateData function, in turn, invokes the DoDataExchange function of the CWnd class.

Table 3-2 Member Variables Associated with Controls in the Form

Control ID	*Member Variable Name*	*Member Variable Type*	*Maximum Characters Allowed*
IDC_FNAME	m_Fname	CString	10
IDC_LNAME	m_Lname	CString	10
IDC_AGE	m_Age	int	Min value=1, Max value=100
IDC_MALE	m_Male	Bool	Not applicable
IDC_FEMALE	m_Female	Bool	Not applicable
IDC_PREF	m_Pref	CString	30

Having added member variables for controls on the form, write the code for the Submit and the Reset buttons. Before you do that, we need to discuss event handling.

Handling events

The controls in a form generate events during user interaction. These events help trap errors and notify the user of any required information. For example, `Edit Control` has an `EN_KILLFOCUS` event that's generated when you move out of the control. You can use this event to ensure that a user enters a valid value in the control.

To find out how to handle events, add an event handler for the `IDC_FNAME` control.

1. **Right-click the `IDC_FNAME` control (the control is placed on your form) and click Add Event Handler from the shortcut menu that appears.**

   The Event Handler Wizard appears. (See Figure 3-13.)

2. **In this dialog box, select an event from the Message Type list and then click the Add and Edit button to edit the code for the event.**

3. **Click EN_KILLFOCUS from the Message Type list and then click the Add and Edit button to edit the code for the `EN_KILLFOCUS` event handler.**

   When you click the Add and Edit button, the wizard adds the event handler to your application and opens the `MFC1View.cpp` file. You can now edit the code for the event handler at the exact location that the wizard specifies.

This is how smart the wizard is: If you try to add an event handler that you've already added, the Edit Code button is enabled instead of the Add and Edit button. Gotta like that!

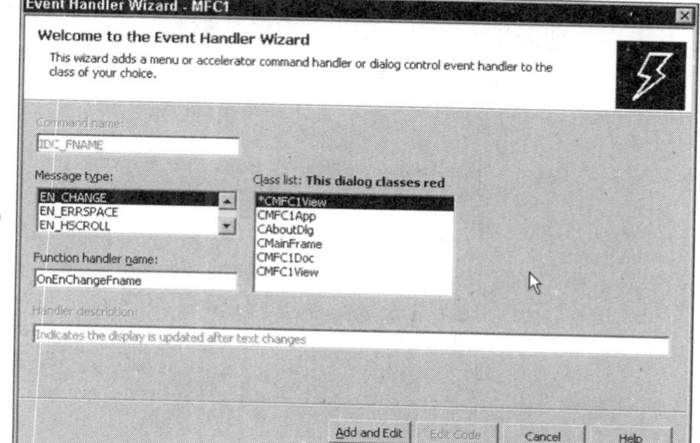

Figure 3-13: Add event handlers with the Event Handler Wizard.

4. **Change the code of the event handler to match the following code:**

```
void CMFC1View::OnEnKillfocusFname()
{
    char m_name[20];
GetDlgItemText(IDC_FNAME,m_name,20);
    if (strlen(m_name)==0)
    {
        MessageBox("Please specify your first name.");
        CEdit *name;
        name=(CEdit*)GetDlgItem(IDC_FNAME);
        name->SetFocus();
    }
}
```

When a user runs your application, the user can't proceed without specifying a value in the First Name text box. If the user attempts to divert from this step, the application displays the message `Please specify your first name`.

The functions used in the above code are

- `GetDlgItemText`: The `GetDlgItemText` function retrieves the text associated with a control. This function accepts the following parameters: ID of the control, destination string, and the maximum number of characters to retrieve.
- `strlen`: This function determines the number of characters in the string supplied to it as a parameter.

- **GetDlgItem:** The GetDlgItem function retrieves a pointer to the specified control.
- **SetFocus:** The SetFocus function provides input focus to the control for which it is invoked.

You can perform all validation at once at the click of a button. This saves you from writing event handlers for each function separately.

Accepting user information and running a form

Code the Submit and Reset buttons to complete your application. The code for these buttons is fairly straightforward. The Reset button initializes all the controls to their original values. To write the code for the Reset button, double-click the button in the form and write the code given below:

```
void CMFC1View::OnBnClickedReset()
{
    SetDlgItemText(IDC_SNO,"");
    SetDlgItemText(IDC_FNAME,"");
    SetDlgItemText(IDC_LNAME,"");
    SetDlgItemText(IDC_PREF,"");
    SetDlgItemText(IDC_AGE,"0");
    CButton *button;
    button =(CButton*)GetDlgItem(IDC_MALE);
    button->SetCheck(0);
    button =(CButton*)GetDlgItem(IDC_FEMALE);
    button->SetCheck(0);
}
```

In this code, we use the SetDlgItemText function to delete the text in each Edit Control. We also use the SetCheck method of the CButton class to deselect the Male and Female radio buttons. That's pretty simple.

The code for the Submit button is also given below. This code ensures that a user has specified values in all fields; subsequently, it displays the name and age of the user.

```
void CMFC1View::OnBnClickedSubmit()
{
//Assign data from controls to member variables
UpdateData(TRUE);
//Determine whether any of the Gender options are selected
CButton *male, *female;
male=(CButton*)GetDlgItem(IDC_MALE);
female=(CButton*)GetDlgItem(IDC_FEMALE);
m_Male=male->GetCheck();
m_Female=female->GetCheck();
if ((m_Male==false) && (m_Female==false))
{
```

```
    MessageBox ("Please specify the gender.");
    return;
}
//Determine whether last name and serial number were speci-
    fied.
if ((strlen(m_Lname)==0) || (strlen(m_Sno)==0))
{
    MessageBox ("Not all details have been specified.
                    Please complete the form.");
    return;
}
//display the message
char message[40];
sprintf(message,"%s %s is aged %dyears",m_Fname,m_Lname,
                m_Age);
MessageBox(message);
}
```

The `UpdateData` and `sprintf` functions used in the code are

- **`UpdateData`:** The `UpdateData` function is used to transfer data between member variables and controls. When the parameter supplied to this function is `TRUE`, data is transferred from the controls to the member variables and vice versa. After data is transferred to member variables, they're examined to check whether the values in controls were specified.
- **`sprintf`:** Use the `sprintf` function to write a formatted output to a string. In the above code block, the `m_Age` variable is of `int` type. Instead of converting this variable to the string type, concatenating it to a string, and then displaying it on the screen, you can perform these steps by using the all-in-one `sprintf` function. In this function, you specify a series of characters that are interjected by arguments. The arguments are replaced by their values when the final output is written. For example, note the `%s`, `%s`, and `%d` arguments in the string supplied to the `sprintf` function. When your application is run, these arguments are replaced by the respective values of `m_Fname`, `m_Lname`, and `m_Age`.

Now, run your application, which is as simple as pressing Ctrl+Shift+B and then pressing F5. After specifying the appropriate values and clicking the Submit button, the output of your application should look like what's shown in Figure 3-14.

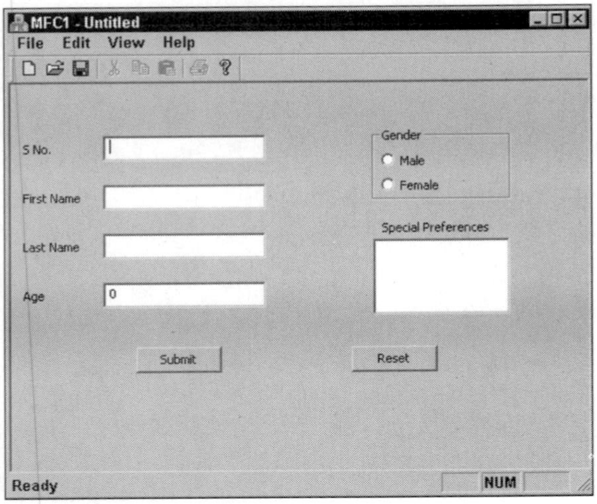

Figure 3-14: The final output of your application looks good!

Chapter 4: Database Programming in Visual C++ .NET

In This Chapter

- ✓ **Creating an application framework**
- ✓ **Managing records in an application**

All applications process data in one form or another. When you create a form-based application, you probably need to retrieve data from a form and store it at a convenient location for future retrieval and analysis — unless you want to display a message box to a user who enters data and be done with it! The most convenient location for storing data is a database.

Visual C++ .NET has several features for efficient data handling. Apart from the usual database classes that enable you to build a data-driven application, it provides new object linking and embedding database (OLE DB) templates that help you connect to new types of data sources, such as XML documents. In this chapter, we walk you through creating an application in which the data entered by a user in a form is stored in a database.

Creating an Application Framework

The Microsoft Foundation Classes (MFC) Application Wizard helps you create a data-driven application easily. With the aid of a few options, you get an easy-to-use and customizable application. In this section, you learn to run the Application Wizard to create an application. Before you begin using the wizard, take a while to explore the simple structure of the database used for our application. In addition, learn about the role of an Open Database Connectivity (ODBC) connection that you use for connecting to a database.

Prerequisites: Database and ODBC

The first prerequisite for a database application is the database itself. (If you're not planning to use a database, reading this chapter is kinda pointless.) You may be lucky enough to have an existing database that matches your requirements. If not, you need to create one by choosing from the popular database management systems, such as Microsoft Structured Query Language (SQL) Server or Microsoft Access.

For this chapter, we create a database in Microsoft Access and then add a table called Party to the database. The Party table is used to store details of guests at a birthday party. You're invited! The final application that you create by using the Party application is available for download at the Hungry Minds Web site at `http://www.dummies.com/extras/VS.NETAllinOne`. The name of the application is Party.

As long as you're using ODBC classes to connect to the database, don't worry about the application to be used to create the database. In an MFC application, data from all types of databases is processed through the ODBC connection, irrespective of the data source.

The structure of the Party table is defined as shown in Table 4-1.

Table 4-1: Structure of the Party Table

Field Name	*Data Type*
`S No`	Number
`First Name`	Text
`Last Name`	Text
`Age`	Number
`Special Preferences`	Text

We also add a record to the database. This record will display in the application that we create.

After you list the database structure, examine the role of an ODBC connection. ODBC acts as a link between an application and a data source. When you execute your application, the following sequence of events enables your application to communicate with the database.

1. **Call to ODBC functions:** The application calls ODBC functions to submit SQL statements to the data source.
2. **Selection of drivers:** The driver manager loads correct ODBC drivers to communicate with the data source.
3. **Calls to the database:** The driver submits SQL requests to the database and returns the resultant data to the application. If necessary, the driver modifies the requests made by the application so that they're compatible with the database application.

The interaction between an application and a database through ODBC drivers is depicted in Figure 4-1.

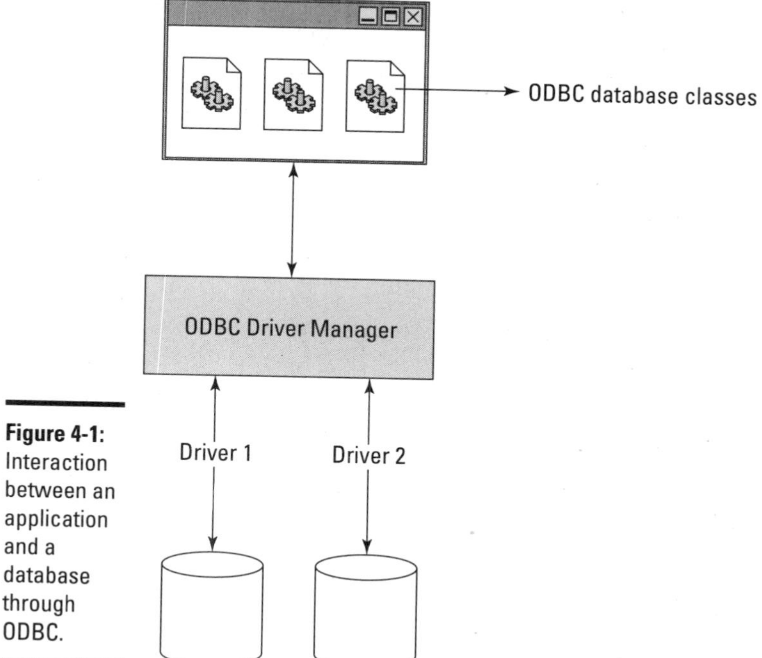

Figure 4-1: Interaction between an application and a database through ODBC.

Selecting database-specific options in the Application Wizard

To run the Application Wizard for creating the database application, follow these steps:

1. **Create an application based on the MFC Application template and then assign the name *Party* to the application.**

   Read more on using the MFC Application Wizard in Book 4, Chapter 3. When you create the new application, the MFC Application Wizard launches and the MFC Application Wizard - Party dialog box appears.

2. **In the MFC Application Wizard - Party dialog box, select the Application Type screen (left side of the screen).**

3. **Select the Single document radio button in the Application Type screen (right side) and then select the Database Support wizard screen (beneath Application Type, left side).**

   Selecting the Single document radio button ensures that your application has a single document interface (SDI).

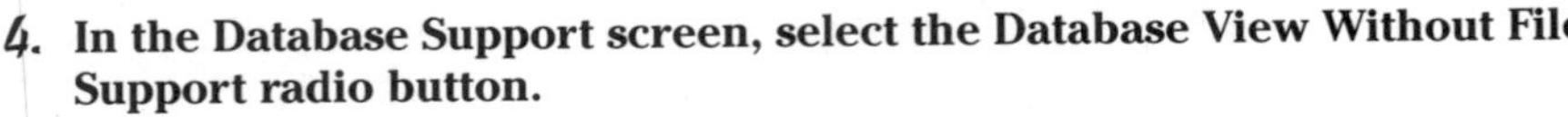

4. **In the Database Support screen, select the Database View Without File Support radio button.**

In a database application, you don't need file support because data is stored in a database. Your application doesn't read and write from a file on the disk; instead, the application performs transactions on a database.

5. **Select the ODBC radio button for the Client type and then click the Data Source button.**

   The Select Data Source dialog box appears. In this dialog box, you specify the ODBC connection to the data source.

6. **Select the Machine Data Source tab in the Select Data Source dialog box.**

   The Machine Data Source tab in the Select Data Source dialog box is shown in Figure 4-2. This tab lists the ODBC connections configured on your computer and allows you to create a new ODBC connection to your database.

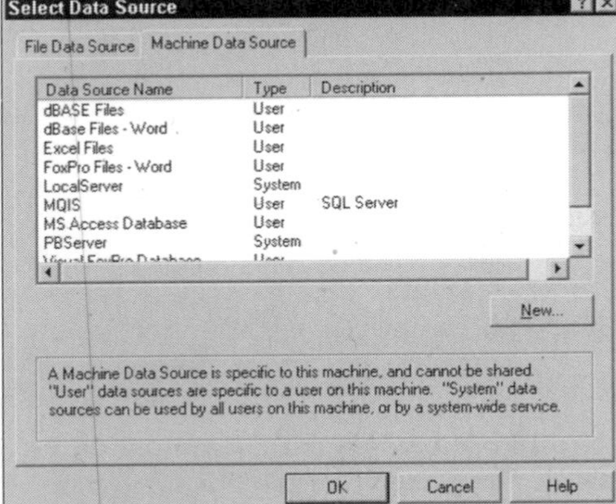

Figure 4-2: Select an ODBC connection or create a new one here.

7. **In the Machine Data Source tab, click the New button.**

   The Create New Data Source wizard appears.

8. **In the first screen of the Create New Data Source wizard, click the Next button.**

   A screen that lists the drivers available for connecting to a data source appears. (See Figure 4-3.)

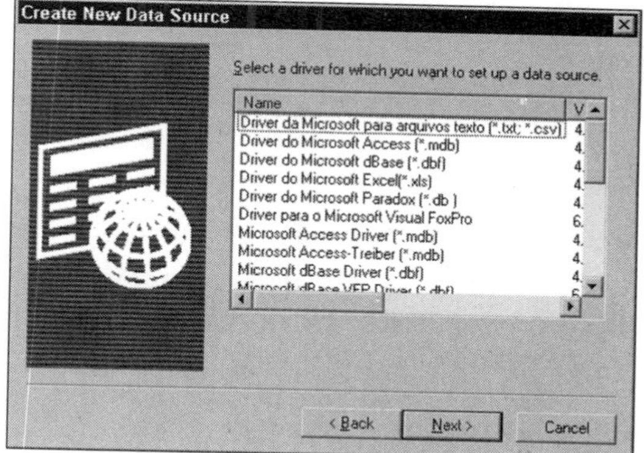

Figure 4-3: Select a driver for your database.

9. **Select Microsoft Access Driver (*.mdb) from the list of available drivers and then click the Next button.**

   The last screen of the wizard appears. This screen lists the details of the ODBC connection that you'll create.

10. **Click the Finish button to finish using the Create New Data Source wizard.**

   When you finish using the Create New Data Source wizard, the ODBC Microsoft Access Setup screen appears, as shown in Figure 4-4. In this screen, you specify the name of the ODBC connection and the path to the Microsoft Access database that you'll use for your application.

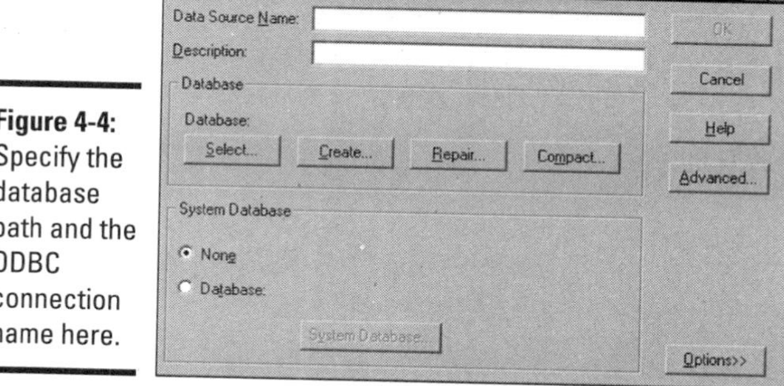

Figure 4-4: Specify the database path and the ODBC connection name here.

11. **In the Data Source Name text box, enter** Party **as the name of the ODBC connection.**

12. **Click the Select button and navigate to the location of the database; after you select the database, click OK to return to the ODBC Microsoft Access Setup screen.**

13. **Click OK to close the ODBC Microsoft Access Setup dialog box.**

    The Select Data Source dialog box reappears. In this dialog box, the ODBC data connection — Party — that you created is selected.

14. **Click OK.**

    The Login screen appears. You don't need to specify any specific log-on information for connecting to the Microsoft Access database.

15. **Click OK to close the Login dialog box.**

    The Select Database Object table dialog box appears. This dialog box displays the database tables that you select, as shown in Figure 4-5.

Figure 4-5: Select a table in the Select Database Object table dialog box.

16. **Click the Party table in the Select Database Object dialog box and click OK.**

    You return to the Database Support screen of the Application Wizard.

17. **Click the Finish button to end using the wizard and create your application.**

Making sense of the Application Wizard-generated code

In Book 4, Chapter 3 we discuss in detail the code generated by the Application Wizard. In this chapter, we cover particular features of the generated code. These features are specific to a database application.

The Application Wizard writes code specific to database operations in the `CRecordset`- and `CRecordView`-derived classes. In this application, this code is written in the `CPartySet` and `CPartyView` classes. Examine the code of these classes and you see that three ODBC classes are involved in database connectivity. These classes, along with their important member functions and member variables, are described below.

CDatabase class

The `CDatabase` class establishes a connection with a database and makes the connection available to your program. The `OpenEx` method of the `CDatabase` class initializes a new `CDatabase` object. After the object is initialized, you can construct a recordset and retrieve data from database tables.

In the MFC application created by the MFC Application Wizard, the `OpenEx` function of the `CDatabase` class isn't used for connecting to the database. Instead, the application uses the `GetDefaultConnect` function of the `CRecordset` class for obtaining the default connection string that you specify while creating the ODBC connection.

CRecordset class

The `CRecordset` class stores records retrieved from a database. An MFC application generated by the Application Wizard uses two functions of the `CRecordset` class to connect to the database and retrieve records from the default table. These functions are

- **`GetDefaultConnect`:** The `GetDefaultConnect` function returns the default connection string to the database that you select for your application. For example, the following code retrieves the connection string to the database:

```
CString CPartySet::GetDefaultConnect()
{
     return
          _T("DSN=Party;DBQ=E:\\applications\\
           Database1.mdb;
          DriverId=25;FIL=MS
          Access;MaxBufferSize=2048;PageTimeout=5;
          UID=admin;");
}
```

Notice the use of the _T macro in the preceding code. This macro is required because different operating systems may use distinct character sets. To design code that's compatible with all operating systems, you use the _T macro to write the code. The code is compiled to the appropriate character set before execution. The compilation is based upon the requirements of the operating system.

✦ `GetDefaultSQL`: The `GetDefaultSQL` function selects a default table and executes a query on the table to retrieve a recordset. Consider the following code:

```
return _T("[Party]");
```

In this code, the application selects the Party table of the database specified by the `GetDefaultConnect` function. Next, the application retrieves all the records from the Party table.

After you select the default table, you can update, add, and delete records from the table. To perform these tasks, you bind data members of your application with the columns in the database.

The application binds data members by the Record Field Exchange (RFX) mechanism, which is implemented in the `DoDataExchange` member function of the `CRecordset` class. Just like the Dialog Data Exchange (DDX) mechanism exchanges data between a form and the application, the RFX mechanism exchanges data between data members and columns of the database.

Database columns may contain different data types. Therefore, distinct RFX functions are available for each data type. For example, the `RFX_Text` function transfers string data and the `RFX_Long` function transfers `long int` data. The code to implement the RFX mechanism for each column in the Party table of your application is given below:

```
void CPartySet::DoFieldExchange(CFieldExchange* pFX)
{
   pFX->SetFieldType(CFieldExchange::outputColumn);
   RFX_Long(pFX, _T("[S No]"), m_SNo);
   RFX_Text(pFX, _T("[First Name]"), m_FirstName);
   RFX_Text(pFX, _T("[Last Name]"), m_LastName);
   RFX_Long(pFX, _T("[Age]"), m_Age);
   RFX_Text(pFX, _T("[Special Preferences]"),
      m_SpecialPreferences);
}
```

Notice that the `DoFieldExchange` function takes the `CFieldExchange` class as a parameter. This class ensures accurate data transfer between the database and the application.

CRecordView class

The `CRecordView` class is derived from the `CFormView` class. The `CRecordView` class implements the DDX mechanism to transfer data between the `CRecordset` class and the form. (You can read about the DDX mechanism in Book 4, Chapter 3.)

The data transfer between the database and an application is illustrated in Figure 4-6.

The `CRecordView` class also facilitates default implementation of record navigation in a form by using an `m_pSet` pointer. The `m_pSet` pointer refers to the `CRecordset`-derived class that's associated with the view. This pointer can be used to manage records in the recordset. You can learn more about using the `m_pSet` pointer in the upcoming section "Managing Records in an Application."

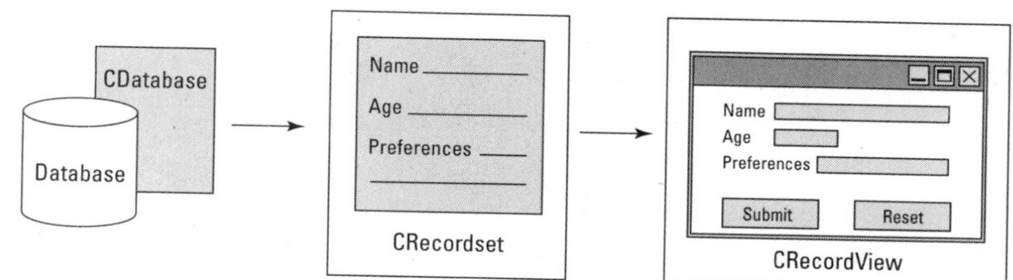

Figure 4-6: Flow of data between a database and an application involves three MFC classes.

Associating database records with a form

The Application Wizard automatically performs most of the tasks that we describe in earlier sections of this chapter. All you need to do is to carry out these two simple steps:

1. **Add controls to the form:** The controls in the form display data that's retrieved from the database.
2. **Implement the DDX mechanism:** The DDX mechanism associates controls with the data members of the `CRecordset` class (accessed by the `m_pSet` pointer).

Adding controls to the form

You need to create a simplified form for displaying data to users identical to the one shown in Figure 4-7. You add controls to the `IDD_PARTY_FORM` form. When you create such a form for the `Static Text` controls, you need to change only the `Caption` property. In case of other controls, use the details listed in Table 4-2.

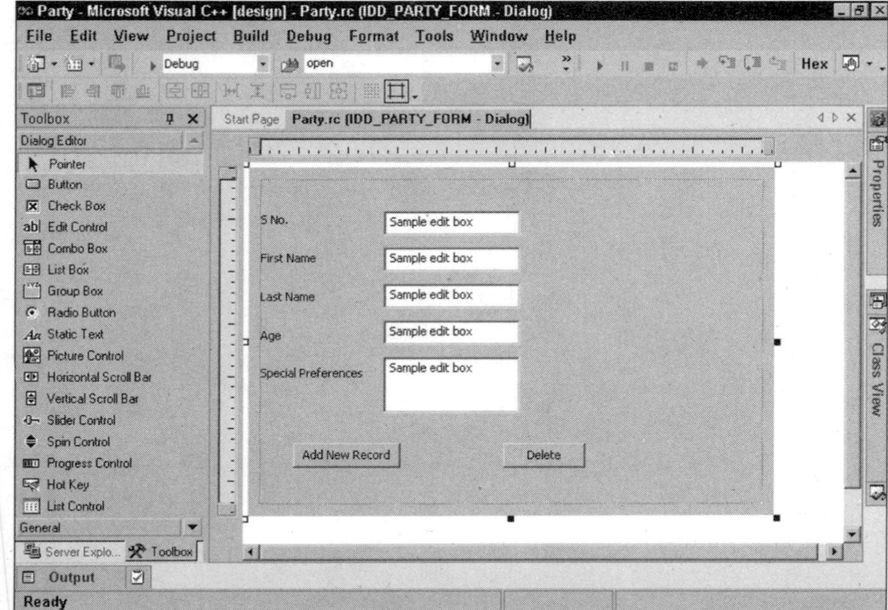

Figure 4-7: Add these five controls to your form.

Table 4-2 Controls Added to the IDD_PARTY_FORM Form

Control	*Control Type*	*Modified Properties*
`S No.` text box	Edit Control	`ID=IDC_SNO`
`First Name` text box	Edit Control	`ID=IDC_FNAME`
`Last Name` text box	Edit Control	`ID=IDC_LNAME`
`Age` text box	Edit Control	`ID=IDC_AGE`
`Special Preferences` text box	Edit Control	`ID=IDC_PREF` and `Multiline=True`
`Add New Record` button	Button	`ID=IDC_ADD`
`Delete` button	Button	`ID=IDC_DELETE`

When you add controls to a form, use the menu options in the Format menu to align and resize controls.

Implementing the DDX mechanism

After you add controls to your form, implement the DDX mechanism to display the database records in the form.

1. **Double-click the `PartyView.cpp` file by using Solution Explorer (press Ctrl+Alt+L to open Solution Explorer).**

2. **Locate the code for the** `DoDataExchange` **function.**

   Find the code written after the message map declaration. (For a description of message maps, refer to Book 4, Chapter 2.) In the `DoDataExchange` function, you need to associate controls with data members of the `CPartySet` class. An easy way to determine the exact name of data members defined in the `CPartySet` class is to use Class View.

3. **Open Class View by choosing View⇨Class View (or press Ctrl+Shift+C).**

4. **In Class View, click the + arrow next to Party and then click the + arrow next to CPartySet.**

   All data members of the `CPartySet` class appear in Class View, as shown in Figure 4-8.

5. **Change the code of the** `DoDataExchange` **function to match the code given below:**

```
void CPartyView::DoDataExchange(CDataExchange* pDX)
{
    CRecordView::DoDataExchange(pDX);
    DDX_FieldText(pDX,IDC_SNO, m_pSet->m_SNo, m_pSet);
    DDX_FieldText(pDX,IDC_FNAME, m_pSet->m_FirstName,
        m_pSet);
    DDX_FieldText(pDX,IDC_LNAME, m_pSet->m_LastName,
        m_pSet);
    DDX_FieldText(pDX,IDC_AGE, m_pSet->m_Age, m_pSet);
    DDX_FieldText(pDX,IDC_PREF,
        m_pSet->m_SpecialPreferences, m_pSet);
}
```

   In the code given above, the data type of the `m_FirstName`, `m_LastName`, and `m_SpecialPreferences` data members is `CStringW`. None of the overloaded implementation of the `DDX_FieldText` function can manage the `CStringW` data type. Therefore, you need to change the data type of these data members to `CString` in the `PartySet.h` header file.

   `CStringW` is a Unicode character string that supports the C runtime. `CStringW` is an implementation of the `CStringT` class, which in turn is the MFC-independent implementation of the `CString` class.

6. **Open the** `PartySet.h` **header file by using Solution Explorer.**

7. **Locate the declaration of the** `m_FirstName`, `m_LastName`, **and** `m_SpecialPreferences` **data members by browsing the code in the** `PartySet.h` **header file and change their data type from** `CStringW` **to** `CString` **by typing** `CString` **instead of** `CStringW`.

8. **Build and run your application.**

   The output of the application is shown in Figure 4-9. We add a sample record; this record is displayed in the form.

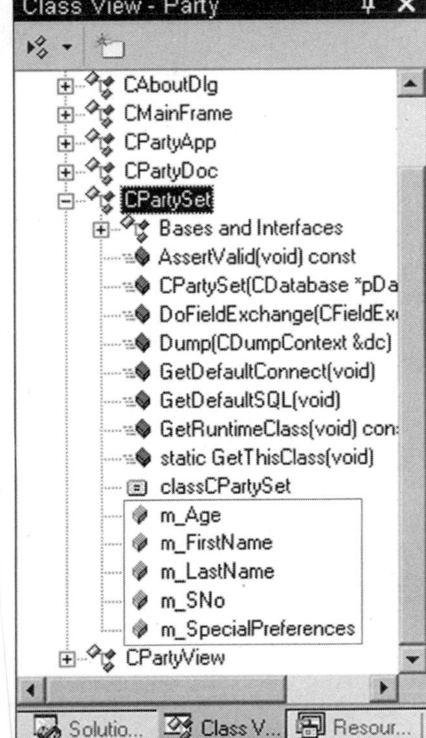

Figure 4-8: Data members of the CPartySet class are visible in Class View.

Disabling the Print-related menu options

The application that you create in this chapter is a data-driven form-based application (as if you didn't already know it!). In a form-based application, you do not need to use the Print menu option. Therefore, you should disable these menu options. To do so, follow these steps:

1. **Press Ctrl+Alt+L to open Solution Explorer.**
2. **In the Solution Explorer, double-click Resource Files.**

   The contents of the Resource Files folder appear.
3. **Under resource files, double-click Party.rc.**

   The Party.rc file opens.

4. **Select the View➪Resource View menu option to switch to the Resource View.**

   The Resource View lists all the icons, bitmaps, dialog boxes, and menus that are associated with your application.

5. **In the Resource View, click the plus (+) sign next to menu and double-click IDR_MAINFRAME.**

   The menu for the application opens.

6. **In the Resource View, click Print to select it and press the delete key to delete the menu option.**

7. **Repeat Step 6 to disable the Print Preview and Print Setup menu options.**

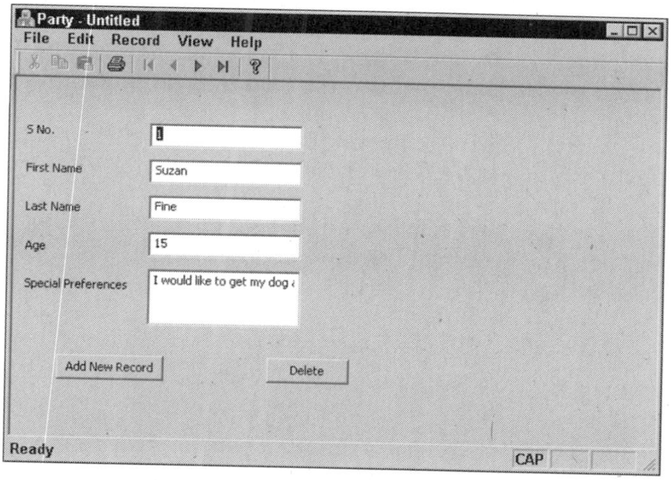

Figure 4-9: The first record displays when you run your form.

Managing Records in an Application

The Application Wizard incorporates most of the functionality required by your application. However, if you need to add or delete records from the database, you need to code the functionality manually. In this section, you learn how to update, add, and delete records from a database.

Updating records in a database

When you move from one record to another, your application automatically saves changes that you made to the initial record. Therefore, we don't include the functionality for updating records in our application. However, if you need to update records manually, you can use the `Edit` and `Update` functions of the `m_pSet` pointer, as shown in the code below:

```
m_pSet->Edit();
UpdateData(TRUE);
m_pSet->Update();
```

Adding and deleting records from a database

To add and delete records from a database, we create the Add New Record and Delete buttons, respectively, in the form. Based upon the user's selection of these buttons, we use them in more than one way.

- **User clicks the Add New Record button:** When a user clicks the Add New Record button, you don't need the Delete button until the user completes specifying the record. Therefore, we change the caption of the Add New Record button to Submit and the caption of the Delete button to Cancel. After the user submits the new record, the button names revert to the original.
- **User clicks the Delete button:** When a user clicks the Delete button, the current record is deleted and the contents of the database are renewed.

To implement the Add New Record button, double-click Add New Record in Dialog Editor. Write the following code for the Add New Record button.

If you cannot view your form in the Dialog Editor, select View⇨Resource View to open the Resource View and double-click the name of the form in the Resource View.

```
void CPartyView::OnBnClickedAdd()
{
   char caption[20];
   GetDlgItemText(IDC_ADD,caption,15);
   if (strcmp(caption,"Add New Record")==0)
   {
      SetDlgItemText(IDC_SNO, "");
      SetDlgItemText(IDC_FNAME, "");
      SetDlgItemText(IDC_LNAME, "");
      SetDlgItemText(IDC_AGE, "");
      SetDlgItemText(IDC_PREF, "");
      SetDlgItemText(IDC_ADD,"Submit");
      SetDlgItemText(IDC_DELETE,"Cancel");
   }
   else
   {
      if (m_pSet->GetRecordCount() > 0)
         m_pSet->MoveLast();
      m_pSet->AddNew();
      UpdateData(TRUE);
      if (!m_pSet->Update())
         MessageBox("Cannot add the new record");
      if (m_pSet->Requery()==0)
         return;
```

```
        UpdateData(FALSE);
        SetDlgItemText(IDC_ADD, "Add New Record");
        SetDlgItemText(IDC_DELETE,"Delete");
    }
}
```

In the above code, you determine whether the caption of the IDC_ADD button is Add New Record. If it is, you initialize all text boxes and change the caption of the Add New Record button to Submit. We also change the caption of the Delete button to Cancel. When the user clicks the Submit button, the application uses the following functions to add a new record:

- MoveLast: You call the MoveLast function to move to the end of the recordset. This function is only called if the number of records in the recordset is greater than zero, as determined by the GetRecordCount function.
- AddNew: You call the AddNew function of the CRecordset class to add a new record to the recordset.
- UpdateData: You call the UpdateData function to update the data members of the CRecordset class with the values in the form.
- Update: You update the new record in the database with the values in the data members of the CRecordset class by calling the Update function.
- Requery: You call the Requery function to refresh the recordset after adding the new record. The application queries the database and reconstructs the recordset to display updated records.

Now code the functionality of the Delete button. The application first checks the caption of the IDC_DELETE button. Here, the two types of situations are

- **When the caption is Delete:** In this case, the application deletes the current record by using the Delete method of the CRecordset class. The application also checks whether the recordset has extended beyond the last record by using the IsEOF function. If it has, the application calls the MoveLast function to move the recordset to the last record and then updates the form.
- **When the caption is Cancel:** While adding a new record, the caption of the IDC_DELETE button is Cancel. In this case, the application refreshes the recordset and changes the caption of the IDC_ADD and IDC_DELETE buttons to Add New Record and Delete, respectively, so that the changes are discarded.

The code for the Delete button is

```
void CPartyView::OnBnClickedDelete()
{
   char caption[20];
```

```
    GetDlgItemText(IDC_DELETE,caption,15);
    if (strcmp(caption,"Cancel")==0)
    {
        if (m_pSet->Requery()==0)
        return;
    UpdateData(FALSE);
    SetDlgItemText(IDC_ADD, "Add New Record");
    SetDlgItemText(IDC_DELETE, "Delete");
    }
    else
    {
        m_pSet->Delete();
        m_pSet->MoveNext();
        if (m_pSet->IsEOF())
        {
            m_pSet->MoveLast();
    }
    UpdateData(FALSE);
  }
}
```

In the code shown above, we haven't validated data before storing it in the database. Read more about data validation in Book 4, Chapter 3. The final output of the application is shown in Figure 4-10.

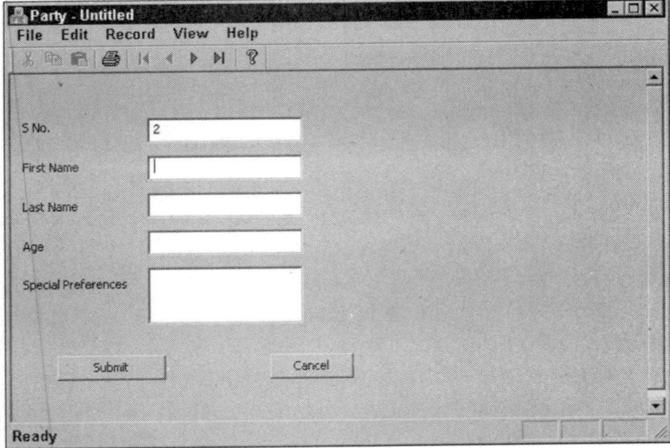

Figure 4-10: Your completed party invitation application.

With that code, you complete your application. Don't forget to fill the form and invite yourself to the party!

Chapter 5: Creating ATL Server Projects

In This Chapter

- **Exploring ATL Server**
- **Creating an ATL Server application**

Web developers face a number of challenges, such as creating high-performance multithreaded Web applications and monitoring Web sites. Microsoft provides a solution for creating high-end Web applications: Internet Services Application Programming Interface (ISAPI).

Programming in ISAPI isn't easy, however, because Visual C++ 6.0 provides limited support for creating ISAPI applications. Keeping this in mind, Microsoft has introduced ATL Server in Visual Studio .NET. ATL Server helps you develop high-end Web applications and Web services. ATL Server also helps you create ISAPI extensions and ISAPI applications easily. In this chapter, you find out the concepts pertaining to ATL Server and how to create an ATL Server application.

Exploring ATL Server

To understand ATL Server, you need to be familiar with the mechanism by which requests from the Internet are forwarded to a request handler that processes the request and yields the required Hypertext Markup Language (HTML) content. The mechanism of processing client requests also involves the use of ISAPI filters and extensions. In this section, we examine how ATL Server uses the ISAPI extension to process requests. We also examine the benefits of ATL Server.

ATL Server 101

ATL Server comprises C++ classes that aid in programming Web applications and Web services. Most of the common-functionality that was coded by Web developers has been packaged in ATL Server.

ATL Server includes several benefits that were not available before the introduction of ATL server. These benefits are summarized below:

- **Internal thread pools:** ATL Server applications can implement internal thread pools. Internal thread pools enable applications to receive multiple client requests and allocate these requests to different threads. When one thread is waiting for information from a client, another thread can continue processing client requests. This results in the high availability of a Web application or Web service.

  The mechanism of thread pools can also be implemented for desktop applications. When you implement such a mechanism for desktop applications, your application can achieve high performance levels.

- **ISAPI extensions:** When you create a project in ATL Server, two separate applications are created. One of the two applications is an ISAPI extension Dynamic Link Library (DLL) that redirects the incoming requests onto the ATL server. You can read more about the mechanism of sending client requests to ATL Server in the next section ("Processing a request in ATL Server"). By redirecting all requests to the ATL Server, ISAPI extensions enable ATL Server to perform the role of a Web server because ATL Server can allocate resources to process requests and send the requested data to the client.

- **Separation of code from HTML:** The output of a Web application is an HTML page that's displayed to the client. However, to create an HTML page, programming logic as well as data from data sources is used. When you write code in languages such as ASP 3.0, the programming code as well as the HTML tags are in the same document. This makes it difficult for you to concentrate on the logic of the program.

  In ATL Server, the programming logic and the HTML that's used to display output to users are defined separately. Therefore, it becomes easier for the application developer to concentrate on the programming logic and interface designer to concentrate on the interface of the application.

Processing a request in ATL Server

To understand how ATL Server processes a request, take a look at the sequence of steps that allow a client application to interact with an ATL Server application. The following interactions take place between a client and an ATL Server application:

1. **Client requests a resource:**

   A client requests a resource in the form of a file. The request is received at the Web server.

2. **The Web server redirects the request to the ISAPI extension:**

   IIS examines the file extension for the requested resource. When the file extension is `.srf`, Internet Information Server (IIS) passes the request to the ISAPI extension that you've designated for handling client requests.

3. **The ISAPI extension responds to the request:**

   An ISAPI extension interacts with the application DLL that's specified in the `.srf` file to retrieve the required data and send it to the client.

In the preceding step, we mention a file that has the `.srf` extension. The `.srf` extension represents the Server Response File (SRF) that's generated by an ATL Server application. The file specifies the application DLL that handles the code for the ATL Server application. The SRF file also contains the HTML code for the file and the data tags that need to be processed by the ISAPI extension DLL. In an SRF file, data tags are responsible for separating programming code from the HTML markup. You can learn more about data tags in the "Adding functionality to the wizard-generated code" section of this chapter.

Getting the benefits of ATL Server

ATL Server offers many benefits over Web applications that are created in other programming languages. We highlight these benefits in the following list:

- **Decision structures and loops:** You can use decision structures in an SRF file to control program flow. For example, you can execute one set of statements if a condition evaluates to true and another set if the condition evaluates to false.

  ATL Server supports only two program flow statements: `if/else` and `while`.

- **Accessibility to source code:** The source code of ATL Server classes is available to all ATL Server application developers. Therefore, you can modify the source code and customize it to meet your business requirements.

- **Accessibility to Windows 2000 performance objects:** Windows 2000 Performance Monitor is accessible from ATL Server applications. Therefore, you can analyze the performance of an ATL Server application.

- **Support for Visual Studio .NET:** ATL Server applications can be coded in Visual Studio .NET. When you code your applications in Visual Studio .NET, you can benefit from the debugging support and the code completion features of Visual Studio .NET. For a description of the debugging features of Visual Studio .NET, refer to Book 4, Chapter 8.

In the next section, we show you how to create your own ATL Server application.

Creating an ATL Server Application

To create an ATL Server application, follow these steps:

1. **Use the ATL Server Project or ATL Server Web Service project to create a new ATL Server project.**
2. **Add functionality to the wizard-generated code for implementing your application.**
3. **Debug the application.**
4. **Deploy the application on IIS Web server.**

Throughout this section, we discuss adding functionality to the wizard-generated code and deploying the application in detail. For more on debugging the application, see Book 4, Chapter 8.

Traversing the ATL Server Project wizard

Visual Studio .NET includes two ATL Server project templates: ATL Server Project and ATL Server Web Service. These project templates include application wizards that help you create an ATL Server application and an ATL Server Web service respectively.

A project template enables you to create a framework for your application on which you can build your application. For example, if you create a new Windows application in Visual C# and Visual Basic .NET, you'll notice that Visual Studio .NET creates a window for you. You can add controls to the window and create your application.

When you create a project by using the ATL Server Project template, Visual Studio .NET adds two applications to your project: the Web application and the ISAPI extension that redirects requests to your Web application. For this example, we use the ATL Server Project template to create a new ATL Server project.

To create a new project, follow these steps:

1. **Launch Visual Studio .NET.**
2. **Choose File⇨New⇨Project.**

   The New Project dialog box appears.
3. **In the New Project dialog box, select the Visual C++ Projects category from the list of project types.**

   The templates in the Visual C++ Projects category appear in the Templates list.

4. **Select the ATL Server Project option from the list of templates.**
5. **Name the project by typing** ATLServer1 **in the Name text box.**

   The completed New Project dialog box is shown in Figure 5-1.

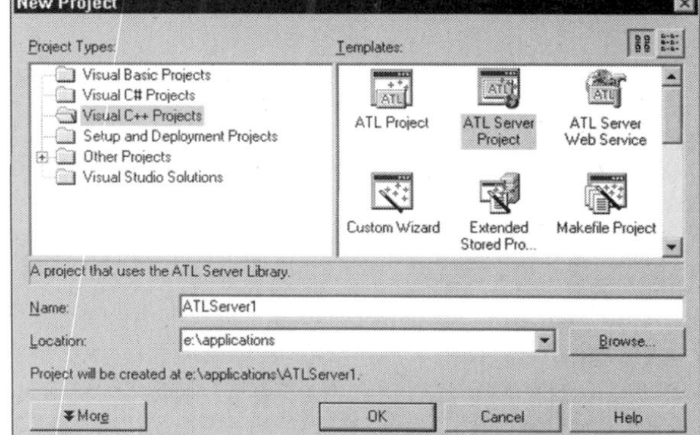

Figure 5-1: Create a new ATL Server project.

6. **Click OK to create the new project.**

   The ATL Server Project Wizard launches. This wizard is composed of five screens. By default, the Overview screen of the wizard opens first, shown in Figure 5-2, summarizing the settings of your new project.

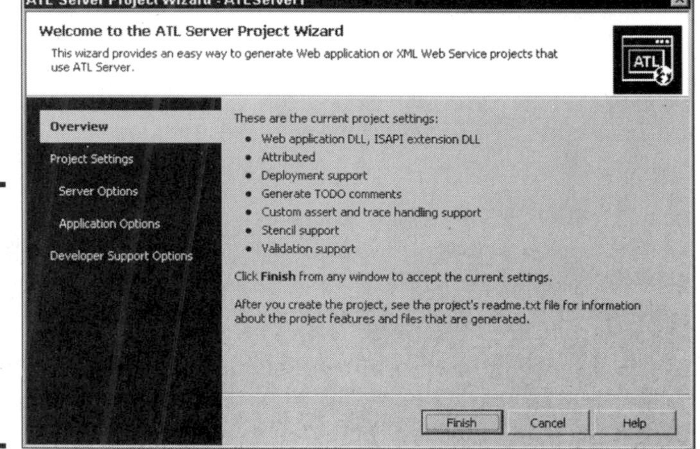

Figure 5-2: The Overview screen of the ATL Server Project Wizard.

Retain the default settings for this project. However, following is a list in which we explain what the other screens are used for:

- **Project Settings:** Use this screen to specify the project types that'll be generated for your project. By default, the Web application and the ISAPI extension are generated for your project. For a description of ATL Web applications and ISAPI extensions, refer to the "Processing a request in ATL Server" section earlier in this chapter. On this screen, you can also specify the name of the virtual root directory for your ATL Server application and the location of the ISAPI extension.
- **Server Options:** On this screen, you can select the caching-related options to implement caching for your Web application. You can also use this screen to add support for creating Performance Monitor counters and storing session-related information between client requests.
- **Application Options:** This screen is where you're able to include validation and stencil support in your application. When you select the Validation support option on this screen, Visual Studio .NET inserts necessary methods to validate forms and request queries. Similarly, stencil support generates a sample tag for your application so that you can use it as a prototype for generating tags in your application.
- **Developer Support Options:** This final screen generates ToDo comments for your application and creates attributed code. ToDo comments specify pending work in an application. When you create attributed code, Visual C++ .NET generates code to add performance monitoring capabilities and Web service request handlers for your application.

7. **Click Finish to retain the default options and create your application.**

   The ATL Server Project wizard creates an ATL Server application.

After you perform the preceding steps, the ATL Server Project creates a number of files for your project. To view these files, open Solution Explorer by pressing Ctrl+Alt+L where the files for your project are visible (see Figure 5-3).

As you can see in Figure 5-3, your project is composed of two applications, `ATLServer1` and `ATLServer1Isapi`. The important files of these applications are

- `ATLServer1`: The `ATLServer1` application is the ATL Server Web application, which includes the following important files:
  - `ATLServer1.h` and `ATLServer1.cpp`: The `ATLServer1.h` and `ATLServer1.cpp` files implement the functionality of the ATL Server Web application. These files include a default request handler for your application. As you code your application, you can add more request handlers to your application in these files.

  - `ATLServer1.srf`: The `ATLServer1.srf` file is the main server response file for your application. The Web server first invokes this file when a client requests resources from your application. The SRF file contains the HTML markup code for displaying a Web page and the data tags to retrieve data from the Visual C++ .NET application.

- `ATLServer1Isapi`: The `ATLServer1Isapi` application contains the ISAPI extension for your application. The ISAPI extension is responsible for routing requests from clients to the ATL Server application. The important files generated for the `ATLServer1Isapi` application are

  - `ATLServer1Isapi.cpp`: The `ATLServer1Isapi.cpp` contains the code that's compiled into the ISAPI extension when you build your project and also includes code to impart exception and trace handling for your ATL Server application.

  - `ATLServer1Isapi.def`: The `ATLServer1Isapi.def` file contains three default functions that are exported to your ISAPI extension: `HttpExtensionProc`, `GetExtensionVersion`, `TeminateExtension`. The `HttpExtensionProc` function provides the entry point for your application, the `GetExtensionVersion` function registers the ISAPI extension version information with IIS, and the `TeminateExtension` function unloads the ISAPI extension from IIS.

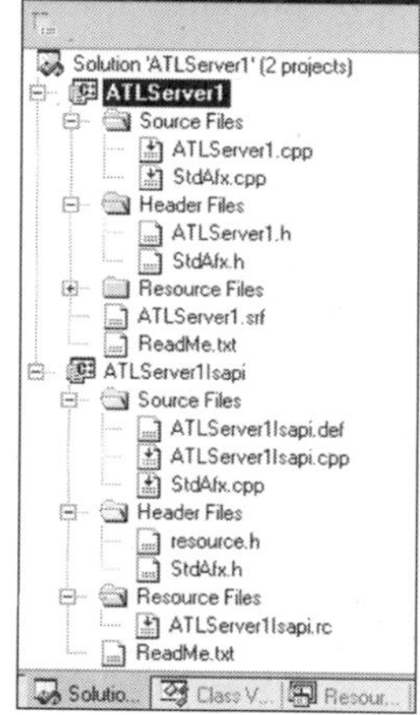

Figure 5-3: The files generated for your application.

Adding functionality to the wizard-generated code

In your application, you write code in the `ATLServer1.h` and the `ATLServer1.srf` files. The application that you create in this chapter uses the system time to compute time across different time zones in the world. For example, we use the time in the Eastern Standard Time (EST) zone to compute in three different time zones: Pacific Time, Greenwich Mean Time (GMT), and Indian Standard Time (IST). You can download this application from the Hungry Minds Web site at `www.dummies.com/extras/VS.NETAllinOne`. To run the application after downloading it, you need to follow the steps in the "Deploying the ATL Server application" section later in this chapter.

In your application, you should first create the application's interface by designing the SRF file and then implement the code required to display the required output on the SRF file. The following steps help you design your SRF file:

1. **Open the** `ATLServer1.srf` **file from Solution Explorer (press Ctrl+Alt+L).**
2. **Delete the existing code in the** `ATLServer1.srf file`**.**
3. **Add the following line of code in the** `ATLServer1.srf` **file:**

   ```
   {{handler ATLServer1.dll/Default}}
   ```

   The preceding line of code is used for declaring the request handler for the SRF file. In this code, we specify the `ATLServer1.dll` file as the default handler for all data tags that'll be used in the SRF file. Notice the double brackets in the preceding code. The double brackets are used to delimit code that needs to be executed by ATL Server from the plain HTML code on a page.
4. **On the next line, add the following code:**

   ```
   Date in New York: {{Date}}
   ```

   In the preceding code, the double brackets around `Date` signify that `Date` is a data tag. A data tag is defined in the header or CPP file that implements an ATL Server application. For example, in your application, you need to define the `Date` data tag in the `ATLServer1.h` file. We add this tag later in this section (Step 3 of the next set of tasks). When your application is running, the `Date` data tag is replaced by the output of the `Date` data tag definition in the `ATLServer1.h` file. Therefore, the output that's redirected to a client is in HTML format, even though you've generated a part of the output by using ATL Server data tags.
5. **Center-align the code from Step 4 by using the Formatting toolbar.**

   Your Web page appears in a Web browser the same way you format it in your SRF file. Therefore, make it look attractive.
6. **Open the Toolbox (press Ctrl+Alt+X) and drag a** `Horizontal Rule` **control from the Toolbox to your SRF file.**

   A horizontal line appears on your SRF page. As you added the `Horizontal Rule` control to your SRF file, you can add other controls to the SRF file from the Toolbox.

At runtime, all controls appear the same on your Web pages as they appear when you design your SRF file.

7. **Specify the following lines of code below the `Horizontal Rule` control:**

```
GMT Time: {{GMT}}

Pacific Time: {{Pacific}}

IST Time: {{IST}}
```

In the preceding code, we declare three data tags: GMT, Pacific, and IST. These data tags are used to display current time in the respective time zones.

8. **Place another `Horizontal Rule` control on your SRF file.**

Refer to Step 6 to place a `Horizontal Rule` Control on the SRF file.

9. **Add the following line of code to display information about when your page was last updated:**

```
Last updated at: {{UpdateTime}} Eastern Time
```

You can format the line that you've added above so that your application is visually appealing. After you perform the preceding steps, your form resembles the form shown in Figure 5-4.

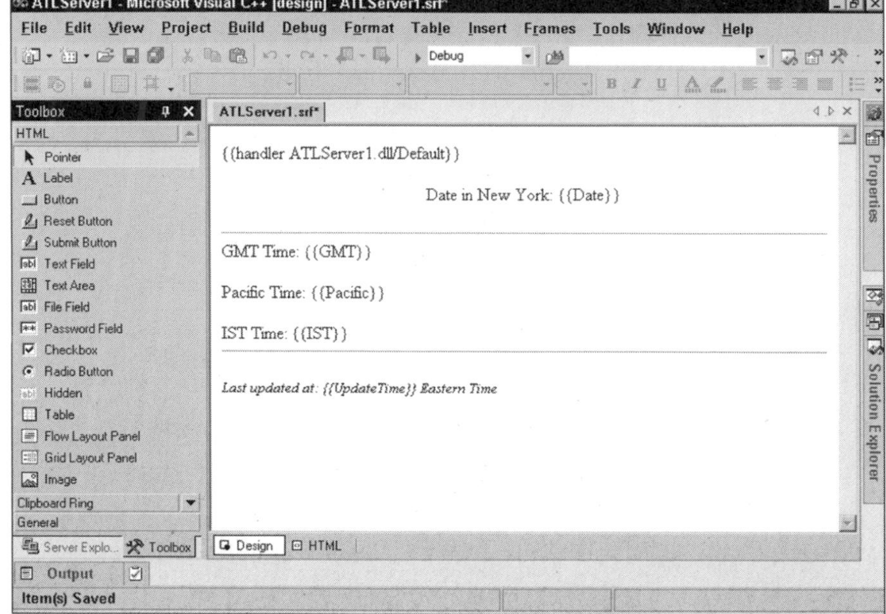

Figure 5-4: Your SRF file should resemble this file.

After you design your SRF file, you can write the code for implementing the data tags that you've used in the SRF file. To implement the data tags, follow these steps:

1. **Open the `ATLServer1.h` file by double-clicking its entry in Solution Explorer.**

   The `ATLServer1.h` file opens in the Code Editor. This file includes a `ValidateandExchange` method that's used to initialize a page before it is displayed to the user. Because we used data tags for all information that we need to retrieve programmatically, we can leave this section as is.

2. **Delete the following code from the `ATLServer1.h` file:**

   ```
   [ tag_name(name="Hello") ]
   HTTP_CODE OnHello(void)
   {
        m_HttpResponse << "Hello World!";
        return HTTP_SUCCESS;
   }
   ```

   The code that you've just deleted was a sample implementation of data tags that was generated when you created your application. However, we recommend that you examine this code so that you know how to implement data tags. In the preceding code, the `tag_name` attribute is used to declare Hello as a request handler for HTTP requests. The `OnHello` function provides the implementation of the `Hello` data tag. In other words, the output of the `Hello` data tag specified by the `m_HttpResponse` data member is displayed instead of the `{{Hello}}` statement in the SRF file.

   The first data tag that we need to implement in our application is the `Date` data tag that displays the current date.

3. **To implement the `Date` data tag, write the following code in the `protected` section of the `ATLServer1.h` file:**

   ```
   [ tag_name(name="Date") ]
   HTTP_CODE OnDate(void)
   {
        CTime ct = CTime::GetCurrentTime();
        CString St = ct.Format("%a, %B %d, %Y");
        m_HttpResponse << St;
        return HTTP_SUCCESS;
   }
   ```

   In the above code, we use the `GetCurrentTime` function of the `CTime` class to retrieve the current time. The time is then formatted into the day, month, year format and returned to the calling data tag by the `m_HttpResponse` data member.

Next, write the code for the UpdateTime data tag to display the last updated time to the user. The last updated time is nothing but the time when the ATL Server last processed a user's request.

4. **Write the following code for the UpdateTime data tag, immediately after the code for the Date data handler:**

```
[ tag_name(name="UpdateTime") ]
HTTP_CODE OnUpdateTime(void)
{
    CTime ct = CTime::GetCurrentTime();
    CString St = ct.Format("%H:%M");
    m_HttpResponse << St;
    return HTTP_SUCCESS;
}
```

In the preceding code, the current time is retrieved by using the GetCurrentTime function of the CTime class. The Format function of the CTime class formats the current time to the hh:mm format and returns it to the user.

Finally, you need to write the code for the GMT, Pacific, and IST data tags. The logic for implementing these data tags is

- Declare a function, GetTimeSpan, that accepts the hours and minutes to add or subtract from a CTime object as parameters.
- Declare an object of the CTimeSpan class and assign the hours and minutes accepted as parameters of the GetTimeSpan function to the object of the CTimeSpan class.
- Add or subtract the time span represented by the object of the CTimeSpan class from the current time.
- Format the output and return it to the function that invoked the GetTimeSpan function.
- Redirect the output from the GetTimeSpan function to the user.

5. **Write the following code for the GetTimeSpan function, immediately below the code that you wrote in Step 4:**

```
CString GetTimeSpan(int hr,int min)
{
    CTimeSpan TimeSpan= CTimeSpan(0,hr,min,0);
    CTime ct = CTime::GetCurrentTime();
    ct=ct+TimeSpan;
    CString St = ct.Format("%H:%M (%B %d)");
    return St;
}
```

6. **Write the following code to implement the GMT, Pacific, and IST data tags:**

   ```
   [ tag_name(name="GMT") ]
   HTTP_CODE OnGMT(void)
   {
        m_HttpResponse << GetTimeSpan(5,0);
        return HTTP_SUCCESS;
   }
   [ tag_name(name="Pacific") ]
   HTTP_CODE OnPacific(void)
   {
        m_HttpResponse << GetTimeSpan(-3,0);
        return HTTP_SUCCESS;
   }
   [ tag_name(name="IST") ]
   HTTP_CODE OnIST(void)
   {
        m_HttpResponse << GetTimeSpan(10,30);
        return HTTP_SUCCESS;
   }
   ```

   The preceding code simply calls the `GetTimeSpan` function and passes the required number of hours and minutes to add or subtract from the current time to get the current time in the required time zone. For example, GMT is ahead of EST by five hours; therefore, you pass five hours and zero minutes as parameters to the `GetTimeSpan` function. Similarly, IST is ten and a half hours ahead of EST and Pacific time is three hours behind EST.

You're done with your application. The next step is to deploy the application so that you can run it and see the output.

Deploying the ATL Server application

After you create an ATL Server application, you need to explicitly deploy it on the IIS Web server. It is only after you deploy your application that you can test and debug it. To build and deploy your application, follow these steps:

1. **Choose Build⇨Build Solution.**

   Visual Studio .NET builds your application and creates a DLL file. You can now deploy the file.

2. **Open Solution Explorer by pressing Ctrl+Alt+L.**

3. **Right-click** `ATLServer1` **and choose Deploy from the shortcut menu.**

   To deploy an ATL Server application, you can also click the name of the application in Solution Explorer and choose Build⇨Deploy.

   Visual Studio .NET deploys your ATL Server application and the ISAPI extension for your project on the IIS Web server.

You've successfully deployed your application. You can now run your application and check out the output. Choose Debug⇨Start to run your application. The output of your application is shown in Figure 5-5.

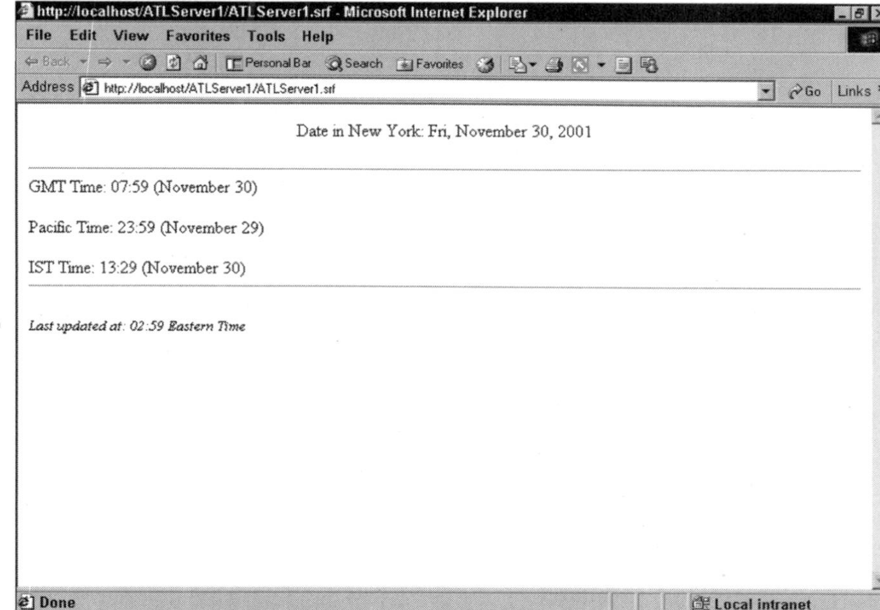

Figure 5-5: The output of your ATL Server application, showing the current time in different time zones.

Chapter 6: Programming in Managed Extensions for C++

In This Chapter

- Discussing application types created in managed extensions
- Using managed extensions to create a console application

Managed extensions are a set of language extensions for Visual C++ .NET. You can use these extensions to create Visual C++ .NET applications that run on the .NET Framework. Although you may not be familiar with Visual C++ programming, creating applications with managed extensions is an effortless task because managed extensions provide an easier alternative to other C++ technology, such as Active Template Library (ATL) and Microsoft Foundation Classes (MFC).

In this chapter, you discover the types of applications that you can create using managed extensions. We also walk you through creating a console application. A console application is an application that's run from the command prompt. For a detailed description of types of applications created in Visual Studio .NET, refer to Book 1, Chapter 4.

While you create your application, we discuss the namespaces and classes provided by managed extensions. We even toss in some details on how to manipulate strings, arrays, and date-time functions.

For a brief description of managed extensions, read through Book 4, Chapter 1. For a description of the .NET Framework, peruse Book 1, Chapter 3.

Discovering Types of Applications

Of all languages in Visual Studio .NET, Visual C++ .NET provides the most elaborate range of templates to create applications. Because templates make it easy for you to create applications, Visual C++ .NET applications are the easiest to create! Templates provided by Visual C++ .NET can be categorized into templates for creating unmanaged applications and templates to create applications using managed applications. (You can learn about unmanaged applications and how to create them in Book 4, Chapters 2–5.)

Visual C++ .NET provides the following templates to create applications using managed extensions:

- **Managed C++ Application**
- **Managed C++ Class Library**
- **Managed C++ Web Service**
- **Managed C++ Empty Project**

Read through the following sections for descriptions of these project templates, when you use them, and the files that are generated when you create a project in each of these templates.

Managed C++ Application template

You use the Managed C++ Application template to create applications that are executed in the managed environment, such as Web services and Windows applications, that need to interact with applications that are developed by using other .NET languages. To create these applications, launch Visual Studio and follow these steps:

1. **Choose File⇨New⇨Project.**

   The New Project dialog box appears.

2. **Click Managed C++ Application from the list of project templates in the Visual C++ Projects category.**

3. **Enter a name for the project in the Name text box and then click OK.**

   Visual Studio .NET creates a new Hello World application in Visual C++. (An application similar to the Hello World application created by the Managed C++ Application template is described in Book 4, Chapter 1.)

To view the files created by the Managed C++ Application template, open Solution Explorer by choosing View⇨Solution Explorer (or press Ctrl+Alt+L). You'll notice the following files in your project:

- `stdafx.h`: The `stdafx.h` file includes commonly used header files in your project. By default, this file is included in all your source files. Therefore, instead of including multiple header files in each source file, you can include them in `stdafx.h` and make them available across all source files.
- `stdafx.cpp`: This file includes any precompiled types that are used by your project. In addition, the file specifies the preprocessor directive for including the `stdafx.h` file (`#include "stdafx.h"`). When you include precompiled types in the `stdafx.h` file, your code compiles faster.

When you compile your project for the first time, the compiler builds precompiled header files for your project. During subsequent compilation, only the files that are changed are recompiled. No precompiled header files are recompiled. This results in faster compilation.

- `AssemblyInfo.cpp`: The `AssemblyInfo.cpp` file specifies assembly information for your application. An assembly stores namespaces and information about types used in your application. For a description of assemblies and namespaces, refer to Book 1, Chapter 2. When you compile your application, it creates an assembly for your application.
- `Application.cpp`: The `Application.cpp` file is executed when you run your application. This file functions as the primary file in your application and all other files in your application support the functionality of this file. The `Application.cpp` file includes a preprocessor directive to include the `mscorlib.dll` file and provides a `main()` function, which is the first function that's executed in your application.

The word *Application* in `Application.cpp` refers to the name of your application. Thus, if you name your application *MyApplication*, this file accordingly gets the name `MyApplication.cpp`.

You have ample opportunity to use this template in this chapter in the section "Creating a Console Application."

Assemblies and assembly attributes

An assembly needs to be assigned certain characteristic identifiers, called *attributes*, which can be used to identify the assembly. These identifiers are defined in the `AssemblyInfo.cpp` file, which imports the `Reflection` namespace into your application. This namespace is used to retrieve information about assemblies and types used in your application.

Assembly attributes, defined in the `AssemblyInfo.cpp` file, store information related to the identity of an assembly, its company and product information, its description, and its strong name. Assembly identity and strong name are discussed below:

- **Identity:** The name, version, and culture of an assembly determine its identity. The *culture* of an assembly determines whether an assembly is a main assembly or a satellite assembly. A *main assembly* is an independent unit of application, and a *satellite assembly* is used to execute another application successfully.
- **Strong name:** The *strong name* of an assembly is used to add a digital signature to an assembly. A digital signature is used to establish the authenticity of information. After you digitally sign an assembly, it's unique. Thus, if two assemblies have the same strong name, their digital signatures are identical — and therefore, the assemblies are also identical.

Managed C++ Class Library template

A *class library* is a collection of classes that you can use in an application. Most of the classes and methods that you use in a managed application are a part of the .NET Framework class library. However, you can also build your own class library for use in your applications. For example, suppose that you want to use some generic functions that validate a user against a data source. Save yourself the effort of writing these functions in all applications by defining them in a class library and using the class library in the required applications.

You can create a class library that uses managed extensions by using the Managed C++ Class Library template. When you create a new application by using this template, Visual Studio .NET generates the following files for your application:

- **stdafx.h, stdafx.cpp, and AssemblyInfo.cpp:** We discuss these files in the previous section "Managed C++ Application template." However, the stdafx.h file in the Managed C++ Class Library template is unique in that it includes the preprocessor directive for importing the mscorlib.dll file (#using <mscorlib.dll>). Therefore, you don't need to include the mscorlib.dll file in the application.h or application.cpp files.
- **Application.h:** The Application.h header file defines a namespace and a class for your project. By default, the name of the namespace is the same as the name of your application, and the name of the class is Class1. You can change these names, if you want the name of the namespace and class to represent your application. For example, if you're creating an application to register employees, you might want to name the namespace EmployeeRegister.

  In the declaration of the class, notice that the __gc class keyword is used, as shown in the following code snippet:

  ```
  namespace Library1
  {
     public __gc class Class1
     {
        // TODO: Add your methods for this class here.
     };
  }
  ```

  The __gc class keyword specifies that the class is created using managed extensions and it should be executed in the common language runtime (CLR) environment. Thus, garbage collection and cross-language interoperability, which are provided by the CLR, are implemented in your program. (You can learn more about garbage collection and CLR in Book 1, Chapter 3.)
- **Application.cpp:** The Application.cpp file is the source file for the class library. This file is used to create the final output of your application.

Managed C++ Web Service template

Use the Managed C++ Web Service template to create a *Web service* — an application that can be accessed by other applications through the Internet. You can learn the details about Web services in several chapters within Book 7.

The Managed C++ Web Service template generates a number of files, some of which are similar to the files generated by the Managed C++ Application and Managed C++ Class Library templates. The additional files generated by the Managed C++ Web Service project template are

- **Disco file:** The name sounds pretty interesting. Your Web service creates a disco file (short for *disco*very, with a `.vsdicso` extension). Web service clients use the disco file to discover the features of your Web service. Just as this book helps you to discover Visual Studio .NET, the discovery file helps Web service clients link to resources that describe the Web service. The description helps the client applications determine the functionality of your Web service, the methods it implements, and the mode of communication best suited to interact with it.
- **Config file:** This file stores the *config*uration settings of your Web service. If you need to change the configuration of your Web service, such as implementing a custom authentication method to authenticate Web service clients, you need to change the configuration settings in this file.
- **`Global.asax` and `Global.asax.h`:** The `Global.asax` file is analogous to the `Global.asa` file in Active Server Pages (ASP) 3.0. `Global.asax` points to the `Global.asax.h` file that contains function declarations for implementing the application-level and session-level events raised by your application.
- **ASMX file:** A file with an `.asmx` extension is created by Visual Studio .NET. This file references the managed classes defined in the `Application.h` file and is responsible for implementing the functionality of a Web service.

Managed C++ Empty Project template

The Managed C++ Empty Project template is the simplest of all templates. It doesn't create any source file for your project, but rather ports existing applications to the managed environment. The template simply provides the necessary configuration settings to compile your application in the managed environment.

To check out the configuration settings specified by the template, right-click the project name in Solution Explorer (press Ctrl+Alt+L to open Solution Explorer) and select Properties from the shortcut menu that appears. The property pages of the project appear, as shown in Figure 6-1. Notice in this figure that the Use Managed Extensions Property option is specified as Yes.

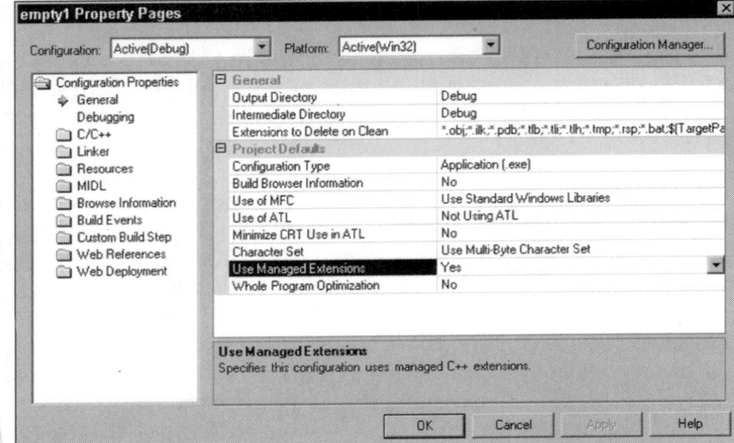

Figure 6-1: View project configuration settings of your application.

If you explore the General option under the C/C++ option in the tree view on the left, you'll notice that the `/clr` switch is enabled. This switch notifies the compiler that the application output will be executed by the CLR. You can learn more about the switches required for executing a managed application in Book 4, Chapter 7.

Creating a Console Application

To create a console application, you use the Managed C++ Application template. Follow along as we create an application that accepts month and a year as parameters to display the calendar for the specified month and year. You can obtain this application from the Hungry Minds Web site at `www.dummies.com/extras/VS.NETAllinOne`. The application is named Cal.

Create a new project in Visual C++ .NET. (Follow the steps in the "Managed C++ Application template" section, earlier in this chapter.) Specify the name of the new project as *Cal*. The new project that you create is, by default, a Hello World application. Look at the existing code of this application before we proceed to create a new project.

Examining the existing code in your application

Note the following code in the `main()` function defined in the `Cal.cpp` file:

```
Console::WriteLine(S"Hello World");
return 0;
```

C++ literals

Traditional C++ literals include variables of the type `String` that are declared with or without the prefix `T`. There is a clear difference between these string variables and the string variables declared with the prefix `S`. Suppose that you have two string variables with the same value. In case of string literals declared with the `S` prefix, these string variables always point to the same object. However, in case of string literals declared with the `T` prefix, the string variables might point to different objects.

In this code, the `WriteLine` method of the `Console` class is used to display the message `Hello World` at the command prompt. (Read more about the `Console` class and its `WriteLine` method in Book 4, Chapter 1.) The `WriteLine` method has a number of overloads that allow you to print multiple data types, such as `float`, `double`, and `String`. Note that the prefix `S` is added to the string `Hello World`. `S` is a new string literal defined in managed extensions. A *string literal* is a language constant that's used to represent strings. Using the `S` string literal in managed code is preferable because it gives better results than the conventional C++ literals.

Now customize your application code and begin to create a calendar application. Start off by deleting the `Console::WriteLine(S"Hello World");` statement from your code.

Tracing the logic of the application

Take a minute to think about the logic of a calendar application before you create it. You need this application to accept the month and year from a user. You begin by calculating the number of days in the month and the first day of the month. By knowing the first day of the month and the number of days in that month, you can create a calendar. You can then store the dates of the month in an array and format the output before it's displayed on-screen.

Employ this same logic to create your application. The first step is to accept a month and a year from a user.

Accepting information from a user

First display a message asking the user to enter the required year and month. (The following code snippet prompts the user to specify a date and month.) You use the `WriteLine` method of the `Console` class to display the message. Next, use the ReadLine method of the Console class to accept the required information. The ReadLine method accepts a sequence of characters from the command prompt. The data accepted by the ReadLine method is in the String format. This information is then stored in the szYear and szMonth String variables.

```
Console::WriteLine("--------------------------");
Console::WriteLine("My own calendar application");
Console::WriteLine("--------------------------");
Console::WriteLine();
Console::Write("Please specify the year: ");
String* szYear=Console::ReadLine();
Console::Write("Please specify the month: ");
String* szMonth=Console::ReadLine();
```

The IntelliSense feature provides a description of possible errors in the code in the status bar, as you type your code. This feature is especially useful when you write code in managed extensions. As you type the code, look at the status bar for clues that tell you whether you're typing correctly. For example, if you type **System.Console** instead of **System::Console** (something that you might do if you're used to another language, such as Visual Basic .NET or Visual C# .NET), you get the message `Could not understand expression to the left of . or ->.`

In the preceding code, note the `Console::WriteLine();` statement without any parameters. This statement is used to draw a blank line on the command prompt.

Determining days and dates in a month

Use the values of the szMonth and szYear variables to determine the first day of a month. To determine what day of the week the first day of the month falls on, follow these steps:

1. **Convert the year and month specified by the user to a specific date.**

   For example, convert 2002 and 12 to 01/12/2001.

2. **Use the .NET Framework to determine the day of the week on the corresponding date.**

   The .NET Framework provides the DateTime structure for date- and time- related operations. You can use the Parse method of this structure to obtain the DateTime equivalent of a date specified as a String data type. Thus, if you supply a variable of String data type, such as 01/31/2002 to the Parse method, the variable gets converted to the DateTime data type — 01/31/2002.

After you obtain the date in the DateTime format, you call the DayOfWeek method of the DateTime structure to obtain the day of the week. This method returns an Integer data type that specifies the day of the week — starting from 0 for Sunday. Thus, if the method returns 6, you know that the day of the week corresponding to the date that you specified is Saturday. For the date 01/31/2002, the function would return 4 because 01/31/2002 was a Thursday.

To use the DateTime structure in your application, follow these steps:

1. **Add the first date of the month (01) to the month and year provided by the user, as given in the following code.**

   You get a specific date. To combine the month, date, and year and form a string, use the Concat method of the String class.

2. **After you get the string format of the specific date, pass the format to an object of the DateTime structure and then retrieve the day of the week for the first day of the specified month and year.**

The complete code for the preceeding sequence of steps is

```
//Specify the date as mm/dd/yyyy
String* szFirstDate="/01/";
String* szDate=String::Concat(szMonth,szFirstDate);
szDate=String::Concat(szDate,szYear);
//determine the first day of the month
int intDayWeek;
DateTime dt;
dt=DateTime::Parse(szDate);
intDayWeek = dt.DayOfWeek;
```

The next step in creating a calendar is to determine the number of days in a month. You use the DaysInMonth method of the DateTime structure to get this information.

The DaysInMonth method accepts the year and month in integer form as parameters. To convert the year and month specified by the user into integers, use the Convert class. The Convert class of the .NET Framework class library provides a variety of functions to convert data types from one type to another. For example, you can use the ToDateTime function to convert a specified value to the DateTime format. Similarly, you can convert a Boolean value to a String by using the ToString function.

In your application, you use the ToInt32 function of the Convert class. This function converts a String data type to a 32-bit signed integer.

The code to convert the year and month specified by a user to `Int32` and to use these values to determine the number of days in the month is

```
//Convert month and year to int
int intNoDays, intYear, intMonth;
intYear=Convert::ToInt32(szYear);
intMonth=Convert::ToInt32(szMonth);
//Determine the number of days in the month
intNoDays=DateTime::DaysInMonth(intYear,intMonth);
```

Building the output

After you gather all the ingredients for building the output of your application, you need to create an array of the days and dates for displaying a calendar on-screen.

To create an array, include the `System::Collections` namespace in your application and use `ArrayList` class of the namespace. To include the `System::Collections` namespace in your application, specify the following code line after the statement `using namespace System;`:

```
using namespace System::Collections;
```

An *array* is a sequence of elements that are grouped and stored together. For example, you can store the numbers 1 to 10 in an array. The numbers in the array are its *elements*.

Instantiate the `ArrayList` class and add elements to it by using the `Add` method of the `ArrayList` class. This method accepts a pointer to the `String` data type as the parameter.

In our running example, first add the days of the week to an array named `cal`. The code for the same is

```
//building the output
ArrayList* cal=new ArrayList();
//Add days of the month to the array
cal->Add(ForArray("  S  "));
cal->Add(ForArray("  M  "));
cal->Add(ForArray("  T  "));
cal->Add(ForArray("  W  "));
cal->Add(ForArray("  T  "));
cal->Add(ForArray("  F  "));
cal->Add(ForArray("  S  "));
```

In the preceding code, note that we include two spaces before and after the day of the week. We're adding two spaces before and after the day of the week to enhance the appearance of the final output of the application. To convert the day of the week to the String data type before adding the day to the array, we use the ForArray function, which is shown below:

```
String* ForArray(char* szDay)
{
        String* strArr = szDay;
        return strArr;
}
```

Just like any other C++ functions, you need to declare the ForArray function outside the main() function. Write the following line before the definition of the main() function:

```
String* ForArray(char* szDay);
```

Next, insert blank spaces in your calendar for the days before the first date of the month. For example, if your month starts on a Thursday, you need to leave out the first four days: Sunday through Wednesday. We use the value in the intDayWeek variable — which specifies the first day of the month — to add the required blank spaces to the cal array. The code for this is

```
int intCnt=0;
intCnt=0;
while (intCnt < intDayWeek)
{
     cal->Add(ForArray("      "));
     intCnt=intCnt+1;
}
```

Now add the required dates to the calendar. These dates are retrieved from the intNoDays variable by using the following code:

```
intCnt=1;
while (intCnt <= intNoDays)
{
    cal->Add(ForArray(intCnt));
    intCnt=intCnt+1;
}
```

Again, we use the ForArray function to add the required number of spaces to the date before assigning it to the array. The definition of this function is

```
String* ForArray(int intDate)
{
      String* strArr=Convert::ToString(intDate);
```

```
        String* strSpace= " ";
        if (intDate < 10)
        {
              strSpace=String::Concat(strSpace,strSpace);
              strArr=String::Concat(strSpace,strArr);
              strArr=String::Concat(strArr,strSpace);
        }
        else
        {
              strArr=String::Concat(strSpace,strArr);
              strSpace=String::Concat(strSpace,strSpace);
              strArr=String::Concat(strArr,strSpace);
        }
        return strArr;
}
```

In the preceding code, we determine whether the date is less than 10. If it is, we insert an extra blank space before the date; otherwise, we insert one blank space before and two blank spaces after the date. That's because if the date is less than 10, the date will contain only one digit. However, if the date is more than 10, it will contain two digits. Adding an extra space before the date compensates the one less digit if the date is less than 10.

Note that the ForArray function used here has a different functionality than the ForArray function we use earlier in this section, when we had converted the day of the week into a String data type. Such an implementation in which two functions accept different parameters and have a different functionality is known as *function overloading*. We overload the ForArray function to operate differently for different data types.

You need to declare all overloads of a function before implementing them so that the compiler can recognize the overloaded functions. You do this by adding another line of code to your application and before the main() function:

```
String* ForArray(int intDate);
```

Displaying the output

Time to display the output of your application. First, add a few blank lines to the application, to enhance the appearance of your application, and then display the month and year for which you're creating the output. This is accomplished with the following code:

```
//displaying the output
Console::WriteLine("");
Console::WriteLine("");
```

```
szMonth=FormatMonth(intMonth);
Console::Write(String::Concat("Calendar for ",szMonth));
Console::WriteLine(String::Concat(", ",szYear));
Console::WriteLine("");
Console::WriteLine("");
```

In the preceding code, the `FormatMonth` function returns the name corresponding to the month number. For example, this function returns `December` for the month `12`. All that you need to do to implement this function is to

1. **Declare the `FormatMonth` function before the `main()` function by writing the following code:**

   ```
   String* FormatMonth(int intMonth);
   ```

2. **Implement the `FormatMonth` function as given below:**

   ```
   String* FormatMonth(int intMonth)
   {
               String* strMonth;
               switch(intMonth)
               {
               case 1:
                     return strMonth = "January";
                     break;
               case 2:
                     return strMonth = "February";
                     break;
               case 3:
                     return strMonth = "March";
                     break;
               case 4:
                     return strMonth = "April";
                     break;
               case 5:
                     return strMonth = "May";
                     break;
               case 6:
                     return strMonth = "June";
                     break;
               case 7:
                     return strMonth = "July";
                     break;
               case 8:
                     return strMonth = "August";
                     break;
               case 9:
                     return strMonth = "September";
                     break;
   ```

```
                    case 10:
                         return strMonth = "October";
                         break;
                    case 11:
                         return strMonth = "November";
                         break;
                    case 12:
                         return strMonth = "December";
                         break;
                    default:
                         return strMonth = "Invalid";
               }
          }
```

In the last step, you read the elements of the array and display a calendar. To do this, use the `get_Item` method, which retrieves a specific element from a collection.

An instance of an `ArrayList` class is a *collection*. A collection is a group of variables that are stored as a single logical unit. Each element in a collection can be accessed by its index value. The index value is the position of an element in a collection. Thus, the first element has the index value 0, the second has the value 1, and so on.

When you retrieve the elements of the array, you use the `Write` function of the `Console` class to write the first six elements of the array in the same line. Every seventh element of the array is written using the `WriteLine` function so that the next element begins in a new line. The code for such an output is given below:

```
int i,j;
i=0;
j=0;
while (i < cal->Count)
{
if (j < 6)
     {
          Console::Write(cal->get_Item(i));
          j++;
     }
     else
     {
Console::WriteLine(cal->get_Item(i));
          j=0;
     }
     i++;
}
Console::WriteLine(" ");
Console::WriteLine(" ");
Console::WriteLine(" ");
```

The lower bound of an array is `0`. Therefore, the first element in the array has the index `0` and can be represented as `cal(0)`. Thus, if you need to retrieve the first six elements, you need to retrieve the indexed elements `0`—`5` of the array.

Your application is now complete. However, if you execute your application, you'll notice that the output disappears as soon as the calendar is displayed. To get around this problem, your application should wait for the user to press any key before it is terminated so that the user can see the output. The steps to halt the application until the user presses a key are given below:

1. **Include the `conio.h` header file into your project by specifying the following line of the code in the `Cal.cpp` file:**

   ```
   #include <conio.h>
   ```

2. **Write the following lines of code before the `return 0;` statement in the `main()` function:**

   ```
   Console::WriteLine("Press any key to continue");
   _getch();
   ```

   In the preceding code, the message `"Press any key to continue"` is displayed on the screen and the application control moves to the `_getch()` function. The `_getch()` waits for the user to press any key. As soon as the user presses a key, the control moves to the end of the function and the application is terminated.

Compile and execute your application by performing these steps:

1. **Compile the application by choosing Build⇨Build.**

   A message appears stating that the build process was successfully completed.

   If you get an error message, look for the error in the Task List, which appears automatically if there is an error. It displays the line in which the error occurred and the description of the error. To know more about the Task List, refer to Book 4, Chapter 8.

2. **Execute your application by choosing Debug⇨Start.**

   The final output of your program appears. The calendar application prompts you to specify a month and year.

3. **Specify a month and a year of your choice to view the calendar.**

   As shown in Figure 6-2, we time-travel back to September, 1850. You can do the same for your month and year of birth.

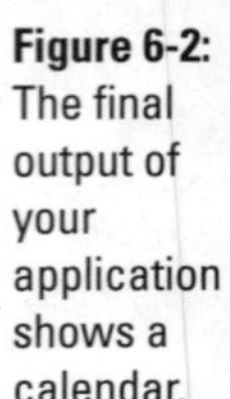

Figure 6-2: The final output of your application shows a calendar.

Chapter 7: Mixing and Matching Managed and Unmanaged Code

In This Chapter

- **Discovering the pros and cons of using managed code**
- **Adding managed code to your application**

In Visual C++ .NET, you can develop applications that are based purely on managed extensions for C++ — see Book 4, Chapter 6 — or based on unmanaged code, such as applications developed by using Microsoft Foundation Classes (MFC) — see Book 4, Chapters 3 and 4 for MFC applications. Applications that are created by using managed extensions utilize the .NET Framework class libraries and run in the common language runtime (CLR) environment. On the other hand, applications that don't use managed extensions are executed outside the CLR environment and cannot reap the advantages of CLR, such as garbage collection and just-in-time compilation.

For a description of CLR and its features, refer to Book 1, Chapter 2.

Consider this scenario: You've written a program without using managed extensions. However, you know that some of the functionality in your program can be easily implemented by using the classes and namespaces of managed extensions. To the rescue, Visual C++ .NET offers you the flexibility to write managed *and* unmanaged code in the same application. Thus, you have the best of both worlds at your disposal, which was not possible before. In this chapter, we embark on a journey creating applications that use managed as well as unmanaged code.

Throughout this chapter, we use the term *managed code* for code written with managed extensions for C++ and *unmanaged code* for code that doesn't use these extensions.

Determining Where to Use Managed Code

In this section, we examine some of the pros and cons of using managed and unmanaged code in the same application. As you can discover, some instances don't warrant using managed extensions; with others, you clearly benefit from using them.

Advantages of using managed extensions

The advantages of using managed extensions in an application that was previously written in unmanaged code are

- **Interoperability:** Applications written with managed extensions easily interoperate with applications developed in other languages of the .NET suite. For example, you may write code interfaces of your application in managed extensions so that these interfaces are easily available in another language, such as Visual Basic .NET.
- **Enhanced exception handling:** Exception handling in managed extensions for C++ is well developed. In managed extensions, exceptions are considered as objects and can be processed independently of the other programming logic. Handle exceptions by specifying `Try` and `Catch` blocks for handling exceptions. When your application throws an exception, the runtime implements the exception handler to handle the exception. If no exception handler is available, a default handler displays the error name and error message along with the method in which the exception was thrown.

  Managed extensions for C++ provide the `System::Exception` class for handling exceptions. You can use this class to identify the location and the cause for an exception and examine the stack trace. The *stack trace* is a list of all methods called by your application. The list specifies the name of the method and line numbers of the application code where the runtime made method calls.
- **Access to CLR:** Managed code is executed by the common language runtime (CLR). Therefore, your managed code benefits from the enhanced features of CLR. These features include cross-language exception handling as well as enhanced versioning and deployment support. You can learn about common language runtime in Book 1, Chapter 2.

Constraints of using managed and unmanaged code in the same application

Using managed and unmanaged code in the same application can lead to some constraints, including the following:

- **Arguments of the `main()` function:** When your application solely uses managed extensions, you can't use arguments of the managed type in the `main()` function. For example, you can't use the `String*` data type as an argument in the `main()` function. Instead, use the `char*` data type.

  Managed types in Visual C++ are either gc types or value types. gc types are managed types that use the common language runtime heap for execution. Therefore, garbage collection is performed on the managed heap. On the other hand, values types are allocated on the call stack.

Therefore, the garbage collector doesn't act on these types. For a detailed explanation on garbage collection and managed heaps, read through Book 1, Chapter 3.

- **Compilation of managed types:** In the debug version of MFC programs, the compiler redefines the `new` operator when you compile your application. Therefore, when you use managed types, the compiler may generate an error stating that placement arguments aren't allowed in new instances of managed classes. However, this error doesn't appear in the Release configuration of your application. (Read more on project configurations in Book 4, Chapter 8.)

When you use the `new` operator, you can also avoid compilation errors in the Debug configuration by using Visual C++ .NET macros. These macros are a part of the Visual C++ class library and allow you to undefine the new operator before creating instances of the managed type. After you've created instances of managed types, you can redefine the new operator.

Managing Your Application

In this section, we discuss how to add managed code to an application. We reuse an application that we create in Book 4, Chapter 2. Even if you haven't read that chapter, you can download the MyFirstApplication application from `www.dummies.com/extras/VS.NETAllinOne`. You can also download the completed application for this chapter from the same Web site. The completed application is in the Managed-Unmanaged application folder.

When you add managed code to an existing application, you first need to change project settings so that the compiler can identify that your code needs to be compiled for the managed environment. After you change the project settings, you can write managed code in your application executed by the common language runtime.

Changing project settings

By changing project settings, you make the `/clr` switch available for compiling your code. The `/clr` compiler option compiles your code into an application that requires the common language runtime for its execution. In addition to enabling the `/clr` switch, you need to disable the switches that are incompatible with the `/clr` switch.

Open the application that has to be compiled for the managed environment and perform the following steps (for performing these steps, you can open the MyFirstApplication application):

1. **Open Solution Explorer by choosing View⇨Solution Explorer.**
2. **In the Solution Explorer window that opens, right-click the name of the project and click Properties on the shortcut menu.**

   The *Application* Property Pages dialog box appears (where *Application* is the name of your project).
3. **Click the C/C++ option beneath Configuration Properties in the tree-view panel (left side of the dialog box).**

   The suboptions of the C/C++ option are now visible in the tree-view panel.
4. **Click the General suboption.**

   See how the MyFirstApplication Property Pages dialog box appears (Figure 7-1) after you make these selections.

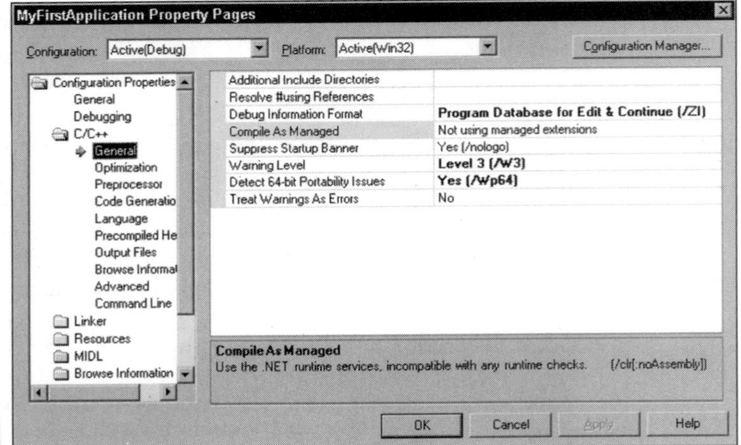

Figure 7-1: Configure your project in the MyFirst-Application Property Pages dialog box.

5. **Click the Compiled as Managed property option and select Assembly Support (/clr) (from the right side of the screen).**

   The `/clr` switch is available for your application. Now, when you run your application, it's run by the common language runtime.

Three compilation switches, `/ZI`, `/RTC1`, and `/Gm`, aren't compatible with the `/clr` switch. You need to disable these switches in your managed application.

The `/ZI` switch builds a single program database for storing debug information of your program, which prevents redundant information and saves disk space. The `/RTC1` switch checks your code for runtime errors, such as loss of data when it's assigned to a variable of lower capacity. The `/Gm` switch enables minimal rebuild, in which only the source code that's changed after the last compilation is recompiled.

Follow these steps to disable the three switches. You're still in MyFirstApplication Property Pages dialog box.

1. **To disable the `/ZI` switch, click Debug Information Format (in the General suboption beneath the C/C++ option) and select the Disabled option from the choices on the right side.**

   The `/ZI` switch is now disabled.

2. **To disable the `/RTC1` switch, first select the Code Generation suboption beneath the C/C++ option in the MyFirstApplication Property Pages dialog box tree view.**

3. **From the right side of the screen, select the Default option for the Basic Runtime Checks property.**

   The `/RTC1` switch is now disabled.

4. **To disable the `/Gm` option, select the No option for the Enable Minimal Rebuild property of your application (you're still in the Code Generation suboption).**

   The `/Gm` switch is now disabled.

   See how the MyFirstApplication Property Pages dialog box looks (Figure 7-2) after you disable these three switches.

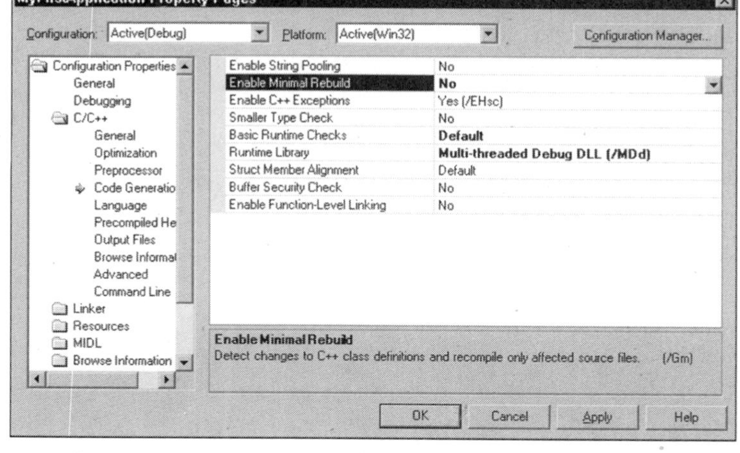

Figure 7-2: Disable non-compatible compilation switches in the MyFirst-Application Property Pages dialog box.

5. **Click the Apply button and then click OK to save your changes and to close the MyFirstApplication Property Pages dialog box.**

Your application is now ready to be executed in a managed environment. Now you need to write managed code for your application.

Writing managed code

The application that we use for this chapter is used to draw geometric figures and display them on-screen. (Read through the development of this application in Book 4, Chapter 2.) In this application, we use the `Rectangle` and `RoundRect` functions of the `CClientDC` class to draw rectangles on the screen. In another version of this application (Book 4, Chapter 2), we draw all figures by using the same blue color.

In this version of the application, we use the `Random` class of the `System` namespace to generate a new RGB (red, green, blue) combination each time. RGB combinations characterize colors; they comprise quantities of red, green, and blue to compose variant colors. Because RGB values range from 0 to 255, when you generate a random value number for each color, you get a different color every time. We load the new color in an object of the `CBrush` class and use the brush to draw figures of a different color each time.

Follow this sequence of steps to add the required code to your application to make the color values change:

1. **Open the `MyFrame.cpp` file and add the following lines after the `#include "MyDialog.h"` directive:**

   You can open the `MyFrame.cpp` file from Solution Explorer. (Press Ctrl+Alt+L to open Solution Explorer.)

```
using namespace System;
__gc class draw
{
   public:
   int GetNumber(int a)
   {
      System::Random *rnd;
      rnd= new System::Random();
      return rnd->Next(a);
   }
};
```

   In the preceding code, the `__gc` keyword for the declaration of the class signifies that garbage collection is performed on the class. This magical keyword ensures that you don't have to write code for destroying objects when they're no longer needed by your program. Although your application runs in the managed environment when you change project properties, .NET-specific features such as garbage collection and JIT (just-in-time) compilation are implemented only when you specify the `__gc` keyword.

Note the following about the code pertaining to the System namespace:

- using namespace System;: The using namespace System; directive imports the System namespace into your application. You can use the methods and classes of this namespace after specifying this directive. (Read more on namespaces in Book 1, Chapter 2).
- GetNumber: In the GetNumber function, you create an instance of the Random class of the System namespace. Next, you call the Next function of the Random class. This function generates a random number that is less than the parameter supplied to the function. Finally, the function returns the generated random number to the calling function.

2. **After specifying the previously given code, change the code of the** OnLButtonUp **function to the one following.**

   The changes that we make to the code are in bold.

```
void CMyFrame::OnLButtonUp(UINT flags,CPoint Point2)
{
    if (flag==true)
    {
        int x,y,z;
        draw* dr = new draw;
        x=dr->GetNumber(256);
        y=dr->GetNumber(256);
        z=dr->GetNumber(256);
        CClientDC CurDC(this);
        newBrush = new CBrush;
        oldBrush = new CBrush;
        newBrush->CreateSolidBrush(RGB(x,y,z));
        oldBrush=CurDC.SelectObject(newBrush);
        switch(shape)
        {
        case 1:
            CurDC.MoveTo(p1);
            CurDC.LineTo(Point2);
            flag=false;
...
...
//The remaining code is the same as before
```

   In the preceding code, notice that we create three variables of type int, instantiate the draw class, and obtain random numbers for each variable. Next, we use the values in the variables of type int to create a brush that's eventually used to draw the figures.

Your application is complete. Compile and run your application. When you draw figures by using the Insert menu, you'll notice that the output is in different colors, as shown in Figure 7-3. (Okay, so it's a black-and white book — different shades of gray. . . .)

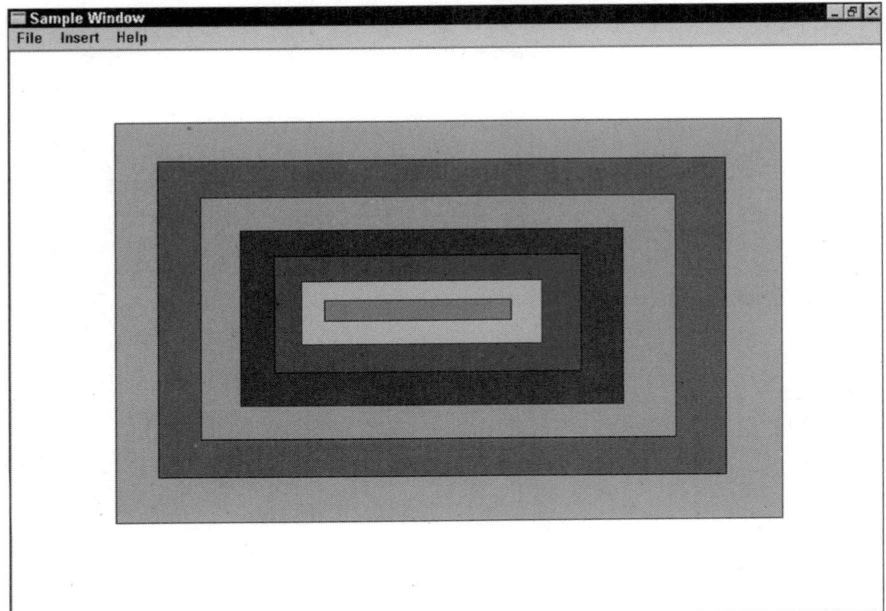

Figure 7-3: The multi-colored output of your application.

Chapter 8: Debugging and Exception Handling in Visual C++ .NET

In This Chapter

- Debugging Visual C++ .NET applications
- Handling exceptions in Visual C++ .NET applications

If you can write a bug-free application in your first attempt, you're a genius. For the rest of us mere mortals, Visual C++ .NET offers debugging tools to make us look like geniuses too. Visual C++ .NET even helps identify and correct user input errors. This safety net really helps you prevent exceptions, which are all the more devilish because you can't control what a user will mess up . . . um, we mean, enter. You'll undoubtedly come across times when users specify incorrect information or specify correct information in an incorrect format, either of which may cause a change in the behavior of an application. Such changes, also referred to as *exceptions*, can lead to erroneous results or may cause your application to collapse. Not good.

In this chapter, we discuss how you can avoid errors in your applications by using debugging tools and exception-handling classes of Visual Studio .NET. Debugging tools enable you to get rid of programming errors, and exception-handling classes ensure that a user specifies correct values.

To get a description of errors that might sneak into your code, check out Book 3, Chapter 9. In this chapter, we get into the nitty-gritty of error handling in Visual C++ .NET. Here, you explore how to debug applications and handle exceptions in applications. We illustrate the concepts in this chapter with the help of a sample application and see how debugging tools and techniques can make the application bug-free.

Debugging Visual C++ .NET Applications

Debugging is the process by which you identify and eliminate bugs in an application. If you're familiar with debugging in Visual C++ 6.0, you'll find debugging in Visual C++ .NET very similar. However, Visual C++ .NET offers a number of new debugging methods and classes to simplify the task of bug elimination. Some of these methods are the use of the Task List and automatic summarization of faulty code that needs to be worked on. In this section, you discover debugging in Visual C++ .NET.

Switching project configuration

Visual Studio .NET provides two types of configurations for compiling projects — Debug and Release.

A *project* comprises a set of files that are compiled to create the final output of an application. All source files, resource files, or header files that you create for your application are included in the project. A project is also referred to as a *solution* in Visual Studio .NET.

When you create a new project, it assumes the Debug configuration by default. Visual Studio .NET makes it easier for you to develop your application in the Debug configuration by providing detailed information about application flow and by offering you a number of debugging tools and classes. (Read about debugging tools and classes later in the section "Using debugging windows.")

When you switch from the Debug to the Release configuration, the compiler optimizes your code. That is, the compiler deletes unnecessary information that may be of use for debugging your application but would reduce the efficiency of your application. We recommend that you develop your application in the Debug configuration because it helps you debug your application easily. You should switch to the Release configuration only after you've debugged your application.

To determine whether your application is in the Debug or Release configuration, see which one appears in the Solution Configuration drop-down list on the Standard toolbar (far-right side), as shown in Figure 8-1.

Solution Configuration drop-down list

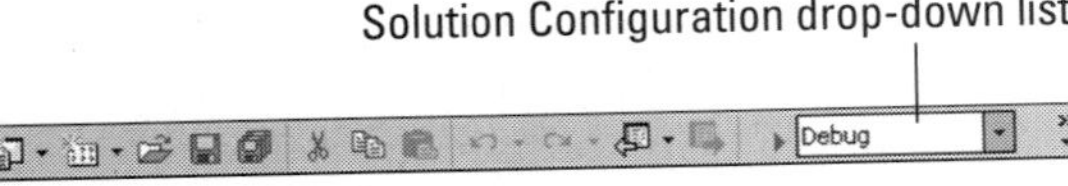

Figure 8-1: The Standard toolbar.

The Standard toolbar, which displays by default, is the first toolbar from the top in Visual Studio .NET. If it isn't visible, choose View➪Toolbars➪Standard.

You can alternatively change the project configuration by performing these steps:

1. **Choose Build⇨Configuration Manager.**

   The Configuration Manager dialog box appears.

2. **Select the Debug configuration in the Active Solution Configuration list and then click the Close button to return to the same screen that was open before Step 1.**

   In this chapter, we use the Debug configuration because we'll be able to use the Debug tools, which are otherwise not available in the Release configuration.

In this chapter, we'll discuss the use of the Debug tools and classes of Visual Studio .NET. Read on as we discuss the major Debug players: the Task List and inserting breakpoints.

Using the Task List

While writing code, you may often feel the need to jot down your thoughts about how you're going to implement your application. Some programmers may first design a prototype and then write the code for the function. For example, you may write a note such as `//Include user validation code here`. Wouldn't it be great if your application could summarize these tasks that you need to complete? Visual Studio .NET comes to the rescue with the Task List feature, which you can use in the following ways. (We detail later in this section how to view, record, and check off finished tasks.)

- **Viewing compilation errors:** This is the most common use of the Task List. The compilation errors that are generated when you compile your application are displayed in the Task List by default. You can even strike out errors in the list as you fix them.
- **Recording user-defined tasks:** When you just gotta capture that one fantastic idea before it slips from your mind, just add a user-defined task to the Task List. Similarly, use the Task List to record suggestions that you may have for other developers on your project so that these suggestions are available for everyone.
- **Viewing a summary of pending work:** When you're aware of specific lines of code that have errors but you're too lazy to debug them at that moment, just add a comment to the line of error. The Task List records your comment so that you can refer to it later and debug the errors at your convenience.

To view all the tasks in the Task List, choose View⇨Show Tasks⇨All. An empty Task List is shown in Figure 8-2.

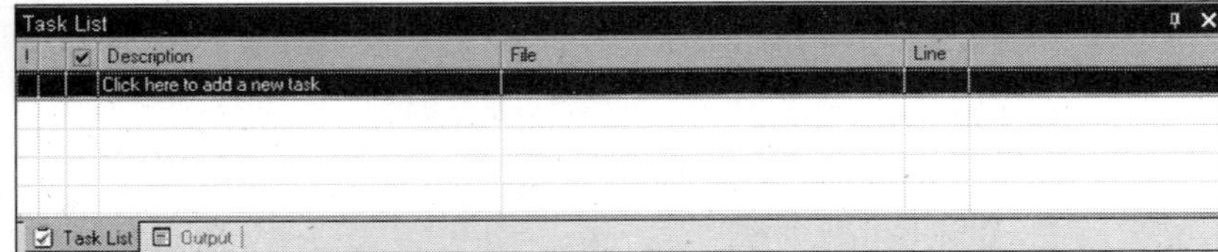

Figure 8-2: Keep yourself on track with the Task List.

Perhaps you've come across another application that provides you with an interface similar to that of the Task List. (Attention, all Microsoft Outlook users in the audience: hint, hint.) For the uninformed, the Task List functions in a manner similar to the Tasks feature of Microsoft Outlook. You can add tasks to specify pending work using the Tasks feature of Microsoft Outlook. Similarly, you can add tasks to the Visual Studio .NET Task List. Also, the look and feel of the Tasks feature of Microsoft Outlook and the Task List in Visual Studio .NET is the same.

To add a user-defined task to the Task List, perform these steps:

1. **Open the Task List by choosing View⇨Show Tasks⇨All.**

   The Task List appears.

2. **Click the highlighted line of text that reads** `Click here to add a new task`.

   The line of text in the description column changes to form a text box.

3. **Write the description of the task in the description column of the Task List.**

4. **Prioritize the task by clicking the far-left column of the new task (look for the exclamation mark symbol) and clicking the appropriate value for priority from the drop-down list, as shown in Figure 8-3.**

   By default, the priority of a task is Normal.

Figure 8-3: Set priorities for your tasks.

The new task now appears in the Task List.

Here's another way to add a task to the Task List — directly from the code of a function:

1. **Open any Visual C++ .NET project.**

   If you don't have any project ready at hand, just create a new Visual C++ .NET project by following the steps listed in Book 4, Chapter 1.

2. **Open a source file of the project by clicking the filename in Solution Explorer (press Ctrl+Alt+L to open Solution Explorer).**

3. **Add the following line of code anywhere in the source file that you open:**

   ```
   // TODO: Create an error handler here.
   ```

   There's no escaping the three inevitables of life: death, taxes, and creating To Do lists.

   As soon as you add this line to your code, a new task appears in the Task List. The exact line and file number of the comment entry is also included along with the task, as shown in Figure 8-4.

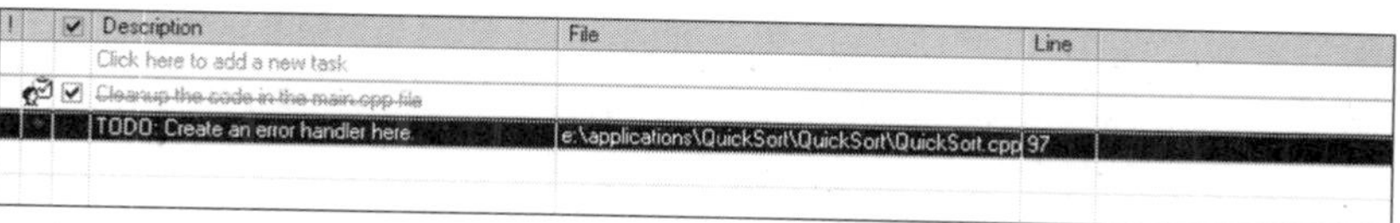

Figure 8-4: Keep tasks in line with TODO comments.

You can keep the Task List open as you add To Do comments to the code. In this way, you can see the additions to the task list as you code your application.

You can delete any task by selecting the check box in the third column (look for the check mark symbol). When you select the check box — check the task off your list, as it were — the description of the task appears in ~~strikethrough~~ to denote that the task is complete. Refer to Figure 8-4 for a peek at what a struckthrough task looks like.

Even after you strikethrough a task to signify that it has been completed, it remains in the Task List until you delete it (by selecting the task and pressing the delete key). In this way, you can keep track of work that has been completed. Smart work!

Just like the comments with the TODO annotation, comments with the HACK and UNDONE annotations also appear in the Task List. You can create the HACK and UNDONE annotations in the same way as you create the TODO annotation (by adding //HACK and //UNDONE statements).

Other key points to know about the Task List:

- **You have to delete comments manually from the code:** You can't delete comments that you add to the Task List by annotating the code directly from the Task List. However, you can delete the annotation of the comment from the appropriate line in the code: Double-click the task entry in the Task List to get to the required line and the comment is no longer in the Task List.
- **You can apply filters to the Task list:** You can apply a number of filters to the Task List to view only those entries that are relevant to you. Some commonly used filters are Comment, Build Errors, and Users. For example, if you want to view tasks only for the currently open file in Visual Studio .NET, right-click the Description column in the Task List and choose Show Tasks⇨Current File. When you do so, notice that the caption of the Task List that denotes that the Task List view is filtered.

If you can't see the tasks that you add to the Task List, ensure that a filter isn't on. Remove a filter by choosing View⇨Show Tasks⇨All menu option.

Inserting breakpoints

Breakpoints in Visual C++ .NET function similar to the breakpoints in Visual C++ 6.0. A *breakpoint* temporarily suspends the execution of an application. This enables you to examine the state of the application, such as the values stored in variables or the functions called in the application. You can also customize the behavior of a breakpoint by specifying parameters, such as the number of times that an application traverses a breakpoint before the application should halt.

To insert a breakpoint in your code, perform these steps:

1. **Position the cursor on the line of code in which you want to insert a breakpoint.**
2. **Choose Debug⇨New Breakpoint (or press Ctrl+B).**

   The New Breakpoint dialog box shown in Figure 8-5 appears. The four dialog box tabs all share a common set of buttons — Condition and Hit Count.

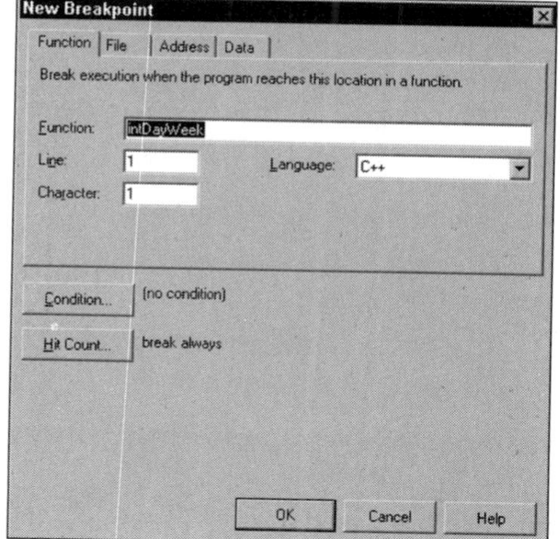

Figure 8-5: Insert breakpoints to help debug a program.

You use the tabbed pages of the New Breakpoint dialog box to determine when to halt executing your application. The tabs comprise

- **Function:** Use the Function tab to specify the name of the function where the execution of the application should be suspended.
- **File:** Use this tab to specify the exact line number of the code where your application should be suspended.

  Notice that the position where you place the cursor in Step 1 is automatically specified in the File tab page in the Line text box.

- **Address:** Use this tab to specify the address space in which you want to suspend your application.
- **Data:** Use the Data tab to specify the name of a variable that you want to monitor for determining when your application should be suspended.

3. **To suspend the execution of your application at a specific line, click the File tab from the New Breakpoint dialog box.**
4. **To specify a hit count, click the Hit Count button.**

   The Breakpoint Hit Count dialog box appears. In this dialog box, to conditionally halt your application, select a condition from the When the Breakpoint Is Hit list. Next, you specify a value in the text box that appears next to the list. In the case of our application, we retain the default option — `break always`.

You specify a hit count to determine the number of times the application should be allowed to pass through the statement before it is halted. You use the hit count in case of loops because an application executes loop statements more than once.

5. **Click OK to close the Breakpoint Hit Count dialog box.**

6. **Click OK to close the New Breakpoint dialog box.**

   A new breakpoint appears next to the statement where you positioned your cursor in Step 1. The breakpoint is represented by a dark brown bullet next to the line of code, as displayed in Figure 8-6.

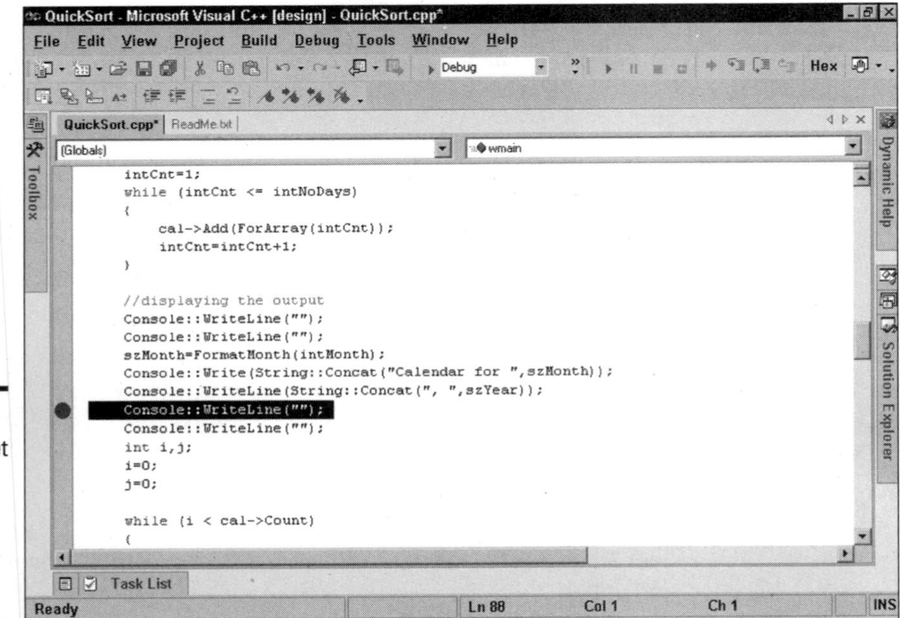

Figure 8-6: A dark bullet next to a highlighted statement is a breakpoint.

You can also specify a condition for a breakpoint. A *condition* enables you to specify that the execution of the program should stop only if the value in one or more expressions has changed or is true. For example, you can specify a condition by using an expression as Month>12, where the variable Month represents a month in a year. In this expression, your application will stop executing only when the value of Month is greater than 12.

To specify a condition — assuming that you're on the screen shown in Figure 8-5 — follow these steps:

1. **Click Condition.**

   The Breakpoint Condition dialog box appears.

2. **Specify an expression in the Condition text box.**

   You can specify a condition as Month>12.

3. **Retain the Is True option to enter the breakpoint only when the condition is true and click OK to close the Breakpoint Condition dialog box.**

   When you click OK, you return to the New Breakpoint dialog box.

When you right-click a breakpoint symbol, a number of options are displayed. For example, if you select the Add Task List Shortcut option, the breakpoint appears in the Task List. Similarly, you select the Disable Breakpoint option to disable the breakpoint.

Run your application and check the output when the application encounters a breakpoint. To execute the application, press Ctrl+Shift+B and then press F5 (assuming that you have no build errors). When the application encounters a breakpoint, the execution halts and the application is said to be in the break mode. See Figure 8-7 to check out an application in the break mode.

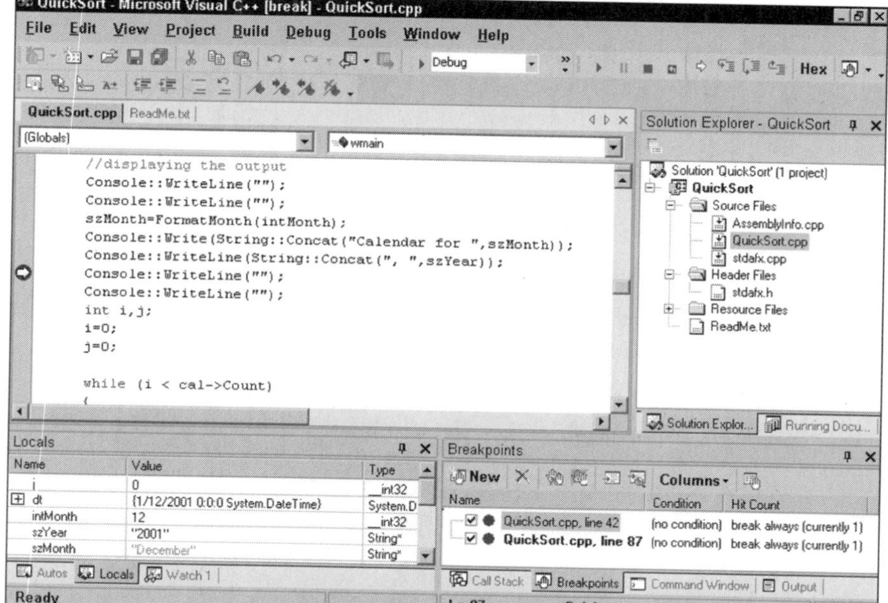

Figure 8-7: During the break mode, an application shows all debugging windows and the breakpoint location.

In Figure 8-7, the Autos, Locals, and Watch panes are *debugging windows*. These windows are visible when you debug your application. Read through the following sections for the scoop on them.

The Watch window comprises four panes: Watch 1, Watch 2, Watch 3, and Watch 4. By default, the first pane, named Watch 1, is visible. You can open other Watch panes by selecting the required pane from the Debug⇨Windows⇨Watch menu option when your application is executing.

Using debugging windows

Visual Studio .NET includes 13 debugging windows. These are the Breakpoints, Running Documents, Watch, Autos, Locals, This, Immediate, Call Stack, Threads, Modules, Memory, Disassembly, and Registers windows.

You can examine a number of features of your application by using these windows. These features include the order in which functions are invoked in your application or the values of expressions. In this section, we examine only the windows that are most commonly used for debugging.

You can open all debugging windows from the Debug⇨Windows menu option. You can also activate these windows from the minimized views at the bottom of the screen. However, the debugging windows (except the Immediate and Breakpoint windows) are available only when your application is in the break mode. Therefore, don't search for windows when your application isn't being executed.

Autos window

The Autos window shows the name and value of the variable involved in the statement of code being currently executed. To use this window, follow these steps:

1. **Open an existing project in Visual C++ .NET.**
2. **Insert a breakpoint in your project.**

   Need a refresher on inserting breakpoints? Check out the aptly named section "Inserting breakpoints" earlier in this chapter.
3. **Execute your application.**

   The application enters the break mode when it reaches the breakpoint.
4. **In the break mode, choose Debug⇨Windows⇨Autos.**

   The Autos window appears.

5. **Traverse one line of code at a time by choosing Debug⇨Step Into (or press F11).**

   Notice that as you move through the code, the value in the Autos window changes and that this value is also based on the statement being executed.

A cool feature of the break mode is that you can determine the value stored in a variable by positioning the mouse pointer over the name of the variable. See Figure 8-8 to view the Autos window and the value of the `szMonth` variable determined by positioning the mouse pointer over the variable name.

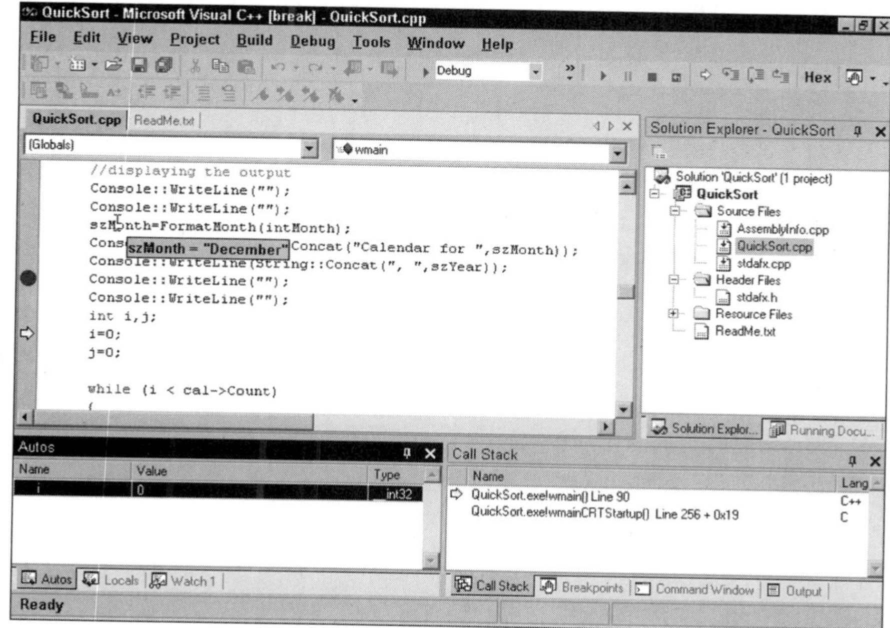

Figure 8-8: View the value of a variable in the break mode via the Autos window.

Breakpoints window

The Breakpoints window lists all the breakpoints in your project. You can use the window to disable breakpoints (by clearing the check boxes next to them) or you can change their properties.

To change the properties of a breakpoint, right-click the breakpoint and select Properties from the shortcut menu that appears. The Breakpoint Properties dialog box appears. You can use various features of this dialog box as we discuss in the earlier "Inserting breakpoints" section of this chapter.

Command Window

The Command Window, also named the Immediate window, allows you to evaluate an expression. For example, specify `? szMonth` in the Command Window and you get the value stored in the variable `szMonth`. The output of the Command Window is shown in Figure 8-9.

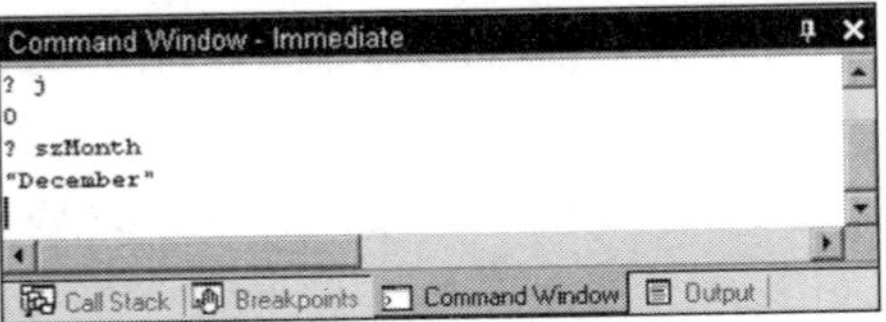

Figure 8-9: Evaluate an expression or retrieve the value of a variable.

Output window

The Output window displays the assemblies and modules that have been loaded by your application. You can trace the order in which these assemblies are loaded by using this window. If your application encounters errors, such as unhandled exceptions, these errors are also recorded in the Output window. (Read more about exceptions and errors in the section "Handling Exceptions in Visual C++ .NET applications.")

Locals, Watch, and Call Stack windows

We describe the Locals, Watch, and Call Stack windows in Book 3, Chapter 9, but here's a brief overview:

- **Locals:** The Locals window specifies the values stored in all variables that are currently in use by your application.
- **Watch:** The Watch window is used to monitor the values of certain variables. You can add variables to the watch window by simply typing the variable name in the Name column of the window or by choosing Debug⇨QuickWatch.
- **Call Stack:** The Call Stack window specifies the order in which the functions in your application have executed before reaching the breakpoint.

Debugging processes

A process represents the executing instance of an application. In Visual Studio .NET, you can debug the running instance of another application. Here we discuss the example of an application originally created using managed extensions. For this example, you can use the `Cal` application from the `www.dummies.com/extras/VS.NETAllinOne` Web site.

To debug the application, launch Visual Studio .NET and follow these steps:

1. **Choose Tools➪Debug Processes.**

   The Processes dialog box appears. As shown in Figure 8-10, this dialog box displays the processes currently executing on your computer.

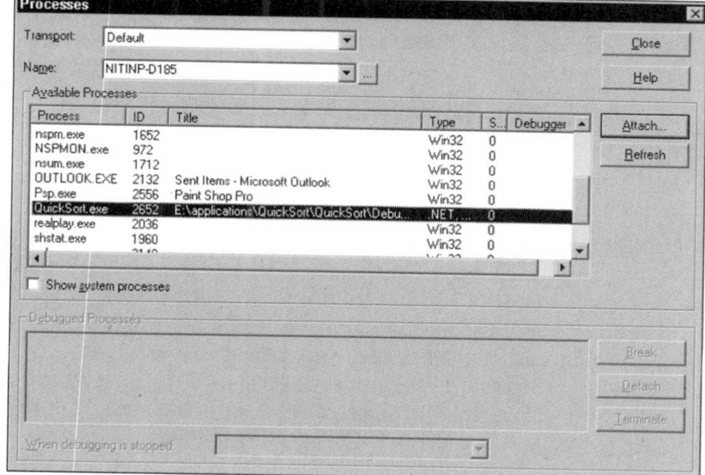

Figure 8-10: Select a process to debug from the Processes dialog box.

2. **Select the managed application that you had initially launched and click the Attach button.**

   The Attach to Process dialog box appears. In this dialog box, specify the type of application that you're debugging by selecting the required values from the Choose the Program Types That You Want to Debug list.

3. **Clear (deselect) all check boxes except Common Language Runtime, as shown in Figure 8-11, and then click OK.**

   A managed extensions application is run on common language runtime (CLR). Therefore, you need to debug only the CLR instance of the application.

   You go back into the Processes dialog box.

4. **Click Close to exit the Processes dialog box.**

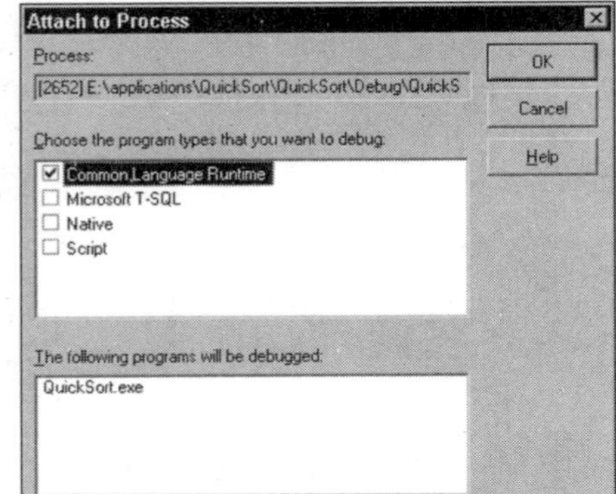

Figure 8-11: Debug an application written using managed extensions.

The debugger is now attached to a process. You can debug the process as you debug any other Visual C++ .NET application.

Handling Exceptions in Visual C++ .NET Applications

An *exception* is an abnormal behavior in an application. An abnormal behavior can arise because of incorrect data types specified by a user or errors in programming logic. For example, if a user specifies *Twelve* as her age instead of *12*, or if your application logic tries to access a nonexistent member of an array, the application throws an exception. If the exception isn't caught, it causes your application to terminate abnormally.

In this section, we describe methods for handling exceptions. Here you discover how to develop applications that handle all types of exceptions, which will help you work with greater efficiency.

Exception-handling classes in Visual C++ .NET

The logic of exception handling in Visual C++ .NET is the same as that in Visual C++ 6.0. However, Visual C++ .NET provides a number of new exception-handling classes that are used to implement the logic. These new classes enable you to represent exceptions as objects so that you can take corrective actions easily.

The .NET Framework class library includes the `Exception` class as the parent class for exception handling. This class belongs to the `System` namespace. The `Exception` class provides properties that help identify the code in which the exception occurred.

Two classes are derived from the `Exception` class — `SystemException` and `ApplicationException`. Your application throws an exception from the `SystemException` class for system-defined exceptions. Similarly, for user-defined exceptions, your application throws an exception from the `ApplicationException` class.

The `SystemException` class further includes child classes that specify the types of exceptions that can be generated. For example, the `FormatException` class specifies an exception that's thrown when a parameter passed to a function isn't in the correct format. As you see later in this section, this class takes care of the problem scenario that we mention earlier where a user specifies *Twelve* instead of *12* as her age.

The exception handling classes of the .NET Framework class library are illustrated in Figure 8-12.

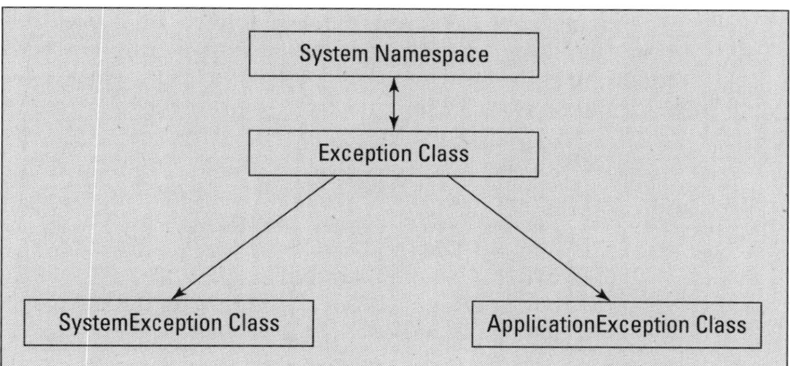

Figure 8-12: Use the classes derived from the Exception class for exception handling in Visual Studio .NET.

Using try and catch statements

Use the `try` and `catch` statements to execute the statements of code that may cause an error. For example, if you're accepting a set of values from a user, the statements used for accepting these values may cause an error if the user doesn't specify correct values. Therefore, you can include these statements in a `try` block.

If the statements executed in a `try` block result in an error, your application throws an exception. Exception handlers are defined with a `catch` statement. The application executes statements in the `catch` block when the `try` block generates an exception of the same type required by the `catch` block.

We use the `try` and `catch` statements to prevent errors in an application example. For this, we use an application that we create using managed extensions in Book 4, Chapter 6. The application accepts the required year and month from users and displays a calendar. The exceptions that can be raised by such a user interaction are

- **`FormatException`:** An exception of the `FormatException` class can occur when the user specifies string data types where integer data types are expected (for the month and year).
- **`ArgumentOutOfRangeException`:** An exception of the `ArgumentOutOfRangeException` class can occur when a user specifies a month value greater than 12 or a year value greater than 9999.

To handle these exceptions in your code, follow these steps:

1. **Create an identifier just before you accept information from a user.**

   The identifier enables you to direct application flow to accept information again from a user in case the user specifies incorrect values. In the following code, we create a `USERINPUT` identifier just before accepting information from a user.

   ```
   USERINPUT:
      Console::WriteLine();
      Console::Write("Please specify the year: ");
      String* szYear=Console::ReadLine();
      Console::Write("Please specify the month: ");
      String* szMonth=Console::ReadLine();
      szDate=String::Concat(szMonth,szFirstDate);
      szDate=String::Concat(szDate,szYear);
   ```

   In the preceding code, we use the `Write` and `WriteLine` methods of the `Console` class to display messages to a user. (Read more about the `Write` and `WriteLine` methods in Book 4, Chapter 6.)

2. **Implement the statements that may generate an exception in a `try` block.**

   In the following code, we implement the statements that may cause exceptions in a `try` block.

   ```
   try
   {
      intYear=Convert::ToInt32(szYear);
      intMonth=Convert::ToInt32(szMonth);
      intNoDays=DateTime::DaysInMonth(intYear,intMonth);
      dt=DateTime::Parse(szDate);
      intDayWeek = dt.DayOfWeek;
   }
   ```

3. **Implement the `catch` block for all exceptions that may be generated by the statements in the `try` block.**

   In the following code, we implement the `catch` statements for the `FormatException` and `ArgumentOutOfRangeException` exceptions. (The `catch` statement accepts a pointer to the exception class as a parameter.)

   ```
   catch(FormatException *e)
   {
      Console::Write("Error in input: ");
      Console::WriteLine(e->Message);
      goto USERINPUT;
   }
   catch(ArgumentOutOfRangeException *e)
   {
      Console::Write("Error in input: ");
      Console::WriteLine(e->ParamName);
       goto USERINPUT;
   }
   ```

   In the preceding code, we use the `Message` property of the `FormatException` class and the `ParamName` property of the `ArgumentOutOfRangeException` class to display an error message to the user. We then accept values again for the specific month and year by directing the user to the statements implemented after the `USERINPUT` identifier.

Make the required changes to the code of your application and execute the application. Your application will now ensure that only valid values are accepted. Error messages on invalid values specified by the user are displayed in Figure 8-13.

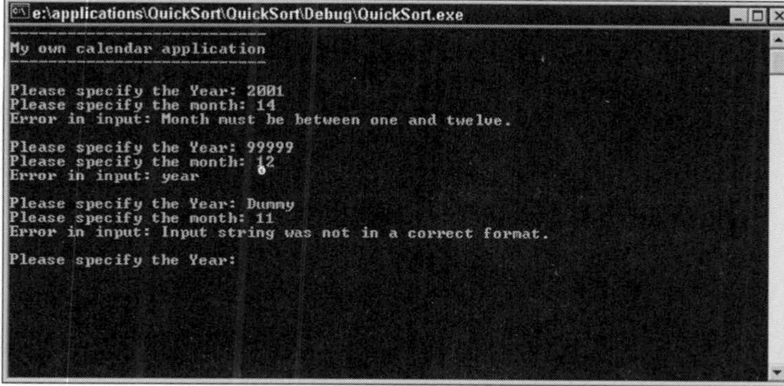

Figure 8-13: Use exception handling to validate user-provided information.

Using the Debug and Trace classes

When you debug your application, we recommend that you make sure that a variable doesn't exceed a given value at any time. For example, the number of hours in a day should never exceed 24. Therefore, if you could determine when the value of the variable representing hours in a day exceeded 24, you could debug the application immediately and resume its execution. One such way is to use a conditional breakpoint. (Read more about conditional breakpoints in the earlier section "Inserting breakpoints.")

Visual Studio .NET provides another quick method for tracking variable values: the `Debug` and `Trace` classes. These classes belong to the `Diagnostics` namespace, which is defined in the `System` namespace. The `Diagnostics` namespace provides a number of classes for analysis and optimization of an application. You can use the classes of this namespace to add reports to the Event Viewer log or analyze the performance of your application by using Performance Monitor.

You can use the `Debug` and `Trace` classes to debug your code and get a notification of a potential bug. The two classes aren't very different except that the `Debug` class can function only in the Debug configuration while the `Trace` class can function in both the Debug as well as Release configuration. (You can read about the Debug and Release configuration in the "Switching project configuration" section of this chapter.)

The `Debug` class is not functional in the Release configuration of your project. Therefore, don't write code by using the `Debug` class that will change variable values or make logical decisions. If you write such a code, application logic and variable value changes will not be made to the Release configuration and errors will be introduced in your application.

The `Assert` method of the `Debug` and `Trace` classes checks for a condition. If the condition is `False`, the method displays a debug assertion failure dialog box. We implement the `Assert` method to ensure that the number of hours in the `hr` variable never exceeds 24. The steps to implement the `Assert` method in a managed application are

1. **Reference the `system.dll` file into your project by specifying the preprocessor directive `#using <system.dll>`.**

   The `system.dll` file includes the `Debug` and `Trace` classes of the `Diagnostics` namespace.

2. **Include the** `System::Diagnostics` **namespace into your application by specifying the following line of code:**

```
using namespace System::Diagnostics;
```

3. **Specify the following line of code where you need to ensure that the value of the** `hr` **variable doesn't exceed** `24`**.**

```
Debug::Assert(hr <= 24, "The value of hr exceeded 24");
```

If the value of `hr` exceeds `24` after you perform these steps, a debug assertion failure dialog box appears, as shown in Figure 8-14.

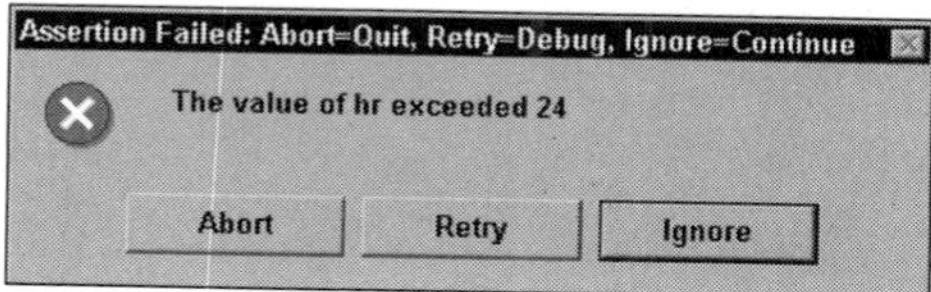

Figure 8-14: Identifying bugs.

Chapter 9: Upgrading Existing Applications to Visual C++ .NET

In This Chapter

- **Preparing an application for upgrade**
- **Upgrading an application to Visual C++ .NET**
- **Finalizing the upgrade process**

If you've worked on earlier versions of Visual C++ .NET, chances are that you may already be using Visual C++ 6.0 applications. We recommend that you upgrade these applications to be able to use the new and enhanced features of Visual C++ .NET, such as programming using managed extensions and enhanced memory management. (Find out more about these features in Book 4, Chapter 1.) In this chapter, we provide you an overview of the main tasks that you need to perform to upgrade your application to the .NET platform.

Getting Ready to Upgrade an Application

Before you upgrade an application to Visual C++ .NET, decide whether you want to upgrade the entire application all at once. You don't have to go whole hog: Alternatively, you can create a new application or just upgrade your application incrementally. Your choice depends on the coding effort involved to upgrade the existing application to Visual C++ .NET and also the features of Visual C++ 6.0 that you want to retain. If you need to retain or enhance most of the Visual C++ 6.0 features, but not write a new application, this chapter is for you.

Read through this chapter as we steer you through the upgrade process, which includes examining the infrastructure for upgrading and testing your application. In this section, we provide some tips to help you plan for these tasks.

Selecting the route to upgrade

To upgrade your application, you have the following options:

- **Create a new application.**

  In Visual C++ .NET, creating a new application is the same as creating one with Visual C++ 6.0. Okay, technically you're creating a new application instead of performing an upgrade. Still, even if you do start from scratch, you're still upgrading what you currently use. To read about creating a new application, read Book 4, Chapter 1 for the scoop.

✦ **Upgrade your application incrementally.**

You can continue to use your existing application but move some of its functionality to .NET. This way, you can take advantage of the .NET Framework enhanced features, such as garbage collection and unified debugging. (Read Book 1, Chapter 3 for a description of garbage collection and unified debugging.) Visual C++ .NET is completely compatible with the Visual C++ 6.0 code. Therefore, you can convert your application with all its existing code to .NET and then, based on your requirements, upgrade only those features that you want to use in Visual C++ .NET.

We recommend that you upgrade your application incrementally if you just want to make minor modifications to your code. These modifications may be just enough to make your application interoperable with other .NET languages or to help you take advantage of some of the enhanced features of Visual C++ .NET, such as enhanced debugging, exception handling, and memory management.

✦ **Upgrade your application completely.**

The third alternative is to completely upgrade your application to the .NET platform and delete the earlier version of your application. When you choose to undertake a complete upgrade, you don't have to worry about any post-upgrade problems pertaining to application performance or interoperability with other languages of the .NET suite.

We recommend that you choose this upgrade route when you want to benefit from using managed extensions and to provide complete interoperability with other programming languages of the .NET suite. (Read about managed extensions in Book 4, Chapter 6.)

Installing the required software

To upgrade your application, first install Visual Studio .NET. You can install Visual Studio .NET on the same computer on which Visual Studio 6.0 is installed. This convenient compatibility exists because these versions of Visual Studio (Visual Studio .NET and Visual Studio 6.0) can coexist. You can read about installing Visual Studio .NET in Book 1, Chapter 6.

Be sure that your computer meets the system requirements for installing Visual Studio .NET. These requirements vary substantially from Visual Studio 6.0. For system requirements to install Visual Studio .NET, again refer to Book 1, Chapter 6.

After you install Visual Studio .NET, you can open Visual C++ 6.0 projects in Visual Studio .NET and upgrade them from there.

Documenting an application

Before you upgrade your application, you should document it — that is, specify the classes and methods that you've coded for implementing the business logic of your application. This documentation is useful especially when you're creating a new application or modifying the code of the existing application. This documentation also comes in handy when you need to test your new application for its required features.

An easy way to document your application is to analyze the code behind user interactions with the application. For example, if your application first displays a log-on screen, you can examine its corresponding code to check for specific database tables and source files that are involved when a user logs on. In this way, you can document your entire application in the form of a flow chart that can be used to build the application logic from scratch when you develop your application.

Even if you aren't building an application from scratch, a flowchart that depicts the application's functionality comes in handy because the flowchart helps you predict the implications of modifying the code of one feature of an application on the other features.

Finalizing a test plan

The concluding phase of documenting an application is the finalization of the test plan. A test plan comprises test cases, and each test case contains the following:

- **Procedure:** A well-defined procedure helps a tester understand how to perform a test.
- **Step-wise output:** The output of each step of the test procedure is listed in the step-wise output section. When you perform a test, you can identify a problem as soon as you discover that you haven't got the required output. For example, if the output of a step was supposed to be your name and you get your age, you know there's something wrong with your application!
- **Set-up instructions:** Any special set-up instructions, such as the instructions to set up Web servers for Active Template Library (ATL) Web applications and Web services, are listed as set-up instructions.

Performing the Upgrade

The following basic steps are the skeleton process that you use to upgrade your application, whether incrementally or completely, to Visual C++ .NET:

1. **Upgrade databases and Web servers.**
2. **Save a new version of the application in Visual Studio .NET.**
3. **Modify necessary code and logic to use the classes and libraries provided by the .NET Framework and Visual C++ .NET.**

Read through the following sections as we discuss each of these steps in detail.

After you upgrade your application to Visual C++ .NET, you'll not be able to open the upgraded application in Visual C++ 6.0.

Upgrading databases and Web servers

If your application involves the use of databases and Web servers, you can upgrade these along with the application. For example, your application may run on Microsoft Access 97 or Microsoft SQL Server 7.0. When you upgrade a database or Web server application, you can upgrade these databases to the later versions: Microsoft Access 2000 or Microsoft SQL Server 2000, respectively.

If you're using a computer other than the one on which your application is installed, you need to create a DSN (data source name) connection to the database so that the database is available to your application. Refer to Book 4, Chapter 4 to know more about creating a DSN connection.

You need to create a DSN connection only for those applications that use a data source. While creating the new DSN connection, use the DSN name that you use in the original application because your upgraded application will use the same DSN name to access your data source (unless you want to take the headache of changing the DSN name in the code of your application).

Saving a new version

After you upgrade your application's database or Web server (if needed), you need to save a new version of the application. To save the new version of your application, follow these steps:

1. **Locate and copy the source files of your application to the computer on which you've installed Visual Studio .NET.**

   The source files will be located in the folder that has the `.dsw` (workspace) file for your application.

2. **Locate the project file (with the extension `.dsw` or `.dsp`) and open it in Visual Studio .NET.**

   As shown in Figure 9-1, the Visual C++ Project dialog box appears, prompting you to upgrade your project to Visual Studio .NET.

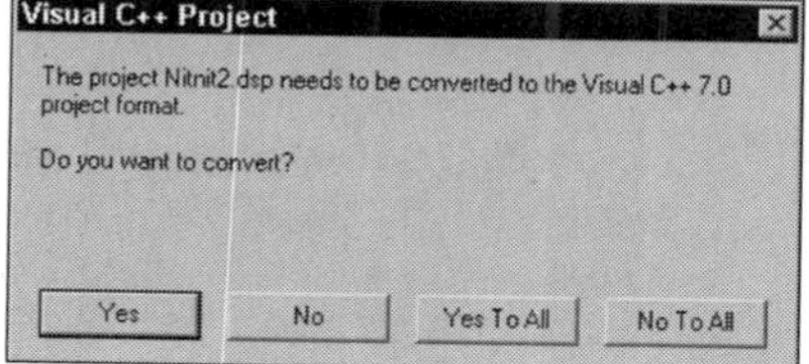

Figure 9-1: Upgrading is easy in Visual C++.

3. **In the Visual C++ Project dialog box, click the Yes button to upgrade your project to Visual C++ .NET.**

In the Visual C++ Project dialog box, if you're opening more than one project, you can click Yes To All to upgrade all projects simultaneously. Similarly, you can click No or No To All to cancel the process of upgrading to Visual C++ .NET. If you select the No or No To All options, Visual Studio .NET prompts you to upgrade your project the next time you open it.

When you click the Yes button to make the upgrade, your project opens in Visual Studio .NET. Visual Studio .NET then creates three additional files for your project:

- `.sln` file: The `.sln` file (Solution file) for your project stores information necessary for Solution Explorer to load your project. This file stores the location of project files on your computer's hard drive so that Visual Studio .NET can load these project files.
- `.suo` file: A `.suo` file (Solution User Options file) stores any customized views that you may have defined for your application. If you leave Solution Explorer or a set of files open before closing your application, you'll notice that Solution Explorer and the set of files will open automatically when you open your application the next time.
- `.vcproj` file: A `.vcproj` file (Visual C++ .NET project file) is the project file for your project. This file is analogous to the `.dsp` or `.dsw` files used in Visual C++ 6.0.

Modifying the required code

After you update your database or Web server and save those changes, it's time to modify the application code and complete the upgrade to Visual Studio .NET.

Key to handling errors

An easy way to determine the cause of an error is to note the error number and view a detailed description of the error in the Visual Studio .NET documentation. The Visual Studio .NET documentation is installed when you install Visual Studio .NET. To open the documentation, choose Start⇨Programs⇨ Microsoft Visual Studio.NET 7.0⇨Microsoft Visual Studio.NET Documentation.

In the example that we discuss in the section "Modifying the required code," you can open Visual Studio .NET, go to the Index tab of the documentation (click Index in the left pane of the documentation), and search for `C4996`.

Another way to find the details of an error in the Visual Studio .NET documentation is by selecting the error in the Task List. Then click the link to the description of the error in Dynamic Help. (Learn more about the Task List in Book 4, Chapter 8 and about Dynamic Help in Book 2, Chapter 1.)

Before you modify the required code, compile your application by pressing Ctrl+Shift+B. If you see compilation errors and warnings, you first need to debug these errors and warnings. For example, the following Microsoft Foundation Classes (MFC) 5.0 code generates a warning when compiled in Visual Studio .NET:

```
#ifdef _AFXDLL
   Enable3dControls();
#else
   Enable3dControlsStatic();
#endif
```

The warning message displaying `warning C4996: 'CWinApp:: Enable3dControls' was declared deprecated` is generated because the `Enable3dControls()` and `Enable3dControlsStatic()` functions of the `CWinApp` class are obsolete. These functions were used in MFC version 5.0 for imparting a three-dimensional appearance to your controls. Although operating systems such as Windows 98 and Windows 2000 do have this functionality, the `Enable3dControls` and `Enable3dControlsStatic` functions are unlikely to be available in the future versions of Visual C++ .NET and thus become obsolete. To avoid the `C4996` warning, comment out the preceding code by adding two slash characters (`//`) before each line of code. When you *comment out* the preceding code, the compiler skips the commented lines of code while compiling your application. Therefore, the code that caused the `C4996` warning isn't compiled, and the warning is suppressed.

After compiling your application, you can modify the necessary code to run your application in the .NET environment. You can use either the updated libraries of Visual C++ .NET or managed extensions in C++ for writing code that's targeted at the .NET Framework. These two methods are

- **Using updated libraries:** If you don't want to use managed extensions for Visual C++ .NET, you can still use the updated libraries of Visual C++ .NET, such as the new MFC libraries and ATL Server. Learn more about MFC and ATL in Book 4, Chapters 3 and 5, respectively. When you use these libraries, you benefit not only from their new and enhanced features but also from the enhanced debugging and exception-handling support of Visual Studio .NET. (Learn more about these features in Book 4, Chapter 8.)
- **Using managed extensions:** If you want to use managed extensions to modify the code of your application to run it in the common language runtime (CLR) environment, change the compiler options to enable the `/clr` switch. After changing the compiler options, you can write *managed code* (the code that targets the CLR) and compile it for execution by CLR. To learn more about setting compiler options and writing managed code in a C++ application, refer to Book 4, Chapter 7.

Performing Post-Upgrade Steps

Before you deploy your upgraded application, you should first test it to ensure that the application can access the latest application data. In this section, we list some post-upgrade steps that enable you to deploy your application successfully.

Testing an application

Create a test plan before upgrading an application. A *test plan* describes the tests that you need to perform to make sure that your application is bug-free. We discuss the components of a test plan in the earlier section "Finalizing a test plan."

After upgrading your application, use your test plan to measure the application's functionality. In Book 1, Chapter 5, we describe some methods — such as black box testing and glass box testing — to test an application's functionality. An application is generally tried in a test environment to simulate the environment in which the application is intended to operate. For example, you may test a Web application on a Web server, simulating the number of client requests that the application may receive. Using this kind of specific test lets you analyze the performance of your application under specific traffic conditions.

Deploying a new application

After you complete the testing and debugging of your application, you're ready to deploy your application. To deploy your application, follow these steps:

1. **Create a deployment project.**

   The deployment project that you create depends upon the type of project. For example, you can deploy a Windows application project by creating a Microsoft Installer (MSI) file. Learn more about MSI files, project types, and deployment projects in Book 7, Chapter 4.

2. **Use the deployment project to install the application in the production environment.**

   A project's *life cycle* consists of the development environment and the production environment. In the development environment, you develop, test, and debug your application. After you finalize the application, you host the application to the production environment, where your application operates according to its functionality and is accessible to users. For example, a Web application is in the development environment when you create and test it in a lab. However, when you host the same application on the Internet, the application is in the production environment.

3. **Import application data to the application's database.**

   While your application is being upgraded, users may add data to the *hosted application* (its earlier version). You need to import this data into the upgraded application.

Importing data into a Microsoft Access database

Although the method you select to import data depends on the Relational Database Management System (RDBMS) that you're using for your application, we describe the procedure to import data into Microsoft Access and Microsoft SQL Server databases here.

To import data into a Microsoft Access database, follow these steps:

1. **Open the database to which you want to import the database.**
2. **Choose File⇨Get External Data⇨Import.**

   The Import dialog box appears, as shown in Figure 9-2.

3. **In the Import dialog box, navigate to the database from which you want to import the tables and click Open.**

   The Import Objects dialog box appears, as shown in Figure 9-3.

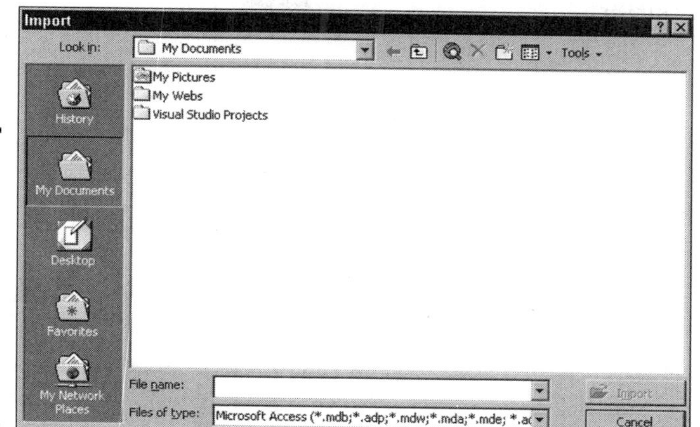

Figure 9-2: Import data into a Microsoft Access database by using the Import dialog box.

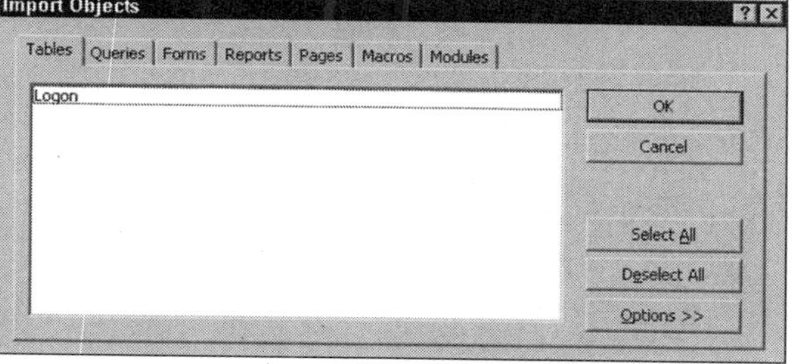

Figure 9-3: Use the Import Objects dialog box to import database objects into your database.

In the Import Objects dialog box, you can select the tables, queries, forms, reports, pages, macros, or modules that you want to import to your database. For example, as shown in Figure 9-3, the Tables tab of the Import Objects dialog box shows the Logon table that you can import to your database.

4. **Select a database object and click OK to import the selected object to your database.**

   The database object is imported into your application.

If you import a database object that has the same name as an existing object in your database, the new object is imported with a different name.

Importing data into an SQL Server database

To import data into an SQL Server database, you use the Data Transformation Services Import/Export wizard. To import data into an SQL Server database, follow these steps:

1. **Launch SQL Server Enterprise Manager by choosing Start➪Programs➪Microsoft SQL Server➪Enterprise Manager.**

   The SQL Server Enterprise Manager window opens.

2. **In the SQL Server Enterprise Manager window, expand Console Root➪Microsoft SQL Servers➪SQL Server Group.**

3. **In SQL Server Group, expand the node for the SQL Server that has the database for your application and navigate to the database.**

   For example, if your database is named `Logon` and is available on the local computer, expand (local) (Windows NT)➪Databases and select Logon.

4. **Right-click the database to which you want to import data and choose All Tasks➪Import Data from the shortcut menu.**

   The Data Transformation Services Import/Export Wizard is launched.

5. **On the welcome screen of the wizard, click Next.**

   The Choose a Data Source screen appears, as shown in Figure 9-4. On this screen, you can select the type of data source from the Data Source list.

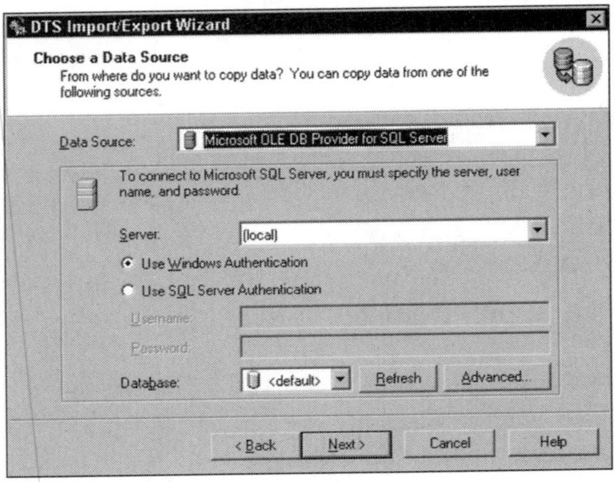

Figure 9-4: Select a data source from the Choose a Data Source screen.

6. **On the Choose a Data Source screen, click Next.**

   The Choose a Destination screen appears. On this screen, you'll notice that the name of the database that you selected in Step 3 is shown in the Database list.

7. **Click Next to continue.**

   The Specify Table Copy or Query screen appears, which is shown in Figure 9-5. On this screen, you select options to copy tables, objects, or use queries to transfer data from one database to another.

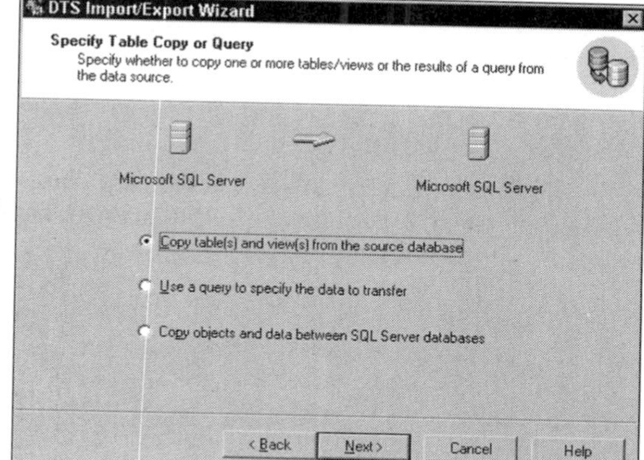

Figure 9-5: Specify how you want to copy data from one database to another.

8. **To copy views and tables from the source database, retain the default option and click Next.**

   The tables and views of the source database appear in the Select Source Tables and Views screen.

9. **Select the tables and views that you want to copy to the destination database and click Next.**

   The Save, schedule, and replicate package screen appears. On this screen, you can save the settings that you've specified in the wizard to run at a later time, or you can run the wizard immediately.

10. **To run the wizard immediately, leave the Run Immediately option selected and click Next.**

    The Completing the DTS Import/Export Wizard screen appears. The screen summarizes the settings that you've chosen in the wizard.

11. **Click Finish to complete the Data Transformation Services Import/Export Wizard.**

    When you click Finish, the Executing Package screen appears. When the required data has been imported into the database, a message appears confirming the same, as shown in Figure 9-6.

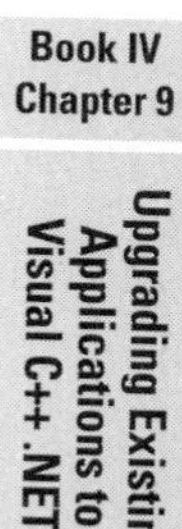

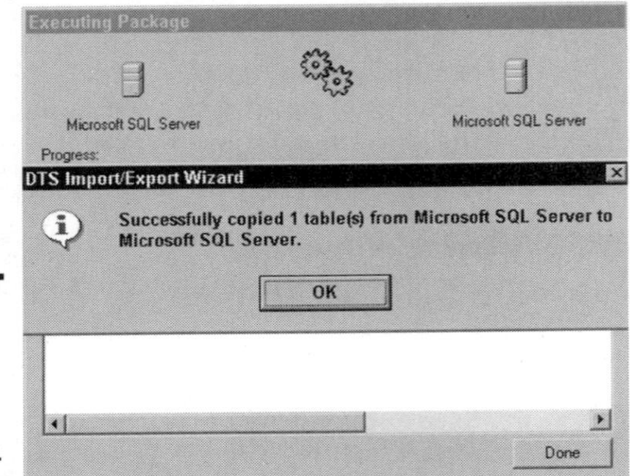

Figure 9-6: The data was imported successfully.

12. **Click OK to close the DTS/Import Export Wizard dialog box and exit the Data Transformation Services Import/Export Wizard.**

You've successfully imported data into an SQL Server database.

Uninstalling and archiving the old application

In the final stages of upgrading your application, you uninstall and archive the earlier version of the application. To uninstall your previous application, follow these steps:

1. **Open the Control Panel by choosing Start➪Settings➪Control Panel.**
2. **In the Control Panel window that appears, double-click the Add/Remove Programs icon.**
3. **In the Add/Remove Programs dialog box that appears, select the application that you need to uninstall and click the Change/Remove button.**

   The application is uninstalled from your computer.

After your application is uninstalled, you may be prompted to manually delete files that could not be deleted by the uninstallation program. To delete these files, you should check the application folder and delete all the files that are no longer needed.

After you've uninstalled an application, you don't need the application's files. Therefore, you can go ahead and delete the files that exist in the application's folder. However, if you want to save certain log files or configuration files that might be useful for a later version of your application, be sure to save these files at a different location.

Finally, you should archive your previous application for record. Archiving isn't mandatory but can help you refer to your application's history as well as trace the versions of your application.

To archive your application, you need to perform the following steps:

1. **Create a configuration plan.**

   The configuration plan is usually created when you create your application. However, if you've not created it already, create it for archiving your application. A configuration plan describes the configurable items in an archive. In a configuration plan, you need to specify all files that you'll archive, which includes the source files, databases, and the database diagrams or schemas that you may have created for your application. The configuration plan also details the steps required to create the application from the source files.

2. **Create the source and object compact disks (CDs).**

   A source CD stores the source files for your application. In simple words, it stores the information required to create the final application. The directory structure and the contents of the source CD are in accordance with the configuration plan. Thus, a source CD doesn't store the final application but the source files to create the final application.

   An object CD contains the compiled application. The object CD should enable a user to install and run the application. Thus, you can store the deployment package for your application in the object CD.

   You can burn more than one source and object CD to ensure that you don't lose data — in case your CD becomes corrupted.

3. **Deposit the source and object CDs.**

   Most organizations house a library where you deposit the source and object CDs to complete the archiving process.

Index

A

B

C

Book V

Visual C# .NET

Contents at a Glance

Chapter 1: Moving to Visual C#

In This Chapter

- **Introducing Visual C#**
- **Understanding a Visual C# program**
- **Building your first Visual C# program**

In Visual Studio .NET, Microsoft introduces yet another programming language: Visual C#. Visual C# combines the best features of C++ and Visual Basic and is the finest programming language available to developers — at least we think so. In this chapter, we introduce you to the features of Visual C#. After you get a grasp of these features, we get you started using Visual C# by creating a small application.

Introducing Visual C#

The good old programming days saw programmers working with C++. This programming language offered high flexibility to developers and helped them build applications that could access low-level system resources with ease. However, using C++ led to lengthy development cycles, which made programming a time-consuming task. The development of Visual Basic simplified programming and led to drastic reduction in development life cycles. However, Visual Basic lacked the flexibility to mesh with low-level system resources, compelling developers to revert to C++.

Visual C# (pronounced Visual *C sharp*) is Microsoft's new generation programming language that integrates the flexibility of C++ with the short development cycle of Visual Basic. These features, along with an array of new features, makes Visual C# more than just the sum of Visual Basic and C++. Visual C# can cater very well to the requirements of an enterprise programmer because it's an object-oriented programming language that enables you to create a wide variety of components ranging from high-level business objects to low-level system applications. In addition, Visual C# enables you to convert these components to eXtensible Markup Language (XML) Web services so that you can make them available over the Internet. Subsequently, any language running on a platform can invoke these components. Visual C# also simplifies development of the COM+ application. A *COM+ application* is an application based on the COM+ technology, which is an advanced development environment used to create distributed applications with ease.

When you use a new programming language, of course you have to learn its syntax and features. However, the learning curve for Visual C# isn't that steep because its syntax is derived from C++. Before we examine the details of Visual C#, here's a little history lesson so that you understand the evolution of Visual C#.

Why was Visual C# necessary?

Microsoft introduced Visual C# to bridge the gaps that existed in previous programming languages. Some of these gaps include

- **Rapid Application Development (RAD):** One of the major factors contributing to the success of a product is how easy it is to understand. In addition, a programming language should help you with tools that make application development faster and produce code that's easy to update and debug.

  Visual C# uses various tools like Garbage Collection and Delegates that make it suitable for rapid application development.

- **Cross-platform deployment:** The languages used for Web development sites must provide the functionality of developing applications that can operate independently of the hardware and software platforms.

  Visual C# compiles the code in byte-stream format, which can be understood by any application irrespective of the hardware and software platform. This format makes cross-platform deployment possible.

- **Access to platform-native resources:** An application may sometimes need to access platform-native resources, such as low-level system calls. This may be required for the optimal performance of the application or for the application to function in conjunction with existing application programming interfaces (API). A language should provide developers with the capability of accessing these resources in their applications.

  Visual C# allows a developer to programmatically view the native code which the developer can use to access the low-level system resources.

- **Support for COM:** Until now, no language supports COM (Component Object Model) comprehensively because providing features to support COM introduces complexity in a language. For example, in C++, you need to create an Interface Description Language (IDL) declaration and a class factory for every COM object that you create. Visual Basic doesn't support low-level COM; although it has overcome the consequent complexity, this has adversely affected the performance of this language.

  Visual C# provides a feature called *attribute* that helps you implement COM in your applications.

What does Visual C# offer?

Visual C# successfully bridges the gaps in the areas listed above and many consider it to be the programming language of the future. The advantages that we like best include

- **Garbage collection:** When you create an object in an application, runtime allocates memory for the object. However, because of limited memory availability, memory allocation can't be done infinitely. Therefore, runtime needs to make some memory available. This is where the Garbage Collector comes into the picture. The Visual C# Garbage Collector checks for the objects not being used by an application and deletes them from memory.

  For more on garbage collection, peruse Book 1, Chapter 3.

- **Value/reference type system:** According to this system, all types are divided into two categories:

  - **Value types:** The standard data types, enumerations, and structures are *value types*. Objects of the value types contain data.
  - **Reference types:** Interfaces, classes, and delegates are *reference types*. Objects of the reference types contain a reference to the location of data storage.

  The value/reference type system provides the advantage of eliminating a number of memory bugs and simplifying object manipulation.

- **Unified declaration and definition of class methods:** Visual C# combines the declaration and definition of methods in a class. This alleviates developers from creating multiple files — one containing declaration (header files) and the other containing definition (source files). In addition, Visual C# automatically determines the location of source files, thus eliminating the need to use statements for including these files in an application.

- **Delegates:** A *delegate* is a type-safe and secure object that contains a reference to a method. *Type-safe* means that a delegate accesses various types, such as classes, in the ways allowed by the compiler. When you invoke a delegate object, the referenced method is also invoked.

  The advantage of using delegates is that they are helpful in *anonymous invocation*: That is, the method to be invoked is not known at compile time. Any method that matches the signature defined in the delegate object can be invoked. In addition, Visual C# allows multiple methods to be attached with a delegate object so that each time you call the delegate object, all the attached methods are called. This is *multicasting*. Delegates are also used for event handling.

- **Simple thread synchronization:** Visual C# helps you build multi-threaded applications. A main disadvantage of multithread applications is that they're error-prone: Because a number of threads may work simultaneously on the same piece of code, you can create a deadlock. To solve this problem, mark important parts of the code and lock them by using the `lock` keyword. This allows only one thread to work on the code at any given time, which is called *thread synchronization*.
- **Versioning:** In Visual C#, you need to explicitly override the members of a base class in a derived class by using the `override` keyword. If you don't mention the `override` keyword, the Visual C# compiler considers the method declared in the derived class as a new method. This eliminates the errors, if any. Moreover, you can add new methods to a base class. This revision creates a new version without affecting the existing program.
- **Interoperability:** Visual C# applications are platform-independent because the Visual C# compiler generates the code in the form of a byte code stream, which you can use across platforms.
- **Access to native code:** Visual C# allows a developer to programmatically view the native code. *Native code* is the code compiled to generate the code understood by the processor. Accessing the native code could help you improve the performance of your application. In addition, you can use the existing APIs.
- **Attributes:** An *attribute* is a declarative tag that you can use to describe various entities in your programs. Consider the example of the methods that you define in a class. You use keywords, such as `Private` and `Public`, with these methods. These keywords provide information regarding accessibility about the methods. Similarly, you can use attributes to describe entities, such as types, fields, properties, and methods. Attributes also enable you to record the name of a file or the name of the developer.

  Using Visual C#, you can create attributes that display declarative information for your applications.

What Constitutes a Visual C# Program?

A Visual C# program comprises a number of components, such as namespaces and classes. A *namespace* is a collection of various types, such as classes. A *class* is a collection of objects that display similar behavior and can be represented by some common features. In this section, we walk you through creating a console-based application and then we discuss the components of a Visual C# program. A console-based application is one that operates from the command prompt and doesn't have a graphical user interface.

You can gather more information on namespaces and classes in Book 1, Chapter 2 and Book 5, Chapter 4 respectively.

Creating a new application

To create a new application in Visual C#, just follow the steps given below.

1. **Launch Visual Studio .NET.**
2. **On the Start Page, click the New Project button.**

   The New Project dialog box appears, as shown in Figure 1-1.

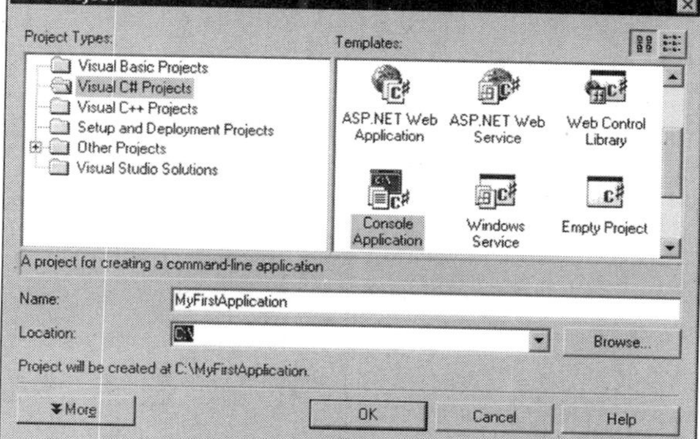

Figure 1-1: Create a new application from the New Project dialog box.

3. **Under Project Types (left side), click the Visual C# Projects folder.**

   Various project templates appear in the Templates list on the right side of the dialog box.

   Read more on templates in Book 4, Chapter 3.

4. **Under Templates (right side), click the Console Application icon.**

   We begin with a console-based application. We discuss form-based applications later in Book 5, Chapter 5.

   You might need to scroll down the Template list to find the Console Application icon.

5. **In the Name text box, enter** MyFirstApplication.
6. **In the Location text field, specify an appropriate location for the application.**

   You can type in this location or click the Browse button to navigate to the location you desire.

7. **Click OK to create the new application.**

   The development environment appears, as shown in Figure 1-2.

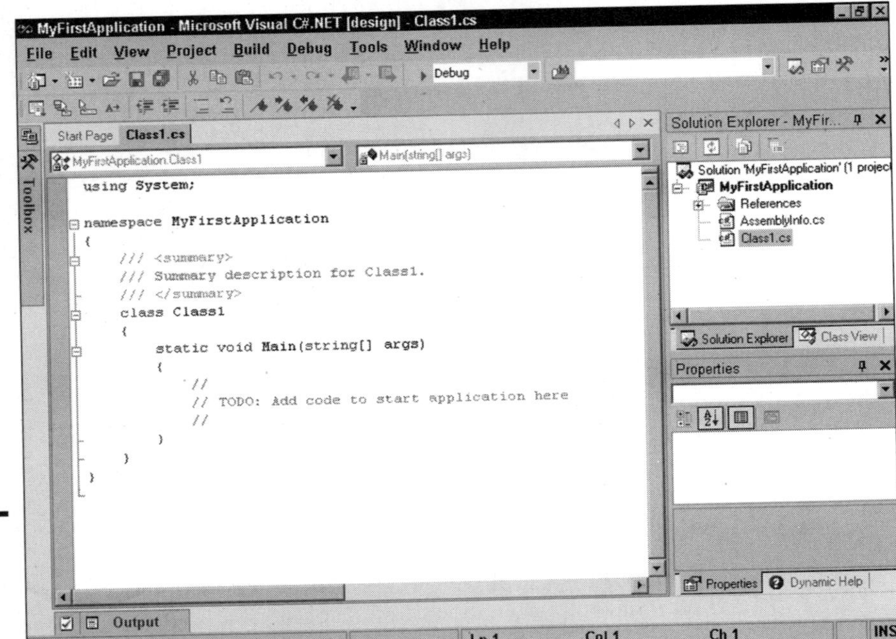

Figure 1-2: It's alive! Your first creation.

Note that the file containing the code is named `Class1.cs`. By default, the file is given the name of the class, but you can change it. The extension of all Visual C# files is `.cs`.

The `Class1.cs` file contains the code generated by Visual Studio .NET. Read on as we analyze this code.

Dissecting the code

Here is the code that Visual C# produces from the sample application we create in the previous section. (Refer to Figure 1-2.)

```
using System;
namespace MyFirstApplication
{
    /// <summary>
    /// Summary description for Class1.
    /// </summary>
    class Class1
```

```
    {
        static void Main(string[] args)
        {
            //
            // TODO: Add code to start application here
            //
        }
    }
}
```

The preceding code creates a class (Class1), which is created in a namespace (MyFirstApplication). The Class1 class contains a method: Main. There are also comments used in the code. In each of the following sections where we dissect the above code, we include a matching snippet so that you can see exactly what we're referencing.

The using directive

Employing the using directive (using System;) specifies a namespace to be used in an application. When you create an application, by default Visual Studio .NET includes certain namespaces, which are helpful in creating that application. You can also include additional namespaces per your developmental requirements. In this case, the System namespace is included by default.

A *namespace* is a container that contains Visual C# classes. To read more about namespaces, see Book 1, Chapter 2.

The System namespace contains various commonly used classes, such as Array and Console, to provide data types, events and event handlers, interfaces, and attributes in your applications. The Array class contains methods to manipulate arrays. The Console class helps read and write characters to the console.

The namespace keyword

Use the namespace keyword (namespace MyFirstApplication) to declare a namespace. When you create a new project, a namespace with the name of that project is created by default. In this case, MyFirstApplication is the namespace that Visual C# creates.

The class keyword

Use the class keyword (class Class1) to declare a class. In this case, Class1 is created by default. To read more about classes, see Book 3, Chapter 8.

The Main method

When you execute a program, the first method to be executed is the `Main` method [`static void Main(string[] args)`]. Your program execution begins and ends with this method. The `Main` method is present within a class or a struct and is static; thus, you don't need to create an instance of the class to execute this method.

A *struct* is used to declare constants, variables, properties, and methods. Read more on structs in Book 5, Chapter 2.

The `Main` method may or may not return a value. If the `Main` method does return a value, that value is of the type `int`. The `Main` method may or may not contain parameters. For more detail on methods, their return values, and parameters, read through Book 3, Chapter 7.

In this case, the `Main` method doesn't return a value. The method contains one parameter, which is a `string` array. This array represents command-line arguments required to invoke the program.

Comments

Comments are the simple English-like statements used to describe the code. In Visual C#, comments start with two front slashes (//). For example,

```
// TODO: Add code to start application here
```

The preceding statement indicates to the user that she should write code to start the application at this point.

Statements starting with three front slashes (///) helps you document the code by using XML. You can use this documentation as a help file. For example,

```
/// <summary>
/// This Class (Class1) stores user information.
/// </summary>
```

The preceding code will store the description of the class `Class1` in an XML document so that a user using your application can refer to this document to learn the functionality of the class.

Say Hello World

All the reading in the world can't replace actually creating an application. Here we help you begin working in Visual C# by creating a standard Hello World application.

After this line of code in the preceding block

```
// TODO: Add code to start application here
```

add this line of code to the `Main` method:

```
Console.WriteLine("Hello World");
```

The preceding line of code displays the message `Hello World` on the console. The `WriteLine` method writes the specified text on the standard output stream. The semicolon (;) is the sentence terminator.

Executing the program

We know, we know: You want to execute your program. Easy enough. Execute the program by choosing Debug➪Start Without Debugging. The output of your program appears in a separate window, as shown in Figure 1-3.

You can also choose Debug➪Start to execute your program. However, the output screen just flashes for a moment without giving you a chance to view the output. What's the fun in that?

Figure 1-3: Your first application in Visual C#.

Chapter 2: Getting Started with Visual C#

In This Chapter

- Storing data in variables
- Converting one type of data to another
- Using operators
- Understanding Visual C# statements

Visual C# — that's *C sharp* — is a derivative of C++. Because Visual C# uses syntax that exactly matches that of C++, use this chapter as a refresher if you've already worked with C++. If you're a novice, this chapter is a stepping stone to learn how to incorporate Visual C# in your applications.

In this chapter, we cover the basics of a programming language, including variables, data types, conversions, operators, and statements. For some practical experience, we then walk you through creating a Visual C# application that accepts and validates certain user-entered values, such as the name, age, and qualifications entered by a job candidate. We also discuss how an application stores such data.

The sample `Variable1` application is available for download from `www.dummies.com/extras/VS.NETAllinOne`.

Storing Data

In an application, you need to store data temporarily: data may be entered by a user or may be the result of a calculation. To store this data, you use *variables*, which you can create in Visual C#.

Identifying variable types

You can create seven types of variables in Visual C#: static, instance, and local variables; array elements; and value, reference, and output parameters. When you see sample code in italic in the following sections on variables, it indicates where the code changes depending on your requirements.

Static variables

A *static variable* is a variable that stores the given value until the program ends. In other words, a static variable is allocated memory when a program begins; this memory is de-allocated when the program ends. To understand the use of static variables, consider an application that asks the user to logon. The application allows a user three attempts, but if all three fail, the application closes. In such a situation, you can declare the counter variable to be static. This variable will retain the value until the application closes.

A static variable is declared at the class level, and all instances of the class share the same copy of the static variable. Moreover, you don't have to create an instance of a class to initialize a static variable.

To declare a variable as static, you use the `static` keyword. The syntax of declaring a static variable is

```
access_modifier static datatype variable_name;
```

An example of a statement with a static variable is

```
public static int StaticVariable;
```

In the preceding statement,

- `access_modifier` is used to specify the accessibility of a variable. *Access modifiers* are keywords that define the scope of variables. Some of the commonly used access modifiers are
  - `public`: Variables with `public` access can be accessed anywhere in the project or outside the project.
  - `protected`: Variables with `protected` access are accessible in the class in which they are declared. You can also access these variables in any class that is derived from this class.
  - `internal`: Variables with `internal` access are accessible to files in the same assembly.
  - `private`: Variables with `private` access can be accessed in the class in which they are declared.

  Read more about classes in Book 5, Chapter 4.

- `datatype` refers to the type of data present in a variable. Some of the commonly used data types are `int`, `char`, `string`, `float`, `decimal`, and `double`. Read more about variables in the upcoming section "Specifying data types."
- `variable_name` is the name of a variable.

Visual C# is case-sensitive, so be careful when you're declaring variables.

Instance variables

A variable declared without the `static` keyword is an *instance* variable. You need to create an instance of a class to initialize an instance variable. Use these variables to store any temporary values, such as the result of a calculation or the values entered by a user. The syntax of creating an instance variable is

```
datatype variable_name;
```

To understand this better, consider the following code statement:

```
int InstanceVariable;
```

Array elements

Each variable present in an array is an *array element*. An *array* refers to the contiguous memory locations that store a number of variables of the same data type. For example, you can store the names of all the employees in a company in an array, where each array element stores the name of a single employee. You refer to an array element by its *index number*, which is the position of the element in the array. The array index starts at 0. The syntax of creating an array is

```
datatype []array_name;
```

For example, the statement

```
int []Myarray;
```

declares an integer array.

You can assign values to an array by using the following statement.

```
int []Myarray = {1,2,3,4,5};
```

Discover more about arrays in Book 5, Chapter 3.

Value parameters

Value parameters are the variables that are passed as parameters to a function. A *parameter* is a value that's passed to a function for some action, such as a calculation. Use value parameters to pass values to a function. Value parameters are initialized only when their corresponding function is invoked. The syntax of a value parameter is

```
MethodName(datatype variable_name) {}
```

For example, the statement

```
SampleMethod (int ValueVariable) {}
```

declares a value parameter.

You can read about the concepts related to parameters in Book 3, Chapter 7.

Reference parameters

The variables that require the use of the `ref` keyword are *reference* parameters. Similar to value parameters, reference parameters are also initialized when their corresponding function is invoked. Use reference parameters to pass reference to the values to a function. The syntax of a reference parameter is

```
MethodName (ref datatype variable_name) {}
```

Here's an example of a statement with a reference parameter.

```
SampleMethod (ref int ReferenceVariable) {}
```

Output parameters

The variables that require the use of the `out` keyword are *output* parameters. Just like value parameters, these variables are also initialized when their corresponding function is invoked. Use output parameters to return multiple values from a function. The syntax of an output parameter is

```
MethodName (out datatype variable_name) {}
```

An example of a statement using an output parameter is

```
SampleMethod (out int ReferenceVariable) {}
```

A reference and an output parameter differ in only one aspect: A value must be assigned to a reference parameter before it's passed to a function. Conversely, an output parameter may or may not contain a value before it's passed to a function.

Local variables

A variable declared within a block, such as the `for` and `switch` blocks, is called a *local variable*. Local variables are initialized only when code enters the block in which the variable is declared. Like instance variables, use local variables to store temporary values. The syntax to declare a local variable is

```
datatype variable_name;
```

The following example shows the declaration of all types of variables.

```
public class SampleClass
{
//Static variable
   public static int Stat_Var;
//Instance variable
   string Inst_Var;
//Value, Reference, and Output parameter
   void SampleMethod(int ValParam, ref string RefParam, out
      long OutParam)
   {
//Local Variable
      int Loc_Var;
//Array
      string []Array_Element = {"Hello","World"};
   }
}
```

When declaring a variable, you need to specify the data type as well as the variable type. We discuss how to specify data types in the next section.

Specifying data types

Variables store a specific type of data, and they come in pretty handy when you need to perform certain operations specific to a particular type of data. For example, you can perform calculations only on numeric type data. To specify the type of data to be stored in a variable, you use data types. In Visual C#, data types are divided into the following two categories:

- **Value types:** A variable declared using a value type stores *data*. Each such variable stores its own copy of data. Value types are of two types: `struct` and `enum`. See the upcoming sections "struct type" and "enum type" for more detail.
- **Reference types:** A reference type variable stores a *reference* to data. Two or more such variables can point to the same data. Some of the common examples of the reference types are `class`, `array`, `delegate`, and `interface`.

In addition to the value and reference types, you can create pointers in Visual C#. Variables declared as *pointers* store memory addresses of other variables. However, you can use pointers in the unsafe code only. *Unsafe code* is marked by the `unsafe` modifier. In other words, unsafe code allows you to write C code in Visual C#.

struct type

You use the `struct` type to declare constants, variables, properties, and methods. Some of the commonly used `struct` types are `string`, `int`, `char`, and `float`. In addition, Visual C# provides a number of predefined `struct` types called *simple types*. Simple types can be divided into the following four sub-categories:

- **integral types:** Visual C# provides nine integral types: `sbyte`, `byte`, `short`, `ushort`, `int`, `uint`, `long`, `ulong`, and `char`.
- **floating point types:** `float` and `double` constitute the floating point types.
- **decimal type:** Use the `decimal` type to store monetary values.
- **bool type:** The `bool` type is used to represent logical values and can store either `true` or `false`.

A *constant* is a variable that contains a fixed value so that the value — once stored in a constant — can't be changed later. You declare a constant by using the `const` keyword. The syntax of declaring a constant is given below.

```
const datatype Constant_Name = value;
```

In the preceding syntax, *`value`* refers to the data that should be present in the constant.

enum type

You use the `enum` type to store named constants. These constants belong to one of the following types: `byte`, `sbyte`, `short`, `ushort`, `int`, `uint`, `long`, or `ulong`. For example, you can create an enumeration that contains colors, such as red, blue, and green, as constants.

Developing an Application

After you're comfortable with variables and data types, practice creating variables. Start by developing an application. In this section, we help you create variables to store detail information about a job candidate; just follow these steps:

1. **Create a new console application and name the application `Variable1`.**

   The `Variable1` application contains a namespace named `Variable1` and a class named `Class1`, which are created automatically by Visual Studio .NET. The following statements will help you identify these:

   ```
   namespace Variable1
   {
       class Class1
       {
   ```

   You can read the detailed steps for creating a new console application in Book 5, Chapter 1.

2. **Create four variables to store the name, age, gender, and qualification of each job candidate.**

   You need to store the name, gender, and qualification in `string` variables and the age in an `int` variable. In this case, we're accepting the age to ensure that the person isn't underage for the job at hand. To create these variables, just add the following code to the `Main` method.

   ```
   string CandName, CandGender, CandQual;
   int CandAge;
   ```

3. **Write the statements to accept and store the values entered by a candidate.**

   Store the values entered by a user in the variables that you created in the previous step. To write the statements, add the following code to the `Main` method.

   ```
   //Accepting the name
   Console.WriteLine ("Enter your name:");
   CandName = Console.ReadLine();
   //Accepting the gender
   Console.WriteLine ("Enter your gender (M/F):");
   CandGender = Console.ReadLine();
   //Accepting the age
   Console.WriteLine ("Enter your age:");
   CandAge = Console.ReadLine ();
   //Accepting the qualifications
   Console.WriteLine ("Enter your qualification (UG/G/PG)");
   CandQual = Console.ReadLine ();
   Console.WriteLine ("Press Enter to continue");
   Console.Read ();
   ```

In the preceding code, the `WriteLine` method is used to write data to the standard output stream. The `ReadLine` method is used to read data from the standard input stream.

The last two lines of the preceding code make the system halt after displaying the result. Otherwise, it might appear for only a second, and you might not be able to see the results properly.

4. **Execute the application.**

   A message box appears (as shown in Figure 2-1) indicating build errors.

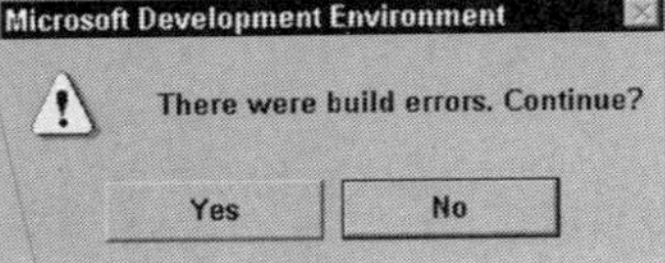

Figure 2-1: Oops! Build errors!

   To learn in detail about the steps for executing an application, read Book 5, Chapter 1.

5. **Click No to close the message box.**

   The Task List, now visible at the bottom of the Visual Studio window (as shown in Figure 2-2), lists the error. The error indicates that you were trying to convert `string` to `int` implicitly. This operation is not accepted by Visual C#. To prevent such errors, you need to convert one type of data to another. Read the next section for information on how to convert one type of data to another.

   In case the Task List is not visible, choose View⇨Show Tasks⇨All.

   To know more about the Task List, read Book 3, Chapter 9.

Applying Type Conversion

Continuing from the previous section with our running example, you encounter an error in your application because Visual C# doesn't allow you to convert a `string` variable to an integer implicitly. One way to rectify this error is to change the data type of the variable `CandAge` to `string`. However, in this case, changing the data type won't help because you may need to check the age of a candidate, which isn't possible with strings. The other alternative is to convert the `string` value to `integer`.

To convert one type of data to another, Visual C# provides you with the `System.Convert` class.

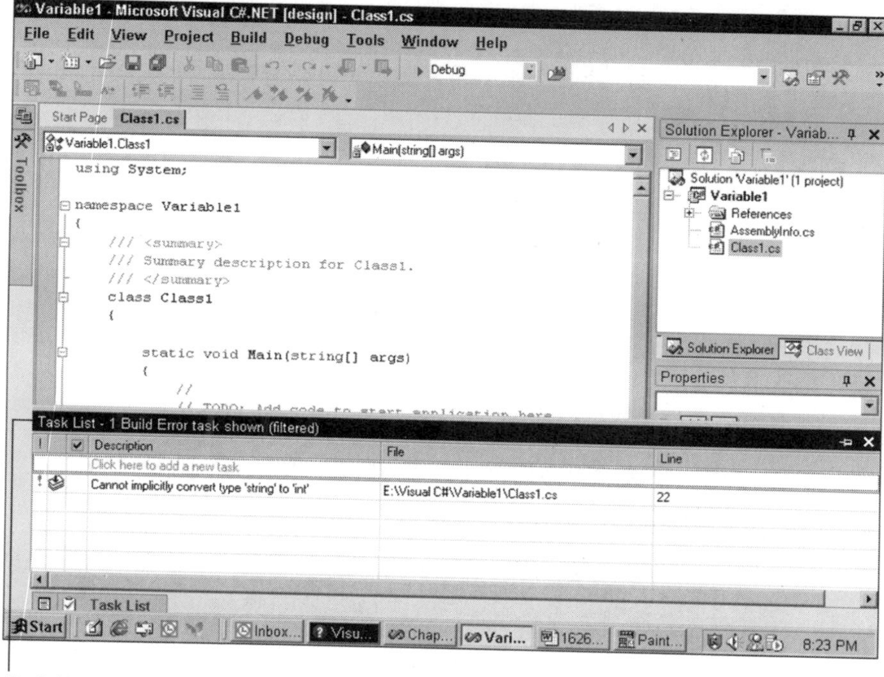

Task List

Figure 2-2: Use the Task List to help you ferret out build errors.

The `System.Convert` class provides methods, such as `ToChar`, `ToString`, and `ToInt32` to convert one type of data to another. The `ToChar` method is used to convert the given data to character type. The `ToString` method is used to convert the given data to string type. Here's the syntax — with `ToInt32` as the example — for using these methods.

```
//Declare and initialize a string variable
string str = "10";
//Declare an integer variable
int i;
//Convert the string value to integer
i =Convert.ToInt32 (str);
```

In the preceding syntax, the `ToInt32` method is used to convert the given string to a 32-bit signed integer. A *signed integer* is a number containing a symbol that indicates whether the number is positive or negative. If the number is positive, you can omit the + symbol.

To rectify the error that was generated in the Variable1 application:

1. **In the Task List, double-click the error.**

   The control moves to the line that generated the error.

   To access the Task List, choose View➪Show Tasks➪All.

2. **Change this line of code to the one given below.**

   ```
   CandAge = Convert.ToInt32 (Console.ReadLine ());
   ```

3. **Execute the application.**

   The application executes without any error, and the console window appears (as shown in Figure 2-3), prompting you to enter your name.

Figure 2-3: Enter details in the console window.

4. **Test the application by entering some values.**

   The application runs successfully without any error.

If you've stayed with us throughout this chapter, you've completed creating your sample application that accepts values from job candidates. Now, write the code for the application to perform certain validations, such as the gender of a candidate. We also need to check that the age of the candidate is not less than 25 years and that the candidates are not undergraduates. To perform these tasks, Visual C# provides operators (such as arithmetic and relational) and statements (such as selection).

Discovering Visual C# Operators

An *operator* is used to perform an operation, such as addition or subtraction, on variables and constants. Visual C# provides a number of operators, including arithmetic, relational, logical, and string concatenation.

Arithmetic operators

Operators used to perform mathematical operations on variables or constants are *arithmetic operators*. Some of the commonly used arithmetic operators are `+`, `-`, `*`, `/`, and `%`.

Relational operators

Operators used to compare two expressions or variables are *relational operators*. Some of the commonly used relational operators are `==`, `!=`, `<`, `>`, `<=`, and `>=`. Consider the following example that uses the `<` operator to check whether the age of a candidate is less than 25 years:

```
if (CandAge < 25)
{
   Console.WriteLine ("You are not eligible for the job!!");
   System.Environment.Exit (0);
}
```

We discuss the `if` statement in the upcoming "Selection statements" section.

Logical operators

Operators used for evaluation of Boolean expressions are *logical operators*. Some of the commonly used logical operators are `&`, `|`, and `!`.

- **&:** Use this operator to perform logical conjunction of two variables. It is the same as the `And` operator in Visual Basic. For example, the following code uses the `&` operator to ensure that the gender entered by a candidate is either M or F:

  ```
  if (CandGender != "M" & CandGender !="F")
  {
     Console.WriteLine ("Incorrect Gender!! Terminating " +
        "Application!!");
  }
  ```

- `|`: Use this operator to perform logical disjunction of two variables. It is the same as the `Or` operator in Visual Basic. The following example uses the `|` operator to ensure that if the qualification of a candidate is either G or PG, she is selected:

```
if (CandQual == "G" | CandQual =="PG")
{
   Console.WriteLine ("You are selected");
}
```

- `!`: Use this operator to perform logical negation of a given variable. It is the same as the `Not` operator in Visual Basic. Consider the following example that uses the `!` operator to check whether the qualification of a candidate is PG:

```
if (!(CandQual == "PG"))
{
   Console.WriteLine ("You are not eligible");
}
```

To understand the concept of logical operators, read Book 3, Chapter 5.

String concatenation operator

The operator used to join two strings is the *string concatenation operator.* You use + to join two strings.

For example,

```
Console.WriteLine ("Hello" + " World");
```

In the preceding statement, the strings `Hello` and `World` are joined and displayed onscreen.

Understanding Visual C# Statements

Statements are instructions that enable your program to execute per specific requirements. Visual C# provides you a number of statements, such as selection, iteration, and jump.

Selection statements

Selection statements enable you to execute a statement(s) based on whether a condition is `true` or `false`. In this manner, selection statements impart decision-making functionality to your application. For example, consider an application in which a candidate has to enter details, such as the name, age, and qualification. Depending on the information entered, the application sends a message informing the candidate about the candidate's eligibility for the job.

Visual C# provides the `if` and `switch` statements as part of selection statements.

if statement

You use the `if` statement to execute a certain statement(s) depending on whether a particular condition is `true` or `false`. For example, an application can use an `if` statement to determine whether the age entered by a candidate is greater than 25 years. The syntax of an `if` statement is

```
if (condition)
{
   statement(s);
}
else
{
   statement(s);
}
```

In the preceding syntax, if the condition is `true`, the statements following `if` are executed; otherwise, the statements following `else` are executed.

Go back to the `Variable1` application and perform gender validation by using the `if` statement. To do this, add the following code after the statement for accepting the gender of a candidate:

```
if (CandGender != "M" & CandGender !="F")
{
   Console.WriteLine ("Incorrect Gender!! Terminating " +
      "Application!!");
   Console.WriteLine ("Press Enter to continue");
   Console.Read ();
   System.Environment.Exit(1);
}
```

In the preceding code, the gender of the candidate is validated using the `!=` (not equal) relational operator. The two conditions are joined by the `&` operator. If both the conditions are `false`, the application enters the `if` statement and terminates by using the `Exit` method of the `System.Environment` class. This method accepts a parameter of the type `int`. This parameter signifies whether the Exit method was called after a successful or unsuccessful operation. In this case, the value 1 signifies that the operation was unsuccessful.

Similarly, specify the validation for the age entered by the candidate. The age of a candidate should not be less than 25 years.

```
if (CandAge < 25)
{
   Console.WriteLine ("You are not eligible for the job!!");
   Console.WriteLine ("Press Enter to continue");
   Console.Read ();
   System.Environment.Exit (1);
}
```

switch statement

The switch statement allows you to execute a set of statements based on the result of an expression. The result of an expression is tested across a number of constants provided using the case statement. For example, in this application, the candidates may differ in their qualifications: They may be graduates or postgraduates. To handle this situation, you can evaluate the expression holding the value entered by the candidate and then test it by comparing with various constants. Look at the syntax of a switch statement:

```
switch (expression)
{
   case ConstantExpression1:
       statement(s)1;
       break;
   case ConstantExpression2:
       statement(s)2;
       break;
   default:
       statement(s);
       break;
}
```

In the preceding syntax, the expression is evaluated and the result is checked across ConstantExpression1. If the two values match, the statement set 1 is executed and the control moves out of the switch statement because of the break statement. If the two values don't match, the result is checked across ConstantExpression2. If none of the constant expressions provide matches with the result, the statements following default are executed.

Now validate the qualification entered by the user. To do this, add the following code after the statement for accepting the qualifications of a candidate:

```
switch(CandQual)
{
    case "UG":
      Console.WriteLine ("Sorry!! You are not eligible.");
      break;
    case "G":
      Console.WriteLine("We'll get back to you shortly.");
      break;
    case "PG":
      Console.WriteLine("You've been short-listed for " +
        "interview.");
      break;
    default:
      Console.WriteLine ("Incorrect value entered");
      break;
}
```

Iteration statements

You use *iteration statements* to repeat a set of statements based on the Boolean value of a condition. Visual C# provides a number of iteration statements, such as `while`, `do`, `for`, and `foreach`.

while statement

You use the `while` statement to execute a set of statements until the given condition becomes `false`. For example, your application might need to accept details of 10 candidates. In such a situation, instead of writing the code statements 10 times, you can write the code once and loop it 10 times by using the `while` statement.

The `while` statement first tests for a condition and then executes the enclosed statements. As a result, there is a possibility that the statements enclosed within the `while` statement may not be executed. The syntax of a `while` statement is

```
while (condition)
{
    statement(s);
}
```

Further modify your application so that it can accept details of 10 candidates. To do this, enclose the existing code within the given statement.

```
//Initializing the counter
int ctr=1;
//Repeat the loop 10 times
while(ctr<=10)
{
   //Already existing code should come here
   //Incrementing the counter
   ctr = ctr +1;
}
```

do statement

You can also use the do statement to execute a set of statements until a given condition becomes false. Good catch if you noticed that this is just like a while statement. However, the two statements differ because the while statement first tests the condition and executes the enclosed statements *only if* the condition is true. Conversely, the do statement executes the statements at least once before testing the condition. Here's the syntax of a do statement:

```
do
{
   statement(s);
} while (condition);
```

You can use the do statement also to accept details of 10 candidates in your application. Check out the following code:

```
//Initializing the counter
int ctr=1;
do
{
   //Already existing code should come here
   //Incrementing the counter
   ctr = ctr +1;
} while(ctr<=10);
```

for statement

You use the for statement to execute a set of statements until a given condition becomes false. For example, you can use the for statement to repeat a set of statements. The syntax of a for statement is

```
for(Initialization_expr; Test_expr;Change_expr)
{
   statement(s);
}
```

In the preceding syntax,

- `Initialization_expr` refers to the statements that initialize the counters used in a loop. This statement is executed only once.
- `Test_expr` is the expression that is evaluated for repeating the enclosed statements.
- `Change_expr` is used to increment or decrement the value of the counters used in a loop.

Here's how this loop works. First, the `Initialization_expr` is executed. This expression initializes the counters used in the loop. The next step is to evaluate `Test_expr`. If the result of the `Test_expr` evaluation is true, the enclosed statement(s) are executed. After executing the statements, `Change_expr` is executed. `Change_expr` increments or decrements the counter of the loop. Next, the `Test_expr` is again evaluated. If the result is `true`, the enclosed statements are again executed; otherwise, the control is transferred outside the loop.

You can also use the `for` statement to accept the details of 10 candidates in your application. Look at the following code to see how to accomplish this task.

```
for each (ctr =1; ctr<=10; ctr = ctr +1)
{
   //Already existing code should come here
}
```

foreach statement

You use the `foreach` statement to execute a set of statements for all the elements of an array or a collection. For example, you can use this statement to display all the elements stored in an array. The syntax of the `foreach` statement is

```
foreach (datatype element in group)
{
   statement(s);
}
```

In the preceding syntax,

- `datatype` refers to the type of the element.
- `element` is a variable that refers to an element of an array or a collection.
- `group` refers to the array or collection.

Consider the following statements as an example:

```
string [] myarr = {"Jan", "Feb", "Mar", "April"};
foreach (string str in myarr)
{
     Console.WriteLine ("The element is " + str);
}
```

In the preceding code, the `myarr` array stores the names of the first four months in a year. The `foreach` statement is then used to display all these elements. We discuss more about arrays in Book 5, Chapter 3. Notice the use of the string concatenation operator (+).

You can read more on loops in Book 3, Chapter 6.

Jump statements

You use jump statements to transfer the control of a program to a particular statement. For example, in an application, if a user enters an incorrect value, the control should move back (jump) to the first statement. Visual C# provides you with a number of jump statements, such as `goto`, `break`, `continue`, and `return`.

goto statement

Use the `goto` statement to transfer the control of a program to a specified label. The syntax of the `goto` statement is

```
goto label;
```

In the preceding syntax, `label` can be a line label, a `case` label in the `switch` statement, or the `default` label of the `switch` statement. The following code sample illustrates the use of the `goto` statement.

```
//Define a line label
CheckGender:
   Console.WriteLine ("Enter your gender:");
   CandGender = Console.ReadLine();
   if (CandGender != "M" & CandGender !="F")
      {
         Console.WriteLine ("Incorrect Gender!!");
         //Move the control to the CheckGender label
         goto CheckGender;
      }
```

break statement

You use the break statement to stop the execution of a loop or a conditional statement. For example, note the switch statement. After every case statement, there is a break statement. This sequence of statements ensures that after the statements specified in a case are executed, the control moves out of the switch statement instead of moving on to the next case. The syntax of the break statement is

```
break;
```

Refer to the earlier section "switch statement" to see the use of the break statement.

continue statement

A continue statement appears in an iteration statement. You use a continue statement to ignore all the statements that follow it and iterate that the loop has to be executed beginning from the first statement. The syntax of a continue statement is

```
continue;
```

return statement

You use the return statement to terminate the execution of a method in which the statement appears. This statement returns control to the calling method. If a method is not of the type void, the return statement is used to return the value of this method. The syntax of a return statement is

```
return;
```

Chapter 3: Working with Arrays

In This Chapter

- Introducing arrays
- Understanding single-dimensional arrays
- Understanding multidimensional arrays
- Creating jagged arrays

In your applications, you may need to store a large amount of similar data together, such as the names of all candidates who apply for a job. If you've already read Book 5, Chapter 2 (on variables), you may be tempted to create variables and store the names. This is a good solution for storing the names of one or two candidates. However, if a large number of candidates apply for this job, you need to create a matching number of variables. The real problem then would be to remember all those variable names. Creating variables isn't the most efficient solution, but you can use an array in Visual C# to solve your problem.

In this chapter, we tell you about single-dimensional and multidimensional arrays. In addition, we also discuss the concept of jagged arrays.

You can download the sample `Array1` application from `www.dummies.com/extras/VS.NETAllinOne`.

Unearthing Arrays

An *array* is a collection of variables of the same data type. The variables contained in the array are *array elements*. You can refer to a particular array element by using its *index number*, which is the position of the element in the array.

In Visual C#, all the arrays are derived from the `System.Array` class. The `System.Array` class contains members, such as `Length` and `Rank`, that ease working with arrays.

You need to declare arrays before using them. An array declaration includes type and rank of array along with the array name. *Type* refers to the data type of elements that the array can contain, and the *rank* refers to the dimensions of the array. Depending on the number of dimensions, arrays can be single-dimensional or multidimensional. In the upcoming sections, we discuss these types of arrays.

Using Single-Dimensional Arrays

A *single-dimensional array* is an array with only one dimension (go figure). The rank of a single-dimensional array is 1. Use these arrays to store the same type of data, such as the names of all candidates applying for a job. The first step in working with arrays is to create them.

Creating single-dimensional arrays

You can divide the process of creating single-dimensional arrays into two parts: declaring the array and assigning memory to it. The syntax to declare a single-dimensional array is

```
array_type [] arrayname;
```

In the preceding statement, `array_type` refers to the data type of elements that the array can contain. The square brackets indicate the rank of an array. In this case, the rank of the array is 1. You know the rank is 1 because the square brackets are empty. Don't worry — we explain the usage of these square brackets in the upcoming section "Using Multidimensional Arrays."

After declaring an array, you need to assign memory to it. To do so, look at the following syntax:

```
//Declare an array
Array_type [] arrayname;
//Assign memory to the array
Arrayname = new Array_type[number_of_elements];
```

In the preceding syntax,

- `new` is used to assign memory to the array. As soon as the memory is allocated to an array, all the elements contained in the array are initialized to the default value of the array data type. For example, if you create an array of data type `int`, all the elements will be initialized to 0.
- `number_of_elements` specifies the total elements that the array can contain. The total number of elements contained in an array is its *array length*.

You can rewrite the syntax that we describe in the previous bullet list in the following manner:

```
Array_type [] arrayname = new Array_type[number_of_elements];
```

Here's an example of how to create an array.

```
//Declare an array
int [] array1;
//Assign memory to the array
array1 = new int [10];
```

You can replace the above statements with the following statement:

```
int [] array1 = new int [10];
```

The preceding statement creates an array named `array1` of type `int`. This array can contain 10 elements. Elements are stored in the array from the index position 0 up to the index position 9.

Initializing single-dimensional arrays

After you create an array, you need to initialize it. You can initialize an array in one of the following ways:

✦ **Declare and initialize arrays in the same statement.**

```
int [] array1 = new int [] {1,2,3,4,5};
```

In the preceding statement, you don't need to specify the number of elements in the array because you're initializing the array with all the elements that you require. You can also rewrite the preceding statement like this:

```
int [] array1 = {1,2,3,4,5};
```

✦ **Declare and initialize arrays in separate statements.**

```
int [] array1;
array1 = new int [] {1,2,3,4,5};
```

✦ **Initialize arrays like the following:**

```
int [] array1 = new int [5];
array1[0] = 1;
array1[1] = 2;
array1[2] = 3;
array1[3] = 4;
array1[4] = 5;
```

When you use the preceding method, you can store data at specific index positions.

Follow along with this example as we walk you through creating an application. In this application, you create arrays to store first name, last name, age, and qualification of the candidates who apply for a job.

1. **Create a new console application named** `Array1`**.**

   Read up on creating a console application in Book 5, Chapter 1.

2. **In the** `Main` **method, write code statements to declare arrays.**

   ```
   //Declare arrays
   string []first_name;
   string [] last_name;
   int []age;
   string [] qualification;
   ```

3. **Prompt the user to specify the number of elements.**

   The following code accepts a value from the user and then creates the required arrays with the specified number of elements.

   After you declare an array, you need to assign memory to it. While assigning memory to an array, you need to specify the number of elements that the array can contain.

   ```
   int num_cand;
   Console.WriteLine ("Enter the number of candidates :");
   num_cand = Convert.ToInt32 (Console.ReadLine ());
   //Assign memory to arrays
   first_name = new string [num_cand];
   last_name = new string [num_cand];
   age = new int [num_cand];
   qualification = new string [num_cand];
   ```

4. **Write code statements to accept values for all the candidates.**

   ```
   //Declare the counter
   int ctr;
   //Accept values from the user
   for (ctr =0; ctr < first_name.Length; ctr = ctr +1)
   {
      Console.WriteLine ("Enter the first name of the " +
        "candidate number " + (ctr+1));
      first_name[ctr] = Console.ReadLine ();
      Console.WriteLine ("Enter the last name of the " +
        "candidate number " + (ctr+1));
      last_name[ctr] = Console.ReadLine ();
      Console.WriteLine ("Enter the age of the candidate " +
        "number " + (ctr+1));
      age[ctr] = Convert.ToInt32 (Console.ReadLine ());
      Console.WriteLine ("Enter the qualification of the " +
        "candidate number " + (ctr+1));
      qualification[ctr] = Console.ReadLine ();
   }
   ```

In the preceding code, the `for` statement is used to accept the details of all the candidates. The expression `ctr+1` is used to display the number of the current candidate. The `Length` property of the `Array` class returns the total number of elements contained in the array. To access this property, you need to create an instance of the `Array` class. Hence, in the preceding syntax, `first_name` array is used to access `Length` property.

TIP

To get more details on the `for` statement, read Book 5, Chapter 2.

5. **Write code statements to display the details stored in these arrays.**

```
for (ctr =0; ctr < first_name.Length; ctr = ctr +1)
{
    Console.WriteLine ("Details of candidate number" +
      (ctr +1));
    Console.WriteLine ("Name :" + first_name[ctr] + " " +
      last_name[ctr]);
    Console.WriteLine ("Age :" + age[ctr]);
    Console.WriteLine ("Qualification :" +
      qualification[ctr]);
//To pause the system after displaying the result
    Console.WriteLine ("Press Enter to continue");
    Console.Read ();
}
```

6. **Execute and test the application.**

Using Multidimensional Arrays

Multidimensional arrays — those with more than one dimension, or a rank greater than 1 — are used to store related data together. For example, you can store the names of the job application candidates along with their ages.

Creating multidimensional arrays

The processes for creating multidimensional and single-dimensional arrays are similar. Here's the syntax to create a two-dimensional array:

```
Array_type [,] array_name;
Array_name = new Array_type[num_elements,num_elements];
```

To understand this syntax better, consider the following example:

```
//Declare array
int [,] array2;
//Assign memory to this array
array2 = new int [5,1];
```

In the preceding syntax, `array2` is a two-dimensional array of type `int`. This array contains five rows and one column. You can rewrite the above-mentioned example in the following form:

```
int [,] array2 = new int [5,1];
```

Similarly, you can create a three-dimensional array, as shown in the following example:

```
int [,,] array3 = new int [5,1,1];
```

Initializing multidimensional arrays

You initialize a multidimensional array just as you initialize a single-dimensional array. Consider the following statement that initializes a two-dimensional array:

```
int [,] array3 = new int [,] {{1,2},{2,3},{3,4},{4,5}};
```

You can replace the preceding statement with this one:

```
int [,] array3 = {{1,2},{2,3},{3,4},{4,5}};
```

You can also initialize a multidimensional array by specifying the index positions.

```
int [,] array2 = new int [5,1];
//Specifying value for element at index position 0,0
array2[0,0] = 1;
//Specifying value for element at index position 0,1
array2[0,1] =2;
//Specifying value for element at index position 1,0
array2[1,0] =3;
//Specifying value for element at index position 1,1
array2[1,1] =4;
```

Now modify your application to include multidimensional arrays. In this case, add a two-dimensional array to the application: This array stores two hobbies of each candidate.

1. **Declare an array named** `hobbies`**.**

   ```
   string [,] hobbies;
   ```

2. **Initialize the array.**

   ```
   hobbies = new string [num_cand, 2];
   ```

3. **Store values in this array by adding the following code to the** `for` **statement (as we discuss in Step 4 of the previous section).**

   ```
   //Accepting hobbies of the candidate
   Console.WriteLine ("Enter first hobby");
   hobbies[ctr, 0] = Console.ReadLine ();
   Console.WriteLine ("Enter second hobby");
   hobbies[ctr ,1] = Console.ReadLine ();
   ```

4. **Write the code statements to display the elements stored in the hobbies array by adding the following code in the end of the** `for` **statement (as we discuss in Step 5 of the previous section).**

   ```
   Console.WriteLine ("Hobbies :");
   Console.WriteLine (hobbies[ctr,0]);
   Console.WriteLine (hobbies[ctr,1]);
   ```

5. **Execute and test the application.**

Understanding Jagged Arrays

In addition to creating single and multidimensional arrays, Visual C# provides you the capability to create jagged arrays. *Jagged arrays* are the arrays that contain other arrays as their elements. You can also define a jagged array as *an array of arrays*. The syntax to declare a jagged array is

```
string [][] details = new string[2][];
```

In the preceding syntax, `details` is a single-dimensional jagged array. This array can contain two elements, which are single-dimensional arrays of the same data type.

After declaring a jagged array, you need to assign values to this array. Use the following syntax:

```
details[0] = new string [] {"a", "b", "c", "d"};
details[1] = new string [] {"aa", "bb", "cc", "dd"};
```

You can also assign values to a jagged array as shown in the following syntax:

```
details [0] = array1;
details [1] = array2;
```

In the preceding syntax, `array1` and `array2` are single-dimensional arrays of type `string`. Assume that `array1` stores elements `a`, `b`, `c`, `d`, and `array2` stores elements `aa`, `bb`, `cc`, `dd`.

To access the elements stored in an array, you can use the following syntax:

```
Console.WriteLine (details [0][1]);
```

In the preceding statement, the first index position refers to `array1` and the second index position refers to the element stored at the index position 1 of `array1`. Hence, the above statement will display `b`.

Following is a complete example of the jagged arrays:

```
//Declare an array that stores first name
string [] FirstName = {"John", "Peter", "Mary", "Michelle"};
//Declare an array that stores corresponding last name
string [] LastName = {"Wilcox", "Smith", "Wilkins",
   "Goldsmith"};
//Declare a jagged array
string [][] Name = new string[2][];
Name[0] = FirstName;
Name[1] = LastName;
//Displays Peter Smith
Console.WriteLine (Name[0][1] + " " + Name[1][1]);
```

In the preceding code sample, `FirstName` and `LastName` represent two single-dimensional arrays. `Name` is a jagged array that stores both the `FirstName` and `LastName` arrays.

Chapter 4: Creating Classes in Visual C#

In This Chapter

- Creating Visual C# classes
- Adding fields, properties, methods, and indexers to a Visual C# class

Visual C# is an *object-oriented* programming language, which means that it allows you to use classes in your programs. In fact, all the code in your application is organized in classes. For a review of classes in applications that we help you create throughout this book, see Book 5, Chapters 2 and 3. In addition to this, Visual C# also lets you take advantage of the classes provided by the .NET Framework. Here we discuss the concept of classes and then we move on to describe how to decorate a class with its members.

In this chapter, we help you develop an application to automate a hotel reservation system. This application needs to accept customer name, check-in date, total days of stay, and type of room — all information that the user provides. To create this application, you use classes.

Understanding Classes

A *class* is a collection of objects that display similar behavior and can be represented by some common features. For example, consider a class named *birds*. This class can contain all kinds of birds — peacocks, pigeons, sparrows, and kingfishers — as *objects*. These objects all share common *features*, such as wings and a hollow bone structure. In addition, all display a common *behavior* — flying. To explain these features and behaviors, a class comprises a number of components, such as fields, properties, methods, and indexers. These components are called *class members*.

Read an in-depth discussion of the concepts relating to classes in Book 3, Chapter 8.

Creating Classes

To begin the sample hotel reservation application that we mention in the beginning of this chapter, you first have to create a class. However, whenever you create an application, a class is added to it by default. Hence, you start with an Empty Project. Here's how to create one.

Creating an Empty Project

Creating an Empty Project is similar to creating a console application. Read more on creating a console application in Book 5, Chapter 1.

1. **Launch Visual Studio .NET, if it is not open already.**
2. **On the Start Page, click the New Project button to display the New Project dialog box.**
3. **Under the Templates list of the New Project dialog box, click the Empty Project item.**

   Under the Project Types list, Visual C# should be selected.
4. **In the Name box of the New Project dialog box, type** Class1 **as the name of your project and then click OK to create the project.**

   Note that your new project contains no files.

Adding a class to a project

After you create the project, add a class to this project. Use the Visual C# Add Class Wizard, which is available only from the Class view of a project. Here are the steps to add a class to a project:

1. **In Solution Explorer, switch to Class View by clicking the Class View tab at the bottom of Solution Explorer.**

   Solution Explorer is present on the right side of the IDE. In case Solution Explorer isn't visible, make it visible by choosing View⇨Solution Explorer. Read more on the functionality of Solution Explorer in Book 2, Chapter 1.
2. **In Class View of Solution Explorer, right-click Class1.**
3. **From the pop-up menu that appears, choose Add⇨Add Class.**

   The C# Add Class Wizard appears, as shown in Figure 4-1. This wizard contain options required to create a class.

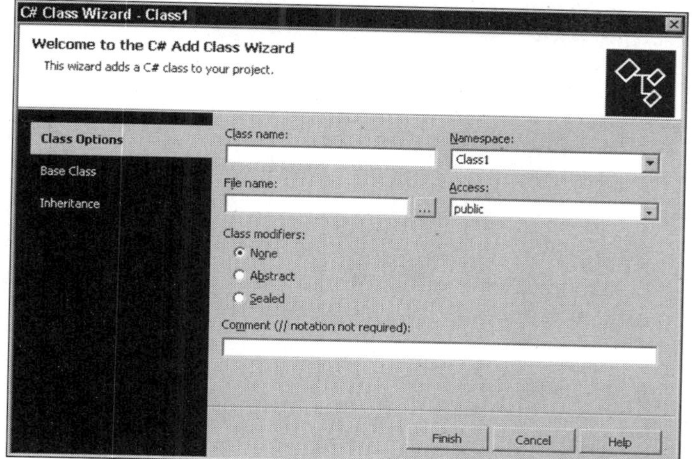

Figure 4-1: Use the Add Class Wizard to add classes to your project.

4. **In the Class Name box, type** Reservation.

   This is the name of the class.

   The Namespace list contains Class1, which means that the Reservation class will be created in the Class1 namespace.

   Note that File Name box now contains `Reservation.cs`, which is the name of the file that contains class definition. You can specify the location of this file by clicking the ellipsis button. The VS Wizards Select File dialog box shows up. Specify an appropriate location for the file in the Save in list and a name for the file in the File Name box. Click Save to save the file and close the dialog box. By default, this file is saved in the Class1 folder.

5. **Specify the accessibility of a class.**

   You use the Access list to specify the option pertaining to the accessibility of a class. This list contains two options:

   - The **public option** specifies that the class can be accessed anywhere within the same project or outside the project.
   - The **internal option** specifies that the class can be accessed only from within the files contained in an assembly.

   Read more on the public and internal keywords in Book 5, Chapter 2.

   In this case, you create a class with public access.

6. **Specify a modifier for a class.**

   These modifiers are used in case of inheritance.

Inheritance is the process of deriving a new class (child class) from an already existing class (base class). Classes created this way inherit all the functionality of the old class. You can read more on inheritance in Book 3, Chapter 8.

You use the radio button options provided under Class Modifiers — None, Abstract, and Sealed — to specify a modifier for your class.

- Select the **None** radio button to specify that the class includes no additional modifiers.
- Select the **Abstract** radio button to specify that the class can only be used as a base class for creating new classes.
- Select the **Sealed** radio button to specify that a class can't be further inherited.

In this case, don't specify any modifiers for the class. Select the None radio button to make sure that no modifiers are selected.

7. **Type** Creating a class using Add Class Wizard **in the Comments text box.**

   You can specify any comments in the Comments text box. These comments are used to generate the eXtensible Markup Language (XML) documentation. These comments also appear in the class file enclosed in the summary tags.

8. **Click the Finish button to complete the class creation.**

   The `Reservation.cs` file appears in the Code Editor. Observe that the class contains a method named `Reservation`. This method is the constructor of the `Reservation` class.

Discussing constructors

A *constructor* is a method that has the same name as the class. For example, if you create a class named `Reservation`, the name of the constructor is `Reservation`. A constructor may or may not accept parameters. However, a constructor can't return a value.

A constructor is invoked as soon as you create an instance of a class. Thus, you can use a constructor to initialize the members declared in a class. A *parameter* is a variable supplied to a method to perform some action.

Visual C# provides three types of constructors: default, instance, and static constructors.

Default constructor

A *default* constructor doesn't take any parameters. This is invoked when you use the `new` operator to create an instance of a class. The syntax of a default constructor is

```
access_modifier class_name()
{}
```

In the preceding syntax, `access_modifier` is the modifier, such as public or internal, to specify the accessibility of the constructor. Using `class_name` specifies that constructor name is same as the class name.

Instance constructor

An *instance* constructor is invoked for every instance of a class, and this constructor can accept parameters. The instance constructor contains statements to initialize the members of a class. The syntax of an instance constructor is

```
access_modifier class_name(parameters)
{
   //initialize the members of a class
   class_member = value;
}
```

Static constructor

A *static* constructor is invoked only once regardless of the number of instances of the class. Use the static constructor to initialize the static members of a class. You declare a constructor to be static by using the `static` keyword. A static constructor doesn't take any parameters. The syntax of a static constructor is

```
access_modifier static class_name()
{
   //initialize the static members of a class
   static_class_member = value;
}
```

Understanding Class Members

A class comprises a number of members, such as fields, properties, methods, and indexers. Read the upcoming sections for more on class members.

Adding fields to a class

A *field* is a variable used to store data related to a class. You can create fields just like you create variables. Use the Visual C# Add Field Wizard to add fields in a class. This wizard contains various options that are required to define a field.

Continuing with our running hotel reservation example, move back to the application Class1. Add four fields to the `Reservation` class, which are used to store the customer name, check-in date, total number of days, and type of room.

1. **In Class View of Solution Explorer, double-click Class1 to expand it.**

   Class1 represents the name of the project. When you double-click it, another Class1 appears, which is the name of the namespace contained in the project. Read more on accessing Solution Explorer and switching to Class View in the earlier section "Adding a class to a project."

2. **Double-click Class1 (namespace) to expand it.**

   The `Reservation` class shows up. You can read more on namespaces in Book 1, Chapter 2.

3. **Right-click Reservation.**

4. **From the pop-up menu that appears, choose Add⇨Add Field.**

   The Add Field Wizard appears, as shown in Figure 4-2.

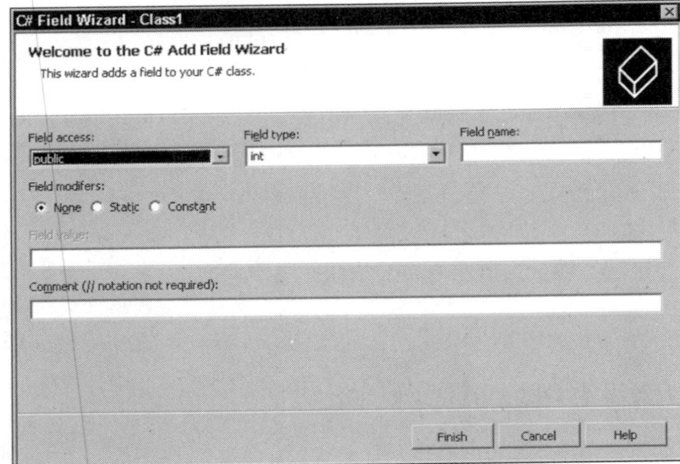

Figure 4-2: Use the Add Field Wizard to create fields in a class.

5. **Specify an access level for the field by selecting the appropriate option from the Field Access list.**

   The various options present in this list are

   * The **public** access modifier specifies that a field can be accessed from any class.

- The **protected** access modifier specifies that a field can be accessed within the class in which it was declared. Also, any class derived from this class can access the field.
- The **private** access modifier specifies that a field can be accessed only within the class in which it was declared.
- The **internal** access modifier specifies that a field can be accessed within the current project.
- The **protected internal** access modifier specifies that a field can be accessed within the current project, or any classes that are derived from the class containing field definition.

In this case, create fields with private access by selecting the private option from the Field Access list.

6. **Specify the type of the field by selecting the appropriate data type from the Field Type list.**

   In this case, select `string`. Other options present in the Field type list are `int`, `char`, `double`, and `bool`, which help you store a specific type of data in a field.

7. **Specify the name of the field by entering the name in the Field name text box.**

   In this case, enter **CName**.

8. **Specify a modifier for the field by selecting an appropriate radio button under Field Modifiers.**

   The following list describes these radio buttons.

   - **None** specifies that no modifier is included.
   - **Static** specifies that the field is a part of the class rather than being a part of the instance of the class. You can access the static fields directly by using the class name instead of creating an instance of the class.
   - **Constant** specifies that the field contains a constant value.

   In this case, select the None radio button.

9. **In the Comment text box, type** Customer Name.

10. **Click the Finish button to complete the wizard.**

    Observe that the `CName` field appears in the code. The syntax of field declaration is similar to a variable declaration, and you can directly type the field declarations in the class. You access these fields like you access variables. For more details on variables, read Book 5, Chapter 3.

Following the above steps, you create one field named CName. Similarly, create three more fields: RDate (string), TDays (int) and RType (string).

Adding properties to a class

Properties are the attributes that describe a class. For example, the bird class that we discuss earlier in the section "Understanding Classes" has properties, such as feathers and hollow bone structure. Properties are like fields, and you can access properties like you access fields. However, properties don't represent storage areas like fields. Instead, the properties contain accessor functions that are executed when you read or write to a property.

In Visual C#, you define a property in two steps:

1. Define a private class member. For this purpose, you can use fields.
2. Define the property by using the get and set accessor functions. The get accessor function is used to read the value stored in the property. The set accessor function is used to assign value to the property.

Here's an example of how to declare a property.

```
private string CName;
public string Name
{
   get
   {
     //Return the stored value
     return CName;
   }
   set
   {
     //Store the value
     CName = value;
   }
}
```

In the preceding syntax, value is an implicit parameter, which is used to assign value to a property. The type of the value parameter is the same as that of a property. After you create a property, you need to access it. Here's an example of how to access a property.

```
//Create an object of the class
Reservation res = new Reservation();
//Assign value to the property
res.Name = "James";
//Read value from the property
string str;
str = res.Name;
```

You can make a property read-only or write-only by including the `get` accessor function or the `set` accessor function, respectively. However, to read and write to a property, you need to include both accessor functions.

You can create properties either by typing the code directly in the class or by using the Add Property Wizard provided by Visual C#. Use the following steps to create properties for your application by using the wizard.

1. **In Solution Explorer, right-click Reservation.**

   Read more on accessing Solution Explorer in the earlier section "Adding a class to a project."

2. **From the pop-up menu that appears, choose Add⇨Add Property.**

   The Add Property Wizard appears, as shown in Figure 4-3. This wizard contain options required to create a property.

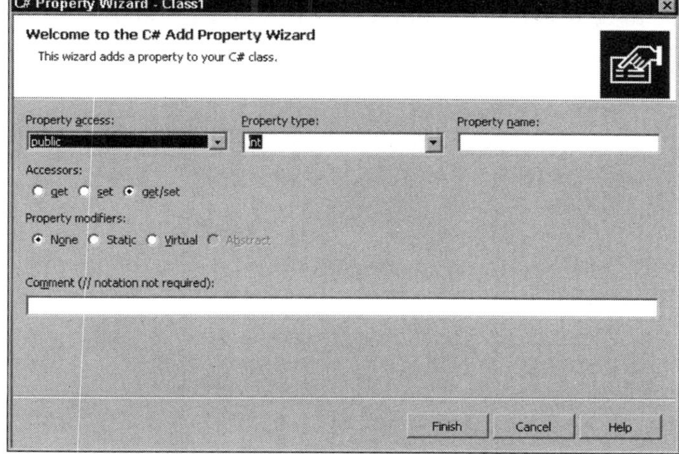

Figure 4-3: Use the Add Property Wizard to add properties to your class.

3. **Specify the access modifier for the property from the Property Access list.**

   In this case, select the public option.

4. **Specify the type of the property from the Property Type list.**

   In this case, select `string`.

5. **Type the name of the property in the Property Name text box.**

   In this case, type **CustomerName**.

6. **Under the Accessors heading, select the Get/set radio button.**

   This imparts the read and write capability to the property.

7. **Under Property Modifiers, select the None radio button.**

   Other radio button options are Static and Virtual. (Read about the Static modifier in the earlier section "Adding fields to a class." The Virtual modifier specifies that you can change the definition of this property by overriding its property in a derived class.)

   The Abstract radio button (grayed out in Figure 4-3) is enabled when you're creating an abstract class. The Abstract modifier specifies that the property doesn't contain any implementation. You need to implement this property in the derived class.

8. **In the Comment text box, type** Property to store name.

9. **Click the Finish button to complete the wizard.**

   The property definition appears in the class. Similarly, create `ReportingDate` (`string`), `TotalDays` (`int`), and `RoomType` (`string`) properties.

After you create all the properties, you need to write the code to implement these properties. For your reference, we implement the code and list it here:

```
//property to store customer name
public string CustomerName
{
   get
   {
      return CName;
    }
    set
    {
      CName = value;
    }
}
//property to store reporting date
public string ReportingDate
{
   get
   {
      return RDate;
   }
   set
   {
      RDate = value;
   }
}
//property to store total days of stay
public int TotalDays
```

```
{
   get
   {
     return TDays;
   }
   set
   {
     TDays = value;
   }
}
//property to store type of room
public string RoomType
{
   get
   {
     return RType;
   }
   set
   {
     RType = value;
   }
}
```

Adding methods to a class

After you add properties to a class, add methods to that class.

A *method* is a set of statements used to perform some specific task. For example, you can create a method that displays current time. In Visual C#, a method may or may not return a value. In case a method returns a value precede the method name with the type it returns. Otherwise, precede the method name with the `void` keyword. Here's an example to declare a method that returns a value.

```
int SampleMethod()
{
int result;
//Code of the method
return result;
}
```

In the preceding syntax, `SampleMethod` returns an `int` value. The value is returned by using the `return` keyword.

In addition, a method may or may not accept parameters. For details on parameters, refer to Book 4, Chapter 2.

In Visual C#, you can create a method either by typing the code in the class or by using the Add Method Wizard. Follow these steps to create a method by using the wizard:

1. In Solution Explorer, right-click Reservations.

2. From the pop-up menu that appears, choose Add⇨Add Method to display the Add Method Wizard.

   The Add Method Wizard (as shown in Figure 4-4) contains various options required to create a method.

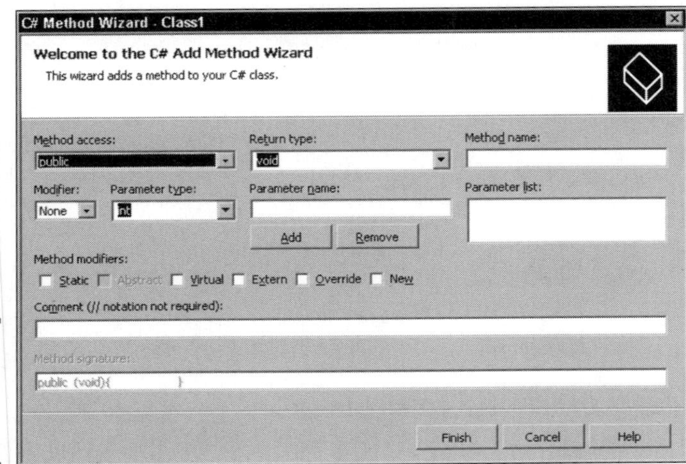

Figure 4-4: The Add Method Wizard.

3. In the Method Access list, select the public modifier.

4. In the Return Type list, select `string`**.**

5. In the Method Name text box, type DisplayDetails**.**

6. Specify parameters for the method.

   1. In the Modifier list, ensure that None is selected.

      The options available are ref and out. Read more about these options in Book 5, Chapter 2.

   2. In the Parameter Type list, select `string` to specify the type of parameter.

   3. In the Parameter Name text box, type **CN**.

   4. Click the Add button to add parameter to the Parameter List.

   5. To add three more parameters — `Date` (`string`), `Num` (`int`), and `Type` (`string`) — repeat the preceding four steps.

7. Select modifiers for the method, if desired.

   • Select the **Extern** modifier check box to specify that a method is implemented externally.

- Select the **Override** modifier check box to specify that a method is to be modified in the child class.
- Select the **New** modifier check box to hide a member that's inherited from a base class.

In this case, don't specify (select) any Method modifiers check box. Because abstract methods can be present only in an abstract class, the Abstract option isn't available.

8. **Click the Finish button to complete the wizard.**

   The method definition appears in the class.

To add functionality to this method, modify it as shown in the following code:

```
public string DisplayDetails(string CN, string Date, int Num,
    string Type)
{
   string result;
   result = "Details of the booking are as follows :";
   result = result + "\r\n" + "\r\n"  + "Name :" + CN;
   result = result + "\r\n"  + "\r\n"  + "Start Date :" +
      Date;
   result = result + "\r\n"  + "\r\n"  + "No of days :" +
      Num;
   result = result + "\r\n"  + "\r\n"  + "Room Type :" +
      Type;
   return result;
}
```

The preceding code joins all the values entered by the user and returns the result.

In the preceding code, `\r\n` is used to insert a new line.

With this, you add fields, properties, and methods to the `Reservation` class. Now write code to implement this functionality by creating the `Main` method. You can either create this method by using the Add Method wizard or type it directly in the class. We provide the definition of this method.

```
public static void Main()
{
   //Creating an object of the class
   Reservation res = new Reservation();
   Console.WriteLine ("Enter the name");
   res.CustomerName = Console.ReadLine();
   Console.WriteLine ("Enter the start date mm/dd/yy");
   res.ReportingDate = Console.ReadLine ();
   Console.WriteLine ("Enter the expected number of days");
   res.TotalDays = Convert.ToInt32 (Console.ReadLine ());
```

```
    Console.WriteLine ("Enter the type of room");
    res.RoomType =Console.ReadLine ();
    string data;
    data = res.DisplayDetails (res.CustomerName
      ,res.ReportingDate, res.TotalDays ,res.RoomType );
    Console.WriteLine (data);
}
```

In the preceding code, we create an object (`res`) of the `Reservation` class. This object is then used to assign values to the properties of the `Reservation` class. The `res` object then calls the `DisplayDetails` method and pass these properties as parameters to this method. The `DisplayDetails` method returns all the details, which are then displayed onscreen.

Adding indexers to a class

One of the latest additions to the list of class members is indexers. You use *indexers* to make your classes appear as virtual arrays. You can then access the instances of the classes just like arrays by using square brackets — `[]` — the array access operator. (Read more on Arrays in Book 5, Chatper 3.) An indexer doesn't have a name: It's identified by its signature. Here's the syntax to declare an indexer:

```
access_modifier data_type this[parameter(s)]
{
    get
    {
      statement(s);
    }
    set
    {
      statement(s);
    }
}
```

In the preceding syntax,

- `access_modifier` represents the modifier to specify the accessibility of an indexer.
- `data_type` refers to the type of indexer.
- `parameter(s)` are any values passed to an indexer.
- `get` and `set` accessor functions are used to read and write the indexer elements, respectively. These accessor functions accept the same parameter as the indexer. In addition, the set accessor function can accept the value implicit parameter.

Looking at the previous syntax, you may think that an indexer is similar to a property. Not so. Look at some differences between the two:

- ✦ A property has a name, but an indexer is identified by its signature.
- ✦ A property is accessed by its name or through the member access, whereas an indexer is accessed like arrays.
- ✦ A property could be a static or an instance member, whereas an indexer can only be an instance member.

Now look at a code sample to understand the usage of indexers. In this code sample, we extend the `Reservation` class that we create earlier. Assume that the hotel for which you're developing this application has 20 rooms, and the manager of this hotel wants to provide the customer with an option to choose the room number. You need to modify the above application so that it stores the choice of rooms and displays it to the customer.

To implement this functionality by using an indexer, follow these steps:

1. **Add a new member to the** `Reservation` **class, which is a string array of size** `20`**.**

   The syntax to do so is

   ```
   private string [] Rooms = new string [20];
   ```

   Add this statement after the definition of the `Reservation` class.

2. **Add the following code to the constructor of the** `Reservation` **class:**

   ```
   public Reservation()
   {
       for (int ctr = 0; ctr<20; ctr++)
       {
           Rooms[ctr] = "Free";
       }
   }
   ```

   You add the code to initialize the `Rooms` array in the constructor so that the array is initialized as soon as the object of the `Reservation` class is created.

3. **Create the indexer by adding the following code to the class.**

   ```
   public string this[int index]
   {
       get
       {
           //Return the value stored at the specified index
           return Rooms[index];
       }
       set
   ```

```
        {
            //Assign value at the specified index
            Rooms[index] = value;
        }
    }
```

4. **Add the following code after the last line in the `Main` method.**

```
int i;
Console.WriteLine ("Enter the room number");
i = Convert.ToInt32 (Console.ReadLine ());
res[i-1] = "Booked";
for(int ctr = 0; ctr<20; ctr++)
{
    Console.WriteLine ("Room number " + (ctr +1) + " is
" +
        res[ctr]);
}
```

The preceding code accepts the room number from the customer because you declare an indexer in the class declaration. You can directly access the elements of the `Rooms` array by using the `res` object. The `for` statement then displays all the elements of the `Rooms` array.

5. **Execute the application.**

Chapter 5: Creating Windows Applications

In This Chapter

- **Creating and customizing a Windows application**
- **Saying Hello to the World**
- **Discovering the `CommonDialog` class**

In Book 5, Chapters 2, 3, and 4, we discuss that Visual C# enables you to create console-based applications. You can also use Visual C# to create superb Windows applications, such as Notepad and Calculator. To create these applications, you use Windows Forms, which is the latest forms package available with Visual Studio .NET.

In this chapter, we introduce you to the basics of creating a Windows application by using Visual C#. We get you started by showing you how to create a Windows Application project. Then we discuss the code automatically generated by Visual Studio .NET. Next we move ahead with the customary Hello World application. In addition, we guide you to implement `CommonDialog` classes in your applications. This chapter requires a basic knowledge of Windows Forms and adding controls to a form. Hence, we recommend that you read Book 3, Chapters 2, 3, and 4 before starting to create Windows applications by using Visual C#.

You can download the sample Windows1 application from the `www.dummies.com/extras/VS.NETAllinOne` site.

Getting Started with a Windows Application

A Windows-based application requires high precision and creativity: precision for using appropriate controls and creativity for displaying these controls in an easy-to-understand format. To create a windows application, you use the Windows Application project template. Select your template from the New Project dialog box. To create a Windows Application project, follow these steps:

1. **Open the New Project dialog box by clicking the New Project button on the Start Page.**
2. **Under Project Types in the New Project dialog box that appears, click the Visual C# folder.**
3. **Under Templates in the New Project dialog box, click Windows Application.**
4. **In the Name text box, type** Windows1 **as the name of the project.**
5. **In the Location box, specify an appropriate location to store the application.**

   You can also specify a location in the Project Location dialog box that opens when you click the Browse button in the New Project dialog box.
6. **Click OK to create the application.**

   The application contains a form that you can use to create a sophisticated user interface. The title bar of the form displays `Form1`, which is the caption of the form.

You may want to alter the appearance of the form according to your preferences. Read the next section to discover how to amend the design of a form.

Tailoring the design of a form

You can make a number of changes to the appearance of a form, including its caption or size. To find out how you can tailor a form, read more on customizing the appearance of a form in Book 3, Chapter 2.

Use the Properties window to modify the appearance of a form, which you access by choosing View⇨Properties Window. Go ahead and check out the Properties window for the application that you create in the previous section: You should be able to see the properties of the file `Form1.cs`.

The Properties window displays all the properties of a selected object. This object could be anything, such as a control or a form. The Properties window also displays the properties of the files and projects present in Solution Explorer.

Assigning a suitable title to a form

You want to assign an appropriate title (caption) to your form — choose a title that helps you identify the function of your form. To specify a title, use the `Text` property. You can specify a value for this property either in the Properties window or the Code Editor. Here we stick with changing the title from the Properties window. To specify an appropriate title for your form, follow these steps:

1. **In the Integrated Development Environment (IDE), click the form to display the properties of this form.**
2. **In the Properties window that opens, edit the Text field to display** `My Windows Form`**.**

   The title bar of the form now displays `My Windows Form`.

Adjusting the size of a form

An extra large or a miniscule form can lead to improper display of controls. Also, a mis-sized form isn't visually appealing. To fine-tune the size of a form, use the `Size` property. The unit of measurement for the `Size` property is in pixels. Just like setting the `Text` property, set the `Size` property in either the Properties window or the Code Editor. Here's how to specify an appropriate size for the form from the Properties window:

1. **Open the Properties window by choosing View➪Properties Window.**
2. **Move to the Size field and look at its specifications.**

   The field displays `300, 300`: This means 300 pixels wide and 300 pixels high.
3. **Change the size to** `500, 500`**.**

   Ta-dah! The size of the form increases.

You can also specify the width and height of a form individually. To do so, in the Properties window, expand the Size field by clicking the + symbol next to it. This displays the Width and Height fields. You can now specify appropriate values in these fields.

After you customize a form, the next logical step is to write code for the application. However, when you create a Windows Application project, Visual Studio .NET automatically generates the code. In the next section, we introduce you to this code.

Understanding the default code

When you create a Windows Application project, Visual Studio .NET automatically generates the code. This code constitutes the basic structure of your application. Read this section to understand the syntax and use of this code.

To view the code generated by Visual Studio .NET, you need to switch to the Code Editor.

1. **Right-click the form.**
2. **From the pop-up menu that appears, choose View Code.**

   The Code Editor appears as shown in Figure 5-1.

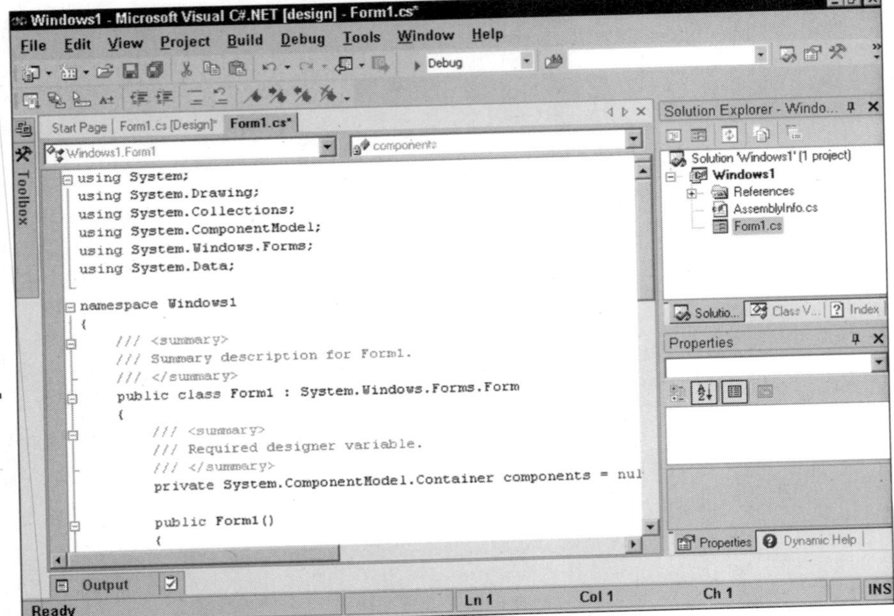

Figure 5-1: Use the Code Editor to write code for your application.

The code contains a number of statements. The functions of these statements are to

- **Include required namespaces**
- **Create a namespace**
- **Define the class that represents the form**
- **Represent the method to initialize resources, such as forms and controls**
- **Represent the method to make resources available**
- **Represent the method to run the application**

Including namespaces

The `using` directive is used to include namespaces in an application. A namespace is a collection of various classes, structures, and enumerations. Read more on namespaces in Book 1, Chapter 2. Here are the statements that are generated in the `Windows1` application:

```
using System;
using System.Drawing;
using System.Collections;
using System.ComponentModel;
```

```
using System.Windows.Forms;
using System.Data;
```

- `System`: The `System` namespace contains classes to provide data types, events and event handlers, interfaces, and attributes.
- `System.Drawing`: The `System.Drawing` namespace contains classes that impart graphics functionality to an application.
- `System.Collections`: The `System.Collections` namespace contains classes and interfaces that are used to define different collections, such as arrays and lists, of the objects.
- `System.ComponentModel`: The `System.ComponentModel` namespace contains classes that are used to implement attributes, convert types, bind controls with data sources, and license components.
- `System.Windows.Forms`: The `System.Windows.Forms` namespace contains classes that help create windows-based applications.
- `System.Data`: The `System.Data` namespace contains classes that represent the components of the ADO.NET architecture.

Creating a namespace

Visual Studio .NET creates a namespace named `Windows1` by using the `namespace` keyword. Look at the following statement for reference:

```
namespace Windows1
```

Defining a class

Every form in your application is represented by a class. In this case, the name of the class is `Form1`. This statement defines the class:

```
public class Form1 : System.Windows.Forms.Form
```

The `Form1` class is derived from the `Form` class, which is present in the `System.Windows.Form` namespace.

The `Form1` class contains a constructor, which calls the `InitializeComponent` method. The definition of the constructor is

```
public Form1()
{
  //Call the InitializeComponent method
  InitializeComponent();
}
```

Read more on classes in Book 5, Chapter 4.

Initializing resources

Initializing resources refers to setting initial values for a form and various controls, such as setting the caption of a form as soon as the form is displayed. Use the `InitializeComponent` method to set initial values for a form and the controls present in the form. One interesting feature of this method is that, as you add, remove, or manipulate controls, the information present in this method changes concurrently to reflect the correct status.

The `InitializeComponent` method is called from the constructor. As a result, as soon as you create an object of the class, the `Initialize-Component` method is invoked and initial values of forms and controls are set. However, you can't see the definition of this method. To view the definition, locate the statement `Windows Forms Designer generated code` in the Code Editor and click the plus (+) sign next to it. The definition of the `InitializeComponent` method appears. Here's the definition of this method:

```
private void InitializeComponent()
{
  //
  // Form1
  //
  this.AutoScaleBaseSize = new System.Drawing.Size(5, 13);
  this.ClientSize = new System.Drawing.Size(492, 473);
  this.Name = "Form1";
  this.Text = "My Windows Form";
}
```

In the preceding code, you can easily infer that no controls exist yet in the form. The various keywords and properties used in this code are

- `this` keyword: Represents the current instance of the form.
- `AutoScaleBaseSize` property: Assigns the base size, which is then used to calculate the scaling factor of the form at display time.
- `ClientSize` property: Specifies the client area of the form. The *client area* is the area excluding the borders and title bar of the form.
- `Name` property: Assigns the name of the form.
- `Text` property: Specifies the caption of the form.

Freeing resources

Freeing resources refers to making available the memory used by the objects that are no longer in use. The `Form1` class contains a method named `Dispose` that makes resources available. This method overrides the `Dispose` method of the `Form` class, which is the base class of the `Form1` class.

The definition of the `Dispose` method is

```
protected override void Dispose( bool disposing )
{
  if( disposing )
    {
      if (components != null)
      {
//Call the dispose method of the Container class
        components.Dispose();
      }
    }
  base.Dispose( disposing );
}
```

In the preceding code, the `Dispose` method of the `Form1` class calls the `Dispose` method of the `Container` class. The `Container` class contains nothing or a few components present in the form.

Running the application

Running the application refers to creating an object of the `Form1` class and displaying the form. To do so, you invoke the `Run` method of the `Application` class from the `Main` method. This method takes an object of the `Form` class, which is to be displayed as a parameter.

```
static void Main()
{
  Application.Run(new Form1());
}
```

Get an in-depth knowledge of using the `Main` method in Book 5, Chapter 1.

Saying Hello World the Visual C# Way

In this section, we move to the practical part of this chapter. We show you how to say Hello to the World — in a new language.

This version of Hello World displays a message to the user. The message displays in a message box and at the click of a button. To do so, perform two simple steps:

1. Add a button to the form.
2. Write the code to display the message at the click of a button.

Adding a button to a form

Use the Toolbox to add controls — such as a button — to a form. The Toolbox contains a number of controls that are grouped into various categories. For detailed information about the Toolbox and its various controls, read Book 3, Chapter 3. To access the Toolbox, choose View➪Toolbox.

To add a control to a form, just click and drag the control from the Toolbox to your form. Alternately, you can double-click the required control in the Toolbox to add it to the form. However, if you follow this latter method, you may need to reposition the control on your form. Perform the following steps to add a button to the form:

1. **Click the Form1.cs [Design] tab present in the IDE to switch to the Design view of the form.**

   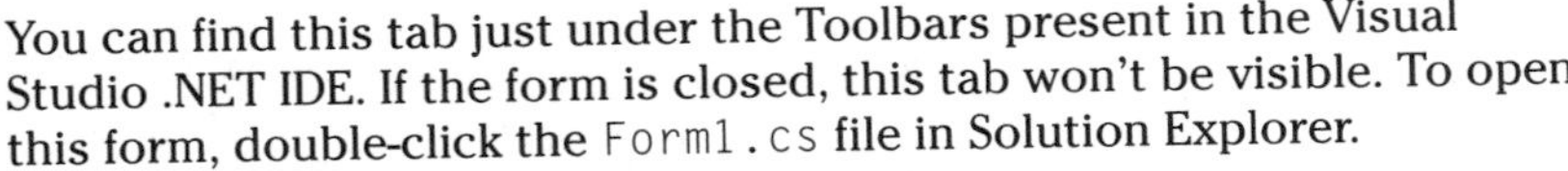

   You can find this tab just under the Toolbars present in the Visual Studio .NET IDE. If the form is closed, this tab won't be visible. To open this form, double-click the `Form1.cs` file in Solution Explorer.

2. **In the Windows Forms tab of the Toolbox, double-click the** `Button` **control to add it to your form.**

   A button appears in your form, as shown in Figure 5-2. The caption of the button is `button1`. Click and drag the button to wherever you want.

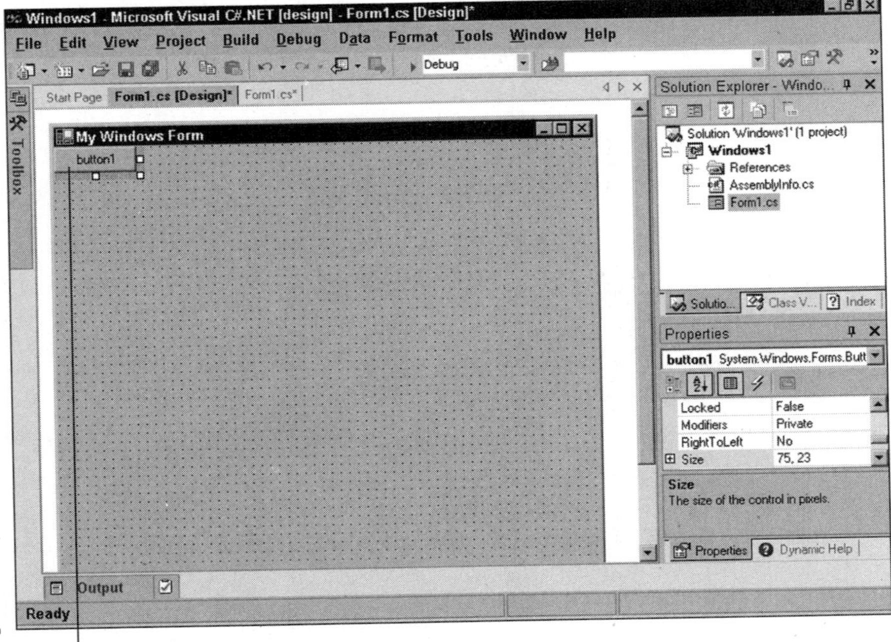

Figure 5-2: Button, button, you've got the button — and where you want it.

3. **In the Properties window, set the `Text` property of the button to `Say Hello`.**

Adding code

Adding code to the `Click` event of this button is simple. To display a message at the click of a button, you need to trap the `Click` event of the button. An *event* is any action that executes a method called an *event handler*. Here's how to add an event and an event handler for a button.

1. **In Design view, double-click the Say Hello button.**

   The Code Editor appears and displays a method named `button1_Click`. This method — an event handler — handles the `Click` event of the button.

2. **To display a message, add the following code to this method:**

   ```
   MessageBox.Show ("Hello World", "Windows App");
   ```

   In the preceding statement, the `Show` method of the `MessageBox` class is used to display `Hello World` to the user. The title bar of the message box displays `Windows App`. Read more about the `MessageBox.Show` method in Book 3, Chapter 4.

3. **Execute the application by choosing Debug⇨Start.**

   The form appears with a `Say Hello` button.

4. **Click the Say Hello button.**

   The message box appears, as shown in Figure 5-3.

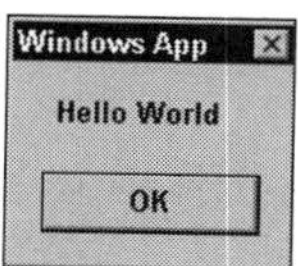

Figure 5-3: Hello World — the Visual C# way.

After you have this simple procedure for creating a Hello World application in Visual C# under your belt, pick up some speed. Read on as we walk you through adding some functionality to make an application display standard Windows dialog boxes, such as Open and Save. You need to utilize the `CommonDialog` class, which we discuss next.

Understanding the CommonDialog Class

You've undoubtedly seen a number of standard Windows dialog boxes, such as Open, Save As, and Font. Your Visual C# applications can also display these. You need to use the `CommonDialog` class, which is the base class for displaying standard dialog boxes. This class contains various classes, such as `FileDialog`, `FontDialog`, and `ColorDialog`, to help you implement these dialog boxes with ease.

To extend your `Windows1` application to display the Save As, Open, Font, and Color dialog boxes, first design the form as shown in Figure 5-4.

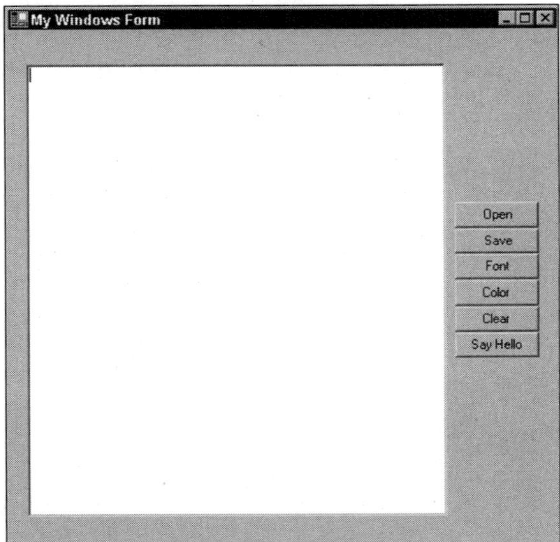

Figure 5-4: Implement dialog boxes in your applications.

The controls used in the form along with their properties are

- One `RichTextBox` control with the following properties:
  - `Name` = Data
  - `Multiline` = True
  - `Text` = ""
- Five buttons with the `Text` property. (Refer to Figure 5-4.) Read how to create the `Say Hello` button in the "Adding a button to a form" section earlier in this chapter.

Read on to discover the various classes present in the `CommonDialog` class.

FileDialog class

Use the `FileDialog` class to display dialog boxes that enable you to select a file. To help you perform these operations, the `FileDialog` class contains the `SaveFileDialog` and `OpenFileDialog` classes.

SaveFileDialog class

Use the `SaveFileDialog` class to display the standard Save As dialog box. You can use this dialog box to implement operations for saving files in your applications. However, you need to write the code for saving the file. The `SaveFileDialog` class provides a number of properties that help you manipulate the Save As dialog box. We describe some of these properties in the following list:

- `CheckFileExists` property: Use this property to determine whether the file specified by the user exists.
- `FileName` property: Use this property to identify the filename selected by the user in the dialog box.
- `Filter` property: Use this property to determine the types of files that will appear in the Save as File Type box in the dialog box.
- `FilterIndex` property: Use this property to determine the index of the filter selected in the dialog box.

The `SaveFileDialog` class provides the `ShowDialog` method to display the Save As dialog box.

To implement this class in your application:

1. **To display the Save As dialog box, add the following code to the `Click` event of the Save button.**

```
SaveFileDialog objSFD;
//Create an object of SaveFileDialog class
objSFD = new SaveFileDialog ();
//Specify the filter
objSFD.Filter ="All Files|*.*|Text Files|*.txt";
//Make All Files the default selection
objSFD.FilterIndex = 1;
//Display the dialog box
//Also check whether the user clicked the Save button
//in the dialog box
if (objSFD.ShowDialog() == DialogResult.OK)
{
   Data.SaveFile(objSFD.FileName,
     RichTextBoxStreamType.PlainText);
   MessageBox.Show("File Saved!!");
}
```

The preceding code sets various properties of the Save As dialog box and then displays the dialog box. In addition, the code enables you to save the file at the click of the Save button.

In the preceding syntax,

1. The `DialogResult` enumeration is used to specify the button that you click to close the dialog box. This enumeration contains various constants, such as `Yes`, `No`, `Cancel`, and `Abort`, that represent commonly used buttons in dialog boxes.

   In this case, you need to check whether the user clicked the Save button. Therefore, you specify `DialogResult.OK`.

2. The `SaveFile` method of the `RichTextBox` control is used to save the contents of the Data box (the `RichTextBox` control) to a text file. This method takes two parameters: name and type of file.

   In this case, the `FileName` property of the `SaveFileDialog` class is used to specify the filename and the `RichTextBoxStreamType` enumeration is used to specify the type in which the file should be saved. In this case, the file is saved as a text file.

2. Execute the application.

3. Type some content in the Data box.

4. Click the Save button.

The Save As dialog box appears as shown in Figure 5-5.

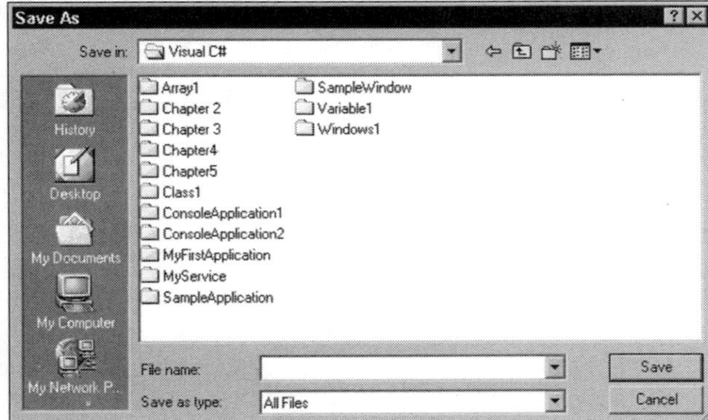

Figure 5-5: Use the SaveFile Dialog class to display the Save As dialog box.

5. Specify an appropriate location (in the Save In box) and name (in the File Name text box) for the file.

6. From the Save As Type list, select Text Files and then click the Save button.

A message box appears, stating that your file was saved.

We create the Clear button on the form because the Clear button helps remove any existing content in the `RichTextBox` control. To do so, add the following code to the `Click` event of this button.

```
Data.Text ="";
```

The next step involves using the `OpenFileDialog` class.

OpenFileDialog class

Use the `OpenFileDialog` class to display the standard Open dialog box through your application. You need to write the code to open the selected file. The `OpenFileDialog` class provides you with a number of properties that help you perform a range of tasks, including

- `Multiselect` property: Use this property to determine whether you can select multiple files in the dialog box.
- `ShowReadOnly` property: Use this property to determine whether the dialog box displays the Open as Read-Only check box.
- `ReadOnlyChecked` property: Use this property to determine the state of the read-only check box displayed in the dialog box. *State* refers to whether this check box is checked (selected) or unchecked (unselected).
- `Filter` property: Use this property to determine the types of files that appear in the Files of Type box in the dialog box.
- `FilterIndex` property: Use this property to determine the index of the filter selected in the dialog box. *Index* is the position number of filters specified by using the Filter property.

Opening a file is not as easy as saving a file; you have to use a number of classes to perform this task. Read the following sections where we discuss these classes.

FileStream class

The `FileStream` class represents a file and helps perform read and write operations.

To utilize the `FileStream` class, you need to create an object of this class. The syntax to do this is

```
FileStream objFS = new FileStream(FileName,
  FileMode, FileAccess );
```

In the preceding syntax, the constructor of the `FileStream` class takes three parameters:

- `FileName`: Refers to the name of the file to be opened.
- `FileMode`: Refers to the mode, such as append or create, in which a file should be opened. To specify the mode of a file, use the `FileMode` enumeration, which contains constants that specify the procedure for opening a file. Some of the constants present in the `FileMode` enumeration are `Append`, `Create`, `Open`, and `OpenOrCreate`.
- `FileAccess`: Refers to the type of access, such as read-only or write-only, granted to a file. To specify the type of access, use the `FileAccess` enumeration, which contains various constants, such as `Read`, `Write`, and `ReadWrite`.

StreamReader class

After specifying a file, you need to read the data (characters) stored in this file. To use the `StreamReader` class, follow these steps:

1. **Create an object of the `StreamReader` class with the following syntax.**

   ```
   StreamReader objSR = new StreamReader(FileStream);
   ```

   In the preceding syntax, `objSR` is the object of the `StreamReader` class. The constructor of the `StreamReader` class takes the file to be read as a parameter. To specify this file, use the `FileStream` object in the steps of the preceding section "FileStream class."

2. **Specify the read/write position by using the `Seek` method.**

   The `Seek` method refers to the position from where a reading or writing operation should start. The syntax is

   ```
   objSR.BaseStream.Seek(Offset, Origin);
   ```

   The `Seek` method accepts two parameters:

   - `Offset`: Refers to the point from where a read/write operation should begin.
   - `Origin`: Is a reference point, such as beginning, end, or current, for the offset. To specify this parameter, use the `SeekOrigin` enumeration, which contains constants, such as `Begin`, `End`, and `Current`, to specify the reference point.

   To understand the `Seek` method better, consider the following example:

   ```
   objSR.BaseStream.Seek(2, SeekOrigin.Begin);
   ```

   In the preceding statement, the `Seek` method sets the read/write position as two characters from the beginning of a file.

3. **Read characters from the file.**

   To do so, you need to use two methods: `Peek` and `ReadLine`.

- Peek: Use the Peek method of the StreamReader class to check the availability of the characters in a file. This method returns a character from a file, and it returns -1 if no other characters are available in the file. The syntax of this method is

  ```
  objSR.Peek();
  ```

- ReadLine: Use the ReadLine method of the StreamReader class to read a line of characters from a given file and return this line as a string.

  ```
  objSR.ReadLine();
  ```

Now implement the OpenFileDialog class in your application.

1. **To implement the OpenFileDialog class in your application, add the following code to the Click event of the Open button:**

   ```
   OpenFileDialog objOFD = new OpenFileDialog ();
   objOFD.Filter ="All Files|*.*|Text Files|*.txt";
   //Make All Files the default selection
   objOFD.FilterIndex = 1;
   //Display the dialog box
   //Also check whether the user clicked the Open button
   in
     //the dialog box
   if (objOFD.ShowDialog() == DialogResult.OK )
   {
      string filename;
      filename = objOFD.FileName;
   //Create a FileStream object
      FileStream objFS = new FileStream(filename,
        FileMode.OpenOrCreate, FileAccess.ReadWrite );
   //Create a StreamReader object
      StreamReader objSR = new StreamReader(objFS);
      // Set read/write position to the beginning.
      objSR.BaseStream.Seek(0, SeekOrigin.Begin);
      Data.Text = objSR.ReadLine ();
      while (objSR.Peek() > -1)
      {
   //Place the contents of the file in the rich text box
        Data.Text = Data.Text + "\r\n" + objSR.ReadLine();
      }
      objSR.Close();
   }
   ```

2. **Execute the application, and click the Open button.**

   The Open dialog box appears as shown in Figure 5-6.

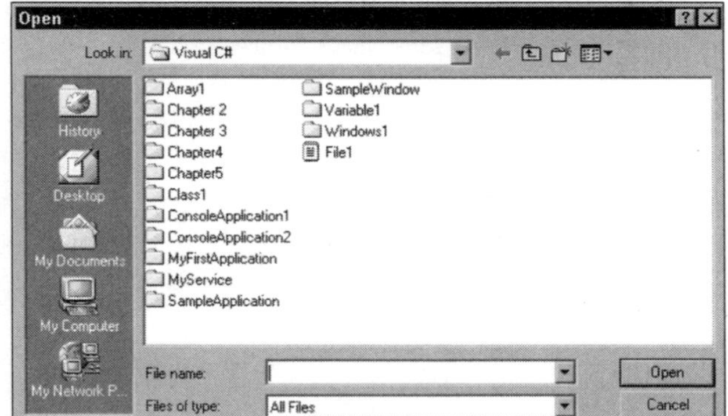

Figure 5-6: Use the OpenFile-Dialog class to display the Open dialog box.

3. **Select the file that you create in the previous section ("SaveFileDialog class") and click Open.**

   The contents of the file appear in the Data box.

FontDialog class

Use the `FontDialog` class to display the standard Font dialog box, from which you can change the font, font style, and size of text. This dialog box displays the fonts currently installed on your system. The `FontDialog` class provides some properties to modify the Font dialog box.

- ✦ `Color` **property:** Use this property to determine the font color selected by the user.
- ✦ `Font` **property:** Use this property to determine the font, style, size, and effects, such as strikethrough and underline.

Use the `ShowDialog` method of the `FontDialog` class to display the Font dialog box.

Here's how to implement the FontDialog class in your application:

1. **To implement the functionality of the `FontDialog` class, add the following code to the `Click` event of the Font button:**

   ```
   FontDialog objFD = new FontDialog ();
   if (objFD.ShowDialog() == DialogResult.OK )
   {
      Data.Font = objFD.Font ;
   }
   ```
2. **Execute the application.**

3. **Type some content in the Data box control.**
4. **Click the Font button.**

   The Font dialog box appears as shown in Figure 5-7.

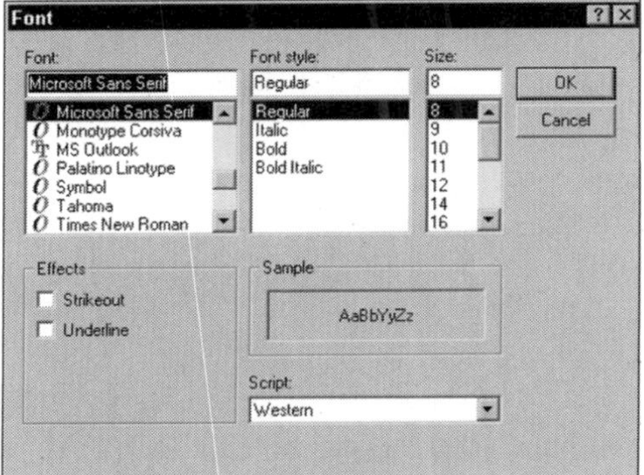

Figure 5-7: Use the FontDialog class to display the Font dialog box.

5. **Make appropriate selection in the dialog box and then click OK.**

   The selections that you make are applied to the text present in the Data box control.

ColorDialog class

Use the `ColorDialog` class to display the Color dialog box. You can use this dialog box to select a color and add colors to a palette. Some properties of this class are

- `Color`: Use this property to determine the color selected by a user.
- `AllowFullOpen`: Use this property to determine whether a user can add custom colors to the dialog box.
- `SolidColorOnly`: Use this property to determine whether a user can use dithered colors. *Dithered colors* are the colors that are composed of various colors.

To implement the `ColorDialog` class in your application, perform the following steps:

1. **To display the Color dialog box, add the following code to the** `Click` **event of the Color button.**

```
ColorDialog objCD = new ColorDialog ();
if (objCD.ShowDialog () == DialogResult.OK )
{
//Apply selected color to the text in the Data box
   Data.ForeColor = objCD.Color ;
}
```

2. **Execute the application, and enter the content in the Data box.**
3. **Click the Color button.**

   The Color dialog box appears as shown in Figure 5-8.

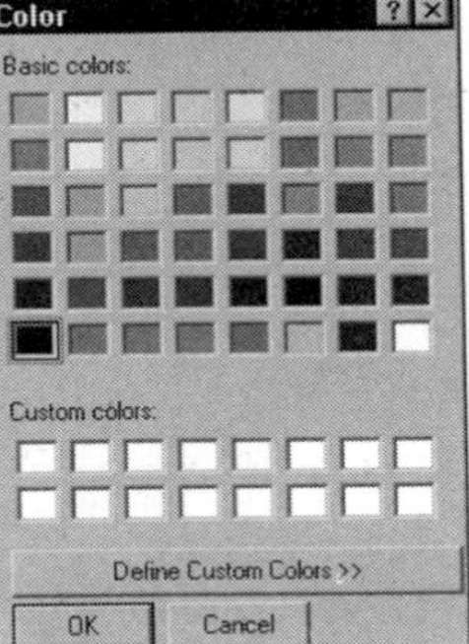

Figure 5-8: Use the ColorDialog class to display the Color dialog box.

4. **Select the appropriate color and click OK.**

   The color that you select is applied to the text present in the Data box.

Your application is now ready to be executed. You can use it to display the contents of a file or save the contents of a rich text box in a file. You can also manipulate the font and color of text. Moreover, you can clear the box by using the Clear button without the need to restart the application to clear the rich text box.

Chapter 6: Creating Windows Services

In This Chapter

- Understanding Windows services
- Creating a Windows service application
- Installing a service
- Administering a service

Windows services work endlessly and perform a number of useful tasks, such as logging all events or monitoring the performance of a system without interfering with your work. Using Visual C#, you can create your own Windows services. Creating these services requires only a few steps and minimal coding. In this chapter, we introduce you to the concepts related to Windows services.

In this chapter, you find out how to create a Windows service. This service accepts a file as a parameter. The service stores various details of this file in a separate text file. These details include the dates when the file was created, last modified, and last accessed. The service also stores the attributes of this file. You then create an application to administer this service. This application displays the contents of the text file in a RichTextBox control.

You can download the sample Windows service from `http://www.dummies.com/extras/VS.NETAllinOne`.

Understanding Windows Services

Windows service is the new name of NT services. These are long-running applications that provide different functionalities. For example, Event Log is a service provided by Windows operating system that is used to log events and messages that are generated by the programs running on your computer or the Windows operating system itself. You can use this information to diagnose problems that might occur while working with various applications. However, these services do not have a user interface, so you can't see them in action. The advantage of using a Windows service is that it doesn't interfere with the users' tasks.

You can administer the services installed on your computer by using a utility called *Service Control Manager*. To view this utility, choose Start⇨Programs⇨Administrative Tools⇨Services. Service Control Manager contains a list of services currently installed on your computer. (Take a look ahead at Figure 6-2 for reference.)

Visual Studio .NET provides you the flexibility to create your own Windows services. Creating a Windows service requires a number of steps. You can refer to these steps as the life cycle of a Windows service. This chapter discusses how to create a Windows service in detail. Let's start our discussion with the life cycle of a Windows service.

Life cycle of a Windows service

To understand a Windows service, you must first understand the events involved in its life cycle. The following list explains the life cycle of a Windows service in brief.

1. The first step to create a service is to create the Windows Service application and specify various properties and methods of the service. You create an application by using the Windows Service template.
2. After you create a Windows service application, you need to install the service. Installing a service comprises the following two steps:
   1. Add installation components to the service. *Installation components* help you install the resources required by a service.
   2. Run the InstallUtil utility to install the service and load the service into Service Control Manager.
3. After you install a service, the next step is to administer it. Visual Studio .NET provides the following three utilities to administer a service.
   - Service Control Manager
   - Server Explorer
   - Code

Let's look at the types of services you can create by using Visual Studio .NET.

Types of services

Visual Studio .NET allows you to create two types of services:

- `Win32OwnProcess`: These are services that run in their own process.
- `Win32ShareProcess`: These are services that run in a shared process.

You already had a brief insight into the life cycle of a Windows service. Now, it's time to get started with creating a Windows service.

Creating a Windows Service Application

The first step toward creating a Windows service is to create an application that would contain this service. This application can contain multiple services. To create the container application, use the Windows Service template. The advantage of using this template is that it includes all of the namespaces and classes that you would require to create the service. Here are the steps to create a Windows Service application:

1. **Open the New Project dialog box.**
2. **Under Templates, select Windows Service to create an application based on this template. Name this application as `Service1`.**

   The design view of the `Service1` application appears.
3. **Double-click anywhere in the design view to switch to the code view.**

   Notice that the project template creates a class named `Service1`, which is derived from the `ServiceBase` class. The `ServiceBase` class is a part of the `System.ServiceProcess` namespace.

Read the upcoming paragraphs for a good understanding of the `ServiceBase` class.

The `ServiceBase` class contains various properties and methods that help you add functionality to your service. This class is contained in the `System.ServiceProcess` namespace. We discuss the properties and methods contained in the `ServiceBase` class.

Properties of the ServiceBase class

In order to specify the features and functions associated with a service, you must set various properties of the service class. The following list describes some of the commonly used properties:

- `ServiceName`: Determines the name of the service
- `CanStop`: Determines whether the service can be stopped
- `CanPauseAndContinue`: Determines whether the service can pause and then continue
- `AutoLog`: Determines whether the Start, Stop, Pause, and Continue steps performed by the service are to be logged into the event log

If you set the properties such as `CanStop` to true, you need to implement the corresponding methods like `OnStop`, `OnPause`, and `OnContinue`, respectively. Not implementing the corresponding methods causes the application to generate an error.

The `Service1` application must log the actions performed by the service in the event log. In addition, the user should be able to stop the service at any point in time. To do so, you set the respective properties of this service by performing the following step.

In the Properties window, set the following properties of the service:

```
ServiceName = FileInfo
AutoLog = True
CanStop = True
```

From the preceding step, you can make out that the name of the service is `FileInfo`, and it can log various actions in the event log. The service can stop.

Methods of the ServiceBase class

The `ServiceBase` class provides a number of methods, which represent various states of a life cycle. Some of the states of a service are start, stop, pause, and continue. You need to override these methods in your service class. Read the following list to understand the methods provided by the `ServiceBase` class.

- `OnStart`: Use this method to specify the steps to be performed when the service starts. This method accepts a parameter, which is an array of type `string`. However, this parameter is optional.
- `OnStop`: Use this method to specify the steps to be performed when the service stops.
- `OnPause`: Use this method to specify the steps to be performed when the service pauses.
- `OnContinue`: Use this method to specify the steps to be performed when the service starts after a pause.

You may or may not implement any of these methods in your application. However, as the `OnStart` method contains the behavior of the service, you should, preferably, implement this method.

The `Service1` application takes a file name as a parameter. The service then generates the details of the file it accepts as parameter and saves the details about the file in a separate file called info.txt. You'll add this functionality in the `OnStart` method of the service. Let's now look at the steps to do so.

1. **Observe the code automatically generated by the Windows Service template.**

   The code contains the structure of `OnStart` and `OnStop` methods. You need to write the code to impart functionality to these methods.

2. **To impart functionality to your service, add the following code to the `OnStart` method:**

```
protected override void OnStart(string[] args)
{
 string flname;
 flname = args[0];
//Check for existence of file
 if(File.Exists(flname))
 {
   //Generate details of file
   string info;
   info = "Created On: " + File.GetCreationTime
(flname) +
     "\r\n";
   info = info + "Last Accessed On: " +
Convert.ToString
     (File.GetLastAccessTime (flname)) +"\r\n";
   info = info + "Last Modified On: " +
Convert.ToString
     (File.GetLastWriteTime (flname)) +"\r\n";
   info = info + "Attributes :" + File.GetAttributes
     (flname) + "\r\n";
   //Write the details to the Info.Txt file
   FileStream fs = new FileStream(@"c:\temp\Info.txt" ,
     FileMode.Create, FileAccess.Write);
   StreamWriter objSW = new StreamWriter(fs);
   objSW.BaseStream.Seek(0, SeekOrigin.Begin );
   objSW.WriteLine("The information for " + flname +"
is:
      " +"\r\n" + info);
   objSW.Flush();
 }
 else
 {
   string info;
   info = args[0];
   FileStream fs = new FileStream(@"c:\temp\Info.txt" ,
     FileMode.Create,    FileAccess.Write);
   StreamWriter objSW = new StreamWriter(fs);
   objSW.BaseStream.Seek(0, SeekOrigin.Begin );
   objSW.WriteLine(info + " Not Found");
   objSW.Flush();
 }
}
```

The preceding code stores the name of the file supplied as a parameter in a `string` variable. Using the `File` class, the code checks whether or not the file exists. If the file exists, all the details about this file are generated using the `File` class. These details are then stored in a separate text file using `FileStream` and `StreamWriter` classes. Otherwise, the message that the file was not found is stored in the same text file.

To make the preceding code work, you need to include the `System.IO` namespace in the `Service1` application.

3. **In this service, you won't implement the `OnStop` method.**

   However, the code contains the structure of the `OnStop` method. This is because you set the `CanStop` property of the service to `true`.

File and StreamWriter classes

The `File` class provides static methods to create, copy, delete, move, and open files. Let's discuss some of the methods of this class.

- `Exists`: Use this method to check whether the given file exists.
- `GetAttributes`: Use this method to retrieve various attributes, such as ReadOnly and Archive, of the given file.
- `GetCreationTime`: Use this method to retrieve the date and time on which the given file was created. This function returns a `DateTime` type value. Therefore, use the `Convert.ToString` method to convert it to string.
- `GetLastAccessTime`: Use this method to retrieve the date and time on which the given file was last accessed. This function also returns a `DateTime` type value.
- `GetLastWriteTime`: Use this method to retrieve the date and time on which the given file was last modified (written onto). This method also returns a `DateTime` type value.

The `StreamWriter` class is used to write characters to a file. Let's look at the steps to write data onto a file by using this class.

The following steps help you understand the working of the StreamWriter class, which you've already implemented in your application.

1. **First, create an object of the `StreamWriter` class by using the following code.**

   ```
   StreamWriter objSW = new
      StreamWriter(fs);
   ```

   In the preceding statement, `fs` is an object of the `FileStream` class.

2. **Next, specify the write position. Use the `Seek` method to do so.**

   ```
   objSW.BaseStream.Seek(0,
      SeekOrigin.Begin );
   ```

   The preceding statement sets the write position to the beginning of the specified file. You can read more on the `Seek` method in Chapter 5.

3. **Use the `WriteLine` method to write the characters at the specified position.**

   The syntax for using this method is given below.

   ```
   objSW.WriteLine(info +
   " Not Found");
   ```

4. **Use the `Flush` method to clear the buffer of the current writer and write the buffered data to the specified file.**

   Use the following syntax as reference.

   ```
   objSW.Flush();
   ```

You can read more about the `FileStream` class in Book 5, Chapter 5.

If you don't provide an implementation of the OnStop method, Service Control Manager stops the service for you.

4. **Observe the Main method: This method calls the Run method of the ServiceBase class.**

```
static void Main()
{
  System.ServiceProcess.ServiceBase[] ServicesToRun;
  ServicesToRun = new
System.ServiceProcess.ServiceBase[]
    { new Service1() };
  System.ServiceProcess.ServiceBase.Run(ServicesToRun);
}
```

The Run method provides an entry point into the executable file containing the service class. This method accepts a parameter of type ServiceBase. This parameter could be a single object or an array of objects of the ServiceBase class. A single object is used when the application contains only one service. In contrast, an array is used when the application contains multiple services.

After you create a Windows service application, the next step is to install this service. "Installing a Service," the next section, introduces you to the concepts related to installing a service.

Installing a Service

A Windows service application, unlike any other Visual Studio .NET application, cannot be executed directly. To execute a Windows service application, you need to install it first. The first step in installing a service is adding installation components to a service. After adding these components, you use the InstallUtil utility to install the service. The following section discusses the installation components.

Adding installation components

Installation components help you install the resources required by a service. In addition, installation components are used to register a service on a computer and update Service Control Manager about it. As mentioned earlier, a service application might contain multiple services. In such a situation, you need to add separate installation components for each service.

To add installation components to the Service1 application, perform the following steps.

1. **In Solution Explorer, double-click Service1.cs to switch back to the design view of the service.**

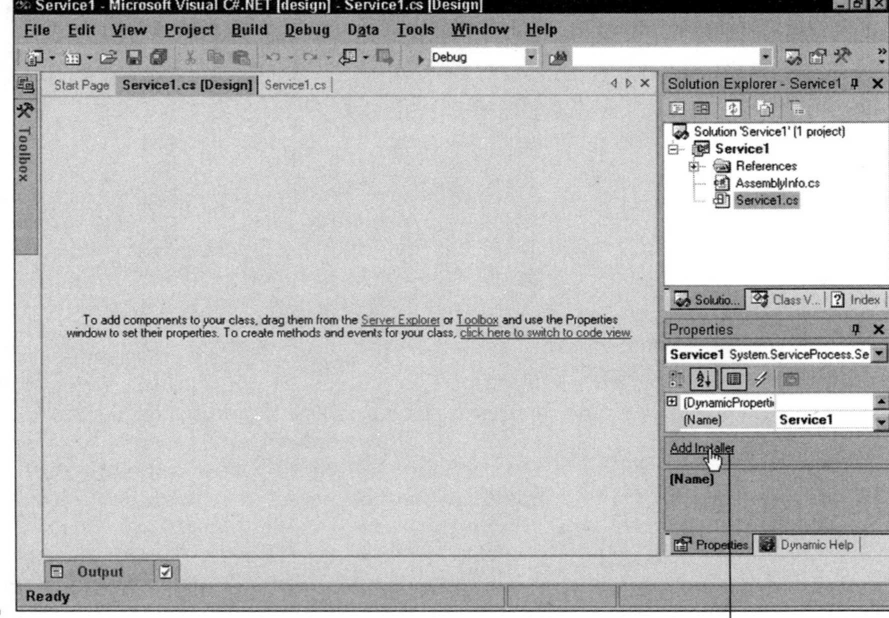

Figure 6-1: Add installers for your service by clicking the Add Installer link.

2. **In the Properties window, click the Add Installer link, as shown in Figure 6-1.**

   A class named `ProjectInstaller` is added to your project. This class is derived from the `System.Configuration.Install.Installer` class and acts as a container for all the required installation components. The `ProjectInstaller` class contains an attribute, which is shown in the following statement:

   ```
   [RunInstaller(true)]
   ```

   The `RunInstaller` attribute specifies whether the installer should be invoked while installing the service.

   The `ProjectInstaller` class contains two installation components, `serviceInstaller1` and `serviceProcessInstaller1`.

   - The `serviceInstaller1` component is used to perform actions specific to a particular service.
   - The `serviceProcessInstaller1` component is used to perform actions common to all the services contained in an application.

   As said earlier, if your application contains multiple services, you need to add separate installation components for each service. However, there is only one `ProjectInstaller` class for all services.

3. **Scroll down to the `InitializeComponent` method. Make the following changes to this method.**

```
//Specify the account under which the service will run
this.serviceProcessInstaller1.Account =
   ServiceAccount.LocalSystem ;
//Specify the password for the user account
this.serviceProcessInstaller1.Password = "password";
//Specify user account under which the service will run
this.serviceProcessInstaller1.Username =
"administrator";
```

A service requires an account to run. By default, a service runs under the System account. This account is not the same as the Administrator account, and you cannot change the rights of this account. However, you can change the account as per the requirement. To do so, use the `ServiceAccount` enumeration to specify a value for the Account property of the `ServiceProcessInstaller` class. This enumeration contains various constants, such as `LocalService`, `LocalUser`, and `User`, which represent various accounts.

In this case, the service will run under the `LocalUser` account. The user name for this account is `administrator` and the password is `password`.

To use the `ServiceAccount` enumeration, you need to include the `System.ServiceProcess` namespace in the application.

```
using System.ServiceProcess;
```

4. **In Solution Explorer, double-click ProjectInstaller.cs to activate the design view of this file.**

5. **Click serviceInstaller1 to select it.**

   The properties of the serviceInstaller1 component appear in the Properties window.

6. **In the Properties window, set the `StartType` property to `Manual`.**

   The `StartType` property is used to specify how and when a service is started. This property can take any of the following three values:

   - `Manual`: Specifies that the service needs to be started manually
   - `Automatic`: Specifies that the service starts automatically each time the computer restarts
   - `Disabled`: Specifies that the service must be enabled before being started

7. **Build the project by choosing Build➪Build.**

   You do so to create the executable file of the application.

After you add installation components to the service application, you need to install this application. To do so, you need to run the InstallUtil utility.

Running the InstallUtil utility

Visual Studio .NET provides the InstallUtil utility to install a service. Let's look at the steps to install a service by using this utility.

1. **Open the Command Prompt window.**

   To do so, choose Start⇨Programs⇨Accessories⇨Command Prompt.

2. **Move to the directory that contains the InstallUtil.exe file by using the following command:**

   ```
   cd c:\winnt\Microsoft.NET\Framework\v1.0.xxxx
   ```

   where xxxx refers to the version number.

3. **Now, execute the following command to install the service.**

   ```
   InstallUtil c:\Service1\Bin\Debug\Service1.exe
   ```

   The drive letter in the preceding command might be different if you created `Service1` in some other drive.

   The result of this command is displayed on the screen, which indicates that the service was successfully created.

You might need to uninstall the service. The following is the command to uninstall a service:

```
InstallUtil /u c:\service1\bin\debug\service1.exe
```

In this section you installed a service. Now, you need to administer this service. Read the following section to know how to administer a service.

Administering a Service

Administering a service involves various operations, such as starting, stopping, or pausing the service. Visual Studio .NET provides you with three options to perform these operations: Service Control Manager, Server Explorer, and the code. The upcoming sections provides details about each of these options.

Starting a service using Service Control Manager

Let's look at the steps to start a service by using Service Control Manager.

1. **Choose Start⇨Programs⇨Administrative Tools⇨Services.**

   The Services window appears, as shown in Figure 6-2. Note that the `FileInfo` service appears in the list. The `FileInfo` service has been selected only for your reference.

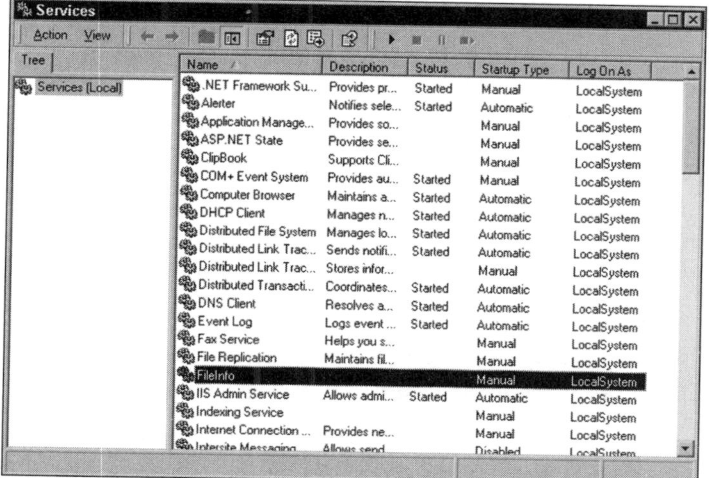

Figure 6-2: The `FileInfo` service appears in the list.

2. **In the Services window, right-click `FileInfo` to display a pop-up menu.**
3. **From the pop-up menu, choose Properties.**

   This displays the property sheets for the `FileInfo` property.
4. **In the Start parameters box, type a valid file name along with the valid path. For example, c:\\MyFile.txt.**
5. **Click the Start button to start the service.**

   A progress bar appears, indicating the progress of the startup procedure of the service.
6. **Click OK to close the property sheet.**

   Notice that the status of the `FileInfo` service has changed to `Started`.
7. **Locate and open the C:\Temp\Info.txt file. This file contains the details about the file that you specified as the parameter for the service.**
8. **Again right-click the service.**
9. **From the pop-up menu, choose Stop to stop the service.**

Let's now learn to use Server Explorer.

Starting a service using Server Explorer

Perform the following steps to start a service by using Server Explorer.

1. **In the Server Explorer, expand the node that contains the server on which you created the service.**
2. **Under this server, expand the Services node and select** `FileInfo`**.**
3. **Right-click** `FileInfo` **and from the pop-up menu that appears, choose Start.**

   Starting a service by using Server Explorer doesn't allow you to specify parameters for the service. Therefore, you can't use this method to start the `FileInfo` service.

Let's now move on to the last part of this chapter that explains how to start a service using code.

Starting a service via code

Visual Studio .NET allows you to start, stop, or manipulate a service using code. However, you should create a different application for starting the service using code. In this application, you will use the `ServiceController` component, which represents the `ServiceController` class. Before we proceed further, let's discuss the `ServiceController` component.

ServiceController component

You use the `ServiceController` component to connect to an existing service. In addition, you can use this component to control the behavior of existing services. To use the `ServiceController` component, you need to add this component to your application and then set certain properties. In Visual Studio .NET, you can add this component to an application in three ways:

- Using the Components tab of the Toolbox
- Manually — by creating a class derived from the `ServiceController` class
- Using Server Explorer

When you add a `ServiceController` component, you need to set at least the following two properties of this component:

- `MachineName`: To specify the name of the computer on which the service is installed. By default, the value is (.), which represents the local computer.
- `ServiceName`: To specify the name of the service to connect to.

However, when you add a `ServiceController` component using Server Explorer, both these properties are automatically set.

In addition to the properties mentioned above, a ServiceController component contains these properties and methods:

- `CanStop` **property**: Use this property to determine whether a service can be stopped.
- `Start` **method**: Use this method to start the service. This method calls the OnStart method of the ServiceBase class.
- `Stop` **method**: Use this method to stop the service. This method calls the OnStop method of the ServiceBase class.

Let's get back to the `FileInfo` service. You'll now create an application that controls this service. To do so, you'll add the `ServiceController` component by using Server Explorer.

Adding the ServiceController component

Let's look at the steps to add a `ServiceController` component by using Server Explorer.

1. **Create a new Windows Application project. Name the project as Controller1.**
2. **In Server Explorer, expand the node that contains the server on which you created the service.**
3. **Under this server, expand the Services node and select `FileInfo`, as shown in Figure 6-3.**
4. **Right-click `FileInfo` and from the pop-up menu that appears, choose Add To Designer.**

   A `ServiceController` component, `serviceController1`, is added to your project.

After you add a `ServiceController` component, you only need to write the code that helps you administer the service. Let's now learn to do that.

Writing code to control the service

The `Controller1` application displays the contents of the file Info.txt, which was created by the `FileInfo` service, in a RichTextBox control . To do so, perform the following steps:

1. **To control the `FileInfo` service, you need to design the form as shown in Figure 6-4 with these controls:**

- TextBox control named `textBox1` and caption `Path\\FileName`.
- RichTextBox named `richTextBox1` and caption `Description`. In addition, it is disabled.

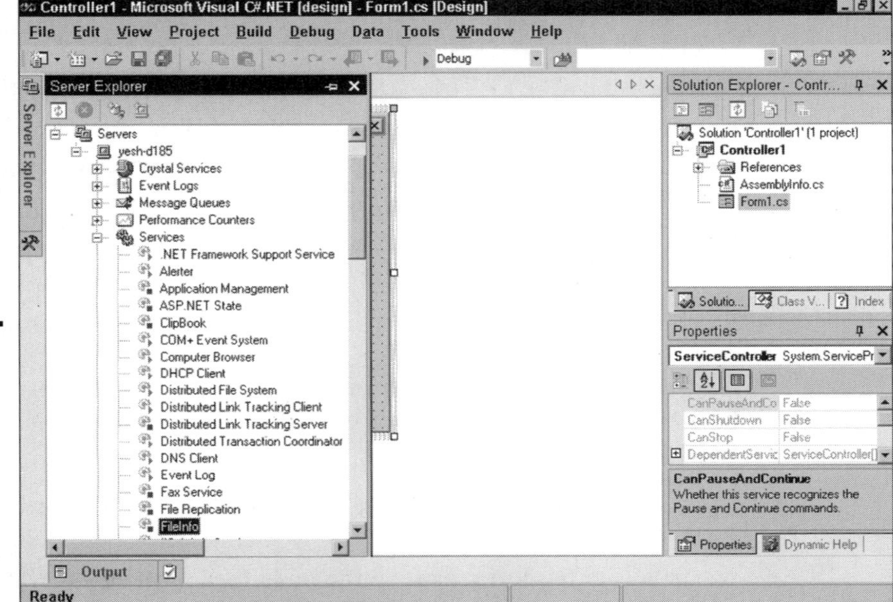

Figure 6-3: Add the `ServiceController` component by using Server Explorer.

To disable a RichTextBox control, in the Properties window, in the Enabled list, select `False`.

- Three buttons with captions `Start` (button1), `Stop` (button3), and `Display Details` (button2).

2. **Add the following code to the `Click` event of the `Start` button.**

```
string [] fname;
fname = new String [1];
fname[0] = textBox1.Text ;
//Start the service
serviceController1.Start (fname);
richTextBox1.Text = "";
MessageBox.Show ("Service Started");
button1.Enabled = false;
button2.Enabled = true;
button3.Enabled = true;
```

In the preceding code, the `Start` method of the `ServiceController` is used to start the service.

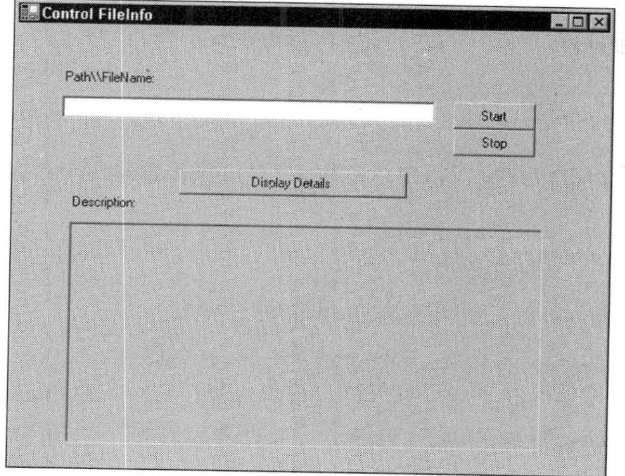

Figure 6-4: Create a form with three buttons and a text box.

3. **Add the following code to the `Click` event of the `Stop` button.**

```
if(serviceController1.CanStop )
{
    //Stop the service
    serviceController1.Stop ();
    MessageBox.Show ("Service Stopped");
}
button3.Enabled =false;
button2.Enabled =true;
```

   In the preceding code, the `Stop` method of the `ServiceController` is used to stop the service.

4. **Add the following code to the `Click` event of the `Display Details` button.**

```
//Display the contents of the file in the rich text box
FileStream objFS = new
FileStream(@"C:\\temp\\info.txt",
  FileMode.OpenOrCreate, FileAccess.Read );
StreamReader objSR = new StreamReader(objFS);
// Set the file pointer to the beginning.
objSR.BaseStream.Seek(0, SeekOrigin.Begin);
richTextBox1.Text = objSR.ReadLine ();
while (objSR.Peek() > -1)
{
  richTextBox1.Text = richTextBox1.Text + "\r\n" +
  objSR.ReadLine();
}
```

```
objSR.Close();
textBox1.Text ="";
button2.Enabled = false;
button3.Enabled = false;
button1.Enabled = true;
```

To make this code work, you need to include the `System.IO` namespace.

In the preceding code, the `CanStop` property of the `ServiceController` class is used to check whether the service can be stopped. If the `CanStop` property returns true, the service can be stopped using the `Stop` method of the `ServiceController` class.

5. **Execute the application and test the service by specifying a file name along with the path in the Path\\FileName text box.**
6. **Click the Start button.**

   A message box appears indicating that the service has started.
7. **Click the Stop button.**

   A message box appears indicating that the service was stopped.
8. **Click the Display Details button.**

   The details of the file that you provided as a parameter appears in the Description box.

This service might not function properly and generate an error, perhaps because of a wrong path or filename. Don't worry; you can make your service handle all these problems with ease by using the exception handling techniques that are discussed in Book 3, Chapter 9.

Viewing the info.txt file

You can also view the contents of the info.txt file directly. To do so, perform the following steps:

1. Choose Start➪Programs➪Accessories➪Windows Explorer.
2. Locate the file info.txt in the c:\temp folder.
3. Double-click info.txt to view its contents.

Index

Symbols

A

B

C

D

E

F

G

H-I

J-K-L

M

N

O

P-Q

R

S

T

U

V

W-X-Y-Z

Book VI

Associated Technologies and Enhancements

Contents at a Glance

Chapter 1: Introducing ASP.NET

In This Chapter

- **ASP.NET: An evolution or a revolution?**
- **ASP.NET platform requirements**
- **ASP.NET programming models**

Here comes good news for all of the Web application developers who are tired of using the same monotonous pattern of creating Web applications — a set of linear applications with logic built inside them. This good news comes with the release of ASP.NET. With ASP.NET, you can break free from the typical mold of Web application development and develop more dynamic Web applications in a new and mature development environment.

ASP.NET offers new features that make Web application development an exciting field. Unlike earlier technologies, such as dbWeb, IDC, and previous ASP versions, ASP.NET offers you an infrastructure that facilitates the development of structured applications. In addition, the introduction of ASP.NET marks the first time that a real framework will be available for developing Web applications. In other words, you can say that ASP.NET has begun a new era of Web application development.

In this chapter, we introduce you to the basic concepts of ASP.NET, the advantages that ASP.NET offers compared to earlier Web application development technologies, and the platform requirements for creating, testing, and deploying ASP.NET applications. In addition, we give you some insight into the ASP.NET architecture and the programming models that you use to create ASP.NET applications. Brace yourself — you're about to discover the world of Web application development with ASP.NET.

ASP.NET: An Evolution or a Revolution?

After its release, a software product undergoes various evolutionary phases. In each evolutionary phase (called *release* or *version*) of a software product, the software vendor provides fixes for the previous version's bugs and usually throws in a few new features. Since the first release of ASP (ASP 1.0, way back in 1996), two more ASP releases (2.0 and 3.0) have been a part of its evolutionary cycle. With each subsequent release, new features have been added, but the basic methodology for creating applications has remained the same. Consequently, users of all these releases follow the same linear model of application development.

Because of the type of features and the application development model available in ASP.NET, calling it the next version of ASP is incorrect. In fact, saying that ASP.NET has started a revolution in the world of Web application development isn't going overboard. ASP.NET provides an altogether unique approach toward application development and, as such, is more than just the latest version of ASP.

So what makes ASP.NET revolutionary? ASP.NET is a Web development technology based on the Microsoft .NET Framework. The .NET Framework, in turn, is based on the CLR, imparting all the CLR benefits to ASP.NET applications. Some of these benefits are automatic memory management, cross-language integration, interoperability with existing code and system, and simplified deployment.

Following are some of the major benefits that ASP.NET provides:

- **Support for multiple programming languages:** The different versions of ASP are restricted to only scripting languages, such as VBScript and JScript. With these scripting languages, you can definitely write applications to perform server-side processing. However, you need to be aware of two major drawbacks — scripting languages are interpreted and are not strongly typed. Because scripting languages are interpreted and not compiled, the errors must be checked at run time affecting the performance of Web applications. Also, scripting languages are not strongly typed indicating that the scripting languages do not have a built-in set of predefined data types. So, developers need to cast the existing objects of the language to their expected data type, which can be validated only at run-time leading to a low performance.

  ASP.NET, which is based on the .NET Framework, continues to support scripting languages. In addition, ASP.NET allows you to use multiple programming languages, such as Visual Basic .NET, Visual C++, and C#, for server-side programming. This feature enables you to select a language according to your level of proficiency and preference.

- **Cross-language development:** When creating objects for different languages, developers using ASP.NET have greater flexibility. If you create an object in C#, you have the flexibility to extend the object to another language — say Visual Basic .NET. This is certainly a marvelous feature that provides you much flexibility and freedom.

- **Content and application logic separation:** In classic ASP, the content to be presented to users (HTML code) and programming logic (ASP scripts) was integrated. This led to several restrictions, including the inability of two people, one proficient in designing a user interface (UI) and the other proficient in programming, to work simultaneously on Web pages. The situation worsens if Web pages are to be frequently updated. And because of the concern regarding the integration of the code and the UI, the use of different design tools is restricted.

With ASP.NET, you can bury all your worries about combining the content with the application logic. ASP.NET separates the content from the application logic, which enables the designer to design the UI while the programmer concentrates on building the programming logic. And, both the designer and programmer can work on the same page simultaneously. Any required updates can be done without any confusion. Also, the designers can use standard design tools to create the UI without worrying about mingling the content with the code.

- **New server processing architecture:** In classic ASP, the content of a page is rendered in the order in which it is written. Therefore, while writing page logic, programmers must take into account the position of the code in the page. ASP also requires you to write code for all actions that occur on your Web page. You need to write code even for displaying HTML output.

  ASP.NET has introduced server-based controls. These controls are declared and programmed on the server-side and are event-driven by the client. This new server processing architecture frees programmers from considering position when designing programming logic, enabling programmers to completely focus on programming logic.

- **Improved caching features:** Compared with classic ASP, ASP.NET provides improved caching features. When working with ASP.NET, you can use

  - *Page-level caching,* which enables you to cache a complete page.
  - *Fragment caching,* which enables you to cache portions of a page.
  - The *Cache API,* which exposes the Cache engine to programmers to cache their own objects.

  Smart use of these caching features results in increased speed and performance of your Web pages. See Book 6, Chapter 15 for more about these.

- **Improved debugging and tracing:** *Debugging* and *tracing* are key elements of application development. You primarily use the `Response.Write` tool to debug and trace your ASP pages. ASP.NET enables you to use the built-in Visual Studio .NET debugging tools and the `Trace` method for tracing your pages (see Book 6, Chapter 7).

- **More control over application configuration:** In addition to the standard IIS settings (which are the same in classic ASP as in ASP.NET), ASP.NET allows you to set application-level configuration information, which is stored in XML format and can be easily accessed. You don't have to touch the registry to modify configuration settings.

- **Greater application security:** You need to frequently authenticate and authorize users of your Web applications. Usually, securing your Web applications is problematic because the users get access to server-based resources, leaving you with little control on the client side of your Web applications. With ASP.NET, you can configure your Web applications to provide security. To find out more about application security, check out Book 6, Chapter 16.
- **Easier application deployment:** Each ASP.NET application, along with its components and configuration information, is self-sufficient. Deploying an ASP.NET application has been highly simplified. You simply need to copy the directory to IIS to deploy an ASP.NET application.

ASP.NET and the .NET Framework SDK

ASP.NET is included in the .NET Framework SDK (Software Development Kit). The .NET Framework SDK consists of the files required to create, build, and test .NET applications. You can download the .NET Framework SDK from `http://msdn.Microsoft.com/downloads`. To use the .NET SDK, you need to install Internet Explorer 5.5 or later on your computer. The following platforms support the .NET Framework SDK:

- Windows NT 4.0 with Service Pack 6a
- Windows 2000
- Windows XP Professional
- Windows Me
- Windows 98

You can create ASP.NET applications on Windows 98 and Windows Me platforms. However, to run ASP.NET applications, you must have a Web server installed. Internet Information Server (IIS) is installed automatically when you install Windows 2000 Server or Windows NT 4.0 (with Service Pack 6a). However, for Windows 98, Windows Me, and Windows XP Professional, you need to explicitly install IIS.

You can use the .NET Framework SDK to develop and test your ASP.NET applications. However, the .NET Framework SDK doesn't provide you with certain features, such as the application development environment and debugging tools. When using the .NET Framework SDK, you can develop ASP.NET applications by using text editors and command line compilers. To deploy your applications, you need to manually copy your files to IIS.

For faster, easier, and convenient application development, you need to install Visual Studio .NET, which provides many handy tools that make application development a rewarding experience. In the following list, we recap some of the tools that Visual Studio .NET provides:

✦ **Intelligent code editors** with statement completion and syntax checking features.

✦ **Visual designers** that allow you to drag and drop controls, saving you time and effort when writing code for the controls. Because you don't need to type code to add each control to your page, using these tools makes designing Web pages more interesting than when using code editors. To learn more about visual designers, check out Book 2, Chapter 1.

✦ **Built-in compilers** and **debuggers** that make using the command prompt for compilation unnecessary. For more information on debuggers, check out Book 6, Chapter 7.

ASP.NET Programming Models

You need the .NET Framework SDK to develop Web applications and the .NET Framework SDK on a platform with IIS is required to run these applications (see previous sections of this chapter). Now, let us understand the ASP.NET architecture, which will help you correlate the different subsystems that are involved in creating, building, testing, and deploying ASP.NET applications. The ASP.NET architecture is shown in Figure 1-1.

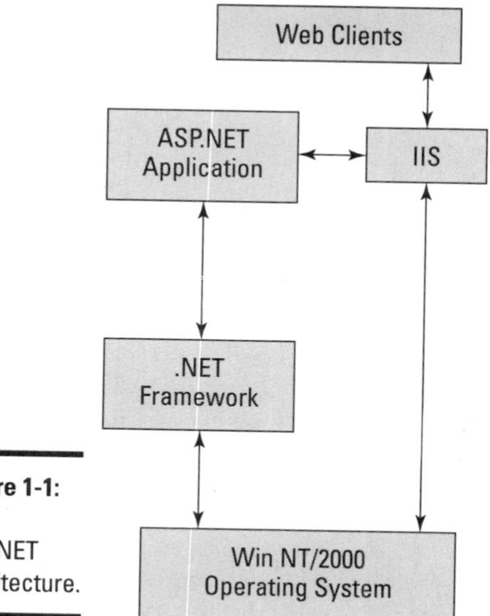

Figure 1-1: The ASP.NET architecture.

As you can see in the Figure 1-1, Web clients communicate with ASP.NET applications through IIS. Therefore, IIS must be installed to run your ASP.NET applications.

ASP.NET provides two programming models to create your Web applications:

- **Web Forms:** Enable you to create Web pages that are form-based. Web Forms are a powerful feature that are used to create dynamic Web pages for Web applications. You can use server controls to create UI components, and then program them at the server side.
- **Web Services:** Enable you to remotely access certain functionality at the server side. Web services play an important role in integrating applications across platforms. Web services are not bound to specific technology or convention. These services enable the exchange of data in a client-server or a server-server environment. To enable this data exchange, Web services use standards such as HTTP and XML messaging.

You can select either of these programming models or use a combination of the two. Both models use the CLR of the .NET Framework and enable you to develop applications that are secure, scalable, and have high performance.

Chapter 2: Getting Started with ASP.NET Applications

In This Chapter

- Getting to know Web Forms
- Creating your first ASP.NET application
- Figuring out IIS applications roots
- Discovering the role of HTML and XML in ASP.NET

In this chapter, we discuss Web Forms ASP.NET applications. Web Forms applications are new aspects of ASP.NET that take the advantage of the .NET framework. Before reading this chapter, however, you might want to take a look at Book 6, Chapter 1 (if you haven't already) for a refresher on the ASP.NET features and programming models. Here we show you how to create your first ASP.NET application, give you some insight about the concepts pertaining to Web Forms and Web Forms page processing, and explain how HTML and XML fit into the ASP.NET picture along the way. We think you'll definitely like the development environment and appreciate the ease with which you can create your Web applications in Visual Studio .NET, so keep reading.

Web Forms

ASP.NET provides the Web Forms technology that enables you to create faster, dynamic, and high speed Web pages. Web Forms enable you to create form-based Web pages. In short, such Web pages are called *Web Forms pages.* Although the pages created by using the ASP.NET Web Forms technology might look like the ones created in the earlier versions of ASP, the overall user experience with Web Forms pages is much better. This is because, the Web Forms pages exploit the CLR and other .NET features. Before we delve into the details of Web Forms, you need to be familiar with its features, which we highlight in the following two lists.

Web Forms

- Use the ASP.NET Page framework, which runs on the Web server to produce dynamic Web Forms pages on the client.

- Take advantage of the features of the CLR, such as type safety and inheritance.
- Provide you with a rich set of controls that you can use to design a rich user interface. In addition, Web Forms are extensible — they provide support for user-created and third-party controls.

Web Forms pages

- Can be designed and programmed by using Rapid Application Development (RAD) tools that Visual Studio .NET provides. The RAD tools allow you to create rich user interfaces quickly.
- Are independent of the client in which they're displayed. In fact, Web Forms pages are compatible with any browser or mobile device. However, you can create Web Forms pages that are compatible to a specific browser client. In this manner, you can take advantage of the features of rich browser clients.

Web Forms components

Separate content and logic is one of the important features of ASP.NET. This feature is implemented by using Web Forms. Web Forms consist of two components:

- **User interface:** Presents content to users. The user interface consists of a file that contains static HTML or XML and server controls. This file is called the `page file` and carries the `.aspx` extension.
- **Programming logic:** Handles user interaction with Web Forms pages. You can use any of the .NET programming languages, such as Visual Basic .NET or C#, to write the logic for your page.
  - You can write page logic in the .aspx file (of course, it is not intermingled with the HTML code as in classic ASP). This model of writing page logic is called the *code inline model.*
  - The other model of writing page logic is the *code-behind model.* In this model, you write page logic in a separate file, which is called the *code-behind file* and carries either the `.aspx.vb` (if you use Visual Basic .NET) or `.aspx.cs` (if you use C#) extension. The choice between the code-inline and code-behind model is just a matter of preference. If you are a programmer who is already used to the usual methodology of application development with ASP, you probably find the code-inline model more convenient. However, once you start using the code-behind file, you may find the code-behind model more convincing.

A page file (`.aspx` file) and a code-behind file (`.aspx.vb` or `.aspx.cs`) together constitute a *Web Forms page*. Figure 2-1 shows the structure of a Web Forms page.

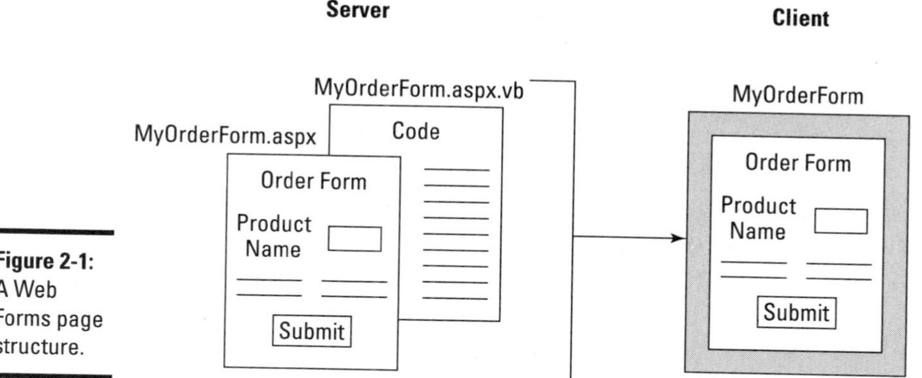

Figure 2-1: A Web Forms page structure.

Web Forms page processing

Before you start creating your ASP.NET applications in a full-fledged manner, you must have a clear picture about what happens when a user interacts with a Web page displayed in a browser. For example, what happens when a user clicks a button or selects an item from a list box? What different events are generated? Who handles these events? The basic understanding of page processing will help you create your Web applications in the long run.

Round trips

A Web Forms page consists of a page file that's presented to users through browsers or any mobile device. When users interact with a page, the page must be *submitted* (posted back) to the server for any server-side processing. After processing on the server, the page must be returned to the client. This sequence is called a *round trip*. To understand round trips better, consider an Orders Web page. A user enters the quantity of a product she wants to buy; the quantity must be validated on the server to check whether or not the quantity entered is available. To accomplish this validation, the page must be posted back to the server for processing. After the validation is performed on the server, the page is returned to the browser for the user to continue using the page. This trip of the page from the client to the server and then back to the client again constitutes a round trip. Figure 2-2 shows a page completing a round trip.

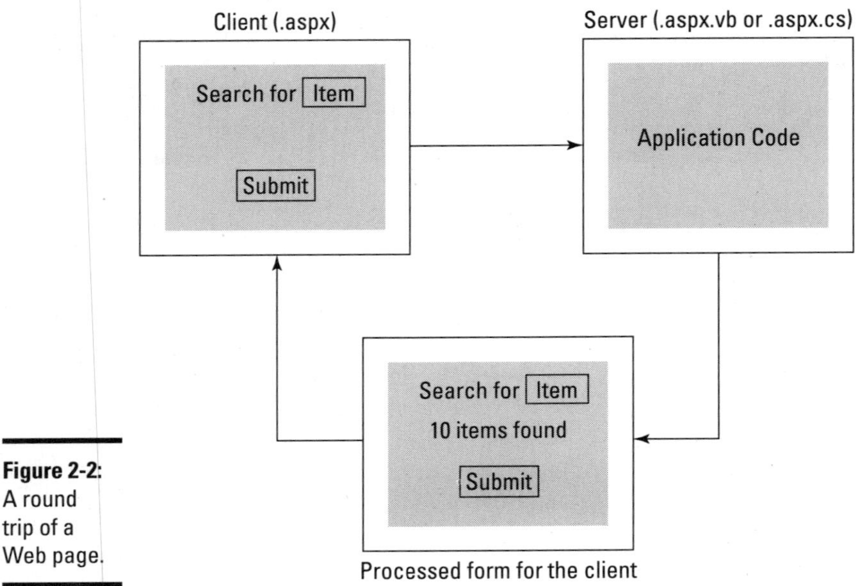

Figure 2-2: A round trip of a Web page.

Not all user interactions with Web pages lead to round trips. Some user interactions, such as input validation (such as validating a user name field for not being empty), don't need server-side processing. To handle such interactions, you can create client scripts in Web Forms.

Page events

If you understand round trips, you're ready for a discussion of the different stages through which a page passes during its life cycle. A Web Form is a class derived from the `Page` class, which in turn is contained in the `System.Web.UI` namespace. For more on namespaces, see Book 1, Chapter 2. Every time you request a Web page (`.aspx` file) from a Web server, the page is compiled into a `Page` object and cached in the server's memory. You can use this `Page` object to manipulate the actions on the page.

ASP.NET uses an event-driven model of programming Web pages. Each time a Web page requires processing on the server side, the page must be posted back to the server and returned to the client for the user to continue using the page. Before the page is returned, it must be re-created. Therefore, with every round trip, a page must be re-created. Each time a page is served from the server to the client, the page follows a sequence of events. Table 2-1 describes these events.

Table 2-1 Page Events

Event	*Generated When*
`Init`	The page is initialized.
`Load`	The page is loaded into the memory.
`Control Event`	A control triggers the page to be reloaded.
`Unload`	The page is unloaded from the memory.

With each event that is raised, you may have some tasks to accomplish. You can accomplish these tasks by writing code in special procedures called *event handling procedures* or simply *event handlers*. For example, you can write the page initialization code in the `Page_Init` or `Page_Load` event. The `Page_Init` is the event handler for the `Init` event of the page, whereas `Page_Load` is the event handler for the `Load` event of the page. There is a small difference between the `Init` and `Load` events. You must note that all controls are guaranteed to be fully loaded in the `Load` event only. During `Init`, the controls that are loaded carry their default values instead of values that are set during postback.

After the `Init` and `Load` events, the page is served to the user. When the user interacts with the page to generate some control event, say the Click event of a button named Submit, the page is posted back to the server and the code in the control's event handler (`Submit_Click`) is executed. After processing, the page is re-created and the page follows the same `Init` and `Load` events. This means that every time a page is requested or posted, the initialization code (in the `Page_Init` and `Page_Load`) is executed. This is silly, isn't it? Moreover, it slows down the loading of your pages. But don't worry — there's a solution to this problem.

The `IsPostBack` property of the page allows you to check if the page is requested for the first time. A false value of the `IsPostBack` property indicates that the page is displayed for the first time. A true value indicates that the page is run as a result of a round trip. Therefore, using the `IsPostBack` property, you can make the page run the initialization code only once when it is requested for the first time (when the `IsPostBack` property is False).

Finally, when a user closes the page or exits from the browser, the page is unloaded from the memory and the `Unload` event is generated. Any de-initialization code can go in the `Page_Unload` event handler.

Now that you know about Web Forms, you're ready to create your first ASP.NET application using Visual Studio .NET, which we show you how to do in the following section.

Creating ASP.NET Web Forms Applications

You've gained a fair knowledge of ASP.NET Web Forms pages and their processing. In this section, we create a simple Web Forms application. Visual Studio .NET provides many tools that enables you to create ASP.NET Web Forms application with ease. Some of these tools include

- ✦ Visual designers
- ✦ Code-aware editors
- ✦ Integrated compilation and debugging

So, let's proceed to create a simple ASP.NET Web Forms applications.

Your first ASP.NET Web Forms application

To get a handle on just how exactly an ASP.NET application is created, you must actually create an ASP.NET Web Forms application. To create an ASP.NET Web Forms application, follow these steps:

1. **In the Visual Studio .NET window, choose File⇨New⇨Project to open the New Project dialog box.**
2. **In the Project Types pane, select project type.**

   Your choices are Visual Basic Projects, Visual C# Projects, or Visual C++ Projects. For this example, select Visual Basic Projects.
3. **In the Templates pane, select ASP.NET Web Application.**
4. **In the Name box, type the name of your project.**

   Choose something descriptive. For our purposes, name the project `MyFirstApplication`.
5. **In the Location box, type the name of the computer on which IIS is installed.**

   Type the location in the format **http://<*computer name*>**, specifying the particular computer.
6. **Click OK to create the Visual Basic ASP.NET Web application.**

   Figure 2-3 shows what the Visual Studio .NET window looks like after you perform these steps.

As you can see in Figure 2-3, the Web application contains a default Web Form, `WebForm1`. Now that you've created the Web Form, you're ready to move on to adding controls and buttons and things — essentially designing the look of the Web Form. We show you how to do this in the following section.

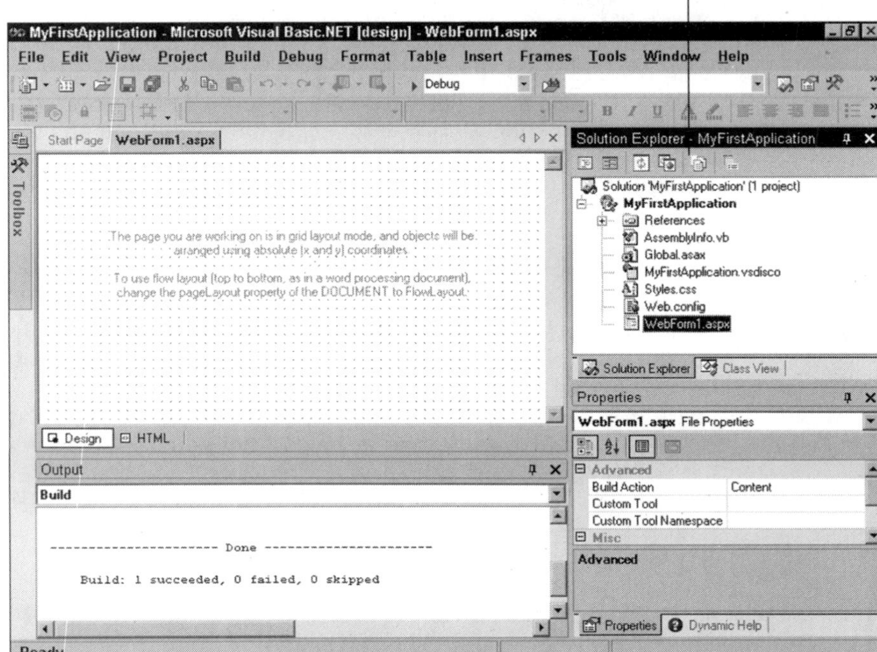

Figure 2-3: The Visual Studio .NET window displaying the newly created ASP.NET Web Forms Application project.

You can rename the Web Form by right-clicking it in Solution Explorer and choosing Rename.

In addition to a Web Form, the ASP.NET Web Application template (see Step 3 in the section "Your first ASP.NET Web Forms application") generates many other files that are listed in Solution Explorer. For more on Solution Explorer, check out Book 2, Chapter1. The files included in an ASP.NET Web application project are

- `AsemblyInfo.vb`: This file contains the information, such as versioning and dependencies, for your assembly.
- `Global.asax`: This file contains application-level event handlers.
- `Licenses.lics`: This file contains license information. Currently, this file is not visible in the Solution Explorer. To see this file, you need to click the Show All Files icon at the top of the Solution Explorer window (See Figure 2-3).
- `MyFirstApplication.vsdisco`: This is an XML file that contains informational links to ASP.NET Web Services to be used in your application. These links provide information about the location of the services and the available functionalities.

- `Styles.css`: This file is used to define default HTML style settings.
- `Web.config`: This file contains application configuration information.

In addition to these files, the ASP.NET Web Application template adds references to namespaces that are contained in the References folder. The bin folder contains the `dlls` for your application. Currently, the bin folder is not visible in the Solution Explorer. To see this folder, you need to click the "Show All Files" icon at the top of the Solution Explorer window (see Figure 2-3).

Designing your form

The page file of this Web Form, `WebForm1.aspx`, is selected in the Solution Explorer window shown in Figure 2-3. By default, this page file appears in the Design view. In the Design view, you can directly place controls on the form from the Toolbox by dragging and dropping. The page contains dots in multiple grids, which help you accurately position the controls. This layout is called the *grid layout*. Another layout that you can apply to your page is the *flow layout*. In flow layout, you can directly add text to the page in the Design view. To change the layout, click the page and press F4 to open the Properties window for the document, and then set the `pageLayout` property to `FlowLayout`.

As you design the form in the Design view, the corresponding HTML code is automatically generated. You can see the HTML code in the HTML view. If you're comfortable working with HTML, you can directly edit the code in the HTML view. In addition to writing HTML code to create the page content, you can even write the page logic in the HTML view. You can switch between the Design and HTML views by clicking the Design or HTML buttons at the bottom of the page file displayed in the Visual Studio .NET window.

Try to recall the file, which constitutes a Web Form, in addition to the page file. Here's the answer: the other component of a Web Form is the code-behind file (bone up on code-behind files in the earlier section "Web Forms components"). At this moment, the code-behind file is not visible. Relax, the code-behind file exists, and you can see it by clicking the Show All File icon in the Solution Explorer window and then clicking the plus button to the left of `WebForm1.aspx`.

You can also view the code-behind file by pressing F7 when the page file is opened. Alternatively, you can select Code from the View menu.

Understanding the automatically generated code

After you've designed the look of your Web Forms page, the next step is to add functionality to it. To do this, you can use either the HTML view of the page file or the code-behind file. Before you can use these files, however, you must understand the automatically generated code that these files contain.

In the HTML mode, the first line of the page displays the following:

```
<%@ Page Language="vb" AutoEventWireup="false"
    codebehind="WebForm1.aspx.vb"
    Inherits="MyFirstApplication.WebForm1"%>
```

The @Page directive is used to specify the page attributes to affect how the page will be created. These different attributes are specified in the preceding code:

- **Language:** Specifies any .NET supported language.
- **AutoEventWireup:** Specifies whether or not the page events are automatically wired. A false value indicates that page events, such as `Load`, must be explicitly enabled by a developer.
- **Codebehind:** Specifies the code-behind file for a page.
- **Inherits:** Specifies the code-behind class that a page inherits. This class can be any class derived from the `Page` class.

The `<Meta>` elements in the `<Head>` element define document information, such as the code language and the default client script.

You can write the page logic within the `<Head>` element. To do this, you need to use the `<Script>` tag. For example, consider the following code snippet that uses the `<Script>` tag:

```
<Script runat="server" language="vb">
   code here
</Script>
```

In this code,

- `runat = "server"` specifies that the code will run at the server side.
- `language = "vb"` specifies that the language used to add programming logic is Visual Basic .NET. Here, the language must be .NET-supported language.

You can add any controls or text that you want to render on the page in the `<Body>` element. Any HTML text or code (in the `<% %>` block) within the `<Body> </Body>` block is rendered on the page when it is displayed in a Web browser.

After you understand of the HTML code, you must also understand the code that's automatically generated in the code-behind file.

The first line of the WebForm1.aspx.vb file contains the following code:

```
Public Class WebForm1
    Inherits System.Web.UI.Page
```

This code indicates that WebForm1 is a class inherited from the Page class. Notice that the Page class is contained in the System.Web.UI namespace.

Next, the Web Form Designer Generated Code section contains two methods, InitializeComponent and Page_Init. The InitializeComponent method contains the code to initialize the page components, such as controls.

The Page_Init method is the event handler for the Init event of the page. This method calls the InitializeComponent method.

After the Web Form Designer Generated Code section, the Page_Load method handles the Load event of the page.

In addition to Page_Init and Page_Load methods, you can add event handlers for the controls that you add to your page.

Creating a simple page that works

After you understand the files (see the section "Your first ASP.NET Web Forms application") and the code (see the preceding section) that's automatically generated by Visual Studio .NET, you're ready to act. In this section, we show you how to create a simple page that displays a welcome message.

Open the Properties window for the WebForm1 Document. Set the bgColor property to #66cccc. (You can set any other color according to your preferences.) Then, open the WebForm1.aspx.vb file. You'll use this file to write any code. In the Page_Load method, write the following code and then press Ctrl+F5 to execute your application:

```
Private Sub Page_Load(ByVal sender As System.Object, ByVal e
         As System.EventArgs) Handles MyBase.Load

    Dim UserName As String
    UserName = Request.QueryString("Name")
    Response.Write("<Center>" + "<B>Hello</B>" + "<B> " +
          UserName + "</B>" + "</Center>" + "<br><br>" +
          "<Center>" + "<B>Welcome to the world of ASP.NET!
          </B >" + "</Center>")

End Sub
```

When you run it, the preceding code displays a welcome message to the user who supplies his/her name in the URL of the page. For example, Figure 2-4 shows the output for the user who enters the URL `http://<computer name>/MyFirstApplication/WebForm1.aspx?Name=Marry`.

Well done! The page runs as required. Check the code once again; do you know about the functions of `Request` and `Response` written in the code? If not, check out the following section "Understanding Request and Response."

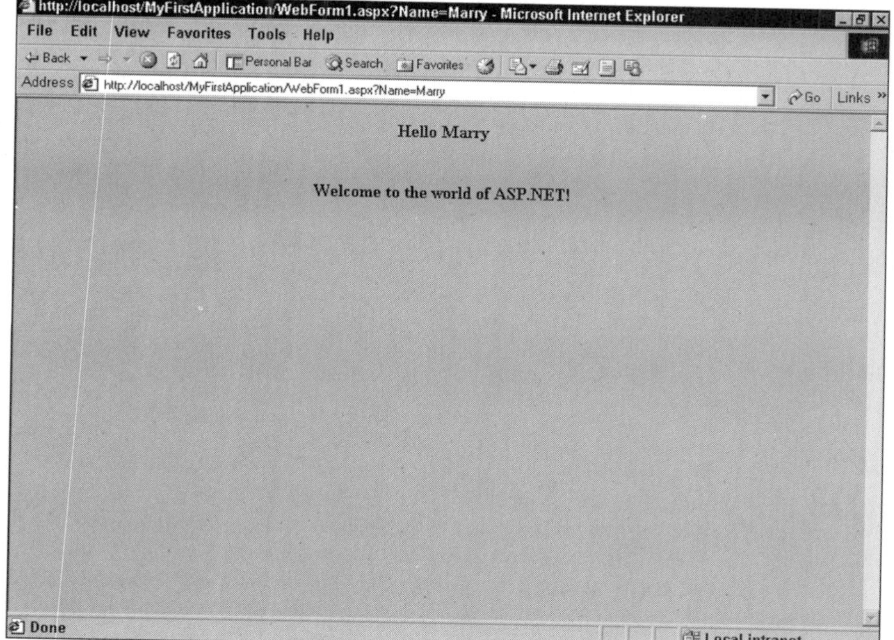

Figure 2-4: Output of the page displaying a welcome message.

Usually, an application contains multiple Web Forms. While you develop an application, you might not want to build the entire application to view a specific page to check whether the page is functioning correctly. In such a case, you can browse only a specific page without building the entire application. You can browse a specific Web Forms page by right-clicking the ASPX file and choosing any of the options:

✦ **View in Browser:** If you choose View in Browser, the page is displayed in the default browser, which is the built-in browser of Visual Studio .NET.

- **Browse With:** On the other hand, if you choose Browse With, you're prompted to choose the browser as Microsoft Internet Explorer or the Internal Web Browser. Here, you can also set Microsoft Internet Explorer as the default browser.
- **Build and Browse:** This option enables you to build the page and display it in the default browser.

Understanding Request and Response

`Request` and `Response` are the properties of the `Page` class. The `Request` property allows you to access the `HTTPRequest` object, which contains information, such as the path of the request, about the HTTP request for the page. The `Response` property allows you to access the `HTTPResponse` object, which in turn allows you to send data to the browser as the result of the request. In fact, the `Request` and `Response` properties map directly to the `HTTPRequest` and `HTTPResponse` objects respectively. Therefore, you can directly access these objects in ASP.NET pages by using the `Request` and `Response` properties.

`QueryString` is the method of the `HTTPRequest` object, which returns the parameter that's passed with the page URL.

The `Write` method of the `HTTPResponse` object is used to display text in a browser. Notice that you can use the HTML formatting elements to format the text.

IIS Application Roots

When you create an ASP.NET application in Visual Studio .NET, you specify the name of the project and the location. You specify the location as `http://localhost` or `http://<computer name>`.

This location may look slightly weird because it has only the name of the computer and no directory path. This makes it tedious for you to trace the application later. But don't worry. When you create an ASP.NET Web Application project, the application root directory (with the same name as that of the project) is created in the default Web site of the IIS server (`http://localhost` or `http://<computer name>`). This application root directory is called the IIS application root and maps to the physical location `c:\inetpub\wwwroot\<project name>`. All Visual Studio .NET-generated files and the files you add to your project are included in the application root directory.

You can trace the application root directory for the application (`MyFirstApplication`) that we showed you how to create in the section "Creating ASP.NET Web Forms Applications." To trace the application root directory, open IIS Microsoft Management Console (MMC) by choosing Start➪Programs➪Administrative Tools➪Internet Services Manager. In the Default Web Site directory, you can find the application root directory for your application (`MyFirstApplication`). Figure 2-5 shows the IIS MMC with the `MyFirstApplication` directory selected (at the bottom of the left pane).

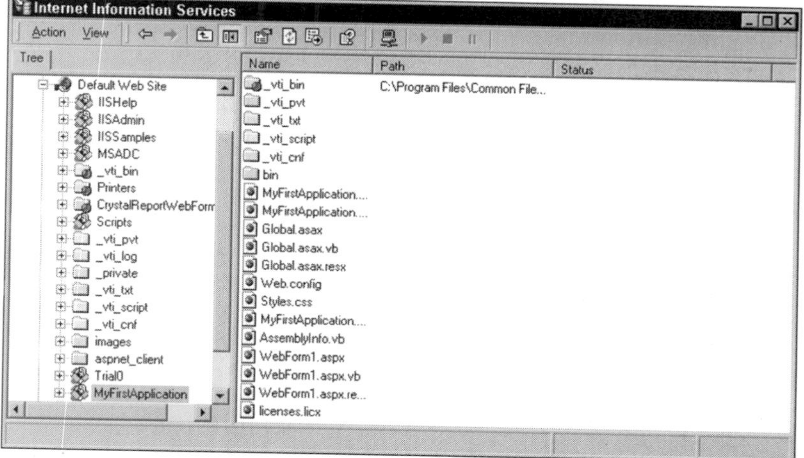

Figure 2-5: IIS MMC displaying an application root directory.

As shown in Figure 2-5, three types of icons show up within the Default Web Site directory:

- **Explorer style folders:** Folders such as `_vti_pvt` and `_vti_txt` exist as physical directories in IIS.
- **Explorer style folders with small globes:** Folders such as `_vti_bin` represent virtual directories (not application roots).
- **Web application folders:** Folders that appear as package icons. When you create a virtual directory, the directory is automatically a Web application folder. For example, if you create an ASP.NET application named MyApplication, the Web application folder named MyApplication is automatically created in IIS.

When you create your ASP.NET application in Visual Studio .NET, the application root is created automatically. However, when you create your ASP.NET applications using a text editor such as Notepad, you'll need to manually create the application root. Every developer would always prefer to use Visual Studio .NET due to the features it offers. However, there might be certain developers who have only the .NET framework installed (without Visual Studio .NET installed). So, they have to rely on text editors to create ASP.NET applications. You can create the application root in one of the following ways:

- ✦ Creating a virtual directory, which is a Web Application folder in IIS
- ✦ Marking a folder as an application

In the following two sections, we show you how to create the application root directory by using each of these ways.

Creating a virtual directory

Suppose you've created a Web Forms page, say `MyPage.aspx` in `C:\MyFolder`. To deploy this page, you need to publish it on a Web site. You can do so by creating a *Web virtual directory*. Web virtual directories are the directories, which are not located at the physical structure of the Web's root directory. The actual directory can be at a completely different physical location (may be on a remote computer). Thus, multiple virtual directories can point to the same set of files. Hence, the virtual directories are useful when you want to create your ASP.NET applications in directories other than the Web's root directory. When you create a Web virtual directory and make it point to your application that is not stored in the Web's root directory, the Web virtual directory becomes your application root directory. You create virtual directories in the IIS MMC; just follow these steps:

1. **Open the IIS MMC and right-click Default Web Site.**
2. **From the context menu, choose New⇨Virtual Directory.**

   The Virtual Directory Creation Wizard starts. Follow the on-screen prompts to complete creating the virtual directory (as we describe in Steps 3-7).
3. **Click Next on the Welcome screen to view the next screen.**

   You're prompted to enter an alias (name) for the virtual directory.
4. **Type a name for your virtual directory; click Next.**

   For this example, use something simple like `MyWeb`. The name you enter appears in the IIS MMC for your virtual directory.

   The next screen that appears asks for the name of the content directory that you want to publish on the Web site.

5. **In the Directory box, type the name of the directory (`C:\MyFolder`) that contains your ASP.NET Web Forms page and other related files; click Next.**

   The next screen that appears asks for the access permissions that you want to set for the virtual directory.

6. **Select the access permissions; click Next.**

   The only required permissions are Read and Run scripts (such as ASP).

   The final screen appears.

7. **Click Finish to complete the process.**

   Figure 2-6 displays the `MyWeb` application root.

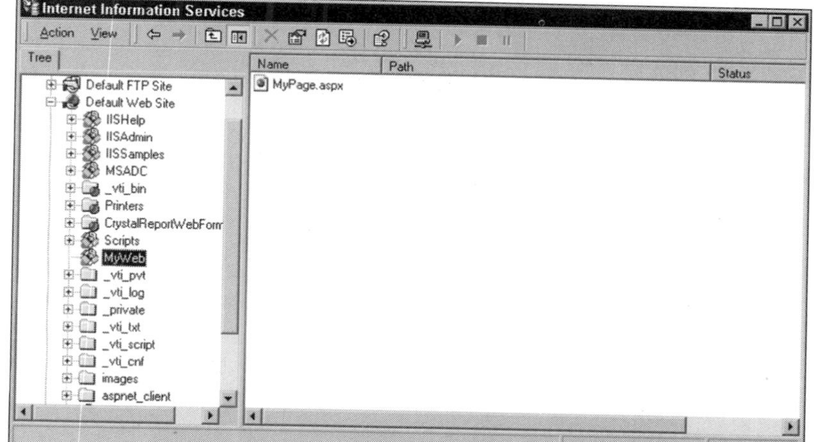

Figure 2-6: The MyWeb application root displays the MyPage.aspx file.

Marking a folder as an application

Another method that you can use to create an application root is by marking a folder containing your ASP.NET application files as an application. To do so, create a folder that you want to mark as an application in `c:\inetpub\wwwroot`. Create the folder and name it `c:\inetpub\wwwroot\MyFolder`. If you open the IIS MMC, you'll notice that `MyFolder` appears under Default Web Site.

If the IIS MMC is already opened, just select Default Web Site and click the Refresh button on the Toolbar. You can also select Refresh from the Action menu.

Next, you'll need to convert this folder to an application. To do so, right-click `MyFolder` and choose Properties from the context menu. The Properties dialog box appears, as shown in Figure 2-7.

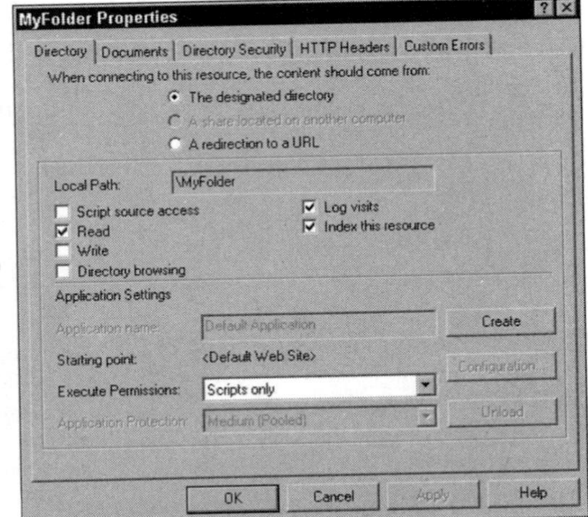

Figure 2-7: The Properties dialog box for the MyFolder folder.

The Properties dialog box displays the local path and permissions for the folder. To create this folder as an application, you simply need to click the Create button under Application Settings. When you click the Create button, the boxes that were not available become available. Click OK to complete the process. At this point, you'll notice that the folder icon for `MyFolder` changes to a package indicating that `MyFolder` is now an application.

HTML and XML in ASP.NET

Presentation of information is a key area and point of concern when developing Web applications. With each new Web development tool, you'll find that the way the applications are created is different. Whatever be the development tool, the basic markup language support needs to be there for presentation of data on the Web. Visual Studio .NET is no exception. In this section, we learn the role of HTML and XML in developing ASP.NET applications in Visual Studio .NET.

HTML

Hypertext Markup Language (HTML) is the de facto standard to present content on the World Wide Web. HTML has been derived from Standard Generalized Markup Language (SGML), which is primarily used to create markup languages. Since its release in 1992, HTML has come a long way, incorporating multiple features, such as Cascading Style Sheets (CSS), advanced linking features, and advanced tables.

Gone are the days when you relied solely on text editors to develop your Web pages. Today, many visual tools are available that you can use for developing Web pages in a WYSIWYG manner. However, even today, some people use text editors. And if you're one of these people, you need a *thorough* understanding of HTML. On the other hand, if you use visual tools or you've switched to using visual tools, you need only a *basic* understanding of HTML, which enables you to make better use of the tools that you use. So whatever tool you use to develop your Web pages, you must have some knowledge of HTML.

Visual Studio .NET provides an efficient Web page editor that allows you to design Web pages in a WYSIWYG manner. This editor provides two views, Design and HTML. You can use the Design view to develop Web pages graphically. The HTML view allows you to directly edit the HTML code. So, a minimal understanding of HTML is all you need to design really dashing Web pages by using Visual Studio .NET.

XML

Another important feature of ASP.NET is the support for eXtensible Markup Language (XML). XML is a standard that provides a way of describing structured data.

Just like HTML, the parent of XML is also SGML. However, unlike HTML, which focuses on displaying data and defining the way the data looks, XML focuses on defining the data types and structure of the data itself. Therefore, HTML is a standard for presenting data while XML is a standard for describing what the data is.

Remember that XML is not a replacement of HTML. In fact, XML and HTML have different goals and each complements the other. HTML focuses on presenting data, while XML focuses on describing data.

Since its release in 1998, XML is gaining popularity day by day. XML has attracted a lot of attention from analysts, reporters, and the development community. Either it is already in use or it is being introduced in many applications today. Visual Studio .NET is no exception!

But how XML fits into the picture of ASP.NET is the question. XML plays a crucial role in the way data is handled in ASP.NET applications. You can create XML documents by using XML editors provided in Visual Studio .NET. Because XML is text-based, writing and reading XML is easy.

The best feature of XML is that it separates data presentation from its description. This feature allows the integration of data from multiple sources. Some of the areas where XML plays a major role are

- ✦ XML is highly flexible in moving the data around. So, it is often used to move data across Internet/intranet applications. Thus, data exchange across different platforms is no longer a tedious task. XML is a standard data representation language that helps you create Enterprise-class Web applications.
- ✦ You can document C# code by using XML. Documenting code using XML is extremely beneficial because it adds more clarity and readability. Also, you can view the code comment documentation separately.
- ✦ XML is used in the discovery documents that are used to locate available Web services, which makes the discovery highly efficient.

Therefore, the success of XML has been correctly exploited in ASP.NET applications. The .NET Framework has an inherent support for XML, and it provides various classes, such as XmlReader and XmlWriter, which enable you to work with XML documents and data.

Chapter 3: Using ASP.NET Web Forms Server Controls

In This Chapter

- **Beginning with server controls**
- **Taking a closer look at Web controls**
- **Using each Web control**
- **Illustrating basic Web controls**

Because users with different know-how and varying levels of computer savvy browse the Internet to visit Web sites, many Web applications are specifically designed with user interfaces that accommodate this range of user profiles. Of course, other multiple factors — such as functionality and performance — help shape and determine the utility and effectiveness of Web applications. However, the user interface design holds primary importance because it creates the first impression of a Web site. A well-organized and well-developed user interface helps you design Web applications that draw in and engage diverse groups of users.

To design a user interface for your Web Forms pages, ASP.NET (Active Server Pages .NET) provides you with a rich set of server controls. Server controls form the core of the ASP.NET technology. These controls enable you to create interactive and dynamic Web Forms pages by adopting a server-side programming model. In this model, users interact with server controls at the client side, raising several events that are handled at the server side.

Visual Studio .NET makes your life easy in designing user interface for your Web applications. In this chapter, we give you an insight into ASP.NET server controls and guide you to use them.

Beginning with Server Controls

Think of a traditional Windows application. A Windows application is completely based on the event-driven approach. You create a user interface by adding several Windows controls on a *form*, such as Text Box or Button. When users interact with different controls on the form, *events* are raised, such as `TextChanged` or `Click`. In response to these events, you perform the required tasks by creating *event handlers*. The code in an event handler is executed when the associated event is generated.

With the advent of the ASP.NET technology, you can create your Web applications as easily as you create Windows applications. When you begin working with server controls, you'll surely appreciate the ease with which you can create your Web applications.

Before you actually take the plunge, you need to understand the significance of server controls. Here we discuss how events raised by server controls handled at server side are beneficial compared with normal HTML controls.

If you're not familiar with the concept of round trips and the different page events that are generated during the life cycle of a page, here's a brief overview. Whenever a browser requests a page, the page is compiled into a `Page` object. All server controls (the controls with the `runat = "server"` attribute) are compiled as objects within this `Page` object. Each time that the page is requested, the server controls are compiled into the page and executed on the server.

This method is a benefit over the normal HTML controls, which have no interaction with the server after they are rendered on the page. So, whenever you need to access a control's properties, methods, and events in server-side code, you must create server controls. Server controls are beneficial over normal HTML controls because they allow accessing the properties, methods, and events of server controls at the server side.

Types of server controls

Broadly speaking, the ASP.NET Framework provides two types of server controls: HTML server controls and ASP.NET Web Forms server controls.

- **HTML server controls:** These controls refer to the HTML elements that can be used in server-side code. These controls exist within the `System.Web.UI.HtmlControls` namespace and are derived from the `HtmlControl` base class. For example, `HtmlInputText` is an HTML server control (derived from the `HtmlControl` class) that renders a text box. For details on namespaces, check out Book 1, Chapter 2. The following code creates an `HtmlInputText` control.

  ```
  <input type = "text" runat = "server" id = "textBox1"
     value = "Welcome">
  ```

  In this code, the `<input type = "text">` HTML tag is used to create the `HtmlInputText` control on the page. Table 3-1 lists HTML server controls and the corresponding HTML tags used to create these controls.

HTML server controls map directly to HTML tags. Therefore, HTML server controls are very useful in migrating your existing ASP pages to ASP.NET, as you simply need to use `runat = "server"` along with controls.

✦ **ASP.NET Web Forms server controls:** These controls, also called Web controls, exist in the `System.Web.UI.WebControls` namespace and are derived from the `WebControl` base class. These controls include basic HTML `<form>` elements, such as `TextBox` and `Button` controls. The following code creates a `TextBox` control:

```
<asp:TextBox id = "TextBox1" runat = "server" Text =
"Welcome"></asp:TextBox>
```

Just like HTML server controls use HTML tags, Web controls use namespaced tags. These tags map to the ASP.NET runtime component. In the preceding code, `asp` is a namespaced tag to represent the `System.Web.UI.WebControls` namespace.

In addition to the basic controls, Web controls also include the following:

- **List controls** are used to build lists. These lists can also be bound to a data source. For example, `ListBox` and `DropDownList` are list controls.
- **Validation controls** are special controls that are used to check and validate the values entered in other controls on a page. For example, `CompareValidator` and `RangeValidator` are validation controls.
- **Rich controls** are special controls with several interesting features that help create task-specific output. For example, `Calendar` and `AdRotator` are rich controls.

Table 3-1 HTML Server Controls and Their Corresponding HTML Tags

HTML Server Control	*HTML Tag*
`HtmlForm`	`<form>`
`HtmlInputText`	`<input type = "text">` and `<input type = "password">`
`HtmlInputButton`	`<input type = "button">`
`HtmlInputCheckBox`	`<input type = "check">`
`HtmlInputRadioButton`	`<input type = "radio">`
`HtmlInputImage`	`<input type = "image">`
`HtmlAnchor`	`<a>`
`HtmlButton`	`<button>`
`HtmlTable`	`<table>`
`HtmlTableRow`	`<tr>`
`HtmlTableCell`	`<td>`

HTML server controls versus Web controls

When you design and develop a Web application, you need to decide between using HTML server controls and Web controls. You choose HTML server controls or Web controls depending on your requirements and the functionality of each server control. You can make this decision only when you're well aware how both types of server controls work. Table 3-2 displays a comparison of the two types of server controls based on specific factors.

Table 3-2 HTML Server Controls versus Web controls

Factor	*HTML Server Controls*	*Web Controls*
Mapping to HTML tags	Map one-to-one with HTML tags. A `runat="server"` attribute converts the traditional HTML tags to server controls. Therefore, they are useful when migrating from ASP pages to ASP.NET.	Do not map directly to HTML tags. This abstraction allows including controls from third party.
Object model	Use a HTML-centric object model. In this model, a control has a set of attributes. The attributes use string name/value pairs, which are not strongly typed.	Use a Visual Basic-like programming model, which uses a consistent object model. Each Web control has a set of standard properties, such as `Font`, `BackColor`, and `ForeColor`.
Target browser	Do not modify the HTML, which they render, depending on the target browser. You are responsible to render your controls in both up-level (that support DHTML) and down-level browsers.	Automatically adjust the rendered output depending on the target browser. This feature allows these controls to render in both the up-level as well as the down-level browsers.

Taking a Closer Look at Web Controls

All Web controls inherit from the `WebControl` class, which exists in the `System.Web.UI.WebControls` namespace. Thus, all controls have a set of common properties, methods, and events that they inherit from the `WebControl` base class. Of course, in addition to the common properties, methods, and events, the controls have their own specific properties, methods, and events. Before we explore specific controls in depth, look at some of the most commonly used properties, methods, and events common to all Web controls. See Table 3-3.

Table 3-3 Properties, Methods, and Events of the WebControl Class

Property/Method/Event	*Description*
`ID` property	Gets or sets the identifier of the control. This property is used programmatically to identify the control.
`Width` property	Gets or sets the width of the control.
`Height` property	Gets or sets the height of the control.
`BorderColor` property	Gets or sets the border color of the control.
`BorderStyle` property	Gets or sets the border style of the control, such as double, solid, or dotted.
`BorderWidth` property	Gets or sets the border width of the control.
`ToolTip` property	Gets or sets the pop-up text displayed when the mouse pointer is over the control.
`AccessKey` property	Gets or sets the keyboard shortcut to access the control.
`Visible` property	Takes a Boolean value. A `True` value indicates that the control is rendered as `UI` on the page, and a `False` value indicates that the control isn't visible.
`TabIndex` property	Gets or sets the tab index of the control.
`Font` property	Get or sets the font information of the control, such as font name and size.
`ForeColor` property	Gets or sets the foreground color of the control.
`BackColor` property	Gets or sets the background color of the control.
`Enabled` property	Takes a Boolean value indicating whether the control is enabled.
`EnableViewState` property	Takes a Boolean value indicating whether the control maintains its viewstate.
`Controls` property	Returns an object of the `ControlCollection` class.
`DataBind` method	Binds data from a data source to a server control and all its child controls.
`DataBinding` event	Is generated when the control is being bound to a data source.

Adding Web controls to forms

You can add server controls to your Web Forms pages either at design time or at runtime. At design time, you have two options to add server controls. First, you can use the Toolbox to add server controls in a WYSIWYG (What You See Is What You Get) manner. For more on Toolbox, see Book 3, Chapter 3. Second, you can use the HTML view of the ASPX file, which is the page file for a Web form. At run time, you add server controls programmatically. You can do so in the ASPX file (using the `<Script>` tag) or in the code-behind file.

Read on to discover how to use the Toolbox, the HTML view of the ASPX file, and the code-behind file to add Web controls to your Web forms.

Using the Toolbox

The Visual Studio .NET Toolbox contains a rich set of controls grouped under different categories for convenient access. The Toolbox appears at the extreme left of the Visual Studio .NET window. If it doesn't, select View➪Toolbox to open the Toolbox. The different categories in the Toolbox include

- **Web Forms** contain all Web controls including validation controls and rich Web controls. You'll frequently use this category of controls to design your Web Forms pages.
- **HTML** contains all HTML server controls.
- **Data** contains data objects, such as `DataSet` and `DataView`, that you can use on your forms to implement data access and manipulation functionality.
- **Component** contains a set of components, such as the `Timer` component, which you use to add time-based functionality to your forms. In addition to the standard available components, you can also add other components, such as EventLog (used to interact with system and custom event logs) and PerformanceCounter (used to interact with performance counters) to this category of toolbox.
- **Clipboard Ring** stores text items in the memory. When you cut or copy any text from the Code Editor, the text is automatically placed in this category. This category is very useful when you want to use multiple code snippets from one part of the Code Editor to another.
- **General** initially displays only a Pointer tool. However, you can add controls to this category, such as TextBox and Button including any custom controls.

To create Web Forms server controls by using the Toolbox, you can either drag or draw controls from the Toolbox (the Web Forms tab) to the form. To drag a control, click the control in the Toolbox and drag it to the form where you want to add the control. The control is added in its default size. The default size of different controls is different.

To draw a control on the form, select the control in the Toolbox. Then click on the form where you want to place the upper-left corner of the control and drag your mouse to make your new control the size you want.

You can also double-click a control in the Toolbox to add the control to a form in its default size and at the default location (0,0) of the form.

When you add controls to the form by using the Toolbox, the corresponding ASP.NET code is automatically generated for the controls in the HTML view of the ASPX file.

Using the HTML view of the ASPX file

You can also write the ASP.NET code directly in the HTML view of the ASPX file of your form to add server controls to the form. For example, to add a TextBox control, use the following ASP.NET code.

```
<asp:TextBox id = "TextBox1" runat = "server" Text =
            "Welcome"></asp:TextBox>
```


While you perform this step, you can switch to the Design view to view the control's rendered output.

Using the code-behind file

You can also add server controls to your form at runtime. To do so, you need to create an instance of the control class — say TextBox — which inherits the WebControl base class. For example, to create a TextBox control at runtime, use the following Visual Basic code.

```
Dim MyTextBox as New TextBox()
Controls.Add(MyTextBox)
```

In the preceding code, the Controls property returns a ControlCollection object. The Add method of the ControlCollection class is used to add a control to the form.

Setting properties of Web controls

In addition to a set of common properties called *base properties*, which are inherited from the WebControl base class, each control has its own set of properties. Again, you can set a control's properties at design time or at runtime. At design time, you can use the Properties window or the ASP.NET code to set a controls' properties. To display the Properties window, right-click the control for which you want to set the properties. Then, from the context menu, select Properties.

You can also display the Properties window of a selected control by selecting Properties Window from the View menu or by pressing the F4 key.

Figure 3-1 displays the Properties window for a TextBox control.

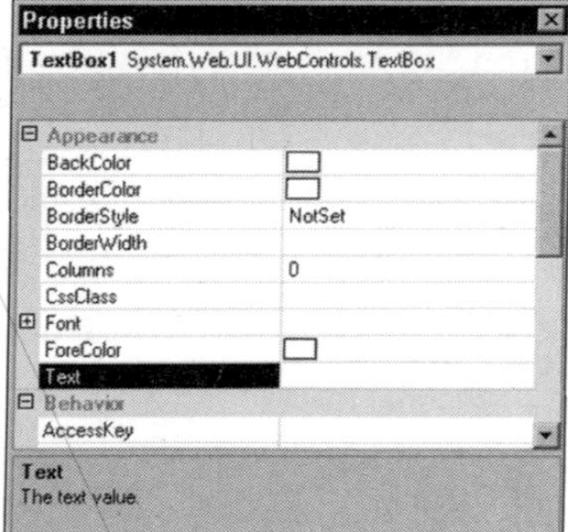

Figure 3-1: Checking out a control's properties.

You can also set the properties of Web controls by directly editing the ASP.NET code in the HTML view of the ASPX file. For example, to set the `Enabled` property of a `TextBox` control to `False` in the ASPX file, use the following code:

```
<asp:TextBox Id = "MyTextBox" runat = "server" Enabled =
          False></asp:TextBox>
```

In addition to setting properties at design time, you may need to set properties at runtime. For example, you might need to display a control only when a certain condition is met. So, you would need to set the `Visible` property of the control to `True` programmatically. To set a control's property programmatically, you use the following syntax:

```
ControlID.PropertyName = Value
```

where

`ControlID` represents the ID of the control.

`PropertyName` represents the property of the control.

`Value` represents the value assigned to the control's property: `PropertyName`.

For example, the following code is used to set the `Enabled` property to `False` of the `TextBox` control with the ID `MyTextBox`:

```
MyTextBox.Enabled = False
```

Handling events of Web controls

In addition to the common set of events inherited from the `WebControl` class, each control has its own set of events. You can handle these events by using either the code-behind file or the ASPX file. To understand this better, consider a Button control. You can handle its Click event either in the code-behind file or the ASPX file. You can open the code-behind file either from the Solution Explorer window or by pressing F7. Next, to write the handler for a control's event, select the name of the control from the Class Name list in the code-behind file. Finally, select the event in the Method Name list.

Another convenient way to associate an event handler with an event is by double-clicking the control.

For example, if the ID of the Button control is SubmitButton, select SubmitButton from the Class Name list and Click from the Method Name list. The following code is automatically generated:


```
Private Sub SubmitButton_Click(ByVal sender As Object, ByVal
          e As System.EventArgs) Handles SubmitButton.Click

End Sub
```

In this code,

- ✦ The procedure SubmitButton_Click is the event handler for the Click event of the button with the ID SubmitButton. The Handles keyword associates the event with the event handler. For more on the Handles keyword, check out Book 3, Chapter 8.
- ✦ The procedure takes two arguments. The first argument contains the event sender. An *event sender* is an object, such as a form or a control that can generate events. The second argument contains the event data.

You can then add code in the event handler to add the desired tasks that you want performed. After you do that, simply test the code by accessing the form from a browser. That looks pretty simple — much like you used to do for Windows applications.

Another way that you can create event handlers for server controls is by using the ASPX file. Consider the same example of a Button control with ID SubmitButton. Creating and associating the event handler with the Click event of the button requires two steps.

1. **In the ASPX file, edit the ASP.NET code for the control to specify the event handler for the Click event.**

   ```
   <asp:Button Id = "SubmitButton" runat = "server"
      OnClick = "SubmitButton_Click"></asp:Button>
   ```

   In this code,

   OnClick = "SubmitButton_Click" is the name of the event handler that must be called when the Click event of the button is generated.

2. **Write the `SubmitButton_Click` event handler in the ASPX file.**

   Any code is written within the `<Script>` tag. The following code illustrates where to add event handlers.

```
<script language="vb" runat="server">
   Sub SubmitButton_Click(sender as Object, e as
   EventArgs)
      Code here
   End Sub
</script>
```

Using Each Web Control in Detail

In this section, we take a closer look at each of the basic Web controls and focus on their specific properties, methods, and events.

Label control

The `Label` control is used to display static text that users can't edit while the Web Forms page is displayed to users. You use this control to display static information, such as instructions or text box names, to users.

The ASP.NET code to add the `Label` control is

```
<asp:Label id = "Label1" runat = "server"
Text = "For Your Information" />
```

You may also need to add a `Label` control and set its properties at runtime. For example, you might need to add a `Label` control and display a message on it when a certain condition becomes true. The following code illustrates how to add a `Label` control and set its `Text` property programmatically.

```
Dim OrderLabel As New Label()
Controls.Add (OrderLabel)
OrderLabel.Text = "This order is processed"
```

TextBox control

The `TextBox` control is used to accept user input, such as text, numbers, and dates. In addition to base properties, the `TextBox` control has a special property called `TextMode`. This property controls the type of the `TextBox` control that is rendered. You can set the `TextMode` property to one of the following values:

- `SingleLine` is the default value that enables users to type characters only in a single line.

✦ `MultiLine` is the value that enables users to type characters in multiple lines.

✦ `Password` is the value that enables users to type characters only in a single line. However, unlike the `SingleLine` value, it masks the characters that are typed and displays them as asterisks (*).

You may already be familiar with the `ID`, `Text`, `Font`, and `TextMode` properties. Some additional properties of the `TextBox` control are listed in Table 3-4.

Table 3-4 Properties of the TextBox Control

Property	*Description*
`ID`	Represents a unique identifier for the `TextBox` control by which it is referred to programmatically.
`Text`	Represents the text to be displayed in the `TextBox` control.
`Font`	Represents the current font for the `TextBox` control.
`TextMode`	Represents the type of the `TextBox` control, such as single-line, multi-line, or password. The control is a single-line text box by default.
`MaxLength`	Represents the maximum number of characters that can be typed in the `TextBox` control.
`Columns`	Represents the width of the `TextBox` control in characters. The default value of this property is `0`. If you set both the `Width` and `Columns` properties, the `Width` property (which takes value in pixels) takes precedence over the `Columns` property.
`Rows`	Represents the height of the `MultiLine TextBox` control and takes value in number of rows. The default value is `0`.
`Wrap`	Represents the word wrap behavior in a `MultiLine` TextBox control. The default value is `True`, indicating that the text wraps automatically. However, if the value is set to `False`, a user must press a carriage return to move to a next line.

Button, LinkButton, and ImageButton controls

The `Button`, `LinkButton`, and `ImageButton` controls are used to submit your Web Forms page along with the user-supplied values in different controls to be processed on a server. All these controls generate a `Click` event, which you can handle to process the post back data on the server.

✦ `Button`: This is a standard button. The ASP.NET code to add a `Button` control is

```
<asp:Button id = "SubmitButton" runat = "server" Text =
   "Submit"></asp:Button>
```

- `LinkButton`: This control is similar to the `Button` control except that it is displayed as a hyperlink on a page. Unlike the HyperLink control, the LinkButton control raises the Click event that you can handle to trap users' action. The ASP.NET code to add a `Button` control is

  ```
  <asp:LinkButton id = "SubmitButton" runat = "server"
     Text = "Submit"></asp:LinkButton>
  ```

- `ImageButton`: This control renders an image on a form. You use the `ImageUrl` property to set the image to be rendered. You can also set the `AlternateText` property to represent the text that is displayed as a tooltip or displayed when the image cannot be loaded. The ASP.NET code to add an `ImageButton` control is

  ```
  <asp:ImageButton id = "SubmitButton" runat = "server"
     ImageUrl = "SubmitImage.gif"></asp:ImageButton>
  ```

HyperLink control

The `HyperLink` control enables users to navigate from one page to another in an application or an absolute URL. To specify the URL to navigate to, you need to set the `NavigateUrl` property. You can use either text (the `Text` property) or an image (the `ImageUrl` property) to act as a hyperlink.

The following ASP.NET code illustrates how to add a `HyperLink` control to a form:

```
<asp:HyperLink id = "HyperLink1" runat = "server" Text =
         "www.msn.com" NavigateUrl = "http://www.msn.com">
         </asp:HyperLink>
```

Image control

Use an `Image` control to render an image on a form. You can set the image to be displayed in this control by setting the `ImageUrl`. You can also set the `AlternateText` property to display the text as a tooltip or display when the image can't be loaded. The following ASP.NET code renders an `Image` control:

```
<asp:Image id = "Image1" runat = "server" ImageUrl =
          "Rose.gif"></asp:Image>
```

DropDownList and ListBox controls

`DropDownList` and `ListBox` controls present a list of choices that users can select from. The `DropDownList` control allows users to select a single value from a list of choices. Similarly, the `ListBox` control also allows users to select only one choice. However, unlike the `DropDownList` control, you can set the `ListBox` control to allow users to select multiple values. To do so, set the `SelectionMode` property to `Multiple`.

The SelectionMode property is not available with the DropDownList control.

You can populate DropDownList and ListBox controls at design time to provide a list of static choices. Also, you can add choices at runtime. To add a choice, you need to set the Items property. The Items property is a collection of items — each item is a separate object with its own properties, such as Text, Value, and Selected.

- **The Text property is the text that is displayed in the list.**
- **The Value property is the value associated with the item and is not displayed in the list.**

  However, when the item is selected, the Value property is stored as the selected value. This property is useful when you don't want the users to know the actual value of the item that's displayed in the list. For example, you can provide a list of product names with the Text property set as the respective product names. However, you can set the Value property to the respective ProductID. When a user selects a product name, the ProductID gets selected.
- **The Selected property is a Boolean value indicating whether the item is selected.**

You can set the Items property by using the Properties window or you can directly write the ASP.NET code. Follow the actual steps to set the Items property later in the chapter (section "Illustrating Basic Web Controls," Step 13) when we discuss using Web controls. The following code illustrates how to add DropDownList and ListBox controls and populate them with a set of static values:

```
<asp:DropDownList id = "ProfessionList" runat = "server">
   <asp:ListItem Text = "Sales" Value = "1" selected =
          "true"/>
   <asp:ListItem Text = "Engineering" Value = "2"/>
</asp:DropDownList>

<asp:ListBox id = "StateList" runat="server" SelectionMode =
          "Multiple">
   <asp:ListItem Text = "Alaska" Value = "1" selected =
          "true"/>
   <asp:ListItem Text = "California" Value = "2"/>
</asp:ListBox>
```

You may need to add the choices to the lists at runtime. For example, you might need to extend the list based on certain conditions at runtime. The following code illustrates how to add choices to the DropDownList at runtime:

```
Dim ListItem1 as New ListItem("Consulting","3")
ProfessionList.Items.Add(ListItem1)
```

In the preceding code, ListItem1 is an object of the ListItem class that represents an item in the Items collection. The ListItem constructor can take one argument (a string to represent the text of the item) or two arguments (a string for the text and another string for the value of the item).

You may need to identify the choice that a user has selected when a page is displayed. You can do so by accessing the SelectedIndex or SelectedItem property of the control.

The SelectedIndex property returns an integer value indicating the index of the selected item (the index of the first item is 0). If nothing is selected, this property returns 0.

```
Dim i As Integer
i=ProfessionList.SelectedIndex()
```

The SelectedItem property returns the list item that is selected. You can then extract the Text, Value, or Selected property of the selected item.

```
Dim ListItem1 As New ListItem()
ListItem1=ProfessionList.SelectedItem()
Dim profession as String
Profession = ProfessionList.SelectedItem.Text
```

CheckBox and RadioButton controls

The CheckBox control renders a check box that users can select (click) to toggle between its selected and cleared states. The ASP.NET code to add a CheckBox control is

```
<asp:CheckBox id = "Subscriptions" runat = "server" Text =
        "Books"></asp:CheckBox>
```

You can use the Checked property of the CheckBox control to get or set the selection state of the control. The Checked property takes a Boolean value; a True value indicates that the check box is selected, and a False value indicates that the check box is cleared.

You can also check the selection state of a check box at runtime. The state of the CheckBox control might change depending on whether a user selects it or clears it. You can identify this state at runtime by writing code. The following code illustrates the same:

```
Dim IsChk as Boolean
IsChk=Subscription.Checked
```

The RadioButton control renders a radio button that users can select (click) to toggle between its selected and cleared states. Thus, a RadioButton control is similar to a CheckBox control. However, the RadioButton control is typically used with other RadioButton controls in a group to provide a set of mutually exclusive choices. You can group a set of radio buttons by setting the GroupName property of the different radio buttons to a same value. The following ASP.NET code renders two radio buttons, which provide mutually exclusive choices: Male and Female. Notice that both the radio buttons belong to the same group: Group1.

```
<asp:RadioButton id = "radio1" runat = "server" Text="Male"
   GroupName="Group1" Checked="true"> </asp:RadioButton>
<asp:RadioButton id = "radio2" runat="server" Text="Female"
   GroupName="Group1"></asp:RadioButton>
```

CheckBoxList and RadioButtonList controls

The CheckBoxList control is a collection of several check boxes, and the RadioButtonList control is a collection of several radio buttons. Like their cousins, CheckBox and RadioButton controls, the RadioButtonList control renders a set of mutually exclusive radio buttons and the CheckBoxList control doesn't.

Just like the DropDownList and ListBox controls, you can set the Items property of the CheckBoxList and RadioButtonList controls to add the choices. The following ASP.NET code illustrates the same:

```
<asp:CheckBoxList id = "SubscriptionList" runat = "server">
   <asp:ListItem Text = "Books" Value = "1" selected =
         "true"/>
   <asp:ListItem Text = "Magazines" Value = "2"/>
</asp:CheckBoxList>

<asp:RadioButtonList id = "SexList" runat = "server">
   <asp:ListItem Text = "Male" Value = "1" selected =
         "true"/>
   <asp:ListItem Text = "Female" Value = "2"/>
</asp:RadioButtonList>
```

When you add different choices in a CheckBoxList or RadioButtonList control, the choices appear vertically by default. This takes up a large area of your form. You can set the choices to appear horizontally by setting the RepeatDirection property to Horizontal.

You can add the list items at runtime when you need to extend the list at run time. Also, you use the SelectedIndex and SelectedItem properties to identify a selected item just like you do for the DropDownList and ListBox controls. (Read more on this in the earlier section "DropDownList and ListBox controls.")

Table control

Tables are a collection of rows and columns. The intersection of a row and a column is a cell that contains data. To render tables in your forms, you use the `Table` control.

Add rows to a table by setting the `Rows` property of the `Table` control. The `Rows` property is a collection of multiple `TableRow` objects; each `TableRow` object represents a row. A `TableRow` object has a property called `Cells`, which in turn is a collection of multiple `TableCell` objects. Think of it this way: If you want to add a table to your form, you need to first add the `Table` control. Then, you need to add rows (each row is represented by a `TableRow` object) by setting the `Rows` property. Finally, within each row, you need to add cells (each cell is represented by a `TableCell` object) by setting the `Cells` property. The steps for this procedure are:

1. **Add a `Table` control to the form and display the control's Properties window (press F4).**
2. **Click ellipsis for the `Rows` property to display the TableRow Collection Editor window.**
3. **In the TableRow Collection Editor window that appears, click the Add button to add a new row.**

   The Properties pane of the window displays the properties of the row that you added.
4. **In the Properties pane, click the ellipsis for the `Cells` property of the row to display the TableCell Collection Editor window.**
5. **In the TableCell Collection Editor window, click the Add button to add a new cell.**

   The Properties pane of the window displays the properties of the cell that you added.

When you finish adding cells to a row, click OK to close the TableCell Collection Editor window. Similarly, when you finish adding rows to the table, click OK to close the TableRow Collection Editor window.

The following ASP.NET code renders a simple table that displays customer details. The table contains two rows; each row contains three cells:

```
<asp:Table id="Table1" runat="server">

   <asp:TableRow ID="Heading">
      <asp:TableCell Text="Customer ID"
           ID="CustomerID"></asp:TableCell>
```

```
        <asp:TableCell Text="First Name"
            ID="FirstName"></asp:TableCell>
        <asp:TableCell Text="Last Name"
            ID="LastName"></asp:TableCell>
    </asp:TableRow>

    <asp:TableRow ID="Record1">
        <asp:TableCell Text="C001"
          ID="Record1ID"></asp:TableCell>
        <asp:TableCell Text="Rita"
          ID="Record1FirstName"></asp:TableCell>
        <asp:TableCell Text="Greg"
          ID="Record1LastName"></asp:TableCell>
    </asp:TableRow>

    <asp:TableRow ID="Record2">
        <asp:TableCell Text="C002"
          ID="Record2ID"></asp:TableCell>
        <asp:TableCell Text="John"
          ID="Record2FirstName"></asp:TableCell>
        <asp:TableCell Text="Anderson"
          ID="Record2LastName"></asp:TableCell>
    </asp:TableRow>

</asp:Table>
```


Apart from adding the `Table` control at design time, you can add the `Table` control and its rows and cells at runtime. To do so, create objects of the `Table`, `TableRow`, and `TableCell` classes as we describe below.

```
Dim Table1 as New Table()
Dim TableRowObj As New TableRow()
Dim TableCellObj As New TableCell()
```

Next, add the `TableCell` object to the `TableRow` object.

```
TableRowObj.Cells.Add(TableCellObj)
```

Finally, add the `TableRow` object to the `Table` control. If the ID of the `Table` control is `Table1`, use the following code to add the `TableRow` object to the `Table` control.

```
Table1.Rows.Add(TableRowObj)
```

After you become comfortable using Web controls, concentrate on understanding two very important concepts: handling post back and using ViewState.

Handling post back

Most user interactions with a Web Forms page result in round trips. And, during each round trip, the page undergoes a cycle of page events. For more on page events, check out Book 6, Chapter 2. Because a single *round trip* involves posting the form to the server for processing and then displaying it again in the browser, the server-control events result in increased cycle time, which affects performance. Therefore, the number of events available with Web controls is kept limited, usually to the `Click` event. For example, the `onmouseover` event is not supported by server controls. However, certain controls do support change events. These change events can result in a *post back*, and thus a round trip, if the `AutoPostBack` property of the control is set to `True`. Table 3-5 displays some of the events associated with Web controls that you use for handling post back.

Table 3-5 Events Associated with Web Controls

Event	*Description*	*Supported By*
`TextChanged`	Generates when the `TextBox` control content is changed.	`TextBox`
`CheckedChanged`	Generates when the `Checked` property value of a `RadioButton` or `CheckBox` control is changed.	`CheckBox` and `RadioButton`
`SelectedIndexChanged`	Generates when the current selection is changed in the list.	`DropDownList`, `ListBox`, `CheckBoxList`, and `RadioButtonList`
`Click`	Generates when a button is clicked.	`Button`, `LinkButton`, and `ImageButton`.

You need to understand how to handle post back when the page is submitted to the server. To handle the post back data for individual controls, the simplest way is to write the event handler for the control's event that caused the post back. One drawback to this remedy is that the code is executed each time that the page is posted back to the server. To avoid this, write the code in the `Page_Load` method. In this method, you can check whether the page is posted back the first time. To do so, use the `IsPostBack` property, as demonstrated in the code below:

```
Private Sub Page_Load(ByVal sender As System.Object, ByVal e
        As System.EventArgs) Handles MyBase.Load
    If MyButton.Page.IsPostBack = True Then
```

```
        YourButton.Visible = False
    End If
End Sub
```

Using ViewState

Use ViewState to understand these essential performance process questions:

Do you know what happens to page information after the page is processed on the server?

Does the server store the page information or discard it?

If the information is maintained at the server side, how does it happen?

If the server discards the page information, how can the information be accessed across subsequent round trips?

With each round trip, the server creates the page from scratch and serves it to the client. After the page is processed and served to the client, the server discards the page information. As a result, in the next round trip, the page information isn't accessible and the page has to be created from scratch.

Because the state of Web Forms pages and controls isn't maintained at the server, the Web Forms pages are called *stateless*. This stateless nature of Web pages was a big problem in traditional Web applications. However, the Web Forms framework provides a workaround for this stateless behavior. The Web Forms framework allows the state of the pages and controls to be saved at the server. To implement this, the Web Forms framework provides two options:

- `ViewState`: With each round trip, the framework automatically saves the state of the page and its current properties and the state of the server controls along with their base properties.
- `State Bag`: Every page maintains a state bag that stores values to be restored in the next round trip.

`ViewState` contains the state of the page and all the server controls between the requests that are sent to the server. This state information is stored in the `System.Web.UI.StateBag` object. The information is stored as name/value pairs in hidden form fields. You can see this state information when the page is displayed in the browser. To do so, select `Source` from the `View` menu of the browser in which the page is displayed. Now the Web Forms pages are no longer stateless. However, using `ViewState` does pose a disadvantage when pages are complex. If pages are complex with many server controls, the state information is also heavy. In that case, maintaining state can affect the performance of pages.

All server controls have an `EnableViewState` property, which is set to `True` by default. Thus, the state maintenance is automatically taken care of by the Page framework. You don't have to do anything explicitly to maintain the state.

You may encounter situations when you can't afford to have the performance of your Web pages be affected because of state maintenance. Also, if you don't need your Web pages to maintain state, you can set the `EnableViewState` property to `False`, as in the following code.

```
<%@ Page EnableViewState = "False" %>
```

Illustrating Basic Web Controls

In this section, you get the opportunity to work with almost every available basic Web control. Here you learn how to work with different controls through a simple subscription form example. Follow along with us in this section to gain hands-on experience on almost each Web control as we walk you through designing three Web forms.

To begin with, create an ASP.NET Web Application project using Visual Basic. After you create this, you'll see a default Web form: WebForm1.aspx. Create two images named SubscribeHome.gif (refer to Figure 3-2) and SubscribeFinal.gif (skip down to Figure 3-5) for your application. Store these graphics in your Web application project.

Next, design WebForm1. To do so, proceed as follows:

1. **Drag the `Image` control from the Toolbox to the form, and display the Properties window for this control (select the Image control and press F4).**
2. **Set the `ImageUrl` property to SubscribeHome.gif.**

   The Image control now displays this image.

   You can also click the ellipsis for the `ImageUrl` property to browse to the image contained within the application or outside the application.
3. **Drag the `Label` control from the Toolbox to the form.**
4. **Set the `Text` property of the `Label` control to `User Name`.**
5. **Drag the `TextBox` control from the Toolbox to the form.**
6. **Set the `ID` property of the `TextBox` control to `UserNameBox`.**

   At this stage, the form should look like the one displayed in Figure 3-2.

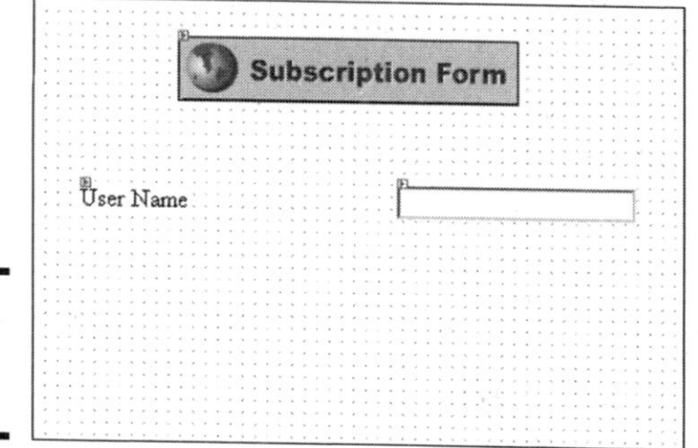

Figure 3-2: A form in the making.

7. **Drag one more `Label` control from the Toolbox, place it below the `User Name` label, and set its `Text` property to `User ID`.**
8. **Drag a `TextBox` control from the toolbox, place it below the first `TextBox` control, and set its `ID` property to `UserIDBox`.**

Instead of dragging a control each time to add it to the form, you can copy the existing control, place it at the desired position, and set its properties. For example, to add the `User ID` label, you can copy (Ctrl+C) the existing `User Name` label, place (Ctrl+V) it below the first label, and set its `Text` property to `User ID`.

9. **Add one more label below the `User ID` label and set its `Text` property to `Password`.**
10. **Add a text box below the `UserIDBox` TextBox and set its `ID` property to `PasswordBox` and its `TextMode` property to `Password`.**
11. **Add another label below the `Password` label and set its `Text` property to `Sex`.**
12. **Adjacent to this label, add a `RadioButtonList` control.**
13. **Set the `ID` property of the `RadioList` control to `SexList`.**

To add individual buttons to this list, you need to set the `Items` property. To do so, click the ellipsis for the `Items` property and follow these steps:

1. In the ListItem Collection Editor window, click the Add button to add an item to the `RadioButtonList` control.

   At this stage, the Members pane of the window displays `ListItem`. Note that `ListItem` is added at position 0. This is the index of the list item. The right pane, ListItem properties pane, displays properties of the item. (See Figure 3-3.)

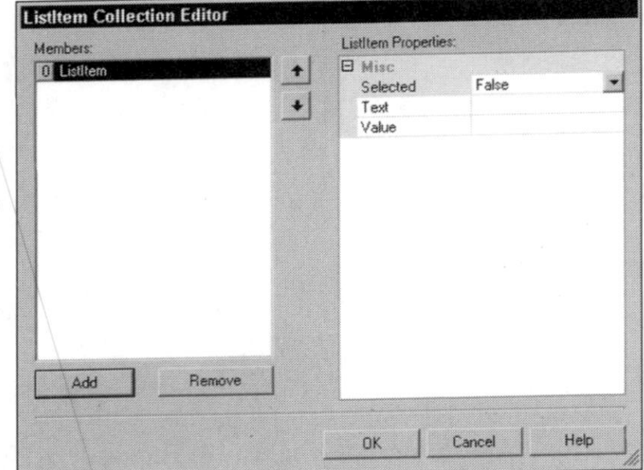

Figure 3-3: View properties in the ListItem Collection Editor window.

2. Set the `Selected` property to `False`. A `True` value in this property indicates that the item would be selected by default.
3. Set the `Text` property to `Male`.
4. When you click in the Value box, note that this property is also set to `Male`. However, you can change this property. Notice that in the Members pane, the `ListItem` now displays `Male`.
5. After adding the `Male` item, add another item, setting its `Text` value to `Female`.
6. Click OK to close the ListItem Collection Editor window. At this stage, note that the `RadioButtonList` now displays two radio buttons: Male and Female.

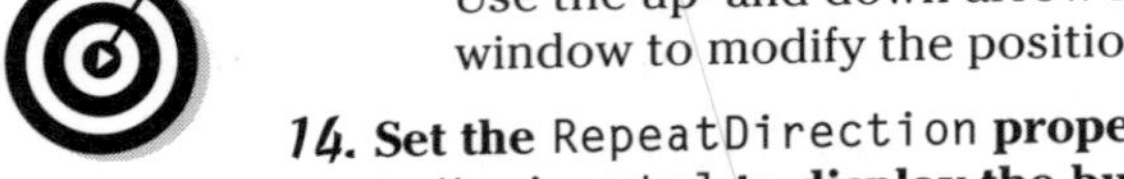

Use the up- and down-arrow keys in the ListItem Collection Editor window to modify the position of list items.

14. Set the `RepeatDirection` property of the `RadioButtonList` control to `Horizontal` to display the buttons in a linear manner.

15. Add another label below the `Sex` label and set its `Text` property to `Occupation`.

16. Adjacent to the `Occupation` label, add a `DropDownList` control and set its `ID` property to `OccupationList`.

To add individual list items, set the `Items` property. Add different items, such as Accounting/Finance, Computer-related, Research, or Student. You can expand this list as and when required.

The item at the 0 (zero) position is always displayed in the `DropDownList` control, even if it's not selected. To avoid this, add a dummy list item — say `[Select your occupation]` — at the position 0.

17. **Add another label below the** `Occupation` **label and set its** `Text` **property to** `E-mail`**.**

    Adjacent to this label, add a `TextBox` control and set its `ID` property to `EmailBox`.

18. **Drag a** `LinkButton` **control from the Toolbox to the form, setting its** `ID` **property to** `NextLinkButton` **and the** `Text` **property to** `Next`**.**

19. **Set a background color of the form by selecting** `Document` **from the Object list of the Properties window and setting the** `bgColor` **property to** `#99cccc`**. This color is a shade of green.**

    At this stage, your form should be ready to display as shown in Figure 3-4.

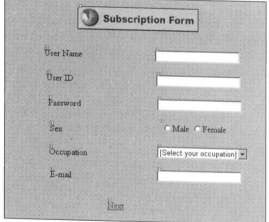

Figure 3-4: A complete subscription form.

The form that you just designed is for collecting user information at the time of subscription. Instead of the default form name, WebForm1, give it a more meaningful name. To do so, right-click the WebForm1.aspx file in Solution Explorer and select Rename from the context menu. If Solution Explorer is not visible, select View⇨Solution Explorer to open it. Rename this file to Subscription1.aspx.

Usually, your Web Application projects contain multiple Web forms. Renaming these forms according to the corresponding information or functions helps you easily identify your forms.

You can switch to the HTML view (by clicking HTML at the bottom of the ASPX file) to see the ASP.NET code (which gets automatically generated) for the controls that you added in the Design view.

Continuing with our running example, you have two more forms to design after you complete the Subscription1 form. Currently, your project contains only one Web Form. To add another Web form, select `Add Web Form` from the `Project` menu. Edit the Name box to read `Subscription2.aspx` and click OK.

Design the Subscription2 form shown in Figure 3-5, using Table 3-6 as a reference for setting the properties of different controls on the form. You only need to set their `Text` properties, which is visible in Figure 3-5.

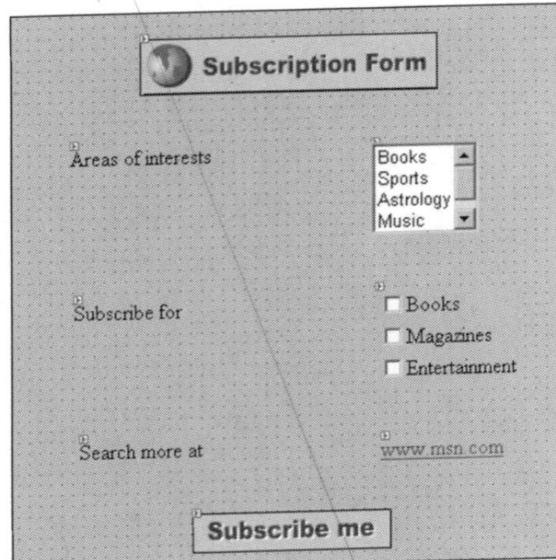

Figure 3-5: The Subscription2 form.

Table 3-6 Properties of the Controls in the Subscription2 Form

Control	*Contains*	*Property*	*Value*
`Image`	Subscription form image	`ImageUrl`	`SubscribeHome.gif`
`ListBox`	Areas of interests	`ID`	`InterestList`
`ListBox`		`Items`	`Books,Sports, Astrology,Music and Movies`
`CheckBoxList`	Subscribe for	`ID`	`SubscriptionList`
`CheckBoxList`		`Items`	`Books,Magazines, Entertainment`

Control	Contains	Property	Value
Hyperlink	Search more at	ID	SearchLink
Hyperlink		Text	www.msn.com
Hyperlink		NavigateUrl	http://www.msn.com
ImageButton	Subscribe me	ID	SubscriptionButton
ImageButton		ImageUrl	SubscribeFinal.gif

After setting the properties of controls, set the background color of the form to #99cccc. This color is a shade of green. With this, you are ready with Subscription2 form.

Next, add another Web form, Subscription3.aspx, to the project. Design the form as shown in Figure 3-6. Refer to Table 3-7 to set the properties of the controls.

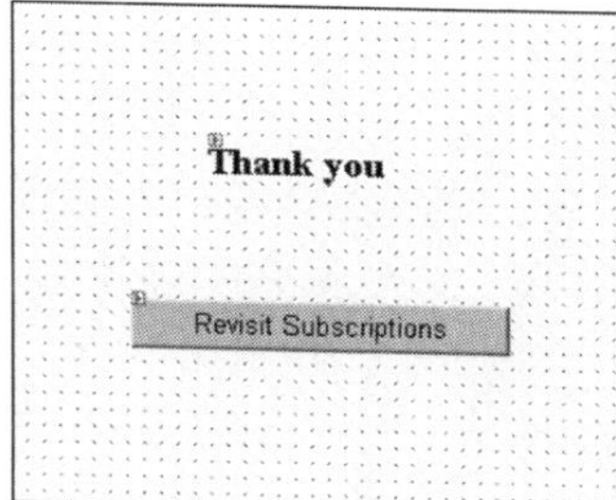

Figure 3-6: The Subscription3 form.

Table 3-7 Properties of the Controls in the Subscription3 Form

Control	Contains	Property	Value
Label	Thank You	Text	Thank you
Button	Revisit Subscriptions	ID	RevisitButton

After you've set the properties of all the controls, set the background color of the form to #ffcccc. This color is a shade of yellow.

Time to move ahead and implement functionality in your forms by handling control events. To do so, follow these steps:

1. **Open the Subscription1 form and select the `NextLinkButton` control.**
2. **Open the code-behind file (Subscription1.aspx.vb) by pressing F7 or double-clicking the `NextLinkButton` control.**

3. **Write the following code in the `Click` event of the `LinkButton` control.**

```
Private Sub NextLinkButton_Click(ByVal sender As
   System.Object, ByVal e As System.EventArgs) Handles
   NextLinkButton.Click
         Response.Redirect("Subscription2.aspx")

End Sub
```

   In this code, the `Redirect` method of the `HTTPResponse` class is used to redirect to a URL. In this case, the control is redirected to the Subscription2 form.

Alternatively, you can create the event handler in the ASPX file.

Next you need to add functionality to the Subscription2 and Subscription3 forms. To do so, write the code to redirect the control to the Subscription3 form in the `Click` event of the `SubscriptionButton ImageButton` control of Subscription2 form:

```
Private Sub SubscriptionButton_Click(ByVal sender As
          System.Object, ByVal e As
          System.Web.UI.ImageClickEventArgs) Handles
          SubscriptionButton.Click
         Response.Redirect("Subscription3.aspx")

End Sub
```

Finally, write the following code in the `Click` event of the `RevisitButton Button` control of Subscription3 form:

```
Private Sub RevisitButton_Click(ByVal sender As
          System.Object, ByVal e As System.EventArgs)
          Handles RevisitButton.Click
         Response.Redirect("Subscription1.aspx")

End Sub
```

After you complete these second and third forms, build and execute the application by pressing Ctrl+F5. When you run the application, the browser displays the Subscription1 form. When you click the Next button, Subscription2 form is displayed. Then, when you supply the details and click the Image button at the bottom, you are directed to the last form displaying a *Thank you* message. If you want to revisit the first form, click the Revisit Subscription button.

Chapter 4: Working with Validation Controls

In This Chapter

- **Discovering validation controls**
- **Using validation controls**
- **Employing multiple validation controls**

Suppose that you have a Web application meant to accept orders from customers worldwide. This application has to include entry areas in which a customer provides name, shipping address, and method of payment. Your order information may also include product information (name and quantity). If any of this information is entered incorrectly, you can imagine the consequences. If a user placing an order forgets to enter the name of the city where the purchase is to be shipped, for example, that's a problem. To prevent forest fires — that is, prevent entry errors — you need to validate user input before processing. You can't presume that anything that a user enters is valid.

In classic Active Server Pages (ASP), you use scripting languages, such as VBScript and JavaScript, to validate user input. Even a simple validation, such as checking whether a field is empty, requires you to write code. The situation worsens if you have to validate user input in multiple controls in a page. Placing a large amount of code in your page for validation (in addition to the already existing code) makes your page more prone to errors. ASP.NET has made your life easier with the inclusion of *validation controls*, which you use to validate user input with minimal coding.

In this chapter, we show you how to use each of the ASP.NET validation controls to validate user input in different controls. You also learn to use multiple validation controls to validate user input in a single control. We hope you come to appreciate the ease with which you can validate the page data. If you've used classic ASP, we predict that you'll appreciate this ease even more.

Introducing Validation Controls

Suppose that you want to validate the user input in a control — say, a text box — but you don't know how to use validation controls to accomplish this goal. Simply put, all you have to do is add a validation control(s) and associate it (them) with the `TextBox` control that you want to validate. (We discuss associating multiple validation controls to another control later in the upcoming section "Using Multiple Validation Controls.") For this section, all you need to know is that you associate a validation control(s) with each control that you want to validate.

ASP.NET has six validation controls, which we detail in Table 4-1. All these validation controls inherit from the `BaseValidator` class. This class serves as an abstract class that provides core implementation for all validation controls. An abstract class provides a set of properties, methods, and events that can be implemented by the classes that inherit from it.

Table 4-1 ASP.NET Validation Controls

Validation Control	*Description*
`RequiredFieldValidator`	Validates a control to check that the control is not empty.
`CompareValidator`	Compares the value in a control with the value in another control or a specific value to check whether the two values match.
`RangeValidator`	Validates the value in a control to check that the value falls in a specified text or numeric range.
`RegularExpressionValidator`	Validates the value in a control to check whether the value matches a specified regular expression.
`CustomValidator`	Allows you to perform validation on a control by using user-defined functions.
`ValidationSummary`	Displays all the validation error messages grouped together.

Before we discuss using each of these validation controls, first understand how validation controls work.

1. When you add a validation control, you must associate it with another control (a text box, for example) that you want to get validated.
2. When a user enters values in different controls and submits a completed form, those values are passed to the appropriate validation controls. That is, the appropriate validation controls are the respective validation controls that are associated with other controls on the form.
3. The validation controls review (test) the values that are passed to them.
4. After the validation tests, the `IsValid` property of each validation control on the page is set to `True` or `False`. A `True` value indicates that the validation test succeeded, and a `False` value indicates a failed validation test. If all controls pass all validation tests, the `IsValid` property of the page is set to `True`. The page data is processed at the server *only when* the `IsValid` property of the page becomes `True`.

If even a single validation test fails, the `IsValid` property of the page becomes `False`. When this happens, the page data is not processed at the server, and the page is sent back to the client with validation errors.

Thus, validation controls always perform validation checks at the server side. In addition to server-side validation, validation controls can also perform validation using client scripts. This client-side validation can be performed only if a user is working in a browser that supports Dynamic HyperText Markup Language (DHTML).

In client-side validation, errors are detected immediately without sending the form to the server, and the error messages are displayed as soon as the user moves out of the control that contains the error. Compared with server-side validation in which the form must be submitted to the server, client-side validation catches errors at the client's end itself — thus reducing cycle time and resulting in improved performance.

Note that when client-side validations are performed, don't assume that server-side validations are skipped. Even if the all client-side validations are successful, validation tests are still performed at the server side also when the form is submitted. This double-check ensures the validity within server-based event handlers. Also, a user who impersonates another user (thus bypassing client-side validation) can't bypass the server-side validation.

Before you can actually start using validation controls, create an ASP.NET Web Application project. Name the project `ValidationSample` and design a basic form that contains several controls to take user input. Design a form named `BookIssue` (use Figure 4-1 as your guide) that takes the necessary information from a user checking out a book from a library. To specify IDs for different controls on the form, use Table 4-2 as a reference. You can check out Book 6, Chapter 3 for a ready reference for form designing.

Working with Validation Controls

User Name

Password

Confirm Password

Number of Books

Telephone Number

Member Card Number

Submit

[MessageLabel]

Figure 4-1: Begin with a sample form with several controls for user input.

Make sure that you are in the Design view of the form. In this view, notice that the label at the very bottom of the form (MessageLabel) is displayed in square brackets. Any control with Visible property set to False appears in square brackets (showing the ID) in the Design mode. Thus, the label appears with square brackets because the Visible property of this label is set to False. Note also that this label is kept invisible. Because this label is supposed to display a message when a user clicks the Submit button, it doesn't make sense to keep it visible at all times on the form. You can make the label visible only when you want to display a message. (Read the upcoming section "Using the RequiredFieldValidator Control" to discover how to display a Hello *User Name* message in your form.)

The more observant readers will also notice that the form contains two horizontal lines at the bottom. These are only for aesthetic purposes. Each horizontal line is actually a horizontal rule (<hr>) HTML control. You can place this control on the form from the HTML tab of the Toolbox. For more on the Toolbox, check out Book 6, Chapter 3.

Table 4-2 Sample Form Control IDs

Control	*Contains*	*ID*
TextBox	User Name	UserNameBox
TextBox	Password	PasswordBox
TextBox	Confirm Password	ConfirmBox
TextBox	Number of Books	BooksNumberBox
TextBox	Telephone Number	TelephoneBox
TextBox	Member Card Number	CardNumberBox
Button	Submit	SubmitButton
Label	Message	MessageLabel

After you create your form, you can start using different validation controls.

Using the RequiredFieldValidator Control

Use the RequiredFieldValidator control to check that the control being validated contains a value. For example, you'd use this control to make sure that a user entered essential information in a required text box, such as name or address. Before we get into the details of the properties of this control, here's how to add a RequiredFieldValidator control to the form (as shown in Figure 4-2). Add the RequiredFieldValidator control from the Web Forms tab of the Toolbox to the form.

Figure 4-2: Use this control to inform users that the field requires a value.

Validation controls aren't rendered on the page unless errors are encountered. Because validation controls are rendered only to display error messages, we recommend that you place validation controls at a position where you can find the source of error.

Set the properties of this control as listed in Table 4-3.

Table 4-3 Setting RequiredFieldValidator Control Properties

Property	*Value*
`ID`	`UserNameRequiredFieldValidator`
`ControlToValidate`	`UserNameBox`
`ErrorMessage`	`You must enter your user name.`
`Display`	`Dynamic`

When you add the `RequiredFieldValidator` control and set its properties, the corresponding ASP.NET code is automatically generated that you can see in the HTML view of the ASPX file. The following is an equivalent code for the `RequiredFieldValidator` control.

```
<asp:RequiredFieldValidator
id="UserNameRequiredFieldValidator" runat="server"
ControlToValidate="UserNameBox"
ErrorMessage="You must enter your user name."
Display="Dynamic">
</asp:RequiredFieldValidator>
```

Although you don't need to write the ASP.NET code for controls while working in Visual Studio .NET, it's good to know about it because you might sometimes need to develop ASP.NET applications using text editors (without the Visual Studio .NET IDE).

After setting the properties of the `RequiredFieldValidator` control, write the following code in the `Click` event of the Submit button.

```
Private Sub SubmitButton_Click(ByVal sender As System.Object,
   ByVal e As System.EventArgs) Handles SubmitButton.Click

        'Checking the IsValid property of the page to
        identify if all validation tests were successful
        If Page.IsValid = True Then
           'Setting a message to be displayed on the label
            MessageLabel.Text = "Hello " + UserNameBox.Text
            'Making the label visible
            MessageLabel.Visible = True
        End If

End Sub
```

After you finish coding, execute the application. Initially, you'll notice that the `RequiredFieldValidator` control isn't rendered on the page. When you click the Submit button without entering any value in the User Name text box, an error message displays — `You must enter your name.` — as shown in Figure 4-3.

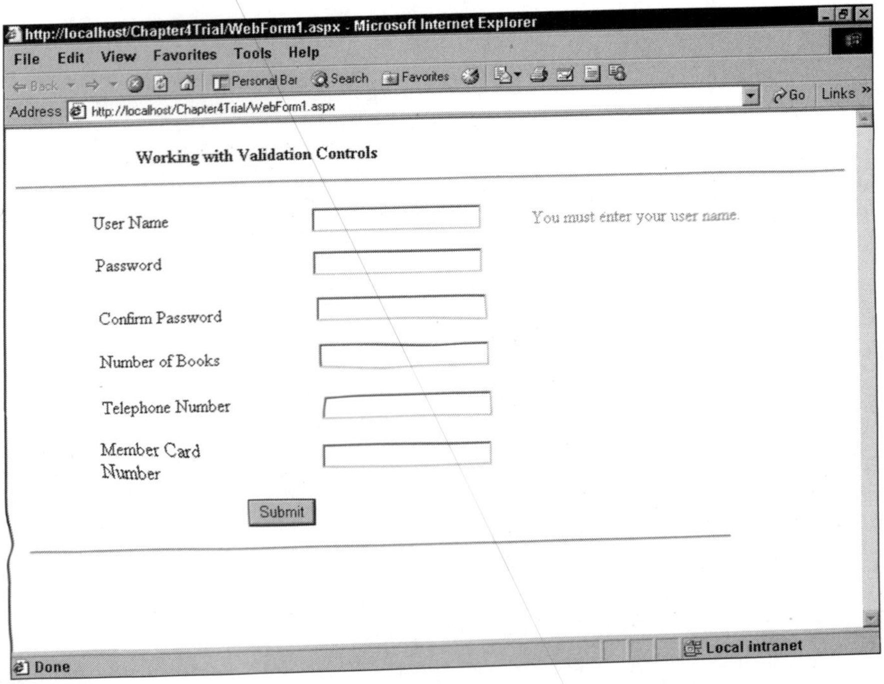

Figure 4-3: An error message displays when a validation test for a required field fails.

Now enter your name in the User Name box and click the Submit button. The server code in the `Click` event of the Submit button runs perfectly without displaying any error message — but you should see a `Hello` message. (See Figure 4-4.)

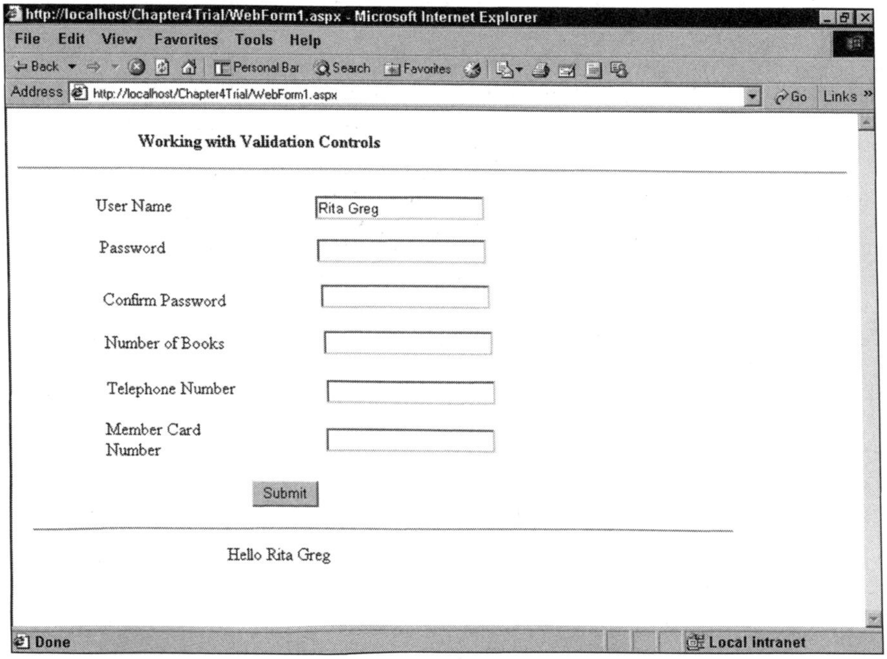

Figure 4-4: Your sample form says "Hello" when this validation test is successful.

Apart from `Id` and `Runat` properties, which are common to all the controls, the most commonly used properties of the `RequiredFieldValidator` control are `ErrorMessage`, `ControlToValidate`, and `Display`. You're probably already familiar with `Id` and `Runat` properties. The `Id` property is used to specify a unique identifier for a control. The `Runat` property is set to `server` to specify that the control runs at the server side. The `ErrorMessage` property is used to get or set the text for error message. Two properties, `ControlToValidate` and `Display`, need a detailed description.

- `ControlToValidate`: Set this property to the ID of the control that you want to get validated. In the previous example, you'd set this property to `UserNameBox`, which is the ID of the `TextBox` control meant to accept the user name.

- `Display`: Set this property to one of the following values to specify the display behavior of the control:
  - `Static`: This is the default value for the `Display` property. A `Static` value indicates that the error message is displayed inline when the validation fails and the validator is a part of the page layout. Because a `Static` value makes the validator a part of the page layout, the layout of the page doesn't change when the validator is visible. Also, if multiple validators are associated with a control, all the validators must be placed at different physical locations.
  - `Dynamic`: A `Dynamic` value indicates that the error message is displayed inline if the validation fails and the validator doesn't always remain as part of the page layout. The validator is a part of the page layout only when it displays the error message. This display behavior enables you to add multiple validators to be placed at the same physical location.
  - `None`: This value indicates that the error message is never displayed inline. You use this value when you don't want to display individual error messages but rather display error messages as a summary by using the `ValidationSummary` control.

Using the CompareValidator Control

Use the CompareValidator control to compare the value entered in a control with the value in another control or to a specific value. You can compare the two values by using any operator available with the control. Some of these operators include `Equal`, `NotEqual`, `GreaterThan`, and `LessThan`. Also, you can compare values of different types, such as `String`, `Integer`, `Double`, `Date`, and `Currency`. By default, the `CompareValidator` control compares string values for equality. In Table 4-4, we describe some of the properties of the `CompareValidator` control.

Table 4-4 Properties of the CompareValidator Control

Property	*Description*
`ControlToValidate`	Gets or sets the ID of the control with the value of which you want to validate.
`ControlToCompare`	Gets or sets the ID of the control with the value of which you want to compare.
`ValueToCompare`	Gets or sets a specific value of which you want to compare.
`Type`	Is the data type of the value with which you want to compare. This property can be `String`, `Integer`, `Currency`, `Date`, or `Double`. The default value is `String`.

Property	*Description*
`Operator`	Is the operator for the comparison. It can be `Equal`, `NotEqual`, `LessThan`, or `GreaterThan`. The default value is `Equal`.
`ErrorMessage`	Gets or sets the text for the error message.
`Display`	Gets or sets one of the values — `Static`, `Dynamic`, or `None`. This property value decides the display behavior of the validator. The default value is `Static`.

Implement the `CompareValidator` control in the `BookIssue` form that we design in the earlier section "Introducing Validation Controls." In this form (refer back to Figure 4-1), we compare the value entered in the Password textbox with the value entered in the Confirm Password box. To implement this, add the `CompareValidator` control to the form, as shown in Figure 4-5.

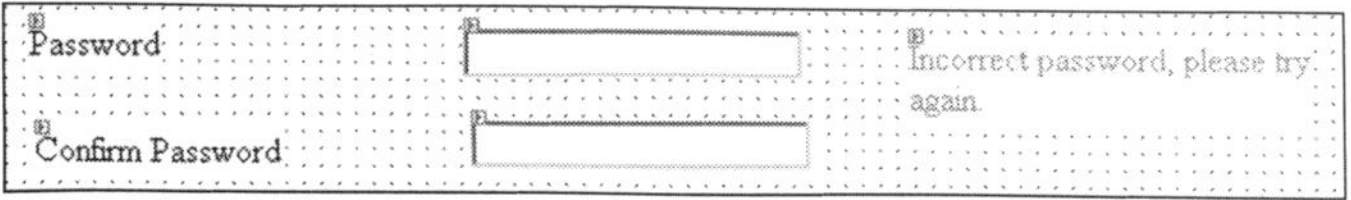

Figure 4-5: A Compare-Validator control on the sample form.

Set the properties of the `CompareValidator` control as listed in Table 4-5.

Table 4-5 Setting CompareValidator Control Properties

Property	*Value*
`ID`	`PasswordCompareValidator`
`ControlToValidate`	`ConfirmBox`
`ControlToCompare`	`PasswordBox`
`ErrorMessage`	`Incorrect password, please try again.`
`Display`	`Dynamic`

You can also write an equivalent ASP.NET code to add the `CompareValidator` control. Here's the equivalent code:

```
<asp:CompareValidator
id = "PasswordCompareValidator" runat = "server"
ControlToCompare = "PasswordBox"
ControlToValidate = "ConfirmBox"
ErrorMessage = "Incorrect password, please try again."
Display = "Dynamic">
</asp:CompareValidator>
```

Next, edit the code in the Click event of the Submit button:

```
Private Sub SubmitButton_Click(ByVal sender As System.Object,
    ByVal e As System.EventArgs) Handles SubmitButton.Click

        'Checking the IsValid property of the page to
        identify if all validation tests were successful
        If Page.IsValid = True Then
            'Setting a message to be displayed on the label
            MessageLabel.Text = "Hello " + UserNameBox.Text +
           ", You are authorized to use the library services."
            'Making the label visible
            MessageLabel.Visible = True
        End If

End Sub
```

Execute the application. Enter your user name and click the Submit button without entering any value in the Password and Confirm Password text boxes. Hmmm . . . no error message displays. Because you didn't enter any value in either password box, the CompareValidator control compared blank values. This wouldn't happen if you made the password text boxes as required fields by using the RequiredFieldValidator control. If you've just gotta know right now how to correct this, skip down to the final section of this chapter ("Using Multiple Validation Controls") to read about implementing multiple validation controls.

Next, enter different passwords in the Password and Confirm Password text boxes and click the Submit button. Notice that the error is displayed on the page, as shown in Figure 4-6.

Enter the same passwords in the Password and Confirm Password text boxes and click the Submit button. Because both the values match, the page doesn't show the error message. Instead, the page displays a message — Hello *User Name*. You are authorized to use the library services. — as shown in Figure 4-7. (*User Name* is the name entered in the User Name textbox.) You can find the code to create this MessageLabel in the previous code block.

The previous example compared the value entered in a control with a string value in another control for equality. In addition, if you want to compare the value entered in a control with a specific value, use the ValueToCompare property instead of the ControlToCompare property. Also, you can use different data types and operators for comparison.

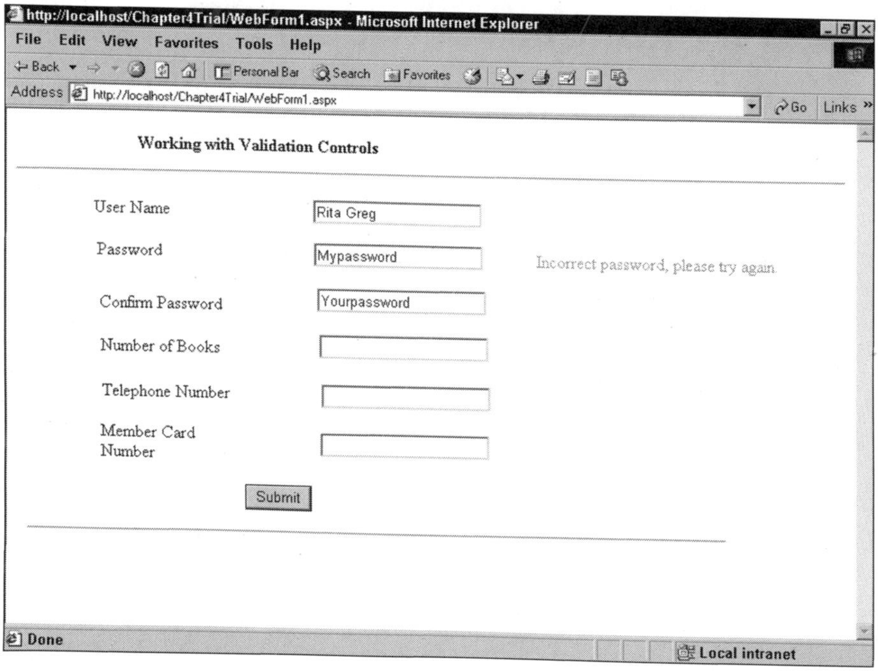
http://localhost/Chapter4Trial/WebForm1.aspx - Microsoft Internet Explorer
File Edit View Favorites Tools Help
Back Personal Bar Search Favorites
Address http://localhost/Chapter4Trial/WebForm1.aspx
Go Links
Working with Validation Controls
User Name
Rita Greg
Password
Mypassword
Incorrect password, please try again.
Confirm Password
Yourpassword
Number of Books
Telephone Number
Member Card Number
Submit
Done
Local intranet

Figure 4-6: Your sample form displays an error message when the validation test fails.

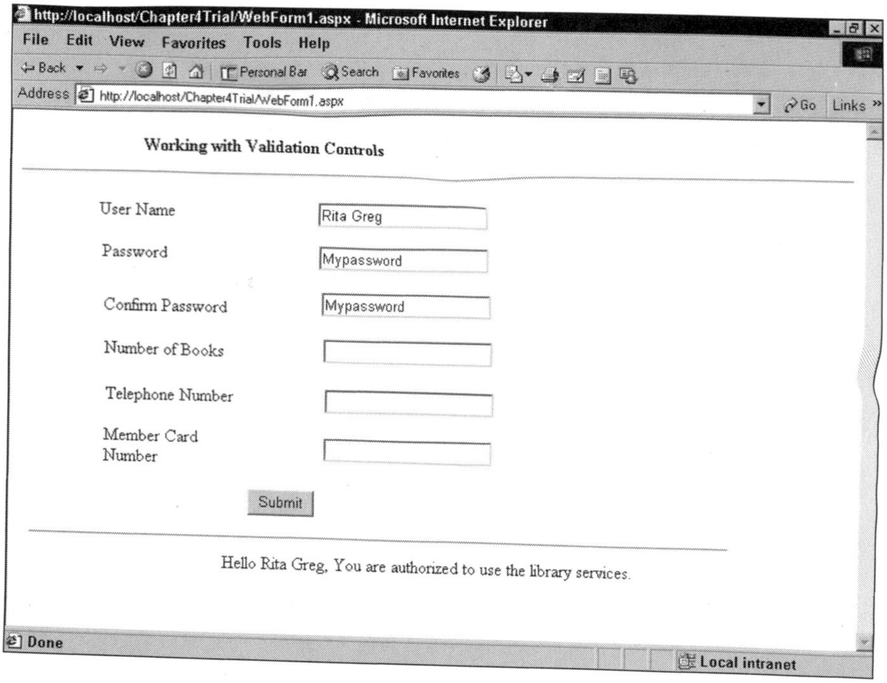
http://localhost/Chapter4Trial/WebForm1.aspx - Microsoft Internet Explorer
File Edit View Favorites Tools Help
Back Personal Bar Search Favorites
Address http://localhost/Chapter4Trial/WebForm1.aspx
Go Links
Working with Validation Controls
User Name
Rita Greg
Password
Mypassword
Confirm Password
Mypassword
Number of Books
Telephone Number
Member Card Number
Submit
Hello Rita Greg, You are authorized to use the library services.
Done
Local intranet

Figure 4-7: Success! Your user validation test works!

Using the RangeValidator Control

Use the RangeValidator control to validate a control to check whether the value falls within a specified range of values. The range is specified by setting maximum and minimum values, which can be constant values or values from other controls.

In addition to the `ControlToValidate`, `ErrorMessage`, and `Display` properties (read about these in the previous section), the `RangeValidator` control has multiple other properties, including

- `MaximumValue`: Gets or sets the upper limit value of the validation range.
- `MinimumValue`: Gets or sets the lower limit value of the validation range.
- `Type`: Gets or sets the data type of the values that are compared. The data type can be `String`, `Integer`, `Double`, `Date`, or `Currency`. The default data type used for comparison is `String`.

After you get the hang of using the `RangeValidator` control, you need to implement the range validation in our `BookIssue` form. (Refer to Figure 4-1 for the form design.) In our running example, we validate the `Number of Books` text box that accepts the number of books. Because the library doesn't allow more than four books to be checked out by one person, we specify the range between one and four.

You add the `RangeValidator` control on the `BookIssue` form, as shown in Figure 4-8. Set the properties of the control as listed in Table 4-6.

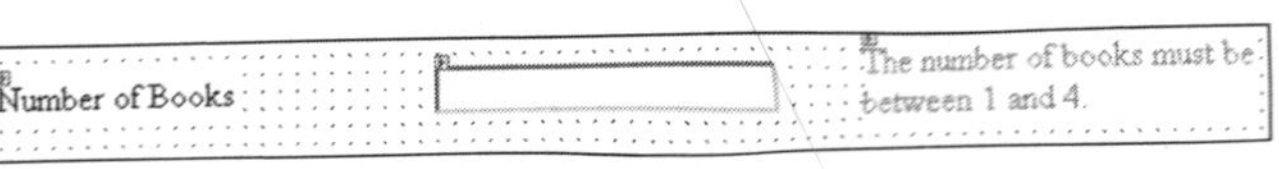
Number of Books
The number of books must be between 1 and 4.

Figure 4-8: Set a book loan amount control on your sample form.

Table 4-6 Setting RangeValidator Control Properties

Property	*Value*
`ID`	`BooksNumberRangeValidator`
`ControlToValidate`	`BooksNumberBox`
`MaximumValue`	`4`
`MinimumValue`	`1`
`Type`	`Integer`

Property	*Value*
`ErrorMessage`	`The number of books must be between 1 and 4.`
`Display`	`Dynamic`

The equivalent ASP.NET code for the `RangeValidator` control is

```
<asp:RangeValidator
id="BooksNumberRangeValidator runat="server"
ControlToValidate="BooksNumberBox"
MaximumValue="4"
MinimumValue="1"
Type="Integer"
ErrorMessage="The number of books must be between 1 and 4."
Display="Dynamic">
</asp:RangeValidator>
```

When you run the application, enter your user name, password (remember to enter the same password in the Password and Confirm Password text boxes), and number of books (outside the range 1–4, say 0 or 5), and then click the Submit button. The page displays the intended output — an error message for the range validation (`The number of books must be between 1 and 4.`). The output is shown in Figure 4-9.

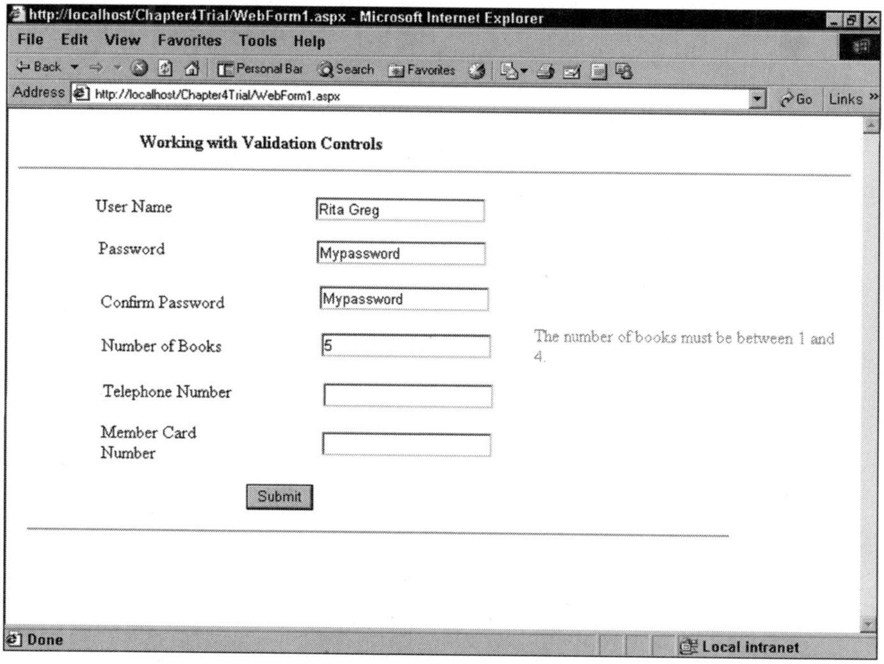

Figure 4-9: Your sample form displays an error message when the range validation test fails.

This time, enter the number of books in the specified range text box (Number of Books) — say 2 — and click the Submit button. Because the value falls in the range (1–4), the range validation is successful and no error message displays.

Using the RegularExpressionValidator Control

Use the `RegularExpressionValidator` control to validate a value entered in a control against some pattern of a regular expression. This regular expression validation is very useful to validate certain data, such as telephone numbers, zip codes, social security numbers, and e-mail addresses.

If you're not familiar with the `ControlToValidate`, `ErrorMessage`, and `Display` properties, read the earlier section "Using the RequiredFieldValidator Control." In addition to these properties, the `RegularExpressionValidator` control has one property for validating user input data against some pattern of a regular expression. This property, `ValidationExpression`, requires a detailed explanation.

Use the `ValidationExpression` property to get or set a regular expression for validation. The validator uses the pattern identified by this regular expression as a criterion for validation. You can either use the standard patterns, such as U.S. Phone Number, available with this property, or add your own pattern. If the value entered in the control being validated matches the regular expression pattern, the validation test is successful. If not, the validation test fails.

In our running example form, we now implement a `RegularExpressionValidator` control in the `BookIssue` form. We implement the regular expression validation for the Telephone Number text box that accepts the user telephone number. This number must be validated against a fixed pattern of US telephone numbers: a three-digit area code, a three-digit prefix, and the remaining four numbers. Additionally, the different parts of the telephone number must be separated by hyphens.

Add the `RegularExpressionValidator` control to the `BookIssue` form as shown in Figure 4-10. Set the control's properties as listed in Table 4-7.

Telephone Number:
Invalid telephone number, please try again.

Figure 4-10: Validate a phone number on your sample form.

Table 4-7 Setting RegularExpressionValidator Control Properties

Property	*Value*
ID	TelephoneRegularExpressionValidator
ControlToValidate	TelephoneBox
ValidationExpression	[0-9]{3}-[0-9]{3}\s[0-9]{4}
ErrorMessage	Invalid telephone number, please try again.
Display	Dynamic

The equivalent ASP.NET code for the RegularExpressionValidator control is

```
<asp:RegularExpressionValidator
id="TelephoneRegularExpressionValidator runat="server"
ControlToValidate="TelephoneBox"
ValidationExpression="[0-9]{3}-[0-9]{3}\s[0-9]{4}"
ErrorMessage="Invalid telephone number, please try again."
Display="Dynamic">
</asp:RegularExpressionValidator>
```


The value [0-9]{3}-[0-9]{3}\s[0-9]{4}, which we specify to the ValidationExpression property, bears further explanation. To break down this value:

- In the first part, **[0-9]{3}-:** [0-9] represents any digit between 0 and 9. {3} means that three digits are required for the [0-9] sequence. The hyphen (-) between 0 and 9 means that a hyphen is required. Thus, this sequence means that the first three digits, followed by a hyphen, are required with each digit in the range 0–9. This represents an area code in a standard US telephone number.
- In the middle part, **[0-9]{3}\s:** \s means a space is required. Thus, this sequence means that the second cluster of three digits, followed by a space, are required with each digit in the range 0–9. This represents the prefix in a standard US telephone number.
- In the final part, **[0-9]{4}:** This pattern dictates a four-digit number with each digit in the range 0–9. (Hope you identified this pattern even before reading the explanation). This represents the last four numbers in a standard US telephone number.

After you set RegularExpressionValidator control in the BookIssue form for the Telephone Number text box, execute the application. When the page is visible in the browser, enter your user name, password (enter the same value in the Password and Confirm Password boxes to avoid comparison validation error), and number of books (enter a value between 1– 4 to avoid range validation error). Then, enter a telephone number that doesn't match the specified regular expression pattern (intentionally for testing purposes) — say 5692354685 — and click the Submit button. Because the telephone number doesn't match the regular expression pattern (no separating hyphens), the page displays an error message as shown in Figure 4-11.

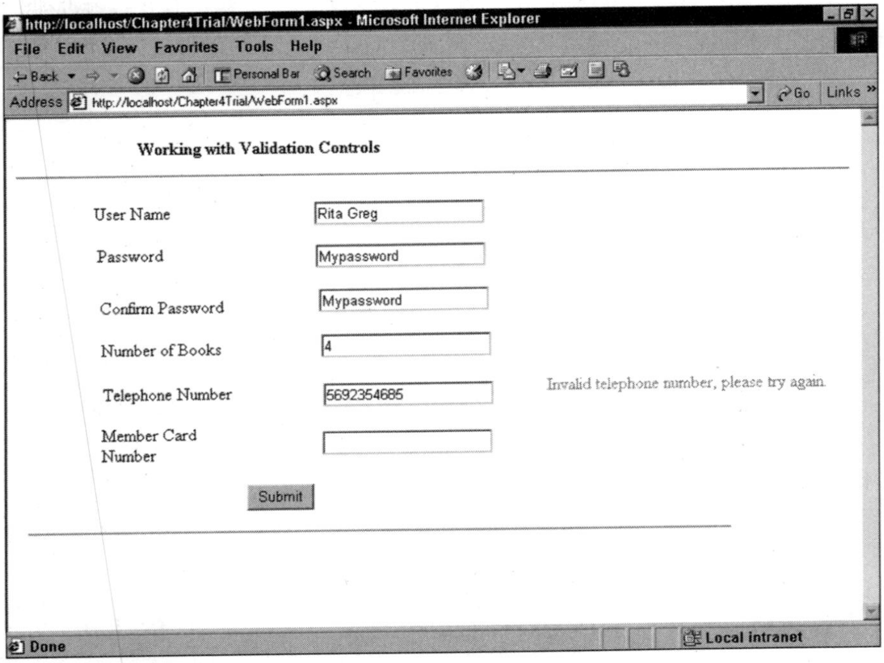

Figure 4-11: You just failed your phone number test.

Now, enter a valid telephone number — say 317-555-4856. This entry does match the specified regular expression because it includes hyphens. Then click the Submit button. Your sample shouldn't show an error message.

Using the CustomValidator Control

Using the `CustomValidator` control enables you to validate a value entered in a control being validated by using a user-defined function. Sometimes none of the validators that we have discussed earlier in this chapter fit your needs. For example, if you want to validate a control to ensure that the control accepts only prime numbers, you can't do so without writing a code for the same. In such situations, the `CustomValidator` controls come in handy.

With the `CustomValidator` control, you can use validation functions at the client side as well as the server side. In addition to several other properties, the `CustomValidator` control has these properties: `ControlToValidate`, `ErrorMessage`, and `Display` — just like the validation controls discussed so far. Additionally, the `CustomValidator` control has a property called `ClientValidationFunction`, which requires detailed description.

Use the `ClientValidationFunction` property to get or set the client script function. This function is called automatically to validate the control that's associated with the validator. You can use any scripting language, such as JavaScript or VBScript, to write the client script function.

The client script functions run in the target browsers. Therefore, the functions must be written in a scripting language supported by the target browsers.

In addition to the client-side validation, the `CustomValidator` control raises an event — `ServerValidate` — for server-side validation. To implement server-side validation, you must write code in the event handler for this control. To do so, you can use either the code-behind file or the HTML view of the ASPX file of the form.

Time to implement the `CustomValidator` control in your `BookIssue` form. You use this validator to validate the Member Card Number text box. Although this is a simple example for custom validation, you'll get a good idea of how to use the `CustomValidator` control in other, more complex applications.

Add the `CustomValidator` control to the `BookIssue` form, as shown in Figure 4-12. Set the properties for the control as listed in Table 4-8.

Member Card Number | Invalid card number, please try again.

Figure 4-12: Set a custom validation control on your sample form.

Table 4-8 Setting CustomValidator Control Properties

Property	*Value*
ID	CardNumberCustomValidator
ControlToValidate	CardNumberBox
ClientValidationFunction	ClientIsCardValid
ErrorMessage	Invalid card number, please try again.
Display	Dynamic

The equivalent ASP.NET code for the CustomValidator control is

```
<asp:CustomValidator
id="CustomValidator1" runat="server"
ControlToValidate="CardNumberBox"
ErrorMessage="Invalid card number, please try again."
ClientValidationFunction="ClientIsCardValid"
Display="Dynamic">
</asp:CustomValidator>
```

The ClientValidationFunction property is set to ClientIsCardValid, which is the name of the client script function. This function gets invoked when the TextBox control with ID CardNumberBox is validated in the target browser. We write this function using VBScript. Thus, write the following validation code in the ASPX file of your BookIssue form:

```
<script language="vbscript">
   Sub ClientIsCardValid(source,arguments)
     if(arguments.Value)="KBL77777" Then
       arguments.IsValid=true
     Else
       arguments.IsValid=false
     End If
   End Sub
</script>
```

The ClientIsCardValid function takes two parameters:

✦ source is the control *being* validated. This parameter seeks the control ID from the ControlToValidate property of the CustomValidator control.

✦ arguments is the actual information about the value entered in the control being validated. The Value property of this parameter is used to access the actual value entered in the control. You use the IsValid property of the arguments parameter to return the result of validation. The fact that the custom validation test is successful or not depends on the value of the IsValid property. If the IsValid property returns true, the validation test succeeds. Otherwise, the validation test fails and the page displays the error message set in the ErrorMessage property of the CustomValidator control.

Thus, in the preceding function, the value entered in the TextBox control with the ID CardNumberBox is matched against a value. If the values match, the IsValid property is set to true. Otherwise, the IsValid property is set to false. If the IsValid property returns true, the validation test at the client side succeeds. If not, the validation test fails.

As we mention earlier in this section, you can implement server-side validation by handling the ServerValidate event of the CustomValidator control. If you want to use the code-behind file to handle the ServerValidate event, you simply need to select the CustomValidator control — in this case, select CardNumberCustomValidator — from the Class Name list and ServerValidate from the Method Name list. Then, write the validation code in this event handler as follows:

```
Private Sub CardNumberCustomValidator_ServerValidate(ByVal
          source As Object, ByVal args As
          System.Web.UI.WebControls.
          ServerValidateEventArgs) Handles
          CardNumberCustomValidator.ServerValidate
        If args.Value = "KBL77777" Then
           args.IsValid = True
        Else
           args.IsValid = False
        End If
End Sub
```

If you prefer to use the ASPX file, you can write the event handler (such as ServerIsCardValid) for the ServerValidate event within the <Script> tag. However, writing the event handler won't call it until you edit the ASP.NET code of the CustomValidator control to include OnServerValidate = "ServerIsCardValid".

After you complete coding to implement custom validation for the TextBox control with ID CardNumberBox, you must edit the code in the Click event of the Submit button to display a message to the user that the books have been issued. Although this isn't a required step to demonstrate the custom validation, we perform this step for the sake of completeness of the application. So, edit the code in the event handler of the Click event of Submit button as follows:

```
Private Sub SubmitButton_Click(ByVal sender As System.Object,
    ByVal e As System.EventArgs) Handles SubmitButton.Click

        'Checking the IsValid property of the page to identify
          if all validation tests were successful
        If Page.IsValid = True Then
            'Setting a message to be displayed on the label
             MessageLabel.Text = "Thank you, " +
           UserNameBox.Text + ". Your books have been issued."
             'Making the label visible
             MessageLabel.Visible = True
        End If

End Sub
```

Execute the application to test how the custom validation works. When the page is displayed in the browser, enter valid data in all the text boxes except for the text box that accepts the Member Card Number. In this text box, enter an invalid value — say KBL55555 — and click the Submit button. The page displays the error message `Invalid card number, please try again`, as shown in Figure 4-13.

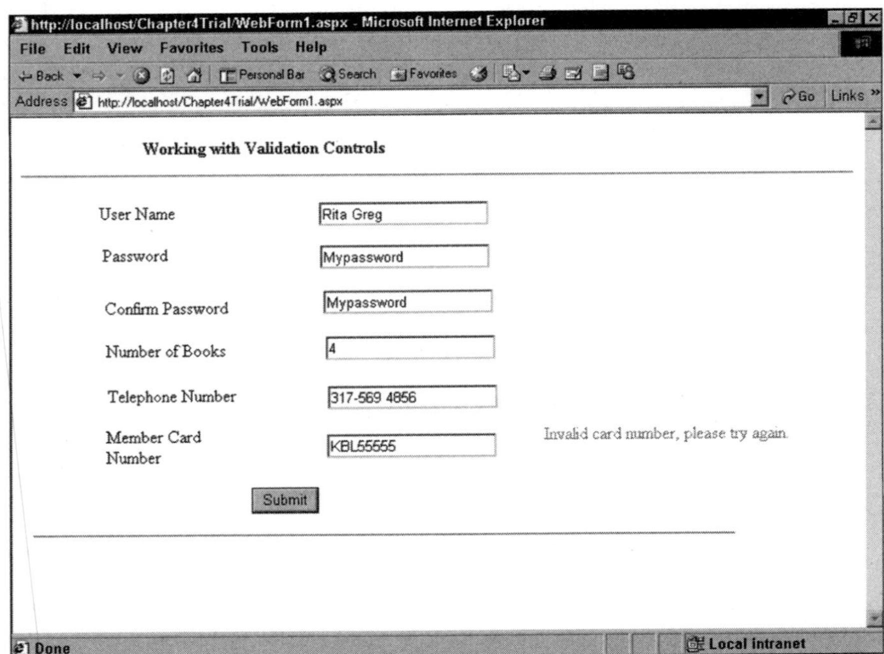

Figure 4-13: You just flunked your credit card number test.

This time, enter valid values in all the boxes and click the Submit button. (A valid value for the Member card Number text box is KBL77777.) Now the page doesn't display an error message. Instead, it displays the message `Thank you, User Name. Your books have been issued.`, as shown in Figure 4-14.

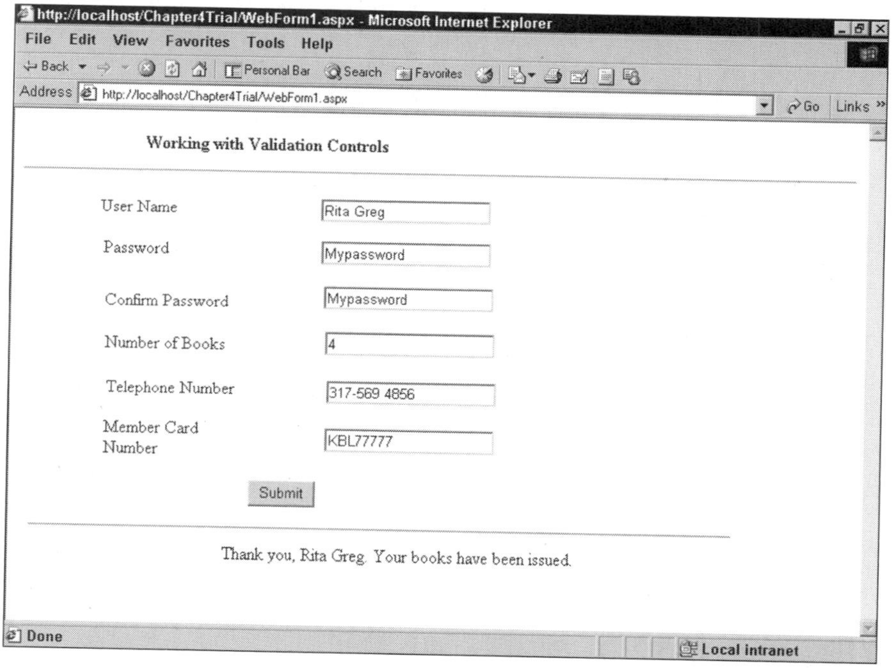

Figure 4-14: Houston, we have a valid credit card.

Using the ValidationSummary Control

Use the `ValidationSummary` control to display all the validation errors in the page in a summary format. You can display the summary of errors in a list, bulleted list, or paragraph format. Also, this control provides you an option to display the summary of errors inline and/or as a pop-up message box.

Before we delve into the implementation part, look at the properties of this control. Table 4-9 lists some of the properties of the `ValidationSummary` control.

Table 4-9	ValidationSummary Control Properties
Property	*Description*
`HeaderText`	Gets or sets the text to be displayed at the top of the validation summary.
`DisplayMode`	Gets or sets the display mode of the validation summary. This property can take one of the three values: `List`, `BulletList`, or `SingleParagraph`. The default value is `BulletList`.
`ShowSummary`	Gets or sets a Boolean value indicating whether the validation summary is displayed inline. The default value is `True`.
`ShowSummaryBox`	Gets or sets a Boolean value indicating whether the validation summary is displayed as a pop-up message box. The default value is `False`.

Add the `ValidationSummary` control to the `BookIssue` form as shown in Figure 4-15. Set the `HeaderText` property to `The following errors were encountered:`.

Figure 4-15: Setting validation errors to display in summary format.

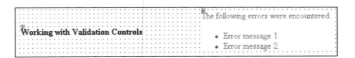

The equivalent ASP.NET code for the `ValidationSummary` control is

```
<asp:ValidationSummary
id="ValidationSummary1" runat="server"
HeaderText="The following errors were encountered">
</asp:ValidationSummary>
```

To display the validation summary as a pop-up message box, set the `ShowSummaryBox` property to `True`. You can alter `DisplayMode` from the default (`BulletList`) to any other mode. Then assign the values to these properties depending on your preferences.

Displaying a validation summary doesn't dictate that the individual error messages of other validators on the page won't show. If you want to display only the validation summary (without those individual errors), set the `Display` property of all the validators on the page to `None`.

Execute the application, enter invalid data in any of the form's text box controls, and click the Submit button. The page displays an inline validation summary, as shown in Figure 4-16.

http://localhost/Chapter4Trial/WebForm1.aspx - Microsoft Internet Explorer

The following errors were encountered:

Working with Validation Controls

- Invalid telephone number, please try again.
- Invalid card number, please try again.

User Name: Rita Greg

Password: Mypassword

Confirm Password: Mypassword

Number of Books: 4

Telephone Number: 3124565678 — Invalid telephone number, please try again.

Member Card Number: KBL55555 — Invalid card number, please try again.

Submit

Done — Local intranet

Figure 4-16: Set your form to display a summary when any validation test fails.

Using Multiple Validation Controls

In earlier sections of this chapter, we discuss how to use each validation control in isolation. For some applications, however, you may require a control for multiple conditions. For example, you may want to test a control's value to be within a specific range. Concurrently, you may also require that the control's value pass a custom validation test. Testing multiple conditions for a control's value requires that you associate multiple validation controls to a single control.

Most commonly, you use the `RequiredFieldValidator` control with other validation controls. For example, consider the example of our running example `BookIssue` form. If you don't enter any value in the two password boxes and then click the Submit button, the comparison validation test does not fail. To avoid such situations, you must use the `RequiredFieldValidator` control along with the `CompareValidator` control.

Using multiple validation controls for the same control is very simple: Just add all the validation controls that you want to associate with a control to the form. Then, set the `ControlToValidate` property of all the validation controls to the ID of the control being validated.

To understand this better, use the `RequiredFieldValidator` along with the `CompareValidator` control and associate it with the text box that accepts the password.

Add another `RequiredFieldValidator` control to the form as shown in Figure 4-17. Set the properties of this control as listed in Table 4-10.

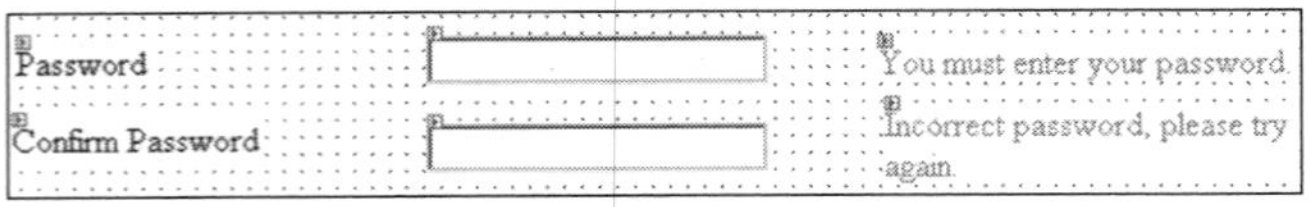

Figure 4-17: You can set multiple required controls on the sample form.

Table 4-10 Setting Properties of a Second RequireFieldValidator Control

Property	*Value*
`ID`	`PasswordRequiredFieldValidator`
`ControlToValidate`	`ConfirmBox`
`ErrorMessage`	`You must enter your password.`
`Display`	`Dynamic`

After you execute the application, enter the data as shown in Figure 4-18, and click the Submit button, the page displays the error message `You must enter your password.`

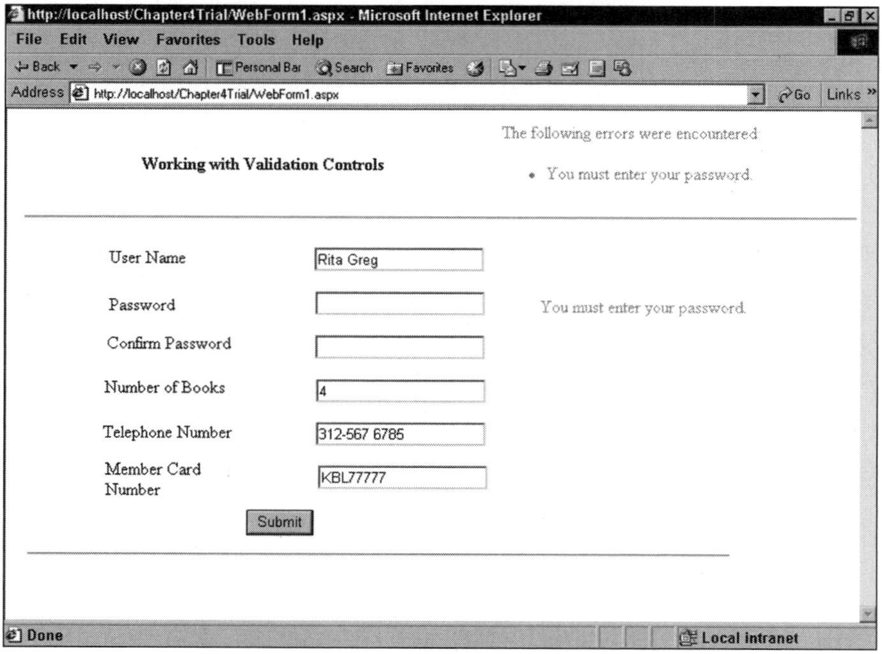

Figure 4-18: Your sample form displays an error message when a second control is invalidated.

Chapter 5: Developing ASP.NET Server Controls

In This Chapter

- ✔ **Developing ASP.NET server controls**
- ✔ **Creating and using Web user controls**
- ✔ **Converting ASP.NET pages to Web user controls**
- ✔ **Creating and using composite controls**

Apart from its built-in Web server controls, Visual Studio .NET has lots more features and tools in store. Use the tools here to develop your own server controls — and in turn, develop applications with greater flexibility.

In this chapter, we build on the elementary requirements for developing ASP.NET server controls. Visual Studio .NET provides templates that you can use to develop server controls with much ease and flexibility. We focus on two types of controls: Web user controls and composite controls. We discuss how to create and use both these types of server controls.

Developing ASP.NET Server Controls

Although ASP.NET does provide you with a rich set of intrinsic Web controls, you'll probably find times when you want or need to develop your own server controls. For example:

- **Recycling:** When you want to reuse the user interface of a Web Forms page in other Web pages.
- **Efficiency:** When you want to combine the functionality of existing server controls, such as `Button` and `TextBox` controls, in your Web pages.
- **Flexibility:** When you want to adapt existing server controls to fit your needs. (You can extend the functionality of an existing server control that fulfills most of your requirements by inheriting from it and overriding its properties, methods, and events.)
- **Customization:** When no existing control fulfills your requirements. (Develop your own control by inheriting from a base control class.)

The primary two types of server controls that you can develop with Visual Studio .NET are

- **Web user control:** This control is a Web Forms page that you can use in other pages. User controls are created using a technique similar to that for creating Web Forms pages (form-based Web pages). You'll need to create Web user controls whenever you need to reuse a Web Forms page in other Web pages. For a detailed coverage of creating Web Forms pages, check out Book 6, Chapter 3.

  Unlike in Web Forms pages, however, you can't call user controls independently. User controls function only when you include them in Web Forms pages.

- **Composite control:** This control is composed of several existing controls that are used as a single control. You can create composite controls by using class composition. When you need to include two or more than two functionalities in a single control, create composite controls. For more on classes, check out Book 3, Chapter 8 and Book 5, Chapter 4.

As a side-by-side comparison, take a look at the dissimilar features of user and composite controls. Table 5-1 lists some of the key differences between these two controls.

Table 5-1 Comparing User Controls and Composite Controls

User Controls	*Composite Controls*
Developing user controls is similar to developing Web Forms pages. Use either ASP.NET syntax or the code-behind file (the file that contains the page logic).	Develop composite controls programmatically by using class composition. Use any .NET-supported programming language, such as Visual Basic .NET or C#.
Complete design-time support is available for developing user controls.	Minimal design-time support is available for developing composite controls.
User controls are stored as text files with an `.ascx` extension.	Composite controls are compiled and stored as assemblies (`.dll`).

Creating and Using Web User Controls

Creating a user control is very similar to creating a Web Forms page. In this section, we walk you through creating a user control that resembles a login form. This control validates the values entered for user name and password against specific values to check for user authorization. See what a basic user control looks like in Figure 5-1.

Login Form
User Name
Password
Validate

Figure 5-1: A basic user control to validate a user log-on.

Creating a Web user control

Creating a Web user control involves designing a user interface and defining the properties, methods, and events of the control.

Designing the user interface

To design the user interface of a Web user control as shown in Figure 5-1, carry out the following steps:

1. **Create an ASP.NET Web Application project by using either Visual Basic .NET or C#.**

   In this case, create a Visual Basic ASP.NET Web Application project. Check out Book 6, Chapter 2 to revise how to create a Web Application project.

2. **In the Name text box, enter** UserControlDemo **as the name of your project.**

3. **Add a Web User Control item by selecting Project⇨Add New Item.**

   The Add New Item - UserControlDemo dialog box displays.

   Alternatively, press Ctrl+Shift+A to open the Add New Item dialog box.

4. **In the Templates pane (right side), select the Web User Control icon and then enter** LoginControl.ascx **in the Name text box to name the control.**

   You may have to scroll down to locate this icon.

   At this stage, the Add New Item dialog box should look as shown in Figure 5-2. Check out the new name's extension (`.ascx`); ASCX files are user control files.

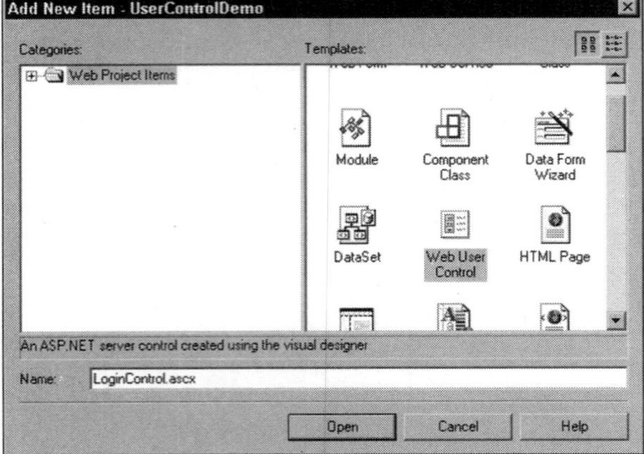

Figure 5-2: Create a Web User control from the Add New Item dialog box.

5. **Click the Open button to open the user control file in the designer window.**

   Here you graphically design the user interface for your user control by using the Toolbox. For more on Toolbox, check out Book 6, Chapter 3.

   - Unlike Web Forms pages, the default layout of a user control is flow layout: That is, when you position controls in this layout, the controls are arranged from top to bottom. You'll modify this newly added Web user control.
   - To position controls accurately, you need to add a Grid Layout Panel control by using the HTML tab of the Toolbox. Then, you can add and place controls within this Grid Layout Panel control.

6. **Design the user interface of your user control as shown in Figure 5-1 and then set the properties of the controls as listed in Table 5-2.**

Table 5-2 Control Properties Used in the User Control

Control	*Contains*	*Property*	*Value*
`Label`	Login Form	`Text`	`Login Form`
		`Font.Bold`	`True`
`Label`	User Name	`Text`	`User Name`
		`Font.Bold`	`True`
`Label`	Password	`Text`	`Password`
		`Font.Bold`	`True`
`TextBox`	User Name	`ID`	`UserNameBox`

Control	Contains	Property	Value
TextBox	Password	ID	PasswordBox
		TextMode	Password
Button	Validate	Text	Validate
		ID	ValidateButton
		Font.Bold	True

That's all there is to designing a user interface for your user control. We love how easy ASP.NET makes designing a user control.

Before we proceed, take a look at the HyperText Markup Language (HTML) code that's generated automatically for the user interface that you design in the above step for your user control.

Switch to the HTML view by clicking the HTML button at the bottom of the designer window. Note that some of the elements usually present in an ASPX file — `<Html>`, `<Head>`, `<Body>`, and `<Form>` — are missing. The HTML code simply contains elements that render the user interface for the user control. In addition to these elements, the HTML view contains the `@Control` directive in the beginning of the code.

```
<%@ Control Language="vb" AutoEventWireup="false"
          Codebehind="LoginControl.ascx.vb"
          Inherits="UserControlDemo.LoginControl" %>
```

The `@ Control` directive indicates that the file is a user control file. For the skinny on the attributes in this snippet, read Book 6, Chapter 2.

Adding properties

After you design a user interface for your user control, add properties to the control. You can add properties to either the ASCX file or the code-behind file of the user control. You can choose any of these ways to add properties — the choice is yours depending on your preferences. Remember, in ASCX file, you need to write the entire code within the `<script>` tag. In our running example, we use the code-behind file and add two properties: `UserName` and `Password`.

Press the F7 key to open the code-behind file (look for the `.ascx.vb` extension) of the user control. Write the following code to create the `UserName` and `Password` properties.

```
'Adding the UserName property
Property UserName() As String
   Get
     Return UserNameBox.Text
```

```
    End Get
    Set(ByVal Value As String)
      UserNameBox.Text = Value
    End Set
End Property
'Adding the Password property
Property Password() As String
    Get
      Return PasswordBox.Text
    End Get
    Set(ByVal Value As String)
      PasswordBox.Text = Value
    End Set
End Property
```

After you add these two properties, you can read (get) or write (set) these properties when you use the user control in a Web Forms page.

The properties that you create in the above code are read-write properties. To add properties that are *read*-only, use only the `Get` accessor. To add a *write*-only property, use only the `Set` accessor.

Adding properties simply requires that you write the corresponding code within the user control class. Similarly, you can write the code to add methods to the user control.

Exposing events

If you want your user control to respond to certain events when used in a Web Forms page, you need to *expose* the events of the user control. For the user control that you design in the earlier section "Designing the user interface," expose the `Click` event of the Validate button.

1. **Write the event declaration code in the declaration section where other controls are declared.**

   Write the following statement to declare the `VaidateClick` event:

```
Public Event ValidateClick()
```

All Web controls are declared using the `WithEvents` keyword.

2. **In the Code Editor, in the Class Name list, select `ValidateButton`; in the Method Name list, select `Click`.**

   The event handler for the `Click` event of the `Button` control with ID `ValidateButton` displays in the Code editor.

```
Private Sub ValidateButton_Click(ByVal sender As Object,
    ByVal e As System.EventArgs) Handles
    ValidateButton.Click
End Sub
```

3. **In the event handler, write the code to raise the `ValidateClick` event.**

```
Private Sub ValidateButton_Click(ByVal sender As Object,
    ByVal e As System.EventArgs) Handles
    ValidateButton.Click
          RaiseEvent ValidateClick()
End Sub
```

The preceding code indicates that each time a user clicks the Validate button of the user control, the control raises the `ValidateClick` event. Then this event can be handled in the Web Forms page in which the user control is used.

Using the Web User Control

After you design the user interface of the user control, add properties to it, and expose an event, your user control is ready to be used in any Web Forms page.

1. **To use your user control (`LoginControl`) on WebForm1, switch to the `WebForm1.aspx` file (click the WebForm1.aspx tab at the top of the designer window).**
2. **Drag `LoginControl.ascx` from the Solution Explorer window to the form. Access the Solution Explorer window by choosing View⇨Solution Explorer.**

   At this stage, the form contains your user control, `LoginControl`. Notice that the ID of the control is set to `LoginControl1` by default. You don't have to use this ID; you can change the default ID in the Properties window of the control.

   Access the properties window by choosing View⇨Properties.

   If you don't drag the user control from the Solution Explorer window to your Web Forms page, you have to write the code manually in the ASPX file of the page to register and add the user control.

3. **Change the default ID `LoginControl1` to `MyLoginControl` by editing the ID field in the Properties window (access the Properties window by selecting the control and then pressing F7).**

   When you add the `LoginControl` user control from Solution Explorer to the form, Visual Studio .NET performs two major tasks in the background: registering the user control and including the user control in the form.

4. **Switch to the HTML view of the `WebForm1.aspx` file (click the HTML button at the bottom of the designer window) to see the details about registering and including the user control in the form.**

   In the beginning of the HTML view, note the `@Register` directive, which registers the user control.

   ```
   <%@ Register TagPrefix="uc1" TagName="LoginControl"
       Src="LoginControl.ascx" %>
   ```

   In the preceding code, the different attributes include

   - `TagPrefix`: This attribute associates a prefix with the user control. This prefix is used in the opening tag of the user control element while adding the element to the Web Forms page.
   - `TagName`: This attribute associates a name with the user control and is also included in the opening tag of the user control element.
   - `Src`: This attribute defines the virtual path of the user control file.

   In addition to registering the user control on the Web Forms page, the HTML code to add the user control is generated automatically.

   ```
   <uc1:LoginControl id="MyLoginControl" runat="server">
      </uc1:LoginControl>
   ```

   In the preceding code, notice that the opening tag of the user control element contains the `TagPrefix` and `TagName` attributes. These attributes are used to register the user control.

5. **Add a `Label` control, setting its ID to `MessageLabel`, its `Text` property to blank (no text), and its `Visible` property to `False`.**

   When a user enters the user name and password and then clicks the Validate button, this label should display a message to indicate whether the log-on process is successful.

To implement this functionality, we handle the `ValidateClick` event of the user control. We expose the event when we create the user control. You can use the ASPX file or the code-behind file. To completely separate code from page presentation, we use the code-behind file.

Perform the following steps to handle the `ValidateClick` event of the user control in your Web Forms page:

1. **Open the code-behind file of the Web form.**

   Press the F7 key to open the code-behind file (look for the `.aspx.vb` extension) of the user control.

2. **Declare the user control in the declaration section of the form.**

   ```
   Public WithEvents MyLoginControl As LoginControl
   ```

   Note that the user control is declared using the `WithEvents` keyword, which indicates that the control's events will be handled in the page.

3. **In the Code Editor, in the Class Name list, select MyLoginControl. In the Method Name list, select ValidateClick.**

   At this stage, the event handler for the `ValidateClick` event of the user control is created as follows.

   ```
   Private Sub MyLoginControl_ValidateClick() Handles
      MyLoginControl.ValidateClick

   End Sub
   ```

4. **Write the code in the `MyLoginControl_ValidateClick` handler to validate the user's log-on information and display the appropriate message.**

   ```
   Private Sub MyLoginControl_ValidateClick()Handles
      MyLoginControl.ValidateClick
      If MyLoginControl.UserName = "John" And
      MyLoginControl.Password = "sweethome" Then
          MessageLabel.Text = "Login successful!"
      Else
          MessageLabel.Text = "Login unsuccessful, try
      again!"
      End If
      MessageLabel.Visible = True
   End Sub
   ```

   As you can see in the preceding code, the `UserName` and `Password` properties of the user control are validated against fixed values. If the values match, the label displays a message indicating that the log-on process was successful. Alternatively, a message indicating an unsuccessful attempt is displayed.

After you add the user control and handle its `ValidateClick` event, you can run the application to test whether all features work correctly. When you enter the user name `John` and the `sweethome` password and then click the Validate button, the page displays the output shown in Figure 5-3.

Instead of continually creating a user control from scratch, you may have already designed a Web Forms page that you want to use as a user control in other forms. Consider a Web Forms page that displays the logo of your company: Because each form of your application must display this logo at the top of the form, you need to use the page containing the company logo as a user control in other forms. Read on as we discuss how to convert an existing Web Forms page into a user control.

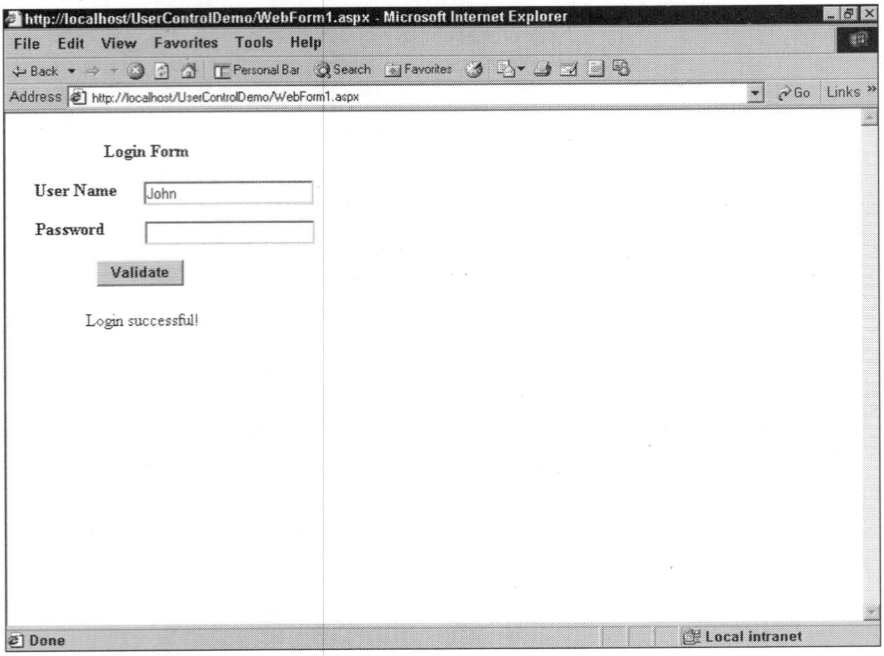

Figure 5-3: Your sample page with user controls.

Converting ASP.NET Pages to Web User Controls

In this section, we convert a Web Forms page displaying a company logo into a user control. During the process, keep in mind that the basic principle of creating a user control remains the same.

Suppose that you have a Web Application project containing a Web form named WebForm1. The form displays the logo of the Shining Stars, Inc. company. (See Figure 5-4.)

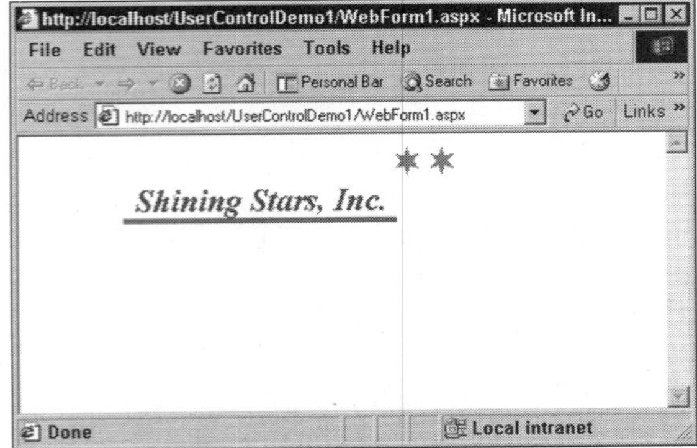

Figure 5-4: Build Web forms with repeating logos.

As you can see in the figure, the form has the following components:

- A **Label control** displaying the name of the company
- An **Image control** displaying an image of two stars
- An **HTML horizontal rule `<hr>` control**

Follow along as we convert the form WebForm1 to a user control — Logo.

1. **Switch to the HTML view of `WebForm1.aspx` (click the HTML button at the bottom of the designer window).**
2. **Delete the HTML tags that include the `<Html>`, `<Head>`, `<Body>`, and `<Form>` tags.**

   At this stage, the HTML view should contain the following code:

```
<%@ Page Language="vb" AutoEventWireup="false"
    Codebehind="WebForm1.aspx.vb"
    Inherits="UserControlDemo1.WebForm1"%>
<!DOCTYPE HTML PUBLIC "-//W3C//DTD HTML 4.0
    Transitional//EN">
<asp:Image id="Image1" style="Z-INDEX: 101; LEFT: 274px;
    POSITION: absolute; TOP: 8px" runat="server"
    ImageUrl="logoImage.tif" Width="49px"
    Height="25px">
</asp:Image>
<asp:Label id="Label1" style="Z-INDEX: 102; LEFT: 86px;
    POSITION: absolute; TOP: 35px" runat="server"
    Width="198px" Height="29px" Font-Bold="True" Font-
    Italic="True" Font-Size="Large" ForeColor="Blue">
     Shining Stars, Inc.</asp:Label>
<HR style="Z-INDEX: 103; LEFT: 77px; WIDTH: 201px;
    POSITION: absolute; TOP: 62px; HEIGHT: 4px"
    width="201" color="#993333" noShade SIZE="4">
```

3. **Change the extension of the Web form from `.aspx` to `.ascx`. The .ascx extension indicates that file is a Web user control.**

   Because we plan to create a user control named Logo, we rename `WebForm1.aspx` to `Logo.ascx`.

4. **Change the `@Page` directive (beginning of the code block) to a `@Control` directive to indicate that the form is now a user control.**

```
<%@ Control Language="vb" AutoEventWireup="false"
   Codebehind="Logo.ascx.vb" %>
```

   The Web form is converted to a user control.

After you convert a Web form to a user control, you can add properties, methods, and events to this control just as you added these when you create a user control from scratch.

For the moment, test this user control in another form. To do so, add a Web form, `Welcome.aspx`, to your project and drag `Logo.ascx` from Solution Explorer to the form. You can switch to the HTML view of the Web form to see that the user control has been registered and added to the form automatically. After you build the project and view the `Welcome.aspx` form in the browser, note that the user control is displayed in the form.

Creating and Using Composite Controls

Composite controls are formed as an aggregate of a number of existing controls. (Jump back to Table 5-1 for a comparison of user controls and composite controls.) The main difference between the two types of controls is that a composite control is compiled into an assembly (`.dll`), which needs to be included in the project in which you want to use the control.

Before we proceed to create a composite control, consider the process in detail. To create a composite control, you need to perform the following steps:

1. **Define a class to implement a composite control.**

   This class must be inherited from the `Control` class. Optionally, you should implement the `INamingContainer` interface when you want the control to

   - Provide data binding. For details on data binding, see Book 6, Chapter 9.
   - Be a templated control. (For a detailed discussion on templates, check out Book 6, Chapter 10.)
   - Route events to its child controls.

2. **Override the `CreateChildControls` method of the `Control` class to create any child controls that are to be rendered as part of the composite control.**
3. **Add the child controls to the `Controls` collection.**

Creating the composite control

In this section, we create a composite control that accepts the date of birth and qualification of a candidate to validate whether the candidate is eligible for a job. We create this composite control by using C#. However, you can use the same programming logic to create the control in Visual Basic .NET.

To create the control in C#, first create a Class Library project in C#:

1. **Display the New Project dialog box of the Class Library project.**

2. **In the Project Types pane, select Visual C# Projects.**
3. **In the Templates pane, select Class Library.**
4. **Name the project MyCompositeControl.**

   After creating the project, note that Visual Studio .NET displays the code for the default class file: `Class1.cs`.

After you create a Class Library project in C#, add a reference to the `System.Web` assembly.

1. **Choose Project➪Add Reference.**

   This displays the Add Reference dialog box.
2. **In the Component Name list of the .NET tab, select `System.Web.dll` and then click the Select button.**

   At this stage, the Add Reference dialog box is displayed as shown in Figure 5-5.

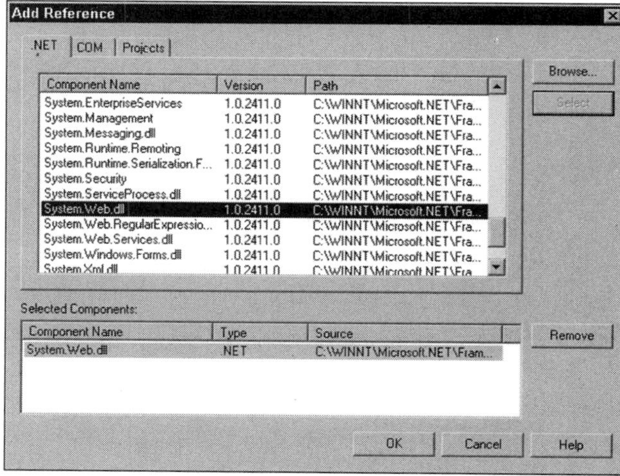

Figure 5-5: Creating a composite control in C#.

3. **Click OK to complete the process.**
4. **Add the code to the class to include the following namespaces within the `System.Web` assembly:**

```
using System;
using System.Web;
using System.Web.UI;
using System.Web.UI.WebControls;
```

Now modify the class code to implement your composite control.

1. **Rename** `Class1.cs` **with a more meaningful name:** `Eligibility.cs`.

   The default name of the class is `Class1`.

2. **Rename** `Class1` **in the Code editor as** `Eligibility` **and the constructor** `Class1()` **as** `Eligibility()`.

3. **Write the code to declare the** `Text` **property of the** `MessageLabel` `Label` **control.**

4. **Create placeholders for the** `CreateChildControls` **method and the event handler for the** `Button` **control with ID** `SubmitButton`.

   The class file should now contain the following code:

```
namespace MyCompositeControl
{
   /// <summary>
   /// Summary description for Class1.
  /// </summary>
   public class Eligibility: Control, INamingContainer
   {
      public Eligibility()
      {
         //
         // TODO: Add constructor logic here
         //
      }
      private Label MessageLabel;
      public string Text
      {
         get
         {
            EnsureChildControls();
            return MessageLabel.Text;
         }
         set
         {
            EnsureChildControls();
            MessageLabel.Text=value;
         }
      }
      protected override void CreateChildControls()
      {
      }
      protected void SubmitButton_Click(object sender,
System.EventArgs e)
      {
      }
   }
}
```

In the preceding code, the `EnsureChildControls()` method of the `Control` class checks whether the server control contains the child controls. If the server control doesn't contain the child controls, this method creates them.

5. **Write the code in the `CreateChildControls()` method to add the child controls that comprise the composite control.**

   In this example, add the `Calendar`, `TextBox`, and `Button` controls.

   TIP

   To display only text, add `Label` controls. To display plain text, add `Label` controls. To insert line breaks, use Literal controls.

```
protected override void CreateChildControls()
{
    Label Label1=new Label();
    Label1.Text="Select your date of birth:";
    Controls.Add(Label1);

    Calendar Cal1=new Calendar();
    Controls.Add(Cal1);

    Controls.Add(new LiteralControl("<Br>"));

    Label Label2=new Label();
    Label2.Text="Enter your qualification:";
    Controls.Add(Label2);

    TextBox QualBox=new TextBox();
    Controls.Add(QualBox);

    Controls.Add(new LiteralControl("<Br>"));

    Button SubmitButton=new Button();
    SubmitButton.Text="Submit";
    Controls.Add(SubmitButton);

//Associating the Click event of the SubmitButton
//control with the event handler, SubmitButton_Click
SubmitButton.Click+=new
System.EventHandler(this.SubmitButton_Click);

    Controls.Add(new LiteralControl("<Br><Br>"));

    MessageLabel=new Label();
    MessageLabel.Height=50;
    MessageLabel.Width=300;
    MessageLabel.Text="Eligibility check"
    Controls.Add(MessageLabel);
}
```

6. **Write the code in the event handler for the** `Click` **event of the** `Button` **control named** `SubmitButton`**.**

   The following code checks the selected date of birth and qualification of candidates against fixed values. If the values match, the user is considered eligible for the job. If the values don't match, the user is denied.

   ```
   protected void SubmitButton_Click(object sender,
   System.EventArgs e)
   {
       EnsureChildControls();
       if (
   (((Calendar)Controls[1]).SelectedDate.Year)<=1976)
       {
           if( ((((TextBox)Controls[4]).Text)=="M.S." ) ||
   ((((TextBox)Controls[4]).Text)=="Doctorate"))
           {
               MessageLabel.Text="You are eligible for the
   job!";
           }
           else
           {
               MessageLabel.Text="You are NOT eligible for
   the job!";
           }
       }
       else
       {
           MessageLabel.Text="You are NOT eligible for the
   job!";
       }
   }
   ```

After you complete the coding part, build the application to create the DLL file for the composite control. After the code is successfully built, you're ready to use the composite control in a Web form.

Using the composite control

In this section, you use the composite control in a Web application. Follow these steps to include the composite control in a Web application:

1. **Create a new ASP.NET Web Application project, CompositeControlDemo, using C#.**

   Or, you can open an existing Web application project.

2. **Choose Project⇨Add Reference.**

   In the Add Reference dialog box that appears, select the Projects tab and browse to the DLL file of your composite control.

3. **Register the composite control in the Web form by switching to the HTML view of the Web form and adding the `@Register` directive.**

   To switch to HTML view, click the HTML button at the bottom of the Designer window.

   ```
   <% @Register TagPrefix="Composite"
   Namespace="MyCompositeControl"
   Assembly="MyCompositeControl" %>
   ```

   In the preceding code, `TagPrefix` is the prefix for the control that is used in the opening tag of the composite control. `Namespace` is the name of the namespace that was created in the project containing the composite control. `Assembly` is the name of the DLL that is generated after you build the project containing the composite control.

4. **Include the composite control in the form by using the following code.**

   ```
   <form id="Form1" method="post" runat="server">
   <Composite:Eligibility id="Eligibility1"
       Text="Eligibility check" runat="server" />
   </form>
   ```


Notice that the `Text` property of the composite control has been set, which in turn sets the `Text` property of the `Label` control named `MessageLabel` within the composite control. After you register and include the composite control in the form, switch to the Design view to check whether the control has been added successfully. Figure 5-6 displays the composite control in the Design view.

Figure 5-6: A composite control included in a Web form.

Build and run the application to test whether the composite control functions in the required manner. To test the functioning of the control, select a birth date earlier than 1976, specify the qualification as *Doctorate*, and click the Submit button. The output of the form with these values is displayed in Figure 5-7.

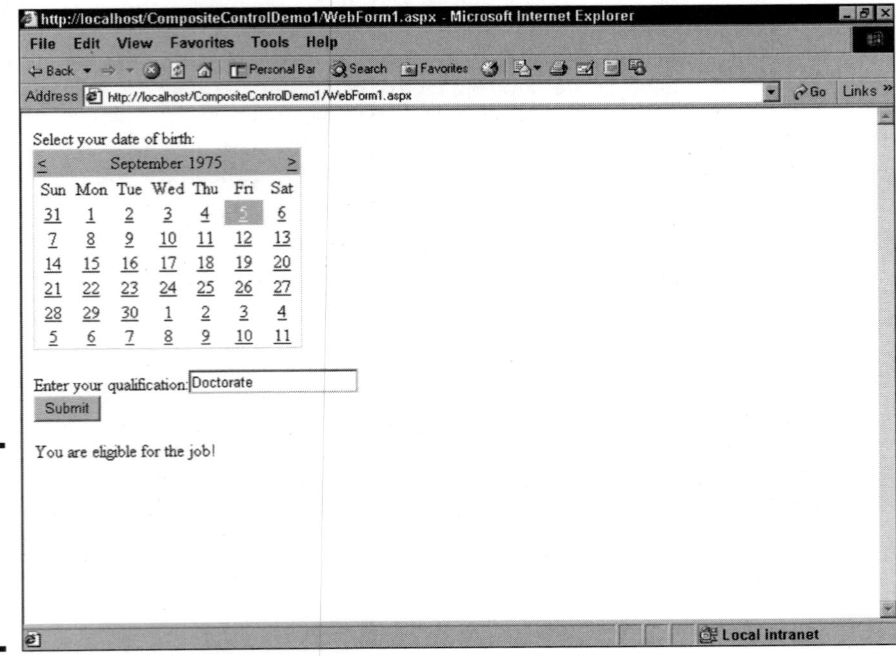

Figure 5-7: Your Web Forms page uses a composite control.

Chapter 6: Using Rich Web Controls

In This Chapter

- **Creating dynamic ads with the `AdRotator` Web server control**
- **Developing interactive calendars with the `Calendar` Web server control**
- **Displaying an XML document with the Xml Web server control**

In this chapter, we show you how to work with rich Web server controls that come with Visual Studio .NET. We call these server controls *rich* because they have additional features compared with the controls that we cover in Book 6, Chapter 3 and Book 6, Chapter 4. Rich Web server controls provide complex functionality. For example, use a `Calendar` Web server control to render a fully functional calendar in a tabular format on a Web page. In this chapter, we explore the `AdRotator`, `Calendar`, and `Xml` Web server controls.

Using the AdRotator Web Server Control

The increase in the popularity of the Internet has resulted in a boom in advertising on the Web. Flashy advertisement banners to draw users' attention abound on most Web sites. Even for the novice, the `AdRotator` Web server control in ASP.NET helps you easily create and display advertisement banners on your Web pages. You can use a single AdRotator control on a page to display and rotate through more than one advertisement.

Similar to other Visual Studio .NET Web server controls, the `AdRotator` control is available in the Web Forms section of the Visual Studio .NET Toolbox. When you add the `AdRotator` control from the Toolbox to your form, the ASP.NET code is automatically generated. For more on Toolbox, check out Book 6, Chapter 3.

```
<asp:AdRotator id="AdRotator1"
   runat="server"></asp:AdRotator>
```

See Figure 6-1 for a typical Web page with an advertisement banner. Although we can only show you one at a time, this banner does display two advertisements: one for e-greetings and the other for a holiday package contest. These two advertisements are displayed in rotation, each one being displayed for a specified time period.

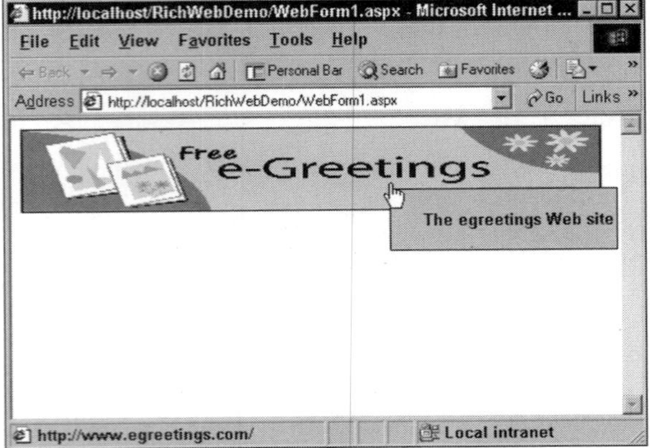

Figure 6-1: Make a Web page come alive with changing ad banners.

When users click an advertisement, they are directed to a specific link on the Web. For example, if a user clicks the advertisement for e-greetings, the user is directed to the Web site `www.egreetings.com`.

AdRotator control properties

The `AdRotator` control has basic control properties (inherited from the `System.Web.UI.Control` class), such as ID and Visible. In addition, this control has some pretty cool toys, including the `KeywordFilter` property. Using this property enables you to set a category by which you can filter advertisements to be displayed *dynamically* — that is, they change by alternating for set periods of time. For example, you can display advertisements for specific products or organizations relevant to specific users.

We really like the `AdvertisementFile` property of `AdRotator`, which specifies the path to a well-formed XML file (well-formed refers to the correct usage of all XML tags) that contains information pertaining to the display of the advertisement. This XML advertisement file contains information about which image is displayed in the advertisement banner and the page to which a user is directed when the user clicks the banner. Which advertisements are shown for how much duration is determined by a weight assigned to the `<Ad>` element through the `<Impressions>` element.

Here's the format of an XML advertisement file.

```
<Advertisements>
  <Ad>
```

```
    <ImageUrl>
      URL of the image to display
    </ImageUrl>
    <NavigateUrl>
      URL of the page to navigate to
    </NavigateUrl>
    <AlternateText>
      Text to be displayed as ToolTip
    </AlternateText>
    <Keyword>
      keyword used to filter
    </Keyword>
    <Impressions>
      relative weighting of ad
    </Impressions>
    <CustomInformation>
      Custom data about advertisement
    </CustomInformation>
  </Ad>


  <Ad>


  </Ad>
</Advertisements>
```

As you can see in the preceding format, the opening and closing `<Advertisement>` tags mark the beginning and end of the advertisement file. Each advertisement is enclosed within the opening and closing `<Ad>` tags.

The data elements for an advertisement are nested between an opening and closing `<Ad>` element. The description of these data elements is listed in Table 6-1.

Table 6-1 Data Elements for an Advertisement in an XML Advertisement File

Element	*Description*
`<ImageUrl>`	This is the URL to an image file that is rendered on the page for the advertisement.
`<NavigateUrl>`	This is the URL of the page to which a user should be directed when the user clicks the advertisement.
`<AlternateText>`	This is the text to be displayed in place of the image when the image specified in the `<ImageUrl>` element can't be downloaded. In some browsers, this text is displayed as a ToolTip for an advertisement.

(continued)

Table 6-1 *(continued)*

Element	*Description*
`<Keyword>`	This is a category, such as *computers* or *books,* for an advertisement by which you need to filter advertisements.
`<Impressions>`	This is a number that indicates the importance of the advertisement compared with other advertisements in the file. The greater the number, more is the importance. This number correlates with the frequency with which the advertisement is displayed.
`<CustomInformation>`	These are custom elements that you want to include for the custom description of an advertisement.

Follow along as we walk you through creating an ad. You create your advertisement file in Notepad and save it as an XML file — say `SiteAds.Xml`. Or, you can create this file in Visual Studio .NET. After that, create an ASP.NET Web Application project. For this example, create an ASP.NET Web Application project using Visual Basic and name it `RichWebDemo`. You also need some graphic files to use in your ad. For this example, name them `Greetings.gif` and `Holidays.gif`. Then add the graphic files `Greetings.gif` and `Holidays.gif` to the project. Now you're ready to create the advertisement file as follows:

1. **Choose Project⇨Add New Item.**
2. **In the Add New Item dialog box that opens, select XML File from the Templates pane.**
3. **Name the XML file `SiteAds.xml` and click the Open button.**

   In the `SiteAds.xml` file, type the following code below the starting XML statement that is automatically generated.

```
<Advertisements>
  <Ad>
    <ImageUrl>
      http://localhost/RichWebDemo/Greetings.gif
    </ImageUrl>
    <NavigateUrl>
      http://www.egreetings.com/
    </NavigateUrl>
    <AlternateText>
      The egreetings Web site
    </AlternateText>
    <Impressions>
      1
    </Impressions>
  </Ad>

  <Ad>
    <ImageUrl>
            http://localhost/RichWebDemo/Holidays.gif
```

```
    </ImageUrl>
    <NavigateUrl>
      http://www.travelholiday.com/
    </NavigateUrl>
    <AlternateText>
      The travelholiday Web site
    </AlternateText>
    <Impressions>
      1
    </Impressions>
  </Ad>
</Advertisements>
```


The preceding file contains two advertisements: one with the `Greetings.gif` image file and the other displaying the `Holidays.gif` image. Clicking the first advertisement takes a user to the `www.egreetings.com` Web site. Clicking the second advertisement takes a user to the `www.travelholiday.com` Web site.

To create the advertisement banner as displayed in Figure 6-1, add an `AdRotator` control from the Toolbox to the form `WebForm1.aspx`. Next, set the `AdvertisementFile` property of the control to the advertisement file (`SiteAds.Xml`). The equivalent ASP.NET code for the `AdRotator` control is

```
<asp:AdRotator id="AdRotator1" runat="server"
   AdvertisementFile="SiteAds.Xml"></asp:AdRotator>
```

AdRotator control events

In addition to the events inherited from the `Control` base class, the `AdRotator` control supports an interesting event: `AdCreated`. This event is fired with each round trip of the page to the server after the control is created but before the page is rendered. You can handle this event by writing its event handler. If the name of the `AdRotator` control is `AdRotator1`, the syntax for the event handler for the `AdCreated` event is

```
Private Sub AdRotator1_AdCreated(ByVal sender As Object,
          ByVal e As
          System.Web.UI.WebControls.AdCreatedEventArgs)
          Handles AdRotator1.AdCreated

    End Sub
```

The event handler for the `AdCreated` event takes two parameters:

- `sender As Object`: Represents the object that raised the event.
- `e As System.Web.UI.WebControls.AdCreatedEventArgs`: Represents the object containing the data related to the event. This object has a set of properties, which describe the event-specific data. Table 6-2 lists these properties.

Table 6-2 AdCreatedEventArgs Object Properties Storing Data Specific to the AdCreated Event

Property	*Description*
`AdProperties`	Obtains a `System.Collections.IDictionary` object that contains the advertisement properties associated with the currently displayed advertisement.
`AlternateText`	Obtains or sets the alternating text displayed instead of the image in the `AdRotator` control when the image can't be downloaded.
`ImageUrl`	Obtains or sets the URL of the image to be displayed in the `AdRotator` control.
`NavigateUrl`	Obtains or sets the URL of the page which the user should be directed to when the user clicks the `AdRotator` control.

Now handle the `AdCreated` event for the `AdRotator` control that you add to the form `WebForm1` in the `RichWebDemo` project. To do so, follow these steps:

1. **From the Toolbox, add a `Label` control below the `AdRotator` control in the `WebForm1` form.**
2. **Open the code-behind file for the form (press F7). For more on code-behind file, check out Book 6, Chapter 2.**
3. **In the Class Name list of the code-behind file, select `AdRotator1`.**
4. **In the Method Name list of the code-behind file, select `AdCreated`.**

   At this stage, the Code editor creates the event handler for the `AdCreated` event.

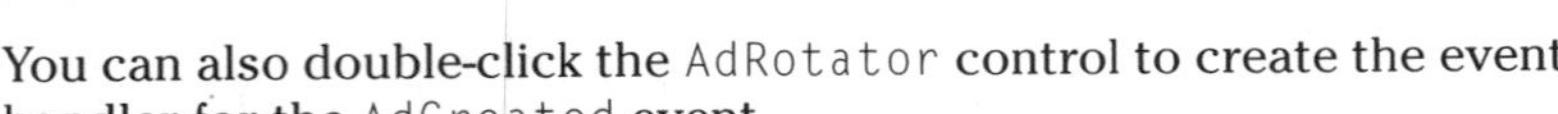

   You can also double-click the `AdRotator` control to create the event handler for the `AdCreated` event.

5. **Add the following code to display the `ImageUrl` and `NavigateUrl` properties of the advertisement that is currently displayed in the `AdRotator` control.**

```
Private Sub AdRotator1_AdCreated(ByVal sender As
   Object,
   ByVal e As System.Web.UI.WebControls.
   AdCreatedEventArgs) Handles AdRotator1.AdCreated

        Label1.Text = "The Url of the image is: " + _
   e.ImageUrl
End Sub
```

When you browse the page, note that the label displays the path of the image file for the advertisement on display (see Figure 6-2).

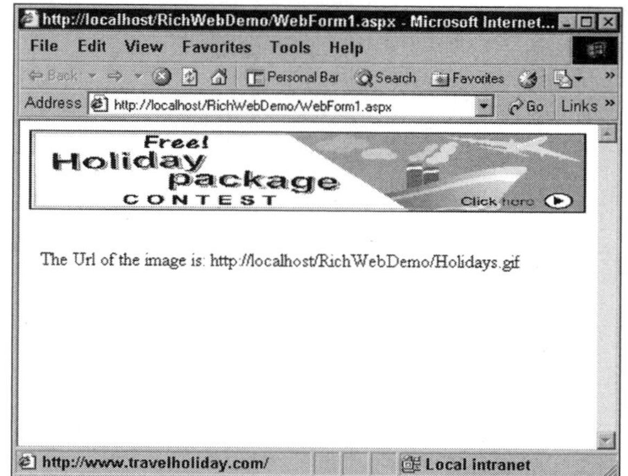

Figure 6-2: Use the AdRotator control to make an AdCreated event.

With the basics under your belt, experiment further to attain expertise. Creating flashy advertisements with ASP.NET isn't a tough task. Just put your creativity and imagination to action.

Using the Calendar Web Server Control

In Book 6, Chapter 5, we demonstrate using a `Calendar` control. In this section, we describe this control in detail.

Use a `Calendar` Web server control to render a fully functional and interactive calendar in your Web pages. The `Calendar` control displays a one-month-at-a-time calendar in a tabular format. You can use this calendar to select a specific day, week, or month and move to previous or next month. When you change the month (move either to previous or next month), the page doesn't need to be reloaded because the control includes client-side code for changing the month. Sweet! This ability saves an incredible amount of development effort.

To use a `Calendar` control, simply drag the control from the Web Forms section of the Toolbox to your form. An equivalent ASP.NET code for a `Calendar` control is

```
<asp:Calendar id="Calendar1" runat="server"></asp:Calendar>
```

Modify the look and feel of the `Calendar` control by setting properties and styles of the control per your requirements. In addition, you can handle several events of the `Calendar` control to trap users' action on the control, such as changing the selection and changing the visible month. In the next two sections, we discuss the properties and events associated with the Calendar control.

Calendar control properties

The Calendar control has several properties and styles that you can set in the Properties window. Of course, you can write the ASP.NET code for the same. Some Calendar control properties are described in Table 6-3.

Table 6-3 Calendar Web Server Control Properties

Property	*Description*
DayNameFormat	This property refers to the day name format. Its default value is Short, which displays day names as Sun, Mon, Tue, and so on.
FirstDayOfWeek	This property refers to the day name displayed as the first day of the week in the calendar. The default value is Default, which displays Sunday as the first day of the week.
NextPrevFormat	This property refers to the format for the next and the previous month hyperlinks in the title head of the Calendar control. By default, the less-than symbol (<) is used for the previous month and the greater-than symbol (>) is used for the next month hyperlink.
SelectedDate	This property refers to the date that appears selected in the calendar when it's rendered in the page. This property defaults to the current date.
SelectionMode	This property enables you to select a day, week, or month of a calendar. By default, the control enables you to select only a day. If you set this property to None, users can't select from the calendar.
ShowDayHeader	This property takes a Boolean value indicating whether the header displaying day names is visible. The default value for this property is True.
ShowTitle	This property takes a Boolean value indicating whether the title displaying the current, previous, and next months is visible. The default value for this property is True.
TitleFormat	This property refers to the format of the title of the calendar. The default format displays the month and the year.

In addition to properties, the Calendar control has several styles available. You can use these styles to change the appearance of the calendar for your requirements and preferences. Styles enable you to modify the appearance of several sections of a calendar, such as the title, day header, or day cells. For example, to set the appearance of the day header, click the + (plus) button in the `DayHeaderStyle` row of the Properties window for the `Calendar` control. The different attributes within this style appear in the expanded form as shown in Figure 6-3.

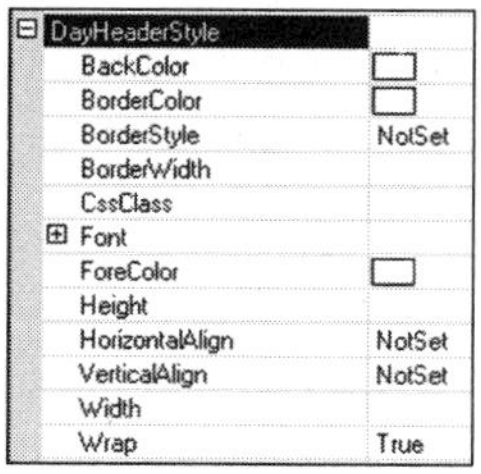

DayHeaderStyle	
BackColor	
BorderColor	
BorderStyle	NotSet
BorderWidth	
CssClass	
Font	
ForeColor	
Height	
HorizontalAlign	NotSet
VerticalAlign	NotSet
Width	
Wrap	True

Figure 6-3: Set styles for the Calendar control here.

You can set several other styles for your `Calendar` control. The scope of this chapter doesn't allow us to go into them all in depth, so we encourage you to explore the different styles in this control. For a detailed coverage of each style, refer to the .NET Framework documentation. This documentation is provided as part of the Visual Studio .NET help.

For another example on using the `Calendar` control, add another Web form — `WebForm2.aspx` — to your `RichWebDemo` project. Then add a `Calendar` control to this form. Experiment with different properties and styles by using the Properties window for the `Calendar` control (select the control and press F4) to see whether you can match the display in Figure 6-4. Notice that this control has a completely different appearance as compared with the default appearance of the control. (Don't cheat and read ahead.)

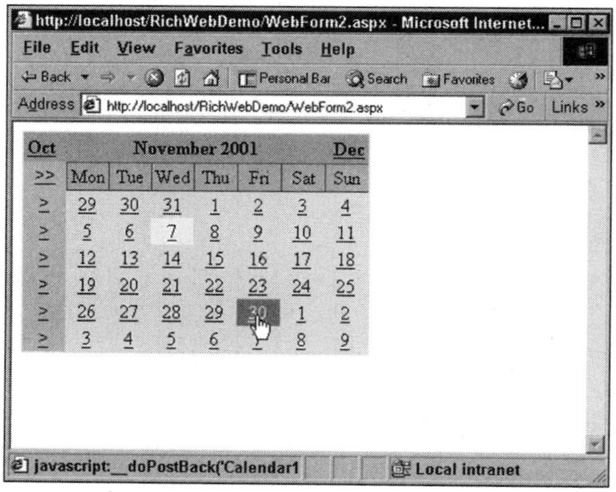

http://localhost/RichWebDemo/WebForm2.aspx - Microsoft Internet...

File Edit View Favorites Tools Help

Address http://localhost/RichWebDemo/WebForm2.aspx

Oct	November 2001						Dec
>>	Mon	Tue	Wed	Thu	Fri	Sat	Sun
>	29	30	31	1	2	3	4
>	5	6	7	8	9	10	11
>	12	13	14	15	16	17	18
>	19	20	21	22	23	24	25
>	26	27	28	29	30	1	2
>	3	4	5	6	7	8	9

javascript:__doPostBack('Calendar1' Local intranet

Figure 6-4: Customize your Calendar control from its Properties window.

The corresponding ASP.NET code for the `Calendar` control displayed in Figure 6-4 is

```
<asp:Calendar id="Calendar1" runat="server"
          FirstDayOfWeek="Monday"
          NextPrevFormat="ShortMonth"
          SelectionMode="DayWeekMonth">
<TodayDayStyle BackColor="Yellow"></TodayDayStyle>
<SelectorStyle BackColor="LightSteelBlue"></SelectorStyle>
<DayStyle BackColor="Aquamarine"></DayStyle>
<DayHeaderStyle BorderWidth="1px" BorderStyle="Ridge"
          BorderColor="Gray"
          BackColor="YellowGreen"></DayHeaderStyle>
<SelectedDayStyle BackColor="DodgerBlue"></SelectedDayStyle>
<TitleStyle Font-Bold="True" ForeColor="Black"
          BackColor="DarkSeaGreen"></TitleStyle>
<WeekendDayStyle HorizontalAlign="Center"
          BackColor="Wheat"></WeekendDayStyle>
</asp:Calendar>
```

Calendar control events

The `Calendar` control supports several events that you can handle to make the control even more interactive. In addition to the basic control events, the `Calendar` control supports the following three events:

- `DayRender`: This event is generated when a day cell is rendered in the `Calendar` control. You can handle this event to modify the format and content of a particular day cell in the calendar. The event handler for the `DayRender` event takes an argument of the type `DayRenderEventArgs`, which contains data specific to the event. The following `DayRenderEventArgs` properties describe the event-specific data:
  - `Cell`: Represents a `TableCell` object, which in turn represents a cell within which the day is rendered.
  - `Day`: Represents the `CalendarDay` object, which in turn represents the day being rendered.
- `SelectionChanged`: This event is generated when a user selects a day, a week, or a month in the calendar. You can handle this event to validate the selected date against some business logic. The event handler takes an argument of the type `EventArgs`, which contains any event-specific data.
- `VisibleMonthChanged`: This event is generated when a user clicks the next and previous month hyperlinks on the title heading of the `Calendar` control. The event handler for this event takes an argument of the type `MonthChangedEventArgs` containing the following event-specific data:

- `NewDate`: Represents the date that determines the currently displayed month in the calendar.
- `PreviousDate`: Represents the date that determines the previously displayed month in the calendar.

Now handle these events for the `Calendar` control that you add in the previous section (refer to Figure 6-4). First, add a `Label` control below the `Calendar` control. Second, open the code-behind file for the form. Third, perform the following steps to add event handlers for the `DayRender`, `SelectionChanged`, and `VisibleMonthChanged` events of the `Calendar` control.

1. **In the code-behind file (press F7), select `Calendar1` from the Class Name list.**
2. **In the code-behind file, select `DayRender` from the Method Name list to create event handler for the `DayRender` event.**
3. **In the event handler for the `DayRender` event, write the following code.**

This code displays today's date if it is today. However, if the selected day is a weekend day, another message — `The selected day is a holiday` — is displayed.

```
Private Sub Calendar1_DayRender(ByVal sender As Object,
    ByVal e As
    System.Web.UI.WebControls.DayRenderEventArgs)
    Handles Calendar1.DayRender
        If e.Day.IsToday Then
            Label1.Text = "Today's date is " +
            e.Day.Date
        ElseIf e.Day.IsSelected And e.Day.IsWeekend
            Then
            Label1.Text = "The selected day is a
            holiday"
        End If
End Sub
```

4. **Create the event handler for the `SelectionChanged` event by selecting `Calendar1` from the Class Name list and `SelectionChanged` from the Method Name list.**
5. **Write the following code, which displays a message if a user selects a date within the month of October.**

```
Private Sub Calendar1_SelectionChanged(ByVal sender As
    Object, ByVal e As System.EventArgs) Handles
    Calendar1.SelectionChanged
        If Calendar1.SelectedDate.Date.Month = 10 Then

            Label1.Text = "Reminder! Appraisal time."
        End If
End Sub
```

6. **Create the event handler for the `VisibleMonthChanged` event by selecting `Calendar1` from the Class Name list and `VisibleMonthChanged` from the Method Name list.**

7. **Write the following code, which displays a message whenever a user clicks the previous month or next month navigation controls on the title heading of the calendar.**

```
Private Sub Calendar1_VisibleMonthChanged(ByVal sender
    As Object, ByVal e As
    System.Web.UI.WebControls.MonthChangedEventArgs)
    Handles Calendar1.VisibleMonthChanged
        If e.NewDate.Month > e.PreviousDate.Month Then
            Label1.Text = "You moved a month forward"
        Else
            Label1.Text = "You moved a month backward"
        End If
End Sub
```

After you complete the coding for the event handlers, test the code.

Before you run the application, remember to set `WebForm2.aspx` (containing the `Calendar` control) as the start-up page; otherwise, `WebForm1.aspx` (containing the `AdRotator` control) will display when you run the application. To set a page as a start-up page, right-click the page in the Solution Explorer window and select Set As Start Page. Setting WebForm2.aspx as a start-up page will eliminate the need to browse the page separately. Simply executing the application will take you to the start-up page.

If you don't want to set `WebForm2.aspx` as the start-up page (simply for the reason that you don't want to execute the application just for testing a single page), browse this page independently without having to build and run the entire application. Simply right-click `WebForm2.aspx` and select Build and Browse (to build and browse the page). Alternatively, select View in Browser (to browse in Internet Explorer) or Browse With (to browse in a selected browser).

When you browse the `WebForm2.aspx` page, it displays the current date on the label. When you move from the current month, another message is displayed informing you whether you moved to the previous month or the next month. And, when you select a date in the month of October, the message on the label changes to a reminder for appraisal. In Figure 6-5, you can see a page displaying the latter message.

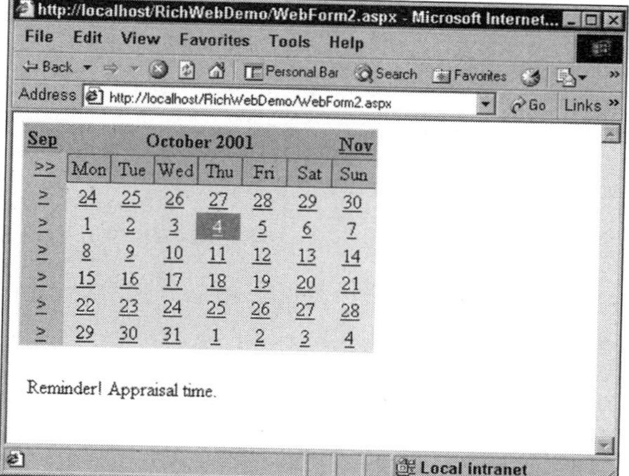

Figure 6-5: Set reminders in your Web pages with the Calendar control.

Using the Xml Web Server Control

Use the `Xml` Web server control to display the contents of an eXtensible Markup Language (XML) document on your Web pages. In addition, this control can perform server-side transformation in the XML document by using an eXtensible Stylesheet Language (XSL) or an eXtensible Stylesheet Language Transformations (XSLT) style sheet. This control supports the following properties:

- `DocumentSource`: Represents the URL of the XML document that you want to display or transform.
- `TransformSource`: Represents the URL of either the XSL or XSLT style sheet that you want to use for transforming the XML document.
- `Document`: Represents a reference to an object of the `System.Xml.XmlDocument` class. This object, in turn, contains the XML document that you want to display or transform.
- `Transform`: Represents a reference to an object of the `System.Xml.XslTransform` class. This object, in turn, contains either the XSL or XSLT style sheet that you want to use for transforming the XML document before displaying the document.

You can add an `Xml` Web server control from the Toolbox. The equivalent ASP.NET code for an `Xml` control is

```
<asp:xml id="Xml1" runat="server"></asp:xml>
```

DocumentSource and TransformSource properties

To demonstrate the Xml control, first create an XML document. To create an XML document in our running example, RichWebDemo, open the Add New Item dialog box by selecting Project➪Add New Item. In the Templates pane of the Add New Item dialog box, select the XML file. Finally, name the XML file Employees.xml and click the Open button.

Write the following code in the Employees.xml file. This file lists the names and designations of two employees.

```
<?xml version="1.0" encoding="utf-8" ?>
<Employees>
   <Title>Employee Details</Title>
   <Employee>
      <EmployeeID>E001</EmployeeID>
      <FirstName>Mary</FirstName>
      <LastName>Dukes</LastName>
      <Designation>Sales Manager</Designation>
   </Employee>

   <Employee>
      <EmployeeID>E002</EmployeeID>
      <FirstName>Rita</FirstName>
      <LastName>Greg</LastName>
      <Designation>Sales Executive</Designation>
   </Employee>
</Employees>
```

After you create this XML document, add a Web form, WebForm3.aspx, to our project and an Xml Web server control to the new form. Next, select the Xml control and press F4 to open the Properties window of the Xml control. Set the DocumentSource property to Employees.xml. When you build and browse this form, the output should look like what's shown in Figure 6-6.

Ick. Is the output that you see in Figure 6-6 what you wanted? We hope not. To get the required output, you should have an XSLT file to transform the XML document before getting displayed in the Xml control.

Now create an XSLT style sheet for the XML document present in the Employees.xml file. Choose Project➪Add New Item; in the Add New Item dialog box, select the XSLT file, name this file Employees.xslt, and click the Open button.

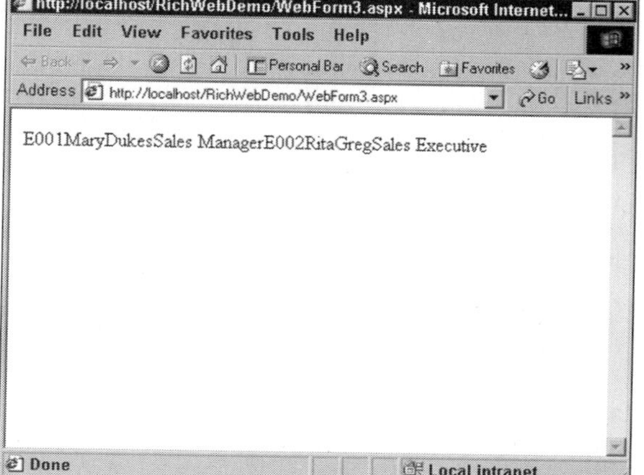

Figure 6-6: Your Web page displays an XML document.

Write the following code to create the style sheet for the `Employees.xml` file:

```
<xsl:stylesheet version="1.0"
         xmlns:xsl="http://www.w3.org/1999/XSL/Transform"
         xmlns="http://www.w3.org/TR/xhtml1/strict">
<xsl:output method="xml" encoding="iso-8859-1" />
<xsl:template match="/">
   <OL>
      <xsl:for-each select='Employees/Employee'>
         <LI>
            <b>
               Employee Id :
                <xsl:value-of select='EmployeeID' /> <br />
            </b>
               First Name :
                <xsl:value-of select='FirstName' /> <br />
               Last Name :
                <xsl:value-of select='LastName' /> <br />
               Designation :
                <xsl:value-of select='Designation' /> <br />
            <hr />
         </LI>
      </xsl:for-each>
   </OL>
</xsl:template>
</xsl:stylesheet>
```

Breaking down the different elements of the preceding style sheet:

- <xsl:template>: This element enables you to create a template to display data in the required format. The match attribute of the template element specifies the element in the XML document from where you want the template to be applied. In this case, "/" specifies that you want the template to be applied from the root element. In the template element, you can use HTML elements to apply formatting to the document.
- <xsl:for-each>: Use the for-each element to perform a task repeatedly. The select attribute is used to specify the element on which the task needs to be repeated. The XML data must be retrieved and displayed in an appropriate format. Therefore, the for-each element is used to retrieve data from the elements included in the <Employee> elements within the <Employees> element of the XML document.
- <xsl:value-of>: Use the value-of element to retrieve the data from individual elements. The select attribute specifies the element in the XML document from which you want to fetch the data. For example, `<xsl:value-of select='EmployeeID' />` element retrieves data from the <EmployeeID> element of the XML document.

After you create the XSLT style sheet, set the TransformSource property of the Xml control to Employees.xslt. Now, when you browse the form containing the Xml control, the output is well-formatted and displays as shown in Figure 6-7.

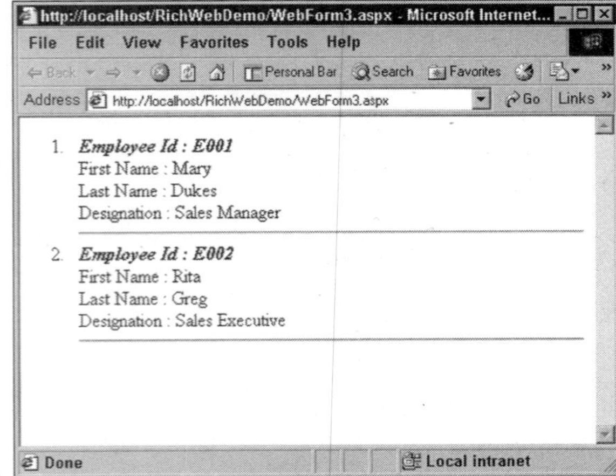

Figure 6-7: Your Web page displaying an XML document after XSLT transformation.

Document and Transform properties

An alternative to displaying XML documents in an Xml control is to use the Document and Transform properties. Before we show you how to use these properties, check your powers of observation. Remember how many properties are available for the Xml Web server control? (Answer: four.) However, the Properties window displays only two properties: DocumentSource and TransformSource. Check it out: Open the Properties window of the Xml control that you added in the previous section.

You can set the Document and Transform properties programmatically. But these properties can't be used during designing because they refer to the XmlDocument and XslTransform objects, which are created at runtime. In this section, we show you how to display an XML document by using the Document and Transform properties.

To demonstrate the use of the Document and Transform properties, first delete the settings for the DocumentSource and TransformSource properties. Then open the code-behind file for the form containing the Xml control. The Document and TransformSource properties refer to the XmlDocument and XslTransform objects. As a result, you must add a reference to the System.Xml assembly by performing these steps:

1. **Choose Project⇨Add Reference.**
2. **From the Add Reference dialog box that appears, select System.Xml.dll in the Component Name list, click the Select button, and then click OK.**

After adding the reference to the System.Xml assembly, import the System.Xml and System.Xml.Xsl namespaces in the code-behind file (press F7) as follows.

```
Imports System.Xml
Imports System.Xml.Xsl
```

Finally, in the Page_Load method, write the following code:

```
Private Sub Page_Load(ByVal sender As System.Object, ByVal e
        As System.EventArgs) Handles MyBase.Load
    'Put user code to initialize the page here
    Dim doc As XmlDocument = New XmlDocument()
    'loading the XML document in the XmlDocument object
    doc.Load(Server.MapPath("Employees.xml"))

    Dim trans As XslTransform = New XslTransform()
    'Loading the XSLT stylesheet in the XslTransform
       object
```

```
        trans.Load(Server.MapPath("Employees.xslt"))
        'Setting the Document and Transform properties of the
           Xml Web control
        Xml1.Document = doc
        Xml1.Transform = trans

End Sub
```

After you set the `Document` and `Transform` properties of the `Xml` control in the `Page_Load` method, build and browse the page. The page displays the XML document as shown in Figure 6-7.

Chapter 7: Debugging ASP.NET Web Applications

In This Chapter

- Tracing ASP.NET applications
- Error-handling in ASP.NET applications
- Discovering how to debug ASP.NET applications

To err may be human, but to recover from errors is an art. Although errors bug you (get it — *bug* you?), they do happen. And because humans are not (sigh) error-free, you must test your applications to check whether they function as you desire.

The Code Editor of Visual Studio .NET is smart enough to catch most syntactical errors in your code. However, in addition to syntactical errors, there are *runtime errors,* which can't be caught at design time and hence pop up at runtime. The worst situation arises when the Code Editor finds no error nor is there any runtime error but you still don't get the required result. Such errors occurring because of fallible programming logic are *logical errors*. The process of finding the root cause of these logical errors is *debugging*.

In addition to built-in ASP.NET debugging tools such as tracing, you can utilize the debugging tools of Visual Studio .NET to debug ASP.NET applications. In this chapter, we discuss the ASP.NET trace functionality and error handling. We also show you how to use the Visual Studio .NET debugger to debug ASP.NET applications. (Also read through Book 3, Chapter 9 and Book 4, Chapter 8 for more details on debugging.)

Tracing ASP.NET Applications

Tracing is an important technique employed for debugging applications. You use this technique to watch how an application progresses and thus find the root cause of any logical errors. Tracing has been a part of the earlier versions of ASP, in which you use the `Response.Write` method to trace applications.

Including Response.Write in your code is an easy technique for debugging. However, this technique leads to the incorporation of unnecessary lines of code in your application. The technique becomes all the more cumbersome when you have to disable tracing by deleting or commenting on all the occurrences of those unnecessary Response.Write statements.

ASP.NET enables you to trace applications in a much simpler manner. Here you use Trace.Write instead of Response.Write for tracing. As you can read in the upcoming section "Writing trace messages," Trace.Write provides a distinct advantage over Response.Write. You can use ASP.NET to either trace an application pagewise (page-level) or trace the entire application (application-level).

Page-level tracing

The trace functionality of ASP.NET is included within the System.Web.TraceContext class. The TraceContext class, a non-inheritable public class provided along with the .NET Framework, captures the execution details of a Web request and presents data to users. While tracing applications, you use the Trace.Write method to display messages within your Web pages. Trace is a public property exposed within the Page object. When you use the Trace property, you're actually working with the TraceContext object. This object has several properties and methods. Two of these properties and methods are described in Table 7-1.

Table 7-1 TraceContext Object Properties and Methods

Property/Method	*Description*
IsEnabled property	Takes a Boolean value indicating whether tracing is enabled for the current Web request.
TraceMode property	Represents the sequence of trace messages displayed in the requesting browser.
Write method	Helps write trace messages in the requesting browser.
Warn method	Helps write trace messages in the requesting browser. This method is similar to the Write method except that the Warn method displays text in red.

The IsEnabled property of the TraceContext object is available at the page level. You can set this property (Trace = "True/False") in the @Page directive of an ASP.NET page. Similarly, the TraceMode property can be set in the @Page directive.

Both the Write and Warn methods use the same syntax and are overloaded (overloaded methods are the ones that are called by the same name and perform different tasks depending on the parameters passed). The three overloaded forms take different numbers of parameters as we describe below:

- **One parameter:** A `String` parameter used to display a message.
- **Two parameters:** Both parameters are of the type `String`. The first parameter displays the trace category, and the second parameter displays the trace message.
- **Three parameters:** The first two parameters are of the type `String` and display the trace category and a message, respectively. The third parameter displays any exception information and is of the type `System.Exception`.

Enabling page-level tracing

For some hands-on page-level tracing experience, first create an ASP.NET application. Specifically, create an ASP.NET Web Application project by using Visual Basic. First name the project `DebuggingDemo`. Then write the following ASP.NET code in the form `WebForm1.aspx` to create a simple page.

The files that have .aspx extension represent page files for Web Forms. Page files represent the user interface component of Web Forms. Read Book 6, Chapter 2 for more details on Web Forms.

```
<body MS_POSITIONING="GridLayout">
   <form id="Form1" method="post" runat="server">
      <b>A sample page to demonstrate ASP.NET tracing! </b>
      <br>
      <asp:Button id="ClickMeButton" style="Z-INDEX: 101;
           LEFT: 351px; POSITION: absolute; TOP: 14px"
           runat="server" Text="ClickMe"></asp:Button>
   </form>
</body>
```

Although the preceding code displays the ASP.NET code for the `Button` server control, you don't have to write this code. You can simply add the `Button` control to the form in the Design view (To access the Design view, click the Design button at the bottom of the Designer window) and the code is automatically generated.

When you browse the preceding page, the output is simple and doesn't do anything. This is a sample page to help you get started with tracing.

Next, modify the `@Page` directive of the form to enable tracing (`Trace = "True"`) for the page.

```
<%@ Page Trace="True" Language="vb" AutoEventWireup="false"
          Codebehind="WebForm1.aspx.vb"
          Inherits="DebuggingDemo.WebForm1"%>
```

Now, if you browse the form (display the form in a browser), the output is displayed as shown in Figure 7-1.

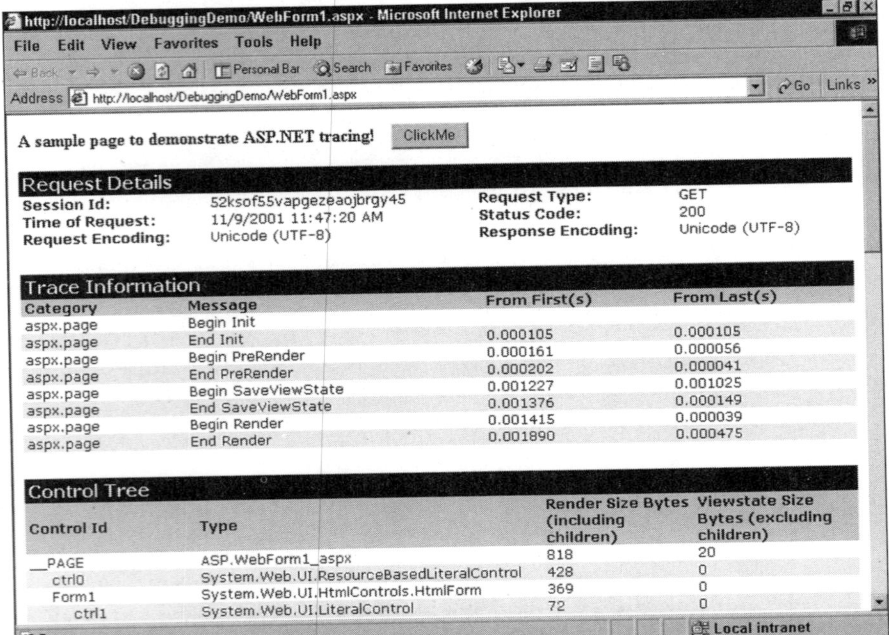

Figure 7-1: Enable tracing on a Web page.

Although you only modify one line of this code, the output displays quite a bit of information. In this page, apart from the original output (a simple message and a button), the information is categorized into different sections, such as Request Details and Trace Information. Because of the screen size constraints, Figure 7-1 doesn't display all these sections. The different sections of the Web page on Figure 7-1 are displayed in Table 7-2.

Table 7-2 Enabled Tracing Web Page Sections

Section	*Description*
Request Details	Contains details regarding the type of request, time of request, request encoding, response encoding, and so on.
Trace Information	Contains details of execution order in a tabular format. The different columns list trace categories, trace messages, and the time taken for execution.
Control Tree	Contains a hierarchical tree of all the controls on the page along with the size of each control.

Section	Description
Cookies Collection	Contains the name, value, and size of each cookie.
Headers Collection	Contains the HTTP header information.
Server Variables	Lists all the server variables along with their values.

Writing trace messages

You can write your own trace messages by using the `Trace.Write` or `Trace.Warn` methods within ASP.NET pages. These trace messages are then displayed in the Trace Information section of the page.

Write trace messages in the form that you create in the preceding section (`DebuggingDemo`). Write the following code in the `Page_Load` method of the form `WebForm1.aspx`.

```
Private Sub Page_Load(ByVal sender As System.Object, ByVal e
         As System.EventArgs) Handles MyBase.Load
       'Put user code to initialize the page here
       Trace.Write("LoadMessage", "In the Page_load method")
End Sub
```

In the event handler for the `Click` event of the button, write the following code:

```
Private Sub ClickMeButton_Click(ByVal sender As
         System.Object, ByVal e As System.EventArgs)
         Handles ClickMeButton.Click
       Trace.Warn("ClickMeButton", "Inside Button click")
End Sub
```

When you browse the form and click the ClickMe button, the output is displayed as shown in Figure 7-2.

Notice that the trace messages are displayed in the Trace Information section of the page. In addition, even though you can't see this in Figure 7-2, the message `Inside Button click` displays in red: It's red because you use the `Trace.Warn` method to write this message. This is a good method to use to attract user attention.

Before proceeding, analyze the advantages of the trace functionality over the `Response.Write method`. In addition to your trace messages, ASP.NET displays different types of trace information when tracing is enabled. When you want to disable tracing, you simply need to remove `Trace = "True"` from the `@Page` directive. Alternatively, you may set the `Trace` property to `False` without deleting or commenting on the `Trace.Write` or `Trace.Warn` statements in your code. The `Trace.Write` method is extremely convenient compared with the `Response.Write` method.

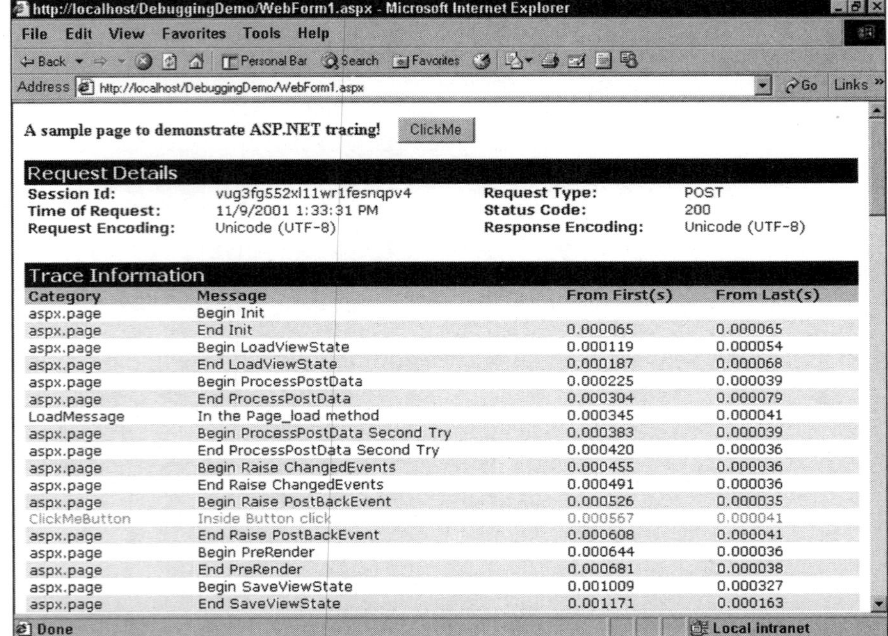

Figure 7-2: Configure your Web page to display custom trace messages.

Application-level tracing

Application-level tracing enables you to track the progress of the entire application as opposed to tracking only a specific page (page-level tracing). In application-level tracing, the trace information for each Web request is collected. You can then optionally display this information on each page or examine this information later.

Getting an overview of the application configuration file

To enable application-level tracing, you need to specify certain settings in the application's configuration file — `Web.config` — which is created automatically when you create an ASP.NET Web application in Visual Studio .NET. `Web.config` is an XML file containing configuration information about all the ASP.NET resources, such as session state and security, required for the application. Check out Book 6, Chapter 13 for a detailed information regarding the ASP.NET configuration. For now, look at enabling application-level tracing by using the `Web.config` file.

You need to modify the `<trace>` element within the `<system.web>` section of the `Web.config` file to enable application-level tracing. Check out the default settings available with the `<trace>` element.

```
<configuration>
   <system.web>
      <trace
        enabled="false"
        requestLimit="10"
        pageOutput="false"
        traceMode="SortByTime"
        localOnly="true"
      />
   </system.web>
</configuration>
```

Before you modify the trace settings, first understand the different attributes used with the `<trace>` element:

- `enabled`: Takes a Boolean value indicating whether application-level tracing is enabled.
- `requestLimit`: Represents the number of HyperText Transfer Protocol (HTTP) requests for which trace information is collected and maintained in a log (*trace log*).
- `pageOutput`: Takes a Boolean value indicating whether the trace information is displayed for each Web page.

  REMEMBER

  If you set the `pageOutput` attribute to `true`, indicating that the trace information is displayed on each Web page, the trace information is still collected and stored in a separate trace log.
- `traceMode`: Represents the sequence in which trace messages are displayed in the Trace Information section.
- `localOnly`: Takes a Boolean value indicating whether the trace information is available only to local clients or is also available to remote clients.

Enabling application-level tracing

After you become familiar with the different attributes of the trace element, you can modify these attributes for application-level tracing. To demonstrate application-level tracing, use the project `DebuggingDemo` that you created in the earlier section "Enabling page-level tracing."

Open the `Web.config` file and scroll down to the trace element. Then set the value of the `enabled` attribute to `true` (to enable application-level tracing). Also, set the `localOnly` attribute to `false` (to display trace information to local as well as remote clients). Thus, the `<trace>` element should appear as follows.

```
<trace
  enabled="true"
  requestLimit="10"
```

```
        pageOutput="false"
        traceMode="SortByTime"
        localOnly="false"
    />
```

Remove the Trace attribute in the @Page directive to implement page-level tracing. When you run the application, the page doesn't display any trace information. To view application-level tracing, you need to navigate to trace.axd in the root directory of the application project. Trace.axd is a special URL intercepted by ASP.NET. Figure 7-3 displays the output when you navigate to trace.axd after executing the application once.

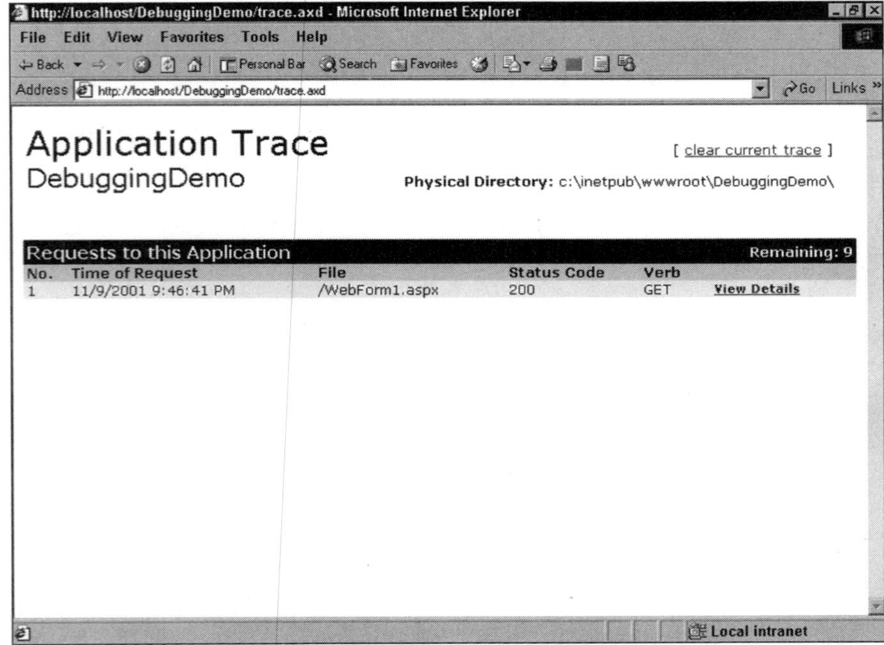

Figure 7-3: View application-level trace information from the root directory.

Because you execute the application once, the number of requests displayed in the preceding figure is only one. Notice the hyperlink View Details to the extreme right of the request: Click this hyperlink to view the trace information pertaining to that Web request.

The maximum number of Web requests for which the trace information is collected is determined by the number specified in the requestLimit attribute of the <trace> element.

As we mention earlier in this section, you can enable application-level tracing in a manner that displays the trace information for each Web request. To implement this, you simply need to set the `pageOutput` attribute of the `<trace>` element in the `Web.config` file to `true`.

Handling Errors in ASP.NET Applications

When runtime errors occur in ASP.NET applications at the server side, the error details are displayed in client browsers. While displaying these error messages, ASP.NET manages security issues by default. For example, ASP.NET ensures that no secure information — such as the source code, remote machine compiler messages, configuration settings, or file names — are displayed in client browsers. In this section, we show you how to handle ASP.NET runtime errors.

Displaying custom error messages

Although ASP.NET displays error messages indicating the source of error and further error details, these error messages are not pretty to look at. Use ASP.NET to display custom error messages, which are easier to read and understand.

Before we walk you through creating and displaying a custom error page, first understand the configuration setting for custom errors. The `<customErrors>` element of the `Web.config` file contains information about custom error messages of ASP.NET applications. The format of the `<customErrors>` element is

```
<customErrors
   defaultRedirect="url"
   mode="On|Off|RemoteOnly">
   <error statusCode="statuscode"
          redirect="url"/>
</customErrors>
```

To use custom error configuration settings, you must have a clear understanding of the different attributes of the `<customErrors>` element:

- `defaultRedirect`: Refers to the URL to which client browsers should be directed when an error occurs.
- `mode`: Refers to the mode in which custom errors function. This attribute can take one of the following values:
  - `On`: Indicates that custom errors are enabled. This value prohibits the display of original error messages in client browsers.

- `Off`: Indicates that custom errors are disabled. This value forces the display of original error messages even if custom error pages are available.
- `RemoteOnly`: Indicates that custom errors are shown only to remote clients.

In addition to the above attributes, the `<customErrors>` element also contains the subelement `<error>`, which is used to define a custom error condition, if any.

To define multiple custom error conditions, you need to include multiple `<error>` subelements.

The `<error>` subelement takes two attributes:

- `statusCode`: Refers to the status code of the error that redirects client browsers to a custom error page.
- `redirect`: Refers to the URL to which client browsers be redirected when an error occurs.

Now create a custom error page and display it in case a runtime error occurs. Implement this in the same application project (`DebuggingDemo`) that you created earlier in this chapter.

First create a custom error page. To do so, add a Web form named `CustomError.aspx` to the project. Then, design the page as shown in Figure 7-4.

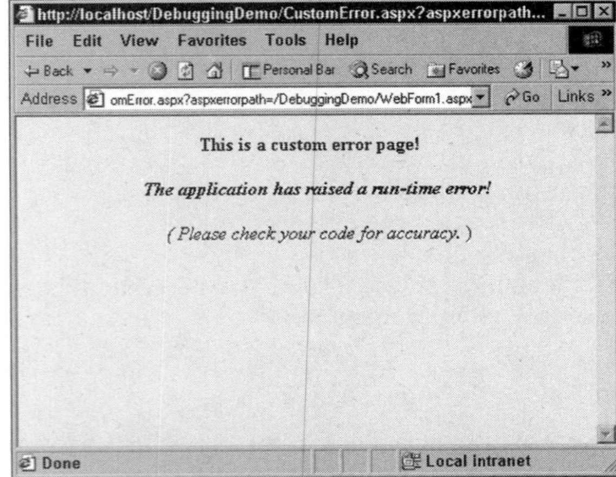

Figure 7-4: Create a custom error page to fit your needs.

Second, open the `Web.config file` and scroll to the `<customErrors>` element. Modify the attributes as follows:

```
<customErrors
mode="On"
defaultRedirect="CustomError.aspx"
/>
```

The preceding settings indicate that custom errors are enabled for the application. Each time that an error occurs, client browsers are redirected to the custom error page `CustomError.aspx`.

Third, to demonstrate the custom error pages, you need to have some fallible code in your application. Open the `WebForm1.aspx` page and switch to its code-behind file (press F7). In the event handler for the `Click` event of the button with caption ClickMe, write the following code:

```
Dim MessageLabel As Label
MessageLabel.Text = "Welcome to error handling!"
```

Notice that the preceding code is incorrect because the object `MessageLabel` has not been allocated any memory. (Of course, we did this deliberately so that we could demonstrate custom errors.) Anticipating a runtime error, go ahead and test whether the custom error page is displayed when a user clicks the ClickMe button. First build and run the application: The output should be shown without any errors. Now click the ClickMe button. The browser window displays the custom error page as shown in Figure 7-4.

Writing error messages to the Event Log

Although errors in an application are displayed to users in client browsers, administrators should also be informed about application errors so that they can identify and rectify the errors. When application errors occur, you can write the error messages in an Event Log, send an e-mail message to administrators, or write to a database. Administrators can then access one of these (Event Log, mail, or the database) to identify and solve the problems associated with the application.

Whenever an application error occurs, the `Application_Error` event is generated. You can handle this event to write the error messages to the Event Log. The event handler for the `Application_Error` event is included in the `Global.asax` file of the application project. The `Global.asax` file is also known as the ASP.NET application file.

The .NET Framework provides the `EventLog` class in the `System.Diagnostics` namespace that you can use to write error messages to the

Event Log. Before we proceed to use this class to write to the Event Log, look at some of the properties and methods of this class, which are listed in Table 7-3.

Table 7-3 EventLog Class Properties and Methods

Property/Method	*Description*
`Entries` property	Obtains the contents of the Event Log.
`Log` property	Obtains or sets the name of the log which to read from or write to.
`Source` property	Obtains or sets the name of the source to register and use when writing to the Event Log.
`Exists` method	Checks whether the log exists.
`SourceExists` method	Searches the computer's registry for an event source.
`CreateEventSource` method	Enables an application to write event information to a particular log on the system.
`WriteEntry` method	Writes an entry in the Event Log.

Now write error messages for the `DebuggingDemo` application (that you created in the earlier section "Enabling page-level tracing") to the Event Log.

First, open the `Global.asax` file. Double-click `Global.asax` in Solution Explorer (If Solution Explorer is not opened, select View⇨Solution Explorer in the Visual Studio .NET window), and the `Global.asax.vb` file is opened in Design view. To switch to the code-behind file, click the hyperlink Click here to switch to code view. Alternatively, you can press F7.

While in the `Global.asax.vb` file, import the `System.Diagnostics` namespace because the `EventLog` class exists in this namespace.

```
Imports System.Diagnostics
```

Now write the following code in the event handler for the `Application_Error` event.

```
Sub Application_Error(ByVal sender As Object, ByVal e As
   EventArgs)
        ' Fires when an error occurs
        Dim PageUrl, Message, LogName As String
        'Creating an object of the EventLog class
        Dim EventLog1 As New EventLog()

        'Retrieving the URL of the Web request
```

```
        PageUrl = Request.Path

        'Creating an error message to write to Event Log
        Message = "The page that generated the error: " &
        PageUrl

        'Specifying a name for the Event Log
        LogName = "MyLog"

        'Creating Event Log if it does not exist
        If (Not EventLog.SourceExists(LogName)) Then
            EventLog.CreateEventSource(LogName, LogName)
        End If

        'Writing to the log
        EventLog1.Source = LogName
        EventLog1.WriteEntry("Application error occured. " +
        Message, EventLogEntryType.Error)

End Sub
```


After coding for the `Application_Error` event, build and run the application. This time, to test for the Event Log, you don't need to write any fallible code in your application because the event handler for the `Click` event of the ClickMe button already contains incorrect code.

When you run the application, `WebForm1.aspx` is displayed in the browser. If you click the ClickMe button, the custom error page is displayed as shown in Figure 7-4. Additionally, the error message is written to the Event Log named `MyLog`.

To view the Event Log, you need to open the Event Viewer. In Windows 2000, choose Start➪Programs➪Administrative Tools➪Event Viewer to open the Event Viewer. In Windows XP, choose Start➪All Programs➪Control Panel. In the Control Panel window, double-click Performance and Maintenance. In the Performance and Maintenance window, double-click Administrative Tools. Finally, in the Administrative Tools window, double-click Event Viewer to open the Event Viewer. In the Event Viewer, the Event Log, MyLog, is listed in the left pane. When you click MyLog in the left pane, a list of all entries in this Event Log appear in the right pane. An entry is created each time that an error occurs in your application. The Event Viewer with MyLog Event Log is shown in Figure 7-5.

You can then double-click an entry to see the error details, as shown in Figure 7-6.

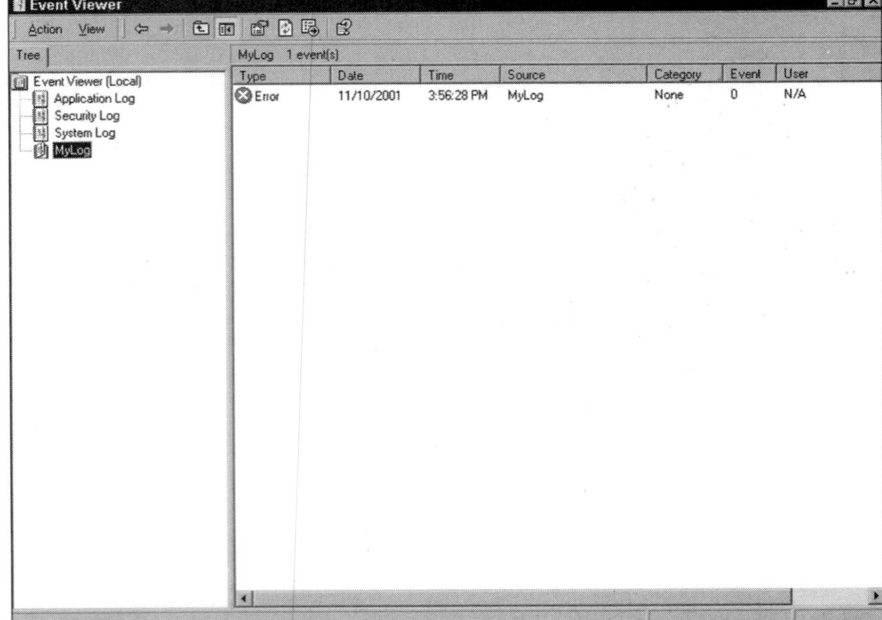

Figure 7-5: Use the Event Viewer to show errors written to the Event Log.

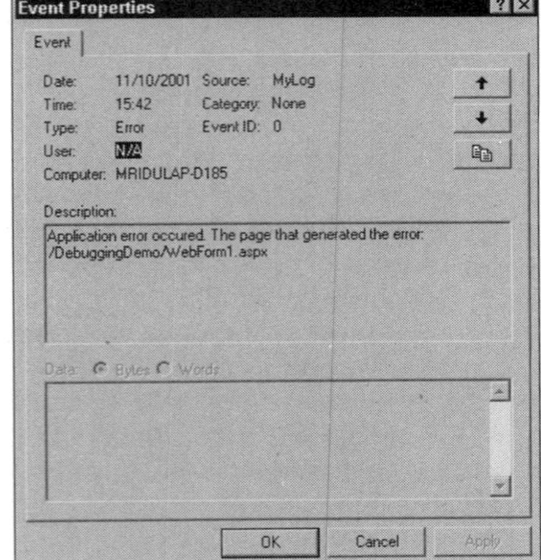

Figure 7-6: Error details display in the Event Properties dialog box.

Notice that the Description box contains the error message that you wrote in the Event Log.

Debugging ASP.NET Applications with the Visual Studio .NET Debugger

Visual Studio .NET provides a common debugger that you can use to debug all types of applications developed in its framework. To debug an application in Visual Studio .NET, you need to set a *breakpoint* at the line of code where you suspect the source of error. When you run the application, the execution halts when the application reaches the breakpoint. At this stage, your application enters a mode called the *break mode*. For more on break points and break mode, read Book 3, Chapter 9 and Book 4, Chapter 8. You can debug your ASP.NET applications by using any of the following methods:

- Using the Debug menu
- Attaching the debugger at runtime

Using the Debug menu

Before you proceed to use the Visual Studio .NET debugger, look at the different options available in the Debug menu that we describe in Table 7-4.

Table 7-4 Debug Menu Options

Option	*Description*
Start	Starts application execution.
Continue	Continues application execution after it halts at breakpoint.
Restart	Restarts the debugging process.
Step Into	Transfers control to the called procedure in the application.
Step Out	Transfers control from the called procedure back to the calling procedure without carrying out execution in the called procedure.
Step Over	Skips a called procedure.
New Breakpoint	Sets a breakpoint on a line of code. Selecting this option opens the New Breakpoint dialog box, which provides you several options for the breakpoint. For example, you can set a condition for a breakpoint.

To demonstrate the use of the Visual Studio .NET debugger, add a new Web form to the `DebuggingDemo` application project (which you created earlier in this chapter). Design this new form as shown in Figure 7-7. Specify the IDs of the different controls on this form as given in Table 7-5.

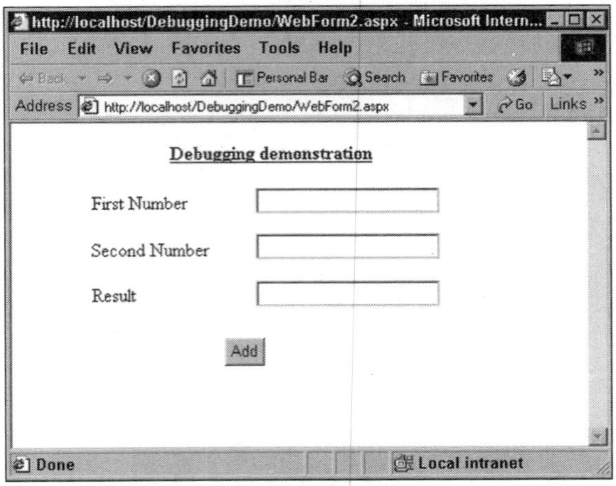

Figure 7-7: A sample form to demonstrate debugging.

Table 7-5	DebuggingDemo ID Controls	
Control	***Contains***	***ID***
`TextBox`	First Number	`FNumBox`
`TextBox`	Second Number	`SNumBox`
`TextBox`	Result	`ResultBox`
`Button`	Add	`AddButton`

After you design the form, open the code-behind file (Press F7) for this form, and write the following code in the event handler of the `Click` event of the Add button.

```
Private Sub AddButton_Click(ByVal sender As System.Object,
          ByVal e As System.EventArgs) Handles
          AddButton.Click
       ResultBox.Text = FNumBox.Text + SNumBox.Text
End Sub
```

Before you run the application, set this form as the start-up form. Next, when you run the application, enter two numbers. For the example, enter **5** in both the First Number and Second Number text boxes. When you click the Add button, the Result box displays `55` instead of `10`. Although there was no syntactical or runtime error, the result is incorrect. Therefore, you conclude that your code contains a logical error. Here's how to use the Visual Studio .NET debugger to resolve this problem.

First set a breakpoint. Typically, a breakpoint is set at the line of code where you suspect an error. In our case, the error occurs when you click the Add button. Therefore, the source of the error is the code in the event handler for the `Click` event of the Add button. Set the breakpoint at this procedure by pressing F9 at the line containing the procedure. The code appears as shown in Figure 7-8.

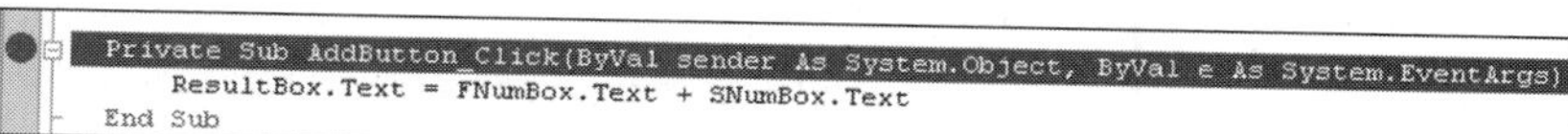
Private Sub AddButton_Click(ByVal sender As System.Object, ByVal e As System.EventArgs)
ResultBox.Text = FNumBox.Text + SNumBox.Text
End Sub

Figure 7-8: Code with a breakpoint.

After you set the breakpoint, choose Debug➪Start. The page is displayed in Internet Explorer. When you enter **5** in both the text boxes and click the Add button to calculate and display the result in the Result box, the application halts execution and enters the break mode. At this stage, the event handler of the `Click` event of the Add button appears highlighted in the Code editor.

Next proceed line-wise to identify the source of the error. Choose Debug➪Step Into to transfer the control to the next line in the code. Choose Debug➪Step Into again to transfer the control to the next line (`End Sub` statement). This is the time to check the values in different text boxes to identify the source of the problem. For any ad hoc querying of variables or control properties, you can use the Immediate window. To display the Immediate window, choose Debug➪Windows➪Immediate. In the Immediate window, type the following line to check the value in the Result text box:

```
?ResultBox.Text
```

After you type this code line and press the Enter key, the Immediate window displays the result `"55"`. The quotes in this number indicate that the result is a string and not a number. Therefore, you can now identify the source of the problem as a data-type conversion. Now, stop debugging the application by selecting Debug➪Stop Debugging.

Remove the breakpoint by placing the cursor at the line where you set the breakpoint and then pressing F9. Then, modify the code in the event handler for the `Click` event of the Add button as follows:

```
ResultBox.Text = CInt(FNumBox.Text) + CInt(SNumBox.Text)
```

After fixing the code, run the application, enter the numbers again — **5** and **5** — and click the Add button. The result `10` is displayed in the Result box.

Attaching the debugger at run time

You can also attach the Visual Studio .NET debugger to an application that's running. Switch to the Visual Studio .NET window where the application is opened and follow these steps.

1. **Choose Debug⇨Processes.**
2. **In the Processes dialog box that opens, confirm that the Show System Processes check box is selected.**
3. **In the Available Processes pane, select** `aspnet_wp.exe`.
4. **Click the Attach button to open the Attach To Process dialog box.**
5. **From the available choices, select Common Language Runtime and Script.**
6. **Click OK and then click the Close button.**

After attaching the debugger, you can proceed to debug your application.

Chapter 8: Data Binding with Server Controls

In This Chapter

- **Understanding data binding**
- **Binding server controls to single-value data sources**
- **Binding server controls to repeated-value data sources**

Visual Studio .NET provides a large number of server controls that you can use to design a user interface for your ASP.NET applications. In addition to taking user input and displaying static text and image, you often need to access data from multiple data stores and display the data values in these controls. You can display values in server controls from multiple data stores, such as arrays, relational databases, or eXtensible Markup Language (XML) data stores. Some of these data stores (arrays) are static, whereas others (relational databases) are dynamic.

In addition to displaying static information, you encounter situations in which you need to display information dynamically. For example, consider an ASP.NET application designed for accepting orders from customers. You can't expect customers to enter the exact names of the products that they want: This could be pretty cumbersome — and inconvenient — for a customer, given the range of products potentially available. Make ordering (and buying) easy for a customer by displaying a list of products directly from a data store.

In other situations, you will need to access and display data values in server controls from different data stores. To meet this requirement, ASP.NET provides you with data binding. *Data binding* enables you to bind server controls to data stores and thus display data dynamically; that is, the displayed values change each time that the values in the data store change.

In this chapter, we describe data binding in detail and the methods to implement data binding with different server controls.

Getting to Know Data Binding

Data binding implies binding a control's property to a data store. To implement data binding, you simply need to tell controls or the page (containing the controls) about the source of the data store (the data source). Subsequently, when you build and run the page, the page or controls extract the data values from the specified data source. Before we begin to discuss the implementation of data binding from different types of data stores, take a look at the data binding syntax:

```
<%# data source %>
```

An example of the syntax to bind a data source with the `Text` property of a `Label` control is

```
<asp:Label id = "Label1" runat = "server" Text = "<%# data
   source %>" />
```

Note that you may specify the data source from where you need to extract values for the property of the control. However, the .NET Framework can't automatically extract the data values from the specified data source when the page is built and run. Therefore, to display data values in controls, simply writing a data binding code for a control isn't enough. You also need to call the `DataBind` method explicitly. The `DataBind` method is supported by the page as well as each control on the page.

When you call the `DataBind` method for a control, it's cascaded to all its child controls. Thus, when you call the `DataBind` method for the page, the method is automatically called for all the controls on the page.

Broadly speaking, you can perform two types of data binding with server controls:

- **Single-value data binding:** Use this when you bind a server control to a data source that has a single value, which may be a control's property or an expression evaluating to a single value. This type of data binding is suitable for controls that display a single value, such as `Label`, `TextBox`, or `Button` controls.
- **Repeated-value data binding:** Use this when you bind a server control to a data source that has multiple values, such as arrays or a recordset from a database. This type of data binding is suited to the controls that display multiple values, such as a list control.

In the subsequent sections of this chapter, we discuss how both these types of data binding is carried out.

Binding Server Controls to Single-Value Data Sources

Single-value data sources are the ones that return only one value. So, these data sources can be bound to controls that display only one value at a time, such as Text Box or Label control. Single-value data sources include

- **Properties**
- **Expressions**
- **Methods**

In this section, we show you how to bind server controls to each of these data sources. First create an ASP.NET Web application by using Visual Basic and name the application project DataBindingDemo. Also rename the default Web form `WebForm1.aspx` as `OrderForm.aspx`.

Remember to give meaningful names to Web forms. Meaningful names help you determine the purpose of Web forms.

Then design the form as shown in Figure 8-1, using Table 8-1 as a reference for setting the IDs (for identifying the different controls programmatically) of different controls on the form. Of course, you can set various other properties (such as `Font`) to improve the form aesthetically.

Figure 8-1: Create a sample order form.

Table 8-1 Order Form Control IDs

Control	*Contains*	*ID*
TextBox	Customer ID	CustIDBox
TextBox	Order ID	OrderIDBox
TextBox	Order Date	OrderDateBox
TextBox	Product Name	ProdNameBox
TextBox	Quantity	QtyBox
TextBox	Price	PriceBox
TextBox	Amount	AmtBox
Button	Calculate Discount	DiscountBox
Label	Discount	DiscountLabel
Label	MessageLabel	MessageLabel
Button	Calculate Amount	AmtButton
Button	Submit	SubmitButton

Set the `Visible` property of the `Label` control with the ID `MessageLabel` to `False`. You use this label to display messages at runtime.

Binding page properties

To demonstrate data binding with page properties, create a read-only property called `OrderDate` — which returns the current date — and bind it with the `Text` property of the `TextBox` control with ID `OrderDateBox`. To implement this data binding, perform the following steps:

1. **Create the property by opening the code-behind file for the form. (Press F7 when the form is opened in the Design view.**

   To access the Design view, click the Design button at the bottom of the designer window.)

2. **In the code-behind file, write the following code (within the class code) to create the read-only property `OrderDate`.**

   ```
   ReadOnly Property OrderDate() As Date
           Get
               Dim CurrentDate As Date
               CurrentDate = Date.Now
               Return CurrentDate
           End Get
       End Property
   ```

   Notice that the property returns the current date and time.

3. **Write the data binding code for the control by switching to the HTML view of the form.**

(To access the HTML view, click HTML at the bottom of the designer window.)

4. **In HTML view, edit the ASP.NET code of the `TextBox` control with ID `OrderDateBox` to include the data binding code:**

```
<asp:TextBox id="OrderDateBox" Text="<%# OrderDate %>"
     runat="server"></asp:TextBox>
```

5. **Call the `DataBind` method for the page by switching back to the code-behind file of the form and writing the following code in the `Page_Load` method:**

```
Private Sub Page_Load(ByVal sender As System.Object,
    ByVal e As System.EventArgs) Handles MyBase.Load
        'Put user code to initialize the page here
        If Not IsPostBack Then
            OrderDateBox.DataBind()
        End If
End Sub
```

Notice that the `DataBind` method has been called explicitly for the text box displaying the order date. You can also call the `DataBind` method for the entire page, in which case the `DataBind` method is called for all the controls on the page. To do so, you can use either the `DataBind` statement or the `Page.DataBind()` statement.

TIP

Also note that before calling the `DataBind` method, the `IsPostBack` property of the page is checked to identify whether the page is requested for the first time. Thus, the preceding code indicates that the `DataBind` method should be called only once when the page is requested for the first time. (This check helps you reduce load on the server for the subsequent requests for the page and hence improve performance.)

When you build and run the application, the page displays the current date in the Order Date text box. (See Figure 8-2.)

Binding control properties

Here we demonstrate how to bind a control's property to another control's property. Bind the `Text` property of the `TextBox` control displaying the product name with the `Text` property of the `Label` control with the ID `MessageLabel`. You set the `Visible` property of this label to `False`.

1. **Switch to the HTML view of the form (click HTML at the bottom of the Designer window) and edit the ASP.NET code for the `Label` control with the ID `MessageLabel` to include the data binding code:**

```
<asp:Label id="MessageLabel" Text='<%# "The product you
   entered is: " + ProdNameBox.Text %>' runat="server"
   Visible="False"></asp:Label>
```

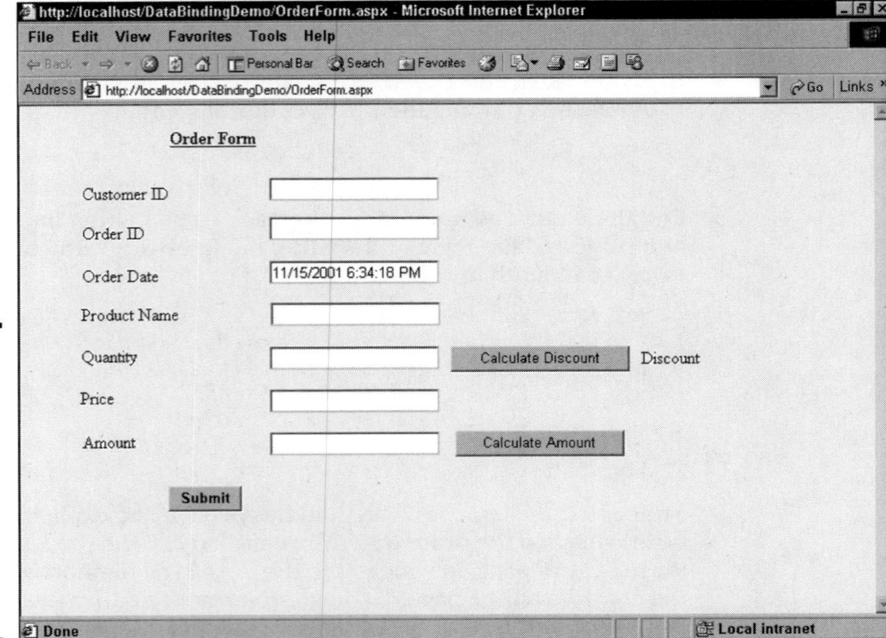

Figure 8-2: The current date displays (from the OrderDate property) in the Order Date text box.

The data binding expression code is included in single quotes instead of double quotes because the data binding code already includes a text message (enclosed within double quotes) and ASP.NET doesn't allow nested quotes.

2. **Switch to the code-behind file for the form (press F7).**
3. **Select SubmitButton in the Class Name list and then select Click in the Method Name list to create the event handler for the `Click` event of the Submit button.**
4. **Write the following code in the event handler:**

```
Private Sub SubmitButton_Click(ByVal sender As Object,
   ByVal e As System.EventArgs) Handles
   SubmitButton.Click
        MessageLabel.DataBind()
        MessageLabel.Visible = True
End Sub
```

   Notice that the `DataBind` method for the `MessageLabel` label has been called explicitly.

When you build and run the application, enter the name of the product and then click the Submit button. The label with the ID `MessageLabel` displays and includes the bound data as shown in Figure 8-3.

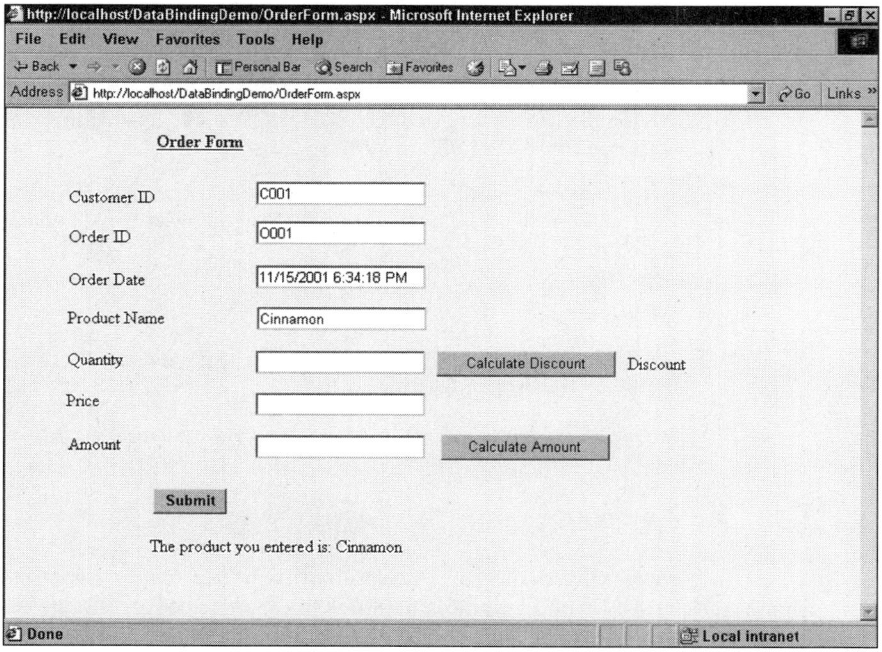

Figure 8-3: The data bound with the Text property of the Product Name displays.

Binding methods

In this section, we create a method named `CalculateDiscount`, which returns the discount based on the quantity of the product ordered. We then bind the method with the label displaying the discount. To see how data binding is performed with methods, follow these steps:

1. **In the code-behind file for the form (press F7), write the following code to create the method named `CalculateDiscount`.**

   This method returns an integer value, `discount`, based on the quantity entered.

   ```
   Function CalculateDiscount() As Integer
    If Val(QtyBox.Text) >= 20 And Val(QtyBox.Text) <= 50
        Then
        Return 20
    ElseIf Val(QtyBox.Text) > 50 Then
        Return 30
    Else
        Return 0
    End If
   End Function
   ```

2. **Select DiscountButton in the Class Name list and then select Click in the Method Name list to create the event handler for the `Click` event of the button labeled `Calculate Discount`.**

3. **Write the following code to call the `DataBind` method explicitly and call the `CalculateDiscount` method:**

```
Private Sub DiscountButton_Click(ByVal sender As Object,
   ByVal e As System.EventArgs) Handles
   DiscountButton.Click
        DiscountLabel.DataBind()
        CalculateDiscount()
End Sub
```

4. **Edit the ASP.NET code of the `Label` control with ID `DiscountLabel` to include the data binding code:**

```
<asp:Label id="DiscountLabel"
Text="<%# CalculateDiscount %>" runat="server">
Discount
</asp:Label>
```

When you build and run the application, enter values for Customer ID, Order ID, Product Name, and Quantity text boxes. Next, click the Calculate Discount button. The `Discount` label displays the discount value as shown in Figure 8-4.

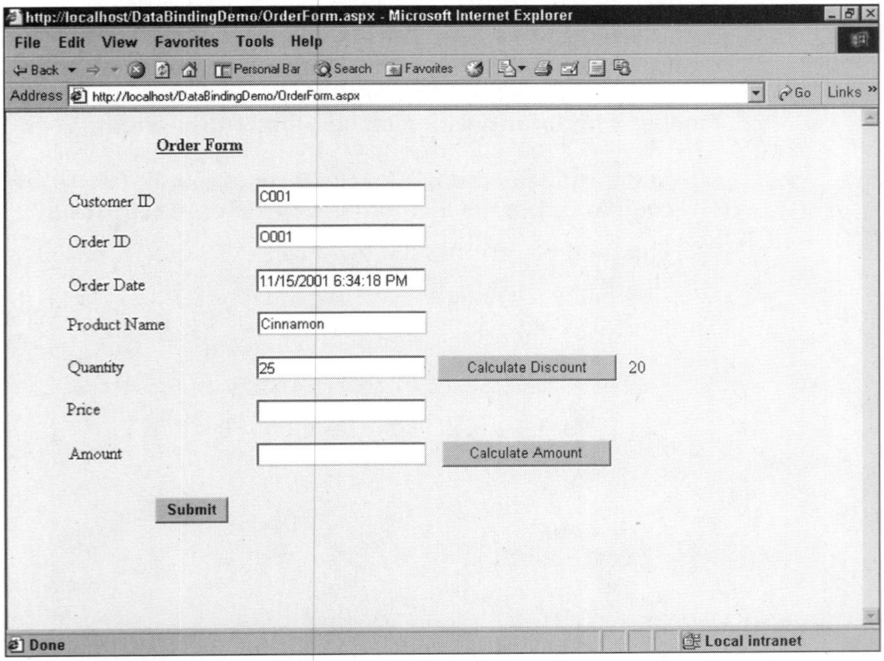

Figure 8-4: The Order form displays the discount returned from the Calculate-Discount method.

Binding expressions

In this section, we demonstrate how to bind a control's property to an expression. Here, we bind the `Text` property of the Amount text box to an expression, which calculates the total order amount. To accomplish this, follow these steps:

1. **In the HTML view (click the HTML button at the bottom of the designer window), edit the ASP.NET code of the `TextBox` control with ID `AmtBox` to include the data binding code.**

   ```
   <asp:TextBox id="AmtBox"
   Text="<%# (Val(QtyBox.Text) * Val(PriceBox.Text)) -
      ((Val(DiscountLabel.Text)/100) *(Val(QtyBox.Text) *
      Val(PriceBox.Text))) %>"
   runat="server">
   </asp:TextBox>
   ```

   Notice that the `Text` property has been bound to an expression, which calculates the order amount keeping into account the discount value.

2. **Switch to the code-behind file for the form.**
3. **In the Class Name list, select AmtButton.**
4. **In the Method Name list, select Click to create the event handler for the `Click` event of the Calculate Amount button.**
5. **Call the `DataBind` method for the `TextBox` control with ID `AmtBox` explicitly.**

   ```
   Private Sub AmtButton_Click(ByVal sender As
        System.Object, ByVal e As System.EventArgs)
        Handles AmtButton.Click
          AmtBox.DataBind()
   End Sub
   ```

When you build and run the application, enter the values for Customer ID, Order ID, Product Name, Quantity, and then click the Calculate Discount button. When you finally click the Calculate Amount button, the page displays an output similar to the one shown in Figure 8-5.

After you master binding control properties with single-value data sources, move on to learn how to bind data from data sources that have multiple values.

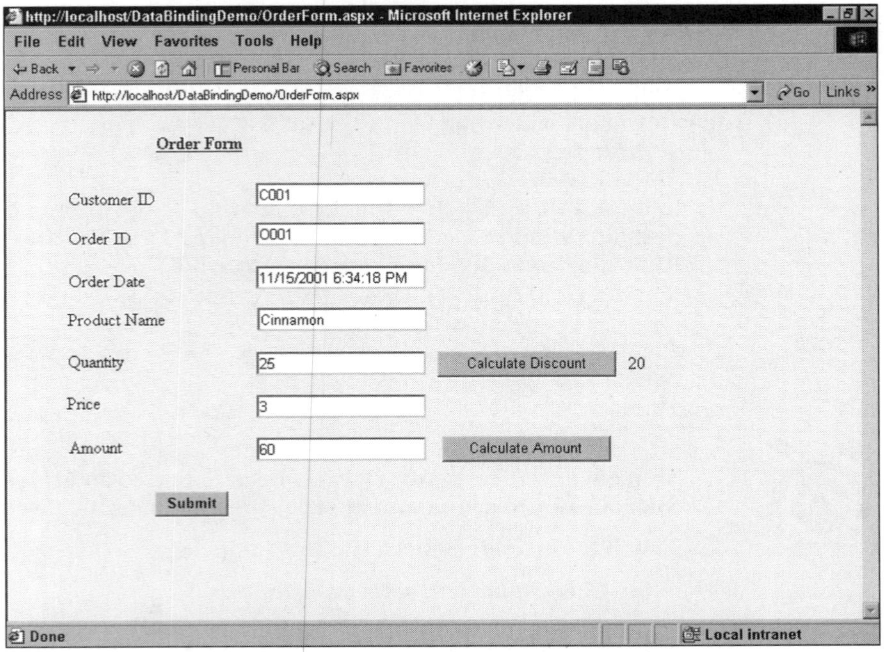

Figure 8-5: The Order form displays the order amount.

Binding Server Controls to Repeated-Value Data Sources

In the earlier section "Getting to Know Data Binding," we discuss that ASP.NET enables you to bind server controls displaying multiple values to repeated-value data sources. Read through that section to become familiar with the controls that display multiple values, such as all the list controls: `ListBox`, `DropDownList`, `CheckBoxList`, and `RadioButtonList` controls.

All list server controls can be bound to data sources that implement the `IEnumerable`, `ICollection`, or `IListSource` interfaces. Such data sources are repeated-value data sources and include `ArrayList`, `HashTable`, and `DataView`. These data sources are independent classes of the .NET framework. Keep reading to learn about implementing data binding with each of these data sources in the subsequent sections of this chapter.

Binding to an ArrayList

The `ArrayList` class represents a simple list of values; the list can be increased dynamically as and when required. In this section, we implement how to bind a `DropDownList` control to an `ArrayList`.

In the beginning of this chapter, we mention the convenience of a customer entering product names by selecting from a list of product names. In this section, we modify the Order form in our running example to implement this functionality.

1. **Modify the Order form to include a `DropDownList` control to display the list of products.**
2. **Delete the `TextBox` control labeled `Product Name` and add a `DropDownList` control in its place. (See Figure 8-6.)**
3. **Set the ID of the `DropDownList` control to `ProdNameList`.**

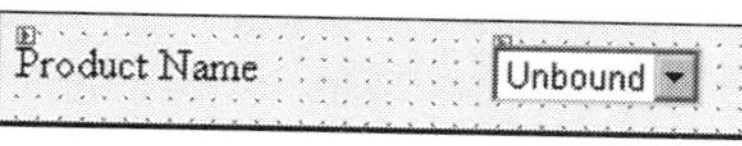

Figure 8-6: Use a DropDown-List control to display product names.

4. **Modify the ASP.NET code for binding the `Text` property of the `MessageLabel Label` control to display the selected item in the `ProdNameList DropDownList` control:**

```
<asp:label id="MessageLabel"
Text='<%# "The product you selected is: " +
   ProdNameList.SelectedItem.Text %>'
runat="server" Visible="False">
</asp:label>
```

5. **Switch to the code-behind file for the form and write the following code in the `Page_Load` method:**

   The following code creates an object of the `ArrayList` class and populates this object with a list of product names:

```
Private Sub Page_Load(ByVal sender As System.Object,
ByVal e As System.EventArgs) Handles MyBase.Load
        'Put user code to initialize the page here
        If Not IsPostBack Then
           'Creating an object of the ArrayList class
            Dim ProdList As ArrayList = New ArrayList()
           'Populating the list with product names
            ProdList.Add("Anise Seeds")
            ProdList.Add("Bay Leaf")
            ProdList.Add("Cinnamon")
            ProdList.Add("Cassia")
            ProdList.Add("Chives")
```

```
                'Binding the DropDownList control to the
                'ArrayList object
                 ProdNameList.DataSource = ProdList
                'Activating the data binding for the list
                 ProdNameList.DataBind()
                'Activating the data binding for the text box
                'displaying order date
                 OrderDateBox.DataBind()
             End If
    End Sub
```

Notice that the `DataSource` property is used for data binding. Then, to reflect the bound data, the `DataBind` method is called explicitly for the `ProdNameList` control.

To display multiple values from the repeated-value data source, you simply need to set the `DataSource` property. The control then automatically displays item for each item in the data source. This is highly convenient because you don't have to write the complete code to map the items in the data source with the display items in the control.

When you build and run the application, the Product Name list automatically gets populated with the names of products. When you select a product from the list, and click the submit button, the `MessageLabel Label` control displays the selected item, as shown in Figure 8-7.

Binding to a HashTable

The `HashTable` class represents a list of items; each item is identified by a `Key` and a `Value` property. The `HashTable` objects are best for data binding with the list controls, where you want the text to be displayed (the `Text` property of the `Item` object in the `Items` collection) and the value to be returned when that item is selected (the `Value` property of the `Item` object in the `Items` collection) to be different. To get more information on the `Text` and `Value` properties of the `Item` object, check out Book 6, Chapter 3.

Each time that you bind a list control to a `HashTable`, the `DataTextField` and `DataValueField` properties need a special attention. These properties are common to all the list server controls:

- **`DataTextField`:** Represents the field or column of a data source, which contains the values to be used for display, such as the `Text` property of `Item` objects in the `Items` collection of a `DropDownList` control. When the data source is a `HashTable` object, set this property to `Key`.
- **`DataValueField`:** Represents the field or column in the data source, which contains the values to be used as the `Value` property of different list items of a list server control. When the data source is a `HashTable` object, set this property to `Value`.

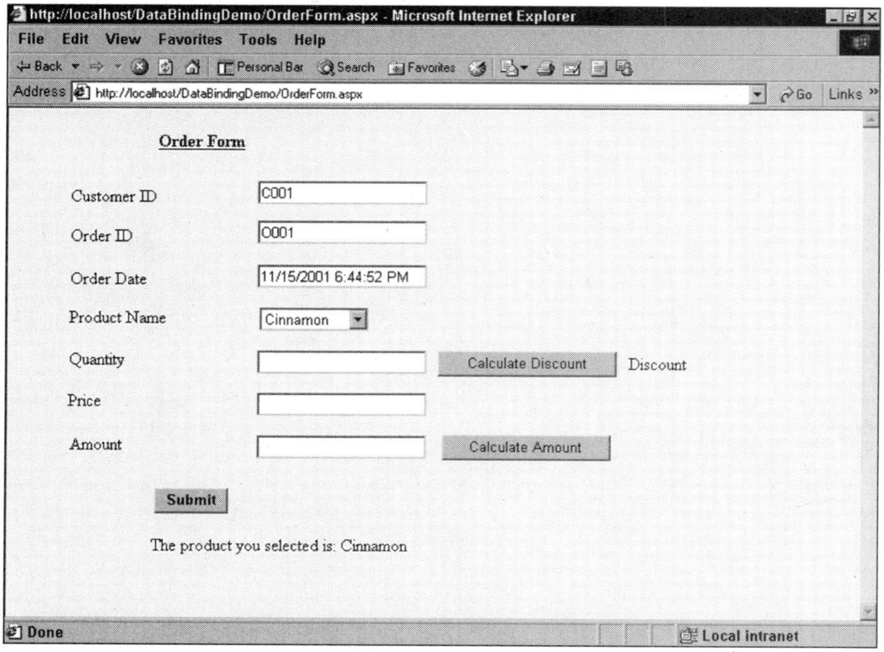

Figure 8-7: The Order form displays a list of products from an ArrayList.

In this section, we implement data binding to a HashTable for the DropDownList control displaying the list of product names. In the previous section, you bind this control to an ArrayList. Usually, order forms display a list of product names from which customers order the required products. However, when a customer selects a product, it translates into the corresponding product ID. This product ID is further used internally for any kind of querying. As a result, to implement different Text and Value properties for the range of items in the product name list, you bind this control to a HashTable.

1. **Switch to the code-behind file for the form and modify the code in the Page_Load method.**

   The Page_Load method should contain the following code:

```
Private Sub Page_Load(ByVal sender As System.Object,
ByVal e As System.EventArgs) Handles MyBase.Load
        'Put user code to initialize the page here
        If Not IsPostBack Then
            'Creating an object of the HashTable class
            Dim ProdList As Hashtable = New Hashtable()
            'Populating the HashTable object with list
            'items. Notice that the Add method takes two
```

```
                'parameters, the syntax being
add("Key","Value")
                ProdList.Add("Anise Seeds", "P001")
                ProdList.Add("Bay Leaf", "P002")
                ProdList.Add("Cinnamon", "P003")
                ProdList.Add("Cassia", "P004")
                ProdList.Add("Chives", "P005")
                'Setting the DataSource property of the
                'control to the HashTable
                ProdNameList.DataSource = ProdList
                'Setting the DataTextField property to "Key"
                ProdNameList.DataTextField = "Key"
                'Setting the DataValueField property to
                '"Value"
                ProdNameList.DataValueField = "Value"
                'Activating data binding for the list
                'displaying product names
                ProdNameList.DataBind()
                'Activating data binding for the text box
                'displaying order date
                OrderDateBox.DataBind()

        End If
End Sub
```

2. **Switch to the HTML view of the form and modify the data binding code of the `MessageLabel Label` control as follows:**

```
<asp:label id="MessageLabel"
Text='<%# "The product name you selected is: " +
   ProdNameList.SelectedItem.Text +
" . The corresponding product ID is: " +
   ProdNameList.SelectedItem.Value %>'
runat="server" Visible="False">
</asp:label>
```

Note that you bind the `Text` property of the `MessageLabel Label` control with both the `Text` and `Value` properties of the selected item of the `ProdNameList DropDownList` control.

Next, you build and run the application. Enter values for Customer ID and Order ID, select a product name, enter values for Quantity and Price for the selected product, and click the Calculate Discount and Calculate Amount buttons to calculate the discount and the payable amount. Finally, click the Submit button. The `MessageLabel Label` control at the bottom of the page displays the `Text` and `Value` properties of the selected item in the list. (See Figure 8-8.)

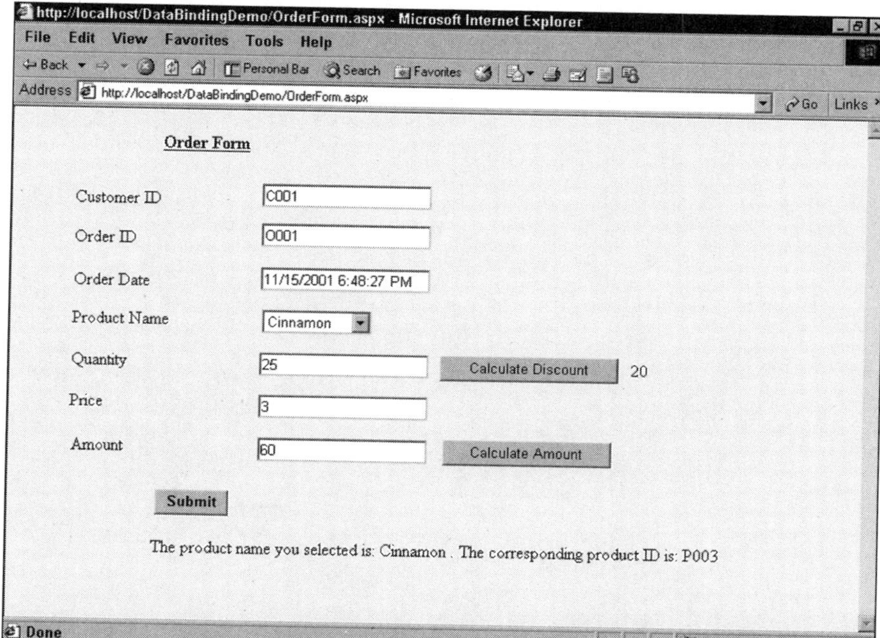

Figure 8-8: The Order form displays data binding to a HashTable.

Binding to a DataView

The `DataView` class represents a custom view of a data table. You can populate the `DataView` object either from a database or manually by using code. In this section, we show you how to bind the `DataView` object to a `DataGrid` server control. The `DataView` object is populated manually by using code. We give a complete description of the `DataGrid` control in Book 6, Chapter 9.

To implement data binding to a `DataView` object, add a new Web form — `SalesOutlets.aspx` — to the DataBindingDemo project. For a complete procedure to add a Web form to a project, check out Book 6, Chapter 3. In this form, add the `DataGrid` control and set its ID as `SalesOutletGrid`. Also, add a `Label` control and set its `Text` property to `Sales Outlets` (just to provide a heading for the form).

The `DataView` class resides in the `System.Data` namespace. For more on namespaces, read through Book 1, Chapter 2. Therefore, to use this class, you must import this namespace. To do so, switch to the code-behind file for the `SalesOutlets.aspx` form and write the following code:

```
Imports System.Data
```

Then, write the following code in the `Page_Load` method to bind the `DataGrid` control with the `DataView` object:

```
Private Sub Page_Load(ByVal sender As System.Object, ByVal e
          As System.EventArgs) Handles MyBase.Load
    'Put user code to initialize the page here
    If Not IsPostBack Then
      'Declaring objects of the DataTable and DataRow classes
      Dim DataTable1 As DataTable
      Dim DataRow1 As DataRow

      'Initializing the DataTable object
      DataTable1 = New DataTable()

      'Adding columns to the DataTable object
      DataTable1.Columns.Add(New DataColumn("City",
           GetType(String)))
      DataTable1.Columns.Add(New DataColumn("State",
           GetType(String)))

      'Creating arrays to store cities and their respective
      'states
      Dim strCity(5) As String
      Dim strState(5) As String
      Dim I As Integer
      strCity(0) = "Chicago"
      strCity(1) = "Hampstead"
      strCity(2) = "Houston"
      strCity(3) = "New York"
      strCity(4) = "Portland"

      strState(0) = "Illinois"
      strState(1) = "New York"
      strState(2) = "Texas"
      strState(3) = "New York"
      strState(4) = "Oregon"

      'Adding rows in the DataTable object
      For I = 0 To 4
        DataRow1 = DataTable1.NewRow()
        DataRow1(0) = strCity(I)
        DataRow1(1) = strState(I)
        DataTable1.Rows.Add(DataRow1)
      Next

      'Setting the DataSource property of the DataGrid
      'control to the DataView representing the
```

```
        'DataTable object
        SalesOutletGrid.DataSource = New DataView(DataTable1)

        'Calling the DataBind() method for the DataGrid control
        SalesOutletGrid.DataBind()
    End If
End Sub
```

When you build the application and browse the `SalesOutlets.aspx` form (right-click the form and select View in Browser from the pop-up menu), the `DataGrid` control displays the cities and states in a tabular format, as shown in Figure 8-9.

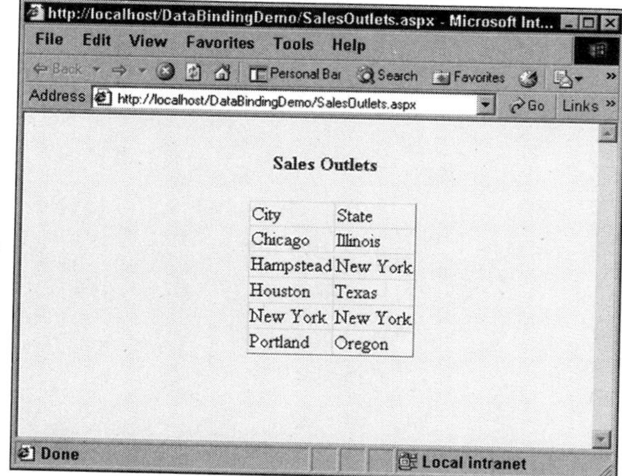

Figure 8-9: A sample form demonstrates data binding to a DataView.

Chapter 9: Working with Web Server Control Templates

In This Chapter

- Understanding Web Server Control templates
- Creating Web Server Control templates
- Using templates with the Repeater, DataList, and DataGrid controls

Each server control provided with Visual Studio .NET has a default look and layout that's determined by a default set of properties and styles applied automatically to the control when you add the control to a form. You can customize the appearance of a control by setting its properties and styles, but you can also use templates to customize the look and layout of server controls. By using these templates, you can tweak styles, properties, and the appearance of individual portions of a control.

In this chapter, we show you what these new Web Server Control templates are and how to create them. Then we walk you through using the templates with the Repeater, DataList, and DataGrid server controls. We love the ease with which you can customize the appearance of individual sections of these controls.

Getting to Know Web Server Control Templates

Three server controls — Repeater, DataList, and DataGrid — all must be bound to some data source to be rendered on a Web form. These controls support a number of templates that you can use to define the look and layout of these controls. Broadly speaking, a *Web server control template* is a combination of HyperText Markup Language (HTML) elements, controls, and embedded server controls. You can customize or create a template by including these elements.

You can create different types of templates to define the appearance of different sections of server controls. In fact, to define the look and layout of each portion of the control — such as a header, separator, or footer — a separate template exists. For example, you can create a HeaderTemplate to define the appearance of the header of a control. Although the names of different templates are self-explanatory, Figure 9-1 gives a clearer picture of the different types of templates.

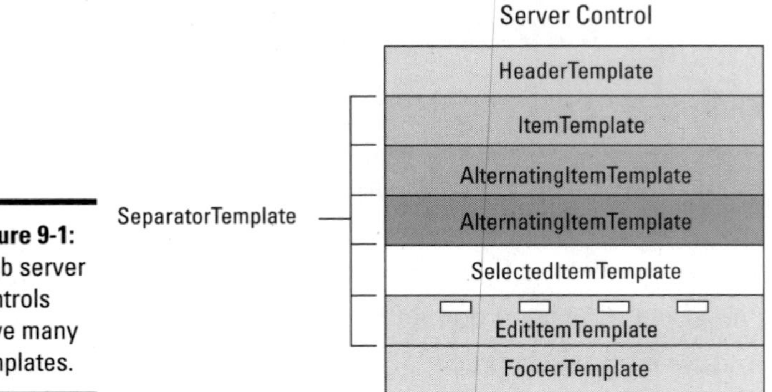

Figure 9-1: Web server controls have many templates.

Although Figure 9-1 displays all the templates, not all these templates are supported by all three server controls (`Repeater`, `DataList`, and `DataGrid`). In Table 9-1, we describe the different templates along with the server controls that support these templates.

Table 9-1 Templates Types and Supporting Server Controls

Template	*Description*	*Supporting Control(s)*
HeaderTemplate	The set of elements and controls that are rendered once before any other item is rendered in the control.	`Repeater`, `DataList`, and `DataGrid`
ItemTemplate	The set of elements and controls that are rendered for each item in the control.	`Repeater`, `DataList`, and `DataGrid`
AlternatingItemTemplate	The set of elements and controls that are rendered once for each alternating item in the control.	`Repeater` and `DataList`
SeparatorTemplate	The set of elements that are rendered as a separator element between items in the control.	`Repeater` and `DataList`
SelectedItemTemplate	The set of elements and controls that are rendered when an item is selected in the control.	`DataList`
EditItemTemplate	The set of elements and controls that are rendered when an item in the control is in Edit mode.	`DataList` and `DataGrid`
FooterTemplate	The set of elements and controls that are rendered once after all the elements are rendered in the control.	`Repeater`, `DataList`, and `DataGrid`

Beginning to Create Templates

Visual Studio .NET provides visual designers to help you design Web forms in a What-You-See-Is-What-You-Get (WYSIWYG) manner. As you design your forms by adding controls and setting their properties, the corresponding ASP.NET code is generated automatically. Similarly, Visual Studio .NET enables you to use visual designers to create and edit templates — in which case, the corresponding ASP.NET code gets automatically generated. However, you can also directly edit the ASP.NET code to create and edit templates. Ultimately, the choice is yours depending on your preferences and convenience. In this section, we discuss how to use the visual designer of Visual Studio .NET to create and edit templates. Also, we cover the corresponding ASP.NET code.

Using the visual designer

The visual designer makes it extremely convenient for you to create and edit templates. Although this feature is available only for the `DataList` control, we bet that you like how easy it is to use. Here are the generalized steps that you need to follow to create or edit a template:

1. **In the Design view (click the Design button at the bottom of the designer window), right-click the server control for which you want to create or edit a template.**
2. **From the pop-up menu that appears, select Edit Template.**
3. **From the available list of templates (the different options represent groups of similar templates — such as Header and Footer Templates and Item Templates), select the group of templates that you want to edit.**

   The control appears in the Edit mode where you can add other HTML elements, controls, or server controls. For example, to edit ItemTemplate (which is grouped within Item Templates) for the `DataList` control, right-click the `DataList` control and choose Edit Template⇨Item Templates.

   Figure 9-2 shows the `DataList` control in the Edit mode for Item Templates. In Edit mode, notice that all the Item Templates (ItemTemplate, AlternatingItemTemplate, SelectedItemTemplate, and EditItemTemplate) appear.

4. **In the template-editing mode, add HTML elements, controls, and server controls to the individual templates in the control.**

   For example, to add a `Label` control to ItemTemplate in the control, drag the `Label` control from the Toolbox to ItemTemplate as shown in Figure 9-3.

   You find the Toolbox in the left bar of the Visual Studio .NET window. If the Toolbox does not appear, choose View⇨Toolbox.

Figure 9-2: Amend the DataList control in Edit mode for Item Templates.

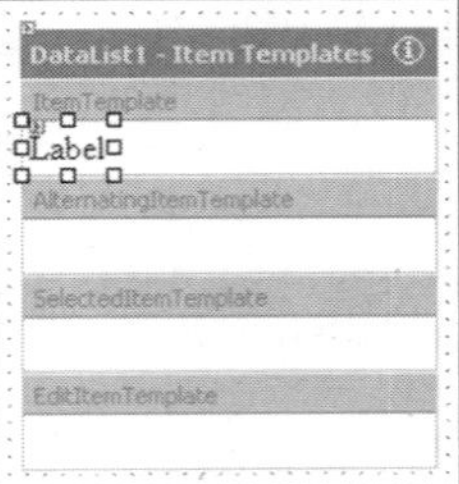

Figure 9-3: Add controls to the individual templates in the DataList control.

5. **From the Properties window (select the control in the template and press F4), set the properties of the controls that you add to the individual templates in the control.**

6. **To finish template editing, right-click the control and select End Template Editing from the pop-up menu that appears.**

After you complete editing the templates in the control, you need to tell this to the visual editor so that the control comes out of the template-editing mode.

Using the ASP.NET code

You can directly edit the ASP.NET code in the HTML view of the ASPX file to create or edit templates. An ASPX file has a .aspx extension, which represents the page file of a Web form. For example, to create ItemTemplate for the `DataList` control, write the following code:

```
<asp:DataList id="DataList1" runat="server">
   <ItemTemplate>
   </ItemTemplate>
</asp:DataList>
```

After you add this code, you can add the controls that you want to include within the template. You can also set the properties of the embedded controls and data bind them. For example, to include a data-bound Label server control in ItemTemplate of the DataList control, write the following code:

```
<asp:DataList id="DataList1" runat="server">
   <ItemTemplate>
     <asp:Label id="Label1"
     Text = "<%# data source %> " runat="server" />
   </ItemTemplate>
</asp:DataList>
```

After you create a template, its controls must be bound to some data source to be rendered in a browser. You can read Book 6, Chapter 8 to refresh your concepts on data binding.

A control's DataSource property is used for data binding. To display rows from the data source in individual items of any of the controls among the Repeater, DataList, or DataGrid controls, you must bind the embedded controls with the data source of the container control. However, you can also use a completely different data source for the embedded controls if you want. To bind the embedded controls to the data source of the container control (Repeater, DataList, or DataGrid), you need to use the DataBinder.Eval method provided with the .NET Framework. The syntax is

```
<%# DataBinder.Eval(Container.DataItem, DataFieldName,
           [FormatString]) %>
```

The three arguments of the DataBinder.Eval method are

- **Container.DataItem:** Represents the container for the individual items to be bound to data rows.
- **DataFieldName:** Represents the name of the field (or column) in the data rows.
- **[FormatString]:** An optional argument that represents the format sting to be used to format individual items.

Using Templates with the Repeater Control

In this section, we discuss the Repeater control in detail and show you how to create templates for this control. The Repeater server control is a data-bound container control that enables you to display data from the bound data source as custom lists. Unlike most server controls, this control has no default layout. Even if you bind the Repeater control with a data source, the control is not rendered on the page until you provide a layout to the control. Therefore, for each item to be rendered in this control, you must at least create ItemTemplate. However, you can enhance the appearance of the control by creating other supported templates, such as HeaderTemplate, FooterTemplate, or AlternatingItemTemplate.

Because the `Repeater` control has no default look and layout, you can create any kind of list with the following formats:

- A comma-delimited list, such as name 1, name 2, name 3, and so on
- A bulleted list
- A numbered list
- A tabular layout

Rendering the Repeater control by using templates

To implement templates with the `Repeater` control, create an ASP.NET Web Application project in Visual Basic and name the project `TemplatesDemo`. Rename the default Web form — `WebForm1.aspx` — to `RepeaterDemo.aspx`. Then, add the `Repeater` control from the Toolbox to the form. When you add the `Repeater` control, the control has no user interface. You need to create templates for this control so as to provide a user interface to the control.

After you create the TemplateDemo application and design the form, open the code-behind file for the form (press F7) and perform the following steps:

1. **Write the following code to import the `System.Data` namespace.**

   For more on namespaces, read through Book 1, Chapter 2.

   Because you use a `DataView` object for data binding with the `Repeater` control, you need to import this namespace.

   ```
   Imports System.Data
   ```

2. **Create a function that includes code for binding the `Repeater` control with a `DataView` object.**

   The `DataView` object has a data table with two columns containing product names and product quantities.

   ```
   Function Bindgrid()
        Dim DataTable1 As DataTable
        Dim DataRow1 As DataRow
        Dim ProdNameStr(5) As String
        Dim ProdQtyInt(5) As Integer
        Dim I As Integer

        ProdNameStr(0) = "Anise Seeds"
        ProdNameStr(1) = "Basil Leaf"
        ProdNameStr(2) = "Cinnamon"
   ```

```
        ProdNameStr(3) = "Cassia"
        ProdNameStr(4) = "Cloves"

        ProdQtyInt(0) = 250
        ProdQtyInt(1) = 300
        ProdQtyInt(2) = 150
        ProdQtyInt(3) = 175
        ProdQtyInt(4) = 400

        'create a DataTable
        DataTable1 = New DataTable()
        DataTable1.Columns.Add(New
        DataColumn("ProductName", GetType(String)))
        DataTable1.Columns.Add(New
        DataColumn("ProductQty", GetType(Integer)))

        'Create rows and put in sample data
        For I = 0 To 4
          DataRow1 = DataTable1.NewRow()
          DataRow1(0) = ProdNameStr(I)
          DataRow1(1) = ProdQtyInt(I)
          DataTable1.Rows.Add(DataRow1)
        Next

        Repeater1.DataSource = New DataView(DataTable1)
        Repeater1.DataBind()
    End Function
```


3. **Write the following code in the** `Page_Load` **method to call the** `Bindgrid` **function to bind the** `Repeater` **control to the** `DataView` **object.**

```
    Private Sub Page_Load(ByVal sender As System.Object,
    ByVal e As System.EventArgs) Handles MyBase.Load
       'Put user code to initialize the page here
       If Not IsPostBack Then
          Bindgrid()
       End If
    End Sub
```

4. **Switch to the HTML view of the form (by clicking the HTML button at the bottom of the designer window) and write the following code to create the different templates:**

```
    <asp:Repeater id="Repeater1" runat="server">
       <HeaderTemplate>
         <table border="2">
           <tr>
             <td>
               <b>Product Name</b>
             </td>
             <td>
               <b>Product Quantity</b>
```

```
            </td>
          </tr>
      </HeaderTemplate>

      <ItemTemplate>
        <tr>
          <td>
            <%# DataBinder.Eval(Container.DataItem,
"ProductName") %>
          </td>
          <td>
            <%# DataBinder.Eval(Container.DataItem,
"ProductQty") %>
          </td>
        </tr>
      </ItemTemplate>

      <AlternatingItemTemplate>
        <tr>
          <td bgcolor="#99cccc">
            <%# DataBinder.Eval(Container.DataItem,
"ProductName") %>
          </td>
          <td bgcolor="#ffcccc">
            <%# DataBinder.Eval(Container.DataItem,
"ProductQty") %>
          </td>
        </tr>
      </AlternatingItemTemplate>

      <FooterTemplate>
        </Table>
      </FooterTemplate>
    </asp:Repeater>
```

In the preceding code, HeaderTemplate contains an HTML table with two columns with headings "Product Name" and "Product Quantity". Notice that the HTML table is not closed in HeaderTemplate because the table is not complete and should include a row for each data row in the data source.

ItemTemplate contains two columns for the table; each column displays data from the data columns in the DataView object. AlternatingItemTemplate renders the same output as displayed in ItemTemplate, but displays each column with a different background color.

FooterTemplate marks the closing of the HTML table indicating that the table contains no more rows.

When you build and run the application, the Repeater control displays the product names and their quantities in a tabular format as shown in Figure 9-4.

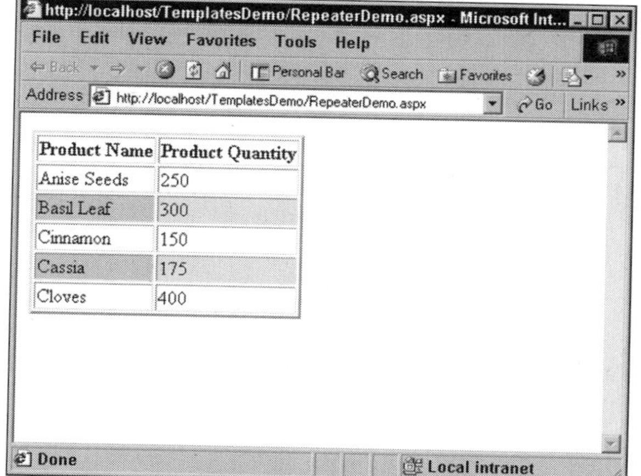

Figure 9-4: Use the Repeater control to display a product list in tabular format.

Handling events of the Repeater control

Among the several events supported by the `Repeater` control, two events need special attention with respect to templates.

- `ItemCreated`: These events are generated each time that individual items are rendered. You can handle this event to customize the item-creation process. For example, you can set certain properties of the items at the time of their creation.
- `ItemCommand`: These events are generated each time that a user clicks a button (a `Button`, `ImageButton`, or a `LinkButton` control) in individual items. You can track the button clicked by a user by accessing the `CommandName` property of the button. This property is passed as one of the arguments of the event handler for the `ItemCommand` event of the `Repeater` control.

The `CommandName` property of the `Button` control is case-sensitive; use only lowercase letters.

In the next section, we demonstrate how to handle each of these events. However, first add a `Label` control below the `Repeater` control in the `RepeaterDemo.aspx` form. Set the ID of this `Label` control to `MessageLabel` and then set the `Visible` property to `False`.

Handling the ItemCreated event

Switch to the code-behind file of the form (by pressing F7). Create the event handler for the `ItemCreated` event of the `Repeater` control by selecting

Repeater1 from the Class Name list and selecting ItemCreated from the Method Name list. Then, write the following code in this event handler:

```
Private Sub Repeater1_ItemCreated(ByVal sender As Object,
            ByVal e As
            System.Web.UI.WebControls.RepeaterItemEventArgs)
            Handles Repeater1.ItemCreated
      MessageLabel.Text = "All items have been created."
      MessageLabel.Font.Italic = True
      MessageLabel.Visible = True
End Sub
```

When you build and run the application, the label displays the message in italic as shown in Figure 9-5.

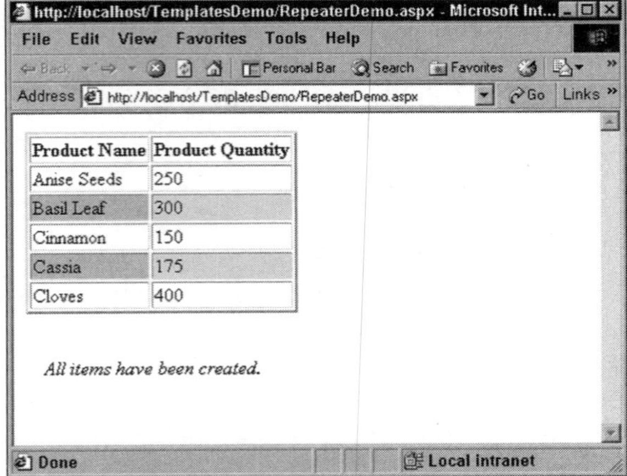

Figure 9-5: A form that demonstrates handling the `ItemCreated` event of the Repeater control.

Handling the ItemCommand event

To handle this event, you must modify the templates of the `Repeater` control to include `Button` controls. Thus, switch to the HTML view of the `RepeaterDemo.aspx` form and write the code in HeaderTemplate to include a column with heading `"Item Status"`. The modified code is given below:

```
<HeaderTemplate>
   <table border="2">
     <tr>
       <td>
         <b>Product Name</b>
       </td>
       <td>
         <b>Product Quantity</b>
       </td>
       <td>
```

```
            <b>Item Status</b>
         </td>
      </tr>
</HeaderTemplate>
```

Then, modify the code in ItemTemplate and AlternatingItemTemplate to include a `Button` control in the third column of the table. The modified code is

```
<ItemTemplate>
   <tr>
      <td>
         <%# DataBinder.Eval(Container.DataItem, "ProductName")
             %>
      </td>
      <td>
         <%# DataBinder.Eval(Container.DataItem, "ProductQty")
             %>
      </td>
      <td>
         <asp:Button ID="StatusButton" CommandName="status"
   Text="Check Status" Runat="server" />
      </td>
   </tr>
</ItemTemplate>

<AlternatingItemTemplate>
   <tr>
      <td bgcolor="#99cccc">
         <%# DataBinder.Eval(Container.DataItem, "ProductName")
             %>
      </td>
      <td bgcolor="#ffcccc">
         <%# DataBinder.Eval(Container.DataItem, "ProductQty")
             %>
      </td>
      <td>
      <asp:Button ID="Button1" CommandName="status"
            Text="Check Status" Runat="server" />
      </td>
   </tr>
</AlternatingItemTemplate>
```

In the preceding code, notice that the `CommandName` property of the `Button` control has been set so that the button clicked by a user can be identified in the event handler of the `ItemCommand` event.

Next create the event handler for the `ItemCommand` event of the `Repeater` control. Switch to the code-behind file for the form, select Repeater1 from the Class Name list, and then select ItemCommand from the Method Name list. Then write the following code to display an appropriate message in the label depending on the button that is clicked:

```
Private Sub Repeater1_ItemCommand(ByVal source As Object,
    ByVal e As
    System.Web.UI.WebControls.RepeaterCommandEventArgs)
    Handles Repeater1.ItemCommand
        If (e.CommandName = "status") Then
            If (e.Item.ItemIndex = 0) Then
                MessageLabel.Text = "We have sufficient stock
                    for this item."
            End If
            If (e.Item.ItemIndex = 1) Then
                MessageLabel.Text = "We have sufficient stock
                    for this item."
            End If
            If (e.Item.ItemIndex = 2) Then
                MessageLabel.Text = "The Reorder Level has
                    been reached. Please place an order for
                    this item."
            End If
            If (e.Item.ItemIndex = 3) Then
                MessageLabel.Text = "The Reorder Level has
                    been reached. Please place an order for
                    this item."
            End If
            If (e.Item.ItemIndex = 4) Then
                MessageLabel.Text = "We have sufficient stock
                    for this item."
            End If
            MessageLabel.Visible = True
        End If

End Sub
```

When you build and run the application and click a button, a message is displayed on the label as shown in Figure 9-6.

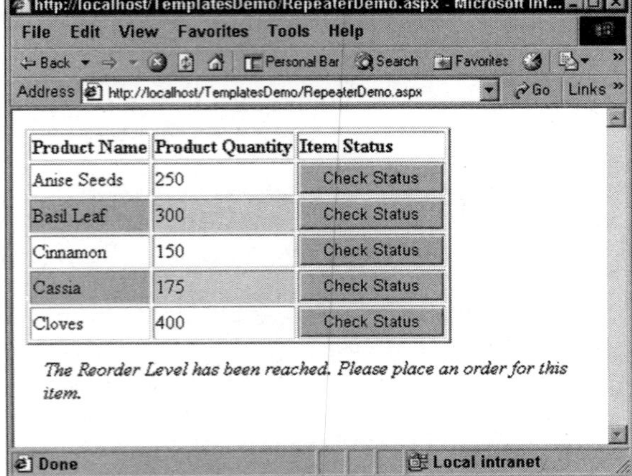

Figure 9-6: Handle the Item-Command event of the Repeater control.

Using Templates with the DataList Control

The DataList control is a data-bound container control that displays data from the bound data source in a format defined using templates. This control displays rows of data from the data source as separate items. To render these rows of data, you must create at least ItemTemplate. The DataList control displays the data rows as a single vertical column by default. However, you can customize the look and layout of this control by using different templates.

Like the Repeater control, the DataList control supports the ItemCreated and ItemCommand events. In addition to these events, this control generates some more events when a user clicks a button in the DataList control. The event generated depends on the CommandName property of the button that is clicked. Different events and the corresponding CommandName properties are listed in Table 9-2. When a button with no predefined CommandName is clicked, the ItemCommand event is generated.

Table 9-2 Button Click Events Supported by the DataList Control

CommandName	*Event*
Edit	EditCommand
Update	UpdateCommand
Cancel	CancelCommand
Delete	DeleteCommand

Rendering the DataList control by using templates

To demonstrate using templates to render the bound data from a data source in the DataList control, add a new Web form — h — to the project TemplatesDemo. To learn how to add a new Web form to a project, read Book 6, Chapter 3. Then, add the DataList control from the Toolbox to the form.

Here we use the same data source that we use for the Repeater control in the earlier section "Rendering the Repeater control by using templates." Switch to the code-behind file for the DataListDemo.aspx form and import the System.Data namespace. Then, create the Datagrid function. You do not need to type the entire code. Simply copy the Bindgrid function from the RepeaterDemo.aspx.vb file and paste it in the DataListDemo.aspx.vb file. Modify the name of the function from Bindgrid to Datagrid. Also, in this function, call the DataBind method for the DataList control: This is the only change in the code from the earlier section "Rendering the Repeater control by using templates." Finally, call the Datagrid method in the Page_Load method.

Then switch to the HTML view of the DataListDemo.aspx form and create ItemTemplate for the DataList control by writing the following code:

```
<ItemTemplate>
   <tr>
     <td>
       <%# DataBinder.Eval(Container.DataItem, "ProductName")
           %>
     </td>
     <td>
       <%# DataBinder.Eval(Container.DataItem, "ProductQty")
           %>
     </td>
   </tr>
</ItemTemplate>
```

Set the DataListDemo.aspx page as the start-up page by right-clicking the page in Solution Explorer and selecting Set As Start Page from the pop-up menu that appears. (Access Solution Explorer by selecting Solution Explorer from the View menu.) When you build and run the application, the page displays the data items as a single vertical column as shown in Figure 9-7.

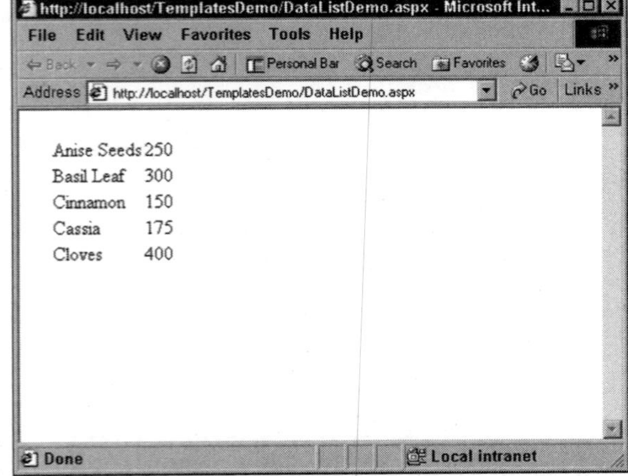

Figure 9-7: Use the DataList control to display bound data items as a single column.

In addition to simply rendering data items from the data source, you can also use the DataList control to select, edit, and update the data rows. In the subsequent sections, we look at these functionalities.

Selecting data rows in the DataList control

To implement the item selection functionality with the `DataList` control, you need to create SelectedItemTemplate and handle the `ItemCommand` event of the `DataList` control. Follow these steps:

1. **Switch to the HTML view of the `DataListDemo.aspx` form and modify ItemTemplate to include a column to add a `Button` control with the `CommandName` property as `select`.**

   The `CommandName` property of the Button control is case-sensitive; use only lowercase letters.

   ```
   <ItemTemplate>
     <tr>
       <td>
         <%# DataBinder.Eval(Container.DataItem,
     "ProductName") %>
       </td>
       <td>
         <%# DataBinder.Eval(Container.DataItem,
     "ProductQty") %>
       </td>
       <td>
         <asp:Button runat="server" Text="Select"
   CommandName="select"></asp:Button>
       </td>
     </tr>
   </ItemTemplate>
   ```

2. **Create SelectedItemTemplate to include text, elements, and controls to be rendered in the data item row when the row is selected.**

   In the following code, we add `TextBox` controls and set their `enabled` property to `False` to prevent users from editing the content although the data won't be updated in the data source if users edit the contents.

   ```
   <SelectedItemTemplate>
      <tr>
        <td>
          <asp:TextBox enabled="False" Runat="server"
   Text='<%# DataBinder.Eval(Container.DataItem,
   "ProductName") %>' />
        </td>
        <td>
          <asp:TextBox enabled="False" Runat="server"
   Text='<%# DataBinder.Eval(Container.DataItem,
   "ProductQty") %>' />
        </td>
        <td>
   ```

```
        <asp:Button runat="server" Text="Edit"
    CommandName="edit" ID="Button1"></asp:Button>
      </td>
    </tr>
</SelectedItemTemplate>
```

3. **Switch to the code-behind file of the `DataListDemo.aspx` form.**
4. **Create the event handler for the `ItemCommand` event of the DataList control by checking the `CommandName` property of the clicked button.**

   If this property is `select`, set the `SelectedIndex` property of the `DataList` control to the index of the item that needs to be selected.
5. **Call the function to bind the `DataList` control with the data source.**

```
Private Sub DataList1_ItemCommand(ByVal source As
Object, ByVal e As
System.Web.UI.WebControls.DataListCommandEventArgs)
Handles DataList1.ItemCommand
        If e.CommandName = "select" Then
            DataList1.SelectedIndex = e.Item.ItemIndex
            Datagrid()
        End If

End Sub
```

To cancel the item selection, set the `Selectedndex` property to `-1`.

When you build and run the application, the `DataListDemo.aspx` form displays the Select button. When you click this button in any row, the corresponding row gets selected as shown in Figure 9-8.

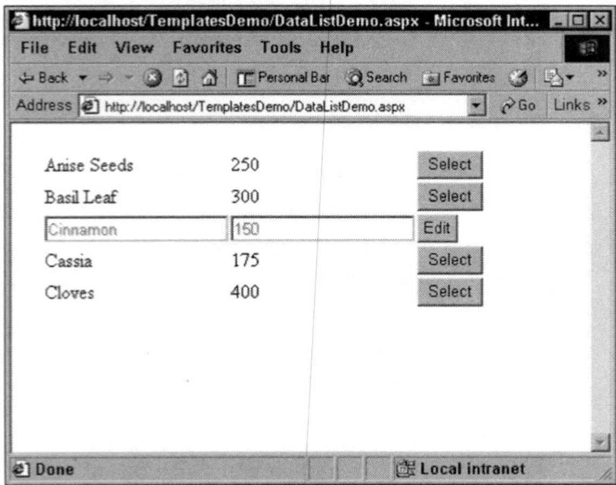

Figure 9-8: Display a selected item in a form.

Editing data rows in the DataList control

To implement data item editing in the DataList control, you create EditItemTemplate and handle the EditCommand, UpdateCommand, and CancelCommand events of the DataList control. To implement this functionality in your DataListDemo.aspx form:

1. **Switch to the HTML view of the DataListDemo.aspx form and create EditItemTemplate to include text, elements, and controls to be rendered in the Edit mode.**

   For this example, include two Text Box controls for editing the product name and product quantity.

2. **Include two Button controls with CommandName property set as update and cancel.**

   The complete code for the EditItemTemplate is given below.

```
<EditItemTemplate>
   <tr>
     <td>
       <asp:TextBox enabled="True" Runat="server"
Text='<%# DataBinder.Eval(Container.DataItem,
"ProductName") %>' ID="Textbox1" />
     </td>
     <td>
       <asp:TextBox enabled="True" Runat="server"
Text='<%# DataBinder.Eval(Container.DataItem,
"ProductQty") %>' ID="Textbox2" />
     </td>
     <td>
       <asp:Button runat="server" Text="Update"
CommandName="update" ID="Button2"></asp:Button>
     </td>
     <td>
       <asp:Button runat="server" Text="Cancel"
CommandName="cancel" ID="Button3"></asp:Button>
     </td>
   </tr>
</EditItemTemplate>
```

3. **Switch to the code-behind file (Press F7) for the DataListDemo.aspx form and create the event handler for the EditCommand event of the DataList control.**

4. **In the event handler, set the EditItemIndex property of the DataList control to the index of the item to be edited.**

5. **Bind the `DataList` control to its data source.**

```
Private Sub DataList1_EditCommand(ByVal source As
   Object,
   ByVal e As
   System.Web.UI.WebControls.DataListCommandEventArgs)
   Handles DataList1.EditCommand
        DataList1.EditItemIndex = e.Item.ItemIndex
        Datagrid()
End Sub
```

When you build and run the application and then click the Select button, the Edit button appears. When you click this Edit button, the Update and Cancel buttons appear. Also, the text boxes in the row become enabled. (See Figure 9-9.)

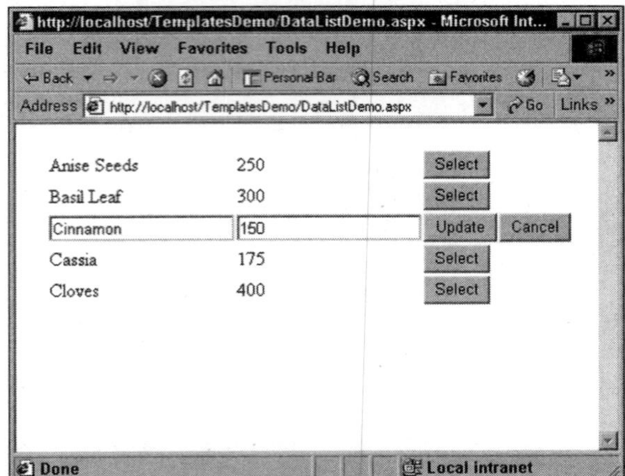

Figure 9-9: Display an item in the Edit mode in a form.

To update the edited data item in the data source, you must write the corresponding code in the event handler of the `UpdateCommand` event of the `DataList` control. If you want to cancel the changes made to the data item, you need to handle the `CancelCommand` event of the `DataList` control; and in the event handler, set the `EditItemIndex` property of the `DataList` control to `-1`. If you want to delete a data item, you need to write the corresponding code in the event handler for the `DeleteCommand` event of the `DataList` control.

Using Templates with the DataGrid Control

The DataGrid control is a data-bound multi-column control that displays the data from the data source in a grid format. Like the Repeater and DataList controls, the DataGrid control is rendered only when you bind the control to a data source and create at least an ItemTemplate. However, you can customize the look and layout of the DataGrid control by creating several other templates, such as HeaderTemplate and FooterTemplate.

With the DataGrid control, you can create different types of columns that enable you to implement item selection, edition, updating, and sorting. In fact, you can completely customize this control to provide desired functionality by creating specific columns called *Template Columns*. The different types of columns are

- **Bound Columns:** Use these to create columns that display data bound to some database fields.
- **Buttons Columns:** Use these to create columns that display one of the buttons to implement item selection, editing, updating, deleting, and cancel editing.
- **Hyperlink Columns:** Use these to create columns that display information as hyperlinks. You can click these hyperlinks to navigate to some other Web page.
- **Template Columns:** Use these to create completely customized columns in the control. In this column, you can include text, HTML elements, and server controls, or you can bind the included controls to a data source. These columns provide you complete flexibility for customization.

Like the DataList control, the DataGrid control supports several events. These events include ItemCreated, ItemCommand, EditCommand, UpdateCommand, DeleteCommand, and CancelCommand. The DataGrid control also supports SortItemCommand event to implement sorting for a data item.

Before proceeding to move ahead and implement templates with the DataGrid control, you may wish to review earlier sections in this chapter that cover the different types of templates and how to select, edit, update, cancel, and delete data items.

To demonstrate the use of templates with the DataGrid control, add another form — DataGridDemo.aspx — to the TemplatesDemo project. Then add the DataGrid control from the Toolbox to the form.

We use the same data source that we use for the `Repeater` and `DataList` controls in the earlier sections "Rendering the Repeater control by using templates" and "Rendering the DataList control by using templates."

Switch to the code-behind file for the `DataGridDemo.aspx` form and import the `System.Data` namespace. Then create the `Datagrid` function. In this function, call the `DataBind` method for the `DataGrid` control. Finally, call the `Datagrid` method in the `Page_Load` method of the form.

Next, switch to the Design view of the `DataGridDemo.aspx` form, select the `DataGrid` control, and display the Properties window (press F4). In the Properties window, click the ellipsis in the Columns property to open the DataGrid1 Properties dialog box as shown in Figure 9-10.

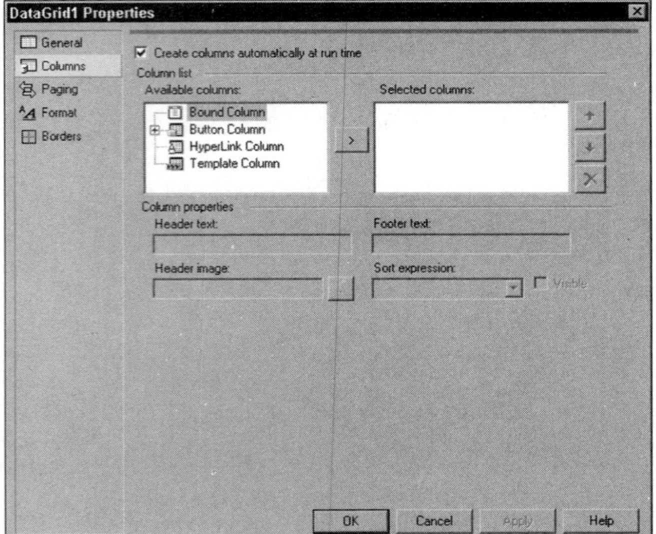

Figure 9-10: Create columns for the DataGrid control in its Properties dialog box.

In the DataGrid1Properties dialog box, select Template Column (from the Available Columns list), enter **Product Category** in the Header Text text box, and click OK to complete the process.

Switch to the HTML view of the `DataGridDemo.aspx` form. Notice that the following code gets automatically generated for the Template column that you create.

```
<Columns>
   <asp:TemplateColumn HeaderText="Product
   Category"></asp:TemplateColumn>
</Columns>
```

You can then create several templates in the Template Column to render and customize the column data values. Write the following code to create ItemTemplate to display a Label control displaying the product category as Spice in the Template column.

```
<asp:TemplateColumn HeaderText="Product Category">
    <ItemTemplate>
      <asp:Label ID="Label1" Runat="server"
          Text="Spice"></asp:Label>
    </ItemTemplate>
</asp:TemplateColumn>
```

Finally, set the DataGrid.aspx page as the start-up page and run the application. The page displays the output shown in Figure 9-11.

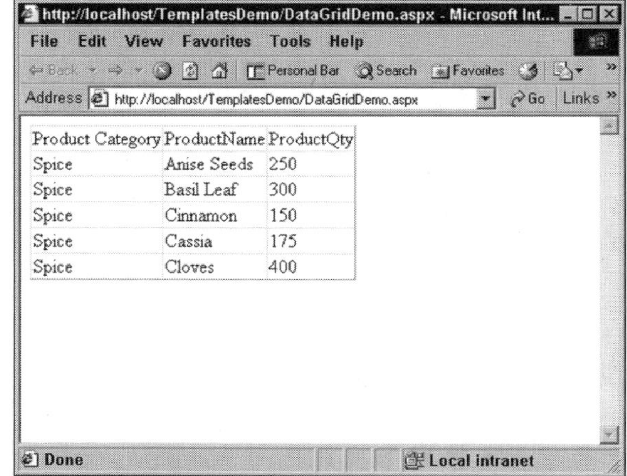

Figure 9-11: Set a DataGrid control to implement a Template column.

Chapter 10: Creating Mobile Web Applications

In This Chapter

- **Preparing the ground for mobile Web applications**
- **Getting started with mobile Web applications**
- **Using validation Mobile Web Forms Controls**
- **Using list Mobile Web Forms Controls**

As the World Wide Web's popularity increases, so does our dependence on it. Today, users want to access the Internet from almost anywhere. No longer do they want to be solely dependent on accessing the Internet through a browser on a PC. To answer this demand, technology has made it possible for users to access the Internet from mobile devices, such as cellular phones or personal digital assistants (PDAs). However, if you've accessed a Web site from any of these mobile devices, you know how hard it is to navigate Web sites on them because reading the output on one of these devices is difficult (for various reasons, but more on that later). By now, you and many other users might have decided that these mobile devices aren't worth the trouble to access the Web from anywhere.

But take heart — as a .NET developer, you can change users' minds about using mobile devices to access Web sites. Visual Studio .NET enables you to develop mobile Web applications that can vary the output depending on the device used for accessing them. So whether you access a Web site from a mobile phone or a PC hardly makes any difference. Wow! This is surely going to make users around the globe happy.

In this chapter, we introduce you to mobile Web applications and show you how to create them by using mobile Web Forms controls. What are you waiting for? Get ready to explore this exciting feature of Visual Studio .NET!

Preparing the Ground for Mobile Web Applications

The ability to access Web sites from mobile devices is a landmark. Perhaps you're curious to know about the technology that has made this access possible: the wireless Internet and the standard communication protocol, Wireless Application Protocol (WAP).

Before we proceed to showing you how to create mobile Web applications (in the section "Getting Started with Mobile Web Applications"), we sate your curiosity by first giving you a quick-and-dirty overview of WAP and the lowdown on the Mobile Internet Toolkit.

Wireless Application Protocol

Compared to browsing the Web from a PC, browsing the Web through a mobile device is difficult because the output is extremely bad. A number of constraints contribute to this bad output:

- Mobile phones are constrained by limited CPU capacity, memory, and battery life that make it difficult for users to access the Internet from a mobile phone.
- Mobile phone Web access requires high bandwidth, which would cause too much overhead when establishing a connection between a client and server.
- Web pages developed for the Internet don't fit on the average mobile phone's tiny screen.

These reasons led to the invention of a new set of protocols that enable wireless devices, such as mobile phones, to access the Internet. WAP Forum, the industry association that includes companies such as Phone.com, Nokia, and Ericsson (among hundreds of others), provides the wireless industry with a single open standard for wireless access: *Wireless Application Protocol (WAP)*. WAP is a communication protocol that allows wireless devices, such as mobile phones, PDAs, and two-way pagers, to connect to the Internet.

As a standard protocol, WAP has made Web browsing through mobile devices a more satisfying — and less aggravating — experience. However, to access the Internet from mobile devices, you must have a device that's WAP-enabled. WAP-enabled mobile devices have *micro-browser* software installed on them. This micro-browser software sends and receives the requests for accessing the Internet. Plus, to access a site with a WAP-enabled device, the site, too, must be WAP-enabled. WAP-enabled sites are created using WML and WMLScript. These languages are used to send and receive information on a mobile phone. The mobile phone, in turn, has a micro-browser (similar to the Web browser in the Web) that displays the received information to the user. Yahoo! and Google are examples of WAP-enabled Web sites. To check out more WAP-enabled sites, visit `www.wap.com`.

Micro-browser software is manufactured on a chip and then sold to mobile handset manufacturers. These manufacturers then integrate the chip with their products. The leading manufacturer of micro-browser software is Openwave Systems, which was formerly known as Phone.com.

Before you can fully understand how WAP-enabled mobile devices connect to the Internet, you must first understand the WAP architecture. WAP architecture is similar to Web architecture. In Web architecture, the client (browser) sends a request to the server, the server acknowledges the request, and then responds to it. The Web server and the client communicate by using Hypertext Transfer Protocol (HTTP). WAP architecture, on the other hand, has a *WAP gateway* present between the client and the server. A WAP gateway is software placed between a network that supports WAP and an IP network, such as the Internet. In the WAP architecture, the process to access an application stored on the server is as follows:

1. The client (mobile device) initiates a connection with the WAP gateway and sends a request for the content.
2. The WAP gateway converts the request into the format that the Internet understands and then forwards the request to the Web server.
3. In response to the request, the Web server sends the content to the gateway, which then translates the content into the WAP format and sends it to the mobile phone.

Web architecture information is hosted in HTML files; in the case of WAP, information is sent to the client as WML (Wireless Markup Language) or WMLScript files. WML and WMLScript are the languages used to write WAP content. These languages are used to send and receive information on a mobile device. The mobile device has a micro-browser — similar to the Web browser in the Web — that displays the received information to the user.

The Mobile Internet Toolkit

When you install Microsoft Visual Studio .NET, it doesn't allow you to create mobile Web applications by default. To be able to create mobile Web applications, you must first install the Mobile Internet Toolkit. Go to `http://msdn.microsoft.com/downloads/` to download the Toolkit for free.

The Mobile Internet Toolkit is based on the Microsoft .NET Framework and enables you to create mobile Web applications in a manner that's similar to creating ASP.NET Web applications. In addition to providing the benefits of the .NET Framework, Mobile Internet Toolkit provides you certain advantages that help you develop mobile Web applications in an easy and efficient manner. The Mobile Internet Toolkit

- Integrates completely with the Microsoft Visual Studio .NET IDE. Therefore, after you install the Mobile Internet Toolkit, the Visual Studio .NET IDE provides you a rich Toolbox for Mobile Web Forms server controls, a rich designer, drag-and-drop server control support, and other features.

- Enables you to create applications that can target a variety of mobile devices. These devices might be HTML-based pocket PC or WML-based cellular phones.
- Enables you to create mobile Web applications that can be accessed from any supported device without requiring you to modify the applications.

Getting Started with Mobile Web Applications

Creating mobile Web applications is similar to creating ASP.NET Web applications. (For everything you ever wanted to know about ASP.NET, check out Book 6, Chapter 3.) Some of the similar points are

- Just as ASP.NET Web applications are based on Web Forms pages, mobile Web applications are based on Mobile Web Forms pages.
- Mobile Web Forms pages have the same extension (`.aspx`) as the Web Forms pages.
- Just as you use Web Forms controls to create ASP.NET Web applications, you use Mobile Web Forms controls to create mobile Web applications.

There are, however, differences in the way the Mobile Web Forms pages are structured. Because of the limitations of mobile devices, this structure is important. Mobile devices offer small screens, so you can structure the Mobile Web Forms pages to contain multiple forms that display one at a time on a mobile device's screen.

When you create mobile Web applications in Visual Studio .NET, viewing the output in your PC's browser is helpful when debugging your applications, but surely you want to view the output on mobile devices. Fortunately, you can display the output of your mobile Web applications on a *WAP device emulator,* so you don't even need an actual mobile device. For this chapter, we use the Microsoft Mobile Explorer 3.0 Emulator (MME Emulator) — the latest version available at time of writing. This emulator acts like mobile phones that run the Microsoft Mobile Explorer micro-browser. The MME Emulator is available from `www.microsoft.com/mobile/phones/mme/mmemulator.asp`.

Then, to enable the emulator to emulate WML devices, you must install the WAP gateway. We recommend downloading the Ericsson Gateway/Proxy Demo 1.0 from the Developer's Zone at `www.ericsson.com`. To install the gateway, simply follow the instructions on the Web site.

After you install the Mobile Internet Toolkit for Microsoft Visual Studio .NET and have a WAP device — or WAP device emulator — you're ready to create and test your mobile Web applications.

Creating a mobile Web Application project

To create a mobile Web Application project, follow these steps:

1. **In the Visual Studio .NET window, choose File⇨New⇨Project to open the New Project dialog box.**
2. **In the Project Types pane, choose either Visual Basic Projects or Visual C# Projects.**

   For this example, choose Visual Basic Projects.
3. **In the Templates pane, choose Mobile Web Application.**
4. **Specify the name and location (`http://<name of the Web server>`) for the project; then click OK to complete the process.**

   For this example, specify the name as `MobileDemo1`.

After you perform the preceding steps, Solution Explorer displays a number of files that are generated automatically as part of the project. Currently, the `MobileWebForm1.aspx` file is selected and displayed in the designer, as shown in Figure 10-1.

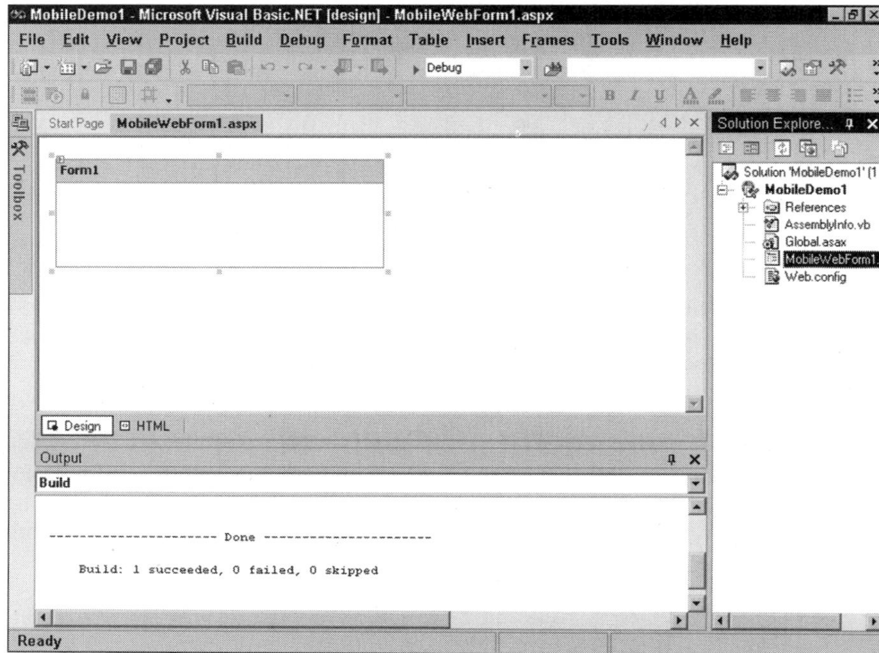

Figure 10-1: A Mobile Web Forms page in the Design mode.

This interface looks similar to the one for the ASP.NET Web applications. The interface for mobile Web applications is very similar to that of ASP.NET Web applications. However, notice that the Mobile Web Forms page already contains a control, `Form1`. In fact, you can have multiple Form controls on a Mobile Web Forms page. When you browse the Mobile Web Forms page, only one Form control is displayed at a time. And the display automatically adapts depending on the device used for browsing the page.

You can add controls to Mobile Web Forms pages from the Mobile Web Forms tab of the Toolbox. Figure 10-2 shows the mobile Web Forms controls available on this tab.

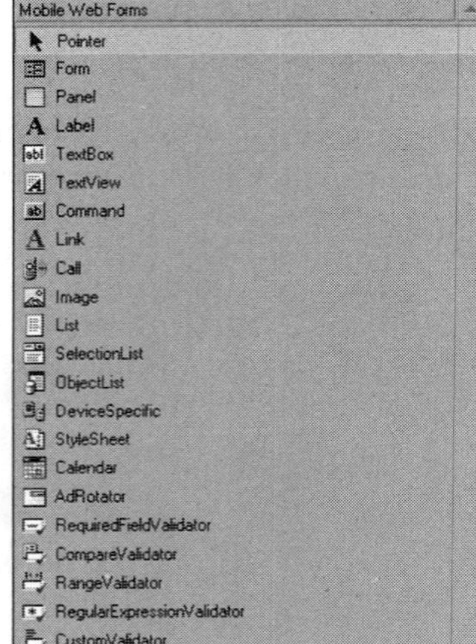

Figure 10-2: The Mobile Web Forms tab of the Toolbox.

One thing to note when adding controls is that you cannot add controls directly to Mobile Web Forms pages. You must place all Mobile Web Forms controls either within Form controls or within Panel controls.

Understanding the automatically generated code

After the Mobile Web Application project is ready, you must understand the code that Visual Studio .NET automatically generates before proceeding. Switch to the HTML view of the page to identify the HTML code that is automatically generated. Notice the first two lines of code:

```
<%@ Page Language="vb" AutoEventWireup="false"
   Codebehind="MobileWebForm1.aspx.vb"
   Inherits="MobileDemo1.MobileWebForm1" %>
<%@ Register TagPrefix="mobile"
   Namespace="System.Web.UI.MobileControls"
   Assembly="System.Web.Mobile" %>
```

The preceding lines of code together are also referred to as the *prolog* of a Mobile Web Forms page. The @Page directive specifies the base class for the page. The @Register directive specifies the Mobile Web Forms controls namespace and assembly. Notice mobile TagPrefix in the preceding code. You use this TagPrefix to add Mobile Web Forms controls to the Mobile Web Forms pages. Because the page already contains one Form control, the corresponding HTML code for this control is contained within the <body> tag, as follows:

```
<mobile:Form id="Form1" runat="server">
```

Next, open the code-behind file for the page by pressing F7. Notice that just like Web Forms pages, the extension for the code-behind file for Mobile Web Forms page is also .aspx.vb (or .aspx.cs for C# applications). The first few lines of code in the code-behind file are the Imports statements. Among these statements, notice that the System.Web.Mobile and System.Web.UI.MobileControls namespaces are imported. These are the namespaces for the framework and controls used for mobile Web applications.

After the Imports statements, the entire code is contained within the class named MobileWebForm1. The class name is the same as the name of the Mobile Web Forms page, MobileWebForm1.aspx, which is added to the project by default. Notice that this class is inherited from the System.Web.UI.MobileControls.MobilePage class. Also, because the page already contains a Form control, the class contains the declaration code for the same, as follows:

```
Protected WithEvents Form1 As
   System.Web.UI.MobileControls.Form
```

If you expand the Web Forms Designer Generated Code section, you'll notice the code for the InitializeComponent and Page_Init methods. The class also contains the code for the Page_Load method.

After taking a look at the designer window and the automatically generated code for the mobile Web application, you might be thinking that creating mobile Web applications is as simple as creating ASP.NET Web applications. This is so true! In fact, creating mobile Web applications is so similar to creating ASP.NET Web applications that you might say, without exaggerating, "If you know creating ASP.NET Web applications, you already know creating mobile Web applications."

Taking the Mobile Web Application project a step further

In this section, we develop a simple mobile Web application using some basic Mobile Web Forms controls so that you get a hang of mobile Web applications. We discuss several Mobile Web Forms controls in the section "Using Validation Mobile Web Forms Controls."

Designing the Mobile Web Forms page

In the section aptly named "Creating a mobile Web Application project," we step you through creating a mobile Web Application project named MobileDemo1, which we now use to show you how to develop a simple mobile Web application.

To design the Mobile Web Forms page shown in Figure 10-3, follow these steps:

1. **Drag the Label control from the Mobile Web Forms tab of the Toolbox to Form1 of the page.**

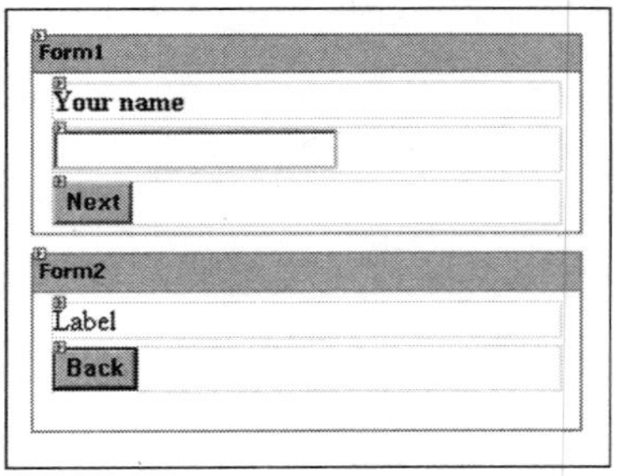

Figure 10-3: A sample Mobile Web Forms page with basic mobile controls in the Design view.

2. **Open the Properties window for this Label control by selecting the Label control and pressing F4.**
3. **Set its Text property to Your name and set the Font.Bold property to True.**
4. **Drag the TextBox control from the Mobile Web Forms tab of the Toolbox to Form1 of the page, open the Properties window, and then set the ID of this TextBox control to NameBox.**
5. **Drag the Command control (similar to the Button Web control) to Form1, open the Properties window, and then set this control's ID property to NextButton, Text property to Next, and Font.Bold property to True.**
6. **Drag the Form control from the Mobile Web Forms tab of the Toolbox to the page.**

   This form is automatically assigned the ID as Form2, which appears at the top of the Form control.

7. **Drag the `Label` control to `Form2`, open the Properties window, and set its `ID` to `DisplayLabel`.**
8. **Drag the `Command` control to `Form2`, open the Properties window, and set its `ID` property to `BackButton`, `Text` property to `Back`, and `Font.Bold` property to `True`.**

After you complete the designing, switch to the HTML view of the page. Notice that as you add controls, the corresponding HTML code for those controls is generated automatically.

Adding functionality to your Mobile Web Forms page

To add functionality to the application, open the code-behind file. You open the code-behind file for a Mobile Web Forms page just as you would in a Web Forms page. The Command controls (which we show you how to add in the preceding section), support the `Click` event that you need to handle. To create the event handler for the `Click` event of the `Next Command` control on `Form1`, double-click the `Command` control. Then write the following code:

```
Private Sub NextButton_Click(ByVal sender As System.Object,
            ByVal e As System.EventArgs) Handles
            NextButton.Click

        Dim UserName As String
        UserName = NameBox.Text
        DisplayLabel.Text = "Hello, " + UserName + ". Welcome
            to the world of mobile Web applications!"
        ActiveForm = Form2

End Sub
```

In the preceding code, `ActiveForm` is the property of the page, which enables you to navigate to another form on the page.

Then, create the event handler for the `Click` event of the `Command` control. To do so, either use the Class Name and Method Name lists in the Code-editor or switch to the Design view and double-click the `Back Command` control on `Form2`. Then, write the following code to navigate to `Form1`:

```
Private Sub BackButton_Click(ByVal sender As System.Object,
    ByVal e As System.EventArgs) Handles BackButton.Click

        ActiveForm = Form1

End Sub
```

Running the application

When you build and run the application, the output is displayed in Internet Explorer. To display the output in MME Emulator, choose View⇨Mobile

Explorer Browser➪Show Browser. Then type the address of the page in the Address box of the Emulator and press Enter. The page is displayed in the Emulator. The page output is shown in Figure 10-4.

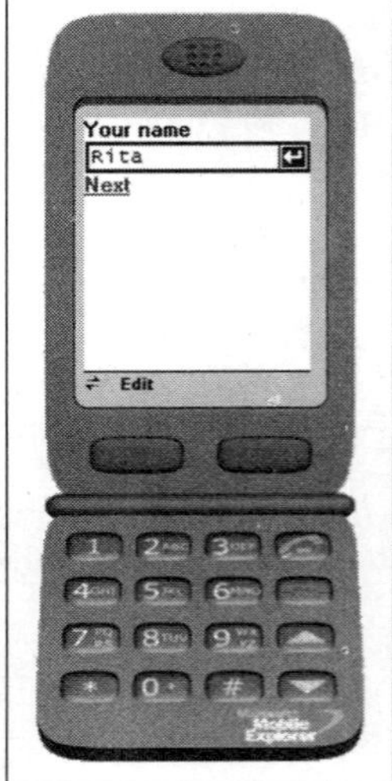

Figure 10-4: Output of a sample Mobile Web Forms page.

After you enter your name and click the `Next Command` control, the page navigates to `Form2`, as shown in Figure 10-5.

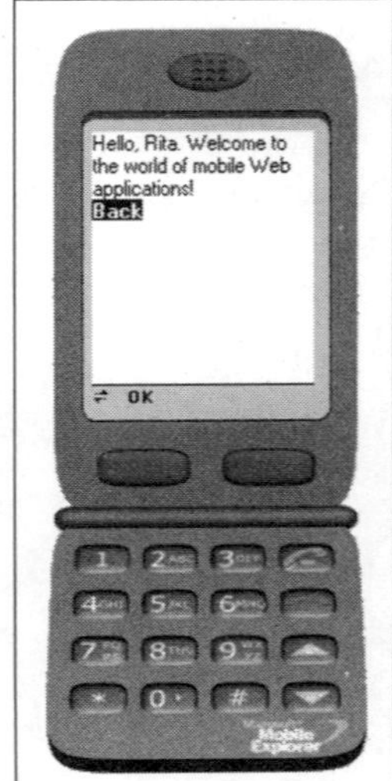

Figure 10-5: Output of a sample Mobile Web Forms page after navigating to Form2.

Using Validation Mobile Web Forms Controls

Just as validation controls are available with Web Forms pages, mobile validation controls are available with Mobile Web Forms pages. Need a refresher on validation controls? Head over to Book 6, Chapter 4. You use validation controls in Mobile Web Forms pages just like you use them in Web Forms pages.

In this section, we use the `CompareValidator` control. To do so, we're using the `MobileDemo1` project that we show you how to create earlier in this chapter in "Creating a mobile Web Application project." Open this project (if it's not open already), and follow these steps:

1. **Choose Project⇨Add New Item to open the Add New Item dialog box.**
2. **In the Templates pane, choose Mobile Web Form and click Open.**

   The form, `MobileWebForm2.aspx`, is added to the project.
3. **Design the page, as shown in Figure 10-6.**

   Use Table 10-1 as a reference for the controls' properties.

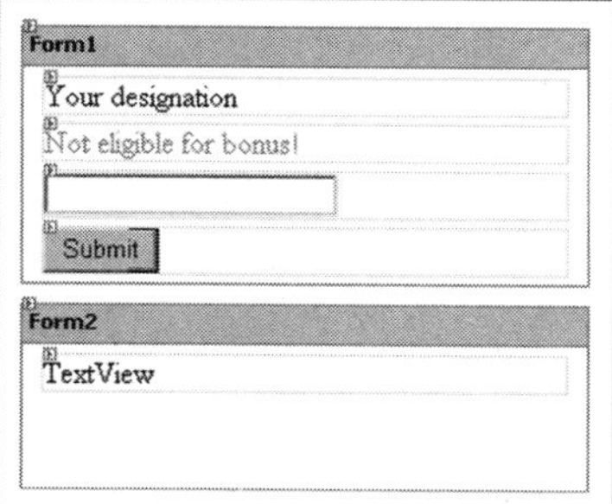

Figure 10-6: A sample Mobile Web Forms page in Design view to demonstrate using validation controls.

Notice the `TextView` control on `Form2` in Figure 10-6. The `TextView` control is used to display large amounts of text and enables you to use some common HTML tags, such as `<B>`, `<I>`, and `<a>`.

4. **In the event handler for the `Click` event of the `Submit Command` control, write the following code:**

```
Private Sub SubmitButton_Click(ByVal sender As
System.Object, ByVal e As System.EventArgs) Handles
SubmitButton.Click
```

```
If Page.IsValid Then
DisplayMessage.Text="<b>You are eligible for the
job!<b> "
ActiveForm = Form2
End If

End Sub
```

When you build the project, browse the `MobileWebForm2.aspx` page in MME Emulator, enter a designation other than Sales Executive, and click the `Submit` control. The page displays the output shown in Figure 10-7. If you enter the designation as Sales Executive and click Submit, the page navigates to `Form2` displaying a message in bold.

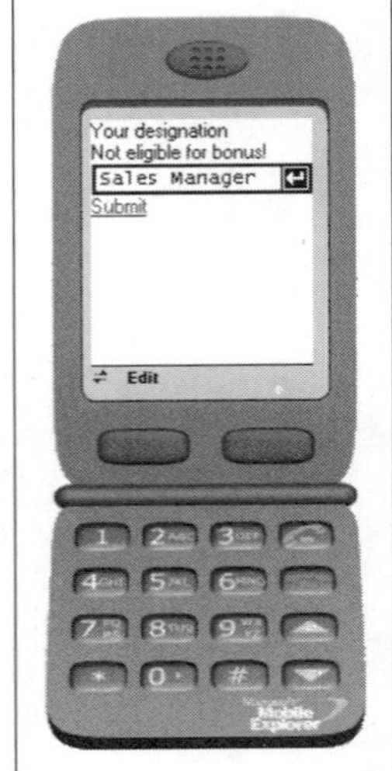

Figure 10-7: Output of a sample Mobile Web Forms page that demonstrates the CompareValidator control.

Table 10-1 Properties of Validation Controls on the Mobile Web Forms Page

Contained In	*Control*	*Property*	*Value*
`Form1`	`Label`	`Text`	Your designation
`Form1`	`TextBox`	`ID`	`DesignationBox`
`Form1`	`CompareValidator`	`ErrorMessage`	`Not eligible for bonus!`
`Form1`	`CompareValidator`	`ControlToValidate`	`DesignationBox`
`Form1`	`CompareValidator`	`ValueToCompare`	`Sales Executive`
`Form1`	`Command`	`ID`	`SubmitButton`

Contained In	Control	Property	Value
Form1	Command	Text	Submit
Form2	TextView	ID	DisplayMessage

Using List Controls in Mobile Web Forms

You can use one of the following List controls in Mobile Web Forms pages:

- `List` control: Used to create menus. You can handle the `ItemCommand` event of this control to perform tasks when an item is selected.
- `SelectionList` control: Used to provide a list of choices in multiple formats, such as check boxes, radio buttons, and drop-down lists. This list is used only to present choices. To submit the list, you must use a separate control explicitly, such as `Command` control.
- `ObjectList` control: Used to display a list of objects and their properties.

To show you how to implement list controls into your projects, the following steps walk you through implementing them to the `MobileDemo1` project from the section "Creating a mobile Web Application project." Just follow these steps:

1. **Add a Mobile Web Form,** `MobileWebForm3.aspx`**, to the** `MobileDemo1` **project.**
2. **Design the page, as shown in Figure 10-8.**

Use Table 10-2 as a reference for setting properties of the controls.

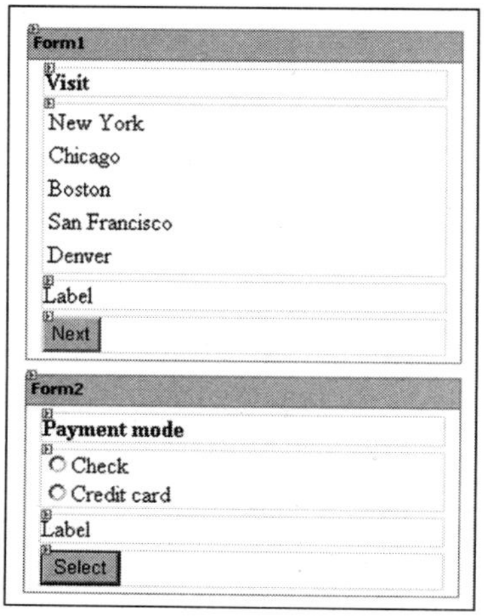

Figure 10-8: A sample Mobile Web Forms page in the Design view to demonstrate list controls.

3. **Create the event handler for the `ItemCommand` event of the `CityList` List control by first opening the code-behind file for the page (press F7), and then, in the `Class Name` list, select `CityList` and in the `Method Name` list, select `ItemCommand`. Finally, write the following code:**

   ```
   Private Sub CityList_ItemCommand(ByVal source As
   Object, ByVal e As
   System.Web.UI.MobileControls.ListCommandEventArgs)
   Handles CityList.ItemCommand

           DisplayLabel1.Text = "You selected to visit " +
   e.ListItem.Text
           DisplayLabel1.Visible = True

   End Sub
   ```

   In the preceding code, the selected item in the list is extracted and displayed in the label.

4. **Create an event handler for the `Click` event of the `Next Command` control to navigate to `Form2`.**

   ```
   Private Sub NextCommand_Click(ByVal sender As
      System.Object, ByVal e As System.EventArgs)
      Handles NextCommand.Click

           ActiveForm = Form2

   End Sub
   ```

5. **Create an event handler for the `Click` event of the `Select Command` control. In this handler, display the selected value from the list in the label.**

   ```
   Private Sub SelectCommand_Click(ByVal sender As
      System.Object, ByVal e As System.EventArgs)
      Handles SelectCommand.Click
    If (PayModeList.SelectedIndex = 0) Then
     DisplayLabel2.Text = "The payment mode is : Check"
    Else
      DisplayLabel2.Text = "The payment mode is: Credit
          card"

    End If
    DisplayLabel2.Visible = True
   End Sub
   ```

After you perform the preceding steps, build the project and browse the page in MME Emulator. When you select a city, the label becomes visible and displays the name of the city that you selected (see Figure 10-9).

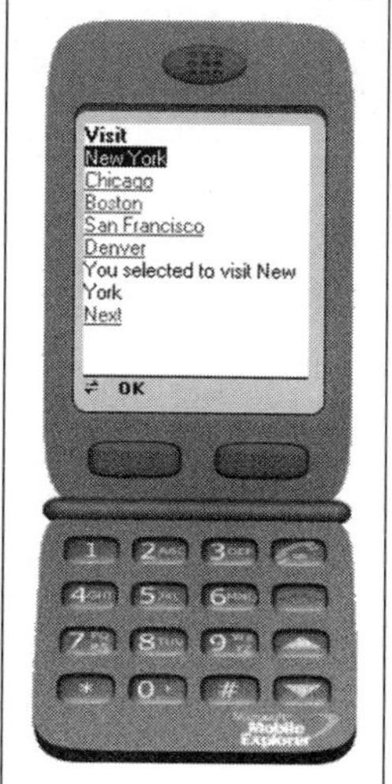

Figure 10-9: Output of a sample Mobile Web Forms page that demonstrates the List control.

Then, when you click the `Next Command` control, the page navigates to `Form2`. When you select a choice for payment mode and click the `Select Command` control, the selected option is displayed on a label, as shown in Figure 10-10.

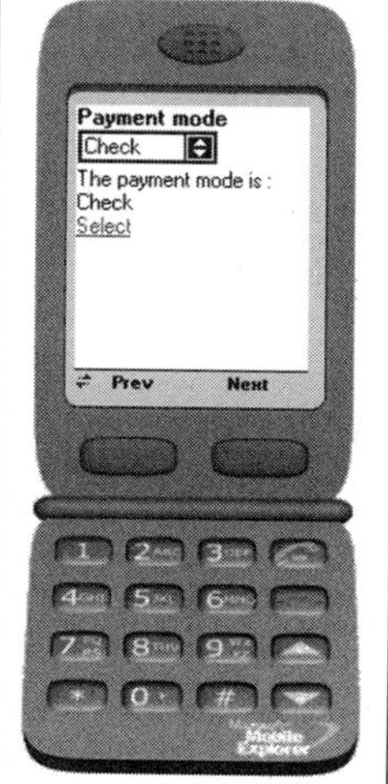

Figure 10-10: Output of a sample Mobile Web Forms page that demonstrates the SelectionList control.

Table 10-2 Properties of List Controls on the Mobile Web Forms Page

Contained in	*Control*	*Property*	*Value*
Form1	Label	Text	Visit
Form1	Label	Font.Bold	True
Form1	List	ID	CityList
Form1	List	Items (Collection)	New York, Chicago, Boston, San Francisco, Denver
Form1	Label	ID	DisplayLabel1
Form1	Label	Visible	False
Form1	Command	ID	NextCommand
Form1	Command	Text	Next
Form2	Label	Text	Payment mode
Form2	Label	Font.Bold	True
Form2	SelectionList	ID	PayModeList
Form2	SelectionList	SelectType	Radio
Form2	SelectionList	Items (Collection)	Check, Credit card
Form2	Label	ID	DisplayLabel2
Form2	Label	Visible	False
Form2	Command	ID	SelectCommand
Form2	Command	Text	Select

Chapter 11: Using ADO.NET with ASP.NET

In This Chapter

- Getting started with ADO.NET
- Figuring out the ADO.NET object model
- Creating your very own data aware application

The introduction of the .NET Framework has made significant changes to the world of programming. Data access in applications has also been affected. Accessing data from virtually any possible data source is mere child's play now — thanks to ADO.NET — and data access is also less time-consuming. The next question that flashes through your mind is: What is this wonderful ADO.NET? *ADO.NET* is a set of classes that handles data access.

In this chapter, we get you started with ADO.NET by discussing the various limitations of ADO (ActiveX Data Objects), the previous version of ADO.NET, and of course its benefits. We also help you to understand ADO.NET by creating an application that accesses data stored in a SQL Server database. Interesting stuff, huh? Keep reading! (For related material on ADO.NET, check out Book 3, Chapter 10.)

Getting Started with ADO.NET

ADO.NET is a successor to ADO and of course is an enhanced version of ADO. ADO.NET provides a flexible architecture that allows you to represent your data in a form that suits your taste. Moreover, ADO.NET is completely based on the Microsoft philosophy of interoperability and, in the process, ensures that an application can access data from any data source or application. To do so, ADO.NET uses XML (eXtensible Markup Language), a widely used industry standard.

Before we delve into the details of ADO.NET, we discuss the reasons that led to the evolution of ADO.NET by explaining the problems posed by ADO and differentiating between the two tools, which we do in the next section.

ADO vs. ADO.NET

Before the development of ADO.NET, ADO was the tool used to access data. However, ADO posed a number of limitations for the data aware applications (applications that access data from a database; more on these in the later section "Creating Data Aware Applications"). In the following subsections, we discuss these limitations along with the remedies that ADO.NET offers.

Recordset vs. DataSet

To store data, ADO uses a *recordset,* which can contain data from multiple tables. However, to do so, you need to use the JOIN clause of SQL. Because the execution of a query containing the JOIN clause consumes a lot of memory and CPU power on the computer storing the database, using it leads to performance-related problems. Moreover, the records contained in a recordset are scanned sequentially, which is time-consuming.

To solve this problem, ADO.NET uses a *DataSet,* a collection of tables that are called *data tables*. A DataSet can also contain other information, such as relationships and constraints, so it makes working with multiple tables easier. Sounds pretty good, doesn't it? But wait, there's more! A DataSet stores the rows in a table as a collection, so you're able to access any row by using its ordinal number or key.

A *collection* is a group of related objects. For example, the Controls collection contains all the controls present on a form.

Connected vs. disconnected architecture

ADO provides *connected* access to data. Translated, that means that after establishing a connection with a database, you need to remain connected until the time you're done working. This is helpful in situations when you require the latest information; for example, an application that performs airline reservations always requires up-to-date information. This kind of architecture might invite trouble, however, when two or more applications need to connect to the same database, which slows access.

ADO.NET uses a *disconnected* architecture for data access, which means that after you retrieve the required data from a database, the connection with the database is terminated, making the database free to handle other requests. The retrieved data is then stored in a DataSet.

COM marshalling vs. XML

ADO uses COM marshalling to transfer data (or recordset) from one application to another. *COM marshalling* is the process of packing, sending, and unpacking data across application boundaries. COM marshalling is limited because it requires the use of data types that are defined by Component

Object Model (COM). Moreover, firewalls are generally configured in such a manner that they prevent COM marshalling, and so the transfer of data by using recordsets might not even happen.

ADO.NET stores data in a DataSet in the eXtensible Markup Language (XML) format, so nothing restricts the use of data types. In addition, XML reads just like HTML, so you don't have to worry about pesky firewalls stopping the transfer of data.

Benefits of ADO.NET

The following list highlights the benefits of creating data aware applications by using ADO.NET:

- **Interoperability:** An application that uses ADO.NET stores and transfers data in XML format. So the only condition for an application to receive this data is the capability to understand XML. As a bonus, this application doesn't have to be an ADO.NET application. This makes Microsoft's dream of interoperable applications a possibility.
- **Maintainability:** ADO.NET believes in dividing an application in layers. For example, you can separate business logic, user interface, and data access. Creating this kind of application is helpful when you need to make some changes to the application. In such a situation, you need to make changes only to the required layer.
- **Programmability:** ADO.NET provides typed programming, which means writing statements that are easier to understand. For example, consider the following statement:

  ```
  Dim EmpSalary As Integer
  EmpSalary = dsEmployees.Employee("Martha").Salary
  ```

  From the preceding statements, you can easily make out that the Salary of an employee named Martha is being stored in a variable named `EmpSalary`. Moreover, typed programming checks for errors at compile-time instead of generating runtime errors.
- **Performance:** ADO.NET doesn't require the conversion of data types used in an application to data types recognized by COM. This significantly reduces processing costs while improving performance.
- **Scalability:** ADO.NET promotes simultaneous data access by multiple users. How? The answer is simple: by providing a disconnected architecture. According to this architecture, the connection with the database is terminated as soon as required data is retrieved in a DataSet, freeing the database for others' use and making the database capable of handling a growing number of users.

Discussing ADO.NET Object Model

Two components comprise the ADO.NET object model: .NET data provider and DataSet. In the upcoming sections, we discuss these components in detail.

Understanding .NET data provider

The .NET data provider acts as a layer between your code and the data source, and it's used to connect to a database, execute commands to add, modify, and delete data, and retrieve results. You can manipulate the results obtained directly or store them in a DataSet for later use. The following four objects make up a .NET data provider:

- `Connection`: Establishes a connection with the data source.
- `Command`: Executes a command, such as inserting, updating, or deleting records.
- `DataReader`: Retrieves forward-only data from a data source. This data is read-only and is useful while creating reports.
- `DataAdapter`: Retrieves data from a data source and plugs it into a DataSet and vice versa.

The .NET data provider comes in two flavors: OLE DB .NET data provider and SQL Server .NET data provider.

OLE DB .NET data provider

The OLE DB .NET data provider accesses data by using — what else? — OLE DB (Object Linking and Embedding Database) technology. *OLE DB* is a programming interface used to access both relational and non-relational data. This includes ISAM/VSAM and hierarchical databases, text, and graphical data.

ISAM stands for *Indexed Sequential Access Method*, and VSAM stands for *Virtual Storage Access Method.*

The OLE DB .NET data provider contains certain classes, described in the following list, that represent the objects of a .NET data provider:

- `OleDbConnection`: Represents the `Connection` object.
- `OleDbCommand`: Represents the `Command` object.
- `OleDbDataReader`: Represents the `DataReader` object.
- `OleDbDataAdapter`: Represents the `DataAdapter` object.

To use these classes in your application, you need to include the `System.Data.OleDb` namespace.

SQL Server .NET data provider

The SQL Server .NET data provider accesses data from a SQL Server data source (but we probably didn't have to tell you that). This data provider connects to the specified SQL Server data source directly without using any OLE DB or Open Database Connectivity (ODBC) layer. However, you can use the SQL Server .NET data provider to access the data sources created only in SQL Server 7.0 or later.

Don't worry: You can still use the data sources created in earlier versions of SQL Server also, but to do so, you need to use the OLE DB .NET data provider.

Like an OLE DB .NET data provider, the SQL Server .NET data provider contains a number of classes to represent the objects of a .NET data provider, as follows:

- `SqlConnection`: Represents `Connection` object.
- `SqlCommand`: Represents `Command` object.
- `SqlDataReader`: Represents `DataReader` object.
- `SqlDataAdapter`: Represents `DataAdapter` object.

To use these classes in your application, you need to include the `System.Data.SqlClient` namespace.

Understanding DataSet

The DataSet is the most important part of the ADO.NET object model. It contains the data retrieved from a data source in a format similar to that of a relational database. This data includes tables, constraints, and relationships among these tables. In ADO.NET, a DataSet is represented by the `DataSet` class. You can read more on the `DataSet` class in Book 3, Chapter 10.

The various components of a `DataSet` object are

- `DataTableCollection` object: A collection of `DataTable` objects (see next bullet) present in a DataSet.
- `DataTable` object: Represents a table in a DataSet. This object contains two other objects, each appropriately named:
  - `DataColumn`: Represents a column in a DataTable.
  - `DataRow`: Represents a row in a DataTable.

✦ `DataRelationCollection` object: A collection of the DataRelation objects, which represent a relation between two DataTable objects.

Creating a Data Aware Application

This section is surely the most exciting part of this chapter because here's where we show you how to create an application that accesses data from a SQL Server database. Of course, we use ADO.NET to do so. First you must identify areas where the components of the ADO.NET object model fit into this application, as we demonstrate in the following list:

1. **Establish a connection with the database.** The .NET data provider component takes care of this part. See "Connecting with a SQL Server database."
2. **Create DataSet.** Some data is obtained as a result of the connection and is stored in a DataSet, which is another component of the ADO.NET object model. See "Creating a DataSet."
3. **Perform certain operations, such as adding, deleting, or modifying records.** This is also performed by using the .NET data provider. See "Accessing and manipulating data" and its subsections.

Don't worry about implementing these steps in your application just yet because we provide guidelines in the upcoming sections that show you just how to do that. Before we move on to these sections, however, we first look at the structure of the table that we use in the application and which, of course, we must build before creating the data aware application. Table 11-1 describes Employees table, which is used to store various employee details, such as name, designation, and department.

Table 11-1 Employees Table

Field Name	*Data Type*	*Size*
EmployeeId	Char	4
FirstName	VarChar	20
LastName	VarChar	20
Department	VarChar	20
Designation	VarChar	15

You can create the `Employees` table in the `tempdb` database. To do so, follow these steps:

1. **Choose Start⇨Programs⇨Microsoft SQL Server⇨Query Analyzer to launch SQL Server.**

2. **In the Connect to SQL Server dialog box that appears, from the SQL Server list, select the appropriate server.**
3. **Also in the Connect to SQL Server dialog box, under Connect using, select the appropriate authentication mode.**
4. **Click OK to connect to the database.**
5. **From the list present in the Toolbar, select** `tempdb`**.**

   This makes `tempdb` the current database.
6. **Type the following code in the Query window.**

   This is the SQL statement necessary to create the Employees Table shown in Table 11-1:

   ```
   Create Table Employees
   (
   EmployeeId char (4) Primary Key,
   FirstName varchar(20),
   LastName varchar(20),
   Department varchar(20),
   Designation varchar(15)
   )
   ```
7. **Press the F5 key to execute the query.**

   A message indicating that the query was executed successfully appears in a lower pane of the window that automatically appears.

Connecting with a SQL Server database

To connect to a SQL Server database, ADO.NET provides the `SqlConnection` and `SqlDataAdapter` classes. You can implement the `SqlConnection` and `SqlDataAdapter` classes in your application by using the `SqlDataAdapter` and `SqlConnection` controls. Add these controls — which you must configure to make them usable — to a form from the Data tab of the Toolbox.

Don't worry about configuring these controls; Visual Studio .NET provides you the Data Adapter Configuration Wizard to configure an `SqlDataAdapter` control. You must appreciate Visual Studio .NET at this point because when you configure a `SqlDataAdapter` control, the `SqlConnection` control is configured automatically.

To connect to a SQL Server, follow these steps:

1. **Create a new Visual Basic Web Application and name it** `SQLDataAccess`**.**
2. **In the Toolbox, click the Data tab.**

3. **Double-click `SqlDataAdapter` to add this control to your project.**

   The Data Adapter Configuration Wizard Appears, showing its welcome screen.

4. **Click Next to move to the next screen of the wizard.**

   Use the screen that appears to establish a connection (which the data adapter uses to access data) with the data source.

5. **Click the New Connection button.**

   The Data Link Properties dialog box shows up. Use this dialog box to specify the server, login details, and the database that contains the required table (see Figure 11-1).

   While specifying details in the Data Link Properties dialog box, the server and login details might differ depending on the setup you're using. However, make sure you select the `tempdb` database.

   You can test the connection by clicking the Test Connection button.

6. **Click OK to close the Data Link Properties dialog box and move back to the wizard.**

7. **Click Next to move to the next screen of the wizard.**

   This screen prompts you to specify the way in which the data adapter should access the database. You can either use SQL queries or stored procedures. A *stored procedure* is a set of SQL statements that are used to perform specific tasks, such as adding or deleting records.

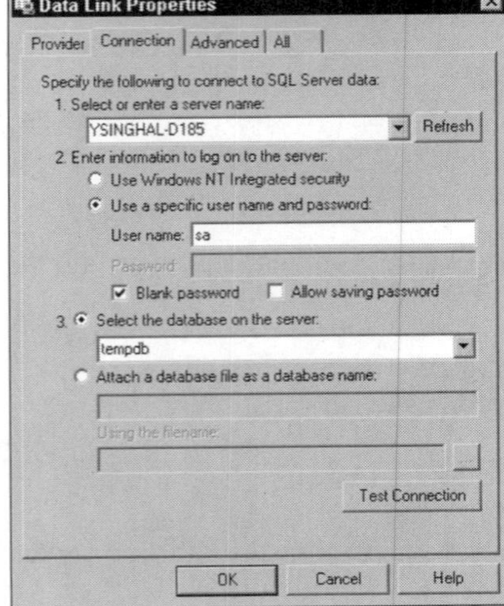

Figure 11-1: Get connected! Using the Data Link Properties dialog box.

8. **Select Use SQL Statements and click Next.**

   The screen that next appears prompts you to specify the SQL statement for retrieving data.

9. **On this screen, type the following statement (see Figure 11-2):**

   ```
   Select * From Employees
   ```

   This statement retrieves all the records stored in the Employees Table (refer to Table 11-1). You can also use the Query Builder to specify this SQL statement. (Don't understand the use of Query Builder? Take a look at Book 3, Chapter 10.)

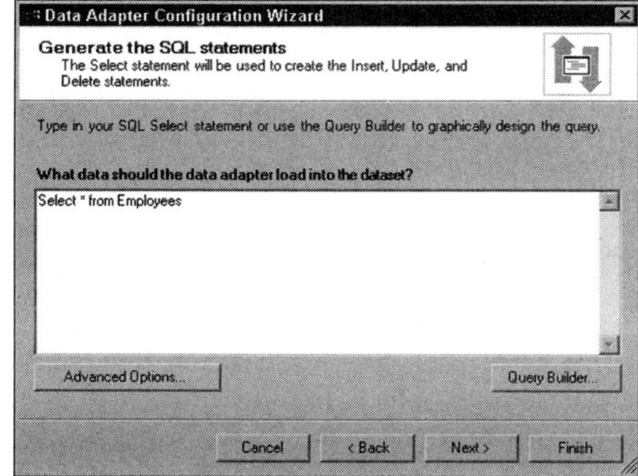

Figure 11-2: Specify the query to retrieve appropriate data.

10. **Click Next to move forward.**

    The corresponding screen displays the results of the Wizard.

11. **Click Finish to complete the wizard.**

    Note that `SqlDataAdapter1` and `SqlConnection1` components appear in the Tray at the bottom of the Web form:

    - The `SqlDataAdapter1` component is used to retrieve the data from a database and store it in a DataSet and vice versa.
    - The `SqlConnection1` component contains the connection information.

Creating a DataSet

After you're connected to a database (see the previous section), you can create a DataSet. When you connect to a database, some data is generated as a result. This data is stored in a DataSet, which you create by following these steps:

1. **Choose Data⇨Generate Dataset.**

   The Generate Dataset dialog box shows up. Use this dialog box to specify a DataSet for your application. You can either use an existing Dataset or create a new one.

2. **Ensure that New is selected and, in the corresponding box, type dsEmployees.**

   This creates a DataSet named `dsEmployees`.

3. **Click OK to close the dialog box.**

   Observe that the `DsEmployees1` component appears in the Tray at the bottom of the Web form.

Accessing and manipulating data

After you connect to the database and create the DataSet (see previous two sections), the fun begins: You now start working on the data. `SQLDataAdapter` class contains various properties that help you add, modify, delete, and search records in a database. These properties are

- `InsertCommand`: Adds new records in the table in a database.
- `UpdateCommand`: Makes changes to the existing records in a table.
- `DeleteCommand`: Deletes records from the table in a database.
- `SelectCommand`: Retrieves records from the table in a database.

In addition to these properties, ADO.NET also provides the `SQLCommand` class that symbolizes the SQL statement to be executed on a database in SQL Server.

To help you better understand these concepts, we show you how to make your application capable of adding, modifying, and deleting records, as well as how to add the capability to search for a particular record. To do so, you need to design the form contained in your application, as shown in Figure 11-3.

The form (`WebForm1.aspx`) contains a number of text boxes. Name the text boxes by using the information in Table 11-2.

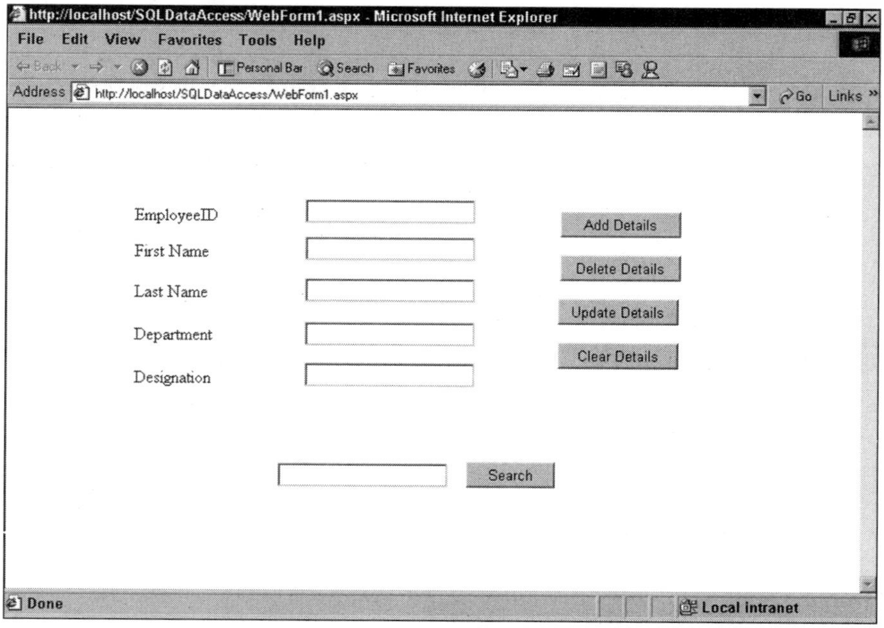

Figure 11-3: Get started with accessing data.

Table 11-2	**Names of Text Boxes**
Caption	***ID***
Employee ID	TxtID
First Name	TxtFName
Last Name	TxtLName
Department	TxtDept
Designation	TxtDesg

In addition to these text boxes, the form also contains a number of buttons. Table 11-3 lists the function of each of these buttons.

Table 11-3	**Function of Buttons**
Caption	***Function***
Add Details	Adds employee details to the table.
Delete Details	Deletes employee details from the table.
Update Details	Modifies employee details in the table.
Clear Details	Clears all the text boxes present on the form.
Search	Searches for the details of an employee with the employee id provided in the text box present next to this button.

Inserting records in a table

After you design the form, the time to start with coding has arrived. We start you off by inserting records in the Employees Table. Before adding the capability to insert new records, however, first revise the SQL statement that you use to insert records in a table:

```
Insert Employees
Values('E001', 'James', 'Brown', 'Sales', 'Executive')
```

The preceding statement inserts the record of an employee in the Employees Table. This statement seems simple. To implement this statement by using ADO.NET, however, you need to perform a number of steps, as follows:

1. **Create the SQL command by using the** `SQLCommand` **class; the necessary syntax follows:**

   ```
   Dim str As String
   //Create the Insert statement
   str = "Insert Into Employees Values (@ID, @FN, @LN," _
      & "@DPT, @DSG)"
   Dim InsCom As New SqlCommand(str, SqlConnection1)
   ```

   In the preceding code:

   - `@ID`, `@FN`, `@LN`, `"@DPT`, `@DSG` are the parameters, which represent the values to be inserted in the table.
   - `InsCom` is an object of the `SQLCommand` class. The constructor of the `SQLCommand` class takes the string containing SQL statement and the object of the `SQLConnection` class as parameter.

2. **Associate the SQL command with the Data Adapter by using the** `InsertCommand` **property of the** `SqlDataAdapter` **class.**

   Here's the syntax:

   ```
   SqlDataAdapter1.InsertCommand = InsCom
   ```

3. **Assign values to the SQL statement that you create in Step 1 by using the** `Parameters` **property of the** `SqlDataAdapter` **class.**

   This property represents the `Parameters` collection, which contains objects of type `SqlParameter`. The working mechanism of the `Parameters` collection is that you add the parameters (which you use in the SQL statement) to this collection, and then you assign values to these parameters. The syntax to perform these steps is as follows:

   - **Add objects to a** `Parameters` **collection by using the** `Add` **method of this collection; here's the syntax:**

     ```
     SqlDataAdapter1.InsertCommand.Parameters.Add(New _
       SqlParameter("@ID", SqlDbType.Char, 4))
     ```

The preceding statement adds a parameter named @ID to the Parameters collection. This parameter is of type Char having a size 4. The SqlDbType enumeration contains constants that specify data types contained in SQL Server.

- **Assign values to these parameters (@ID) by using the Value property of the Parameters collection; the syntax follows:**

```
SqlDataAdapter1.InsertCommand.Parameters("@ID"). _
  Value = _   txtID.Text
```

4. **Next open the connection by using the Open method of the SqlConnection class:**

```
SqlConnection1.Open()
```

5. **Execute the completed command on the database by using the ExecuteNonQuery method:**

```
SqlDataAdapter1.InsertCommand.ExecuteNonQuery()
```

6. **Close the connection after the query is executed by using the Close method:**

```
SqlConnection1.Close()
```


After you complete the preceding six steps, you have the complete code that will insert records into a table. To make this code work, add it to the Click event of the Add Details button present on WebForm1.aspx.

To find out more about trapping the Click event of a button, read the "Adding Code" section of Book 5, Chapter 5.

```
Dim str As String
str = "Insert Into Employees Values (@ID, @FN, @LN," _
   & "DPT, @DSG)"
Dim InsCom As New SqlCommand(str, SqlConnection1)
SqlDataAdapter1.InsertCommand = InsCom
SqlDataAdapter1.InsertCommand.Parameters.Add(New _
   SqlParameter("@ID", SqlDbType.Char, 4))
SqlDataAdapter1.InsertCommand.Parameters.Add(New _
   SqlParameter("@FN", SqlDbType.VarChar, 20))
SqlDataAdapter1.InsertCommand.Parameters.Add(New _
   SqlParameter("@LN", SqlDbType.VarChar, 20))
SqlDataAdapter1.InsertCommand.Parameters.Add(New _
   SqlParameter("@DPT", SqlDbType.VarChar, 20))
SqlDataAdapter1.InsertCommand.Parameters.Add(New _
   SqlParameter("@DSG", SqlDbType.VarChar, 15))
SqlDataAdapter1.InsertCommand.Parameters("@ID").Value = _
   txtID.Text
SqlDataAdapter1.InsertCommand.Parameters("@FN").Value = _
   txtFName.Text
SqlDataAdapter1.InsertCommand.Parameters("@LN").Value = _
```

```
   txtLName.Text
SqlDataAdapter1.InsertCommand.Parameters("@DPT").Value = _
   txtDept.Text
SqlDataAdapter1.InsertCommand.Parameters("@DSG").Value = _
   txtDesg.Text
SqlConnection1.Open()
SqlDataAdapter1.InsertCommand.ExecuteNonQuery()
SqlConnection1.Close()
```

Modifying records in a table

The time has come to fiddle with (and otherwise modify) the already existing records in the Employees Table. Before you proceed further, revise the SQL statement to update records in a table:

```
Update Employees
set Department = 'HR', Designation = 'Manager'
where EmployeeId = 'E001'
```

The preceding statement updates the `Department` and `Designation` field of the employee with `EmployeeId` E001.

To implement this statement in your application, you need to add the following code to the `Click` event of the `Update Details` button:

```
Dim str As String
str = "Update Employees set Department = "@DPT, " & _
   & "Designation = @DSG where EmployeeId =@ID"
Dim UpdCom As SqlCommand
UpdCom = New SqlCommand(str, SqlConnection1)
SqlDataAdapter1.UpdateCommand = UpdCom
SqlDataAdapter1.UpdateCommand.Parameters.Add(New _
   SqlParameter("@DPT", SqlDbType.VarChar, 20))
SqlDataAdapter1.UpdateCommand.Parameters.Add(New _
   SqlParameter("@DSG", SqlDbType.VarChar, 15))
SqlDataAdapter1.UpdateCommand.Parameters.Add(New _
   SqlParameter("@ID", SqlDbType.Char, 4))
SqlDataAdapter1.UpdateCommand.Parameters("@DPT").Value = _
   txtDept.Text
SqlDataAdapter1.UpdateCommand.Parameters("@DSG").Value = _
   txtDesg.Text
SqlDataAdapter1.UpdateCommand.Parameters("@ID").Value = _
   txtID.Text
SqlConnection1.Open()
SqlDataAdapter1.UpdateCommand.ExecuteNonQuery()
SqlConnection1.Close()
```

Deleting records from a table

To delete records from a table, revise the SQL statement as shown in the following lines of code:

```
Delete from Employees
where EmployeeId = 'E001'
```

The preceding statement deletes the record of the employee with the `EmployeeId` E001.

To implement this statement in your application, add the following code to the `Click` event of the `Delete Details` button:

```
Dim str As String
str = "Delete From Employees where EmployeeId = @ID"
Dim DelCom As SqlCommand
DelCom = New SqlCommand(str, SqlConnection1)
SqlDataAdapter1.DeleteCommand = DelCom
SqlDataAdapter1.DeleteCommand.Parameters.Add(New _
   SqlParameter("@ID", SqlDbType.Char, 4))
SqlDataAdapter1.DeleteCommand.Parameters(0).Value = _
   txtID.Text
SqlConnection1.Open()
SqlDataAdapter1.DeleteCommand.ExecuteNonQuery()
SqlConnection1.Close()
```


Searching records in a table

Searching for a particular record in the table? Revise the SQL statement to search for you:

```
Select * from employees
where EmployeeId = 'E002'
```

To implement this statement in your application, add the following code to the `Click` event of the `Search` button:

```
Dim str As String
str = "Select * From Employees where EmployeeId = @ID"
SqlDataAdapter1.SelectCommand.CommandText = str
SqlDataAdapter1.SelectCommand.Parameters.Add(New _
   SqlParameter("@ID", SqlDbType.Char, 4))
'txtSearch text box is located next to the Search button
SqlDataAdapter1.SelectCommand.Parameters("@ID").Value = _
   txtSearch.Text
SqlConnection1.Open()
SqlDataAdapter1.SelectCommand.ExecuteNonQuery()
SqlConnection1.Close()
```

The preceding code executes the SQL statement and generates the desired result. Now, you need to display this result in the controls on your form by binding controls with the fields of the table.

Displaying results on your form

To display results on your form, you need to bind controls with the fields present on the form of the table; just follow these steps:

1. **Populate the DataSet with the resulting values by using the `Fill` method of the `SqlDataAdapter` class, as shown here:**

   ```
   SqlDataAdapter1.Fill(DsEmployees1)
   ```

2. **Display the values stored in the DataSet on the various controls present on the Web form (your last task!) by binding these controls with columns of the table present in the DataSet.**

   The `Eval` method of the `DataBinder` class helps you do so. To understand the usage of this method, consider the following statement:

   ```
   txtID.Text = CStr(DataBinder.Eval(DsEmployees1, _
      "Tables[Employees].DefaultView.[0].EmployeeId"))
   ```

   In the preceding statement, the `EmployeeId` field of the Employees Table is bound with the `Text` property of the `txtID` text box.

Now write the complete code to bind text boxes present on the Web form with fields of the Employees Table. Append this piece of code to the already existing code in the `Click` event of the `Search` button:

```
SqlDataAdapter1.Fill(DsEmployees1)
'Bind EmployeeId with txtID
txtID.Text = CStr(DataBinder.Eval(DsEmployees1, _
   "Tables[Employees].DefaultView.[0].EmployeeId"))
'Bind FirstName with txtFName
txtFName.Text = CStr(DataBinder.Eval(DsEmployees1, _
   "Tables[Employees].DefaultView.[0].FirstName"))
'Bind LastName with txtLName
txtLName.Text = CStr(DataBinder.Eval(DsEmployees1, _
   "Tables[Employees].DefaultView.[0].LastName"))
'Bind Department with txtDept
txtDept.Text = CStr(DataBinder.Eval(DsEmployees1, _
   "Tables[Employees].DefaultView.[0].Department"))
'Bind Designation with txtDesg
txtDesg.Text = CStr(DataBinder.Eval(DsEmployees1, _
   "Tables[Employees].DefaultView.[0].Designation"))
```

This completes the coding part. Your application is now ready to manipulate the Employees table. Execute the application and try out various operations on the table. The Employees table that you created doesn't contain any record, so you must start inserting some records. After you add some records, try updating, deleting, and searching for details of an employee.

Chapter 12: Working with XML in Visual Studio .NET

In This Chapter

- **Getting to know XML basics**
- **Presenting XML-related specifications**
- **Converting data from the relational format to the XML format**
- **Data binding with XML documents**

With its worldwide presence, the Internet has gained importance as an efficient medium for communication and information exchange. As a result, most companies are conducting business over the Web, leading to the increased need of dispersing data to business groups and partners located across the world. To meet this need, Web applications have to present data in a standard format that's compatible with a majority of hardware and software platforms. Providing standardized data representation might sound like an enormous task, but the solution lies in one of the latest — and most hyped — Web technologies, eXtensible Markup Language (XML). XML, a markup language defined by the World Wide Web Consortium (W3C), provides a format for describing data. Because XML is standardized by the W3C, the data presented in the XML format remains uniform and independent of applications or vendors.

XML has been a tremendous success since its introduction in 1998. Most upcoming software supports XML; Visual Studio .NET is no exception. XML plays a key role in the way data is handled in Visual Studio .NET.

To understand the role that XML plays in Visual Studio .NET, read Book 6, Chapter 2. In this chapter, we present an overview of XML and the XML designer provided with Visual Studio .NET. Next, we show you how to convert data from the relational format to the XML format. Finally, we discuss performing data binding of server controls with XML documents. Read on to explore the application of XML in Visual Studio .NET!

Getting to Know XML

XML, defined by the World Wide Web Consortium (W3C), provides a format to present structured data, which is stored in XML documents. These documents, like databases, enable you to store data. However, unlike databases,

XML documents store data as plain text, which can be understood across platforms, serving as a standard interface for interchanging data across Web applications.

You can access the W3C Web site at www.w3.org.

XML versus HTML

Like HTML, XML uses tags to define data. However, unlike HTML, which focuses on presenting data, XML focuses on describing what data is. HTML consists of a set of predefined tags that focus on the appearance of data. For example, the data enclosed within the <B> </B> (bold) tag is displayed as bold in a browser. The browser doesn't care what's within the tags. On the other hand, XML enables you to create your own tags to define the structure of data, and there is no provision for predefined tags. For example, to present data pertaining to the employees of a company, you can create a tag called <EmployeeId> to enclose employee IDs within this tag. Thus, tags in XML focus on structuring data rather than focusing on the appearance of data.

To make this difference between HTML and XML clearer, consider an example where you create the following HTML document named Employees.html (in Notepad) to display employee details in a numbered list:

```
<HTML>
<HEAD> <TITLE> Employee Details </TITLE> </HEAD>
<BODY>
<OL>
    <LI> <B> Employee Id: </B> E001  <B> Employee Name : </B>
          Rita Greg </LI>
    <LI> <B> Employee Id: </B> E002  <B> Employee Name : </B>
          Robert Brown </LI>
</OL>
</BODY>
</HTML>
```

When you open this HTML document in a Web browser, you see the output shown in Figure 12-1.

Create an XML document named Employees.xml (in Notepad) to describe the data (in a structured manner) as displayed in the preceding HTML document:

```
<?xml version="1.0"?>
<Employees>
   <Employee>
       <Id> E001 </Id>
       <LastName> Greg </LastName>
       <FirstName> Rita </FirstName>
   </Employee>
```

Figure 12-1: A sample output of an HTML document.


```
   <Employee>
        <Id> E002 </Id>
        <LastName> Brown </LastName>
        <FirstName> Robert </FirstName>
   </Employee>
</Employees>
```

In the preceding code, the first line `<?xml version= "1.0"?>` is an XML declaration statement that notifies the browser that the document being processed is an XML document. When you open this XML document in Internet Explorer, the document appears as shown in Figure 12-2.

You'll notice that the document in Figure 12-2 is displayed in a structured manner, in the form of a tree. Each tag (which contains sub tags) can be expanded or collapsed. All XML documents are displayed in a similar manner.

Visual Studio .NET provides you with the XML designer that you can use to create and edit XML documents. So you don't need to use an external editor to create XML documents; instead, you can create them in Visual Studio .NET.

To use the XML designer of Visual Studio .NET to create XML documents, follow these steps:

1. **Create an ASP.NET application project by using Visual Basic; name the project** `XMLDemo`**.**

   We show you how to create an ASP.NET project in Book 6, Chapter 2.

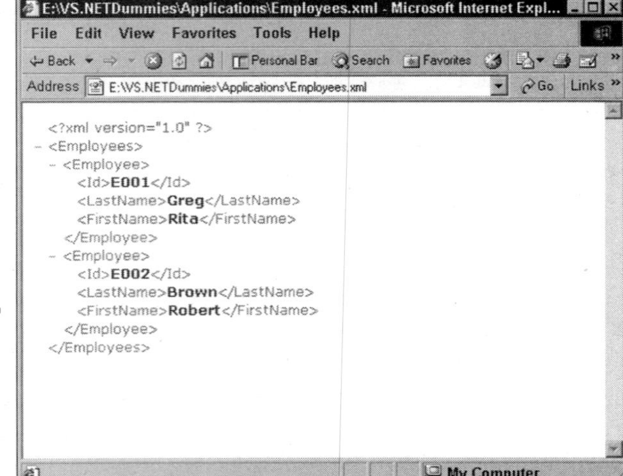

Figure 12-2: A sample output of an XML document.

2. **Choose Project⇨Add New Item to open the Add New Item dialog box.**
3. **In this dialog box, select XML File in the Templates pane.**
4. **Enter the name of the file as `Employees.xml` and click OK.**

   The file opens within the XML designer. At the bottom of the designer window are two tabs, XML and Data. The XML view is used to directly edit the XML code while the Data view displays the XML data represented by the XML document. You can edit the XML data directly in this view. Currently, the XML view is active.

5. **In the XML view, write the XML code that you wrote for the `Employees.xml` file (using Notepad) earlier in this section.**
6. **Switch to the Data view.**

   The data is displayed as shown in Figure 12-3.

Data for Employee

	Id	LastName	FirstName
▸	E001	Greg	Rita
	E002	Brown	Robert
*			

Figure 12-3: The Data view of the XML designer.

Basic rules for a well-formed XML document

In the preceding section, we show you how an XML document is created and displayed in a browser; now we quickly discuss the basic rules that you must follow while creating an XML document. All XML documents that conform to these rules are called *well-formed* XML documents. It's important that you remember the following basic rules:

- **Tag names are case-sensitive.** The tag `<Employees>` is not the same as the tag `<employees>`.
- **All opening tags must have corresponding closing tags.** Otherwise, the browser reports an error. For example, the opening tag `<Employees>` must have the corresponding closing tag `</Employees>`.
- **All empty tags must be closed by including a forward slash (/) before the closing angular bracket of the tag.** For example, include an empty tag, the `<Image>` tag, in an XML document by using the following code:

  ```
  <Image src = "MyPicture.gif" />
  ```

- **Values of all attributes of an element must be enclosed within quotation marks.** See code snippet in the preceding bullet.
- **All inner tags must be closed before closing the outer tags.** For example, consider the following code:

  ```
  <Employee>
       <LastName> Greg </Employee>
  </LastName>
  ```

  The preceding code causes an error because the outer tag `<Employee>` has been closed before closing the inner tag `<LastName>`.

Presenting XML-Related Specifications

Throughout this section, we tell you all about XML-related specifications. DTDs specify the rules for XML documents that make it easier for everyone to understand the structure and logic of your XML documents. XML schemas, which can be considered a subset of DTDs, are another XML specification that defines the structure of XML documents.

Sometimes, your XML documents are too long and use multiple elements. When numerous elements are used, you might have a situation where names of certain elements conflict. To avoid these situations, XML namespaces are used. To format XML documents, W3C has specifically provided a style sheet for XML documents. This style sheet is called Extensible Stylesheet Language Transformations (XSL/T).

When you want to access XML documents programmatically, you need to use the Document Object Model (DOM).

Document Type Definition

As its name suggests, Document Type Definition (DTD) represents a set of rules that define the structure of XML documents. The documents that store these rules are called DTD documents and carry the extension `.dtd`. These DTD documents (DTDs) add structure and logic to your XML documents. To understand DTDs better, compare them with the `Create Table` SQL statement. The `Create Table` statement is used to specify the columns included in a table, the data types for different columns, the conditions under which a column can hold null values, and so on. In a similar manner, a DTD specifies the tags and attributes that can be used in XML documents. You can think of DTDs as the grammar for XML documents.

It's not essential for you to create a DTD for your XML documents. However, a DTD can be important to users who need to understand the structure of your XML documents or who need to create an XML document similar to the one you've already created. These users can refer to your DTD document to understand the structure and logic of your XML documents.

When you include a DTD document in an XML document, the XML document is checked against the rules specified in the DTD document. If the XML document is well-formed and follows all the DTD rules, the document is considered valid. Otherwise, your XML document fails.

To understand how DTDs work, create the following DTD document named `Employees.dtd` (in Notepad):

```
<!ELEMENT Employees (Employee)+>
<!ELEMENT Employee (Id, LastName, FirstName)>
<!ELEMENT Id (#PCDATA)>
<!ELEMENT LastName (#PCDATA)>
<!ELEMENT FirstName (#PCDATA)>
```

The preceding DTD declares five elements: `Employees`, `Employee`, `Id`, `LastName`, and `FirstName`. Each element declaration statement specifies the element name and the type of content of that element. For the `Employees` element, the content type is `(Employee)+`, which means that this element can contain one or more `Employee` elements. Similarly, the `Employee` element contains three elements: `Id`, `LastName`, and `FirstName`. The `Id`, `LastName`, and `FirstName` elements can each contain character data, and this type of data is represented as `(#PCDATA)`.

Including a DTD in an XML document is pretty simple. You can include the previous DTD document in an XML document by using the following statement:

```
<!DOCTYPE Employees SYSTEM "Employees.DTD">
```

Next, create the following XML document named `TestingDTD.xml` (in Notepad):

```
<?xml version="1.0"?>
<!DOCTYPE Employees SYSTEM "Employees.DTD">
<Employees>
    <Employee>
          <Id> E001 </Id>
          <Name> Rita Greg </Name>
    </Employee>
</Employees>
```

When you open this XML document in a browser, the browser reports an error because the XML document isn't valid. According to the DTD, the `<Employee>` element contains the three elements `<Id>`, `<LastName>`, and `<FirstName>`. However, the XML document doesn't conform to this rule and thus doesn't pass the validation test.

XML namespaces

When creating XML documents, you define your own elements to describe the data. You can also use elements that are defined outside your XML document. For example, when defining the data structure to present employee details, you might end up defining the `<Name>` element twice, once to qualify the employee name and a second time to qualify the department name. This might lead to name collisions. To avoid such situations, W3C recommends the use of *XML namespaces,* which are a collection of unique elements. XML namespaces are identified by Uniform Resource Identifiers (URI) and are declared by using the keyword `xmlns`. For example, you can declare an XML namespace for the `<Name>` element that defines the department names, as follows:

```
xmlns:DepartmentName="http://www.dn.com/dn"
```

Next, when you want to use the `<Name>` element that qualifies a department name, you must prefix it with the alias `DepartmentName`.

```
<DepartmentName: Name>
```

When you specify a namespace URI, the URI or the documents at the specified URL are not searched by the browser. In fact, the URI just serves as a unique identifier for tags from different vocabularies.

XML schemas

You may be aware of database schemas that define and validate the tables, columns, and data types that make up the database. XML schemas are similar to these database schemas in that *XML schemas* also define and validate the content and structure of XML documents and can be used to maintain consistency among various XML documents defining different types of XML data. In fact, organizations can use XML schemas as a contract for exchanging data between different applications. XML schema files have the `.xsd` extension.

If you're thinking that XML schemas must be similar to DTDs, which are also used to define the structure of XML documents, you're correct! In fact, you can think of an XML schema as a superset of a DTD. By using XML schemas, however, you gain a couple of advantages over using DTDs:

- ✦ DTDs help you specify whether an element can be empty or can contain character data or other elements. In contrast, XML schemas enable you to specify whether an element can contain an integer, float, or string value.
- ✦ Unlike DTDs, which have their own syntax, XML schemas use the XML syntax, so you don't have to learn a new syntax to create XML schemas.

To understand the concept of XML schemas better, we use the XML designer to create an XML schema for the `Employees.xml` document. To do so, we use the same project `XMLDemo` that we create in the step list in the section "XML versus HTML" earlier in this chapter. Just follow these steps:

1. **Open the Add New Item dialog box by choosing Project⇨Add New Item.**
2. **Select XML Schema in the Templates pane, enter the name of the file (`Employees.xsd`), and click OK.**

   The designer opens in the Schema view. In this view, you can design the schema visually by using the Toolbox. The designer also provides the XML view that you can use to write the XML code to create the XML schema.
3. **Switch to the XML view and write the following code to define the structure of the XML data represented in the `Employees.xml` document:**

```
<?xml version="1.0" encoding="utf-8" ?>
<xsd:schema
xmlns:xsd="http://www.w3.org/2001/XMLSchema">
   <xsd:element name="Employees" type="EmployeeInfo" />
     <xsd:complexType name="EmployeeInfo">
```

```
            <xsd:sequence>
              <xsd:element name="Employee" type="Details"
minOccurs="0" maxOccurs="unbounded" />
            </xsd:sequence>
        </xsd:complexType>

        <xsd:complexType name="Details">
            <xsd:sequence>
              <xsd:element name="Id" type="xsd:string" />
              <xsd:element name="LastName"
type="xsd:string" />
              <xsd:element name="FirstName"
type="xsd:string" />
            </xsd:sequence>
        </xsd:complexType>
</xsd:schema>
```

In the preceding code,

- The XML schema elements (`.xsd`) are defined in the `XMLSchema` namespace.
- The `<xsd:element>` element describes the data that it contains.
- The `<xsd:complexType>` element can contain additional elements and attributes.

4. **Switch to the Schema view.**

   You see the schema as shown in Figure 12-4.

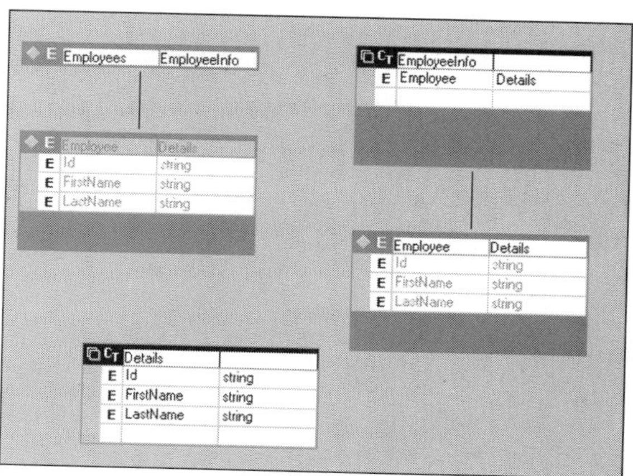

Figure 12-4: The XML schema for the Employees.xml document in the Schema view.

Extensible Stylesheet Language Transformations (XSL/T)

The basic aim of XML is to describe structured data rather than to focus on the presentation of data. XML documents do not contain any tags that define the format of the data to be displayed. This has its unique advantage because XML documents do not have any user-viewable format. As a result, you can apply any format to the data and display the same data in multiple formats.

W3C has specified a stylesheet — called *Extensible Stylesheet Language Transformations* (XSLT) — specifically designed for XML documents. You can check out information about XSL/T in Book 6, Chapter 6. To create this stylesheet in Visual Studio .NET, use the XSL or XSLT template in the Add New Item dialog box. For example, the following code defines a stylesheet named `Employees.xslt` for the `Employees.xml` document:

```
<xsl:stylesheet version="1.0"
   xmlns:xsl="http://www.w3.org/1999/XSL/Transform"
   xmlns="http://www.w3.org/TR/xhtml1/strict">
<xsl:output method="xml" encoding="iso-8859-1" />
<xsl:template match="/">
   <OL>
      <xsl:for-each select='Employees/Employee'>
         <LI>
             <b>
                Employee Id :
                 <xsl:value-of select='Id /> <br />
             </b>
                Last Name :
                 <xsl:value-of select='LastName' /> <br />
                First Name :
                 <xsl:value-of select='FirstName' /> <br />
             <hr />
         </LI>
      </xsl:for-each>
   </OL>
</xsl:template>
</xsl:stylesheet>
```

In the preceding code:

- The `<xsl:template>` element allows you to create a template to display the data in the required format.
- The `<xsl:for-each>` element is used to perform a task repeatedly.
- The `<xsl:value-of>` element is used to retrieve the data from individual elements.

After you create the .xslt file, combine this file with your XML file to apply the format by opening the Employees.xml file in the XML view and, after the first line, adding the following line:

```
<?xml-stylesheet type="text/xsl" href="Employees.xslt"?>
```

When you browse the Employees.xml file in a browser, the output looks formatted and appears as shown in Figure 12-5.

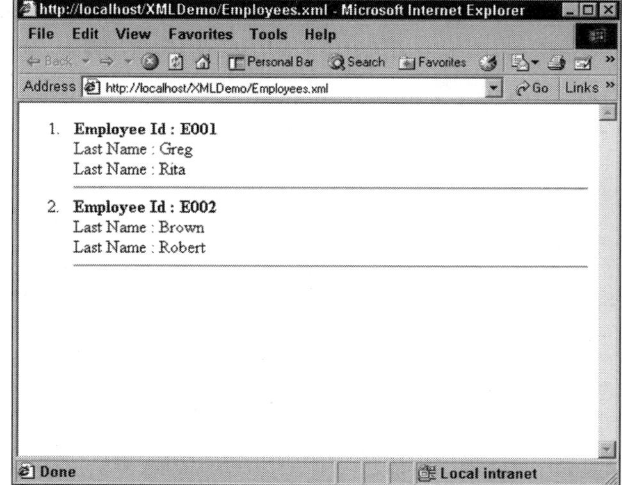

Figure 12-5: The Employees.xml file after applying the stylesheet Employees.xslt.

XML Document Object Model

When you want to access and display the XML data in your Web applications, use the Xml Web server control and set its specific properties at the design time. (Read more about the Xml Web server control in Book 6, Chapter 6.) In certain situations, you may need to display the XML data based on some conditions. In such cases, you'll have to access the XML data programmatically. To do that, you must employ the use of the *XML Document Object Model* (DOM), which is an in-memory representation of an XML document and represents data as a hierarchy of object nodes.

At the top of the hierarchy lies the XML document. To implement XML DOM, the .NET Framework provides a set of classes — which enable you to access the XML data programmatically — included in the System.Xml namespace. Some of the classes in the System.Xml namespace are as follows:

- XmlDocument: Represents a complete XML document.
- XmlDataDocument: Enables you to store and manipulate XML and relational data into a data set. This class is derived from the XmlDocument class.
- XmlDocumentType: Represents the DTD used by an XML document.
- XmlTextReader: Represents a reader that performs a fast, noncached, forward-only read operation on an XML document.
- XmlTextWriter: Represents a writer that performs a fast, noncached, forward-only generation of streams and files that contain XML data.
- XmlElement: Represents a single element from an XML document.
- XmlAttribute: Represents a single attribute of an element.

Converting Data from the Relational Format to the XML Format

Suppose your Web application accesses data from a SQL database. Consider also that you need your application to share data with other Web applications, which may be running on another platform. In such a case, the best solution is to convert relational data to the data in the XML format, which then can be shared across platforms.

To convert data from the relational format to the XML format, create a table named Employees in the tempdb database of your SQL server. The SQL statements for the table are as follows:

```
Create Table Employees
(
EmployeesId char (4) Primary Key,
LastName varchar(20),
Firstname varchar(20),
Designation varchar(15)
)
```

Then, add some records to this table. The following SQL statements add two records to the Employees table:

```
Insert Employees
Values('E001', 'Greg', 'Rita', 'Sales Manager')

Insert Employees
Values('E002', 'Brown', 'Robert', 'Sales Executive')
```

Next, you'll display the data from the Employees table in an Xml server control in XML format. To do so, follow these steps:

1. **Add the Xml server control from the Toolbox to the Web form (in Design mode).**
2. **Open the code-behind file for the Web form and import the following namespaces so that you can use the required classes:**

   ```
   Imports System.Data
   Imports System.Data.SqlClient
   Imports System.Xml
   ```

3. **In the `Page_Load` method, write the following code:**

   ```
   Dim Connection As New
   SqlConnection("server=localhost;uid=sa;pwd=;database=
   Pubs")
   Dim Mycommand As New SqlDataAdapter("SELECT * FROM
       Employees", Connection)
   Dim dsEmployees As New DataSet()
   Mycommand.Fill(dsEmployees, "Employees")
   'Creating an object of the XmlDocument class. Notice
   'that the constructor takes the dataset as its parame-
   'ter. Thus, the dataset fetched from the SQL database
   'is converted to an XmlDocument object.
   Dim XmlDoc As XmlDocument = New
   XmlDataDocument(dsEmployees)
   'Setting the Document property of the Xml server control
   'to the object of the XmlDocument class
   Xml1.Document = XmlDoc
   XmlDoc.Save("Employees1.xml")
   ```

4. **Switch to the HTML view of the Web form, and add the following attribute to the `@Page` directive:**

   ```
   ContentType="text/xml"
   ```

   This attribute indicates that the page content represents an XML document.

When you build and run the application, the page displays the data in the XML format, as shown in Figure 12-6.

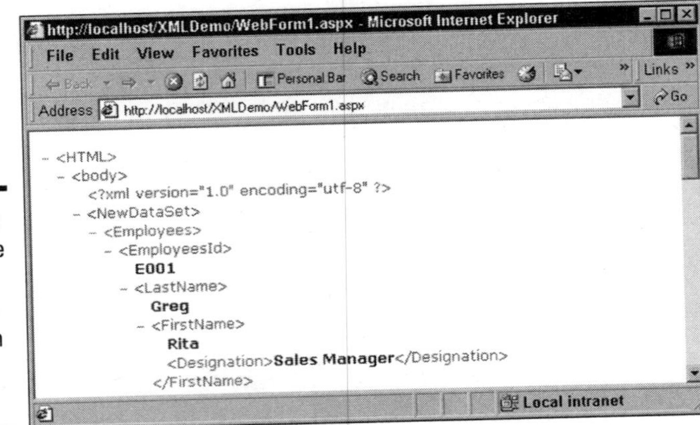

Figure 12-6: A Web page displaying data from a SQL table in the XML format.

Data Binding with XML Documents

You can bind server controls to data from different sources, such as a control's property, method, or a `DataView` object. Data binding enables you to bind server controls to data stores and thus display data dynamically; that is, the displayed values change each time that the values in the data store change. To refresh your knowledge about data binding, check out Book 6, Chapter 8. In this section, we show you how to implement data binding with XML documents.

An XML document cannot be directly bound to server controls. To implement data binding, you first need to load the XML document into a dataset. Then, you can bind a server control with this dataset. In this section, we use the `Employees.xml` document (which you create in the section "XML versus HTML" earlier in this chapter) for data binding. We bind the `<Id>` element of the XML document to a `DropDownList` control to populate the list with employee Ids. When you select an employee Id at run time, the corresponding details are displayed in a `DataGrid` control. To implement this functionality, follow these steps:

1. **Add a new Web form to the** `XMLDemo` **project, and set this form as the startup page for the project.**
2. **Add a** `Label` **Web server control from the Toolbox to the form, and set the** `Text` **property of the control to** `Select Employee Id`**.**
3. **Add a** `DropDownList` **Web server control to the form, and set its properties by using Table 12-1 as reference.**

Table 12-1 Properties of the DropDownList Web Server Control

Property	*Value*
`ID`	`EmployeeIDList`
`DataTextField`	`Id`
`DataValueField`	`Id`
`AutoPostBack`	`True`

Notice that the `DataTextField` and `DataValueField` properties are set to the `<Id>` element of the `Employees.xml` document. The `AutoPostBack` property is set to `True`, indicating that each time a user selects a value from the list, the page is posted back to the server.

4. **Add a `DataGrid` control to the form and set its ID to `DetailsGrid`.**
5. **Open the code-behind file for this form, and import the following namespaces:**

```
Imports System.Data
Imports System.IO
```

The `System.IO` namespace contains classes that are required to read the XML document into a dataset.

6. **In the `Page_Load` method, write the following line of code to create an object of the `FileStream` class, which is used to open or create a file:**

```
Dim EmpFile As New
FileStream(Server.MapPath("Employees.xml"),
FileMode.Open, FileAccess.Read)
```

The constructor of the `FileStream` class takes three parameters:

The first parameter represents the path of the file, which is set to the `Employees.xml` file.

The second parameter indicates the mode in which the file needs to be opened.

Finally, the third parameter indicates how the file should be accessed.

In this example, the `EmpFile` object represents the `Employees.xml` file, which is opened with read access.

7. **To create a dataset and load the `Employees.xml` file in this dataset, write the following lines of code in the `Page_Load` method:**

```
Dim dsEmpData As New DataSet()
dsEmpData.ReadXml(EmpFile)
```

The `ReadXml` method is used to load the XML file (represented as an object of the `FileStream` class) in a dataset.

8. **Write the following code to bind the data with the `DropDownList` control the first time a user requests the page.**

```
If Not IsPostBack Then
   'Set the DataSource property of the DropDownList
   EmployeeIDList.DataSource =
dsEmpData.Tables(0).DefaultView()
   'Bind the data with the control
   EmployeeIDList.DataBind()
Else
   'Create a DataView object from the dataset for the
   'Employees.xml document
   Dim dvEmpView = New DataView(dsEmpData.Tables(0))
   'The RowFilter property of the DataView object
   'filters the bound data by the Employee Id
   dvEmpView.RowFilter = "Id='" +
EmployeeIDList.SelectedItem.Text + "'"

   DetailsGrid.DataSource = dvEmpView
   DetailsGrid.DataBind()
End If
```

In case of subsequent requests, the `DataGrid` control should be data bound.

When you run the application, and select an employee Id from the drop-down list, the corresponding employee details are displayed in the `DataGrid` control, as shown in Figure 12-7.

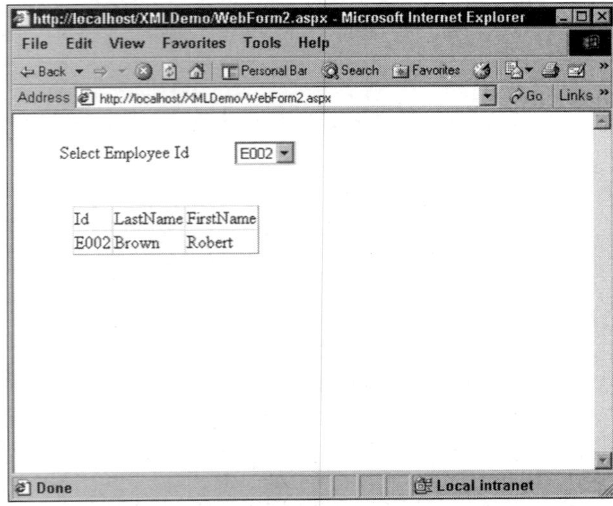

Figure 12-7: A Web page displaying data from an XML document.

Chapter 13: Configuring ASP.NET Applications

In This Chapter

- **Getting the basics of ASP.NET configuration**
- **Examining ASP.NET configuration in-depth**
- **Setting up configuration**

While creating an application, you usually provide certain details that define the behavior of the application. This information is called *configuration information*. To understand it better, take the analogy of Microsoft Outlook. When you install Microsoft Outlook, you specify the address of the mail server, user profile information, and so on. Thus, configuring an application involves defining certain settings that in turn define the manner in which the application behaves. Now, further extend this concept of configuration information and behavior to Web applications. Configuring Web applications involves specifying the details, such as the session timeout (the time after which the session expires), security options, the way errors should be handled and logged, and so on.

In this chapter, we discuss the ASP.NET configuration concepts and tell you about the advantages that ASP.NET configuration offers over its predecessor ASP. We observe and analyze the format of the configuration files that will ultimately help you in setting your own configuration options. Finally, we show you some common configuration settings for Web applications. So keep reading to uncover this feature of ASP.NET!

Getting an Overview of ASP.NET Configuration

The properties and behavior of ASP.NET applications are determined by the settings contained within specific files called *configuration files*. These files are XML-based, which enables you to access and set the configuration settings in a manner that's extremely convenient and hence doesn't require you to write scripts for configuration settings. The complete ASP.NET configuration system stands on the pillars of these configuration files. In this section, we give you the lowdown about these files so that you'll know how these files make the ASP.NET configuration system work. We also look at the advantages that the ASP.NET configuration system offers.

ASP.NET configuration files

The ASP.NET configuration system supports two types of configuration files, Machine.config and Web.config, which form the backbone of the ASP.NET configuration system:

- **Machine.config:** When you install Visual Studio .NET, the Machine.config file gets automatically installed on the server in the `%windir%\Microsoft.NET\Framework\[version]\Config` file. The Machine.config file is at the highest level and contains the default configuration settings for all the Web applications that are hosted on the server. Being at the highest level, this file is also called the *machine-level configuration file.*
- **Web.config:** When you create an ASP.NET Web Application project, some files get automatically created. One of these is the Web.config file, which is created in the application's root directory and contains the settings specific to an individual application. Because the Web.config file is specific to an application, this file is also called *application-level configuration file*. The application-level configuration file inherits settings from the machine-level configuration file. However, you can override the default settings by editing application-level configuration files.

While only one Machine.config file exists, there can be multiple Web.config files on the server with each file existing in individual application root directories or the directories within the root directory.

The hierarchical configuration system

The complete configuration system revolves around two types of configuration files, Machine.config and Web.config. But how are the configuration settings applied when a browser requests a Web application from a server? When an application is requested, the configuration settings are checked in both files (Machine.config and Web.config) in a hierarchical manner.

To understand the *hierarchical configuration system*, consider an example. As you can see in the directory structure shown in Figure 13-1, the Application Root represents the virtual directory for a Web application. The application has two more directories, Sub Directory 1 and Sub Directory 2, within the root directory.

When a browser requests for this application from the server, the settings are checked in the configuration files hierarchically. To understand this hierarchical checking, consider a configuration setting that defines the user access to the application resources. The default settings in the Machine.config file enable all users to access application resources. If you want all users to have access to the resources on the Web site, but you want only specific users accessing the resources in Sub Directory 1, you can create a Web.config file in Sub Directory 1. The Web.config file helps override the default settings of the Machine.config file. The configuration settings for the application root are the same as the settings in the Machine.config file because they're applied automatically to all Web applications unless overridden. Thus, with the hierarchical configuration system, you can control the settings at different levels of an application.

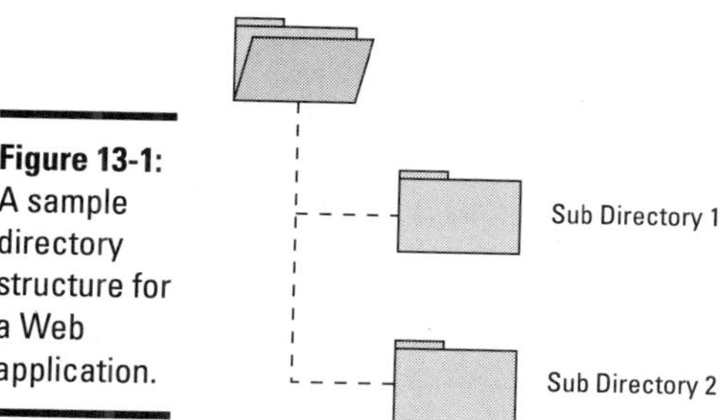

Figure 13-1: A sample directory structure for a Web application.

Advantages of the ASP.NET configuration system

You'll better appreciate the advantages of the ASP.NET configuration system when you understand the configuration system of its predecessor ASP. In ASP, all the configuration information is stored in a binary format on IIS in a special repository called *metabase*. Whenever you need to modify configuration settings, you need to modify the metabase. To modify the metabase, you either need to write scripts or use the IIS Microsoft Management Console (MMC) snap-in. In addition, after you modify the IIS metabase to modify the configuration settings, you must restart the Web server for the changes to take effect. All this requires a lot of effort as opposed to using the XML-based configuration files in ASP.NET.

Configuring your Web applications in ASP.NET is far more convenient and efficient. Some of the advantages are

- ✦ ASP.NET configuration files are XML-based, making them easy to read and write. Modifying configuration settings simply requires you to edit the XML-based configuration files.
- ✦ Any modifications made to the configuration files take effect immediately. Unlike ASP, you need not restart the Web server.
- ✦ The ASP.NET configuration settings are applied in a hierarchical manner. Thus, you can have different settings for different applications and different settings for different parts of the same application.

✦ Last but not least, the ASP.NET configuration system is extensible, meaning that you can create custom configuration handlers. This extensibility feature can then be used at runtime to affect the processing of the HTTP requests.

As we move ahead and look at the format of the configuration files, this elementary knowledge about configuration in ASP.NET will prove useful.

Taking a Closer Look at ASP.NET Configuration

Both Machine.config and Web.config configuration files have the same format. The only difference is in the location of these files in the file system and the support for some settings. Open a configuration file and observe its format. You can find the Machine.config file in the `%windir%\Microsoft.NET\Framework\[version]\Config` directory. Web.config files can be found in specific Web application projects. The following code provides a general format of a configuration file:

```
<?xml version="1.0" encoding="UTF-8" ?>

<configuration>
     <configSections>
         <section name="{sectionName}" type="{Class}" />

         more section declarations
         <sectionGroup name="{sectionGroup}">
             <section name="{sectionName} type="{Class}" />

             more section declarations
         </sectionGroup>

         more section declarations
     </configSections>

     <{sectionName} attribute="{value}"/>

         more sections
     <{sectionGroup}>
          <{sectionName} attribute="{value}" />

          more sections
     </{sectionGroup}>
</configuration>
```

Notice the *camel-casing convention* used to name the different configuration sections. In this naming convention, the first letter of the first word is in lowercase, and the first letters of subsequent words are in uppercase — as in `<configSections>`. Remembering these conventions is important because the ASP.NET configuration system is case-sensitive.

As you can see in the preceding format, the root element of the configuration file is `<configuration>`. All the elements are enclosed within this element. The different elements are called *configuration sections* and represent configuration settings.

Logically, the complete file can be divided into two parts:

✦ **Configuration section handler declarations:** All the elements included within `<configSections>` and `</configSections>` tags are collectively referred to as the configuration section handler declarations. This part contains the declaration of all other configuration sections that are used in the configuration file. To organize sections, multiple sections are declared within section groups. When a section is declared, the type attribute specifies the .NET class that's responsible for handling the configuration settings at runtime in addition to other details, such as the version.

All of the configuration sections must be declared only once for all applications. This is because all applications inherit the configuration settings in the Machine.config file and, therefore, the sections need not be declared again in the Web.config files.

✦ **Actual configuration section settings:** This part contains the actual configuration sections. All tags defined in this section control the behavior of the ASP.NET runtime. This section is a great way to control, change, and manage the behavior of Web applications. There is one configuration section for each declaration in the `<configSections>` part. These configuration sections contain subsections with attributes that contain the settings for that section.

To understand the configuration file format, consider the example of the `<trace>` section in the code that follows. You can read Book 6, Chapter 7 to revisit the practical implementation of the `<trace>` section.

```
<?xml version="1.0" encoding="UTF-8" ?>

<configuration>
    <configSections>


        <sectionGroup name="system.web">


<section name="trace"
   type="System.Web.Configuration.TraceConfigurationHandler,
   System.Web, Version=1.0.2411.0, Culture=neutral,
   PublicKeyToken=b03f5f7f11d50a3a" />


        </sectionGroup>
```

```
    </configSections>
</configSections>


<system.web>

    <trace
      enabled="false"
      localOnly="true"
      pageOutput="false"
      requestLimit="10"
      traceMode="SortByTime"
    />
</system.web>
</configuration>
```

In the preceding code:

- The `<trace>` section is declared within the `<configSections>` section. When declaring the `<trace>` section, the type attribute specifies the class that handles the configuration settings related to tracing in addition to other details, such as version. Notice that the `<trace>` section is declared within a section group named `system.web`.
- Outside the `<configSections>` section, the `<trace>` element is actually defined. Here, the `<trace>` section contains several attributes that define the configuration settings pertaining to the trace functionality.

Now that you know the configuration file format, you're ready to move on to some of the most commonly used configuration sections, which we discuss in the next section.

Discussing Configuration Settings

The configuration file contains several sections that describe the configuration settings, such as tracing, custom errors, security, and compilation. Throughout this section, we take a look at some of the configuration sections and their implementations.

The <httpRuntime> section

General HTTP runtime settings include the time for which a request is processed before being timed out, the maximum length of a Web request, and whether or not to use the fully qualified URLs for client redirects. The default settings for this section as specified in the Machine.config file are as follows:

```
<httpRuntime
      executionTimeout="90"
      maxRequestLength="4096"
      useFullyQualifiedRedirectUrl="false"
      ---
      ---
/>
```

In the following list, we discuss each attribute of the `<httpRuntime>` section in some detail:

- `executionTimeout`: Represents the time for which a Web request is processed before the application times out. The default value is `90`, which means that a Web request is processed for 90 seconds. If the processing isn't complete within this time limit, the application times out. If you think that your Web applications will take more time to process — for example, in the case of an application that accesses a large database — you can increase this value.
- `maxRequestLength`: Represents the maximum size of a Web request in kilobyte (KB). The default value, `4096 KB`, indicates that the maximum size of a Web request is 4096 KB. If the content for the Web requests for your Web applications is larger than this default size, however — for example, in the case of upload sites — you can increase this value.
- `useFullyQualifiedRedirectUrl`: Represents whether or not fully qualified URLs may be used for client redirects. This attribute takes a Boolean value. By default, the attribute is set to `false`, indicating that fully qualified URLs cannot be used for client redirects. For example, if your Web application named `MyApplication` redirects to the page `Details.aspx`, the redirect URL is set to `/MyApplication/Details.aspx`. On the other hand, if you set this attribute to `true`, the redirect URL would be `http://<server name>/MyApplication/Details.aspx`.

The <appSettings> section

Suppose you have several pages in your application that access a database. Wouldn't it be nice if you could store the data source name (DSN) somewhere at the application level and then access the DSN whenever needed? You specify such custom settings in the `<appSettings>` section. This section uses a set of key value pairs, which in turn populates a hashtable that you can access from your application.

To understand the implementation of the `<appSettings>` section, create an ASP.NET Web Application project by using VB and name it `ConfigurationDemo`. Then, open the Web.config file. Because this file isn't listed in the Solution Explorer window initially, click the Show All Files button at the top of the Solution Explorer window to see the Web.config file. In the Web.config file, create the <appSettings> section as follows:

```
<configuration>
   <appSettings>
       <add key="DSN"
   value="server=localhost;uid=sa;pwd=;database=Pubs" />
       <add key="empTable" value="Select * from Employees" />
   </appSettings>
</configuration>
```

In the preceding code, the <appSettings> section has two keys, DSN and empTable. The DSN key takes the value as the connection string to the Pubs database on a SQL server. The empTable key takes the value as the string for a SQL query that retrieves all rows from the Employees table.

In the preceding code, notice that the <appSettings> section is not declared in the <configSections> section before specifying the actual configuration settings. Actually, you don't have to declare this section in the Web.config file because the section is already declared in the Machine.config file, and the Web.config file inherits from the Machine.config file.

Next, to demonstrate how to access these custom settings in the application named ConfigurationDemo that you just created, add a DataGrid control to the Web form in the project. Then, switch to the code-behind file for the form and import the following namespaces:

```
Imports System.Data
Imports System.Data.SqlClient
```

Then, in the Page_Load method, write the following code:

```
Private Sub Page_Load(ByVal sender As System.Object, ByVal e
    As System.EventArgs) Handles MyBase.Load
         'Put user code to initialize the page here
         Dim dsn, sqlEmp As String
         dsn = ConfigurationSettings.AppSettings("DSN")
         sqlEmp =
    ConfigurationSettings.AppSettings("empTable")
         Dim connection As New SqlConnection(dsn)
         Dim command As New SqlDataAdapter(sqlEmp, connection)
         Dim dsEmployees As New DataSet()
         command.Fill(dsEmployees, sqlEmp)
         DataGrid1.DataSource = dsEmployees
         DataGrid1.DataBind()
End Sub
```

In the preceding code, ConfigurationSettings.AppSetings is used to access the custom settings in the <appSettings> section.

When you build and run the application, the page displays the records from the Employees table in the Pubs database, as shown in Figure 13-2.

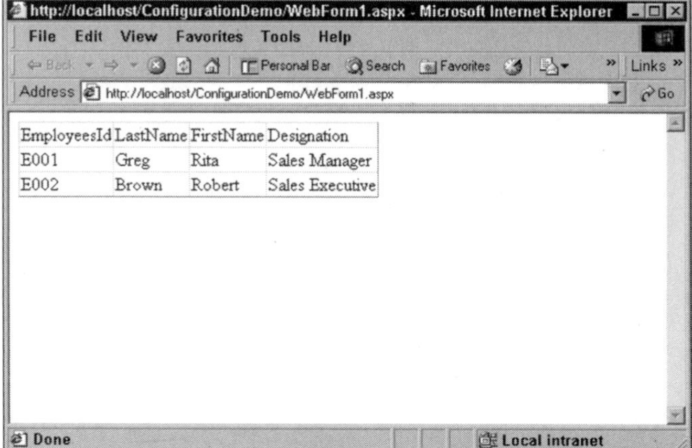

EmployeesId	LastName	FirstName	Designation
E001	Greg	Rita	Sales Manager
E002	Brown	Robert	Sales Executive

Figure 13-2: A sample page that accesses configuration settings in the <appSettings> section of the Web.config file.

The <compilation> section

The `<compilation>` section is where you specify the settings related to the compilation of ASP.NET applications. Some of the settings that you can specify include the default language to be used for dynamic compilation and whether or not to enable the explicit declaration feature of VB. In addition, the `<compilation>` section also enables you to add additional CLR compilers, such as COBOL in the `<compiler>` subsection and to specify the assemblies to link to during compilation.

The default settings that are available in the `<compilation>` section in the Machine.config file are as follows:

```
<compilation debug="false" explicit="true"
   defaultLanguage="vb">

   <compilers>
     <compiler language="c#;cs;csharp" extension=".cs"
   type="Microsoft.CSharp.CSharpCodeProvider, System,
   Version=1.0.2411.0, Culture=neutral,
   PublicKeyToken=b77a5c561934e089" />
     <compiler language="vb;visualbasic;vbscript" exten-
   sion=".vb" type="Microsoft.VisualBasic.VBCodeProvider,
   System, Version=1.0.2411.0, Culture=neutral,
   PublicKeyToken=b77a5c561934e089" />
     <compiler language="js;jscript;javascript"
   extension=".js"
```

```
    type="Microsoft.JScript.JScriptCodeProvider,
    Microsoft.JScript" />
    </compilers>

    <assemblies>
      <add assembly="mscorlib"/>
      <add assembly="System, Version=1.0.2411.0, Culture=neu-
    tral, PublicKeyToken=b77a5c561934e089"/>
      <add assembly="System.Web, Version=1.0.2411.0,
    Culture=neutral, PublicKeyToken=b03f5f7f11d50a3a"/>
      <add assembly="System.Data, Version=1.0.2411.0,
    Culture=neutral, PublicKeyToken=b77a5c561934e089"/>
      <add assembly="System.Web.Services, Version=1.0.2411.0,
    Culture=neutral, PublicKeyToken=b03f5f7f11d50a3a"/>
       <add assembly="System.Xml, Version=1.0.2411.0,
    Culture=neutral, PublicKeyToken=b77a5c561934e089"/>
       <add assembly="System.Drawing, Version=1.0.2411.0,
    Culture=neutral, PublicKeyToken=b03f5f7f11d50a3a"/>
       <add assembly="*"/>
    </assemblies>
</compilation>
```

In the preceding code:

- The `<compilers>` subsection lists the CLR-supported compilers. This subsection takes the following three attributes:
  - `language` (specifies the language to be used)
  - `extension` (specifies the extension of the code-behind file for the page)
  - `type` (specifies the class to be used for compilation)
- The `<assemblies>` subsection lists the assemblies that are used during compilation. You can also use this subsection to add and remove assemblies.

The <customErrors> section

All settings related to custom error messages can be specified in the `<customErrors>` section. It'll be a good idea to revisit the concepts on error handling in Book 6, Chapter 7. For now, look at the format of the section:

```
<customErrors
   defaultRedirect="url"
   mode="On|Off|RemoteOnly">
   <error statusCode="statuscode"
          redirect="url"/>
</customErrors>
```

In the following list, we dissect the preceding section and quickly revisit the different attributes used:

- `defaultRedirect`: The URL to which client browsers should be directed when an error occurs.
- `mode`: The mode in which custom errors function. This attribute can take one of the following values:
  - `On`: Custom errors are enabled. This value prohibits the display of original error messages in client browsers.
  - `Off`: Custom errors are disabled. This value forces the display of original error messages even if custom error pages are available.
- `RemoteOnly`: Custom errors are shown only to remote clients.

In addition to the attributes that we list in the preceding bulleted list, the section also contains a subsection called `<error>`. This subsection takes two attributes, `statusCode` and `redirect`. The `statusCode` attribute represents the status code of the error that redirects client browsers to a custom error page. The `redirect` attribute represents the URL to which client browsers should be redirected when an error occurs. To see the implementation of the `<customErrors>` section, check out Book 6, Chapter 7.

The <trace> section

Tracing, a new feature of ASP.NET, enables you to trace the execution of Web applications. For a detailed discussion on tracing, check out Book 6, Chapter 7. To trace the execution of individual pages in a Web application, you set `Trace = "true"` in the `@Page` directive. However, if your Web application consists of a number of pages that you want to trace, adding `Trace = "true"` could be a cumbersome task. ASP.NET eases this for you by providing the `<trace>` section in the configuration file. You set the various attributes of the `<trace>` section for performing application-level tracing. The default settings contained in this section are as follows:

```
<configuration>
   <system.web>
       <trace
           enabled="false"
           requestLimit="10"
           pageOutput="false"
           traceMode="SortByTime"
           localOnly="true"
       />
   </system.web>
</configuration>
```

Now to quickly review the different attributes of the `<trace>` section:

✦ `enabled`: Indicates whether or not application-level tracing is enabled. This attribute takes a Boolean value. The default value is `false` indicating that application-level tracing is not enabled. You can set this attribute to `true` to enable application-level tracing.

Although application-level tracing is disabled by default, you can enable page-level tracing by setting `Tracing = "true"` in the `@Page` directive.

✦ `requestLimit`: Indicates the maximum number of trace requests to be stored in the server cache. The default value is `10`.

✦ `pageOutput`: Indicates whether or not the trace information is displayed for each page in the application for which tracing (application-level) is enabled. The default value is `false` indicating that the page-level trace information isn't displayed for each page in the application. Instead, the trace information for each page is stored in the server cache, which is available via `trace.axd`.

✦ `traceMode`: Indicates the sequence in which trace messages are displayed. This attribute takes either the `SortByTime` or `SortByCategory` value; the default value is `SortByTime`.

✦ `localOnly`: Indicates whether the trace messages are available for only client requests (using `http://localhost`) or also for remote client requests. The default value is `true`. Usually, you use tracing for debugging purposes wherein you need to display trace messages for local client requests. Hence, we advise leaving this attribute set to `true`.

You can check out the implementation of the `<trace>` section in Book 6, Chapter 7.

The <sessionState> section

Usually, numerous users access Web applications simultaneously. While an application runs and users interact with it, you might need to track and maintain data for different users and isolate the data of one user from others. For example, you might want to track the duration for which an ad banner is displayed to a user. You can perform this user-wise data maintenance and tracking by using the `Session` object provided with ASP.NET. This object enables you to store the session state data as key/value pairs.

The configuration settings pertaining to the session state are contained in the `<sessionState>` section. The default settings contained in this section are:

```
<configuration>
   <system.web>
       <sessionState
           mode="InProc"
           stateConnectionString="tcpip=127.0.0.1:42424"
           sqlConnectionString="data source=127.0.0.1;user
```

```
    id=sa;password="
            cookieless="false"
            timeout="20"
        />
    </system.web>
</configuration>
```

Now look at each attribute and its purpose:

- mode: This attribute specifies where to store session state data and takes one of these four values:
    - Off: Indicates that the session state isn't enabled and thus no user session data is maintained and tracked.
    - Inproc: Indicates that the session state data is stored within the ASP.NET process. This is the default value for the mode attribute. Because session state data is stored within the ASP.NET process, you reap the performance benefits. Additionally, this value is the best choice for applications that are hosted on a single server.
    - StateServer: Indicates that the session state data is stored outside the ASP.NET process on some remote server (Windows NT service). Because the separate process where the session state data is stored is reliable for managing the state of multiple servers, this value is the best choice when Web applications are hosted on several servers (Web farms).
    - SqlServer: Indicates that the session state data is stored outside the ASP.NET process on a SQL server. Because the data is stored on the SQL server, this value is the best choice when the reliability of the data is of the utmost importance.
- stateConnectionString: This attribute specifies the TCP/IP address and the port number of the remote server where the session state data is stored. You must set this attribute when the mode is StateServer.
- sqlConnectionString: This attribute specifies the connection string for the SQL server where the session state data is stored. You must set this attribute when the mode is SqlServer.
- cookieless: This attribute takes a Boolean value and indicates whether or not the session state should be enabled for clients that do not support HTTP cookies. The default value is false indicating that the session state is disabled for those clients who don't support HTTP cookies.
- timeout: This attribute indicates the time in minutes for which a session can remain idle (the duration for which a user doesn't interact with the application). After this time limit is crossed, the session is abandoned automatically. The default value is 20.

To understand the implementation of the `<sessionState>` element, consider the situation in which the `cookieless` attribute is set to `true`. When you set this attribute to `true`, ASP.NET extracts the session ID from the cookie and passes it with the URL of the Web request. This feature of embedded session ID with the URL enables the session state data to be stored as per the mode attribute.

In the `ConfigurationDemo` project, add a Web form and design it as shown in Figure 13-3. Use Table 13-1 as a reference for setting the properties of different controls on the form.

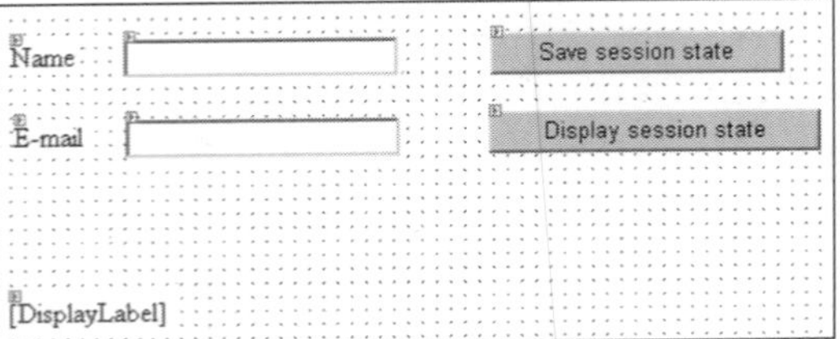

Figure 13-3: A sample form in Design mode.

Table 13-1 Properties of the controls on the sample form

Control	Contains	Property	Value
`Label`	Name	`Text`	`Name`
`TextBox`	Name	`ID`	`NameBox`
`Label`	E-mail	`Text`	`E-mail`
`TextBox`	E-mail	`ID`	`EmailBox`
`Button`	Save session state	`Text`	`Save session state`
`Button`	Save session state	`ID`	`SaveButton`
`Button`	Display session state	`Text`	`Display session state`
`Button`	Display session state	`ID`	`DisplayButton`
`Label`	DisplayLabel	`Text`	`Blank`
`Label`	DisplayLabel	`ID`	`DisplayLabel`
`Label`	DisplayLabel	`Visible`	`False`

In the event handler for the `Click` event of SaveButton, write the following code:

```
Private Sub SaveButton_Click(ByVal sender As System.Object,
   ByVal e As System.EventArgs) Handles SaveButton.Click
       Session("UserName") = NameBox.Text
       Session("UserEmail") = EmailBox.Text
```

```
        DisplayLabel.Text = "The session data stored is: " +
    "User Name: " + Session("UserName") + " and E-mail: " +
    Session("UserEmail")
        DisplayLabel.Visible = True
End Sub
```

In the preceding code, note that the session data is stored as a key/value pair in the Session object. The name and e-mail address of the user interacting with the application is stored in UserName and UserEmail keys.

Next, in the event handler for the Click event of DisplayButton, write the following code:

```
Private Sub DisplayButton_Click(ByVal sender As
           System.Object, ByVal e As System.EventArgs) Handles
           DisplayButton.Click
    If ((Session("UserName") Is Nothing) Or
           (Session("UserEmail") Is Nothing)) Then
        DisplayLabel.Text = "Session data lost"
        DisplayLabel.Visible = True
    Else
        DisplayLabel.Text = "Session data retrieved:" + "User
           Name: " + Session("UserName") + "E-mail: " +
           Session("UserEmail")
        DisplayLabel.Visible = True
    End If
End Sub
```

In the preceding code, note that the values stored in keys in the Session object are retrieved.

Then, in the Web.config file, navigate to the <sessionState> section and set the cookieless attribute to true. Finally, when you build the project and browse the form, notice that the session ID appears embedded in the URL of the Web request. When you supply user details in the text boxes and click the Save Session Data button, the session data is stored in the Session object as key/value pairs. Next, when you click the Display Session State button, the session state data is retrieved and displayed, as shown in Figure 13-4.

The <authentication> section

You use the <authentication> section to define the settings related to authentication of Web requests on the server. *Authentication* involves establishing an identity between the server and the request. In fact, we recommend that you read Book 6, Chapter 16 where we discuss in detail the ASP.NET security concepts.

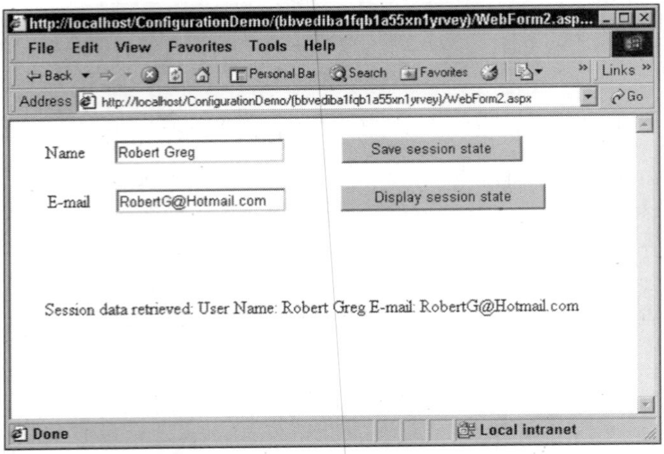

Figure 13-4: A sample form that displays the session state data for cookieless sessions.

The format of the `<authentication>` section is as follows:

```
<authentication mode="Windows|Forms|Passport|None">

   <forms name="name" loginUrl="url"
      protection="All|None|Encryption|Validation"
      timeout="30" path="/" >

      <credentials passwordFormat="Clear|SHA1|MD5">
         <user name="username" password="password" />
      </credentials>

   </forms>

   <passport redirectUrl="internal"/>

</authentication>
```

The only attribute that the `<authentication>` section supports is the `mode` attribute, which controls the default authentication mode for an application. The `mode` attribute can take any one of the following values:

- `Windows`: Indicates Windows authentication as the default authentication mode. This is the default value and is the right choice when using any form of IIS authentication.
- `Forms`: Indicates the ASP.NET forms-based authentication as the default authentication.
- `Passport`: Indicates Microsoft Passport authentication as the default authentication.

✦ None: Indicates no authentication. Usually, this value is used when only anonymous users are expected to access a Web application.

If the mode attribute is set to Forms, the behavior of the forms-based authentication can be defined in the <forms> subsection, which takes the following attributes:

✦ name: Represents the name of the HTTP cookie to be used for authentication. The default value is .ASPXAUTH.

✦ loginUrl: Represents the URL to which the user is redirected for login when no valid cookie is found. The default value is default.aspx. However, if you want to provide some other filename, you must also provide the complete implementation for login in this file.

✦ protection: Represents both the data validation and encryption of the HTTP cookie used for forms-based authentication. This attribute can take one of these values:

  - All: Indicating that both the data validation and encryption of the cookie is performed, this is the default and recommended value.
  - None: Indicates that neither data validation nor encryption of the cookie is performed. This value can be used when cookies are used only for personalization. However, because of security issues, this value is not recommended.
  - Encryption: Indicates that the encryption of the cookie is enabled, but the data validation isn't performed.
  - Validation: Indicates that the data validation of the cookie is enabled, but the encryption isn't performed. Use this value to validate if the value stored in the cookie isn't modified during the transit.

✦ timeout: Represents the time in minutes after which the cookie expires. The default value is 30.

✦ path: Represents the path of the cookie. The default value is "/", which indicates the root of the server.

In addition to the preceding attributes, the <forms> subsection has one subsection, <credentials>, within it. The <credentials> subsection can be used to define username and password in the configuration file and takes one attribute, passwordFormat, which specifies the encryption format for storing passwords. The valid values for this attribute are MD5, SHA1 and Clear. The Clear value indicates that the passwords are not encrypted. The <credentials> subsection supports another subsection named <user> to specify the username and password. For specifying the username and password, the <user> subsection provides two attributes, name and password.

For the practical demonstration of the <authentication> section, check out Book 6, Chapter 16.

The <authorization> section

By default, all Web applications allow all users to access the application resources. Of course, there can be multiple situations where you don't want all users accessing your application resources. ASP.NET enables you to allow or deny access to your application resources by using the <authorization> section. This section supports two subsections, <allow> (to allow access) and <deny> (to deny access). These subsections allow or deny access based on the values in the following attributes:

- users: Specifies a comma-separated list of users who are given access to the resources. The default value is "*" indicating that all users are allowed access to resources. To specify anonymous users, "?" is used.
- roles: Specifies a comma-separated list of roles who are given access to the resources.
- verbs: Specifies a comma-separated list of HTTP transmission methods, such as GET, HEAD, or POST, that are given access to the resources.

Consider the following settings contained in the <authorization> section:

```
<configuration>
  <system.config>
    <authorization>
      <allow users="John, Rita, Robert"
          roles="Administrator, Manager" />
      <deny users="?" roles="Customer" />
    </authorization>
  </system.web>
</configuration>
```

You can see from the preceding settings that all anonymous users and users with role Customer are denied access to application resources. Users named John, Rita, and Robert and all users with roles as Administrator and Manager are allowed access to resources. For more on authorization, check out Book 6, Chapter 16.

The <httpHandlers> section

ASP.NET Runtime is responsible for handling all the Web requests during the execution of Web applications. To handle different Web requests, such as requests for .aspx files, requests for .ascx files, or requests for Web requests by using a specific HTTP verb, ASP.NET Runtime uses the <httpHandlers> section. The <httpHandlers> section contains the mappings of different types of Web requests to the respective class and assembly, which in turn handles the request. For a detailed discussion on HTTP handlers, check out Book 6, Chapter 14.

In the <httpHandlers> section, you can create your own mappings for some custom Web requests with the respective class and assembly. To do so, the section supports a subsection named <add>, which supports three attributes:

- verb: Specifies a comma-separated list of the HTTP verbs, which should be mapped to the class or assembly specified in the type attribute. A * value indicates that the mapping should be performed for all the HTTP verbs.
- path: Specifies the URL path (/MyApplication/Greetings.aspx) or a wildcard string (*.aspx) for which mapping should be performed.
- type: Specifies a comma-separated list of class and assembly combination that implement the HTTP handler code.

The <httpHandler> section also enables you to remove the entries for mapping Web requests with the respective handler class and assembly. To do so, use the <remove> subsection, which takes two attributes: verb and path. The <httpHandler> section also provides another subsection named <clear> to remove all the handler entries in the configuration file. The complete format of the <httpHandler> section is as follows:

```
<httpHandlers>
   <add verb="[verb list]"
      path="[path/wildcard]"
      type="[type,assemblyname]" />
   <remove verb="[verb list]"
      path="[path/wildcard]" />
   <clear />
</httpHandlers>
```

The <globalization> section

Usually, Web applications are targeted toward a wide audience who may belong to different countries, speak different languages, and follow different cultures. These applications, which cater to the international audience, are usually referred to as *international-ready applications*. Such applications adapt automatically to the locale in which they're used. So you don't need to develop different versions of the same application for different locales. To be precise, a *locale* refers to the language and to the region in which that language is spoken. For example, English/US is a locale that refers to an audience who speaks English and who lives in the United States. Likewise, French/France is another locale. You can access and specify locale-specific configuration information in the <globalization> section of the configuration file. Here's the format of this section:

```
<configuration>
   <system.web>
```

```
    <globalization
        requestEncoding = "{a valid encoding string}"
        responseEncoding = "{a valid encoding string}"
        fileEncoding = "{a valid encoding string}"
        culture = "{a valid culture string}"
        uiCulture = "{a valid culture string}"
    />
  </system.web>
</configuration>
```

To help you understand the configuration settings available with the <globalization> section, here are the details of each of its attributes:

- `requestEncoding`: Represents the way the request data is encoded. The default value of this attribute is set to `"utf-8"`, which indicates an encoding system that represents a character as a sequence of 8-bit bytes. If no request encoding is specified to this attribute, the attribute defaults to the computer's Regional Options locale setting. The different encoding systems that you can use to set this attribute are available in the `System.Text` namespace.
- `responseEncoding`: Represents the way the response data is encoded. This attribute is also set to `"utf-8"` by default. If no response encoding is specified, the attribute defaults to the computer's Regional Options locale settings. You can find the different encoding systems to be used to set this attribute in the `System.Text` namespace.
- `fileEncoding`: Represents the way the ASPX, ASMX, and ASAX files are encoded.
- `culture`: Represents the culture string that is used to set the localized settings, such as the user interface language, the date/time format, and fonts for the application. For example, the culture string `en-US` represents the `English/US` locale. Similarly, `fr-FR` represents the `French/France` locale. You can find all the available culture strings that you can use for this attribute in the `System.Globalization.CultureInfo` class.
- `uiCulture`: Represents the culture string to be used to search for resources.

To specify locale-specific configuration settings at the application level, ASP.NET provides you the <globalization> section. To set the locale-specific settings at the page level, you can simply use the `@Page` directive, as shown in the following code line:

```
<%@Page ... responseEncoding="UTF-7"%>
```

Next, to understand the use of the `<globalization>` section and see it in action, follow these steps:

1. **Open the project `ConfigurationDemo` that we have you create earlier in this chapter.**
2. **Switch to the Web.config file and scroll to the `<globalization>` section.**

   For this example, suppose that a French audience is currently accessing this application.
3. **Edit the `<globalization>` section as follows:**

```
<configuration>
   <system.web>
     <globalization
          requestEncoding="utf-8"
          responseEncoding="utf-8"
          culture="fr-FR"
          uiCulture="fr-FR"
     />
   </system.web>
</configuration>
```

4. **Add a new Web form to the project.**
5. **In the Design view of this form, add a `Literal` control and set its `Text` property to `The application is accessed on:`; then, add a `Label` control and set its `ID` to `DisplayLabel`.**
6. **Open the code-behind file for the form and write the following code in the `Page_Load` method to display the current date and time:**

```
Private Sub Page_Load(ByVal sender As System.Object,
ByVal e As System.EventArgs) Handles MyBase.Load
        'Put user code to initialize the page here
        '"U" represents the date time format.
        DisplayLabel.Text = DateTime.Now.ToString("U")
End Sub
```

   When you build the application and browse the form, it displays the date and time in a format for the French audience, as shown in Figure 13-5.

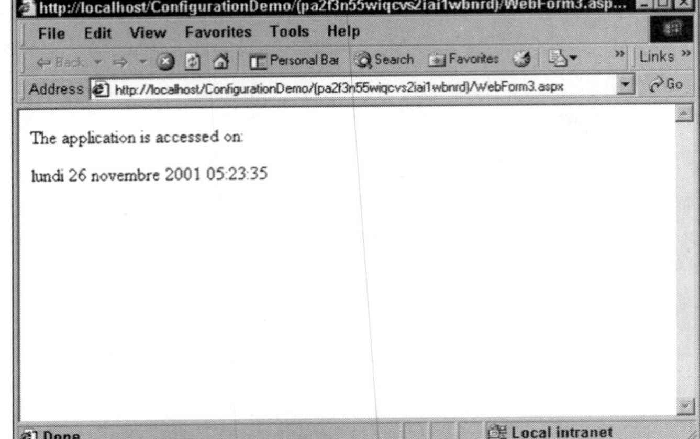

Figure 13-5: A form that displays the date and time for the fr-FR culture.

Chapter 14: Building ASP.NET HTTP Handlers

In This Chapter

- Building ground for HTTP handlers
- Understanding classes and interfaces required for building HTTP handlers
- Building custom HTTP handlers

Hypertext Transfer Protocol (HTTP) is the underlying protocol to communicate over the World Wide Web (WWW). Clients send requests to Web servers, which in turn respond to these requests by using HTTP. In addition to handling standard Web requests, there might be situations in which you want special requests to be handled in a specific manner at the server side. For example, suppose that you're developing an application that displays customized pages to users. To be able to provide customized output, you must capture user information and direct the user to several other pages, based on the entered information. To handle such custom HTTP requests, ASP.NET provides you with custom components called *HTTP handlers*.

In this chapter, we introduce you to HTTP handlers, explore the background behind them, and tell you about the HTTP runtime in this context. Then, we show you the classes and interfaces that are required for building HTTP handlers, finally putting your knowledge to the test by having you build a custom HTTP handler.

Building Ground for HTTP Handlers

Internet Information Server (IIS) processes Web requests based on HTTP transmission methods also called *HTTP verbs* that are used to build Web requests. Some of the various HTTP verbs are

- `GET`: This method is used when a Web page needs to be retrieved from the server. For example, when you type the URL in the Address box of a browser or click a hyperlink of a page, the `GET` method is used. Usually, the `GET` method is used to get the pages that do not alter the state of a database.

- `POST`: This method is used when you request resources that interact with a database.
- `HEAD`: This method is used when you request the information about a Web page rather than the page itself.

In addition to this standard processing based on HTTP verbs, IIS provides the *Internet Server API (ISAPI)*, which enables you to have a low-level control on processing Web requests. With ISAPI, you can create your own dynamic-link libraries (DLLs) that specify the tasks that must be performed in response to specific Web requests. IIS enables you to create two types of DLLs:

- **ISAPI filters:** These DLLs load into the IIS process when the Web server starts and remain in memory until the server shuts down. For each HTTP request that IIS receives, a number of events are generated in a specific sequence. For example, the `SF_NOTIFY_URL_MAP` event is generated while IIS is converting a URL to a physical path and after the `SF_NOTIFY_PREPROC_HEADERS` event is generated, which indicates that the server has completed preprocessing HTTP header information. Likewise, there are many other events that are generated in a specific sequence. You can use the ISAPI filters to receive a number of event notifications and perform processing at that stage. This ability of ISAPI filters makes them highly flexible and powerful. They're usually used to facilitate the processing of applications that perform tasks, such as custom authentication, encryption, and logging.
- **ISAPI extensions:** These DLLs may be loaded both as part of the IIS process or as a separate process. After ISAPI extensions are loaded, the entire HTTP request is handled by these extensions, with IIS only playing as an intermediary.

Although the ISAPI DLLs enable you to have a lower level control on the processing of Web requests, creating these DLLs isn't easy because it requires knowledge of C++ and multithreaded programming. Moreover, because these DLLs are loaded in the same process as IIS, there's always the threat of IIS being shut down in case the DLLs crash.

In ASP.NET, HTTP handlers have eliminated the difficulties of implementing custom HTTP request processing. HTTP handlers are implemented within the HTTP runtime, which in turn is built upon the Common Language Runtime (CLR) of the .NET Framework. Thus, in ASP.NET, the HTTP runtime replaces ISAPI under IIS.

The HTTP runtime can perform several tasks, such as receiving requests, resolving the address in the requested URL, and redirecting the request to specific applications for their processing. Plus, HTTP offers you the following advantages:

- HTTP runtime can receive multiple requests simultaneously improving the performance to handle multiple requests.
- Different applications (that handle different requests) run in different address spaces thereby improving reliability. Thus, failure of a single application doesn't affect the working of the HTTP runtime.
- HTTP runtime is easy to implement. To create HTTP handlers, you don't need to know C++; you simply need to know any CLR-supported language.

Hence, ASP.NET prefers the HTTP runtime model to handle Web requests over the ISAPI under IIS.

In a nutshell, HTTP handlers are special HTTP runtime components that are meant to handle Web requests. HTTP handlers are mapped to the Web requests that they're supposed to handle, and these mappings are listed in the `<httpHandlers>` section of the Web.config file. This section already contains a set of mappings, so whenever a client makes an HTTP request, the corresponding HTTP handler is loaded to handle the request in a specific manner. If you don't want the default handler (the one already listed in the `<httpHandlers>` section) to handle a specific request, however, you can create your own handler and create an entry for the same in the configuration file.

With this background knowledge about HTTP handlers, we can now proceed to the classes and interfaces that are required to build HTTP handlers. In the next section, we elaborate on these classes and interfaces.

Understanding Classes and Interfaces Required for Building HTTP Handlers

Creating an HTTP handler requires you to create a class that implements the `IHttpHandler` interface contained in the `System.Web` namespace. The `IHttpHandler` interface allows processing of HTTP requests using custom HTTP handlers. After you create a handler class (the one that implements the `IHttpHandler` interface), you must create an entry in the `<httpHandlers>` section of the Web.config file to map the class with the Web request. Later, when the client makes the request (the one you mapped with a handler class), the corresponding class is loaded to handle the request. Before you create an HTTP handler, however, you need to look at the required classes and interfaces.

The IHttpHandler interface

The `IHttpHandler` interface must be implemented to create HTTP handlers. The class that implements the `IHttpHandler` interface must override a method named `ProcessRequest` and a property named `IsReusable`.

The ProcessRequest method

For each Web request that a client makes, the `ProcessRequest` method of the custom handler (the class that implements the `IHttpHandler` interface) for the request is called automatically. Thus, it is in this method that you write any processing code for the Web request.

The following is the Visual Basic syntax for the `ProcessRequest` method:

```
Sub ProcessRequest (ByVal context As HttpContext)

End Sub
```

In the preceding syntax, the `ProcessRequest` method takes an object of the `HttpContext` class. The `HttpContext` object provides a reference to server objects, such as `Request`, `Response`, `Session`, and `Server`. You can use these server objects to process Web requests. We describe the `HttpContext` class later in this section.

The IsReusable property

The `IsReusable` property is a read-only property that gets a Boolean value indicating whether or not the instance of the custom HTTP handler (the class that implements the `IHttpHandler` interface) is reusable. A reusable instance of an HTTP handler is the one that can be used to process another Web request. If the property returns `true`, the instance of the custom handler is reusable. On the other hand, if the property returns `false`, the instance of the custom handler is not reusable and therefore can process only one Web request. The Visual Basic syntax for the `IsReusable` property is

```
ReadOnly Property IsReusable As Boolean
```

You must override this property and set its value explicitly.

The IHttpHandlerFactory interface

A Web request is processed by an `IHttpHandler` instance. When the server receives a Web request, the request must be resolved to the respective `IHttpHandler` instance (as specified in the `<httpHandlers>` section) for the request to be processed. This resolution of a Web request to its respective handler is performed by the class that implements the `IHttpHandlerFactory` interface. In fact, the class that implements the `IHttpHandlerfactory` interface has no specific behavior except that it creates new handler instances dynamically. You'll appreciate what we're saying here when you find out about two methods that this interface supports:

- `GetHandler`: Returns an `IHttpHandler` instance that processes the request.
- `ReleaseHandler`: Releases an `IHttpHandler` instance to enable reuse of an existing handler.

Thus, the `IHttpHandlerFactory` instance does nothing except dynamically create `IHttpHandler` instances. We discuss these methods in the next couple of subsections.

The GetHandler method

The `GetHandler` method returns an instance of the class that implements the `IHttpHandler` interface. In other words, this method returns an `IHttpHandler` instance that's used for processing a Web request. The following is the Visual Basic syntax of the `GetHandler` method:

```
Function GetHandler( ByVal context As HttpContext, ByVal
    requesttype As String, ByVal url As String, ByVal path-
    translated As String ) As IHttpHandler

End Function
```

As you can see in the preceding syntax, the `GetHandler` method returns an `IHttpHandler` instance. The different parameters that are passed to the method are

- `context`: Represents an `HttpContext` instance that provides references to intrinsic server objects, such as `Request`, `Response`, `Session`, and `Server`.
- `requesttype`: Is a string value that represents the HTTP verb (`Get` or `Post`) that is used in the Web request.
- `url`: Is a string value that represents the URL of the Web request.
- `pathtranslated`: Is a string value that represents the actual physical path of the application's root directory.

The ReleaseHandler method

The `ReleaseHandler` method enables an `IHttpHandler` instance to be released so that it can be made available to process another Web request. The Visual Basic syntax of this method is

```
Sub ReleaseHandler( ByVal handler As IHttpHandler)

End Sub
```

As you can see in the preceding syntax, the method takes one parameter — an IHttpHandler instance — to be released.

The HttpContext class

The HttpContext class provides reference to intrinsic server objects, such as Request, Response, Session, and Server, which are used for processing Web requests. The HttpContext class references these objects through its properties. We describe some of these properties in Table 14-1.

Table 14-1 Properties of the HttpContext class

Property	*Description*
Request	Gets an object of the HttpRequest class for the current Web request.
Response	Gets an object of the HttpResponse class for the current Web request.
Session	Gets an object of the SessionState object for the current Web request.
Server	Gets an object of the HttpServerUtility object for the current Web request. This class, in turn, provides certain utilities that can be used when processing the request. For example, the MachineName property gets the name of the server machine.
Application	Gets an object of the HttpApplicationState class for the current Web request.

HttpRequest and HttpResponse classes

The HttpRequest instance enables you to access information, such as the path of the request, and the HttpResponse instance enables you to send data to the browser in response to the request. To be precise, we can say that the HttpRequest instance handles the communication from a browser to a Web server and the HttpResponse instance handles the communication from the Web server to the browser. We describe some of the properties of the HttpRequest and HttpResponse classes in Table 14-2 and Table 14-3 respectively.

We also discuss the HttpRequest and HttpResponse classes in Book 6, Chapter 2.

Table 14-2	Properties of the HttpRequest class
Property	*Description*
`ApplicationPath`	Gets the virtual path of the application root directory of the current application.
`PhysicalApplicationPath`	Gets the physical path of the current application.
`Browser`	Gets the details pertaining to the capability of the browser that made the request. To retrieve the browser capabilities, this property references the `HttpBrowserCapabilities` class.
`FilePath`	Gets the virtual path of the current request.
`RequestType`	Gets or sets the HTTP transmission method used by the browser.
`QueryString`	Gets a collection of HTTP query string variables that are passed along with the request.
`Url`	Gets the information related to the URL, such as URL port and URL protocol, of the current request.

Table 14-3	Properties of the HttpResponse class
Property	*Description*
`BufferOutput`	Gets or sets a Boolean value indicating whether or not to buffer the output and send it after the entire page is finished processing.
`Cache`	Gets the policy information, such as the expiration time of a Web page.
`ContentEncoding`	Gets or sets the HTTP character set of the output from the server.
`IsClientConnected`	Gets a Boolean value indicating whether or not the client is connected to the server.

Building Custom HTTP Handlers

If you've read the previous sections of this chapter, you now have a fair knowledge of the classes and interfaces required to create HTTP handlers. The time for creating a custom HTTP handler has come.

Building custom HTTP handlers requires you to create a class that implements the `IHttpHandler` interface and then to create an entry in the `<httpHandlers>` section. In this section, we create a simple HTTP handler to process a Web request that contains a query string variable in the URL of the request. In addition, the handler displays additional information pertaining to the requesting browser and the processing server.

Creating a custom HTTP handler

To create a custom HTTP handler that displays a welcome message to the user who passes his/her name in the URL of the request, follow the steps that we outline in this section. Additionally, the handler also displays information related to the requesting browser and the processing server.

1. **Create an ASP.NET Web Application project.**

   Create the project by using VB and name it `HttpHandlersDemo`.

2. **Rename the default form from `WebForm1.aspx` to `Welcome.aspx`.**
3. **Add a class to the project by choosing Project⇨Add Class.**
4. **In the Add New Item dialog box that appears, name the class `SampleHandler.vb`.**

   In the code editor for this class file, you're going to write the code to create a class that implements the `IHttpHandler` interface, and you're also going to override the `ProcessRequest` method and the `IsReusable` property of the `IHttpHandler` interface.

5. **Write the following code in the code editor for the `SampleHandler.vb` class file:**

```
'Importing the System.Web namespace
Imports System.Web

'Creating a namespace
Namespace HttpHandlers

   'Creating a class that implements the IHttpHandler
   'class
    Public Class SampleHandler : Implements
       IHttpHandler

   'Implementing the ProcessRequest method of the
   'IHttpHandler interface
    Public Sub ProcessRequest(ByVal Context As
    HttpContext) Implements IHttpHandler.ProcessRequest

      'Using the Write method of the Response method
      'to display a welcome message
       Context.Response.Write("<h2> Welcome " +
Context.Request.QueryString("UserName") + "</h2>")

      'Using the write method of the Response object
      'to display a message in a browser.
      Context.Response.Write("<b>This is a demo on HTTP
handlers</b>")
      Context.Response.Write("<Br><Br>")
```

```
        'Using the Browser property of the Request object
        'to get an object of the
        'HTTPHttpBrowserCapabilities class
        Dim browserCa As HttpBrowserCapabilities =
Context.Request.Browser

        'Displaying the name and version of the browser
        Context.Response.Write("<b>Browser capabili-
             ties:</b><br>")
        Context.Response.Write("Name = " &
browserCa.Browser & "<br>")
        Context.Response.Write("Version=" &
browserCa.Version & "<br>")

        'Using the PhysicalApplicationPath and the
         'Applicationpath properties of the Request
         'object
         'to get the physical path and the virtual path
         'of
         'the application respectively
             Dim pPath As String
             Dim vPath As String
             pPath =
Context.Request.PhysicalApplicationPath
             vPath = Context.Request.ApplicationPath

          'Displaying the virtual and physical path of
          'the application
           Context.Response.Write("<Br><b>Virtual path
of the application:</b><Br>")
             Context.Response.Write(vPath & "<br>")

             Context.Response.Write("<Br><b>Physical
path of the application:</b><Br>")
             Context.Response.Write(pPath & "<Br>")

             'Using the IsClientConnected property of
             'the Response object to determine whether
             'the client is connected to the server
             Dim connect As Boolean
             Dim connectStr As String
             connect =
Context.Response.IsClientConnected
             connectStr = connect.ToString

             Context.Response.Write("<Br><b>Client con-
nection status:</b><br>")
             Context.Response.Write(connectStr)

        End Sub

        'Implementing the IsReusable method of the
```

```
            'IHTTPHttpHandler interface


            Public ReadOnly Property IsReusable() As
    Boolean Implements IHttpHandler.IsReusable
                Get
                    Return True
                End Get
            End Property
        End Class

    End Namespace
```

6. **Build the project to create the DLL for the handler class by choosing Build➪Build.**

   This creates `HttpHandlersDemo.dll` in the bin directory of the project.

After you create the DLL, the HTTP handler is ready to be used. In the next section, we show you how to use this handler.

Using the custom HTTP handler

Using a custom HTTP handler requires you to add an entry in the `<httpHandlers>` section of the Web.config file. Additionally, you must add a reference to the DLL for the handler class. To use the handler that we show you how to create in the previous section, follow these steps:

1. **Open the Web.config file of the** `HttpHandlersDemo` **project.**
2. **Navigate to the** `<httpHandlers>` **section and add an entry as follows:**

   ```
   <httpHandlers>
   <add verb="*" path="Welcome.aspx"
   type="HttpHandlersDemo.HttpHandlers.SampleHandler,HttpH
   andlersDemo" />
   </httpHandlers>
   ```

3. **Add a reference to the DLL for the handler class by choosing Project➪Add Reference.**

4. **In the Add Reference window that appears, click the Browse button and navigate to the bin directory of the** `HttpHandlersDemo` **project.**

5. **Select** `HttpHandlersDemo.dll` **and click Open; then, click OK to complete the process.**

6. **After adding the reference to the DLL, browse the Welcome.aspx page and pass your name in the** `UserName` **query string variable.**

   Thus, the URL of the page should appear like this:

```
/HttpHandlersDemo/Welcome.aspx?UserName=John
```

The page output is shown in Figure 14-1.

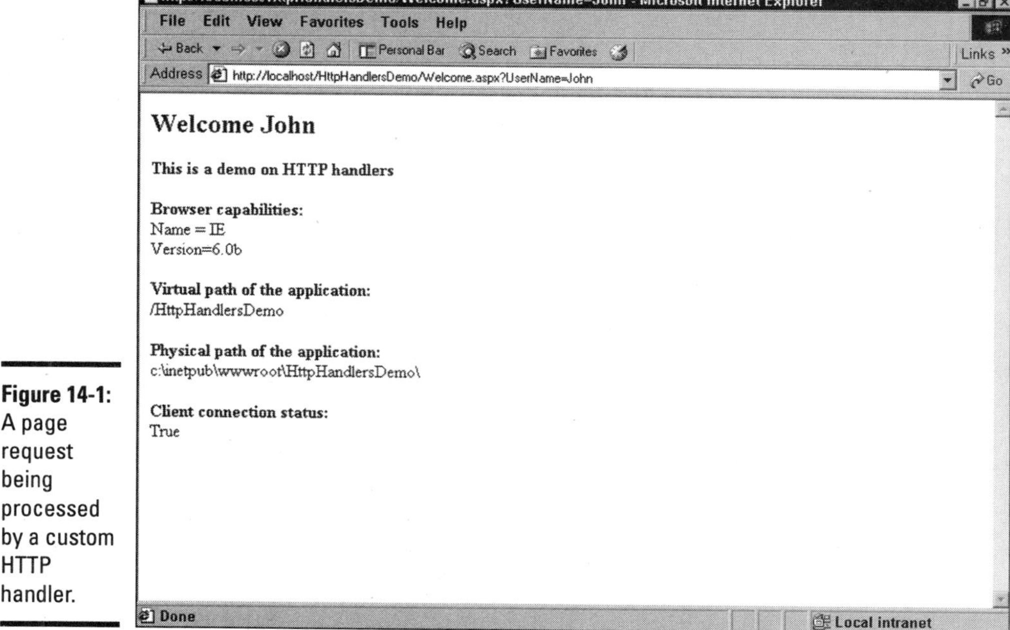

Figure 14-1: A page request being processed by a custom HTTP handler.

Chapter 15: Caching in ASP.NET

In This Chapter

- **Finding out about caching**
- **Putting output caching to work**
- **Including fragment caching in your applications**
- **Using data caching**

Do you want to visit a Web site that provides excellent content and services, but is extremely slow? Of course not. Everyone wants to visit good Web sites — but only if they are fast. A slow-loading Web site irritates users, so speed of loading can make your Web site a tremendous success or a complete failure.

Usually, while you're testing Web applications, fully simulating a real-life situation is difficult because in a real-life scenario, a Web application will be accessed simultaneously by a far greater number of users than most stress testing involves. The simultaneous access increases the load on the server, which in turn results in slow access. Besides the number of simultaneous users, access speed is also determined by a number of other factors, such as the speed of the telephone line, Internet connection, and modem. However, investing heavily on hardware isn't necessarily the solution because the load on the server isn't consistent. One effective solution provided by ASP.NET to this situation is caching, which helps improve your Web applications' performance.

Caching improves performance by storing frequently accessed data in memory. Thus, frequently used pages and page data are retrieved from the cache directly instead of by re-creating the page or page data. This surely reduces the load on the server and improves performance. In this chapter, we explore caching in ASP.NET and show you how to implement different types of caching in your Web applications.

Introducing Caching

ASP.NET caches or stores the frequently accessed data in memory or on local hard disks for later retrieval. As a result, requests are processed only once from the Web server on which the application resides and cached for future use. After that, the subsequent requests are processed from the cache instead of from the Web server, saving time and improving performance. In this section, we introduce you to the caching features of ASP.NET.

Cache locations

You know that caching involves storing frequently accessed data for later retrieval. But where is the cached data stored? You can have your application cache frequently accessed data either at the client side or at the server side. The following are locations at which data may be cached:

- **Client:** The frequently accessed data is stored in temporary files on the client computer's hard disk or in memory. Any subsequent requests for the cached data is served directly from the system memory or the local hard disk of the client. Most Web browsers perform client-side caching, this type of caching does have one drawback: Client-side cached data can't be shared among multiple users.
- **Dedicated server:** Client-side caching is taken care of by most Web browsers. But, to share the cached data among multiple servers, you must specify a dedicated server to cache the frequently accessed data. In most cases, *proxy servers* (such as Microsoft Proxy Server) are used for caching and act as an intermediary between the Internet and the client users' workstations. When a client requests a Web page, the proxy server checks the cache for the requested Web page. If the page is available in the cache, the page is served from the cache. Otherwise, the proxy server directs the request to the Internet, which then serves the request.
- **Reverse proxy:** Having a single dedicated proxy server to cache the frequently accessed data from all the servers on the Internet increases the load on the proxy server. When most requests are made to a specific server, say S1, you can balance the load on the dedicated proxy server by having a proxy server just in front of that S1 server. When users send Web requests to the S1 server, the proxy server in front of that server acts as an intermediary. This type of proxy service is called *reverse proxy*.

Because caching enhances performance without requiring a big hardware investment, it offers you a great advantage. However, you may be wondering what happens when the data at the server, which hosts the application, gets updated. The answer to this question lies in the *expiration policy* of the requested page, which determines the time at which the cache becomes invalid. The data is cached only for a specific duration — the expiration time. When that time is reached, the cached data expires, and then the request is served directly from the Web server instead of from the cache.

Types of caching

ASP.NET supports three types of caching that you can implement for your Web applications to enhance their performance:

- **Output caching:** Caches the contents of the entire page. Imagine a Web page that accesses data from a large database. If this page is to be re-created each time the page is requested, the load on the server and the network traffic increases in the same proportion. However, output caching minimizes the re-creation of the page — pages are re-created only after the expiration time is reached — thus improving the throughput.
- **Fragment caching:** Caches only specific sections of the page instead of the entire page. This type of caching is useful when you want only some portion of the page to be cached, or when you want different portions of the page to be cached for different lengths of time. For example, consider a Web page that extracts data from a database and an XML file and which also contains user-specific data. You can perform fragment caching if you want to cache data from the database and the XML file for different lengths of time, say 10 minutes and 15 minutes respectively, while you don't need to cache the user-specific data.
- **Data caching:** Caches frequently accessed data in memory variables at the server-side. This type of caching is performed programmatically. In fact, ASP.NET provides a complete Cache API to perform data caching.

In the remaining sections of this chapter, we show you how to implement each type of caching in Web applications.

Implementing Output Caching

Output caching enables the entire page output to be cached. To implement this type of caching in your Web pages, you must specify the expiration policy for the pages, which designates the time for which the cache data remains valid. Specify the expiration policy by using the `@OutputCache` directive at the page level. The `@OutputCache` directive takes several attributes to define the behavior of the output cache; here are three of the `@OutputCache` directive's attributes:

- `Duration`: Specifies the time in seconds after which the cache expires. For example, if this attribute is set to 300, the cached data remains only for 5 minutes. After this time limit is reached, the cache expires and the subsequent request is served directly from the Web server and not from the cache.
- `Location`: Specifies the cache location. This attribute can take one of the following values:
  - `Client`: Indicates that the output cache is located on the client browser that sent the request.
  - `Downstream`: Indicates that the output cache is located on the server downstream to the server (similar to proxy caches), where the request is processed.

   - `Server`: Indicates that the output cache is located on the Web server, where the request is processed.
   - `Any`: Indicates that the output cache can be located on the client browser, the downstream server, or the Web server where the request is processed. This is the default value.
   - `None`: Indicates that the output caching isn't enabled for the current page.

- `VaryByParam`: Specifies a list of strings separated by semicolons that are used to vary the Output cache. These strings represent the query string values sent with the `GET` request or the `POST` parameters. Setting this attribute enables you to cache different versions of the same page — each version for a specific string value.

Implementing Output caching without query string parameters

To implement Output caching in a Web application, follow these steps:

1. **Create an ASP.NET Web Application project using VB and name it `CachingDemo`.**
2. **Rename the default form from `WebForm1.aspx` to `OutputCaching.aspx`.**
3. **Access data from a SQL table and display it in a `DataGrid` control on the page.**
4. **To identify the time when the page was cached, display the time when the page was first created. So, add a DataGrid control and a Label control to the form in Design mode.**
5. **Set the ID of the DataGrid control to `EmployeesGrid` and ID of the Label control to `DisplayLabel`.**
6. **Switch to the HTML view and write the following statement at the top of the page to set the cache expiration time to five minutes (in increments of seconds):**

   ```
   <%@ OutputCache Duration="300" VaryByParam="none" %>
   ```

7. **Open the code-behind file for the form and import the `System.Data` and `System.Data.SqlClient` namespaces by using the following code:**

   ```
   Imports System.Data
   Imports System.Data.SqlClient
   ```

8. **Write the following code in the `Page_Load` method to display data from the Employees table in the tempdb database.**

   For more information about the design and data of the Employees table, check out Book 6, Chapter 11.

The code also displays the time when the data was cached.

```
Private Sub Page_Load(ByVal sender As System.Object,
    ByVal e As System.EventArgs) Handles MyBase.Load
        'Put user code to initialize the page here
        Dim dsn, sqlEmp As String
        dsn =
    "server=localhost;uid=sa;pwd=;database=tempdb"
        sqlEmp = "Select * from Employees"
        Dim connection As New SqlConnection(dsn)
        Dim command As New SqlDataAdapter(sqlEmp,
    connection)
        Dim dsEmployees As New DataSet()
        command.Fill(dsEmployees, sqlEmp)
        EmployeesGrid.DataSource = dsEmployees
        EmployeesGrid.DataBind()
        DisplayLabel.Text = "Page cached at: " +
    DateTime.Now.ToString("G")
End Sub
```


When you build and run the application, the page displays the data from the Employees table and also displays the time when the page was created (the time when the page was cached). Because you've specified 300 seconds (five minutes) as the cache expiration time (in Step 6), if you refresh the page within this time limit, the time displayed doesn't change. This indicates that the page is retrieved from the cache and not the server. The output is shown in Figure 15-1.

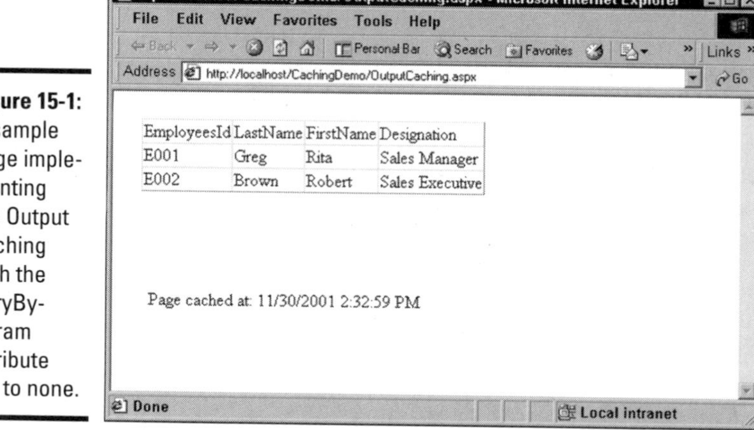

Figure 15-1: A sample page implementing the Output caching with the VaryBy-Param attribute set to none.

Implementing Output caching using query string parameters

In this section, we implement Output caching when the `VaryByParam` attribute takes a query string parameter. The page should cache the data based on the designation of the employee that's passed as a query string variable to the page URL. To implement this, simply modify the application that we show you how to create in the previous section by following these steps:

1. **Switch to the HTML view of the form and modify the `@OutputCache` directive as follows:**

   ```
   <%@ OutputCache Duration="300"
   VaryByParam="Designation" %>
   ```

2. **Modify the code in the `Page_Load` method to read as follows:**

   ```
   Private Sub Page_Load(ByVal sender As System.Object,
       ByVal e As System.EventArgs) Handles MyBase.Load
           'Put user code to initialize the page here
           Dim dsn, sqlEmp, querystring1 As String
           Dim connection As SqlConnection
           Dim command As SqlDataAdapter
           querystring1 =
           Request.QueryString("Designation")
           dsn =
       "server=localhost;uid=sa;pwd=;database=tempdb"

           If querystring1 = Nothing Then
               sqlEmp = "Select * from Employees"
           Else
               sqlEmp = "select * from Employees where
       Designation = '" + querystring1 + "'"

           End If
           connection = New SqlConnection(dsn)
           command = New SqlDataAdapter(sqlEmp,
           connection)
           Dim dsEmployees As New DataSet()
           command.Fill(dsEmployees, sqlEmp)
           EmployeesGrid.DataSource = dsEmployees
           EmployeesGrid.DataBind()
           DisplayLabel.Text = "Page cached at: " +
       DateTime.Now()

   End Sub
   ```

When you build and run the application, the page displays the output as shown in Figure 15-1. However, when you pass the employee designation as a query string variable in the URL as shown here, the page displays only the respective record, shown in Figure 15-2:

```
/CachingDemo/OutputCaching.aspx?Designation=Sales Manager
```

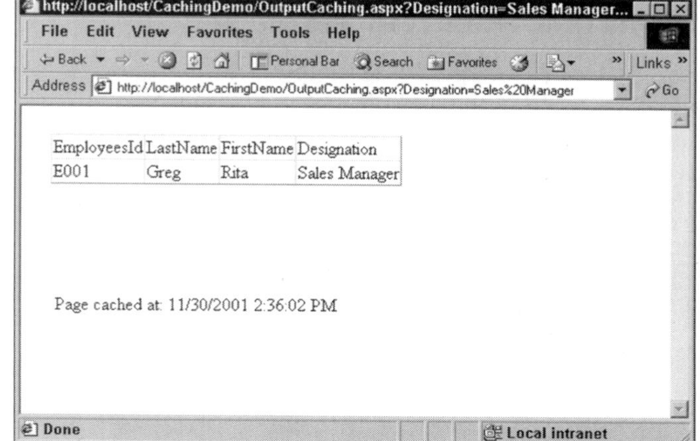

Figure 15-2: A sample page that implements the Output caching using query string parameters.

When you refresh the page after some time, but not before the five-minute limit, the time displayed on the page doesn't change. This indicates that the page output has been cached for the query string value `Designation=Sales Manager`.

Implementing Fragment Caching

Fragment caching enables you to cache different portions of a page. In this section, we create a user control, which in turn displays data from the Employees table. In addition to the employee details, the control displays the time at which the control was created. Then, we use this user control in a page, which doesn't implement Output caching. This page displays the time when it was created.

To implement Fragment caching, first create a Web user control in the `CachingDemo` project. For a detailed discussion on user controls, check out Book 6, Chapter 5. To create a user control, follow these steps:

1. **Open the Add New Item dialog box by choosing Project⇨Add Web User Control and name the control** `MyControl.ascx`**.**
2. **From the HTML tab of the Toolbox, drag the Grid Layout Panel control to the user control in the Design mode.**
3. **From the Web Forms tab of the Toolbox, drag the DataGrid control to the user control and place it on the Grid Layout Panel control.**

You'll have to resize the Grid Layout Panel control so that the DataGrid control fits into it.

4. **Drag the Label control within the Grid Layout Panel control, resizing the Grid Layout Panel control as necessary.**
5. **Set the ID of the DataGrid control to** `EmployeesGrid` **and set the ID of the Label control to** `DisplayLabel`**.**
6. **In the HTML view of the user control, write the** `@OutputCache` **directive as follows:**

```
<%@ OutputCache Duration="300"  VaryByParam="none" %>
```

7. **Open the code-behind file for the user control and import the namespaces as follows:**

```
Imports System.Data
Imports System.Data.SqlClient
```

8. **In the** `Page_Load` **method of the user control, write the following code:**

```
Private Sub Page_Load(ByVal sender As System.Object,
    ByVal e As System.EventArgs) Handles MyBase.Load
        'Put user code to initialize the page here
        Dim dsn, sqlEmp As String
        dsn =
    "server=localhost;uid=sa;pwd=;database=tempdb"
        sqlEmp = "Select * from Employees"
        Dim connection As New SqlConnection(dsn)
        Dim command As New SqlDataAdapter(sqlEmp,
        connection)
        Dim dsEmployees As New DataSet()
        command.Fill(dsEmployees, sqlEmp)
        EmployeesGrid.DataSource = dsEmployees
        EmployeesGrid.DataBind()
        DisplayLabel.Text = "Control cached at: " +
    DateTime.Now.ToString("G")
End Sub
```

Now the user control is ready to be used in a Web form.

9. **Add another form (**`FragmentCaching.aspx`**) to the project. (To add a Web form, choose Project⇨Add Web Form.)**
10. **Add the user control** `MyControl.ascx` **from the Solution Explorer window to this form, and also add a Label control to this form and set its ID as** `DisplayLabel`**.**
11. **Write the following code in the** `Page_Load` **method of this form:**

```
DisplayLabel.Text = "Page created at: " +
DateTime.Now.ToString("G")
```

Build the project and browse the `FragmentCaching.aspx` form. You'll notice that when you refresh the page, the time when the control was cached doesn't change while the page when the page was created gets updated, as shown in Figure 15-3. This happens because only the section of the page that contains the user control had Output caching enabled.

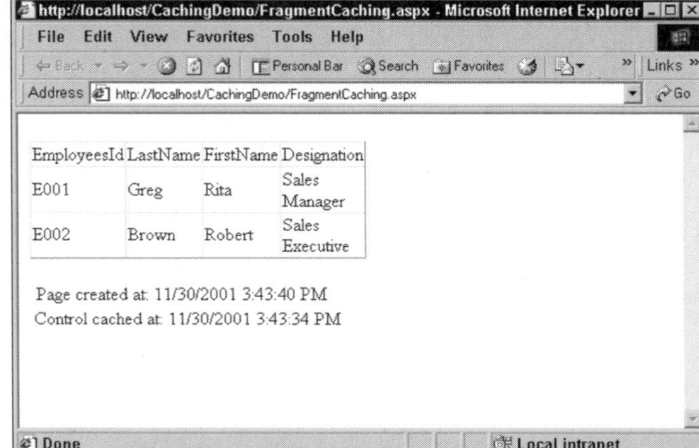

Figure 15-3: A sample page implementing fragment caching.

Implementing Data Caching

Data caching enables you to cache frequently accessed data programmatically in memory variables at the server-side. ASP.NET encapsulates data caching in the `Cache` class, which cannot be inherited, and you use the object of the `Cache` class directly to cache the frequently accessed data. Each item in the `Cache` object is stored as key/value pairs. For example, to store a value stored in the `UserName` variable of an application in the `Cache` object, use the following code:

```
Cache("UserNameKey")=UserName
```

Then, to retrieve the value from the `Cache` item, you simply need to write the following code:

```
UserName= Cache("UserNameKey")
```

Note that the `Cache` object is private to each application. The `Cache` object exists only while the application runs. When the application is restarted, the `Cache` objects get re-created. Thus, the lifetime of the `Cache` object associated with an application is the same as the lifetime of the application.

To implement Data caching, follow these steps:

1. **Add another Web form, `DataCaching.aspx`, to the `CachingDemo` project.**
2. **Add DataGrid and Label controls to this form; set the ID of the DataGrid control to `EmployeesGrid` and the ID of the Label control to `DisplayLabel`.**
3. **Open the code-behind file for the `DataCaching.aspx` form and import the `System.Data` and `System.Data.SqlClient` namespaces as follows:**

```
Imports System.Data
Imports System.Data.SqlClient
```

4. **In the `Page_Load` method of this form, write the following code:**

```
Private Sub Page_Load(ByVal sender As System.Object,
    ByVal e As System.EventArgs) Handles MyBase.Load
        'Put user code to initialize the page here
        Dim EmpSource As DataView
        ' Check the Cache object for the item. If the
        'item is available, retrieve it from the
        'cache. Otherwise, add the item to the cache.

        EmpSource = Cache("EmpSourceKey")

        If EmpSource Is Nothing Then

            Dim connection As SqlConnection
            Dim command As SqlDataAdapter

            connection = New
SqlConnection("server=localhost;uid=sa;pwd=;database=te
mpdb;")
            command = New SqlDataAdapter("select * from
Employees", connection)

            Dim ds As New DataSet()
            command.Fill(ds, "Employees")

            EmpSource = New
DataView(ds.Tables("Employees"))
            'Storing the item in the cache for later
            'retrieval
            Cache("EmpSourceKey") = EmpSource

            DisplayLabel.Text = "Data accessed from the
database"
        Else
```

```
                DisplayLabel.Text = "Data retrieved from
                        cache"
            End If

            EmployeesGrid.DataSource = EmpSource
            EmployeesGrid.DataBind()
        End Sub
```

When you build the project and browse the DataCaching.aspx form, notice that the form displays data from the Employees table and the label displays the text Data accessed from the database. And if you refresh the page, the label displays the text Data retrieved from cache, as shown in Figure 15-4. Thus, when the application runs for the first time, the data is directly accessed from the database. For all subsequent requests, the data is retrieved from the cache.

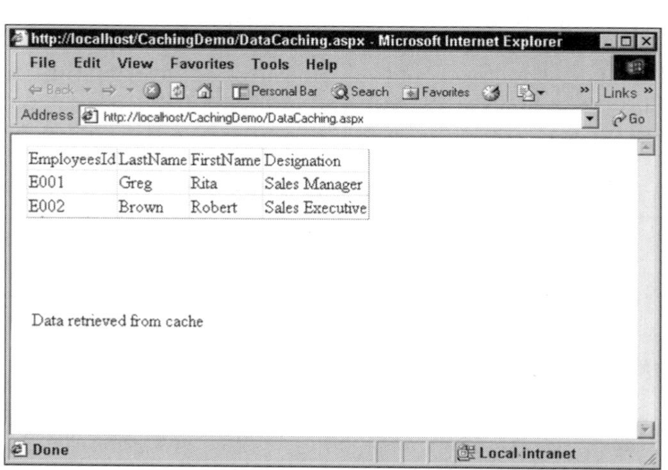

Figure 15-4: Implementing data caching.

At this juncture, you might be wondering, and rightly so, what happens when the application data is updated during the lifetime of the application. The cache items (key/value pairs), once inserted in the Cache object, remain in the cache throughout the lifetime of the application. To enable you to control the data stored in cache based on any changes in the application data, the Cache class supports three types of dependencies, which we describe in the following three subsections. You can invalidate a specific item within the cache depending on the changes to files or other Cache item keys. You can also invalidate a specific Cache item at a specific point of time.

File-based dependency

File-based dependency invalidates a specific cache item based on the changes made to a file on the disk. To create a dependency, you must create an object of the CacheDependency class. Then, you can use the Insert method of the Cache class to create a Cache item that depends on a file. For example, if you have an XML file (say Employees.xml), you can create a Cache item that depends on this file by using the following code:

```
Dim dom As XmlDocument()
dom.Load(Server.MapPath("Employees.xml")
Dim dependency as new
   CacheDependency(Server.MapPath("Employees.xml"))
Cache.Insert("EmployeesDataKey", dom, dependency)
```

In the preceding code,

- dom represents an XML document that contains the Employees.xml file.
- dependency is the object of the CacheDependency class. Notice that the constructor of the CacheDependency class takes a string parameter, which represents the path of the file.
- The Insert method is used to create a Cache item that depends on the file. Notice that the Insert method takes three parameters: key, value, and dependency.

When you specify a file-based dependency, the cache must be re-created whenever the file gets updated.

Key-based dependency

Key-based dependency invalidates a specific Cache item based on the changes made to another Cache item. However, you might wonder when you would need this kind of dependency. Consider a situation in which an application caches data from two data sets, EmployeeSalaries and EmployeePerformance. Because employee salaries depend on employee performance, you'd certainly want to invalidate the Cache item that stores the data from the EmployeeSalaries data set based on the Cache item that stores data from the EmployeePerformance data set. In such a situation, you can rely on key-based dependency. We can create the Cache item for EmployeeSalaries data set and make it dependent on the Cache item for the EmployeePerformance data set in the following manner:

```
Dim dependencyKey(1) As String
dependencyKey(0) = "PerformanceDataKey"
Dim PerformanceDataDependency As new CacheDependency(nothing,
   dependencyKey)
Cache.Insert("SalariesDataKey",
   LoadDataSet("EmployeeSalaries"),
   PerformanceDataDependency)
```

In the preceding code,

- `dependencyKey` is an array to store `Cache` keys. This array contains only one key for the EmployeePerformance data set.
- `PerformanceDataDependency` is an object of the `CacheDependency` class. Notice that the constructor takes two parameters. Both the parameters are string arrays. The first parameter represents an array of file paths. Because we haven't specified any file dependency, we set this parameter to `nothing`. The second parameter represents an array of `Cache` keys. This parameter is set to the array that contains the cache key to be monitored.
- The `Insert` method of the `Cache` class is used to create a `Cache` item for the EmployeeSalaries data set, which depends on the `Cache` item for the EmployeePerformance data set.

When you specify key-based dependency for a `Cache` item, the `Cache` item must be re-created whenever the `Cache` item, which is monitored, gets updated.

Time-based dependency

A time-based dependency simply terminates the `Cache` data at a specific time. You can create a time-based dependency using either of the following options:

- **Absolute expiration:** Represents the time when the `Cache` item is removed from the cache. For example, if you specify absolute expiration time as five minutes, the cache item expires five minutes after the page is requested for the first time.
- **Sliding expiration:** This option resets the cache expiration time with each request. For example, if you set this option as five minutes, the value is reset to five minutes each time the page is refreshed.

You can use another form of the `Insert` method, which is an overloaded method of the `Cache` class to create a time-based dependency. The overloaded `Insert` method takes five parameters: `key`, `value`, `dependency`, `absolute expiration`, and `sliding expiration`. The absolute expiration value should be passed as an object of the `DateTime` class and the sliding expiration value should be passed as an object of the `TimeSpan` class.

Consider the following code, which sets the absolute expiration time as five minutes for a `Cache` item for the EmployeeSalaries data set:

```
Cache.Insert("SalariesData", LoadDataSet("EmployeeSalaries"),
    nothing, DateTime.Now.AddMinutes(5), nothing)
```

To set the sliding expiration time, you can use the following code:

```
'Create an object of the TimeSpan class. Notice that the
'constructor takes three parameters to specify time in hours,
'minutes, and seconds. Here, we've specified the sliding
'expiration time to 5 minutes.
Dim span As New TimeSpan(0,5,0)

Cache.Insert("SalariesData", LoadDataSet("EmployeeSalaries"),
   nothing, nothing, span)
```

Thus, when you specify a time-based dependency for a `Cache` item, the `Cache` item must be re-created whenever the expiration time is reached.

Chapter 16: ASP.NET Application Security

In This Chapter

- Discovering ASP.NET security mechanisms
- Using Forms authentication in a Web application
- Employing Windows authentication in a Web application

The security aspect of a Web application often requires your maximum planning and effort. Not only do you need to protect your Web application against hackers, you also need to ensure that the content accessible to users is restricted. For example, an unauthenticated user shouldn't be allowed to view the Web forms that allow an authenticated user to change his or her profile.

This chapter covers the necessary concepts to help you implement authentication in a Web application. We also discuss the different methods of authenticating users and how you can implement each of these methods.

Understanding Security Mechanisms

An ASP.NET application is deployed on Internet Information Server (IIS). Therefore, any security feature that's available on IIS is automatically available to your Web application. Additionally, ASP.NET provides its own security mechanism that can help you further secure your Web application. In this section, we present the security mechanisms provided in both IIS Server and ASP.NET.

IIS security mechanisms

IIS Server 5.0 provides built-in support for authenticating clients. You can implement four types of security mechanisms by using IIS Server:

- **Anonymous authentication:** Anonymous authentication allows a user to browse a Web application without using a username and password. Anonymous authentication is the default mechanism of authentication used by IIS. In this authentication mechanism, IIS uses a default logon name and password to request for resources from a Web application.

- **Basic authentication:** Basic authentication requires users to specify a logon name and password for accessing Web applications.

  When IIS uses this authentication mechanism, a user's password is sent over the Internet in an unencrypted form, making the password vulnerable.

- **Integrated Windows authentication:** Integrated Windows authentication requires users to have a valid account with the Windows 2000 domain. You would preferably deploy this mechanism in business-to-business (B2B) Web applications, where the number of users accessing your application is relatively few.
- **Digest authentication:** The Digest authentication mechanism is similar to basic authentication but more secure. Digest authentication employs the same mechanism as basic authentication but sends the user's password over the Internet in an encrypted form.

In addition to the authentication mechanisms that we describe here, you can also use IIS to limit access to resources used by a Web application. For more details on implementing IIS authentication mechanisms and limiting access to resources, read Book 7, Chapter 3.

ASP.NET security mechanisms

For the form-level and Web application-level security, ASP.NET provides three authentication mechanisms — Forms authentication, Passport authentication, and Windows authentication.

Forms authentication

The Forms authentication mechanism, also called cookie-based authentication, is based on a single log-on form that can be accessed anytime that a user needs to log on. You may have visited Web applications that enable you to browse Web forms without requiring you to log on. When you proceed to make purchases on the Web application, however, or use any feature that requires you to log on — like when you edit user profiles — then you're redirected to a log-on form. After you successfully log on, you're redirected back to the form that you were originally visiting.

This type of authentication is *Forms authentication,* in which a designated log-on form is invoked whenever an unauthenticated user requests for a Web form. You can read how to implement Forms authentication in the upcoming "Implementing Forms Authentication" section of this chapter.

Passport authentication

Passport authentication is a centralized authentication service provided by Microsoft. When you use the Passport authentication service, you require less hardware infrastructure and fewer people to run your Web application and your application caters to a larger audience compared with the forms authentication service.

The Passport authentication service is the authentication service used by Microsoft for its Web sites, such as Passport, MSN, and Hotmail. You can subscribe to this service by signing a contract with Microsoft through its Web site at `www.microsoft.com/myservices`.

Passport authentication functions in a manner similar to Forms authentication. Use the following basic steps to authenticate a user by using the Passport authentication service:

1. When a user requests a resource that requires authentication, the user is redirected to the Passport log-on service. The details of the resource that a user requests is also passed along to the Passport log-on service.
2. After the user successfully logs on by using his or her passport account, the log-on server redirects the user to the original resource that the user requests. The server also passes an encrypted authentication ticket of the user to the ASP.NET application.

To use the Passport authentication service, you need to download the Passport software development kit (SDK) and use the documentation provided along with the SDK to implement Passport authentication. You can download the Passport SDK (for a fee) from `www.passport.com/business`.

Windows authentication

Windows authentication is the authentication mechanism in which users are authenticated against their accounts in the Windows 2000 domain. To implement this mechanism, you must change the Web application's configuration file. For details about configuring this file, refer to the upcoming section "Implementing Windows Authentication."

Implementing Forms Authentication

ASP.NET, unlike ASP 3.0 that uses only the IIS security mechanism, enables you to store information about the configuration of any Web application in an eXtensible Markup Language-based file in the root directory. You can change the authentication mechanism used by your application in this XML-based file.

In this section, we show you how to configure the Forms authentication mechanism in a Web application by changing the settings in the XML-based file — `Web.Config` — and then implementing the necessary code.

Changing configuration information

The `Web.Config` file stores the configuration information for a Web application; the file itself is stored in the root directory of a Web application. You can have different `Web.Config` files for subdirectories in an application so that different permissions are applied to Web forms in the subdirectory.

A `Web.Config` file for storing the configuration information of a Web application is automatically created by Visual Studio .NET. However, if you want to have different permissions for different subdirectories, you need to create separate `Web.Config` files for subdirectories.

The `authentication` and `authorization` elements of the `Web.Config` file are used for authentication. When you create a new ASP.NET Web application, the existing code of these elements in the `Web.Config` file is

```
<authentication mode="Windows" />
<authorization>
   <allow users="*" />
</authorization>
```

In the default setting of the `authentication` and `authorization` elements, all users are allowed to access the Web application and the authentication mode is set to Windows authentication. To implement form-based authentication on your Web application, consider an example in which only one user is allowed to access pages in the directory of the Web application. The username and the password are *Joe*. To implement form-based authentication in the Web application, you must make the following changes in the `Web.Config` file:

1. **Set the authentication mode of the `Web.Config` file to `forms` by using the following statement:**

```
<authentication mode="Forms" />
```

   The preceding line must be specified instead of the statement `<authentication mode="Windows" />`.

   You find the `Web.Config` file in the root directory of a Web application.

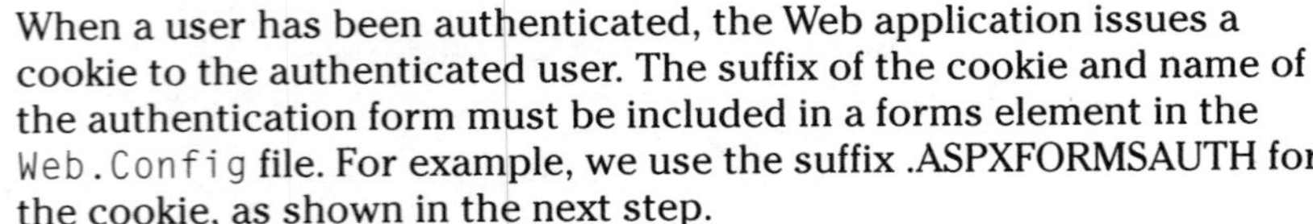

   When a user has been authenticated, the Web application issues a cookie to the authenticated user. The suffix of the cookie and name of the authentication form must be included in a forms element in the `Web.Config` file. For example, we use the suffix .ASPXFORMSAUTH for the cookie, as shown in the next step.

2. **Immediately after the line of code that you add in Step 1, define the forms element as following:**

```
<forms loginUrl="login.aspx" name=".ASPXFORMSAUTH" />
```

3. **Deny unauthenticated access to Web forms by changing the authorization section as follows:**

```
<authorization>
   <deny users="?" />
</authorization>
```

ASP.NET provides two special user types: * and ?. The * user type represents all users, similar to the *.* wildcard in file types. The ? user type represents anonymous users — that is, those users who haven't been authenticated by the Web application.

Creating the login.aspx form

After changing the Web application's configuration in the `Web.Config` file, you must create the `login.aspx` form, which enables users to log on to the Web application. To create the `login.aspx` form, open the Web application to which you want to add the form and perform the following steps:

1. **Choose Project⇨Add Web Form.**

   The Add New Item - WebAuthentication dialog box appears, as shown in Figure 16-1.

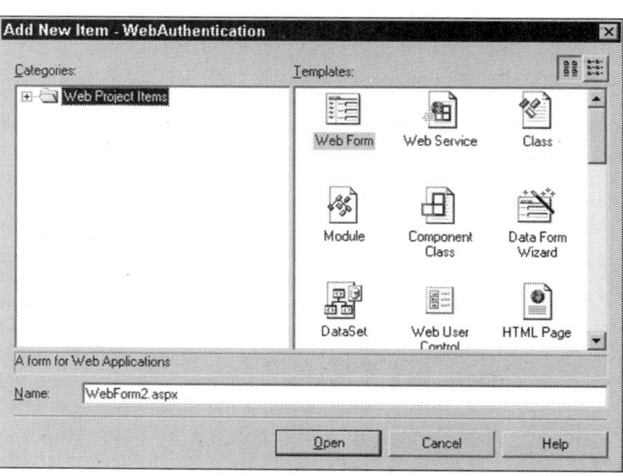

Figure 16-1: Beginning the authentication process.

The name of our sample Web application is *Web authentication*. If you use a different name for your application, the title of the Add New Item dialog box changes accordingly.

2. **Click the Web Form icon from the Templates list, type** login.aspx **as the name of the form in the Name text box, and then click Open.**

   A new Web form, `login.aspx`, is added to your application.

3. **Design the `login.aspx` form as shown in Figure 16-2.**

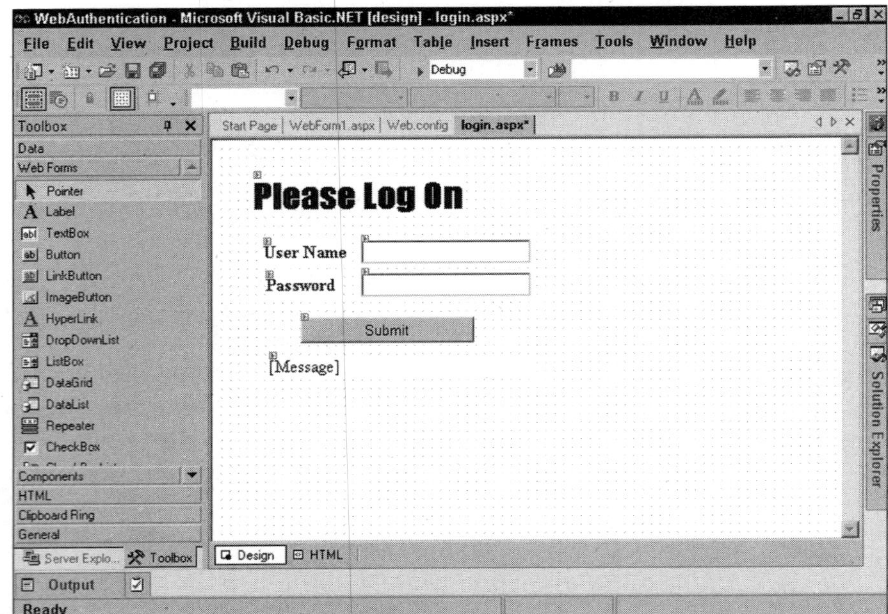

Figure 16-2: Design your new Web log-on form.

To design the form in Figure 16-2, you can add the controls listed in Table 16-1 to your form.

Table 16-1 Web Form Controls to Add

Add this Control	*Control Type*	*Properties*
Add a label to prompt a user to log on	`Label`	`Text`=Please Log On `Font` properties `Bold`=True `Name`=Impact `Size`=X-Large
Add a label for the User Name text box	`Label`	`Text`=User Name `Font:` `Bold`=True
Add a label for the Password text box	`Label`	`Text`=Password `Font:` `Bold`=True
Add a User Name text box	`TextBox`	`ID`=UserName

Add this Control	Control Type	Properties
Add a Password text box	`TextBox`	`ID`=Password `TextMode`=Password
Add a Submit button	`Button`	`ID`=ButtonSubmit `Text`=Submit
Add a label to display messages	`Label`	`ID`=Message `Text`=""

Now write the code to implement the authentication mechanism in your Web application.

All classes in Visual Studio .NET involved in authentication are available in the `System.Web.Security` namespace. (Read Book 1, Chapter 2 for more on namespaces.) In particular, for authenticating a user, you need to use the `FormsAuthentication` class. Some of the commonly used methods of the `FormsAuthentication` class are listed in Table 16-2.

Table 16-2 Common FormsAuthentication Class Methods

Method	Description
`Authenticate`	Checks the given username and password against a data source to verify whether they're valid.
`RedirectFromLoginPage`	Redirects a user to the form that the user initially requests after authentication. This method accepts the user name and a Boolean value to create the authentication ticket. If the Boolean value is `true`, the cookie generated by this method is valid across user sessions.
`RenewTicketIfOld`	Updates an authentication ticket before it expires so that the continuity of a session is maintained.
`SignOut`	Logs a user off the system by removing the authentication ticket that was issued to the user.

Now use the `FormsAuthentication` class methods in Table 16-2 to authenticate a user; just follow these steps:

1. **Double-click the `login.aspx` form in Design view to open the Code Editor.**

   To open a form in Design view, double-click the form in Solution Explorer. (Press Ctrl+Alt+L to open Solution Explorer.)

2. **Import the `System.Web.Security` namespace into your application by specifying the following line of code in the beginning of the `login.aspx.vb` file:**

   ```
   Imports System.Web.Security
   ```

   The System.Web.Security namespace is included in your application.

3. **Add the following code in the `Click` event of the Submit button:**

   To write the code for this event, double-click the Submit button in the Design view of the form, as shown here:

   ```
   Private Sub ButtonSubmit_Click(ByVal sender As
      System.Object, ByVal e As System.EventArgs) Handles
      ButtonSubmit.Click
         If ((UserName.Text = "Joe") And (Password.Text =
              "Joe")) Then
              FormsAuthentication.RedirectFromLoginPage
                  (UserName.Text, False)
         Else
              Message.Text = "Invalid User Name or
                   Password. Please try again"
         End If
   End Sub
   ```

   The preceding code ensures that the username and password specified by the user are both *Joe*. If they are, an authentication ticket is issued to the user, and the user is redirected to the original form that was requested.

After you modify the preceding code, compile your application and run it (press Ctrl+Shift+B and then press F5). You're directed to the `login.aspx` form, shown in Figure 16-3.

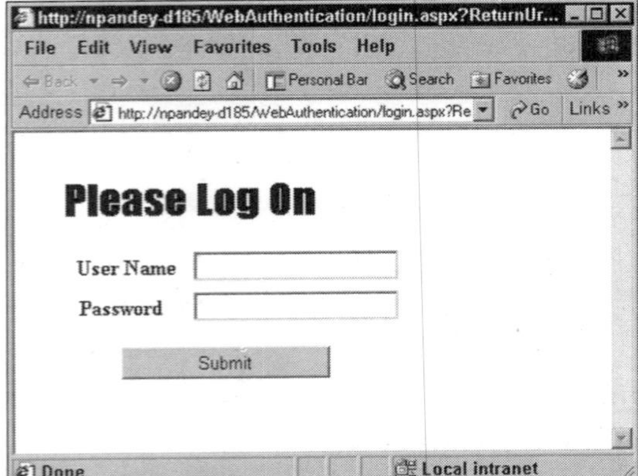

Figure 16-3: The login.aspx form appears if you aren't authenticated.

On the `login.aspx` form, after you specify a valid username and password, you're redirected to the default form in your Web application, whichever you specify.

Retrieving user details

After a user is authenticated by your Web application, you can retrieve the details of the user by using the `User.Identity` property of the `User` object. `User.Identity` provides the following important properties to authenticate a user:

- `AuthenticationType`: The `AuthenticationType` property determines the authentication mechanism that was used to authenticate a user. For example, in Forms authentication, the value returned by this property is `Forms`.
- `IsAuthenticated`: This property determines whether a user is authenticated.
- `Name`: The `Name` property returns the username of the user currently logged on.

To retrieve the username of the authenticated user, you can use the `User.Identity.Name` property:

```
strUserName= User.Identity.Name
```

Validating users against a data source

The Forms authentication mechanism (see the earlier section "Implementing Forms authentication") has one drawback: It uses the same username and password to authenticate all users. In a real-life scenario, you'll probably use a database that stores usernames and passwords to validate individual users. To implement such a mechanism, just change the `login.aspx` file to retrieve data from the database and compare a user's credentials with the data retrieved. You can read in detail about this mechanism in Book 7, Chapter 1.

You may also want to implement a functionality to allow new users to create a user ID. In this case, you need to make the following modifications to your Web application:

1. **Create a subdirectory in your application's root — such as NewLogin.**
2. **Add an `AddUser.aspx` form to the subdirectory.**
3. **Implement the functionality to create a new user ID on the `AddUser.aspx` form.**

   For details on how to implement this functionality, peruse Book 7, Chapter 1.
4. **Add a new configuration file — `Web.Config` — to the NewLogin subdirectory.**

You add a new configuration file to the subdirectory because you need to allow all users to access the AddUser.aspx form. If you don't add a new configuration file to the subdirectory, the Web forms in the subdirectory will inherit permissions from the parent directory, thus barring all unauthenticated users from accessing the Web form.

5. **Assign permissions to all users for accessing the Web forms in the NewLogin directory by specifying the following code:**

```
<configuration>
   <system.web>
      <authorization>
         <allow users="*" />
      </authorization>
   </system.web>
</configuration>
```

   Notice the `<allow users ="*" />` directive in the preceding code, which gives permissions to all users for accessing the AddUser.aspx Web form.

After completing the preceding steps, you can register new users in a Web application.

Implementing Windows Authentication

In the Windows authentication mechanism, users are validated against their Windows 2000 domain accounts. Although it appears to be a complex mechanism initially, read the following sections to discover just how simple it really is.

Modifying the Web.Config file

To implement Windows authentication in your Web application, you need to make the following changes to the Web.Config file:

1. **Double-click the Web.Config file in Solution Explorer.**

   Press Ctrl+Alt+L to open Solution Explorer.

   The Web.Config file opens in the Code Editor.

2. **Change the authentication mode to Windows by changing the authentication element using the following code:**

```
<authentication mode="Windows" />
```

If you haven't changed the Web.Config file since you created your project, the authentication mode is Windows by default.

3. **Allow access to the required users by specifying their domain and usernames in the `allow users` list of the `authorization` element, as shown in the following code:**

   ```
   <allow users="ltbokh\yeshs, ltbokh\mridulap" />
   ```

   In the above code, users with the usernames `yeshs` and `mridulap` have access to the Web application.

4. **To deny permissions to all other users, specify the following code after the code that you enter in Step 3:**

   ```
   <deny users="*" />
   ```

Unless you deny permissions to users, all users are allowed to access your Web application. Therefore, if you permit only two users to use your Web application but don't deny permission to everyone else, *anyone* can access your Web application — of course, including the two who have the permissions.

Running the application

We continue with our running example with the two users *yeshs* and *mridulap*. When you run the application after making the changes in the `Web.Config` file (read the earlier section "Modifying the Web.Config file"), only these two users can log on to the Web application. Now run the application to see the output:

1. **Choose Build⇨Build Solution to build your application.**
2. **Choose Debug⇨Start to run your application.**

Because you're not logged on as *yeshs* or *mridulap*, you see the Enter Network Password window, as shown in Figure 16-4.

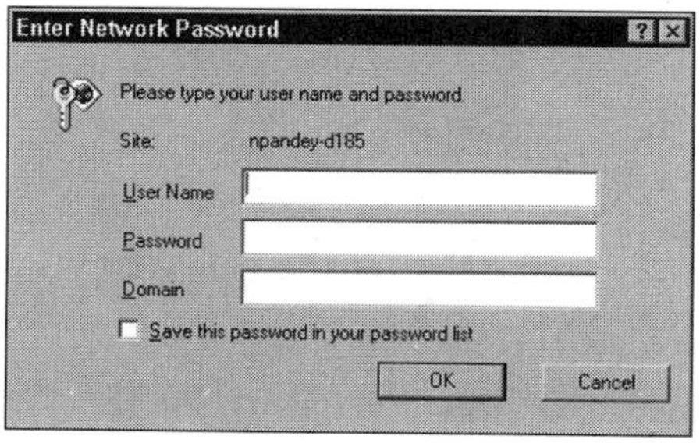

Figure 16-4: In Windows authentication, use an authorized user account to open the Web application.

If you specify a username that's different from the ones specified in the `allow users` list of the `authorization` element three times, an Access is Denied window appears, as shown in Figure 16-5.

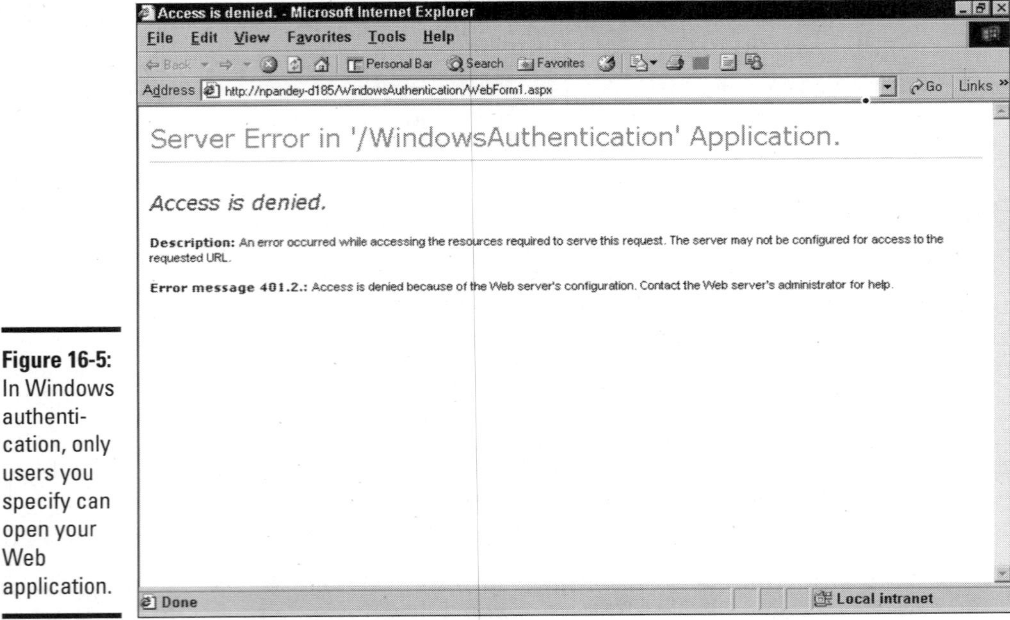

Figure 16-5: In Windows authentication, only users you specify can open your Web application.

Chapter 17: Migrating from ASP to ASP.NET

In This Chapter

- Preparing for migration
- Migrating to ASP.NET
- Optimizing the site

ASP.NET offers a number of benefits over ASP 3.0, such as the separation of programming code from the HTML code and use of the garbage collector feature to manage memory resources. These two advantages are only the tip of the iceberg. For other important advantages, refer to Book 6, Chapter 1 and Book 6, Chapter 2.

In order to experience the advantages of ASP.NET first-hand, why not migrate existing Web sites to ASP.NET? We've geared this chapter to accomplishing that end. After completing this chapter, you'll be able to migrate an existing ASP 3.0 Web site to ASP.NET. So get started!

Preparing for Migration

ASP.NET provides backward compatibility with ASP 3.0 to quite an extent. However, backward compatibility isn't 100 percent. Some coding conventions that you follow in ASP 3.0 won't work in ASP.NET. In addition, the new class library for ASP.NET doesn't support some variables, declarations, and methods that you can use in ASP 3.0. Therefore, it is necessary to modify the existing ASP code to successfully migrate your Web site to ASP.NET.

In this section, you look at some tasks that help you decide the route to migration and prepare your site for migration to ASP.NET.

Choosing the migration route

Before making any migration plans, you first need to determine the viability of migrating a Web site. You need to estimate the time and effort required to migrate the site. Sometimes, migrating an application to a new platform requires greater effort than creating a new application.

You should choose migration when your existing Web site meets the following conditions:

- ✦ You need to improve the performance of your Web site, especially when many users visit your Web site.
- ✦ Rebuilding the application code to build a new ASP.NET Web application for your Web site would be too time-consuming.
- ✦ Your Web developers have adequate expertise in both ASP as well as ASP.NET so that you're able to reduce the costs involved in training your staff.

If you're convinced that the requirement to migrate your Web site is absolute, let's get going.

Replicating the ASP 3.0 Web site

Instead of modifying your ASP 3.0 Web site, you must first make a copy of the Web site and migrate the copy to ASP .NET. This copy ensures that, if something goes wrong during migration, you won't be without a Web site for the remaining portion of this chapter. (If you lost your Web site entirely, you wouldn't need this chapter anymore because you'd be starting from scratch!) Copying a Web site for migration is simple; just follow these steps:

1. **Make a copy of the ASP pages of the Web site.**

   Make a copy of the ASP pages in the same way as you copy other files in Windows (select the files and copy them by using the Edit menu).

2. **Replicate the database for the Web site.**

   For example, to replicate a Microsoft Access database, you can copy the database file and paste it at a different location.

3. **Use the replicated database for running the replica of your Web site.**

Migrating to ASP.NET: The Basics

Migration of ASP 3.0 pages to ASP.NET broadly involves the following steps:

1. Change the file extension from `.asp` to `.aspx`.
2. Modify the code that's incompatible with ASP.NET.
3. Manage user and application state information.

Throughout the following sections, we examine each of these steps in detail.

Changing the file extension

The .NET Framework can, at runtime, determine which ASP pages need to be executed in the .NET Framework by examining the file extensions. Because ASP.NET pages have a different file extension (`.aspx` or `.asmx`) from ASP 3.0 pages (`.asp`), ASP.NET Web applications can coexist with ASP 3.0 Web sites. You can also have a mix of pages with the `.aspx` extension and `.asp` extension for the same Web application.

You need to change the extension of the ASP file to `.aspx` so that your ASP file can be executed in the runtime environment of the .NET Framework.

Just as you must change the `.asp` extension of ASP 3.0 to `.aspx` for migrating these pages to ASP.NET, you must also rename the `global.asa` file to `global.asax`.

Modifying incompatible code

Your ASP 3.0 code might be incompatible with the ASP.NET code because of syntactical and language changes in the ASP.NET language. In this section, we discuss these two types of changes.

Syntactical changes

To counter incompatibility caused by syntactical changes in ASP.NET, consider these points:

- **Use brackets:** In ASP 3.0, you can call methods without using brackets. However, brackets are mandatory in ASP.NET. For example, consider the following code:

  ```
  if selection="vendor" then
  Response.Write "<h3>" &vendortech & "</h3>"
  else
  Response.Write "<h3>Application: " & vendortech &
  "</h3>"
  end if
  ```

  When migrating the preceding code in ASP.NET, you must use brackets in the `Response.Write` function, as shown in the following:

  ```
  if selection="vendor" then
  Response.Write ("<h3>" &vendortech & "</h3>")
  else
  Response.Write ("<h3>Application: " & vendortech &
           "</h3>")
  end if
  ```

✦ **Discard Render functions:** Render functions provide an efficient way to write code in ASP 3.0. However, render functions are no longer supported in ASP.NET. Therefore, you must do away with these functions in ASP.NET. For example, consider this code:

```
<%Sub rendertext()%>
<H1> Requests received in the year 2000-2001 </H1>
<table width="112%" height="36" bordercolor="#CCFFFF">
<tr>
   <td width="22%">
      <div align="right"><b><%=summary%>"</b></div>
   </td>
</tr>
</table>
<%End Sub%>
```

An easy way to do away with the render functions used in the preceding code is to create a subroutine and to use the `Response.Write` method to yield the required output, as shown here:

```
<script language="vb" runat="server">
Sub rendertext()
    Response.Write("<H1> Requests received in the year_
    2000-2001 </H1>")
    Response.Write("<table width='112%' height='36'_
    bordercolor='#CCFFFF'>")
    Response.Write("<tr><td width='22%'>")
    Response.Write("<div align="right"><b>" + _
    summary + "</b></div></td></tr></table>")
End Sub
</script>
```

As you can see, your code becomes more manageable when you use a function instead of the render mechanism. If you examine the preceding code carefully, you'll notice that a script block has been used (identifiable by the `<script>` and `</script>` tags) instead of the code declarations (`<%` and `%>`); see the next syntactical change.

✦ **Use script blocks:** In ASP 3.0, you can declare your function within code delimiters. However, in ASP.NET, you must use the script block to declare all functions and variables. For an example on how to write functions in the script block, refer to the preceding bullet's code.

Language changes

Apply the following directives to migrate your ASP code to ASP.NET:

✦ **Use the `Page` directive:** In ASP 3.0, you declare a directive by using the following syntax:

```
<%@LANGUAGE="JSCRIPT" CODEPAGE="932"%>
```

In ASP.NET, you need to use the Page directive with the Language directive. The corresponding code in ASP.NET is as follows:

```
<%@Page Language="JScript" CodePage="932"%>
```

- **Use specific functions to retrieve values:** In the .NET Framework, Request.QueryString and Request.Form functions return an object of the NameValueCollection class, which represents a collection of string values. Thus, to retrieve specific values from a Request query, you need to use the GetValues function of the NameValueCollection class. Following is the code in ASP 3.0:

  ```
  Request.QueryString("Qty")
  ```

  The preceding statement would return 10 for the query string: http://localhost/Test/qty.asp?Qty=10.

  To retrieve the same value in ASP.NET, use the following syntax:

  ```
  Request.QueryString.GetValues("Qty")
  ```

- **Use ByRef explicitly:** In Visual Basic 6.0, all parameters are passed by reference. However, in Visual Basic .NET, all parameters are passed by value. Therefore, if you're relying on a function to change the value of the parameter that's passed to it, you need to explicitly use the ByRef keyword. For example, the following code would produce the output 10 in Visual Basic 6.0 but 20 in Visual Basic .NET:

  ```
  Value1=10
  ChangeNumber(Value1)
  Response.Write(CStr(Value1))
  'the Value1 parameter used below is ByRef in
  'Visual Basic 6.0 and ByVal in Visual Basic .NET.
  Sub ChangeNumber(Value1)
      Value1=20
  End Sub
  ```

  To get the output 20 from the preceding code in a Visual Basic .NET application, pass the value Value1 — by reference — by writing the following code:

  ```
  Value1=10
  ChangeNumber(Value1)
  Response.Write(CStr(Value1))
  'the Value1 parameter used below is ByRef in
  'Visual Basic 6.0 and ByVal in Visual Basic .NET.
  Sub ChangeNumber(By Ref Value1)
      Value1=20
  End Sub
  ```

In general, you can use Visual Basic .NET, JScript, or C# to write ASP.NET pages. Each of these languages uses the .NET Framework class library. Any consideration that applies to one language applies equally to other languages of Visual Studio .NET.

Managing state information

Although ASP 3.0 and ASP.NET pages can coexist on a Web site, you cannot share state information between these pages. You store state information on a Web site in `Session` and `Application` objects:

- `Session` object: Maintains user information while a user is still logged on to your Web site. For example, you might have retrieved a user profile and stored it in a `Session` object. The user profile may be used to customize the pages of the Web site.
- `Application` object: Declares global variables and makes them available to the Web site. For example, when your application starts, you may connect to a data source and make the connection available to all of the pages on your Web site.

When you rely heavily on state information, you have to migrate your Web site in such a way that this information is still available across ASP and ASP.NET subsystems. An easy way to do this is to migrate one unit of the site at a time and base that unit upon the new state information.

To understand this point, consider an example. Suppose that you've deployed a Web site that displays products in a catalog, allows a user to select a product and to shop for it. In this case, you may utilize `Application` and `Session` objects in the following manner:

- `Application` object: To create a connection to a Catalog database in the `Application` object and to make the connection available to all ASP pages on your Web site. You also connect to the Customer table and make the connection available to all ASP pages so that the details of a logged on customer can be retrieved.
- `Session` object: To store the user profile of the logged on customer. The profile may be required to select a shipping and billing address for the customer.

In the preceding scenario, you can first migrate the unit of your Web site that interacts with customers to ASP.NET. You'll only need to replicate the state information pertaining to the connection to the Customer table and retrieval of the customer's profile. Therefore, the information about catalogs and customers is spread across two subsystems.

Optimizing Your Web Site as You Migrate

When you complete migrating your Web site to ASP.NET, start calling it a Web application instead of a Web site! Ensure that you test your Web application completely before you deploy it. You can read about the methods to test applications in Book 1, Chapter 5.

In the preceding two sections, we specify the bare minimum that you need to do to successfully migrate your Web site to ASP.NET. However, to optimize your Web site as you migrate it, read the practices that we describe (and recommend) in this section.

Using custom Web controls

ASP.NET provides a number of Web controls to simplify your tasks. Instead of depending upon the `Response.Write` function to draw your Web pages, try using the Web controls of ASP.NET. Writing code for ASP.NET by using these customer Web controls isn't only easy — you'll also realize the amount of redundant code that previously existed in your application. For more on how to use custom controls for your Web application, refer to Book 6, Chapters 3 and 4.

Employing the Web.Config file

In ASP.NET, all configuration settings for an application can be stored in the `Web.Config` file. Instead of relying upon the IIS configuration mechanism, you can use the `Web.Config` file to configure your application. The `Web.Config` file also enables you to implement elaborate security mechanisms to secure your Web application. To know how to configure the `Web.Config` file, refer to Book 6, Chapter 16. If you're reluctant to get rid of IIS for configuring your application, you can read about doing so through IIS in Book 7, Chapter 3.

Declaring variables explicitly

The `Option Explicit` directive is used by ASP.NET by default. We recommend that you continue to use this directive because it ensures that all variables in your code are declared before they're used by your application. Better still, you can use the `Option Strict` directive, which forces you to specify the variable type along with the declaration. The `Option Strict` directive ensures that you declare all variables of the required data type in your application, thus avoiding errors that pertain to the use of incorrect data types. To use the `Option Strict` directive, follow these steps:

1. **Right-click the name of the project on Solution Explorer and select the Properties menu option. (Press Ctrl+Alt+L to open Solution Explorer.)**

   The property pages for the project appear.

2. **In the Project Properties dialog box, select the Build suboption from the Common Properties option.**

   The Option Strict directive appears in the right side of the dialog box.

3. **In the Option Strict option, select On to enable the** `Option Strict` **directive.**

   The completed Property Pages for a project, UniversalLogon, are shown in Figure 17-1.

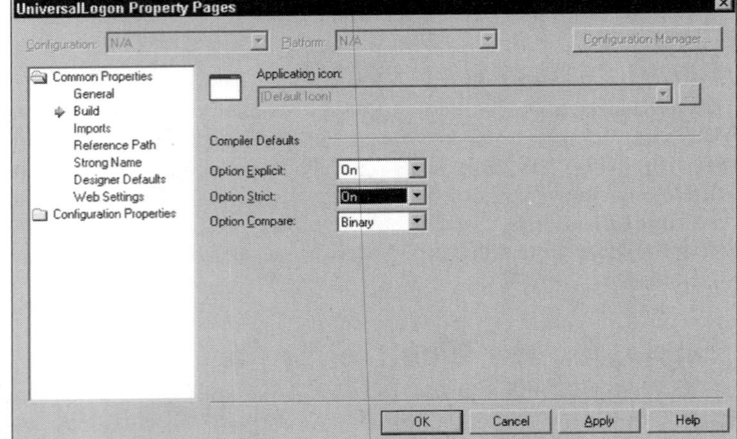

Figure 17-1: Change the project settings in the property pages for the project.

4. Click Apply and then click OK to save your changes and close the dialog box.

Separating code from HTML

In ASP.NET, you can separate the code of your application from HTML content. Not only does this make your code easier to read, but it also allows you to focus on the programming logic instead of worrying about how your code would appear on-screen. To read more about how you can separate your code from HTML, refer to Book 6, Chapter 2.

You can also continue with the process of separating your code from content after you've migrated your Web site. That'll probably be your next step, after you've finished migrating your site and when you can begin the process of optimizing it. Happy coding!

Index

A

B

C

D

E

F

G

H

I

K-L

M

Book VII

Creating and Deploying Web Services and Other Visual Studio .NET Solutions

"Can't I just give you riches or something?"

Contents at a Glance

Chapter 1: Creating ASP.NET Web Services

In This Chapter

- Exploring Web services
- Creating Web services
- Finalizing Web services

Visual Studio .NET offers a significant advantage of allowing you to create Web services. *Web services* are applications that run on the Internet. They provide one or more methods that can be accessed by other applications by using XML as the language of communication. An example of a Web service is the Microsoft Passport authentication service, which enables you to utilize the Microsoft Passport mechanism for authenticating users on your Web application.

Web services were developed to cater to the increasing need for businesses to interoperate. By implementing Web services, businesses are able to share customer data, provide complete solutions to meet customer requirements, and achieve common business objectives.

In this chapter, we include concepts and procedures necessary for creating a Web service. We also show you how to create a Web service in the language of your choice, Visual Basic .NET or Visual C#.

Exploring Web Services

With the development of Web services, creating a solution that comprises different applications that might be created on different platforms is easy because Visual Studio .NET solutions, unlike Visual Studio 6.0 solutions, can use XML to communicate. ASP.NET Web services use XML to communicate with one another and also with client applications that access these Web services. XML is platform independent. Thus, you need not worry about the platform that utilizes the Web service.

When you create Web services by using the templates provided by Visual Studio .NET, your application comprises a number of preconfigured files that are used for coding the functionality of the Web service. In this section, we examine the files generated by the ASP.NET Web Service template. We also describe concepts pertaining to creating a Web service so that you can successfully develop your own Web service.

Web service templates

Visual Studio .NET provides the ASP.NET Web Service and ATL Server Web Service templates for creating Web services. To get a detailed description of the ATL Server Web Service template, refer to Book 4, Chapter 5. In this section, we examine the ASP.NET Web Service template.

By using the ASP.NET Web Service template, you can create Web services in Visual Basic .NET or Visual C#. The template incorporates most of the basic functionality required to create a Web service. To examine the files created by the ASP.NET Web Service template, first create a project by following these steps:

1. **Select the File➪New➪Project option.**

   The New Project dialog box appears. The ASP.NET Web Service template is available in the Visual Basic .NET and Visual C# project types. For this example, use the Visual Basic .NET project type to create the Web service.

2. **Select Visual Basic Projects from the Project Types list.**

   The templates in Visual Basic Projects appear in the Templates list.

3. **Select ASP.NET Web Service and click OK.**

   Visual Studio .NET creates a Web service for you. The default name of the Web service is `WebService1`.

4. **Open Solution Explorer by pressing Ctrl+Alt+L and view the files created by the template.**

If you create a Web service in Visual C#, the only difference from the preceding steps is that, in Step 2, you select the ASP.NET Web Service template from the Visual C# applications.

Notice the following files:

- `AssemblyInfo.vb`: Contains information about the assemblies in a Web service. *Assemblies* contain executable code that can be run by the common language runtime (CLR). Every assembly needs to specify certain information, such as its name and version. The `AssemblyInfo.vb` file provides this information.

If you create a Web service in Visual C#, the extension of the file that specifies assembly information is `.cs` so that the name of the file is `AssemblyInfo.cs`.

✦ `Global.asax`: Analogous to the `Global.asa` file in ASP 3.0, the `Global.asax` file contains code for executing application-level events, such as the `OnStart` and `OnEnd` events.

✦ `Service1.asmx`: The entry point for the Web service, this file provides the code for implementing a Web service and the `WebService` processing directive, which identifies the class where the code for the Web service is implemented.

✦ `Web.Config`: You can change the configuration settings of your Web site in the `Web.Config` file, which specifies the mode of authenticating users and a list of valid user accounts for the Web service.

✦ `WebService1.vsdisco`: Also referred to as the discovery document, the `WebService1.vsdisco` file provides a description of the Web service that enables client applications to access the Web service. A discovery document enables Web service client applications to identify a Web service on the Internet. (Learn more about how Web service clients communicate with Web services in Book 7, Chapter 2). The *discovery document* describes the interfaces and methods implemented by the Web service so that an application developer can understand how to communicate with these methods and interfaces.

You code the discovery document in the Web services description language (WSDL) syntax, which is an XML-based industry standard. After a client application locates a Web service by using its discovery document, the application can view the description of the Web service in the WSDL format, and decide whether or not it wants to implement the Web service. For this reason, the description of the Web service is often referred to as the *contract* for the Web service.

The discovery document for the Web service is optional. If you want to implement a Web service that's accessible to clients within your enterprise but inaccessible to public enterprises, you can omit the discovery document.

Basics of creating a Web service

To ensure that client applications can access and use your Web service easily, you need to follow certain procedures, which we explain briefly in this section. To create a Web service and make it easily available on the Internet, follow these steps:

1. **Code the methods for the Web service.**

   A Web service comprises a number of methods that can be accessed by remote clients. Therefore, as the first step, you create a Web service project and code its methods. To expose these methods to clients, you use the WebMethod attribute, which needs to be placed before the public declaration of the method. For example, the following method is accessible through the Internet because it has the WebMethod attribute associated with it:

```
<WebMethod(Description:="This method ensures that the
username and password are unique and creates a new
user.")> _
Public Function AddUser(ByVal UserName As String, ByVal
      Password As String) As String
End Function
```

The underscore (_) symbol in Visual Basic .NET code implies that the line is a continuation of the preceding line. The symbol adds readability to your code. The compiler interprets the two lines as a single statement.

For more about using the WebMethod attribute, see the section "Adding functionality to a Web service project."

2. **Create a discovery file.**

   Web services communicate through XML-based messages. The types of messages generated by a Web service depend upon the methods implemented by the Web service. For example, a Web service that authenticates users will generate messages different from the messages generated by a Web service that retrieves a list of products in a catalog — the two Web services use different logic for implementing the required functionality.

   The discovery (.disco) file for a Web service provides details of the methods available in a Web service and the procedure for invoking these methods. This file is written in WSDL. To write files in this format, you can use the Universal Description, Discovery, and Integration mechanism (UDDI). A Web service client uses the discovery document to discover a Web service. After the Web service client discovers the Web service, the client uses the Simple Object Access Protocol (SOAP) to communicate with the Web service. The complete cycle of recognizing a Web service and communicating with it is shown in Figure 1-1.

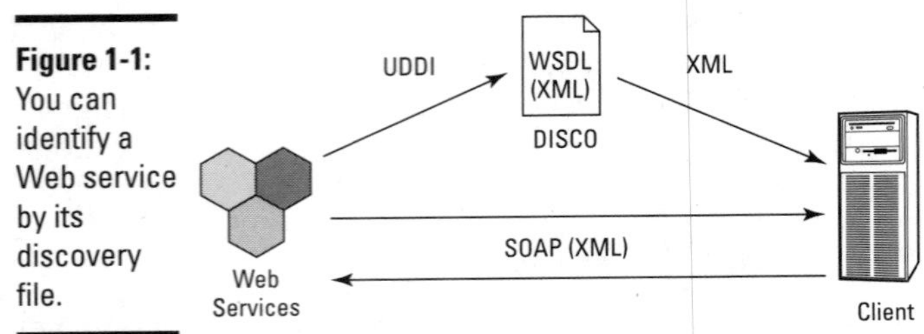

Figure 1-1: You can identify a Web service by its discovery file.

3. **Host the Web service on the Internet.**

   You need to host a Web service before a client application can access it through the Internet. Visual Studio .NET offers several options for hosting a Web service. As the first option, you can create an installer for your service. This installer automatically creates the required virtual directories for hosting your application. Another option for hosting a Web service is to copy project files and move them to a destination computer. You can find out more about creating installation files in Book 7, Chapter 5. The "Replicating Web service project files" section of this chapter includes the procedure for hosting an application by copying project files.

Creating a Web Service

The simplest way to create a Web service is to use the ASP.NET Web Service template, which you use to create a Web service in Visual Basic .NET as well as in Visual C#. In this section, you use the ASP.NET Web Service template in Visual Basic .NET to create a Web service that authenticates users against a data source.

Creating a project

To create a project based on the ASP.NET Web Service template, follow these steps:

1. **Launch Visual Studio .NET and choose File⇨New⇨Project.**

   The New Project dialog box appears.

2. **Select Visual Basic Projects from the Project Types list and select ASP.NET Web Service from the list of templates for Visual Basic .NET, as shown in Figure 1-2.**

   The same Web service would have been created in Visual C# had you selected the ASP.NET Web Service template from Visual C# projects in this step.

3. **Specify the name of the project as** `UniversalLogon` **in the Name text box and click OK.**

   Visual Studio .NET creates a new Web service called `UniversalLogon`.

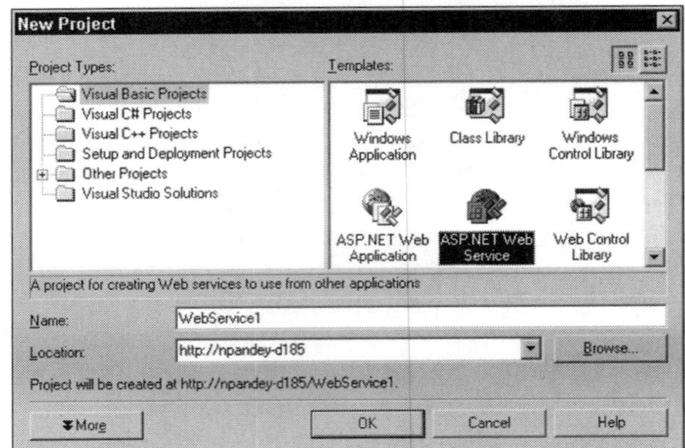

Figure 1-2: Select ASP.NET Web Service from the list of available templates to create a Web service.

When you create a new Web service, the Web service project opens in the Component Designer view, as shown in Figure 1-3. You can add components, such as data access controls and performance counter controls, to the Component Designer. You can also double-click anywhere in the Component Designer view to open the Code Editor. (You use the Code Editor to code the functionality of the Web site.)

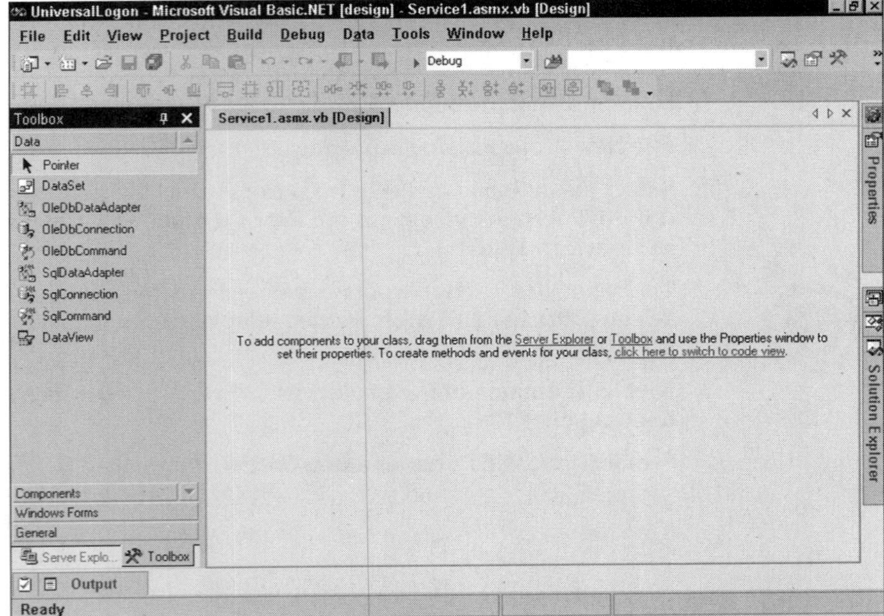

Figure 1-3: Use the Component Designer view to add controls to your Web service.

The Web service that you create by using the ASP.NET Web Service template is just a building block for the Web service. You need to code the methods of the Web service to make it functional, which we explain how to do in the following sections.

Adding functionality to a Web service project

After creating a new Web service, you code its functionality. To make your task of coding a Web service easier, Visual Studio .NET provides Web controls that can be added to the Web service. (For a description of the ASP.NET Web controls, refer to Book 6, Chapter 6).

In your Web service, you'll make use of Web controls to create a Web service easily. In the following numbered steps, we summarize the tasks you need to perform to create the Web service:

1. **Access data from the data source.**

   In your Web service, you need to authenticate users against a data source. To connect to the data source, you should use the following data controls provided by Visual Studio .NET:

   - `OleDbDataAdapter`: Transfers data to and from a data source.
   - `OleDbConnection`: The data adapter (`OleDbDataAdapter`) uses a data connection (`OleDbConnection` control) to connect to the data source.
   - `OleDbCommand`: After connecting to the data source, use the `OleDbCommand` control to access data from the data source.
   - `DataSet`: After retrieving data from the data source, you store the data in a `DataSet` control. You can modify this data or use it for analysis.

   Find out more about data adapters, data connections, and data sets in Book 3, Chapter 10.

2. **Define functions for implementing the Web service.**

   After adding data controls to the Web service, you need to define functions to process requests from clients. You can define the following functions:

   - `AddUser`: Adds a new user to the data source.
   - `EnsureUnique`: Ensures that the user ID supplied to the Web service is unique.
   - `ValidateUser`: Validates an existing user against a data source.

Adding data controls to the Web service

After you access the data and define the functions (see preceding section), you must next add data controls to the Web service. To add a `DataAdapter` control to your project, follow these steps:

1. **Open the Toolbox by selecting View⇨Toolbox.**

   The Toolbox appears in the left side of the screen.

2. **In the Toolbox, click Data to activate the Data tab.**

   The controls in the Data tab are now visible.

3. **Drag the `OleDbDataAdapter` control from the Toolbox to the Component Designer.**

   When you add the `OleDbDataAdapter` control to the Component Designer, the Data Adapter Configuration Wizard starts, displaying its Welcome screen.

4. **Click Next.**

   The Choose Your Data Connection screen of the Data Adapter Configuration Wizard appears, which enables you to specify the data connection that you want to use for your service.

5. **Click New Connection to specify a new data source.**

   The Data Link Properties dialog box appears. By default, the Connection tab of this dialog box is displayed. However, you must first select the correct OLE DB driver for your data source. For this example, select Microsoft Jet 4.0 OLE DB Provider.

   If you're using SQL Server for developing your application, the only difference in setting up the connection with the data source and accessing data is that you need to use the Microsoft OLE DB Provider for SQL Server.

6. **To select an OLE DB driver, click the Provider tab of the Data Link Properties dialog box.**

   The list of OLE DB drivers installed on your computer appears in the Provider tab, as shown in Figure 1-4.

7. **Select Microsoft Jet 4.0 OLE DB Provider from the list of OLE DB drivers and click Next.**

   The Connection tab of the Data Link Properties dialog box is activated (see Figure 1-5).

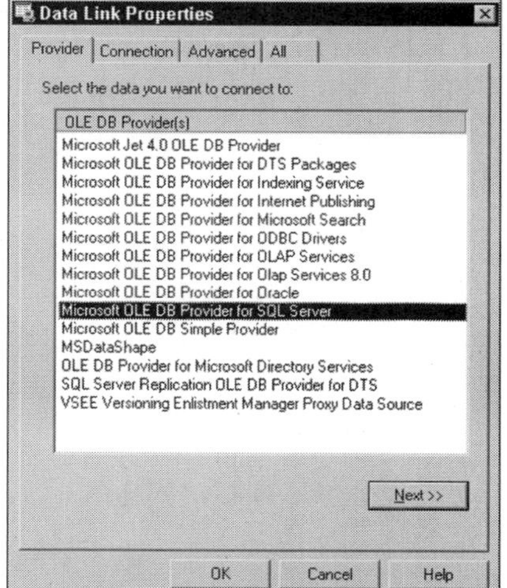

Figure 1-4: Selecting an OLE DB driver.

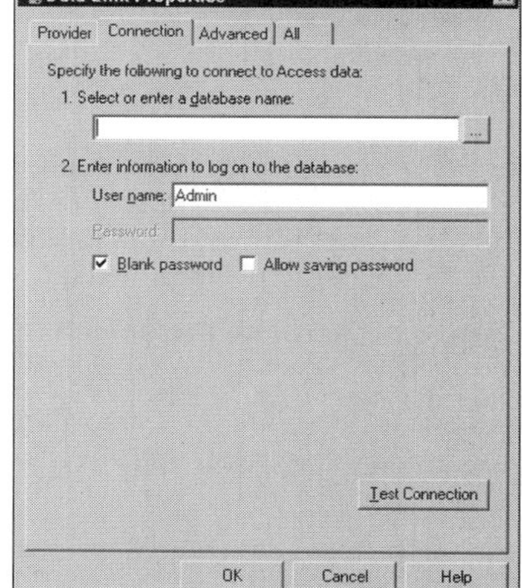

Figure 1-5: Specify the path to a database on the Connection tab.

8. **Specify the name and path of the database in the Select or Enter a Database Name text box and click OK.**

   For Step 8, you select the database that you've created for the Web service. For example, we've specified the database as `e:\applications\Logon.mdb`. The Data Link Properties dialog box closes, and you return to the Choose Your Data Connection screen of the Data Adapter Configuration Wizard. The data connection that you create in the preceding steps appears on this screen, as shown in Figure 1-6.

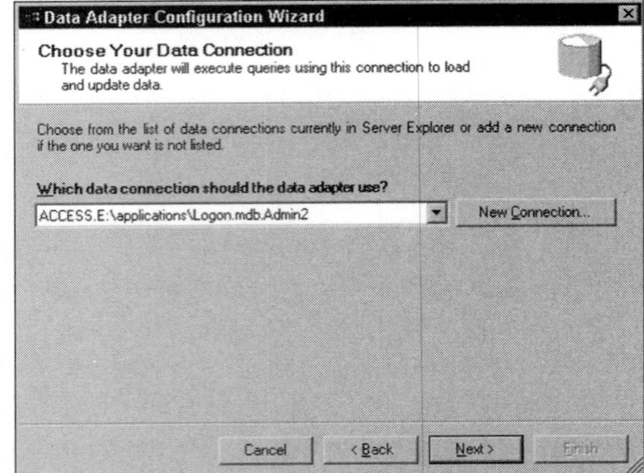

Figure 1-6: View the data connection that you've specified.

9. **Click Next.**

   The Choose a Query Type screen appears. In this screen, you specify whether you want to use Structured Query Language (SQL) to communicate with the data source or you want to use stored procedures. For this example, retain the default option Use SQL Statements.

10. **In the Choose a Query Type screen, retain the default option and click Next.**

    The Generate the SQL statements screen of the Data Adapter Configuration wizard appears. On this screen, you specify the SELECT query to retrieve data from the database.

11. **Type the following statement in the What Data Should the Data Adapter Load into the Dataset? text box.**

    ```
    SELECT LogonName, Pwd FROM Logon
    ```

    By specifying the preceding query, you retrieve the values of the LogonName and Pwd fields of the Logon table.

    Ensure that the Logon table with the two fields LogonName and Pwd exists in the database before you specify the query. To save yourself the effort of writing the query, use the Query Builder to create your query. For details, refer to Book 3, Chapter 10.

12. **Click Next to proceed.**

    The View Wizard Results screen appears.

13. **Click Finish to close the Data Adapter Configuration Wizard.**

When you close the Data Adapter Configuration Wizard, it automatically creates and configures an `OleDbConnection` control for your project. Saves you from doing this work! The `OleDbConnection` control, named `OleDbConnection1` by default, stores the connection settings for the database.

Next, you need to add an `OleDbCommand` and `DataSet` control to the Component Designer. The `OleDbCommand` control specifies SQL statements to manage data in the database while the `DataSet` control stores data that's retrieved from the database. To add the `OleDbCommand` and `DataSet` controls to the Component Designer, follow these steps:

1. **Drag the** `OleDbCommand` **control from the Toolbox to the Component Designer.**
2. **Select the control in the Component Designer and press F4 to invoke the Properties window.**
3. **Specify** `OleDbConnection1` **for the Connection property, as shown in Figure 1-7.**

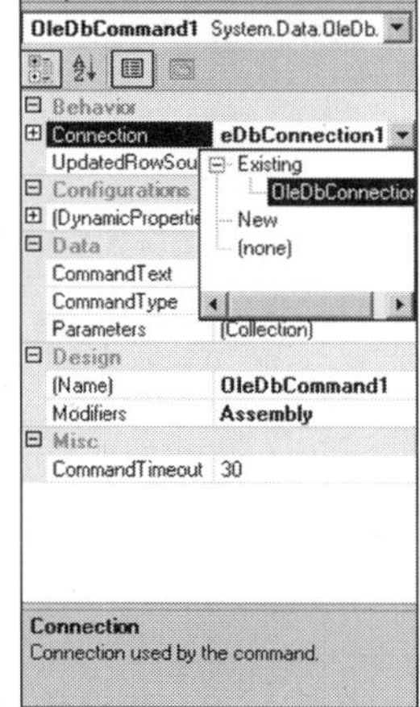

Figure 1-7: Associate a connection to an OleDb-Command control by using the Properties window.

4. **Select the Data⇨Generate DataSet menu option.**

   The Generate DataSet dialog box appears, shown in Figure 1-8, which enables you to specify the tables that you want to include in your `DataSet` control. Notice that the only table in the Logon database is automatically selected.

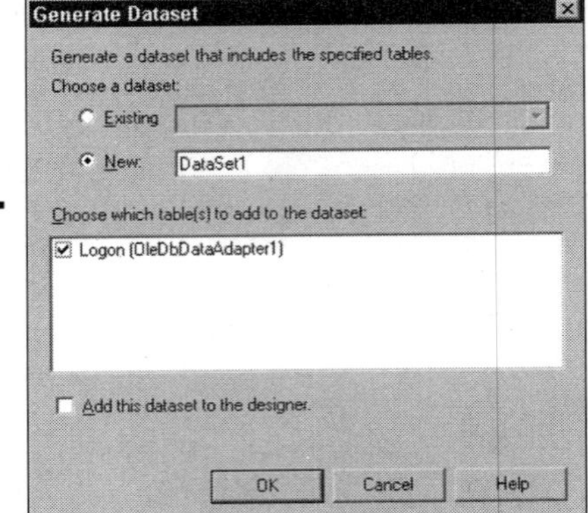

Figure 1-8: Specify the tables that you want to add to the DataSet control.

5. **In the Generate DataSet dialog box, check the Add This Dataset to the Designer box and click OK.**

   A new DataSet control, `DataSet11`, is added to your Web service.

The four controls that you've added to your Web service are now visible in the Component Designer, as shown in Figure 1-9.

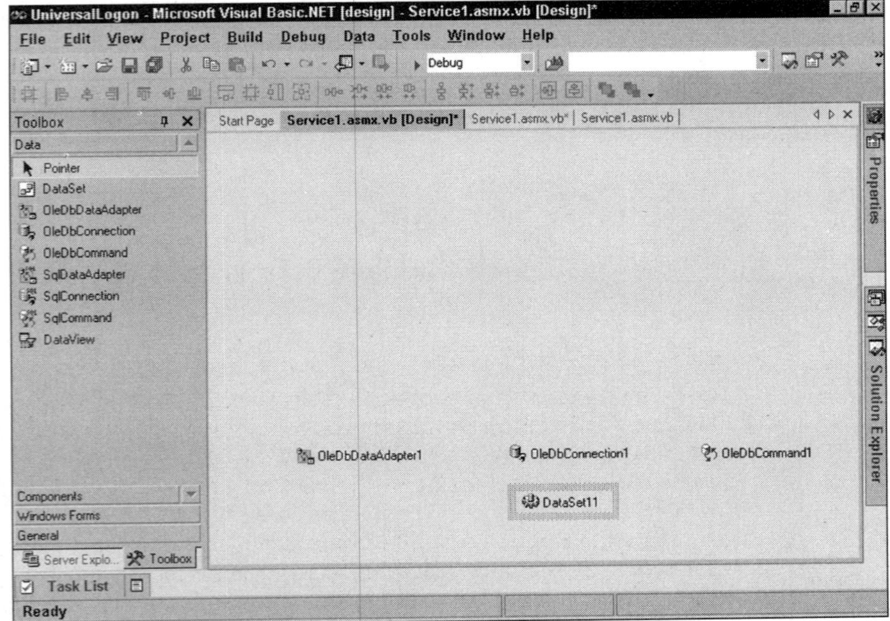

Figure 1-9: Controls that you add to your form are visible in the Component Designer.

Attention Visual C# fans: All steps given here are equally valid for Visual C# Web services.

You've added the required data controls to your Web service. The next thing you need to do is to complete the Web service by coding its methods — Web methods that are accessible to Web service clients and methods that are used to implement the Web service logic but not accessible to Web service clients. We write the code for these methods in the following sections.

Defining methods for the Web service

To complete your Web service, the last thing you must do is code its functions. Before you begin doing that, however, add a description for your Web service by using the `<WebService>` attribute. You can specify the namespace and description of the Web service by using the `<WebService>` attribute. Follow these steps to add the `<WebService>` attribute:

1. **Double-click the Component Designer to open the Code Editor window.**

   The `Service1.asmx.vb` file opens. You create functions for your Web service in this file. Notice that the file's first statement, `Imports System.Web.Services`, imports the `Web.Services` namespace into your application. The `Web.Services` namespace comprises the classes required for creating a Web service. For example, the namespace includes a `WebService` class. If you want to access ASP.NET objects in your Web service, you can inherit your Web service class from this class.

2. **Below the line that specifies** `Imports System.Web.Services`**, add the following line of code:**

   ```
   <WebService(Namespace:="http://WebServices/UnivLogon",
       Description:="This Web Service validates logon
       credentials.")> _
   ```

   The preceding line of code describes your Web service and associates it with the `http://WebServices/UnivLogon` namespace.

Adding the AddUser function

To add a new user to the Logon database, write the code for the `AddUser` function. The function should accept two parameters, the logon name and password. After ensuring that the logon name does not exist in the Logon table of the database, the `AddUser` function adds a new record to the table.

The syntax of Visual C# is different from Visual Basic .NET. Therefore, the syntax of the functions described here changes in Visual C#. The programming logic remains the same. You can check out the syntax of Visual C# in Book 5, Chapter 1.

Here's the code for the AddUser function:

```
<WebMethod(Description:="This method ensures that the user
           name and password are unique and creates a new
           user.")> _
Public Function AddUser(ByVal UserName As String, ByVal
           Password As String) As String
    'Remove blank spaces from username and password
    UserName = UserName.Trim
    Password = Password.Trim
    If UserName.Length < 4 Or UserName.Length > 10 Or
           Password.Length < 4 Or Password.Length > 10 Then
        Return "You've specified an invalid length of user
           name or password!"
    End If
    'Ensure that the username is unique, by using the
    'EnsureUnique function
    Dim ValidUserName As Boolean
    ValidUserName = EnsureUnique(UserName)
    If (ValidUserName = False) Then
        Return "Sorry, the user name already exists. Please
           try again."
    Else
        Try
            'Open the connection to the database
            OleDbConnection1.Open()
            'Insert the new record into the Logon table
            OleDbCommand1.CommandText = "INSERT INTO Logon
               (LogonName, Pwd) VALUES ('" + UserName + "',
                '" + Password + "')"
            'Use the ExecuteNonQuery function to execute the
            'Insert query
            OleDbCommand1.ExecuteNonQuery()
            OleDbConnection1.Close()
            'Return the username.
            Return "Hi! " + UserName
        Catch err As System.Exception
            'If there is an error, return the error message
            Return err.Message
        End Try
    End If
    End Function
```

The preceding code uses the Try and Catch statements to handle any exceptions that might be generated when your code is run. Want to know more about exceptions and exception handling? Check out Book 4, Chapter 8. The following highlights the logical flow of the AddUser function:

1. **Formats the input string.**

   The AddUser function uses the Trim method of the String class to remove trailing and leading blank spaces from the username and password. For example, if you specify the username as   John   , it gets changed to John.

2. **Checks the number of characters in the logon name and password.**

   The AddUser function ensures that the number of characters in the logon name and password fall in the range 4–10.

3. **Ensures that the logon name is unique.**

   The EnsureUnique function ensures that the logon name does not exist in the Logon table. The function accepts a logon name as a parameter and returns True if the logon name doesn't exist in the Logon table. Give us a while and we explain the code of the EnsureUnique function immediately after completing the description of the AddUser function.

4. **Adds the new user's credentials to the Logon table.**

   Finally, you add the new user's credentials to the Logon table by following these steps:

   - Open the connection specified by OleDbConnection1.
   - Specify the SQL query to add a new record to the database.
   - Execute the SQL query by using the ExecuteNonQuery method of the OleDbCommand class.
   - Close the connection specified by OleDbConnection1.

You can add the OleDbConnection1 class to your project by adding the OleDbDataAdapter control to your project. When you add the OleDbDataAdapter control to your project, the Data Adapter Configuration Wizard launches, which in turn adds the OleDbConnection1 class to your project. For details, read "Adding functionality to a Web service project" earlier in this chapter.

Adding the EnsureUnique function

The EnsureUnique function, which is used in the AddUser function, is used to ensure that the user name supplied to it is unique. The code for the EnsureUnique function is given below:

```
Protected Function EnsureUnique(ByVal UserName As
String)
        As Boolean
    OleDbConnection1.Open()
    OleDbCommand1.CommandText = "Select * from Logon
where
        LogonName= '" + UserName + "'"
    OleDbDataAdapter1.SelectCommand = OleDbCommand1
    OleDbDataAdapter1.Fill(DataSet11, "Logon")
    OleDbConnection1.Close()
    If (DataSet11.Tables(0).Rows.Count = 0) Then
```

```
            DataSet11.Reset()
            Return True
        Else
            DataSet11.Reset()
            Return False
        End If
    End Function
```

We didn't use the `<WebMethod>` attribute in the `EnsureUnique` function because this function isn't exposed by the Web service. The function is used only to implement the Web service logic. You may also notice that the `Protected` declaration of the function is also included for the same purpose.

The previous code functions to retrieve records from the Logon table. This code retrieves only the records that have the same logon name as the parameter supplied to the `EnsureUnique` function. If any rows are returned, the number of rows in the `DataSet` is greater than zero and the function returns `False`. Alternatively, the function returns `True`.

Adding the ValidateUser function

The function `ValidateUser` validates a user's credentials. The following code adds the `ValidateUser` function to the project:

```
<WebMethod(Description:="This method accepts the user name
           and password of a user as parameters and validates
           the user against a data source.")> _
    Public Function ValidateUser(ByVal UserName As String,
   ByVal Password As String) As String
        UserName = UserName.Trim
        Password = Password.Trim
        OleDbConnection1.Open()
        OleDbCommand1.CommandText = "Select * from Logon
           where LogonName= '" + UserName + "'"
        OleDbDataAdapter1.SelectCommand = OleDbCommand1
        OleDbDataAdapter1.Fill(DataSet11, "Logon")
        OleDbConnection1.Close()
        If (DataSet11.Tables(0).Rows.Count = 0) Then
            DataSet11.Reset()
            Return "That's an invalid user name!"
        Else
            If Password = DataSet11.Tables(0).Rows(0)("Pwd")
           Then
                Return "Welcome " + UserName
            Else
                Return "That's an invalid password!"
            End If
        End If
    End Function
```

The `ValidateUser` function is very similar to the `EnsureUnique` function. In the `ValidateUser` function, you retrieve a record from the Logon table that has the logon name as specified by a user. When you attempt to retrieve such a record from the database, any of the following possibilities may occur:

- **The specified logon name doesn't exist in the table.**

  When the specified logon name doesn't exist in the Logon table, the `ValidateUser` function returns the message, "That's an invalid user name!"

- **The specified logon name exists, but the password stored in the table doesn't match the one specified by the user.**

  When the specified logon name exists in the Logon table, but the password is incorrect, the `ValidateUser` function returns the message, "That's an invalid password!"

- **The specified logon name exists in the table, and the password matches the one specified by the user.**

  If both the logon name and the password match, the `ValidateUser` function returns the message, "Welcome *username*."

Finalizing a Web Service

After you've coded the methods of the Web service, it is ready to be tested and hosted. Testing a Web service is important because it ensures that all the service's methods yield the required output. There are a number of methods to test a Web service. For a full description of these methods, refer to Book 1, Chapter 5. In this section, we look at some of the ways to test a Web service for yielding the required output.

After you test your Web service, you can host it. The best way to host a Web service is to use the deployment projects that are available in Visual Studio .NET. We include these projects in Book 7, Chapter 5. However, an easy way to host a Web service is to replicate its project files, which we discuss in this section.

Testing a Web service

You might have realized that your Web service doesn't have an interface. It doesn't need one because the Web service simply processes requests from client applications, which in turn don't require communication interfaces.

However, to test a Web service, you need an interface that can be used for sending parameters to Web methods and for viewing the resultant output.

Visual Studio .NET provides such an interface to help you test your Web service. Let's see what this interface is all about. To test your Web service, follow these steps:

1. **Choose Build⇨Build to build your Web service.**

   A message appears (hopefully!) in the Output window to convey that your Web service was compiled successfully.

2. **Choose Debug⇨Start to start debugging your Web service.**

   The `Service1` Web Service window appears, containing information about the Web service and its Web methods, as shown in Figure 1-10.

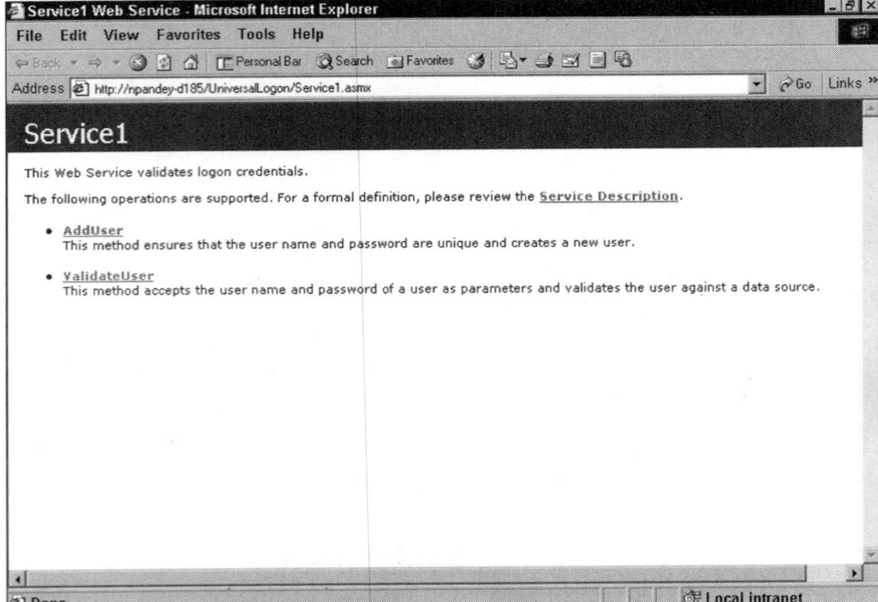

Figure 1-10: When you debug a Web service, you can view the description of its methods in the startup screen.

3. **Click the AddUser link to test the `AddUser` function.**

   The `AddUser` method screen appears, providing the UserName and Password text boxes that enable you to specify the logon name and password, as shown in Figure 1-11.

The UserName and Password text boxes are available because your Web function accepts two parameters — UserName and Password. If your Web function accepts other parameters, the title and number of text boxes change accordingly.

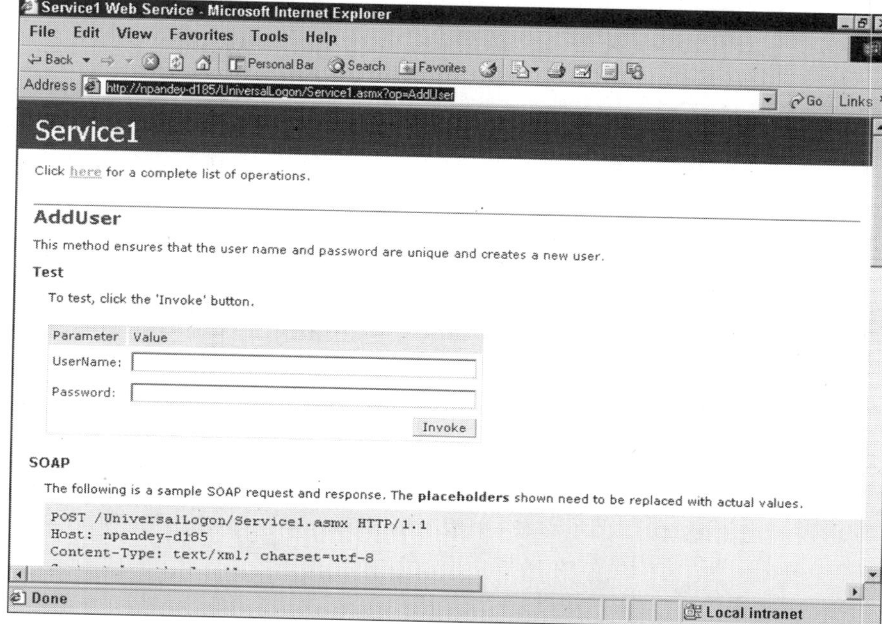

Figure 1-11: Use the text boxes to enter parameters to a Web method and test it.

4. Specify Suzan and password in the UserName and Password text boxes, respectively, and click Invoke.

The `AddUser` function adds Suzan to the Logon table and returns a string `Hi! Suzan` as the output, as shown in Figure 1-12.

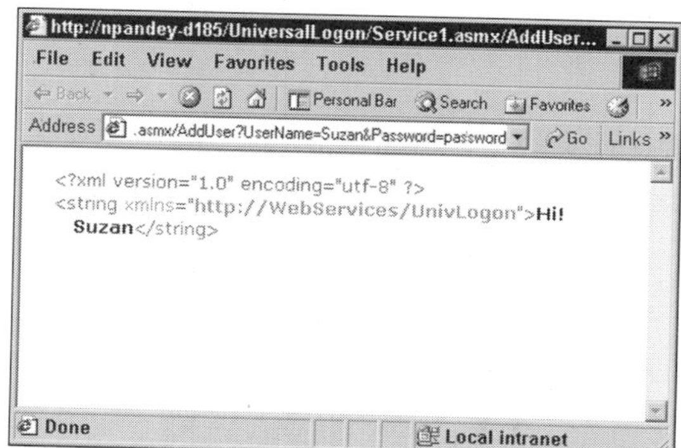

Figure 1-12: When you test your Web service, you can view the output of a function in the XML format.

Similarly, you can test the `ValidateUser` function to ensure that it operates perfectly. The output of the `ValidateUser` function, after you specify the logon name and password for Suzan, is shown in Figure 1-13.

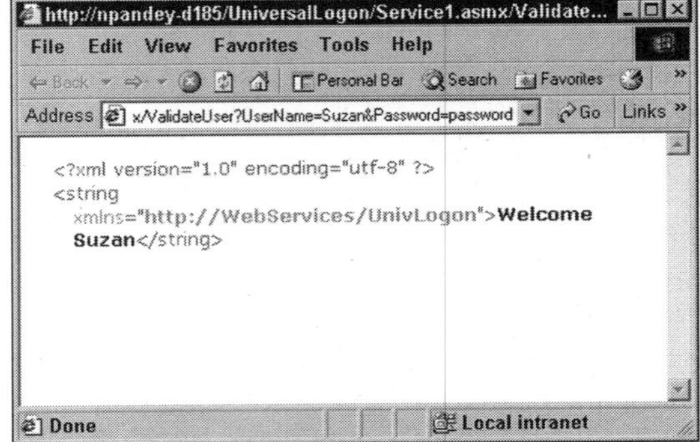

Figure 1-13: Ensure that all functions of your Web service display the required output.

Replicating Web service project files

After testing your Web service, you can host it on the Internet so that client applications across the world can use it. An efficient way to host your Web service is to create an *installer file,* which can create the necessary virtual directories on a computer. You can read about creating an installer file for deploying Web services in Book 7, Chapter 5.

Another easy way to host your Web service is to replicate it. By replicating a Web service, we mean that you copy the source files and output from one computer to another. You might need to replicate your project files to another Web server that has access to the Internet so that your Web service can be accessed by applications over the Internet; to copy project files from Visual Studio .NET for this purpose, follow these steps:

1. **Choose Project⇨Copy Project.**

   The Copy Project dialog box appears, as shown in Figure 1-14.

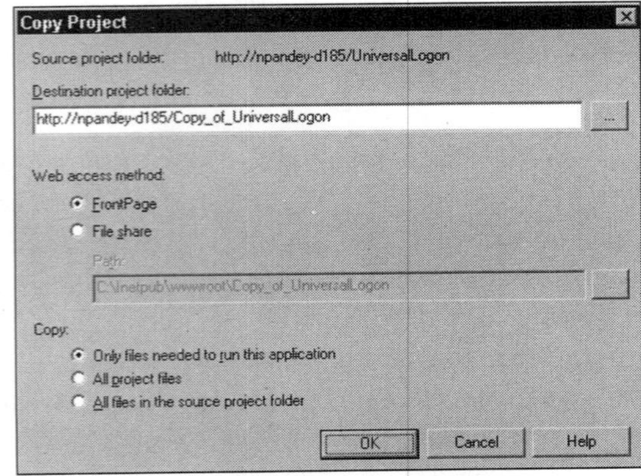

Figure 1-14: Use the Copy Project dialog box to copy project files.

2. **Specify the name and location of the virtual directory to which you want to copy your project files.**

   For example, we've specified the virtual directory as `http://yesh-d185/UnivLogon`.

3. **Select an option from one of the Copy options to specify the files that you want to copy.**

   You can select one of the following options:

   * **Only files needed to run this application:** Select this option if you want to copy only those files that are needed to run your application on the destination computer. You might select this option when your application is complete and only needs to be deployed.
   * **All project files:** Select this option when you want to copy all project files, including the source and output files of your application.
   * **All files in the source project folder:** Use this option to copy all project files and any additional files that you might have stored in the source project's folder.

4. **Click OK to copy the project files to the destination directory.**

If you don't have administrator rights for the destination computer, Visual Studio .NET prompts you for a different logon name when you try to copy your project to the destination folder.

After you carry out the preceding steps, the project files that you select are copied to the destination computer, and you can then access your Web service by specifying the path to the Web service on the destination computer.

Chapter 2: Creating ASP.NET Web Service Clients

In This Chapter

- **Web service clients 101**
- **Creating a Web service client**

Web services help you integrate business processes. You can either create a Web service for your organization or use a Web service provided by another organization. To implement a Web service, you require a Web service client.

A Web service client is a Windows or Web application that communicates with a Web service through the Internet. The Web service client connects to a Web service and invokes its functions. The output of a function of a Web service is either displayed to a user or is further processed by the Web service client.

In Book 7, Chapter 1, we give you the basics on Web services and how to create one. In this chapter, we focus on the concepts and procedures necessary to help you create a Web service client.

Web Service Clients 101

You might already be aware of the importance of a Web service client. If not, we guarantee that by the end of this chapter, you will appreciate the idea of a Web service client because of all the opportunities that Web services bring you. We discuss these opportunities in the following section and then move on to how a Web service and its client communicate in the section "How a Web service client accesses data."

Later in this chapter, in the section appropriately titled "Creating a Web Service Client," we show you everything you need to know to create a Web service client.

Web service clients: Immense possibilities

A Web service client holds immense possibilities for you as a Web developer. In this section, we elaborate upon a few of these possibilities. Suppose that you're hosting a retail Web site for your bookstore. The following items can broadly define the requirements of your Web site, which are easily fulfilled by using Web service clients:

- **You need to provide a catalog of books for your customers.**

  Suppose that you stock books that are published by several publishing houses. If each publishing house hosts a Web service that provides details of the products in its catalog, your job is half done. Now, you just need to create a Web service client that queries each Web service for an updated list of products and displays it on the Web site.

- **The catalog should provide a separate listing for new book releases.**

  After you've implemented the Web service client, fulfilling this requirement isn't a problem. You can sort books on the basis of their publishing dates and display only those books that were published in a specific time period.

- **A customer should be able to log on to the Web site and make purchases.**

  To validate users, you can create a Web service or use an existing one. You must use a Web service that adds new users and validates the existing ones. (Go to Book 7, Chapter 1 to see how to create such a Web service.)

  You can use the authentication service provided by another organization, such as the Microsoft Passport authentication service, to authenticate users on your Web site. You benefit from subscribing to such a service because users registered on these services automatically become the registered users of your Web site.

- **Even if a customer doesn't want to make purchases, the customer should be able to select a list of books and save them to buy later.**

  To display sorted books to customers and allow customers to store books in a shopping basket, you can create a database to associate books in a shopping basket with the customer's profile.

- **Based on a customer's purchase history, the site should present a customized list of books to the customer.**

  For example, if you bought *Visual Basic .NET For Dummies*, the Web site should suggest *Visual Studio .NET All-in-One Desk Reference For Dummies* when you shop the next time.

You have a composite solution that uses data from different Web services and its own applications to fulfill business requirements. Such a solution is shown in Figure 2-1. Makes your job so much simpler, doesn't it?

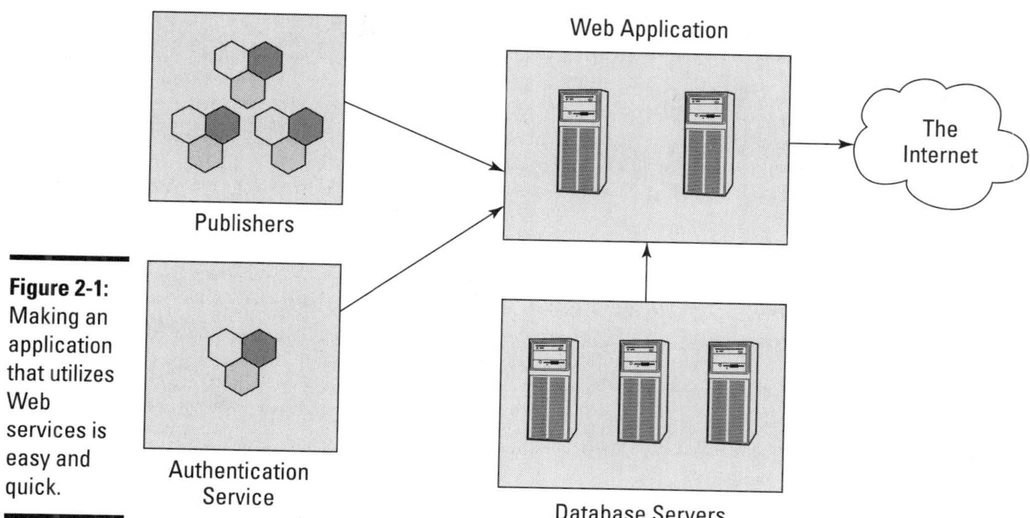

Figure 2-1: Making an application that utilizes Web services is easy and quick.

How a Web service client accesses data

You access a Web service by using standard Internet protocols, such as HTTP (Hypertext Transfer Protocol). To access a Web service by using XML (eXtensible Markup Language), you use Simple Object Access Protocol (SOAP). The SOAP specification defines the rules for representing data and calling procedures from a remote client.

In Visual Studio .NET, you don't have to worry about how to access functions from Web services. You can access functions from Web services easily by using the Add Web Reference feature of Visual Studio .NET. In addition to making data accessible, the Add Web Reference feature

- **Locates a Web service:** The Add Web Reference feature uses the discovery document provided by Web services to locate them. (To discover more about the discovery document, look up Book 7, Chapter 1.) After Visual Studio .NET identifies the accessible services, which are installed on your computer or are available through the Internet, you can select the required service from the list.
- **Downloads the description of the Web service:** After you select a Web service, Visual Studio .NET downloads a description of the service to your computer and creates a proxy class for the Web service. The proxy class includes proxy functions for all Web methods of the Web service. (Find out more about Web methods in Book 7, Chapter 1.) Therefore, you can use the classes and functions of the Web server as if they're locally available on your computer.

A proxy class for a Web service is a representation of the actual class in a Web service. For example, consider a Web service that has a class — `Class1` — that has two Web methods, `Method1` and `Method2`. The proxy class on your computer for this Web service is `Class1` and has the same Web methods. However, the two Web methods don't have the actual code of the Web service methods, but they identify the required input and output parameters so that you can easily use these methods in your application.

As shown in Figure 2-2, Visual Studio .NET helps you locate a Web service by using its discovery document and downloads the description of the Web service to create a proxy class (shown by dotted lines in the right). The proxy class can be used to develop the Web service client.

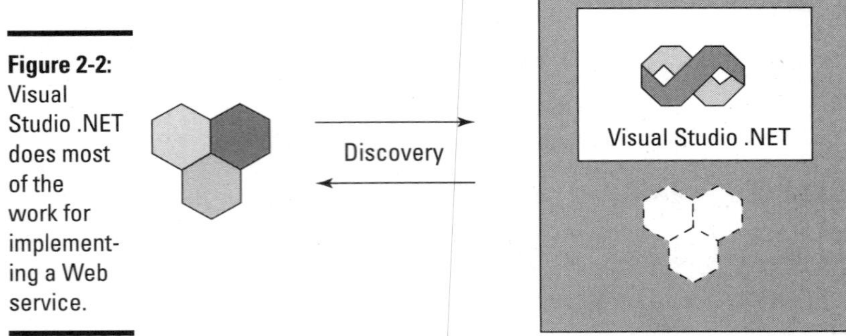

Figure 2-2: Visual Studio .NET does most of the work for implementing a Web service.

Creating a Web Service Client

The best way to learn to create a Web service client is to create one, so in this section, we show you how to do that. First, you need a Web service to which the Web service client can connect. For this example, we use a Web service that we show you how to create in Book 7, Chapter 1. We have included the code of the `Service1.asmx.vb` file of the Web service (`UniversalLogon`) on the `www.dummies.com/extras/VS.NETAllinOne` Web site. The code is in the `UniversalLogon.txt` file. If you've not gone through the previous chapter, you can copy the code of the file to the source file of your Web service.

To create a Web service client, you perform the following steps:

1. **Create a new Web service client project.**
2. **Add one or more Web references to the project, depending upon the number of Web services you want to connect to.**

3. **Implement the methods of the Web service in your application.**
4. **Test and deploy the Web service client.**

Throughout the following subsections, we walk you through each of the preceding steps in painstaking detail.

Creating a new Web service client project

You can create a Web service client that connects to a Web service with any project type. You can use one Web service in another Web service. When you use one Web service in another, the Web service that utilizes the services of the other Web service is the client. You can also utilize a Web service in a Windows application.

However, the most common implementation of a Web service is in an ASP.NET Web application because the primary objective of a Web service is to make applications communicate (mostly over the Internet). Therefore, in this example, we create a Web service client application by using the ASP.NET Web Application template.

To create a Web application in ASP.NET, follow these steps:

1. **Launch Visual Studio .NET.**
2. **Choose File⇨New⇨Project.**

   The New Project dialog box appears.
3. **To create a Web service client in Visual Basic .NET, select Visual Basic Projects from the Project Types list.**

   The templates for Visual Basic .NET projects appear in the Templates list.
4. **Select ASP.NET Web Application from the list of templates.**

   After completing the preceding steps, the New Project dialog box appears.
5. **To name the project, append** WebClient **as the location of the project in the Location text box, and click OK. The completed New Project dialog box is shown in Figure 2-3.**

   Visual Studio .NET creates a new Web application for you.

For a description of the ASP.NET Web application template, refer to Book 6, Chapter 2. You can now utilize a Web service in your new Web application.

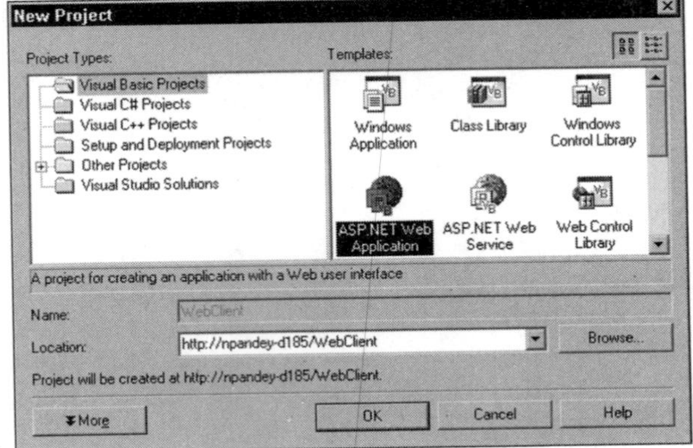

Figure 2-3: Create a new project.

Adding Web references to the project

Visual Studio .NET provides the Add Web Reference feature to utilize a Web service. When you use this feature, Visual Studio .NET creates a proxy class of the Web service for your application so that you can write the application code by using the functions exposed by the Web service.

To add a Web reference to your project, follow these steps:

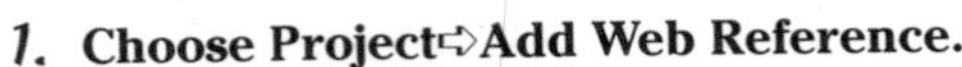

1. **Choose Project⇨Add Web Reference.**

   You can also right-click the name of your project in the Solution Explorer and select the Add Web Reference option from the shortcut menu.

   The Add Web Reference dialog box appears, as shown in Figure 2-4.

   The Add Web Reference dialog box enables you to locate Web services on your local computer as well as in the Microsoft UDDI (Universal Description Discovery and Integration) directory. Alternatively, you can also specify the address of the discovery document of a Web service to locate it.

   UDDI is a mechanism for Web service providers to publicize a Web site. (For more details of UDDI, refer to Book 7, Chapter 1.)

2. **To select a Web service that's installed on the local computer, click the Web References on Local Web Server link in the Add Web Reference dialog box.**

   The details of Web services that are available on the local computer appear in the Available references list, as shown in Figure 2-5.

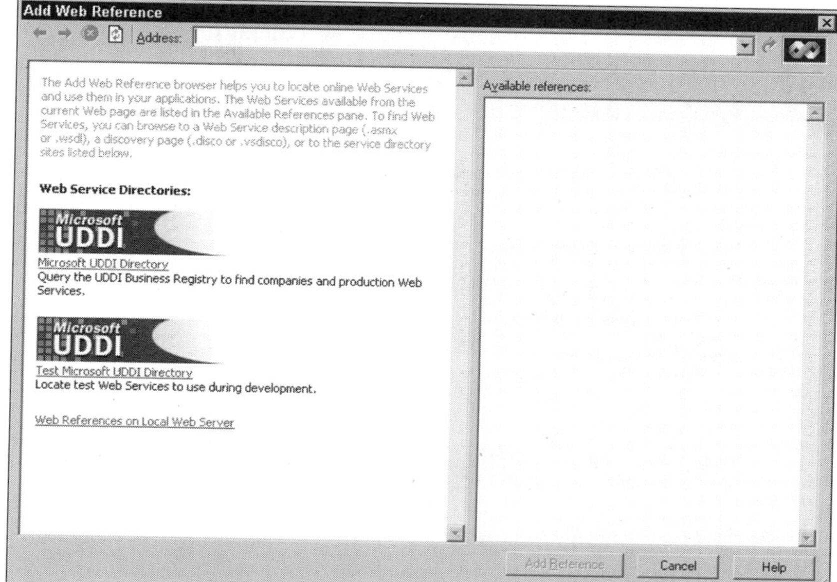

Figure 2-4: Add a reference to a Web service.

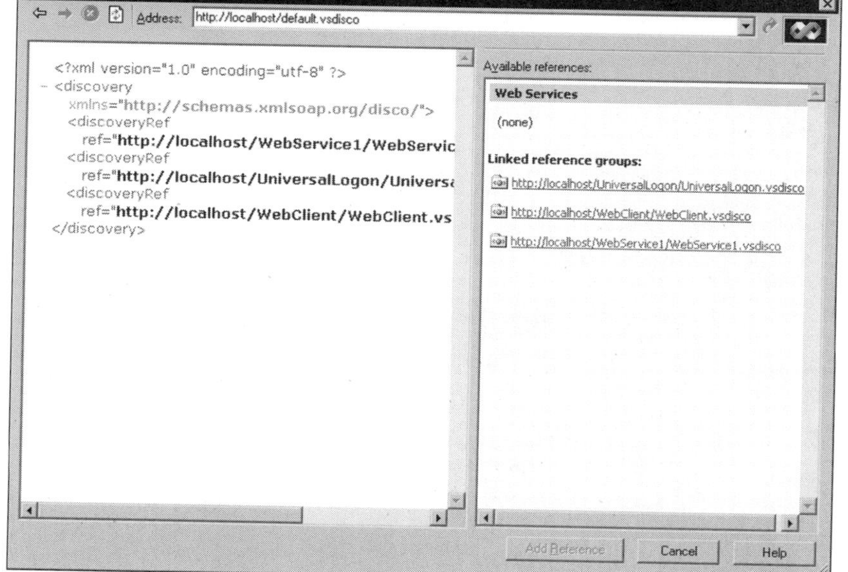

Figure 2-5: Select a Web service from the Available references list.

If your Web service isn't installed on the local computer but on another computer on the network, you can type the path to the discovery document in the Address text box. For example, to access a Web service on the computer John, type **http://john/default.vsdisco** in the Address box; `default.vsdisco` is the name of the discovery document.

3. **Select a Web service from the list of available Web services.**

   For example, if you've installed the Web service that we create in Book 7, Chapter 1, click the link to the `UniversalLogon.vsdisco` file.

   When you click the link to a Web service, the links to the contract and documentation of the Web service appear in the Add Web Reference dialog box, as shown in Figure 2-6. Check out the sidebar "Web service contracts" elsewhere in this chapter.

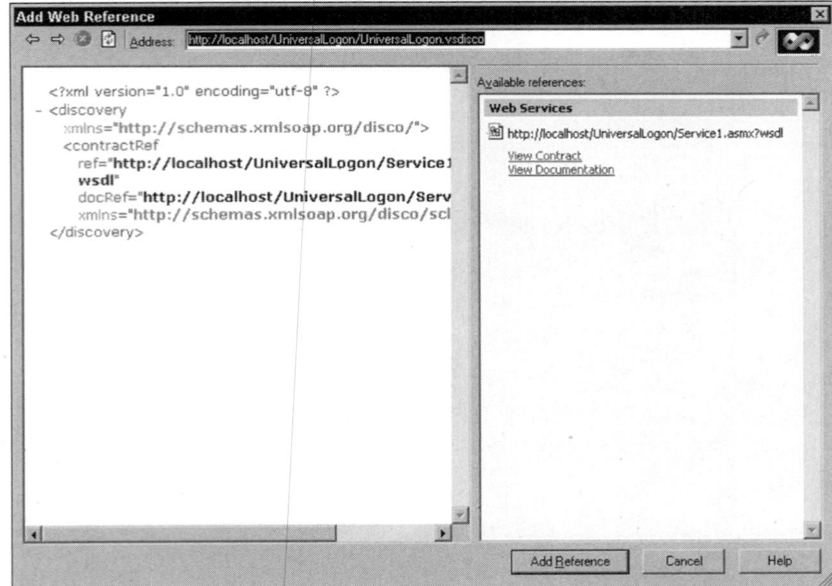

Figure 2-6: View the contract information and a description of the Web service.

4. **To add a Web reference to the Web service that you selected in Step 3, click Add Reference in the Add Web Reference dialog box.**

   A Web reference to the Web service is added to your project.

You can verify that the reference to the Web service is added successfully by opening Solution Explorer (press Ctrl+Alt+L) and viewing the project node. The reference to the UniversalLogon Web service, which appears as localhost, is highlighted in Figure 2-7.

Web service contracts

A *Web service contract* is the discovery document that provides detailed information about the methods implemented by the Web service and how you should interact with it. A Web service contract specifies the target applications for the Web service and the methods implemented by the Web service.

Another resource that helps you understand a Web service is the Web service documentation. To implement a Web service successfully, the Web service documentation lists the methods exposed by the Web service and the parameters necessary to implement those methods. The documentation of a Web service is the same Web page that appears when you debug your Web service. For details about the documentation of a Web service, refer to Book 7, Chapter 1.

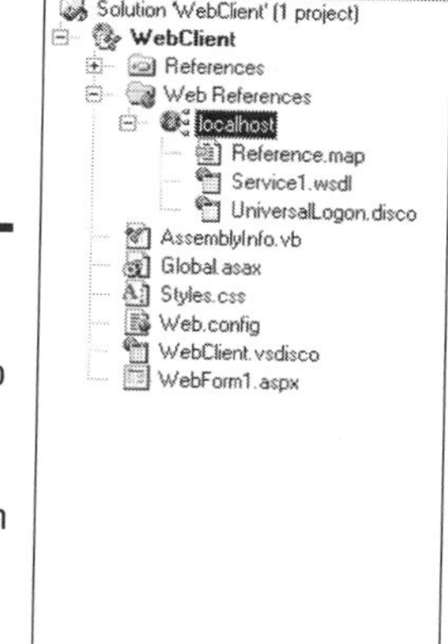

Figure 2-7: The reference to a Web service can be viewed in Solution Explorer.

You can change the name of the reference to a Web service so that it's easier to recognize the service in your program by following these steps:

1. **Right-click** `localhost` **and select the Rename option from the shortcut menu.**
2. **Type** UniversalLogon **as the name of the Web service and press Enter.**

   The name of the reference to the Web service changes to `UniversalLogon`.

You're now ready to implement the methods of the Web service in your application.

Implementing Web methods in an application

After adding Web references to your application (see the previous section), you can use the methods of the Web service in the same way as you use methods from class libraries installed on your computer. To implement the methods of the UniversalLogon Web service, you first need to create the user interface for your Web service client. The UniversalLogon Web service, which you'll utilize in this application, enables you to validate existing users and to add new users to a database.

So to get started, create a Web Form that allows existing users to log on and new users to register. Table 2-1 lists the controls that you add to the form.

Table 2-1 Controls to Add to Your Web Page

Control	*Control Type*	*Properties*
Label to prompt a user to sign-in	`Label`	`Text=`Please Sign-In `Font:` `Bold=`True `Name=`Impact `Size=`X-Large
Label for the Logon Name text box	`Label`	`Text=`Logon Name `Font:` `Bold=`True
Label for the Password text box	`Label`	`Text=`Password `Font:` `Bold=`True
Logon text box	`TextBox`	`ID=`LogonName
Password text box	`TextBox`	`ID=`Password `TextMode=`Password
Sign-In button	`Button`	`ID=`ButtonSignIn `Text=`Sign-In
Add new user button	`Button`	`ID=`ButtonAddNew `Text=`AddNewUser
Label to display messages	`Label`	`ID=`Message `Text=`""

After adding the controls from Table 2-1 to your Web Form, your form appears as shown in Figure 2-8; if you used your designing skills, it might look even better!

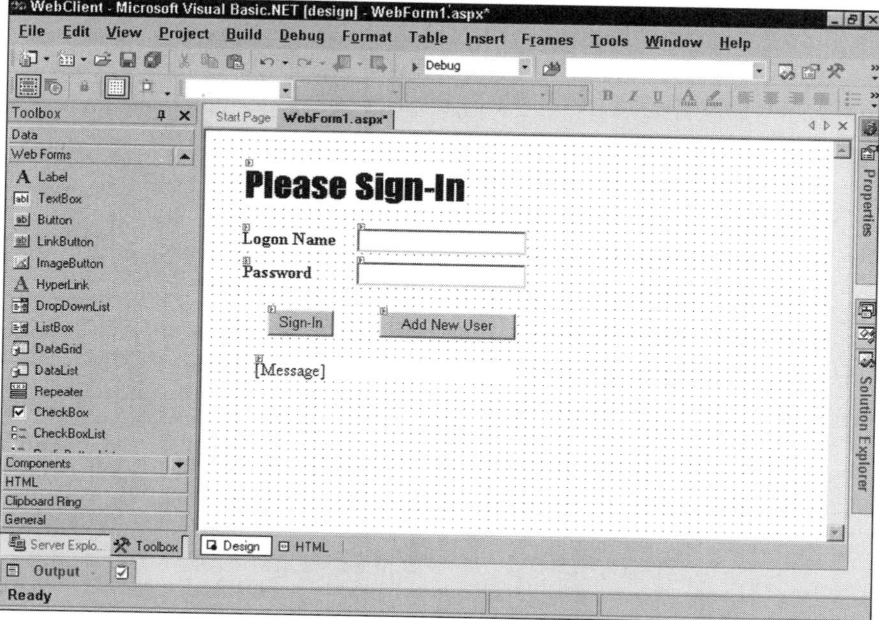

Figure 2-8: Your completed form should resemble this form.

After you've added the controls to your form, you're ready to add functionality to your Web application, which is an easy task when you use a Web service. To allow existing users to log on, follow these steps:

1. **Create an instance of the Web service class.**
2. **Call the** `ValidateUser` **function of the Web service, supplying the logon name and password specified by the user in the two text boxes as parameters.**
3. **Display the returned value of the** `ValidateUser` **function in the Message label.**

The following code, which you write after double-clicking the Sign-In button in the design view of the form, enables you to let users log on:

```
Private Sub ButtonAddNew_Click(ByVal sender As System.Object,
          ByVal e As System.EventArgs) Handles
          ButtonAddNew.Click
    Dim UL As New UniversalLogon.Service1()
    Message.Text = UL.ValidateUser(LogonName.Text,
          Password.Text)
End Sub
```

The code for adding a new user is very similar to the preceding code. The only difference is that you need to call the `AddUser` method of the Web service instead of the `ValidateUser` method. To add a new user, write this code:

```
Private Sub ButtonSignIn_Click(ByVal sender As System.Object,
        ByVal e As System.EventArgs) Handles
        ButtonSignIn.Click
    Dim UL As New UniversalLogon.Service1()
    Message.Text = UL.AddUser(LogonName.Text, Password.Text)
End Sub
```

That's all you need to do for implementing your Web service. Of course, you might want to enhance your Web service client application by adding some Web forms to it. The basic purpose of authentication is to establish a user's credentials before allowing the user to view restricted pages on your Web site. There are several ways to authenticate a user. For example, you can issue a cookie to an authenticated user to identify the user. You can read about these methods in Book 6, Chapter 16.

To run your Web service client application, follow these steps:

1. **Choose Build⇨Build Solution.**
2. **Debug any errors that appear in the Output window.**
3. **Choose Debug⇨Start to start your application.**

   The output of your application, after you add a user, is shown in Figure 2-9.

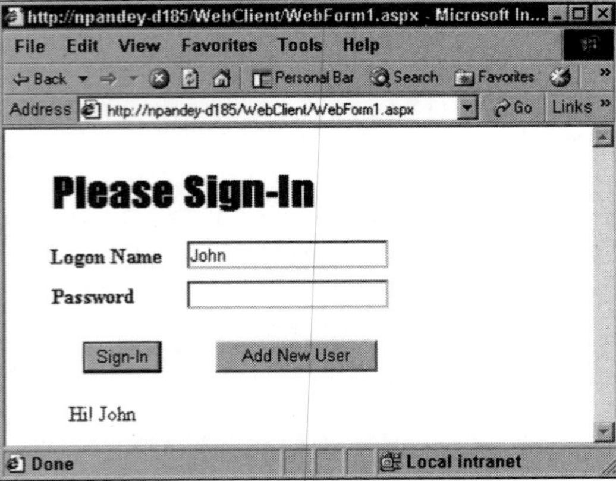

Figure 2-9: The output of your application after you add a new user.

Testing and deploying the Web service client application

Testing and deploying a Web service client application isn't any different from testing and deploying other applications. Depending upon the type of Web service client application that you've created, you can read Book 4, Chapter 8 for testing and debugging Windows applications and Book 6, Chapter 7 for testing and debugging Web applications. You can also look up general concepts on testing and debugging in Book 1, Chapter 5.

For deployment of Windows applications and Web applications, look up Book 7, Chapter 4 and Book 7, Chapter 5, respectively.

Chapter 3: Securing Web Services

In This Chapter

- Restricting access to a Web service
- Managing the Web service directory

A Web service is an ASP.NET application that's deployed over Internet Information Server (IIS). The security concepts and procedures that we discuss in Book 6, Chapter 16 for securing Web applications hold true for securing Web services as well. We therefore recommend that you read that chapter before reading this one because, by doing so, you'll be able to consolidate your learning about Web services and Web application security.

Some security considerations hold special importance for Web services, such as access permissions on files and folders and configuration settings of IIS. Therefore, in this chapter, we show you how to configure an IIS Web server for securing a Web service.

The concepts that we discuss in this chapter pertain only to security mechanisms implemented on the IIS Web server. ASP.NET offers various security mechanisms, such as forms authentication and Passport authentication. We deal with these concepts in detail in Book 6, Chapter 16.

Broadly, you can use IIS to secure a Web service in two ways:

- By restricting access to the Web service itself
- By preventing users from modifying or deleting content of the Web service folder

In this chapter, we discuss how you can implement both these security aspects in a Web service.

Restricting Access to a Web Service

You can limit access of your Web service to a group of users or to specific IP addresses by using IIS. You can also configure the authentication mode for your Web service. An *authentication mode* is the type of data source used to authenticate users on your Web site. In this section, we discuss how to implement different authentication modes and grant access to a specific IP address only. Before doing that, however, we examine where your Web services are installed in IIS.

Web services in IIS

When you create a Web service in Visual Basic .NET or Visual C#, Visual Studio .NET automatically creates an IIS virtual directory for your Web service. However, when you create a Web service in Visual C++ .NET, a virtual directory is created only when you run your Web service. In both cases, by default, the virtual directory is created on the default Web site. To help you understand the default Web sites better, go to IIS Service Manager by following these steps:

1. **Choose Start⇨Settings⇨Control Panel.**
2. **Select Administrative Tools from the Control Panel window that appears.**
3. **In Administrative Tools, double-click Internet Services Manager.**
4. **In the Internet Information Services window that appears, click the plus sign next to your computer's name.**

   The Internet Information Services window, after opening the first node, is shown in Figure 3-1.

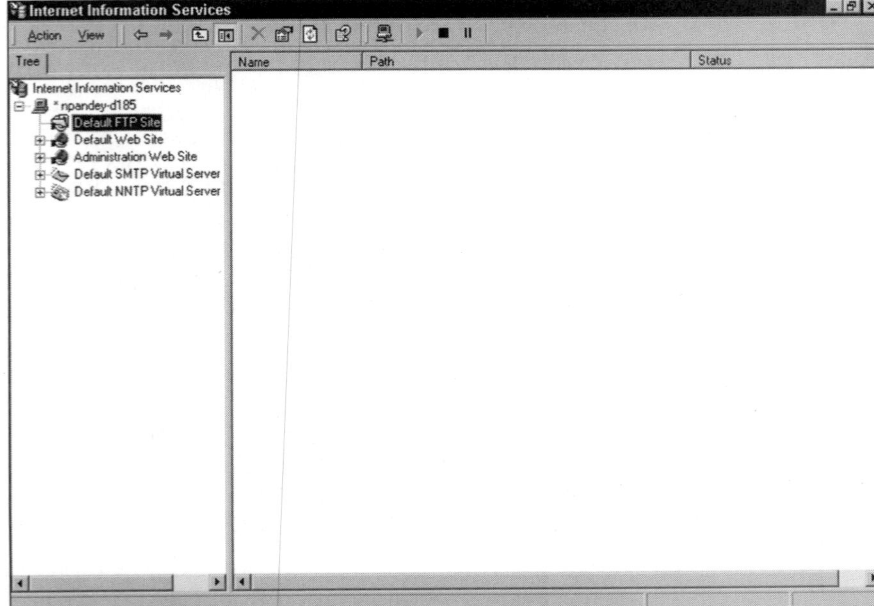

Figure 3-1: Configure your Web applications and services in IIS.

5. **Click the plus sign next to the Default Web Site option.**

   A list of Web applications and Web services that you've created on your computer appear in the Default Web Site section of the Web service, as shown in Figure 3-2.

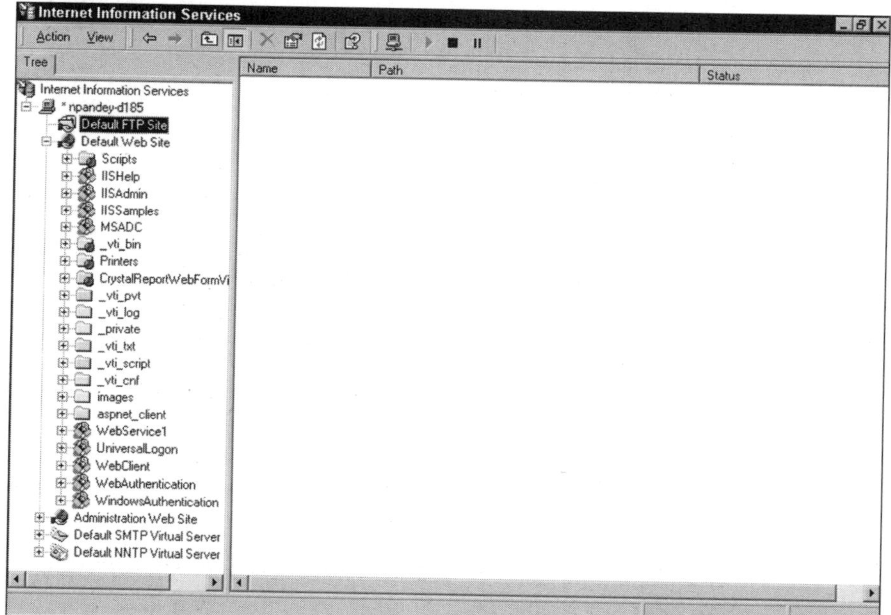

Figure 3-2: All Web applications and services that you've created on the local computer appear in the Default Web Site section of IIS.

In Figure 3-2, notice the default Web site section of IIS. Every computer that has IIS 5.0 installed on it has a default Web site. By default, the address of this Web site is `http://` followed by your computer name. Thus, if your computer is named Suzan, the address of the computer is `http://Suzan`. The default Web site hosts all Web applications and Web services on your computer. Therefore, if you've hosted the UniversalLogon Web service on the computer Suzan, the address of the Web service is `http://Suzan/UniversalLogon`.

By using the Internet Information Services window, you can restrict access to your Web applications and Web services. You can specify these restrictions at the Web site level, or you can restrict access individually for each Web service. When you specify these restrictions at both levels, the settings that are more restrictive take precedence.

Hosting a Web site on the Internet

When you host a Web site on the Internet, you assign an IP address to your Web server and specify the Uniform Resource Locator (URL) of the Web site. For example, refer to Figure 3-2, where you can see that all Web services and applications are hosted on the default Web site. When on the default Web site, these applications are accessible from the local intranet.

To host applications on the Internet, you acquire a domain name and assign the domain name to the default Web site. So that you're able to independently configure and manage each Web application, we recommend that you create different Web sites for different applications. Thus, instead of using two Web applications — `www.mywebsite.com/retail` and `www.mywebsite.com/business` — on the same site, you can use two totally different Web sites — `www.myretailwebsite.com` and `www.mybusinesswebsite.com` — and manage them independently.

Restricting anonymous access

You might want to provide access to your Web service only to select Web service clients. For example, if you've created a Web service for your organization, only computers that belong to your organization should be able to access the Web service. In this circumstance, you need to restrict anonymous access to your Web site.

Restrict anonymous access to your Web server by using Internet Information Services. To begin, open the Internet Information Services window; see the steps in the preceding section. Then, to restrict anonymous access to your Web service, follow these steps:

1. **Right-click the Web service to which you want to restrict access and select Properties.**

   For example, to configure the UniversalLogon Web service, right-click UniversalLogon in the Internet Information Services window and select Properties. The UniversalLogon Properties dialog box appears.

2. **In the UniversalLogon Properties dialog box, click the Directory Security tab; see Figure 3-3.**

3. **To restrict anonymous access to the Web site, click Edit in the Anonymous Access and Authentication Control group box.**

   The Authentication Methods dialog box appears, as shown in Figure 3-4. By default, the Anonymous access option is selected, which enables users to log on anonymously.

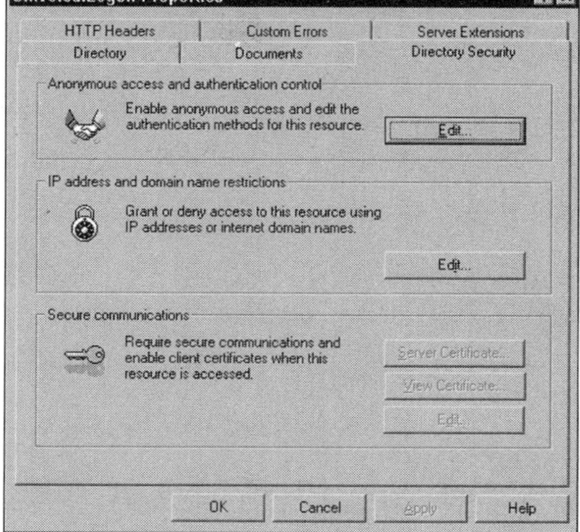

Figure 3-3: Use the Directory Security tab to restrict access to your Web service.

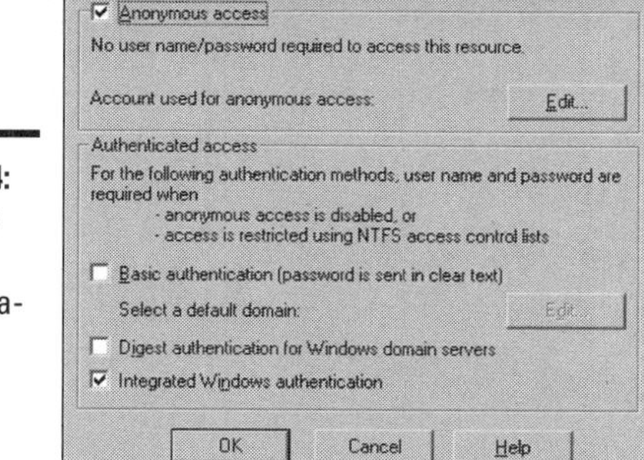

Figure 3-4: Configure user authentication for a Web service.

If you click the Edit button in the Anonymous Access group box and view the Anonymous User Account dialog box, you'll notice a username IUSR_*machinename* listed for anonymous access to the Web site. (In IUSR_*machinename*, *machinename* is the name of the computer on which you're viewing IIS configuration.) This account is used by IIS to send requests on behalf of the anonymous user. Thus, IIS acts on behalf of the user to retrieve content from the Web service. Such a process is referred to as *impersonation*.

4. **To disable anonymous access on the Web site, clear the Anonymous Access option.**

   Anonymous access to your Web site is disabled.

5. **Click OK to close the Authentication Methods dialog box, and then click OK again to close the UniversalLogon Properties dialog box.**

IIS provides three types of authentication mechanisms: Basic authentication, Digest authentication, and Integrated Windows authentication. These can also be configured from the Authentication Methods dialog box (refer to Figure 3-4). For a detailed description of these authentication mechanisms, take a look at Book 6, Chapter 16.

Granting access to IP addresses

When you implement a Web service on your corporate network, you might have some predefined computers that need to access the Web service. To ensure that only specific computers are able to access your Web service, you can grant access to those computers by using their IP addresses and restricting access to all other computers. To grant access to specific computers only, follow these steps:

1. **Open Internet Information Services.**

   For the steps to do so, refer to the "Web services in IIS" section earlier in this chapter.

2. **Right-click the Web service for which you want to grant access to specific computers and select Properties from the shortcut menu.**

   The Web Service Properties dialog box appears.

3. **Click the Directory Security tab; see Figure 3-5.**

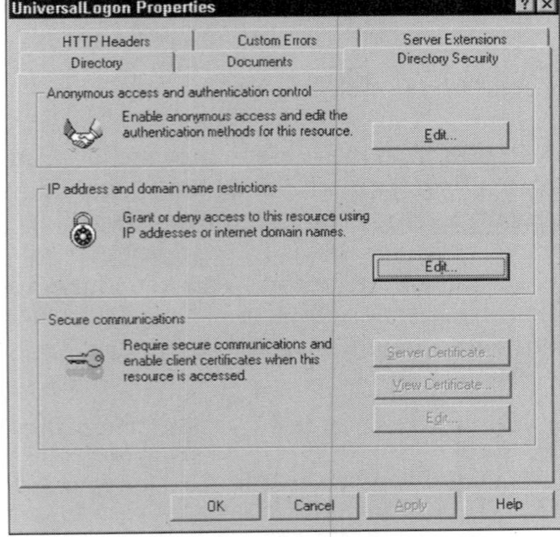

Figure 3-5: The Directory Security tab of the Universal-Logon Properties dialog box.

4. **Click Edit in the IP Address and Domain Name Restrictions group box.**

   The IP Address and Domain Name Restrictions dialog box appears, shown in Figure 3-6, where you can specify the IP addresses of computers that you'll allow to access the Web service.

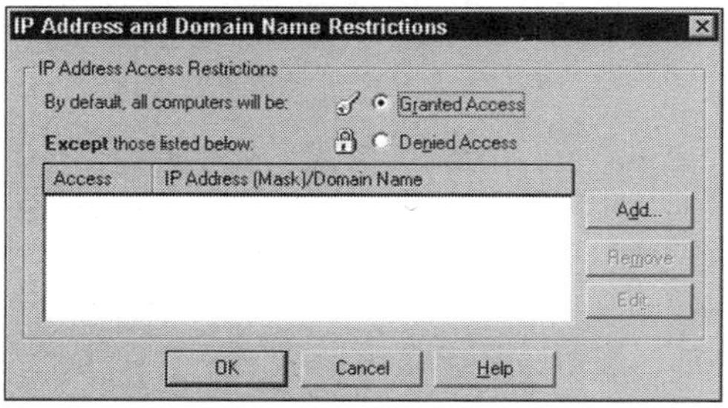

Figure 3-6: Restrict access to your Web service.

5. **Select the Denied Access option to deny access to all computers except those that you specify in the Except Those Listed Below list.**
6. **Click Add to add an IP address to the list of computers to which you want to grant access.**
7. **In the Grant Access On dialog box that appears, specify the IP address of the computer to which you want to grant access, and then click OK.**

   The IP address of the computer that you selected in the Grant Access On list appears in the Except Those Listed Below list, as shown in Figure 3-7.

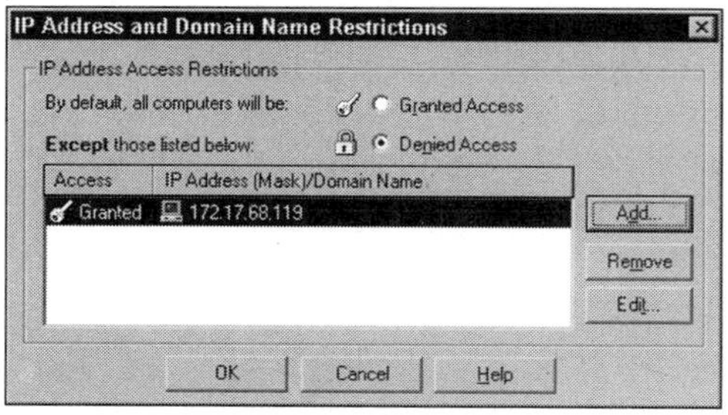

Figure 3-7: The list of computers to which you've granted access.

8. **Click OK to close the IP Address and Domain Name Restrictions dialog box, and click OK again to close the Web Service Properties dialog box.**

Computers other than the computer that you added in the Grant Access On list are denied access to the Web service. If computers to which access is denied try to access the Web service, the You Are Not Authorized to View This Page window appears, as shown in Figure 3-8.

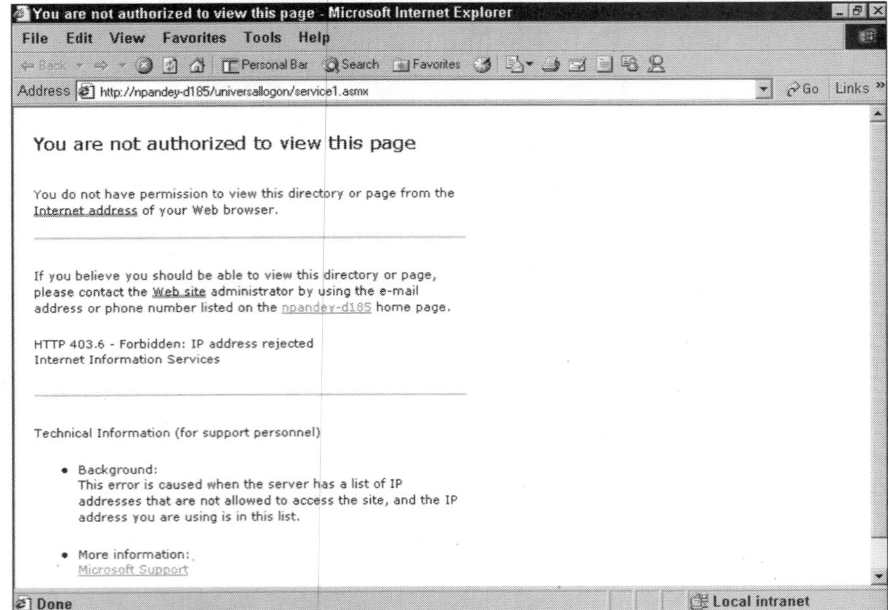

Figure 3-8: Computers to which you deny access receive this message.

Managing the Web Service Directory

To prevent unauthorized users from uploading harmful content into the Web site directory, you can secure the Web service directory. Restricting users from executing files on your computer is also possible. In this section, we detail the steps to enforce such restrictions, and we also look at the steps necessary to redirect a user to another Web site.

Securing the Web service directory

You configure the Web service by using the Internet Information Services window (see "Web services in IIS" earlier in this chapter). Then, to secure your Web service directory, follow these steps:

1. **Right-click the Web service that you want to configure and select Properties from the shortcut menu.**

2. **On the Directory tab of the Web Service properties dialog box that appears, specify the rights to the Web site directory in the options listed below the Local path list.**

   Select from the following list of options:

   - **Script source access:** Allows users to access the source code of ASP.NET applications.
   - **Read:** Default selection; allows users to read and download files from the root directory of your Web service.
   - **Write:** Allows users to upload files to the root directory of your Web service.
   - **Directory browsing:** Allows users to list files and subdirectories in the directory of your Web service.
   - **Log visits:** Default selection; logs details about the users who visit your Web site. By default, all Web server logs are stored in the `C:\winnt\system32\LogFiles` folder.
   - **Index this resource:** Default selection; Microsoft Indexing Service can create an index of the Web site. Select the Index This Resource option to include the Web service directory in the index created by the Microsoft Indexing Service.

3. **Click OK to close the Web Service Properties dialog box.**

After you select one or more of the options that we describe in the preceding list, the permissions corresponding to the selected options are applied to your Web site.

Redirecting users to another URL

Often, because of changing business requirements, such as the addition of a new Web service or reconfiguration of a Web service, you might need to change the virtual directory of a Web service. When you do so, you might assign another location to your Web service.

If you relocate your Web service to another location, you might want to redirect users visiting the original site to the new site. IIS makes it simple for you to redirect users to another site. To redirect the user to another site, follow these steps:

1. **Open Internet Information Services.**
2. **Right-click the Web service from which you want to redirect a user and properties.**

3. **On the Directory tab of the Web Service Properties dialog box that appears, select the A Redirection to a URL option.**

   The Redirect to text box gets enabled.

4. **In the Redirect to text box, specify the address to which you want to redirect the user.**

5. **Click Apply, and then click OK to save the changes and close the Web Service Properties dialog box.**

Any requests to your Web service are now automatically directed to the new address that you've specified in the preceding steps.

Chapter 4: Deploying Windows Applications

In This Chapter

- Discovering deployment basics
- Creating a deployment application
- Adding files to a deployment project
- Tweaking and testing your deployment project

Any application that you create in Visual Studio .NET isn't necessarily confined to the computer on which you create it. You often distribute your application as an installation (or deployment) program that users can run to install your application. Installation programs create a folder structure on the end user's computer and then make some modifications to the registry so that the application runs successfully. In Visual Studio .NET applications, the installation program also makes the common language runtime (CLR) files available for successful execution of an application.

To ensure that all prerequisites for running your application are fulfilled and your application loads successfully, you create an installation program. In this chapter, we show you how to deploy Windows applications by using an installation program. We also walk you through fine-tuning and testing your deployment applications.

Discovering the Basics of Deployment

You can create an installation program for your application by using a deployment project, which is similar to other projects in Visual Studio .NET. In this section, we explore the types of installation programs that you can create for your project and the location where you can deploy the installation program files.

Types of installation programs

Depending on your deployment needs, you can create the following three types of installation programs for your application:

- **Microsoft Windows Installer files**
- **Merge modules**
- **Cabinet files**

Read through the next three sections to see which best fits your situation.

Microsoft Windows Installer files

Microsoft Windows Installer files, also called MSI (Microsoft Installer) files, enable you to install applications by using the Microsoft Installer service. The Microsoft Installer service was introduced with Microsoft Windows 2000.

To optimize project deployment, Microsoft introduced this service that enables you to reinstall application files that you may have accidentally deleted — *without* adversely affecting the application. Common examples of Microsoft products that are installed by using the Microsoft Installer service are Microsoft Office 2000 and Microsoft Commerce Server 2000. In Microsoft Office 2000, you may have noticed a Windows Installer dialog box that pops up every time that you attempt to use a feature that's not available. (See Figure 4-1.) It pops up because the files required to use the required feature aren't present. Windows Installer restores the missing application files and enables you to use the feature.

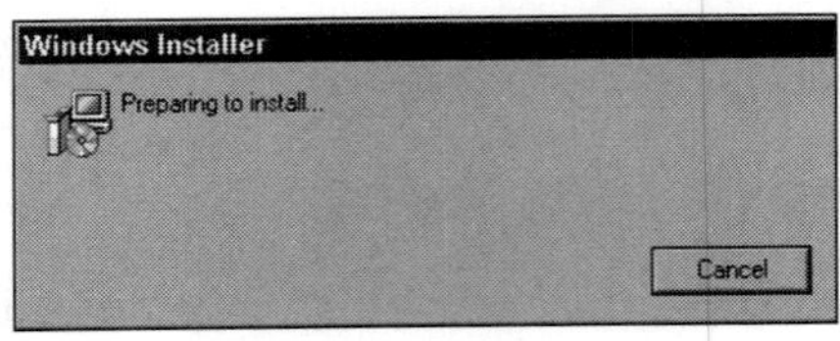

Figure 4-1: The Windows Installer service restores missing files.

When you compile a deployment project for a Windows application, Visual Studio .NET creates an MSI file, which also includes the .NET runtime files required to run your application.

To create the most elementary installation program, you need to simply add the project output to the deployment project and compile the project to create the MSI file. We describe this procedure in the upcoming "Adding Files to a Deployment Project" section.

Merge modules

You create merge modules for packaging components that need to be shared across applications. For example, consider that you have a set of dynamic link library (DLL) files that are to be used in three applications. Instead of adding the DLL files in the deployment project for all three applications, you can create a merge module for the DLL files and then add that merge module to the deployment project for the three applications.

Cabinet files

A cabinet (CAB) file can be used to package ActiveX controls that a user can download and install from a Web site. Visual Studio .NET provides basic support for creating a CAB file by enabling you to do the following:

- **Create a CAB file deployment project:** You can add a CAB file deployment project to your application by using the Cab Project template. (Refer to Book 7, Chapter 6 for details.)
- **Implement Authenticode signing:** You can sign an ActiveX control to establish its authenticity. Authenticode signing is also referred to as *digitally signing* a control. When an ActiveX control is signed, a user can determine its source and verify that the control has not been tampered with.

  If you don't digitally sign an ActiveX control, users may not be able to download it if their browser settings don't permit the download of unsigned ActiveX controls.

- **Define compression levels:** A CAB file compresses the data stored in it, and you can specify the compression levels for a CAB file. As a general rule, with an increase in file compression, file creation takes longer but file download is quicker.

Mad about merge modules

Merge modules provide an important benefit by enabling you to add components to a deployment project. The MSI file, which is generated by compiling the deployment project to which the merge module is added, stores information about the version of the module. When you install the application, the information related to the version is added to a Windows Installer database. This database ensures that when a component is used by multiple applications and you uninstall one of the applications, the component is not uninstalled.

Storage of installation programs

Depending on your deployment needs, you can store installation programs for your application at the following locations:

- **Shared folders:** When you store an installation program in shared folders on a network, other users can access the program and install your application. This method is usually employed for distributing applications within a corporate organization where user computers are connected over a network.
- **Installation media:** This method is commonly employed to distribute your application by using storage media, such as CD-ROMs, Digital Versatile Disks (DVD-ROMs), and floppy disks.
- **Web sites:** You can also host the installation program of your application on a Web site from where users can access and download it.

Creating a Deployment Project

The first step to deploy an application is to create a deployment project. Next, you add this project to another existing project to be deployed. You can simultaneously create and add a deployment project to an existing project.

1. **Open the project for which you want to create an installation program.**

   You can download sample applications from `www.dummies.com/extras/VS.NETAllinOne` and use them to practice the steps listed here. Preferably, use an application that involves the use of .NET runtime files, such as the Visual C# Windows1 application.

2. **Choose File⇨Add Project⇨New Project to add a new project to the existing project.**

   The Add New Project dialog box appears.

3. **In the Add New Project dialog box, select Setup and Deployment Projects in the Project Types list.**

   The project templates available for creating a deployment project appear in the Templates section of the Add New Project dialog box as shown in Figure 4-2.

4. **Click the Setup Project template icon in the Templates list.**

   A Setup Project template creates an MSI file for deploying a Windows application.

5. **Enter** MySetup **in the Name text box as the name of the project and then click OK.**

   A new deployment project is added to your project.

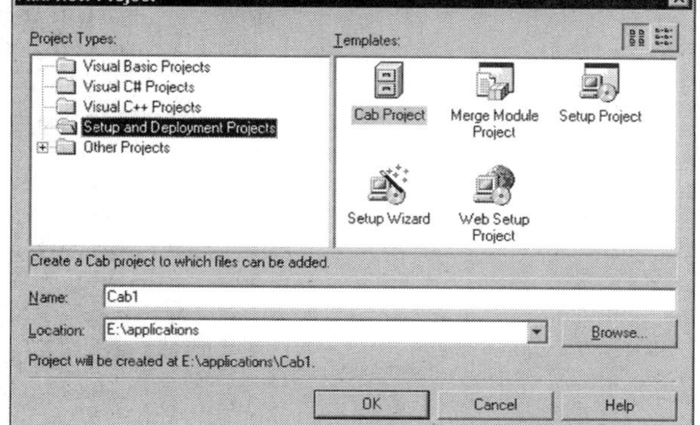

Figure 4-2: Choose deployment project templates here.

A deployment project comprises a number of editors. When you add a new deployment project to your solution, Visual Studio .NET opens the File System editor by default. The File System editor is shown in Figure 4-3.

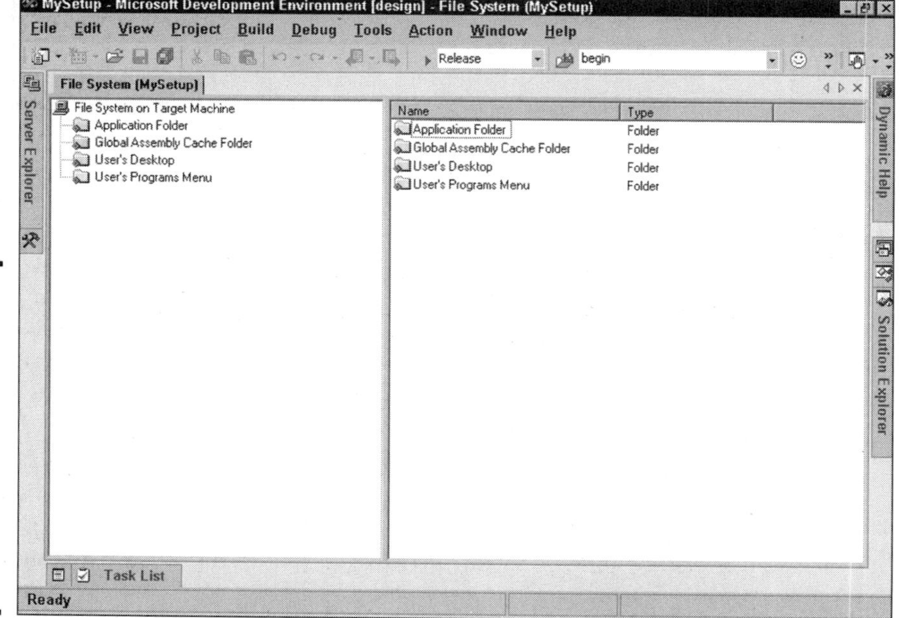

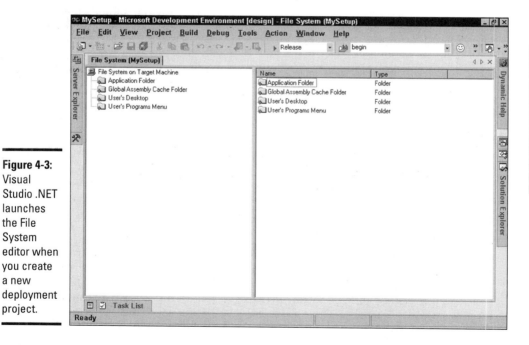

Figure 4-3: Visual Studio .NET launches the File System editor when you create a new deployment project.

In addition to the File System editor, Visual Studio .NET includes five other editors that come in handy for creating deployment projects: File System, Registry, File Types, User Interface, and Custom Actions.

File System editor

You use the File System editor to design the folder structure of your application as it should appear on a user computer. You also use this editor to add the final output of an application to your project and to create shortcuts to the output file. You can read how to use this editor in the upcoming section "Adding Files to a Deployment Project."

Registry editor

In case of an application, you often need to add data to the system registry. For example, you may want to store the name of a registered user or the version of an application in the system registry.

The *system registry* is a complex structure that consists of a number of nodes and subnodes. The Registry editor displays the nodes and subnodes of the registry in a hierarchy. This simplifies your task of specifying a subnode where information specific to your application should be added.

File Types editor

To associate file extensions with your application, you use the File Types editor. After you associate a file type with your application, your application launches each time that a user opens the file. For example, the `.txt` file extension is associated with Notepad.

User Interface editor

Most installation programs have a user interface that enables you to select a destination directory and specify user information before an application is installed. The Setup project template provides a set of standard screens that you can add to a deployment project. These screens are displayed sequentially when a user runs the installation program generated by the deployment project. You can read more about the User Interface editor in the "Fine-Tuning a Deployment Project" section later in this chapter.

Custom Actions editor

You may want to configure an application after installing it on a user computer. For example, you may need to create a database by running Structured Query Language (SQL) scripts or register a set of DLL files after your application is installed. Such tasks that aren't a part of the standard setup process but are essential for the functioning of your application are *custom actions*.

You can create custom actions in batch files or DLL files. Then you can include the files into your deployment project by using the Custom Actions editor. When you include custom actions in your deployment project, these actions are executed as soon as a user installs your application.

Launch Conditions editor

The Launch Conditions editor is used to check a user's computer for software or hardware that's required to install your application. For example, a user should be able to install a Web service only if the user has IIS 5.0 installed on the computer. Similarly, you can use the editor to check the destination computer for .NET runtime files that are required for Visual Studio .NET applications, if you're not packaging these files with your application. You also use this editor to verify hardware configuration, such as the Random Access Memory (RAM) on the destination computer.

To check the destination computer for the prerequisite software, you can add launch conditions to the deployment project by using the Launch Conditions editor. You can read about using this editor in Book 7, Chapter 5.

Adding Files to a Deployment Project

After you add a deployment project to your application, you need to add the output of your application to the deployment project. Next, you need to specify the location of application shortcuts to make your application easily accessible by users.

In the forthcoming sections, we cover all this and more. After going through this section, you should be able to configure the template-generated deployment project to deploy your application successfully.

Adding application output

The output of a Windows application is the executable file that's used to run the application. When you add the executable file of your application to a deployment project, Visual Studio .NET automatically determines the dependencies for your project and adds the required assemblies and DLL files to your application. For example, if you're creating an application that uses the Microsoft Word 9.0 object library, you don't need to explicitly locate and add the MSO9.DLL file to your project. Visual Studio .NET performs these tasks for you when you add the executable file of your application to the deployment project.

To add your application's output to the deployment project, follow these steps:

1. **Choose Project⇨Add⇨Project Output.**

   The Add Project Output Group dialog box appears as shown in Figure 4-4.

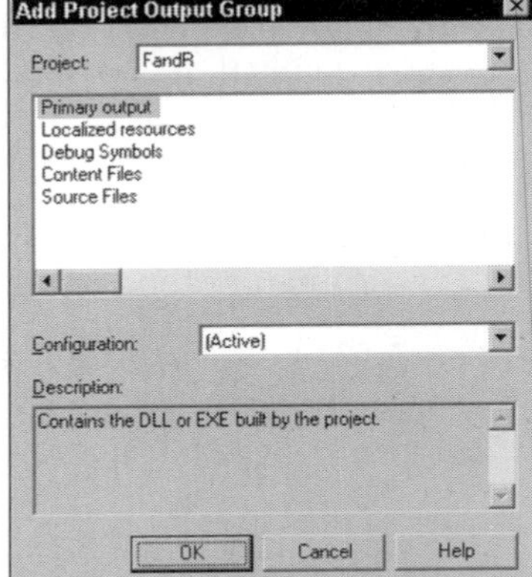

Figure 4-4: Select project output to add to the deployment project.

2. **In the Add Project Output Group dialog box, retain the default options for all settings and click OK.**

   The default options denote that you're adding the primary output of your application to the deployment project.

   When you click OK, the Add Project Output dialog box closes and you return to the File System editor.

3. **Double-click the Application Folder in the File System on Target Machine node.**

   The contents of the Application Folder are displayed in the right pane of the File System editor.

The Application Folder in the File System on Target Machine node represents the folder for your application on a user computer. In fact, all folders in the File System on Target Machine node represent the folders on a user computer. Therefore, if you need to store any shortcuts on the desktop of a user computer where your application is installed, store the shortcuts in the User's Desktop folder. The installation program will ensure that the required shortcuts are stored on the user's computer desktop when the user installs your application.

Look at the contents of Application Folder and note that the runtime files required by your project are automatically added to the folder. One of the files added to Application Folder is the primary output of your application. You can create shortcuts to this file so that the user doesn't have to access Application Folder to execute the application.

Adding shortcuts to user folders

To enable end users to access your application conveniently, include shortcuts to the primary output of your application on the user's computer desktop or in the Programs menu. To add these shortcuts, follow these steps:

1. **View the contents of the Application Folder in the File System editor (choose View⇨Editor⇨File System to open the File System editor).**
2. **Right-click the file for the primary output of your application and then select the Create Shortcut to the *<file name>* menu option (where *<file name>* is the name of the file for the primary output).**

   In the case of our example application, the name of the project file is `FandR`. Therefore, you right-click Primary Output from FandR (Active) and then select the Create Shortcut to Primary Output from FandR (Active) menu option, as shown in Figure 4-5.

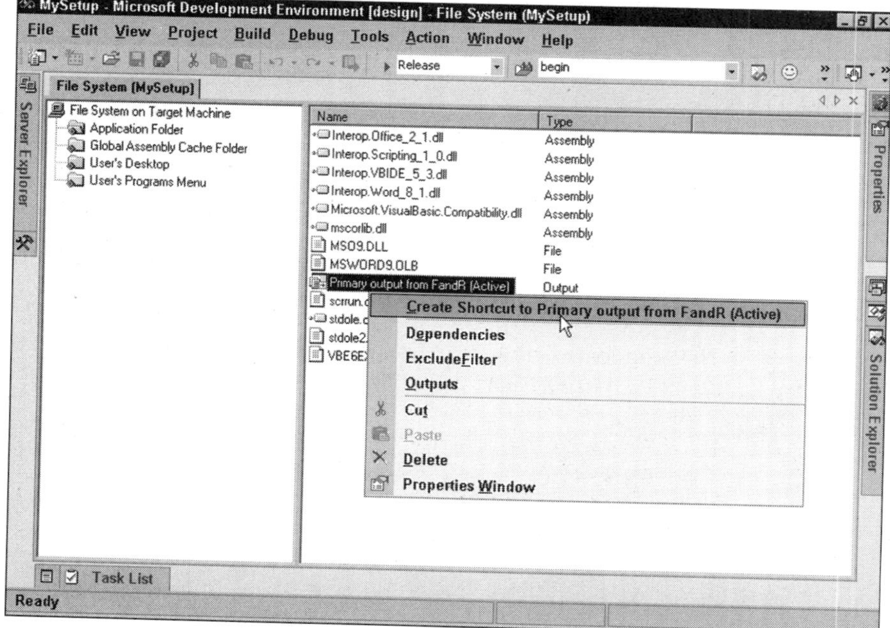

Figure 4-5: Add a shortcut to a file in the deployment project.

A shortcut appears below the file to which you want to add the shortcut. The name of the shortcut is highlighted so that you can change it.

3. **Type a name for the shortcut.**

When you create the new shortcut, the name of the shortcut is highlighted by default. You can change the name of the shortcut so that it helps end users identify your application. For example, our application relates to finding and replacing text, so we name the shortcut *FindAndReplace*.

4. **Drag the shortcut to the User's Desktop folder in the File System on Target Machine node.**

The shortcut is stored on a user's computer desktop when the user installs your application.

Just like you can create a shortcut to the user's computer desktop, you can also create a shortcut to the user's program menu. As shown in Figure 4-6, we add the FindAndReplace folder to the User's Program Menu folder and then add the shortcut to this subfolder.

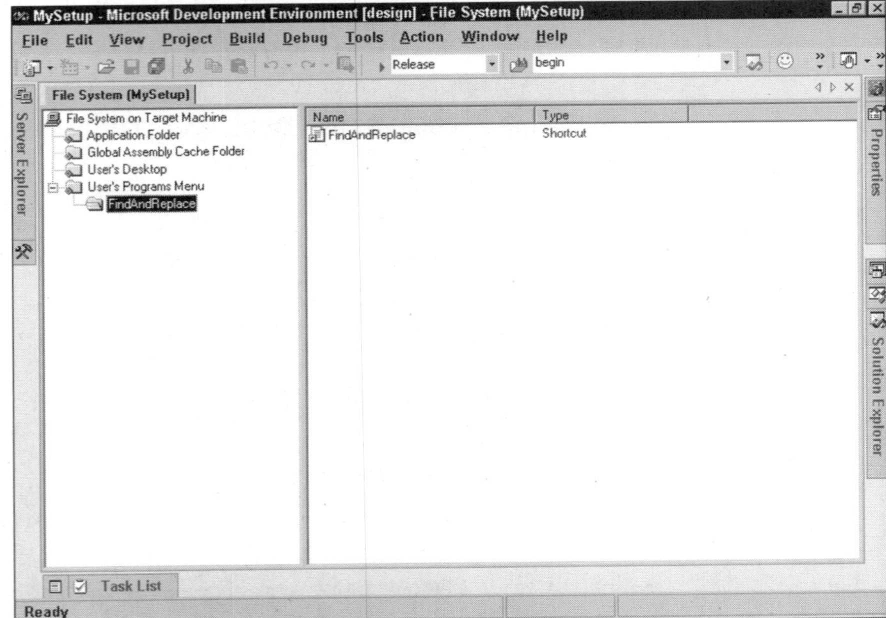

Figure 4-6: Add a subfolder to the User's Program Menu folder and then add your shortcut.

Fine-Tuning a Deployment Project

In earlier sections of this chapter, we describe the bare minimum that you need to perform for deploying your application. However, we recommend that you enhance your deployment projects by adding icons for your application and by optimizing project performance. In this section, we show you how to add icons for your application and change deployment project properties to ensure that users without the latest version of Windows Installer can also install your application. Finally, we take a look at adding screens to the deployment project to optimize it for our application.

Adding icons to your application

Shortcuts to the primary output of your application are represented as standard Windows executable file icons. Imagine the plight of a user who has to routinely use these generic, hard-to-identify icons to launch your application. Instead, use an icon that describes your application. In the following steps, we change the icons for our sample application's shortcuts to things that a user might relate the application to:

1. **Select Application Folder from the File System editor.**
2. **Choose Project⇨Add⇨File.**

   The Add Files dialog box appears.
3. **Navigate to the location of the icon file and click Open.**

   The icon is added to your deployment project.

   An icon file has `.ico` as its file extension.
4. **Right-click an application shortcut and select Properties Window from the shortcut menu that appears.**

   (To perform this step, you can use the shortcut that we create in the previous section, "Adding shortcuts to user folders.")
5. **In the Properties window, select the (Browse) option from the Icon list.**

   The Icon dialog box appears. (See Figure 4-7.)
6. **Click the Browse button to navigate to the location where the icon for your project is stored.**

   The Select Item in Project dialog box appears. Recall that you've already added the icon to Application Folder (Step 3).

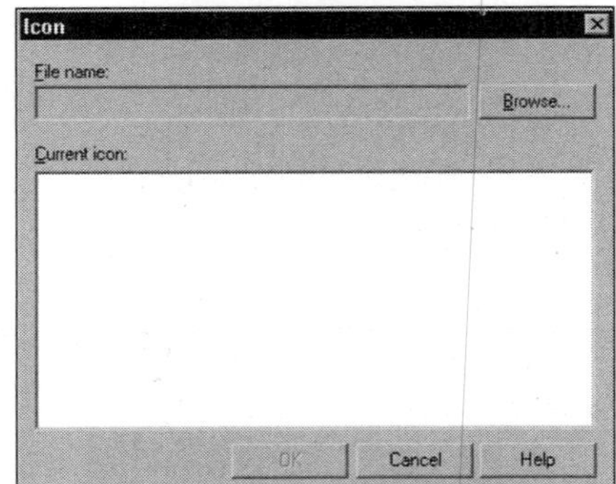

Figure 4-7: Browse to the location of your project's icon.

7. **In the Select Item in Project dialog box, double-click Application Folder.**

   The name of the icon appears in Application Folder.

8. **Click OK to move the selected icon to the Icon dialog box.**

   The icon that you selected in Step 8 appears in the Current Icon list of the Icon dialog box.

9. **Click OK to close the Icon dialog box and assign the icon to the shortcut for your application.**

Repeat Steps 1–9 to add icons to all your application shortcuts.

Adding screens to the user interface

The Setup Project template provides a set of standard screens for creating a set-up project. In addition to the default screens, you can add your screens so that the installation procedure is customized according to your application. For example, your company policy may make it mandatory to include a license agreement screen for your application.

Visual Studio .NET provides a predefined template with which you can add a license agreement screen to your application. To add this screen to your deployment project, you need to use the User Interface editor. To open this editor, choose View➪Editor➪User Interface.

The User Interface editor is shown in Figure 4-8. Notice the two types of installations: Install and Administrative Install.

The Install installation type is used for installing an application to the local computer. The Administrative Install installation type is used by system administrators to install an application on a network. After a system administrator installs the application on the network, users can install the application from the network. This saves users from using the application package every time they need to install the application.

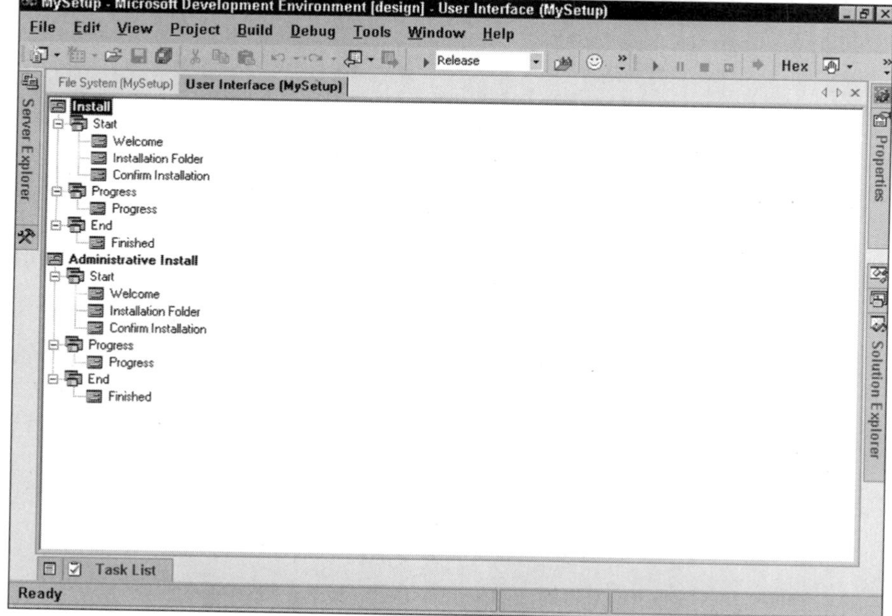

Figure 4-8: Use the User Interface editor to add screens to your deployment project.

In a deployment project, some screens are associated with specific stages of deployment. For example, it's absurd to arrange for the Installation Folder screen to appear after the Progress screen. To avoid such lapses, Visual Studio .NET allows you to add only selected screens for each stage of deployment. The scheme that Visual Studio .NET follows is

- **Start stage:** In the Start stage, you can add the Splash, Welcome, License Agreement, RadioButtons, Checkboxes, Textboxes, Installation Folder, and Confirm Installation screens. We recommend that you add the required screens in the order listed here.
- **Progress stage:** In the Progress stage, when your application is being installed and there is no user interaction, you can add only the Progress screen.
- **End stage:** In the End stage, you can add only the Register User and Finished screens.

In our running example, add the License Agreement screen to your project. Before adding this screen, you need to include the license agreement file into your project. You can do this just like you include an icon in your application. The only difference is that here you import the rich text format (RTF) file with the license agreement. Refer to "Adding icons to your application" to find out more about adding files to your application.

After you add the license agreement file to your application, follow these steps to add the License Agreement screen to your application:

1. **Click the Start stage in the User Interface editor (choose View➪Editor➪User Interface).**

   The Action menu appears in the menu bar.

2. **Choose Action➪Add Dialog.**

   The Add Dialog dialog box appears.

3. **In the Add Dialog dialog box, select License Agreement and then click OK.**

   The License Agreement screen appears at the end of the Start stage of the Install installation type in the User Interface editor. The License Agreement screen conventionally appears after the Welcome screen so that the user can exit from the installation program if the user chooses not to install your application.

4. **Move the License Agreement screen to the Welcome screen.**

   The License Agreement screen is positioned below the Welcome screen. Now you need to associate the License Agreement screen with the text file that you import for the license agreement.

5. **Right-click the License Agreement screen and then select Properties Window from the shortcut menu that appears.**

   The Properties window appears.

6. **Select the (Browse) option in the LicenseFile list.**

   The Select Item in Project dialog box appears, as shown in Figure 4-9.

7. **If you use a text file as the file for the license agreement, select All Files (*.*) from the Files of Type list and then double-click Application Folder.**

8. **Select the license agreement file from Application Folder and then click OK.**

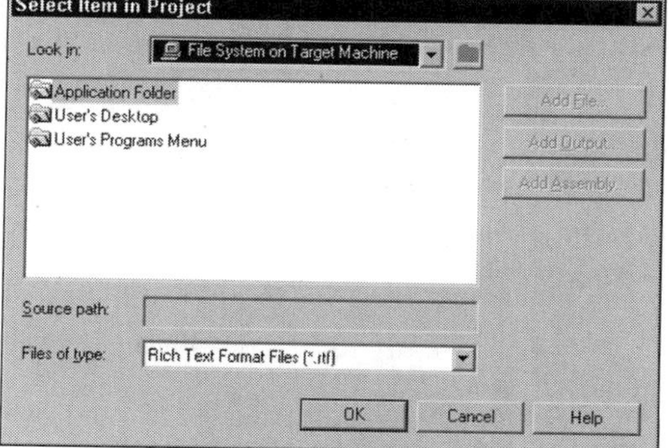

Figure 4-9: Select the location of the license agreement file here.

The license agreement is now included in the Start stage of the installation program. Repeat Steps 1–8 to include the license agreement in Administrative Install as well, so that the license agreement is displayed in both the Install as well as the Administrative Install installation type.

Adding the Windows Installer bootstrapper

Assume that you develop your application using the latest technology, which may be different from the technology installed on the computers of your end users. For example, Windows Installer 1.5 won't install on end user computers with a version of Windows earlier than Windows XP. Therefore, if you're techno-current, users can't run the installation program — and in turn, your application. Not good.

To enable users with earlier versions of Windows to install your application, you should include the latest version of Windows Installer with your application. You do this by including the Windows Installer bootstrapper with your application by changing the project properties. To include the Windows Installer bootstrapper:

1. **Open Solution Explorer by choosing View⇨Solution Explorer.**
2. **Right-click the name of the deployment project and then select Properties.**

   For example, if you specify the name of the project as MySetup, right-click MySetup and then select Properties.
3. **The MySetup Property Pages dialog box appears (assuming that MySetup is the name of your project).**

4. **To include the Windows Installer bootstrapper, select the Windows Installer Bootstrapper option from the Bootstrapper list, as shown in Figure 4-10.**

   The Windows Installer bootstrapper, required to install Windows Installer 1.5 on a computer, is added to your project.

5. **Click the Apply button and then click OK to close the MySetup Property Pages dialog box.**

Your deployment project is now ready to be compiled.

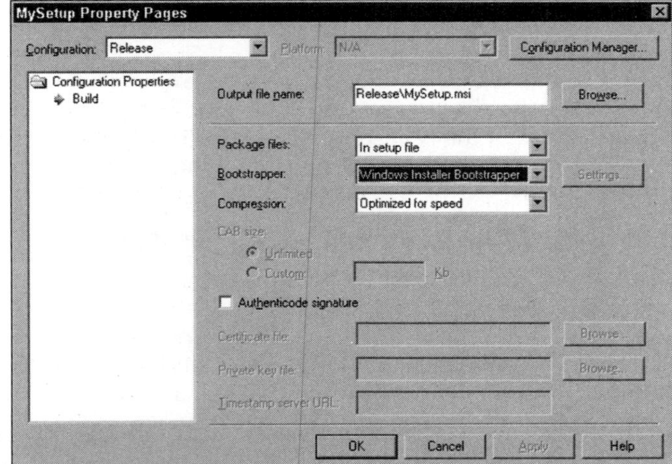

Figure 4-10: Specify properties in the MySetup Property Pages dialog box.

Testing the Deployment Project

In the final stages of creating a deployment project, you compile your application and the deployment project to create the MSI installation file. After creating the MSI file, you test it by deploying your application on a test platform. In this section, we describe the procedure for compiling and testing your deployment project.

Compiling the application

All through the development stage, you develop your application in the Debug configuration. After you finalize your application, you should compile it in the Release configuration and then create an installation program. The Release configuration ensures that your application is optimized for speed and performance. Read more about the Debug and Release configurations in Book 4, Chapter 8.

To compile your application in the Release configuration:

1. **Choose Build⇨Configuration Manager.**

   The Configuration Manager dialog box appears.
2. **Select Release from the Active Solution Configuration list.**
3. **Click the Close button to close the Configuration Manager dialog box.**
4. **Choose Build⇨Build Solution.**

   The Visual Studio .NET compiler creates the MSI file for your application. You can access the file from the Release subfolder in the deployment project's folder.

Installing the application

To ensure that your application has been packaged correctly, install the application on a test computer by performing the following steps:

1. **Double-click the MSI file to start the installation program.**

   The Welcome screen appears.
2. **Click the Next button to continue.**

   The License Agreement screen appears.
3. **Select the I Agree option to accept the license agreement and then click the Next button.**

   The Select Installation Folder screen appears.
4. **To install your application in the Default folder, click the Next button.**

   The Confirm Installation screen appears.
5. **Click the Next button to install your application.**

   The Progress screen appears. When your application is installed, the installation program moves to the next screen — the Installation Complete screen.
6. **Click the Close button to complete the installation of your application.**

After you successfully test your application, you're ready to distribute it.

Chapter 5: Deploying Web Applications

In This Chapter

- **Creating and customizing a deployment project**
- **Testing your installation program**

Visual Studio .NET provides the Web Setup Project template for deploying Web applications. When you create an installation program by using this template, the set-up program first ensures that the software required for installing a Web application is available, and then it installs the Web application.

In this chapter, we show you how to deploy Web applications by using the Web Setup Project template. Then we walk you through testing your program.

Creating a Deployment Project

The fundamental steps to create a deployment project are

1. **Add a deployment project to your application.**
2. **Add the primary output of your application to the deployment project.**
3. **Customize the deployment project to meet your application needs.**
4. **Compile the deployment project to create an installation program.**

Read this section for a detailed discussion of these steps.

Adding a deployment project

Use the Web Setup Project template to create Web applications. When you use this template to deploy your Web application, Visual Studio .NET generates a Microsoft Installer (MSI) file that can be used for installing the application on the end user's computer. Read more about MSI files in Book 7, Chapter 4.

Follow these steps to add a Web Setup Project template to your application:

1. **Open an existing Web application.**
2. **Choose File⇨Add Project⇨New Project.**

   The Add New Project dialog box appears.
3. **Click Setup and Deployment Projects in the Project Types list and then select Web Setup Project from the list of available templates, as shown in Figure 5-1.**

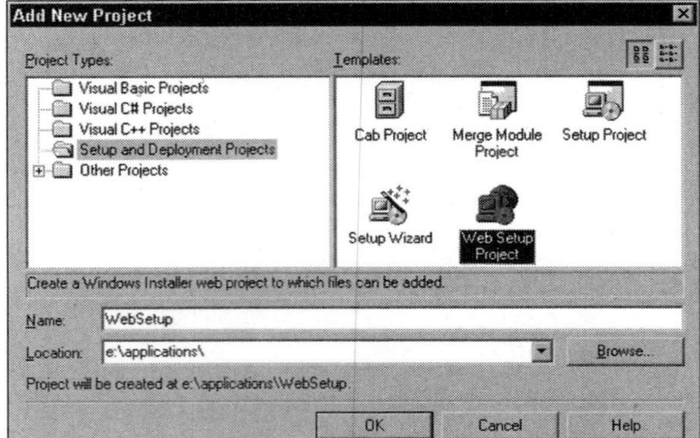

Figure 5-1: Select a Web Setup Project template in the Add New Project dialog box.

4. **In the Name text box, enter** WebSetup **as the name of the project and then click OK.**

   A new deployment project is added to your Web application.

Adding the application's primary output

After adding a deployment project to your application, you add the primary output of your application to the deployment project. You can do this by using the File System editor, which is launched by default when you add the deployment project to your Web application.

Visual Studio .NET provides six editors to simplify the deployment of applications: File System, Registry, File Types, User Interface, Custom Actions, and Launch Conditions. You can read about these editors in Book 7, Chapter 4.

Follow these steps to add the output of your application to the deployment project:

1. **Choose Project⇨Add⇨Project Output.**

   The Add Project Output Group dialog box appears, as shown in Figure 5-2.

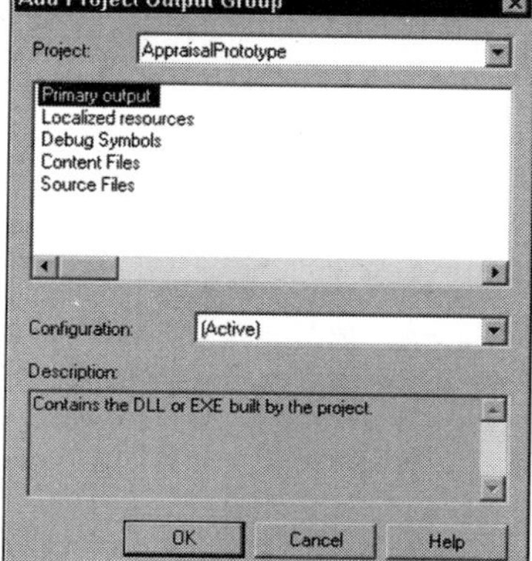

Figure 5-2: Add your program's primary output to the deployment project.

2. **Retain the default options in the Add Project Output Group dialog box and then click OK.**

   The primary output of your application is added to the application.

After adding the output of your application to the deployment project, you can view the contents of the Web Application Folder to confirm that the output was added successfully.

Access the Web Application Folder by double-clicking the Web Application Folder icon in the File System editor.

Customizing the deployment project

You can customize your deployment project to fit your application requirements. For example, if your application demands a minimum of 128MB RAM for successful execution, you may not want users to install your application if their computers don't have the required RAM. You can accomplish this and more by customizing your project with one or more deployment editors. In this section, we discuss common ways to customize a project.

Specifying a name for the virtual directory

Web applications are installed in virtual directories on the Internet Information Services (IIS) Web server. Your application has a default virtual directory name, which is the same as the name of your application. To change this name:

1. **Right-click Web Application Folder in the File System editor and select Properties Window from the shortcut menu.**

   The Properties window for the Web application folder appears.

   The File System editor is launched by default when you add the deployment project to your Web application.

2. **Change the `VirtualDirectory` property of the Web application folder to specify a name of your choice.**

   A user can always change the name of the virtual directory while installing your application. The name that you specify in the `VirtualDirectory` property is just a default name that appears when the user runs the installation.

Reducing the size of the installation program

The installation program that you create by using the deployment tools of Visual Studio .NET is typically 18–25MB in size. An application this size is often cumbersome to deploy because it's too large to copy to a floppy disk and it takes a long time to download over the Internet.

You can drastically reduce the size of your application by excluding the .NET runtime files. The only limitation of excluding runtime files is that your application can't be run on computers that don't have these runtime files already installed. However, as more and more users switch to .NET, this limitation dissipates. Here's how to compress your installation program by excluding the .NET runtime files:

1. **Open Solution Explorer by choosing View⇨Solution Explorer.**
2. **Locate the `dotnetfxredist_x86_enu.msm` file under the deployment project node.**

   The `dotnetfxredist_x86_enu.msm` file includes the .NET runtime files into your application. Excluding this file from your project enables you to compile your project without these runtime files.

3. **Right-click the `dotnetfxredist_x86_enu.msm` file and then select Exclude from the shortcut menu, as shown in Figure 5-3.**

   The runtime files are now excluded from your project.

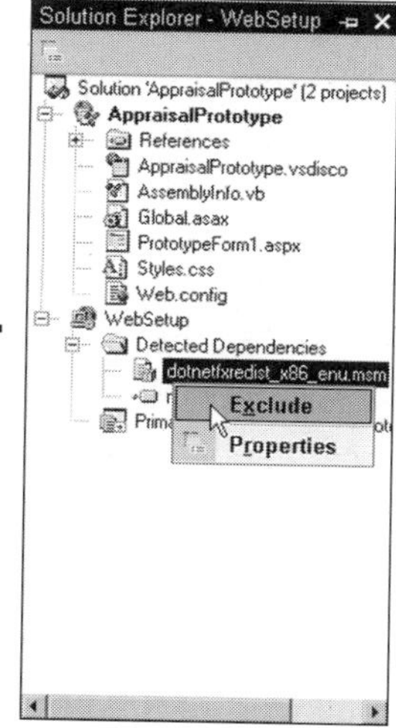

Figure 5-3: Exclude .NET runtime files to reduce your deployment project size.

Compile your application after excluding the runtime files — see how much faster the compilation is? Then compare the size of the installation program sans runtime files with your application with the .NET runtime files included. For more details, refer to the "Testing the Installation Program" section later in this chapter.

You can also use Solution Explorer to add the Windows Installer bootstrapper to your application. The bootstrapper enables you to install your application on computers that don't have Windows Installer version 1.5. (To add the Windows Installer bootstrapper to your application, you need to choose the Windows Installer Bootstrapper option from the Bootstrapper list in the deployment project's property pages. For more details, refer to Book 7, Chapter 4.)

Checking for prerequisite software and hardware

A Web application or a Web service needs IIS Server for successful deployment. In addition, if you've excluded the .NET runtime files from your installation program, these files need to be available on the end user's computer for the successful deployment of your application.

When you create deployment projects in Visual Studio .NET, you can specify launch conditions to determine whether the required software is available on the destination computer before a user proceeds with installing the software. This ensures that end users don't end up installing the application if they aren't able to use the application.

Properties in Visual Studio .NET

PhysicalMemory is an operating system property provided by Visual Studio .NET that helps you determine the amount of RAM installed on a computer. Visual Studio .NET provides a number of properties that help you determine the state of a computer and the details of users logged on. For example, the ScreenX property determines the width of the screen in pixels. Similarly, the SourceDir property specifies the root directory for the source files of an application. You can obtain a complete list of properties available in Visual Studio .NET by viewing the Property Reference section in the Visual Studio .NET documentation.

To ensure that the following hardware and software requirements are fulfilled on the end user's computer before your application is installed, add the following launch conditions to your project:

- **IIS Version 5.0**
- **.NET runtime files**
- **Physical memory, RAM (Random Access Memory), greater than or equal to 256MB**

To confirm that these requirements are fulfilled, you use the Launch Conditions editor. Follow these steps to open the Launch Conditions editor and add launch conditions to it:

1. **Choose View➪Editor➪Launch Conditions.**
2. **Select the Requirements on Target Machine node (leave it selected if it's already highlighted).**
3. **Choose Action➪Add .NET Framework Launch Condition.**

   A launch condition is added to your project for ensuring that the .NET Framework runtime files are available, as shown in Figure 5-4.
4. **Right-click the launch condition that you added in the previous step and then select the Properties Window option from the shortcut menu that appears.**

   The Property window for the condition appears. Notice that the Condition property for the launch condition is specified as `MsiNetAssemblySupport`. This condition ensures that the .NET runtime files are available before your application is installed. The Message property of this window specifies the message that displays to a user when the required condition isn't met. The default message is [VSDNETMSG], which is a message that's translated into different languages by the Visual Studio .NET installation program based upon the language in which a user is operating the application.

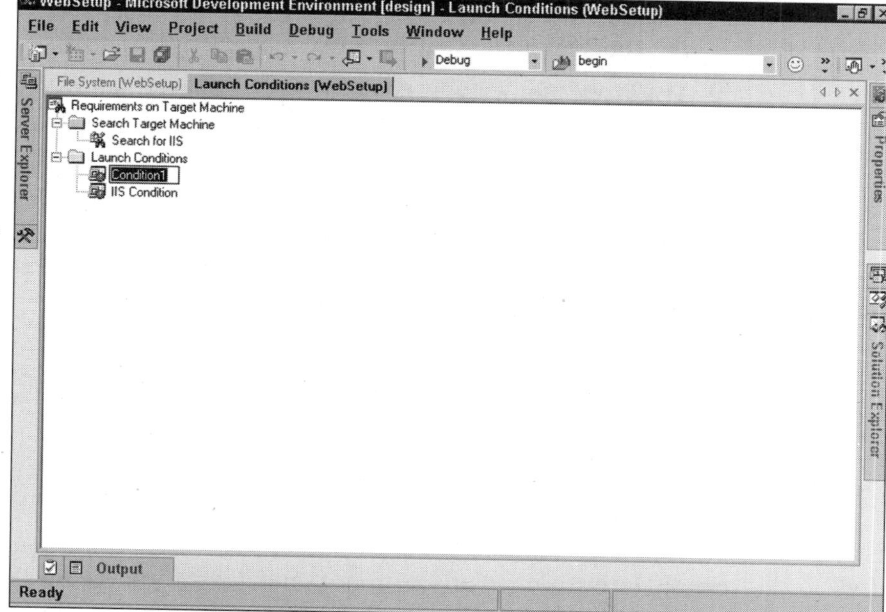

Figure 5-4: Launch conditions enable you to confirm that the end-user's computer fulfills a set of requirements.

You can change the default message displayed to a user when launch conditions aren't fulfilled. However, if you change the default message, Visual Studio .NET can't translate it into a localized language that a user might be using on his or her operating system.

The launch condition that ensures the availability of IIS on the user's computer is already added to the deployment project when you create a new project. Now add a launch condition to ensure that the RAM available is more than 256MB.

1. **In the Launch Conditions editor (choose View⇨Editor⇨Launch Conditions), right-click the Launch Conditions node, and then select Add Launch Condition from the shortcut menu that appears.**

   A new launch condition appears below the launch conditions node, and it is named Condition1. The name of the launch condition is highlighted so that you can change it.

2. **Enter RAM Condition as the name of the launch condition in the name of the launch condition that's highlighted.**

   A blue wavy line appears for the condition that you add to your project. The wavy line appears because you haven't specified the condition that your launch condition needs to check.

3. **Right-click RAM Condition and then select Properties Window from the shortcut menu that appears.**

   The Properties window appears.

4. **Specify** `PhysicalMemory >="256"` **in the Condition property.**

   The condition `PhysicalMemory >="256"` ensures that the installation program proceeds with the installation only when the RAM available is equal to or greater than 256MB.

5. **Enter the following text in the Message property:** You need to have a minimum of 256 MB RAM to install this application. Please upgrade your hardware.

   After you specify the message property, the setup displays an error message if the RAM available on the user's computer is less than 256MB.

Testing the Installation Program

After you configure your deployment project, you need to compile it to create the installation program. You should test the installation program on a test computer to verify that your application is being installed correctly. In this section, we look at the steps to create an installation program and test it.

Compiling the deployment project

To compile your application, follow these steps:

1. **Choose Build⇨Configuration Manager.**

   The Configuration Manager dialog box appears.

2. **Select Release from the Active Solution Configuration list.**

   The Configuration Manager dialog box after selecting the Release configuration is shown in Figure 5-5.

   The configuration of the project is set to Release. The Release configuration optimizes the speed and performance of your application. Learn more about the Debug and Release configurations in Book 4, Chapter 8.

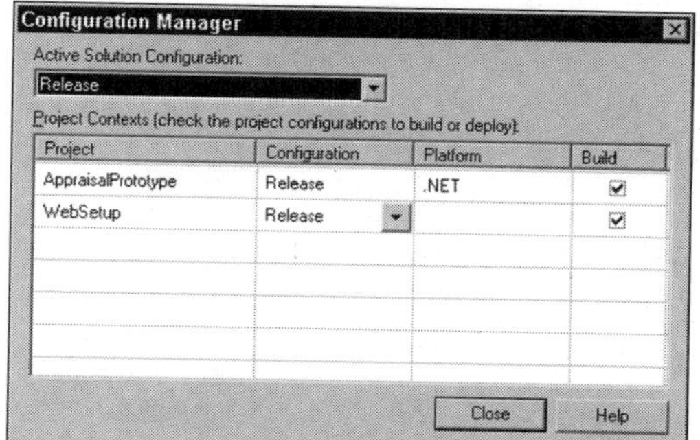

Figure 5-5: Change the configuration of your project to Release.

3. **Click the Close button to close the Configuration Manager dialog box.**
4. **Choose Build⇨Build Solution.**

   Your project is compiled; errors, if any, are displayed in the Output window.

After your application is successfully compiled, the MSI file for your application is created in the Release subfolder of the deployment project's folder. Note that the size of the MSI file is in the range of 1–3MB, which is much smaller than the file would've been if you had included the .NET runtime files.

To quantify the difference in size, we created two deployment projects: one without the .NET runtime files and the other after including these files. In the first case (no .NET runtime files), the size of the MSI file is 1.8MB. When the .NET runtime files were included, the size of the file is 19MB.

Making a successful deployment

To test your application, copy the MSI file to a test computer. Double-click the file to start the installation and follow these steps:

1. **On the Welcome screen, click Next.**

   The Select Installation Address screen appears. On this screen, you can retain the default name of the virtual directory or specify a new name.
2. **Retain the default name of the Virtual Directory as shown in Figure 5-6 and then click the Next button.**

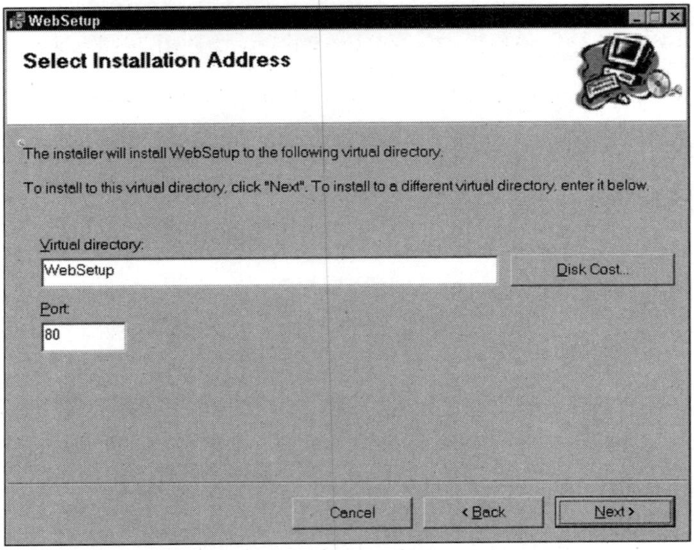

Figure 5-6: Specify the Virtual Directory name for installing your application.

3. **On the Confirm Installation screen, click the Next button to begin installing your application.**

   The installation program installs your application.

4. **On the Installation Complete screen, click the Close button to complete the installation.**

You can't perform these steps if your computer doesn't have IIS, .NET runtime files, or a minimum of 256MB RAM. For example, if we perform the same steps on a machine with 128MB RAM, an error message is displayed, as shown in Figure 5-7.

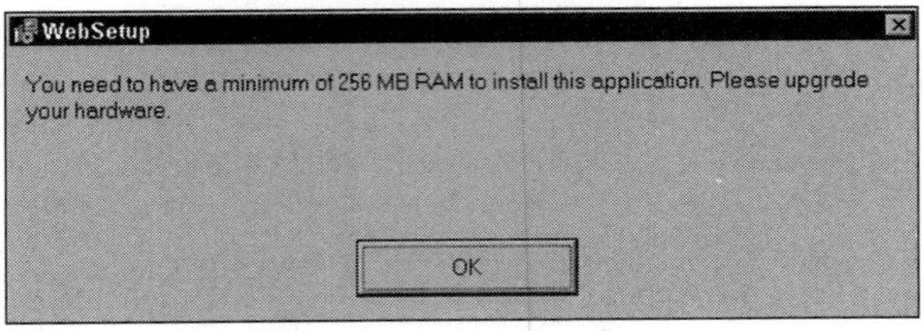

Figure 5-7: Rats. Not enough RAM.

Chapter 6: More Deployment Options

In This Chapter

- **Configuring merge module projects**
- **Configuring cabinet files**

Visual Studio .NET provides a number of deployment options. You can deploy Windows and Web applications by using Microsoft Installer (MSI) files. In addition, you can package components into merge modules and ActiveX controls into cabinet (CAB) files.

For a detailed explanation of deployment of Windows and Web applications, read through Book 7, Chapters 4 and 5. In this chapter, we show you how to create merge modules and CAB files for deploying application components and ActiveX controls, respectively.

Configuring Merge Module Projects

You create merge modules for components that shouldn't be used by users directly. Instead, these modules are meant for developers who want to add components to existing projects. Instead of adding components directly to an application, you can create a merge module and then add the required module to your project.

Defining merge modules

Windows Installer provides merge modules as a standard for sharing components between applications. A merge module in Visual Studio .NET contains a component such as a class library or a custom control.

When you use a merge module to add components to an application, the version, resources, and registry entries for the component are preconfigured. Therefore, you need to pay attention to the functional requirements of the component. Moreover, when you install an application that contains a merge module, Windows Installer records the details of the merge module in its database so that the component isn't accidentally deleted as long as it's in use by one application or the other. (Read more about the Windows Installer service in Book 7, Chapter 4.)

Creating an MSM file

Merge modules are compiled into merge module (MSM) files. These files are equivalent to MSI files but can't run in a standalone mode. (Read more about MSI files in Book 7, Chapter 4.) To create an MSM file, follow these basic steps:

1. **Create a merge module project.**
2. **Add the application's output to the merge module project.**
3. **Compile the deployment project.**

Creating a merge module project

To create a merge module project, we use a custom control created in Visual C#. *Custom controls* are user-defined controls that can be included in a project in the same way that you include other Visual Studio .NET controls. To know more about custom controls, refer to Book 6, Chapter 5.

Let's walk through the steps to create a merge module project. For the steps listed here, you can use any Visual Studio .NET project. You can also download one of the sample projects from `http://www.dummies.com/extras/VS.NETAllinOne`. Follow these steps to add a merge module project for your application:

1. **Open the project to which you want to add a merge module.**

   (To open the project, double-click the `.sln` file for the project in Windows Explorer.)

   The `.sln` extension stands for a Visual Studio .NET Solution file. This file defines how the source files of a project are organized in a project.

2. **Choose File➪Add Project➪New Project.**

   The Add New Project dialog box appears.

3. **In the Add New Project dialog box, click Setup and Deployment Projects in the Project Types list, and then click the Merge Module Project template in the Templates list.**

4. **Retain the default name of the project and click OK.**

   A merge module deployment project is added to your application.

Adding application output to the merge module project

After you add the merge module deployment project to your application — in this case, a custom control — you need to add your application's output to the deployment project. You add your application's output to the deployment project by using the File System editor, which is one of the four editors provided by Visual Studio .NET for a merge module project. Read about these four editors in Book 7, Chapter 4.

Okay, you caught us. If you've already read Book 7, Chapter 4, we list six editors. In case you're wondering where the other two Visual Studio .NET editors went, the Launch Conditions and User Interface editors aren't available for the merge module project. These editors are required only when you perform a standalone installation of the deployment file. A merge module deployment file isn't installed as a standalone file; it's always associated with an MSI file. Therefore, these other two editors aren't required.

The File System editor is open by default when you add the deployment project to your application. If you close it accidentally, choose View⇨Editors⇨File System. When the File System editor is open, perform these steps:

1. **Choose Project⇨Add⇨Project Output.**

   The Add Project Output Group dialog box appears.

2. **To add the primary output of the application to the merge module, select Primary Output from the Add Project Output Group dialog box and click OK.**

   The primary output of your application is added to the Common Files Folder in the File System editor, as shown in Figure 6-1.

The Common Files Folder stores the components that are shared across applications. Project output for components that you add to the Common Files Folder are automatically added to the Common folder on an end user's computer. The contents of this folder are shared across all applications.

If you don't add the primary output of your application to the Common Files Folder, you can specify an alternate location of the merge module in the Module Retargetable Folder.

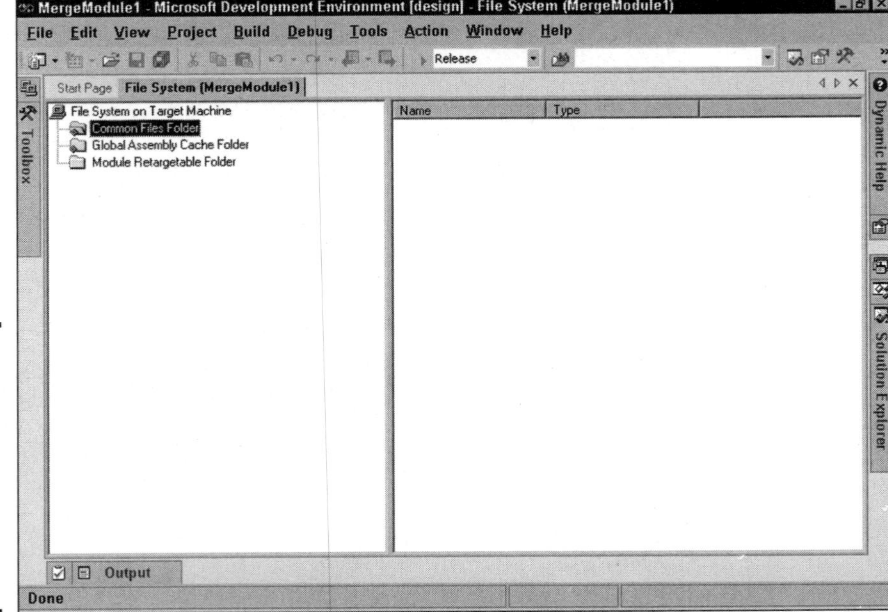

Figure 6-1: Add the primary output of your application to the Common Files Folder.

Compiling the deployment project

After you add the primary output of the custom control to the merge module, you compile your custom control to create the MSM file. However, before you create the MSM file, you can exclude the .NET runtime files from your project to decrease the size of the MSM file.

Because you don't use the MSM file in a standalone mode, you don't include the .NET runtime files in the merge module. Instead, if you want to include the runtime files, include them in the final deployment project that you use to deploy your application.

To exclude the .NET runtime files from your project and compile your deployment project, follow these steps:

1. **Right-click the** `dotnetfxredist_x86_enu.msm` **file in Solution Explorer (press Ctrl+Alt+L) and then select Exclude from the shortcut menu that appears.**

   The .NET runtime files are excluded from your deployment project. (For a detailed step-by-step procedure, you can refer to Book 7, Chapter 5.)

2. **Change the project configuration to Release by selecting the Release option from the Solution Configuration drop-down list on the standard toolbar.**

   For a detailed explanation on project configurations, refer to Book 4, Chapter 8.

3. **Choose Build⇨Build Solution (or press Ctrl+Shift+B).**

   The MSM file for your custom control is generated in the Release subfolder of the deployment project's folder.

Adding a merge module to another project

After you create a merge module, you need to add it to a new or an existing deployment project. The deployment project to which you add the merge module can access its components. Following are the steps to add a merge module file to an existing deployment project. (You can create a deployment project by following the steps listed in Book 7, Chapter 5.)

1. **Open the deployment project to which you want to add the merge module.**
2. **Choose Project⇨Add⇨Merge Module.**

   The Add Modules dialog box appears, as shown in Figure 6-2.

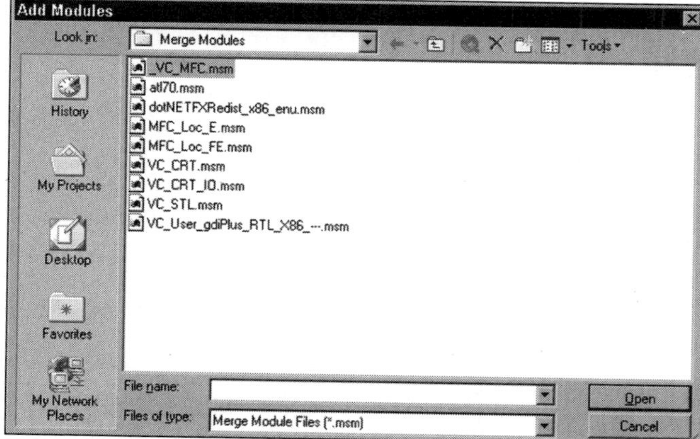

Figure 6-2: Select a merge module to add to your project from the Add Modules dialog box.

3. **Navigate to the Release subfolder of the merge module deployment project and then select the merge module that you want to add to the existing project.**

To create a merge module file, you should first compile your application. For details on how to create the merge module file, refer to the earlier section "Creating an MSM file."

4. **Click Open to add the merge module file to your deployment project.**

   The merge module is added to your deployment project. You can confirm that the merge module was added to your project in Solution Explorer, as shown in Figure 6-3.

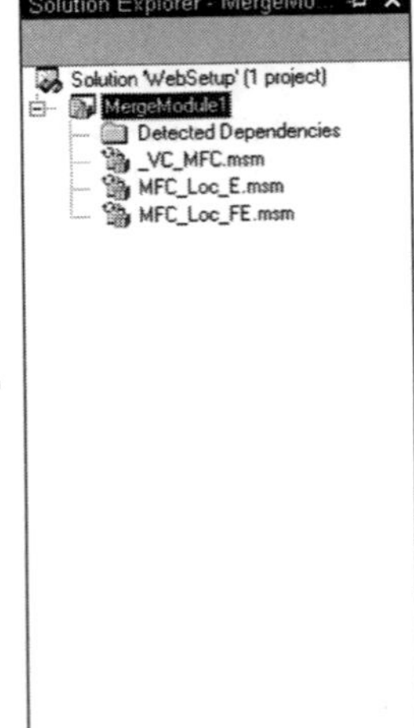

Figure 6-3: View merge modules that you add to a project in Solution Explorer.

After you add the merge module to a deployment project, compile the project to create an MSI file. When an end user deploys the MSI file, your component — that was a part of the merge module — is automatically deployed.

Configuring CAB Files

CAB file projects are the simplest of all deployment projects available in Visual Studio .NET. In this section, you can read about CAB files and the procedure to create them.

Understanding CAB files

You can relate a CAB file to a compressed file with added functionality. A *CAB file* is a single file that stores a number of compressed files. By storing files in a CAB file, you conserve disk space.

Apart from saving disk space, CAB files allow you to deploy ActiveX controls easily. When you add ActiveX controls (files with an `.ocx` extension) to CAB files, you can deploy these controls on end user computers through a Web site. All you need to do is to include a reference to the CAB file on your Web site, and your control is downloaded on a user's computer when the user visits your Web site.

Creating CAB files

To create a CAB file, follow these steps:

1. **Launch Visual Studio .NET.**
2. **Choose File➪New➪Project.**

   The New Project dialog box appears.
3. **Click Setup and Deployment Projects from Project Types and then select the Cab Project template from the list of templates.**
4. **Specify a name for the CAB file in the Name text box, or retain the default name, and then click OK.**

   A new deployment project based on the CAB Project template is created for you.

After creating the new CAB deployment project, add files to the project by following these steps:

1. **Choose Project➪Add➪File.**

   The Add Files dialog box appears, as shown in Figure 6-4.

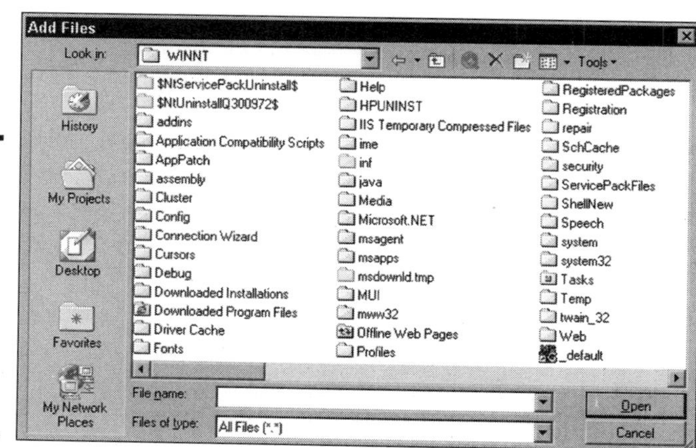

Figure 6-4: Add files to your CAB file deployment project by using the Add Files dialog box.

2. **Navigate to the location of the file that you want to add to the deployment project, select the file, and then click Open to add the file to your deployment project.**

   The file that you select is added to your application.

Next, change the project configuration to Release and compile the deployment project. You can read about changing project configurations and compiling projects in the "Compiling the deployment project" section of this chapter.

After you compile the deployment project, the CAB file is generated in the Release subfolder of the deployment project's folder.

Index

A

B-C

D

Q-R

S

T-U

V

W

X-Y-Z

Index

Numbers & Symbols

A

B

C

D

E

F

G

H

J

K

L

M

N

O

R

T

W

X-Y-Z